A People and A Nation

Brief Eighth Edition

A People and A Nation

A HISTORY OF THE UNITED STATES

Volume 2 Since 1865

Brief Eighth Edition

MARY BETH NORTON
Cornell University

CAROL SHERIFF
College of William and Mary

DAVID M. KATZMAN
University of Kansas

DAVID W. BLIGHT
Yale University

HOWARD P. CHUDACOFF
Brown University

FREDRIK LOGEVALL
Cornell University

BETH BAILEY
Temple University

DEBRA MICHALS
Merrimack College

 WADSWORTH
CENGAGE Learning

Australia • Brazil • Japan • Korea • Mexico • Singapore • Spain • United Kingdom • United States

WADSWORTH
CENGAGE Learning™

A People and A Nation: A History of the United States Volume 2 Since 1865, **Brief Eighth Edition**

Mary Beth Norton, Carol Sheriff, David M. Katzman, David W. Blight, Howard P. Chudacoff, Fredrik Logevall, Beth Bailey, Debra Michals

Sponsoring Editor: Ann West

Development Manager: Jeffrey Greene

Assistant Editor: Megan Curry

Editorial Assistant: Megan Chrisman

Senior Editor: Lisa Ciccolo

Senior Marketing Manager:
Katherine Bates

Marketing Coordinator:
Lorreen Pelletier

Marketing Communications Manager:
Christine Dobberpuhl

Content Project Manager, Editorial
Production: Aimee Chevrette Bear

Art and Design Manager: Jill Haber

Print Buyer: Miranda Klapper

Senior Rights Acquisition Account
Manager: Katie Huha

Text Designer: Cia Boynton

Senior Photo Editor:
Jennifer Meyer Dare

Photo Researcher: Bruce Carson

Cover Design Manager: Tony Saizon

Cover Image: Malvin Gray Johnson,
Self-Portrait, 1934

Cover Credit: Smithsonian American
Art Museum/Art Resource, NY

Compositor: Macmillan Publishing
Solutions

For product information and technology assistance, contact us at
**Cengage Learning Academic Resource Center,
1-800-423-0563**

For permission to use material from this text or product,
submit all requests online at **www.cengage.com/permissions.**
Further permissions questions can be e-mailed to
permissionrequest@cengage.com

Library of Congress Control Number: 2008933839

Student Edition:

ISBN-13: 978-0-547-07560-7

ISBN-10: 0-547-17560-4

Wadsworth
25 Thomson Place
Boston, MA 02210
USA

Cengage Learning products are represented in Canada by Nelson Education, Ltd.

For your course and learning solutions, visit
www.cengage.com.

Purchase any of our products at your local college store or at our preferred online store **www.ichapters.com.**

Printed in the United States of America
1 2 3 4 5 6 7 13 14 12 11 10

Brief Contents

Contents

Maps

Figures

Tables

CREATION OF THE BRIEF EDITION

Nearly three decades have passed since the publication of the first brief edition of *A People and a Nation*. In that initial brief edition as well as each subsequent one, the intent was to preserve the uniqueness and integrity of the complete work while condensing it. This Brief Eighth Edition once again reflects the scholarship, readability, and comprehensiveness of the full-length version. It also maintains the integration of social, cultural, political, economic, and foreign relations history that has been a hallmark of *A People and a Nation*.

Starting with this edition, a new editor, Dr. Debra Michals, has worked with us, ensuring that the changes in content and organization incorporated in the full-length Eighth Edition were retained in the condensation. The authors attained reductions by paring down details rather than deleting entire sections. The Brief Eighth Edition thus contains fewer statistics, fewer quotations, and fewer examples than the unabridged version. A sufficient number of quotations and examples are retained, however, to maintain the richness in style created by the authors.

The Brief Eighth Edition is available in both one-volume and two-volume formats. The two-volume format is divided as follows: Volume 1 contains Chapters 1 through 16, beginning with a discussion of three cultures—American, African, and European—that intersected during the exploration and colonization of the New World and ending with a discussion of the Reconstruction era. Volume 2 contains Chapters 16 through 33, beginning its coverage at Reconstruction and extending the history of the American people to the present. The chapter on Reconstruction appears in both volumes to provide greater flexibility in matching a volume to the historical span covered by a specific course.

CHANGES IN THIS EDITION

While the following Preface to the full-length Eighth Edition elaborates on specific content changes, we note here that the authors paid increased attention to the following: the history of children and childhood; the environment, including the past impact of hurricanes; the American West, subject of a completely new chapter; and the social and religious diversity of America's population, developed through territorial incorporation as well as through immigration. We have further widened our lens to include more coverage of America's place in the world. These emphases as well as the updated scholarship on which they are based, are fully retained in the Brief Eighth Edition. New to this edition are focus questions that follow each chapter's introduction to call students' attention to key issues in the chapter. These questions are answered at the end of each chapter.

Although each author feels answerable for the whole of *A People and a Nation*, we take primary responsibility for particular chapters: Mary Beth Norton, Chapters 1–8; Carol Sheriff, Chapters 9, 11–13; David Blight, Chapters 10, 14–16;

Howard P. Chudacoff, Chapters 17–21 and 24; Fredrik Logevall, Chapters 22, 23, 26, 28, and shared responsibility for 30–33; Beth Bailey, Chapters 25, 27, 29, and shared responsibility for 30–33.

LEARNING AND TEACHING AIDS

This edition of *A People and a Nation* includes a number of useful learning and teaching aids. These ancillaries are designed to help students get the most from the course and to provide instructors with useful course management and presentation tools.

Website Tools

The **Instructor Website** features the **Instructor's Resource Manual** written by George C. Warren of Central Piedmont Community College. For each chapter, there is a brief list of learning objectives, a comprehensive chapter outline, ideas for classroom activities, discussion questions and several suggested paper topics, and a lecture supplement. Also available on the Instructor Website are primary sources with instructor notes in addition to hundreds of maps, images, audio and video clips, and PowerPoint slides for classroom presentation created by Barney Rickman of Valdosta State University. The **HM Testing™** CD-ROM provides flexible test-editing capabilities for the Test Items written by George Warren.

HistoryFinder, a new Houghton Mifflin technology initiative, helps instructors create rich and exciting classroom presentations. This online tool offers thousands of online resources, including art, photographs, maps, primary sources, multimedia content, Associated Press interactive modules, and ready-made PowerPoint slides. HistoryFinder's assets can easily be searched by keyword, or browsed from pull-down menus by topic, media type, or by textbook. Instructors can then browse, preview, and download resources straight from the website.

The **Student Website** contains a variety of tutorial resources including the **Study Guide** written by George Warren, ACE quizzes with feedback, interactive maps, primary sources, chronology exercises, flashcards, and other interactivities. The Website for this edition of *A People and a Nation* features **Audio Summaries,** audio files that are downloadable as MP3 files. These audio summaries help students review each chapter's key points.

Please contact your local Houghton Mifflin sales representative for more information about these learning and teaching tools in addition to the **Rand McNally Atlas of American History,** WebCT and Blackboard cartridges, and transparencies for United States History.

ACKNOWLEDGMENTS

Author teams rely on review panels to help create and execute successful revision plans. For the revision of this Brief Eighth Edition, we were guided by the many historians whose thoughtful insights and recommendations helped us with the preparation of the full-length Eighth Edition. Their names appear in the preface to that edition that follows.

Finally, we want to thank the many people who have contributed their thoughts and labors to this work, especially the talented staff at Houghton Mifflin.

For the authors, Mary Beth Norton, coordinating author.

Preface to the Full-Length Eighth Edition

In this eighth edition, *A People and a Nation* has undergone both reorganization and revision, while still retaining the narrative strength and focus that have made it so popular with students and teachers alike. In the years since the publication of the seventh edition, new materials have been uncovered, new interpretations advanced, and new themes have come to the forefront of American historical scholarship. All the authors—joined by one new member, Carol Sheriff—have worked diligently to incorporate those findings into this text.

Like other teachers and students, we are always re-creating our past, restructuring our memory, and rediscovering the personalities and events that have influenced us, injured us, and bedeviled us. This book represents our continuing rediscovery of America's history—its diverse people and the nation they created and have nurtured. As this book demonstrates, there are many different Americans and many different memories. We have sought to present as many of them as possible, in both triumph and tragedy, in both division and unity.

ABOUT A PEOPLE AND A NATION

A People and a Nation, first published in 1982, was the first major textbook in the United States to fully integrate social and political history. From the outset, the authors have been determined to tell the story of *all* the people of the United States. This book's hallmark has been its melding of social and political history, its movement beyond history's common focus on public figures and events to examine the daily life of America's people. All editions of the book have stressed the interaction of public policy and personal experience, the relationship between domestic concerns and foreign affairs, the various manifestations of popular culture, and the multiple origins of America and Americans. We have consistently built our narrative on a firm foundation in primary sources—on both well-known and obscure letters, diaries, public documents, oral histories, and artifacts of material culture. We have long challenged readers to think about the meaning of American history, not just to memorize facts. Both students and instructors have repeatedly told us how much they appreciate and enjoy our approach to the past.

As has been true since the first edition, each chapter opens with a dramatic vignette focusing on an individual or a group of people. These vignettes introduce key themes, which then frame the chapters in succinct introductions and summaries. Numerous maps, tables, graphs, and charts provide readers with the necessary geographical and statistical context for observations in the text. Carefully selected illustrations—many of them unique to this book—offer readers visual insight into the topics under discussion, especially because the authors have written the captions. In this edition, as in all previous ones, we have sought to incorporate up-to-date scholarship, readability, a clear structure, critical thinking, and instructive illustrative material on every page.

THEMES IN THIS BOOK

Several themes and questions stand out in our continuing effort to integrate political, social, and cultural history. We study the many ways Americans have defined themselves—gender, race, class, region, ethnicity, religion, sexual orientation—and the many subjects that have reflected their multidimensional experiences. We highlight the remarkably diverse everyday lives of the American people—in cities and on farms and ranches, in factories and in corporate headquarters, in neighborhoods and in legislatures, in love relationships and in hate groups, in recreation and in work, in the classroom and in military uniform, in secret national security conferences and in public foreign relations debates, in church and in voluntary associations, in polluted environments and in conservation areas. We pay particular attention to lifestyles, diet and dress, family life and structure, labor conditions, gender roles, migration and mobility, childbearing, and child rearing. We explore how Americans have entertained and informed themselves by discussing their music, sports, theater, print media, film, radio, television, graphic arts, and literature, in both "high" culture and popular culture. We study how technology has influenced Americans' lives, such as through the internal combustion engine and the computer.

Americans' personal lives have always interacted with the public realm of politics and government. To understand how Americans have sought to protect their different ways of life and to work out solutions to thorny problems, we emphasize their expectations of governments at the local, state, and federal levels; governments' role in providing answers; the lobbying of interest groups; the campaigns and outcomes of elections; and the hierarchy of power in any period. Because the United States has long been a major participant in world affairs, we explore America's participation in wars, interventions in other nations, empire-building, immigration patterns, images of foreign peoples, cross-national cultural ties, and international economic trends.

WHAT'S NEW IN THIS EDITION

Planning for the eighth edition began at a two-day authors' meeting at the Houghton Mifflin headquarters in Boston. There we discussed the most recent scholarship in the field, the reviews of the seventh edition solicited from instructors, and the findings of our own continuing research. For this edition, we added a new colleague, Carol Sheriff, who experienced the intellectual exhilaration and rigor of such an authors' meeting for the first time. Sheriff, a member of the History Department at the College of William and Mary, has written extensively on antebellum America, especially in the north, and she has taken on the responsibility for those chapters in the eighth edition.

This edition builds on its immediate predecessor in continuing to enhance the global perspective on American history that has characterized the book since its first edition. From the "Atlantic world" context of European colonies in North and South America to the discussion of international terrorism, the authors have incorporated the most recent globally oriented scholarship throughout the volume. Significantly, the eighth edition includes an entirely new chapter on the American west in the years before the Civil War and the discussion of the west has been expanded throughout. The treatment of the history of children and childhood has been increased, as has the discussion of environmental history, including the devastating impact of hurricanes in North America and the Caribbean from the earliest days of European settlement. As in the seventh edition, we have worked to strengthen our treatment of the diversity of America's people by examining differences within the broad ethnic categories commonly employed and by paying greater attention to immigration, cultural and intellectual infusions from around the world, and America's growing religious diversity. We have also stressed the incorporation of different peoples into the United States through territorial acquisition as well as through immigration. At the same time, we have integrated the discussion of such diversity into our narrative, so as not to artificially isolate any group from the mainstream. We have added three probing questions at the end of each chapter's introduction to guide students' reading of the pages that follow.

As always, the authors reexamined every sentence, interpretation, map, chart, illustration, and caption, refining the narrative, presenting new examples, and bringing to the text the latest findings of scholars in many areas of history, anthropology, sociology, and political science. More than one-third of the chapter-opening vignettes are new to this edition.

"LEGACIES" AND "LINKS TO THE WORLD"

Each chapter contains two brief feature essays: "Legacies" (introduced in the sixth edition) and "Links to the World" (introduced in the seventh edition). Legacies follow chapter summaries and offer compelling and timely answers to students who question the relevance of historical study by exploring the historical roots of contemporary topics. New subjects of Legacies are: Kennewick Man/Ancient One, Blue Laws, women's political activism, the township and range system, descendants of early Latino settlers, "Big Government," the Lost Cause, the Cowboy myth, recorded music, Guantanamo Bay, atomic proliferation, and the all-volunteer military. Numerous other Legacies have been updated.

"Links to the World" examine both inward and outward ties between America (and Americans) and the rest of the world. The "Links" appear at appropriate places in each chapter to explore specific topics at considerable length. Tightly constructed essays detail the often little-known connections between developments here and abroad. The topics range broadly over economic, political, social, technological, medical, and cultural history, vividly demonstrating that the geographical region that is now the United States has never lived in isolation from other peoples and countries. New to this edition are Links on smallpox inoculations, the Amistad case, Russian Populism, European influence on American workers' compensation, and *National Geographic*. Each Link highlights global interconnections with unusual and lively examples that will both intrigue and inform students.

SECTION-BY-SECTION CHANGES IN THIS EDITION

Mary Beth Norton, who had primary responsibility for Chapters 1 through 8 and served as coordinating author, augmented her discussion of the age of European expansion with new information on Muslim power and the allure of exotic spices; she also expanded the treatment of Spanish colonization and settlements in the Caribbean. She incorporated extensive new scholarship on early Virginia into Chapter 2. In addition to reorganizing part of Chapter 3 to bring more coherence to the discussion of the origins of slavery in North America, she added demographic information about enslaved people (both Indians and Africans) and those who enslaved and transported them, stressing in particular the importance of African women in South Carolina rice cultivation. She added material on transported English convicts, Huguenot immigrants, Acadian exiles, iron-making, land riots, the Stono Rebellion, the Seven Years' War in western Pennsylvania, the experiences of common soldiers in the Revolution, Shays's Rebellion, and the Jay Treaty debates. In Chapter 8 she created new sections on Indians in the new nation and on revolutions at the end of the century, including among them the election of Thomas Jefferson.

Carol Sheriff completely reorganized the contents of Chapters 9, 11, and 12, clarifying chronological developments and including much new material. Chapter 9 now covers politics through 1823 in order to emphasize the impact of the War of 1812 in accelerating regional divisions. It has expanded coverage of popular political practice (including among non-voters), the separation of church and state, the Marshall Court, the First and Second Barbary Wars, and the incorporation of the Louisiana Territory and its residents into the United States. Chapter 11, retitled "The Modernizing North," consolidates information previously divided between two chapters and augments it with new discussions of daily life before commercial and industrial expansion, rural-urban contrasts, children and youth culture, male and female common laborers, and the origins of free-labor ideology. Chapter 12 focuses on reform and politics in the age of Jackson, with expanded attention to communitarian experiments, abolitionism (including African Americans in the movement), women's rights, and religion, including revivalism in general and the Second Great Awakening in particular. The entirely new Chapter 13, "The Contested West," combines material that was previously scattered in different locations with a great deal of recent scholarship on such topics as the disjunction between the ideal and reality of the West, exploration and migration, cultural diversity in the West, cooperation and conflict among the West's peoples, and the role of the federal government in regional development. In all her reorganized chapters she relied on a base created by David M. Katzman, an original member of the author team who had responsibility for this section in the seven earlier editions.

David W. Blight, who had primary responsibility for Chapters 10 and 14 through 16, extensively reorganized Chapter 10 (previously Chapter 13), on the South, in part to reflect its new chronological placement in the book. The chapter now covers material beginning in 1815 rather than 1830 and contains a section on Southern expansion and Indian removal. In his chapters he has added material on the Taos revolt, enslaved children, "Bleeding Kansas," Harriet Scott, Louisa May Alcott, union sentiment in the South, the conduct of the war, and economic and social conditions in the postwar North and South. He has revised Chapter 16 to emphasize economic as well as political change in the era of Reconstruction.

Howard P. Chudacoff, responsible for Chapters 17 through 21 and 24, has increased the coverage of Indians, Exodusters, and Hispanics in the West, and of western Progressivism. His treatment of popular culture now stresses its lower-class, bottom-to-top origins. He added information on the history of childhood, vaudeville, and the movies; and he revised discussions of monetary policy, Progressivism, Populism, and urban and agrarian protests. He also has included more coverage of racism and those who combated it, such as Ida B. Wells, and on women and the Ku Klux Klan. Business operation and regulation receive new attention in his chapters, as do Calvin Coolidge, consumerism, and baseball.

Fredrik Logevall, with primary responsibility for Chapters 22, 23, 26, and 28, continued throughout his chapters to work to establish the wider international context for U.S. foreign affairs. He added considerable new material on the Middle East (especially in Chapter 28) and incorporated recent scholarship on the Vietnam War. He also updated the treatment of the Spanish-American War with new information on the sinking of the *Maine* and on the Philippine insurrection. His discussion of World War I now includes consideration of the antagonistic relationship of Woodrow Wilson and V.I. Lenin; and he has given more attention to American economic and cultural expansion in the 1920s and 1930s. He has furthermore expanded his treatment of American reactions to the Spanish Civil War.

Beth Bailey, primarily responsible for Chapters 25, 27, and 29, added information on women, the left, and popular culture (especially film and the production code) during the 1930s. She expanded coverage of the European front in World War II and of divisions within the United States during the war. In Chapter 29, she thoroughly reorganized the section on civil rights to clarify the chronology and key points of development, and she also included new information on emerging countercultures and the beats, union activities, and the Eisenhower administration.

Bailey and Logevall shared responsibility for Chapters 30 through 33. In Chapter 30 Freedom Summer is given enhanced attention and the section on civil rights has been reorganized to emphasize a clear chronology. These chapters contain new material on the women's movement and the barriers women faced before 1970s reforms, recent immigration, neoconservatism, anti-Vietnam War protests, Nixon's presidency, the Supreme Court, the 1982 Israeli invasion of Lebanon, and the 1991 Iraq War. Chapter 33 in particular has been thoroughly revised to include the latest demographic data on Americans and their families, along with discussions of the struggles over science and religion, hurricane Katrina, the Bush administration's domestic policies, and especially the Iraq War.

TEACHING AND LEARNING AIDS

The supplements listed here accompany the Eighth Edition of *A People and a Nation*. They have been created with the diverse needs of today's students and instructors in mind.

FOR THE INSTRUCTOR

- Houghton Mifflin's **HistoryFinder** is a new online tool developed to help instructors create rich and exciting presentations for the U.S. history survey class. HistoryFinder offers thousands of online resources, including art, photographs, maps, primary sources, multimedia content, Associated Press interactive modules, and ready-made PowerPoint slides. HistoryFinder's assets can easily be searched by keyword topic, media type, or by textbook chapter. It is then possible to browse, preview, and download resources straight from the website into the instructor's own PowerPoint collection.

- **The Instructor Website**, at HM HistorySPACE(tm), includes a variety of resources that will help instructors engage their students in class and assess their understanding inside and outside the classroom. The Instructor Website includes the **Instructor's Resource Manual,** written by George C. Warren, of Central Piedmont Community College. For each chapter, there is a brief list of learning objectives, a comprehensive chapter outline, ideas for classroom activities, discussion questions and several suggested paper topics, and a lecture supplement. Also available on the Instructor Website is a complete set of PowerPoint slides created by Barney Rickman of Valdosta State University, to assist in instruction and discussion of key topics and materials for each chapter.
- The **HM Testing™ CD-ROM** provides flexible test-editing capabilities for the Test Items written by George Warren of Central Piedmont Community College. Included in the Test Bank are multiple choice, identification, geography, and essay questions.
- Houghton Mifflin's **Eduspace Course** for *A People and a Nation* offers a customizable course management system powered by Blackboard along with homework assignments that engage students and encourage in-class discussion. Assignments include gradable homework exercises, writing assignments, primary sources with questions, and Associated Press Interactives. Eduspace also provides a gradebook and communication capabilities, such as live chats, threaded discussion boards, and announcement postings. The Eduspace course also includes an interactive version of *A People and a Nation* with direct links to relevant primary sources, quizzes, and more.

FOR THE STUDENT

- The **Student Website,** at HM HistorySPACE™, contains a variety of review and self-assessment resources to help students succeed in the U.S. history survey course. ACE quizzes with feedback, interactive maps, primary sources, chronology exercises, flashcards, and other activities are available for each chapter. Audio files provide chapter summaries in MP3 format for downloading and listening to at any time.
- **Study Guides** (Volumes I and II), written by George Warren, provide learning objectives, vocabulary exercises, identification suggestions, skill-building activities, multiple choice questions, essay questions, and map exercises in two volumes.

Please contact your local Houghton Mifflin sales representative for more information about these learning and teaching tools in addition to the **Rand McNally Atlas of American History,** WebCT and Blackboard cartridges, and transparencies for United States History. Your sales representative can also provide more information about **BiblioBase for U.S. History,** a database of hundreds of primary sources from which you can create a customized course pack.

ACKNOWLEDGMENTS

The authors would like to thank the following persons for their assistance with the preparation of this edition: Shawn Alexander, Marsha Andrews, Edward Balleisen, Philip Daileader, Katherine Flynn, John B. Heiser, Danyel Logevall, Daniel Mandell, Clark F. Norton, Mary E. Norton, Anna Daileader Sheriff, Benjamin Daileader Sheriff, Selene Sheriff, Seymour Sheriff.

At each stage of this revision, a sizable panel of historian reviewers read drafts of our chapters. Their suggestions, corrections, and pleas helped guide us through this momentous revision. We could not include all of their recommendations, but the book is better for our having heeded most of their advice. We heartily thank:

Marynita Anderson, Nassau Community College/SUNY
Stephen Aron, UCLA and Autry National Center
Gordon Morris Bakken, California State University, Fullerton
Todd Forsyth Carney, Southern Oregon University
Kathleen S. Carter, High Point University
Robert C. Cottrell, California State University, Chico
Lawrence Culver, Utah State University
Lawrence J. DeVaro, Rowan University
Lisa Lindquist Dorr, University of Alabama
Michelle Kuhl, University of Wisconsin, Oshkosh
Martin Halpern, Henderson State University
John S. Leiby, Paradise Valley Community College
Edwin Martini, Western Michigan University
Elsa A Nystrom Kennesaw State University
Chester Pach, Ohio University
Stephen Rockenbach, Northern Kentucky University
Joseph Owen Weixelman, University of New Mexico

The authors once again thank the extraordinary Houghton Mifflin people who designed, edited, produced, and nourished this book. Their high standards and acute attention to both general structure and fine detail are cherished in the publishing industry. Many thanks, then, to Patricia Coryell, vice president, publisher, history and social science; Suzanne Jeans, publisher, history and political Science; Sally Constable and Ann West, senior sponsoring editors; Ann Hofstra Grogg, freelance development editor; Jeff Greene, senior development editor; Jane Lee, senior project editor, Katherine Bates, senior marketing manager; Pembroke Herbert, photo researcher; Jill Haber, art and design manager, Charlotte Miller, art editor; and Evangeline Bermas, editorial assistant.

M.B.N.
C.S.
D.B.
H.C.
F.L.
B.B.

Reconstruction: An Unfinished Revolution

The lower half of secession's seedbed, Charleston, South Carolina, lay in ruin when most of the white population evacuated on February 18, 1865. A prolonged bombardment by Union forces around Charleston harbor destroyed many of the low-country planters' town homes. Fires broke out everywhere, ignited in bales of cotton stockpiled in public squares. To many observers, the flames were the funeral pyres of a dying civilization.

The Union's Twenty-first U.S. Colored Regiment received Charleston's surrender from its mayor. For black Charlestonians, most of whom were former slaves, this was a time to celebrate freedom and rebirth. The city's freedpeople converted Confederate ruin into a vision of Reconstruction based on Union victory and black liberation.

During the war's final year, the Confederates transformed the planters' Race Course, a horseracing track, and its famed Jockey Club, into a prison. Kept outdoors in the middle of the track, 257 Union soldiers died of exposure and disease and were buried in a mass grave behind the judges' stand. After the city fell, in April more than twenty black workmen reinterred the dead in marked graves. On the archway over the cemetery's entrance they painted the inscription Martyrs of the Race Course.

On May 1, 1865, ten thousand people marched around the planters' Race Course, led by three thousand children carrying roses and singing "John Brown's Body." Black women with baskets of flowers and wreaths, came next and then black men. The parade concluded with black and white Union regiments and white missionaries and teachers. At the gravesite, five black ministers read from Scripture, and a black children's choir sang "America," "We'll Rally 'Round the Flag," "The Star-Spangled

This icon will direct you to interactive activities and study materials on A People And A Nation, Brief Edition website: **www.cengage.com/history/norton/ peoplenationbrief8e**

Chronology

1865	Johnson begins rapid and lenient Reconstruction.
	Confederate leaders regain power.
	White southern governments pass restrictive black codes.
	Congress refuses to seat southern representatives.
	Thirteenth Amendment, abolishing slavery, is ratified.
1866	Congress passes the Civil Rights Act and renewal of the Freedmen's Bureau over Johnson's veto.
	Congress approves the Fourteenth Amendment.
	Most southern states reject the Fourteenth Amendment.
	In *Ex parte Milligan* the Supreme Court reasserts its influence.
1867	Congress passes the First Reconstruction Act and Tenure of Office Act.
	Seward arranges the purchase of Alaska.
	Constitutional conventions called in the southern states.
1868	House impeaches and Senate acquits Johnson.
	Most southern states readmitted to the Union under the Radical plan.
	Fourteenth Amendment is ratified.
	Grant is elected president.
1869	Congress approves the Fifteenth Amendment (ratified in 1870).
1871	Congress passes the second Enforcement Act and Ku Klux Klan Act.
	Treaty with England settles the *Alabama* claims.
1872	Amnesty Act frees almost all remaining Confederates from restrictions on holding office.
	Grant is reelected.
1873	*Slaughter-House* cases limit the power of the Fourteenth Amendment.
	Panic of 1873 leads to widespread unemployment and labor strife.
1874	Democrats win a majority in the House of Representatives.
1875	Several Grant appointees are indicted for corruption.
	Congress passes a weak Civil Rights Act.
	Democratic Party increases control of the southern states with white supremacy campaigns.
1876	*U.S. v. Cruikshank* further weakens the Fourteenth Amendment.
	Presidential election is disputed.
1877	Congress elects Hayes president.
	"Home rule" returns to three remaining southern states not yet controlled by Democrats; Reconstruction is considered over.

Banner," and Negro spirituals. When the ceremony ended, the crowd retired to the Race Course for speeches, picnics, and military festivities.

African Americans founded this Decoration Day—now Memorial Day—as a day to remember those who perished in the war. In their vision, it was the Independence Day of a Second American Revolution.

The Civil War and its aftermath wrought unprecedented changes in American society, law, and politics, but the underlying realities of economic power, racism, and judicial conservatism limited Reconstruction's revolutionary potential. The nation had to determine the nature of federal-state relations, whether confiscated land could be redistributed, and how to bring justice to freedpeople and aggrieved white southerners. Americans also had to heal psychologically from a bloody and fratricidal war. How they negotiated the relationship between healing and justice would determine the extent of change during Reconstruction.

The turmoil wrought by Reconstruction was most evident in national politics, as Lincoln's successor, Andrew Johnson, fought with Congress over Reconstruction policies. Although a southerner, Johnson disliked the South's wealthy planters, and his early moves suggested that he would be tough on "traitors." By late 1865, however, Johnson became the protector of southern interests. Jefferson Davis stayed in prison for two years, but Johnson pardoned other rebel leaders and allowed them to occupy high offices. He also ordered plantations returned to the original owners, including the abandoned coastal lands of Georgia and South Carolina on which forty thousand freed men and women settled early in 1865, by order of General William Tecumseh Sherman.

Johnson imagined a rapid restoration of the South to the Union rather than the fundamental reconstruction that Republican congressmen favored. Between 1866 and 1868, the president and the Republican leadership in Congress battled over how to put the United States back together again. Before it ended, Congress impeached the president and enfranchised freed men and gave them a role in reconstructing the South. The nation also adopted the Fourteenth and Fifteenth Amendments, ensuring equal protection of the law, citizenship, and universal manhood suffrage. But the cause of equal rights for African Americans fell almost as fast as it had risen.

By 1869 the Ku Klux Klan employed extensive violence to thwart Reconstruction and undermine black freedom. As white Democrats in the South took over state governments, they encountered little opposition. Moreover, the wartime industrial boom created new opportunities and priorities. The West, with its seemingly limitless potential and its wars against Indians, drew American resources as never before. Political corruption became a nationwide scandal, and bribery a way of doing business.

The white South's desire to reclaim control of its states and of race relations overwhelmed the national interest in stopping it. Thus Reconstruction became a revolution eclipsed, leaving legacies with which the nation has struggled ever since.

- **Should the Reconstruction era be considered the Second American Revolution? By what criteria should we make such a judgment?**
- **What were the origins and meanings of the Fourteenth Amendment in the 1860s? What is its significance today?**
- **Reconstruction is judged to have ended in 1877. Over the course of the 1870s, what caused its end?**

WARTIME RECONSTRUCTION

Reconstruction of the Union was an issue in 1863, well before the war ended. Specifically, four vexing problems compelled early thinking and would haunt the Reconstruction era. First, who would rule in the South once it was defeated? Second, who would rule in the federal government—Congress or the president? Third, what were the dimensions of black freedom, and what rights under law would freed men enjoy? And fourth, would Reconstruction be a preservation of the old republic or a second revolution, inventing a new republic?

Lincoln's 10 Percent Plan

Abraham Lincoln had never been antisouthern. His worst fear was that the war would collapse into guerrilla warfare by surviving bands of Confederates. Lincoln insisted on leniency for southern soldiers once they surrendered. In his Second Inaugural Address, delivered a month before his assassination, Lincoln promised "malice toward none; with charity for all."

Lincoln planned early for a swift and moderate Reconstruction process. In his 1863 Proclamation of Amnesty and Reconstruction, he proposed to replace majority rule with "loyal rule" to reconstruct southern state governments, and to pardon ex-Confederates except the highest-ranking military and civilian officers. Once 10 percent of a given state's voting population in the 1860 general election had taken an oath to the United States and established a government, the new state would be recognized. Lincoln did not consult Congress in these plans, and "loyal" assemblies (known as Lincoln governments) were created in Louisiana, Tennessee, and Arkansas in 1864, states largely occupied by Union troops on which they depended for survival.

Congress and the Wade-Davis Bill

Congress responded with hostility to Lincoln's moves to readmit southern states quickly. Led by Pennsylvania's Thaddeus Stevens in the House and Massachusetts's Charles Sumner in the Senate, Radical Republicans were strong proponents of emancipation and aggressive prosecution of the war and now proposed a longer and harsher Reconstruction. Stevens advocated a conquered provinces theory, arguing that southerners organized as a foreign nation to make war on the United States. They, therefore, must be treated as conquered foreign lands and returned to the status of unorganized territories before their readmission could be entertained.

In July 1864, the Wade-Davis bill, sponsored by Ohio senator Benjamin Wade and Maryland congressman Henry W. Davis, emerged from Congress with three specific conditions for southern readmission.

1. There had to be a majority of white male citizens participating in the creation of a new government.
2. To vote or be a delegate to constitutional conventions, men had to take an iron-clad oath declaring that they never aided the Confederate war effort.
3. All officers above the rank of lieutenant and all civil officials in the Confederacy would be disfranchised and deemed "not a citizen of the United States."

Lincoln pocket-vetoed the bill and issued a conciliatory proclamation that he would not be inflexibly committed to any one plan of Reconstruction.

This exchange occurred when the war's outcome and Lincoln's reelection were still in doubt. On August 5, Radical Republicans issued the "Wade-Davis Manifesto" to newspapers, accusing Lincoln of usurpation of presidential powers and disgraceful leniency toward an eventually conquered South. Lincoln saw Reconstruction as a means of weakening the Confederacy and winning the war; the Radicals saw it as a transformation of the nation's political and racial order.

Thirteenth Amendment

In early 1865, Congress and Lincoln joined in two important measures that recognized slavery's centrality to the war. On January 31, Congress passed the Thirteenth Amendment, which first, abolished involuntary servitude and second, declared that Congress shall have the power to enforce this outcome by appropriate legislation. When the measure passed by 119 to 56, just 2 votes more than the necessary two-thirds, Congress rejoiced.

The Thirteenth Amendment emerged from congressional debate and considerable petitioning and public advocacy. One of the first and most remarkable petitions for a constitutional amendment abolishing slavery was submitted in 1864 by Elizabeth Cady Stanton, Susan B. Anthony, and the Women's Loyal National League. Women throughout the Union accumulated thousands of signatures. It was a long road from the Emancipation Proclamation to the Thirteenth Amendment, through treacherous constitutional theory about individual property rights, beliefs that the sacred document (the Constitution) ought never be altered, and partisan politics.

Freedmen's Bureau

On March 3, 1865, Congress created the Bureau of Refugees, Freedmen, and Abandoned Lands—the Freedmen's Bureau, an unprecedented federal agency of social uplift. With thousands of refugees in the South, the government continued what private freed men's aid societies started in 1862. In its four-year existence, the Freedmen's Bureau supplied food and medical services, built several thousand schools and some colleges, negotiated several hundred thousand employment contracts between freed men and their former masters, and tried to manage confiscated land.

The bureau was a controversial aspect of Reconstruction. Southern whites hated it, and politicians divided over its constitutionality. Some bureau agents were devoted to freed men's rights; others exploited the chaos of the postwar South. The war prompted an eternal question of republics: what are the social welfare obligations of the state toward its people, and what do people owe their governments in return? Apart from conquest and displacement of the eastern Indians, Americans were inexperienced at the Freedmen's Bureau's task—social reform through military occupation.

Ruins and Enmity

In 1865, with the war's devastation, America was a land with ruins. Some of its cities lay in rubble; large stretches of the southern countryside were depopulated and defoliated; and thousands of people, white and black, were refugees. Many white refugees faced starvation. Of the approximately 18,300,000 rations distributed across the South in the first three years of the Freedmen's Bureau, 5,230,000 went to whites.

In October 1865, after a five-month imprisonment in Boston, former Confederate vice president Alexander H. Stephens rode a train southward. When he reached northern Georgia, his native state, he expressed shock: "War has left a terrible impression. . . . Fences gone, fields all a-waste, houses burnt." A northern journalist visiting Richmond that fall observed a city "mourning for her sins . . . in dust and ashes." Every northern traveler experienced hatred from white southerners. A North Carolina innkeeper told a journalist that Yankees killed his sons, burned his house, and stole his slaves and left him "one inestimable privilege . . . to hate 'em."

THE MEANINGS OF FREEDOM

Black southerners entered life after slavery with hope and circumspection. A Texas man recalled his father's telling him, "Our forever was going to be spent living among the Southerners, after they got licked." Often the changes freed men and women valued most were personal—alterations in employer or living arrangements.

The Armed Slave, William Sprang, oil on canvas, c. 1865. This remarkable painting depicts an African American veteran soldier, musket with fixed bayonet leaning against the wall, cigar in hand indicating a new life of safety and leisure, and reading a book to demonstrate his embrace of education and freedom. The man's visage leaves the impression of satisfaction and dignity. (Civil War Museum of Philadelphia)

The Feel of Freedom

For America's former slaves, Reconstruction meant a chance to explore freedom. Former slaves remembered singing into the night after federal troops, who confirmed rumors of their emancipation, reached their plantations. A few people gave in to the desire to do what was forbidden before. One angry grandmother dropped her hoe and confronted her mistress with, "I'm free! Ain't got to work for you no more!" Another man recalled that he and others "started on the move," either to search for family members or just to start fresh.

As slaves they learned to expect hostility from white people; they did not presume it would instantly disappear. Many freedpeople evaluated potential employers carefully. After searching for better circumstances, a majority of blacks eventually settled as agricultural workers on their former farms or plantations. But they relocated their houses and tried to control the conditions of their labor.

Reunion of African American Families

Throughout the South, former slaves focused on reuniting their families, separated during slavery by sale or hardship and during the war by dislocation and emancipation. By relying on the black community for help and by placing ads in black newspapers well into the 1880s, some succeeded, while others searched in vain.

Husbands and wives who belonged to different masters could finally establish homes together and raise their own children. When her old master claimed a right to whip her children, a mother informed him that "he warn't goin' to brush none of her chilluns no more." Freed men and women were tired of punishment.

Blacks' Search for Independence

Many black people wanted to minimize contact with whites because, as Reverend Garrison Frazier told General Sherman in January 1865, "There is a prejudice against us . . . that will take years to get over." As such, blacks abandoned slave quarters and fanned out to distant corners of the land they worked. Some described moving "across the creek" or building a "saplin house . . . back in the woods." Other rural dwellers established small, all-black settlements that still exist along the South's back roads.

Freedpeople's Desire for Land

In addition to a fair employer, freed men and women most wanted to own land, which represented self-sufficiency and compensation for generations of bondage. General Sherman's special Field Order Number 15, issued in February 1865, set aside 400,000 acres in the Sea Islands for exclusive settlement by freedpeople. Hope swelled among ex-slaves as forty-acre plots and mules were promised. But President Johnson ordered them removed in October and the land returned to its original owners under army enforcement. The U.S. government eventually sold thousands of acres in the Sea Islands, 90 percent of which went to wealthy northern investors.

Most members of both political parties opposed land redistribution to the freed men. Even northern reformers who administered the Sea Islands during the war showed little sympathy for black aspirations. The former Sea Island slaves wanted to establish small, self-sufficient farms. Northern soldiers, officials, and missionaries of both races brought education and aid to the freed men but also insisted that they grow cotton. They emphasized profit, cash crops, and competitive capitalism.

Black Embrace of Education

Blacks hungered for education that previously belonged only to whites. With freedom, they started schools, and on log seats and dirt floors, freed men and women studied in old almanacs and discarded dictionaries. Young children brought infants to school with them, and adults attended at night or after "the crops were laid by." Despite their poverty, many blacks paid tuition, typically $1 or $1.50 a month—which constituted major portions of a person's agricultural wages and totaled more than $1 million by 1870.

In its brief life, the Freedmen's Bureau founded over four thousand schools, and northern reformers established others through private philanthropy. The Yankee schoolmarm—selfless and religious—became an agent of progress in many southern communities. By 1877, more than 600,000 African Americans broke with their past by enrolling in elementary school.

Blacks and their white allies also established colleges and universities to train teachers, ministers, and future leaders. The American Missionary Association founded seven colleges, including Fisk and Atlanta Universities, between 1866 and 1869. The Freedmen's Bureau helped establish Howard University in Washington, D.C., and northern religious groups, such as the Methodists, Baptists, and Congregationalists, supported seminaries and teachers' colleges.

During Reconstruction, African American leaders were often highly educated members of the prewar elite of free people of color. Francis Cardozo, who held various offices in South Carolina, attended universities in Scotland and England. P. B. S. Pinchback, who became lieutenant governor of Louisiana, was the son of a planter who sent him to school in Cincinnati.

Growth of Black Churches

Freed from slavery's restrictions, blacks could build their own institutions. The secret churches of slavery came into the open; in communities throughout the South, ex-slaves started a *brush arbor*—a shelter with leaves for a roof, where freed men and women worshiped.

Within a few years, independent branches of the Methodist and Baptist denominations attracted most black Christians in the South. By 1877 in South Carolina, the African Methodist Episcopal (A.M.E.) Church had one thousand ministers, forty-four thousand members and a school of theology, while the A.M.E. Zion Church had forty-five thousand members. In these churches, some of which became the wealthiest and most autonomous institutions in black life, freedpeople created enduring communities.

Rise of the Sharecropping System

Since most former slaves lacked money to buy land, they preferred the next best thing: renting. But the South had few sources of credit, and few whites would rent to blacks. Consequently, black farmers and white landowners turned to sharecropping, a system in which a landlord or merchant furnished food and supplies, such as draft animals and seed, to farmers who worked the land. The owners and merchants were repaid with part of the crops. Although landowners tried to set the laborers' share at a low level, sharecroppers would resist or move from year to year. As the system matured during the 1870s and 1880s, most sharecroppers worked on *halves*—half for the owner and half for themselves.

The sharecropping system, which materialized as early as 1868, originated as a compromise between former slaves and white landowners. It eased landowners' problems with cash and credit and provided a permanent, dependent labor force; blacks accepted it because it freed them from daily supervision. But sharecropping proved to be a disaster. Owners and merchants developed a monopoly over the agricultural economy, as sharecroppers faced ever-increasing debt.

The fundamental problem was that southern farmers still concentrated on cotton. In freedom, black women often stayed away from cotton picking to concentrate on domestic chores, especially given the diminishing incentives of the cotton system. By 1878 the South recovered its prewar share of British cotton purchases. But even as southerners grew more cotton, their reward diminished. Cotton prices began a long decline, as world demand fell off.

Thus southern agriculture slipped into depression. Black sharecroppers struggled under growing debt which bound them to landowners and to furnishing merchants almost as oppressively as slavery had bound them to masters. Many white farmers gradually lost their land and became sharecroppers. By the end of Reconstruction, over one-third of all southern farms were worked by sharecropping tenants, white and black.

JOHNSON'S RECONSTRUCTION PLAN

Many people expected President Andrew Johnson's Reconstruction policies to be harsh. Throughout his career in Tennessee he criticized wealthy planters and championed small farmers. When an assassin's bullet thrust Johnson into the presidency, former slaveowners feared their treatment in Johnson's hands. When northern Radicals suggested the exile or execution of ten or twelve leading rebels, Johnson replied, "How are you going to pick out so small a number?"

Andrew Johnson of Tennessee

Like Lincoln, Johnson moved from obscurity to power. With no formal education, he became a tailor's apprentice. But from 1829, while in his twenties, he held nearly every office in Tennessee politics: alderman, state representative, congressman, two terms as governor, and U.S. senator by 1857. Although elected as a Democrat, Johnson was the only senator from a seceded state who refused to leave the Union. Lincoln appointed him war governor of Tennessee in 1862, hence his symbolic place on the ticket in the president's 1864 bid for reelection.

Although a Unionist, Johnson's political beliefs made him an old Jacksonian Democrat. Before the war, he supported tax-funded public schools and homestead legislation, fashioning himself as a champion of the common man. Johnson advocated limited government and was an ardent states' rightist. His philosophy toward Reconstruction may be summed up his slogan: "The Constitution as it is, and the Union as it was."

Through 1865 Johnson alone controlled Reconstruction policy; Congress recessed before he became president in April and did not reconvene until December. Johnson formed new state governments in the South by using his power to grant pardons and extended easy terms to former Confederates.

Johnson's Racial Views

Johnson had owned house slaves, although he was not a planter. He accepted emancipation but did not believe that black suffrage could be imposed on a southern state by the federal government; this set him on a collision course with the Radicals. Johnson was a thoroughgoing white supremacist. He declared in his annual message of 1867 that blacks possessed less "capacity for government than any other race of people. . . . Wherever they have been left to their own devices they have shown a constant tendency to relapse into barbarism."

Such racial views affected Johnson's policies. Where whites were concerned, however, Johnson proposed rules that would keep the wealthy planter class at least temporarily out of power.

Johnson's Pardon Policy

White southerners were required to swear an oath of loyalty to gain amnesty, but Johnson barred from the oath former federal officials, high-ranking Confederate officers, and political leaders or graduates of West Point or Annapolis who joined the Confederacy. He also added ex-Confederates whose taxable property was worth more than $20,000. These individuals had to apply to the president for pardon. The president, it seemed, sought revenge on the old planter elite and the promotion of a new yeomen leadership.

Johnson appointed provisional governors, who began the Reconstruction process by calling state constitutional conventions. The delegates had to draft new constitutions that eliminated slavery and invalidated secession. After ratification, new governments could be elected, and states would be restored to the Union. But only southerners who had taken the oath of amnesty and were eligible to vote on the day the state seceded could participate. Thus unpardoned whites and former slaves were ineligible.

Presidential Reconstruction

The old white leadership proved resilient; prominent Confederates won elections and turned up in appointive offices. Then Johnson started pardoning planters and leading rebels. By September 1865, hundreds of pardons were issued in one day. These pardons, plus the return of planters' abandoned lands, restored the old elite to power and made Johnson seem the South's champion.

Why did Johnson allow the planters to regain power? He may have enjoyed turning proud planters into pardon seekers. He also sought a rapid Reconstruction to deny the Radicals an opportunity for more thorough racial and political changes in the South. Plus, Johnson needed southern support in the 1866 elections; hence, he declared Reconstruction complete only eight months after Appomattox. In December 1865, many Confederate congressmen claimed seats in the U.S. Congress, including former Confederate vice president Alexander Stephens, who was now Georgia's senator-elect.

Black Codes

Furthermore, to define the status of freed men and women and control their labor, some legislatures substituted the word *freedmen* for *slaves* in the old slave codes. These new black codes compelled former slaves to carry passes, observe a curfew, and live in housing provided by a landowner. Vagrancy laws and restrictive labor contracts bound freedpeople to plantations, and antienticement laws punished anyone luring these workers to other employment. State-supported schools and orphanages excluded blacks.

It seemed to northerners that the South was intent on returning African Americans to servitude and that Johnson's Reconstruction policy held no one responsible for the war. Thus the Republican majority in Congress halted Johnson's plan, and the House and Senate did not admit newly elected southern representatives. Instead, they challenged the president's authority and established a joint committee to investigate a new direction for Reconstruction.

THE CONGRESSIONAL RECONSTRUCTION PLAN

The Constitution mentioned neither secession nor reunion, but it gave Congress the primary role in admitting states. Moreover, the Constitution declared that the United States shall guarantee to each state a "republican form of government." This provision, legislators believed, gave them the authority to devise Reconstruction policies.

The key question: What had rebellion done to the relationship between southern states and the Union? Congressmen who favored vigorous Reconstruction measures argued that the war had broken the Union and that the South was subject to the victor's will. Moderate congressmen held that states forfeited their rights through rebellion and thus came under congressional supervision.

The Radicals

Northern Democrats, weakened by their opposition to the war in its final year, denounced racial equality and supported Johnson's policies. Conservative Republicans, despite their party loyalty, favored a limited federal role in Reconstruction. Although a minority, the Radical Republicans, led by Thaddeus Stevens, Charles Sumner, and George Julian, sought to democratize the South, establish public education, and ensure freedpeople's rights. They favored black suffrage and some land confiscation and redistribution and were willing to exclude the South from the Union for years to achieve their goals.

The Radicals brought a new civic vision to American life; they wanted to create an activist federal government and the beginnings of racial equality. A large group of moderate Republicans, led by Lyman Trumbull, opposed Johnson's leniency but wanted to restrain the Radicals. They were, however, committed to federalizing the enforcement of civil, if not political, rights for the freedmen.

With the 1866 elections looming, Johnson and the Democrats sabotaged the possibility of a conservative coalition by refusing to cooperate with conservative or moderate Republicans. They insisted that Reconstruction was over, that the new state governments were legitimate, and that southern representatives should be admitted to Congress. The Radicals' influence grew with Johnson's intransigence.

Congress Versus Johnson

Republicans believed they reached a compromise with Johnson in spring 1866 in which Johnson would modify his program by extending the Freedmen's Bureau for another year and passing a civil rights bill to counteract the black codes. This would force southern courts to practice equality under scrutiny of the federal judiciary. Its

In 1866, as Congress reviewed the progress of Reconstruction, news from the South had a considerable impact. Violence against black people, like the riot in Memphis depicted here, helped convince northern legislators that they had to modify President Johnson's policies. (Library of Congress)

provisions applied to public, not private, acts of discrimination. The Civil Rights Bill of 1866 was the first statutory definition of the rights of American citizens.

Johnson, however, vetoed both bills; they became law when Congress overrode his veto. Because the civil rights bill defined U.S. citizens as native-born persons who were taxed, Johnson claimed that it discriminated against "large numbers of intelligent, worthy, and patriotic foreigners . . . in favor of the negro."

All hope of presidential-congressional cooperation was dead. In 1866 newspapers reported daily violations of blacks' rights in the South and carried alarming accounts of antiblack violence. In Memphis, forty blacks were killed and twelve schools burned by white mobs, and in New Orleans, the toll was thirty-four African Americans dead and two hundred wounded. Violence convinced Republicans and the northern public that more needed to be done. A new Republican plan focused on the Fourteenth Amendment to the Constitution.

Fourteenth Amendment

Of the five sections of the Fourteenth Amendment, the first would have the greatest legal significance. It conferred citizenship on "all persons born or naturalized in the United States" and prohibited states from abridging their constitutional "privileges and immunities" (see the appendix for the Constitution and all amendments). It also barred states from taking a person's life, liberty, or property "without due process of law" and from denying "equal protection of the laws." These phrases have become powerful guarantees of African Americans' civil rights and the rights of all citizens, except Indians, who were not granted citizenship rights until 1924.

Republicans almost universally agreed on the amendment's second and third sections. The fourth declared the Confederate debt null and void and guaranteed the United States' war debt. Northerners rejected paying taxes to reimburse those who financed a rebellion, and business groups agreed on the necessity of upholding the U.S. government's credit. The second and third sections barred Confederate leaders from holding state and federal office. Only Congress, by a two-thirds vote of each house, could remove the penalty, thereby guaranteeing some punishment for Confederate leaders.

The second section of the amendment also dealt with representation and embodied the compromises that produced the document. Northerners disagreed about whether blacks should have the right to vote. In truth, public will, North and South, lagged behind the amendment's egalitarian spirit. Many northern states still maintained black disfranchisement laws during Reconstruction.

Emancipation ended the three-fifths clause for the purpose of counting blacks, which would have increased southern representation. Thus the postwar South stood to gain power in Congress, and if white southerners did not allow blacks to vote, former secessionists would derive the political benefit from emancipation. Consequently, Republicans determined that, if a southern state did not grant black men the vote, their representation would be reduced proportionally.

The Fourteenth Amendment specified for the first time that voters were male. As such, it damaged the women's rights movement. Advocates of women's equality worked with abolitionists for decades, often subordinating their cause to the slaves'. During the drafting of the Fourteenth Amendment, however, some leaders, such as

Elizabeth Cady Stanton and Susan B. Anthony, ended their alliance with abolitionists and fought for women, infusing new life into the women's rights movement. Other women activists, however, argued that it was "the Negro's hour." Many former male abolitionists, white and black, were willing to delay woman's suffrage to secure freed men the vote.

The South's and Johnson's Defiance

Johnson tried to block the Fourteenth Amendment. He urged state legislatures in the South to vote against ratification, and all but Tennessee rejected the amendment by a wide margin.

To present his case to northerners, Johnson organized a National Union Convention. He boarded a special train for a "swing around the circle" that carried his message into the Northeast, the Midwest, and then back to Washington. Increasingly, audiences rejected his views, jeering at him. Johnson handed out American flags with thirty-six rather than twenty-five stars, declaring the Union already restored, and he labeled the Radicals traitors for attempting to take over Reconstruction.

In the 1866 elections radical and moderate Republicans whom Johnson denounced won reelection by large margins, and the Republican majority grew to two-thirds of both houses of Congress. The North had spoken clearly: Johnson's policies of states' rights and white supremacy were giving the advantage to rebels and traitors. Thus Republican congressional leaders won a mandate to pursue their Reconstruction plan.

But nothing could be accomplished as long as the Johnson governments existed and the southern electorate remained exclusively white. Republicans resolved to form new state governments in the South and enfranchise the freed men.

Reconstruction Acts of 1867–1868

After embittered debate, the First Reconstruction Act passed in March 1867. This plan, under which the southern states were readmitted to the Union, incorporated only part of the Radical program. Union generals, commanding small garrisons and charged with supervising elections, assumed control in five military districts in the South (see Map 16.1). Confederate leaders designated in the Fourteenth Amendment were barred from voting until new state constitutions were ratified and freed men were guaranteed the right to vote. In addition, each southern state was required to ratify the Fourteenth Amendment and its new constitution by majority vote and submit that constitution to Congress for approval (see Table 16.1).

The Second, Third, and Fourth Reconstruction Acts, passed between March 1867 and March 1868, provided the details for voter registration boards, the adoption of constitutions, and the administration of good faith oaths by white southerners.

Failure of Land Redistribution

The Radicals halted Johnson, but they had hoped Congress could do much more. Thaddeus Stevens, for example, argued that economic opportunity was essential to the freedmen. He drew up a plan for extensive confiscation and redistribution of land, but it was never realized.

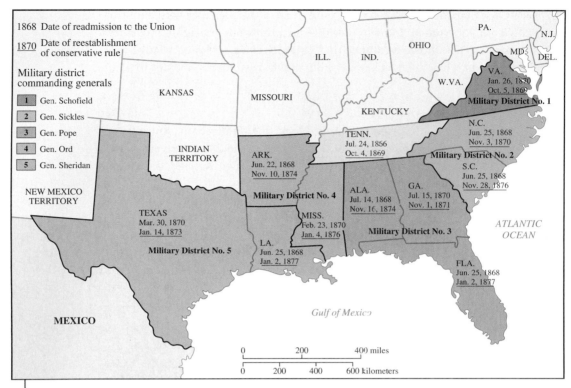

Map 16.1 The Reconstruction

This map shows the five military districts established when Congress passed the Reconstruction Act of 1867. As the dates within each state indicate, conservative Democratic forces quickly regained control of government in four southern states. So-called Radical Reconstruction was curtailed in most of the others, as factions within the weakened Republican Party began to cooperate with conservative Democrats.

TABLE 16.1 Plans for Reconstruction Compared

	Johnson's Plan	Radicals' Plan	Fourteenth Amendment	Reconstruction Act of 1867
Voting	Whites only can vote; high-ranking Confederate leaders must seek pardons.	Give vote to black males.	Southern whites may decide but can lose representation if they deny black suffrage.	Black men gain vote; whites barred from office by Fourteenth Amendment cannot vote while new state governments are being formed.
Officeholding	Many prominent Confederates regain power.	Only loyal white and black males are eligible.	Confederate leaders barred until Congress votes amnesty.	Fourteenth Amendment in effect.
Time Out of Union	Brief.	Several years; until South is thoroughly democratized.	Brief.	3–5 years after war.
Other Change in Southern Society	Little; gain of power by yeomen not realized; emancipation grudgingly accepted, but no black civil or political rights.	Expand public education; confiscate land and provide farms for freedmen; expansion of activist federal government.	Probably slight, depending on enforcement.	Considerable, depending on action of new state governments.

Racial fears and an American obsession with the sanctity of private property made land redistribution unpopular. Thus black farmers were forced to seek work in a hostile environment in which landowners opposed their acquisition of land.

Constitutional Crisis

To restrict Johnson's influence and safeguard its plan, Congress passed several controversial laws. First, it limited Johnson's power over the army by requiring the president to issue military orders through the general of the army, Ulysses S. Grant. Then Congress passed the Tenure of Office Act, which gave the Senate power to approve changes in the president's cabinet. Designed to protect Secretary of War Stanton, a Radical sympathizer, this law violated the tradition of presidents controlling cabinet appointments. All of these measures, along with the Reconstruction Acts, were passed by a two-thirds override of presidential vetoes.

In response, Johnson limited the power of military commanders in the South and increased the powers of the civil governments he created in 1865. Then he removed military officers who were enforcing Congress's new law, preferring commanders who allowed disqualified Confederates to vote. Finally, he tried to remove Secretary of War Stanton, pushing the confrontation to its climax

Impeachment of President Johnson

Impeachment is a political procedure provided for in the Constitution as a remedy for crimes or serious abuses of power by presidents, federal judges, and other high government officials. Those who are impeached (judged or politically indicted) in the House are then tried in the Senate. Twice in 1867, the House Judiciary Committee considered impeachment of Johnson, first rejecting it and then recommending it by a 5-to-4 vote, which was defeated by the House. After Johnson tried to remove Stanton, however, a third attempt to impeach him carried in early 1868. The indictment concentrated on his violation of the Tenure of Office Act, though modern scholars regard his efforts to obstruct enforcement of the Reconstruction Act of 1867 as a more serious offense.

Johnson's trial in the Senate lasted more than three months. The prosecution, led by Radicals, attempted to prove that Johnson was guilty of "high crimes and misdemeanors." But they also argued that the trial was a means to judge Johnson's performance. The Senate rejected such reasoning, which could have made removal from office a political weapon against any chief executive who disagreed with Congress. The prosecution fell one vote short of the necessary two-thirds majority needed to convict Johnson. He remained in office, politically weakened.

Election of 1868

In the 1868 presidential election, Ulysses S. Grant, running as a Republican, defeated Horatio Seymour, a New York Democrat. Grant was not a Radical, but his platform supported congressional Reconstruction and endorsed black suffrage in the South. (Significantly, Republicans stopped short of endorsing black suffrage in the North.) The Democrats denounced Reconstruction and preached white supremacy, conducting the most openly racist campaign in American history. Both

A Republican Party brass band in action during the 1868 election campaign in Baton Rouge, Louisiana. The Union regimental colors and soldiers' caps demonstrate the strong federal presence in the South at this pivotal moment in radical Reconstruction.
(Andrew D. Lytle Collection, Louisiana and Lower Mississippi Valley Collections, LSU Libraries, Louisiana State University, Baton Rouge, Louisiana)

sides waved the "bloody shirt," blaming each other for the war's sacrifices. By associating with rebellion and Johnson's repudiated program, the Democrats were defeated in all but eight states, though the popular vote was close. Blacks voted en masse for General Grant.

In office Grant vacillated in dealing with the southern states, sometimes defending Republican regimes and sometimes currying favor with Democrats. Occasionally Grant called out federal troops to stop violence or enforce Congressional acts, but he never imposed a military occupation on the South. Rapid demobilization reduced a federal army of more than 1 million to fifty-seven thousand within a year of the surrender at Appomattox. Thereafter, the number of troops in the South declined until in 1874 there were only four thousand in southern states outside Texas. The legend of military rule, so important to southern claims of victimization during Reconstruction, was steeped in myth.

Fifteenth Amendment In 1869 the Radicals pushed through the Fifteenth Amendment, the final major measure in Reconstruction's constitutional revolution. It forbade states to deny the right to vote "on account of race, color, or previous condition of servitude." Such wording did not guarantee the right to vote and left states free to restrict suffrage on other grounds. Northern states could deny suffrage to women and certain men— Chinese immigrants, illiterates, and those too poor to pay poll taxes. With passage of the Fifteenth Amendment in 1870, many Americans, especially northerners, considered Reconstruction completed.

RECONSTRUCTION POLITICS AND ECONOMY IN THE SOUTH

From the start, white southerners resisted Reconstruction and opposed emancipation, as evident in the black codes. The former planter class proved especially unbending because of their tremendous financial loss in slaves. For many poor whites who never owned slaves, destitution, plummeting agricultural prices, disease, and the uncertainties of a growing urban industrialization drove them off land, toward cities, and into hatred of black equality.

White Resistance Some planters attempted to postpone freedom by denying or misrepresenting events. Former slaves reported that their owners didn't tell them it was freedom or wouldn't let them go. To hold onto their workers, some landowners claimed control over black children and used guardianship and apprentice laws to bind black families to the plantation. While a few planters divided up plots among their slaves, most condemned the notion of blacks as landowners.

Adamant resistance by whites soon manifested itself in other ways, including violence. A local North Carolina magistrate clubbed a black man on a public street, and in several states bands of Regulators terrorized blacks who displayed any independence. After President Johnson encouraged the South to resist congressional Reconstruction, many white conservatives captured the new state governments, while others boycotted the polls to defeat Congress's plans.

Black Voters and the Southern Republican Party Enthusiastically blacks went to the polls, voting Republican, as one man said, to "stick to the end with the party that freed me." Illiteracy did not keep them (or uneducated whites) from making intelligent choices. Mississippi's William Henry could read only "a little," but he said, "We saw D. Sledge vote; he owned half the county. We knowed he voted Democratic so we voted the other ticket so it would be Republican." Women, who could not vote, encouraged husbands and sons, and preachers exhorted congregations to use the franchise.

Thanks to a large black turnout and the restrictions on prominent Confederates, a new southern Republican Party came to power in the 1868–1870 constitutional conventions. Republican delegates consisted of a sizable black contingent (265 of the more than 1,000 delegates throughout the South), northerners who moved to the South, and native southern whites seeking change. The new constitutions they drafted were more democratic than anything previously adopted in the South. They eliminated property qualifications for voting and holding office, turned many appointed offices into elective posts, and provided for public schools and institutions to care for the mentally ill, the blind, the deaf, the destitute, and the orphaned.

The conventions broadened women's rights in property holding and divorce. Usually the goal was not equality but providing relief to thousands of suffering debtors. Since husbands usually contracted the debts, giving women legal control over their own property provided some protection for their families.

Triumph of Republican Governments

Under these new constitutions, southern states elected Republican-controlled governments. For the first time, state legislators in 1868 included black southerners. Contrary to what white southerners later claimed, Republican state governments did not disfranchise ex-Confederates as a group. James Lynch, a leading black politician from Mississippi, saw disfranchising whites as foolish. Landless former slaves "must be in friendly relations with the great body of the whites in the state," he explained. "Otherwise . . . peace can be maintained only by a standing army." Despised and lacking power, southern Republicans strove for safe ways to gain a foothold in a depressed economy.

Far from being vindictive toward the race that enslaved them, most southern blacks appealed to whites to be fair. Hence, the South's Republican Party condemned itself to defeat if white voters would not cooperate. Within a few years most fledgling Republican parties in the southern states would be struggling for survival against violent white hostility.

Industrialization and Mill Towns

Reconstruction governments promoted industry via loans, subsidies, and short-term exemptions from taxation. The southern railroad system was rebuilt and expanded, and coal and iron mining made possible Birmingham's steel plants. Between 1860 and 1880, the number of manufacturing establishments in the South nearly doubled.

This emphasis on big business, however, produced higher state debts and taxes, drew money away from schools and other programs, and multiplied possibilities for corruption. The alliance between business and government often operated at the expense of farmers and laborers. It also doomed Republicans to failure in building support among poorer whites.

Poverty remained the lot of many southern whites. The war caused a massive loss of income-producing wealth, such as livestock, and a steep decline in land values. From 1860 to 1880, the South's share of per capita income fell to 51 percent of the national average. In many regions the old planter class still had the best land and access to credit or markets.

As poor whites and blacks found farming less tenable, they moved to cities and mill towns. Industrialization did not sweep the South as it did the North, but it laid deep roots. Attracting textile mills to southern towns became a competitive crusade. In 1860 the South counted some 10,000 mill workers; by 1880, the number grew to 16,741; and by century's end to 97,559. Many poor southerners moved from farmer to mill worker or other low-income urban wage earner job.

Republicans and Racial Equality

Whites who controlled the southern Republican Party were reluctant to allow blacks a share of offices proportionate to their electoral strength. Aware of their weakness, black leaders did not push hard for revolutionary change. Instead, they led efforts to establish public schools, though without pressing for integrated facilities. In 1870 South Carolina passed the first comprehensive school law in the South. By 1875, 50 percent of that state's black school-age children were enrolled in school, and approximately one-third of the three thousand teachers were black.

Those African American politicians who did fight for civil rights and integration were typically from cities such as New Orleans or Mobile, where large populations of light-skinned free blacks existed before the war. Their experience made them sensitive to issues of status. Laws requiring equal accommodations were passed but often went unenforced.

Economic progress, particularly land ownership, was a major concern for most freedpeople. Land reform failed because in most states whites were the majority, and former slaveowners controlled the best land and financial resources. Much land did fall into state hands for nonpayment of taxes and was sold in small lots. But most freedmen had too little cash to bid against investors or speculators. Any widespread redistribution of land had to arise from Congress, which never supported such action.

Myth of Negro Rule

Within a few years, white hostility to congressional Reconstruction increasingly prevailed. Conservatives who long wanted to fight Reconstruction through economic pressure and racist propaganda began to do so. Charging that the South had been turned over to ignorant blacks, conservatives used black domination as a rallying cry for a return to white supremacy.

Such attacks were part of the growing myth of Negro rule, which would become a central theme in battles over the memory of Reconstruction. African Americans participated in politics but hardly dominated. They were a majority in only two of ten state constitutional conventions. In the state legislatures, only in South Carolina's lower house did blacks constitute a majority. Sixteen blacks won seats in Congress before Reconstruction was over. Only eighteen served in a high state office, such as lieutenant governor, treasurer, superintendent of education, or secretary of state, but none became governor.

Some four hundred blacks served in political office during the Reconstruction era, an enormous achievement. Elected officials, such as Robert Smalls in South Carolina, labored for cheaper land prices, better healthcare, access to schools, and the enforcement of civil rights. In this way, the black politicians of Reconstruction took heroic first steps in America's long civil rights movement.

www.cengage.com/history/norton/peoplenationbrief8e

Carpetbaggers and Scalawags

Conservative propaganda also assailed the allies of black Republicans. They denounced northern whites as *carpetbaggers*, greedy crooks planning to pour stolen tax revenues into their luggage made of carpet material.

In fact, most northerners who settled in the South had come seeking business opportunities, as schoolteachers, or to find a warmer climate; most never entered politics. Those who did generally wanted to democratize the South and introduce northern ways, such as industry and public education.

In addition to tagging northern interlopers as carpetbaggers, conservatives invented the term *scalawag* to discredit native white southerners cooperating with the Republicans, as many, including wealthy men, did. Most scalawags were yeoman farmers from mountain areas and nonslaveholding districts who were Unionists under the Confederacy. They hoped to benefit from the education and opportunities Republicans promoted. Sometimes joining with freed men, they pursued common class interests to make headway against long-dominant planters. Initially promising, over time most of these black-white coalitions floundered due to racism.

Tax Policy and Corruption as Political Wedges

Republicans wanted to repair the war's destruction, stimulate industry, and support such new ventures as public schools, all of which required tax monies. But the Civil War damaged the South's tax base. Hundreds of thousands of citizens lost much of their property—slaves, money, livestock, and buildings—to the war. Tax increases (sales, excise, and property) were necessary for even traditional services. Inevitably, Republican tax policies aroused strong opposition, especially among yeomen.

Corruption charges also plagued Republicans. Many carpetbaggers and black politicians engaged in fraudulent schemes or sold their votes, participating in what scholars recognize as a nationwide corruption surge in an age ruled by spoilsmen. Corruption crossed party lines, but the Democrats pinned the blame on unqualified blacks and greedy carpetbaggers among southern Republicans.

Ku Klux Klan

Republican leaders also allowed factionalism along racial and class lines to undermine party unity. At the same time, the Ku Klux Klan, a secret veterans' club that began in Tennessee in 1866, spread through the South, quickly becoming a terrorist organization. Klansmen sought to frustrate Reconstruction and keep the freed men in subjection with ongoing nighttime harassment, whippings, beatings, rapes, and murders.

Although the Klan tormented blacks, its main purpose was political. Lawless nightriders targeted active Republicans, killing leading whites and blacks in several states. After freed men who worked for a South Carolina scalawag started voting, terrorists visited the plantation and, as one victim noted, "whipped every . . . [black] man they could lay their hands on." Klansmen also attacked Union League clubs—Republican organizations that mobilized the black vote—and schoolteachers who aided freed men.

Specific social forces shaped and directed Klan violence, with Alamance and Caswell Counties in North Carolina receiving the worst of it. Slim Republican majorities there rested on cooperation between black voters and white yeomen. Together, these black and white Republicans ousted long-entrenched officials. The wealthy and powerful men who lost their accustomed political control were the Klan's county officers and local chieftains. By intimidation and murder, the Klan weakened the Republican coalition and restored a Democratic majority.

Klan violence injured Republicans across the South. One of every ten black delegates to the 1867–1868 state constitutional conventions was attacked, seven fatally. In one judicial district of North Carolina, the Ku Klux Klan was responsible for twelve murders, over seven hundred beatings along with many cases of rape and arson. A single attack on Republicans in Eutaw, Alabama, left four blacks dead and fifty-four wounded. According to historian Eric Foner, the Klan "made it virtually impossible for Republicans to campaign or vote in large parts of Georgia."

Thus Republican mistakes, racial hostility, and terror brought down the Republican regimes. In most states, Radical Reconstruction lasted only a few years (see Map 16.1). The most enduring failure of Reconstruction, however, was that it did not alter the South's social structure or its distribution of wealth and power.

RETREAT FROM RECONSTRUCTION

During the 1870s, northerners lost the political will to sustain Reconstruction, as they confronted vast economic and social transformations in their region and the West. Radical Republicans like Albion Tourgée, a former Union soldier who moved to North Carolina and was elected a judge, condemned Congress's timidity. He and many African Americans believed that, during Reconstruction, the North "threw all the Negroes on the world without any way of getting along." As the North lost interest in the South's dilemmas, Reconstruction collapsed.

Political Implications of Klan Terrorism

Whites in the old Confederacy referred to this decline of Reconstruction as southern redemption. During the 1870s, "redeemer" Democrats claimed to be the South's saviors from alleged black domination and carpetbag rule, as the party regained control of the South.

Meanwhile, in 1870 and 1871 the Ku Klux Klan's violent campaigns forced Congress to pass two Enforcement Acts and an anti-Klan law. These laws made actions by individuals against the civil and political rights of others a federal criminal offense. They also provided for election supervisors and permitted martial law and suspension of the writ of habeas corpus to combat murders, beatings, and Klan threats. In 1872 and 1873, Mississippi and the Carolinas saw many prosecutions; but in other states, the laws were ignored. Southern juries sometimes refused to convict Klansmen; less than half of the 3,310 cases ended in convictions. Although many Klansmen fled their state to avoid prosecution, and the Klan officially disbanded, paramilitary organizations known as Rifle Clubs and Red Shirts often took the Klan's place.

Still, there were ominous signs that the North's commitment to racial justice was fading, as some influential Republicans opposed the anti-Klan laws. Rejecting other Republicans' arguments that the Thirteenth, Fourteenth, and Fifteenth Amendments made the federal government the protector of citizens' rights, dissenters charged that Congress was infringing on states' rights. This foreshadowed a general revolt within Republican ranks in 1872.

Industrial Expansion and Reconstruction in the North

Immigration and industrialization surged in the North. Between 1865 and 1873, 3 million immigrants entered the country, most settling in the industrial cities of the North and West. In that eight-year period, industrial production increased by 75 percent. For the first time, nonagricultural workers outnumbered farmers, and wage earners outnumbered independent craftsmen. Government policies encouraged this rapid growth, as low taxes on investment and high tariffs on manufactured goods helped create a new class of powerful industrialists, especially railroad entrepreneurs.

From 1865 to 1873, 35,000 miles of new track were laid; this fueled the banking industry and made Wall Street the center of American capitalism. Eastern railroad magnates, such as Thomas Scott of the Pennsylvania Railroad, created economic empires with the assistance of huge government subsidies of cash and land. Railroad corporations also bought up mining operations, granaries, and lumber companies. Big business now employed lobbyists to curry favor with government. Corruption ran rampant, with some congressmen and legislators paid retainers of major companies.

As captains of industry amassed unprecedented fortunes, gross economic inequality polarized American society. The workforce, worried a prominent Massachusetts business leader, was in a "transition state . . . living in boarding houses" and becoming a "permanent factory population." In New York and Philadelphia, workers increasingly lived in unhealthy tenement housing. Thousands would list themselves on the census as common laborer or general jobber. Concerned, in 1868 Republicans passed an eight-hour workday bill that applied to federal workers. The labor question (see Chapter 18) now preoccupied northerners far more than the southern or the freed men question.

Then the Panic of 1873 ushered in over five years of economic contraction. Three million people lost their jobs, especially in cities. Workers and farmers desperately needed cash and sought easy-money policies to spur economic expansion. Businessmen, disturbed by the strikes and industrial violence that accompanied the panic, defended property rights and demanded sound money policies. The chasm between wealthy industrialists and farmers and workers widened.

Liberal Republican Revolt

Disenchanted with Reconstruction, a largely northern group calling itself the Liberal Republicans bolted the party in 1872 and nominated Horace Greeley, editor of the New York Tribune, for president. A varied group, Liberal Republicans included foes of corruption and advocates of a lower tariff. Two popular and widespread issues united them: distaste for federal intervention in the South and an elitist desire to let market forces and the "best men" determine policy.

The Grants' Tour of the World

On May 17, 1877, two weeks after his presidency ended, Ulysses S. Grant and his wife Julia embarked from Philadelphia on a twenty-six month world tour. Portrayed as a private vacation, the trip was meant to help dissipate the taint of corruption in Grant's second term. The small entourage included John Russell Young, a reporter for the *New York Herald* who recorded the journey in the two-volume, illustrated *Around the World with General Grant.*

The Grants spent months in England attending an array of banquets, one with Queen Victoria. In Newcastle, thousands of workingmen conducted a massive parade in Grant's honor. Grant was viewed as the savior of the American nation, the liberator of slaves, and a celebrity.

Every royal or republican head of a European state hosted the Grants, including the heads of state of Belgium, France, Switzerland, Italy, Russia, Poland, Austria and Spain. The Grants next went to Egypt and then traveled by train to the Indian Ocean, where they embarked for India. They encountered British imperialism in Bombay, and that of the French in Saigon. The grand excursion went to China and Japan. The Grants enjoyed a rare audience with Japan's Emperor Mutsuhito and found Japan "beautiful beyond description."

The Grants landed in San Francisco in late June 1879. The reason for the prolonged trip: Grant sought publicity abroad to convince his countrymen back home that they should reelect him president in 1880. But he developed no compelling reason why Americans should choose him again. He spent his final years a war hero and a national symbol. No American president would again establish such personal links to the world until Woodrow Wilson after World War I.

On their tour of the world, Ulysses and Julia Grant sat with companions and guides in front of the Great Hypostyle Hall at the Temple of Amon-Ra in Karnak at Luxor, Egypt, 1878. The Grants' extraordinary tour included many such photo opportunities, often depicting the plebeian American president's presence in exotic places with unusual people. Whether he liked it or not, Grant was a world celebrity. (Library of Congress)

The Democrats also nominated Greeley in 1372, but it was not enough to keep Grant from reelection. Greeley's campaign for North-South reunion was a harbinger of the future in American politics. Organized Blue-Gray fraternalism (gatherings of Union and Confederate veterans) began as early as 1874. Grant continued to avoid confrontation with white southerners and in 1875 refused a desperate request from Mississippi's governor for troops to quell racial and political terrorism there.

Grant made several poor appointments that fueled public dissatisfaction with his administration. His secretary of war, his private secretary, and officials in the Treasury and Navy Departments were involved in bribery or tax-cheating scandals. Instead of exposing the corruption, Grant defended the culprits. In 1874, the Democrats recaptured the House of Representatives, signaling the end of the Radical Republican vision of Reconstruction.

General Amnesty

Democratic gains in Congress weakened legislative resolve on southern issues. Congress already lifted the political disabilities of the Fourteenth Amendment from many former Confederates. In 1872 it adopted an Amnesty Act, which pardoned most of the remaining rebels. In 1875 Congress passed a Civil Rights Act, partly in tribute to the recently deceased Charles Sumner, purporting to guarantee black people equal accommodations in public places, but the bill was watered down and contained no enforcement provisions. (The Supreme Court later struck down this law;)

Democrats regained control of four state governments before 1872 and eight by late January 1876 (see Map 16.1). In the North, Democrats successfully stressed the failure and scandals of Reconstruction governments. Sectional reconciliation now seemed crucial for commerce. The nation was expanding westward, and the South was a new investment frontier.

The West, Race, and Reconstruction

As the Fourteenth Amendment and other enactments granted blacks the beginnings of citizenship, other nonwhites faced continued persecution. Across the West, the federal government pursued a containment policy against Native Americans. In California, where white farmers and ranchers often forced Indians into captive labor, some civilians practiced Indian hunting. By 1880, thirty years of violence left an estimated forty-five hundred California Indians dead at the hands of white settlers.

In California and other states of the Far West, few whites objected to the Chinese immigrants who did the dangerous work of building railroads through the Rocky Mountains. But when the Chinese competed for urban, industrial jobs, conflict erupted. Anticoolie clubs appeared in California in the 1870s seeking laws against Chinese labor, inciting racism, and organizing brutal attacks on Chinese workers and the factories that employed them. Western politicians sought white votes by pandering to prejudice, and in 1879 the new California constitution denied Chinese the vote.

Viewing America from coast to coast, the Civil War and Reconstruction years dismantled racial slavery and fostered a volatile new racial complexity, especially in the West. Some African Americans, despite generations of mixture with Native Americans, asserted that they were more like whites than uncivilized Indians, while others, like the Creek freed men of Indian Territory, sought an Indian identity. In Texas, whites, Indians, blacks, and Hispanics had mixed for decades, and by the 1870s forced reconsideration in law and custom of who exactly who was white.

America was undergoing what one historian has called a reconstruction of the concept of race itself. The turbulence of the expanding West reinforced the new nationalism and the reconciliation of North and South based on a resurgent white supremacy.

Foreign Expansion

In 1867 new expansion pressures led Secretary of State William H. Seward to purchase Alaska from Russia, adding vast new territory to the United States (see Chapter 22). Opponents ridiculed Seward's $7.2 million venture, but Seward convinced important congressmen of Alaska's economic potential, and other lawmakers favored the dawning of friendship with Russia.

Also in 1867 the United States took control of the Midway Islands, a thousand miles northwest of Hawai'i. Through diplomacy, Seward and his successor, Hamilton Fish, resolved wartime grievances with Great Britain by arranging a financial settlement for damage done by the *Alabama* and other cruisers built in England and sold to the Confederacy. Sectional reconciliation in Reconstruction America would serve new ambitions for world commerce and expansion.

Judicial Retreat from Reconstruction

Meanwhile, the Supreme Court played its part in the northern retreat from Reconstruction. During the Civil War, the Court was cautious and inactive. Reaction to the *Dred Scott* decision (1857) was so vehement and the Union's wartime emergency so great, that the Court had avoided interference with government actions. But that changed in 1866 when *Ex parte Milligan* reached the Court.

Lambdin P. Milligan of Indiana plotted to free Confederate prisoners of war and overthrow state governments. Consequently, a military court sentenced Milligan, a civilian, to death. Milligan challenged the military tribunal's authority, claiming he was entitled to a civil trial. The Supreme Court declared that military trials were illegal when civil courts were functioning. It seemed the Court intended to reassert its authority.

In the 1870s the Court renewed its challenge to Congress's actions when it narrowed the meaning of the Fourteenth Amendment. The *Slaughter-House* cases (1873) began in 1869, when the Louisiana legislature granted one company a monopoly on livestock slaughtering in New Orleans. Rival butchers sued, and their attorney, former Supreme Court justice John A. Campbell, argued that Louisiana violated the rights of some citizens in favor of others. The Fourteenth Amendment, Campbell contended, had brought individual rights under federal protection.

But in the *Slaughter-House* decision, the Supreme Court dealt a blow to the scope of the Fourteenth Amendment. It declared state citizenship and national citizenship separate. National citizenship involved only matters such as the right to travel freely from state to state, and only such narrow rights, held the Court, were protected by the Fourteenth Amendment.

Shrinking from a role as "perpetual censor upon all legislation of the States, on the civil rights of their own citizens," the Court's majority declared that the framers of the recent amendments had not intended to "destroy" the federal system, in which the states exercised "powers for domestic and local government, including the regulation of civil rights." Thus the justices severely limited the amendment's potential for safeguarding the rights of black citizens—its original intent.

The next day the Court decided *Bradwell v. Illinois,* a case in which Myra Bradwell, a female attorney, was denied the right to practice law in Illinois because she was married woman, and hence not a free agent. Using the Fourteenth Amendment, Bradwell's attorneys contended that the state had unconstitutionally abridged her "privileges and immunities" as a citizen. The Supreme Court disagreed, declaring it was a woman's "paramount destiny . . . to fulfill the noble and benign offices of wife and mother."

In 1876 the Court further weakened the Reconstruction era amendments. In *U.S. v. Cruikshank* the Court overruled the conviction under the 1870 Enforcement Act of Louisiana whites who attacked a meeting of blacks and conspired to deprive them of their rights. The justices ruled that the Fourteenth Amendment did not give the federal government power to act against these whites. The duty of protecting citizens' equal rights, the Court said, "rests alone with the States." Such judicial conservatism blunted the revolutionary potential in the Civil War amendments into the next century.

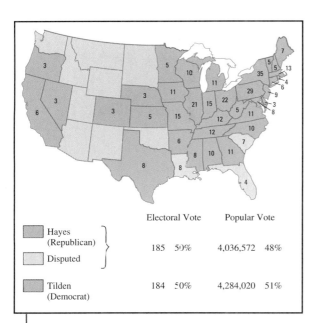

	Electoral Vote	Popular Vote
Hayes (Republican)	185 50%	4,036,572 48%
Disputed		
Tilden (Democrat)	184 50%	4,284,020 51%

Map 16.2   Presidential Election of 1876 and the Compromise of 1877

In 1876 a combination of solid southern support and Democratic gains in the North gave Samuel Tilden the majority of popular votes, but Rutherford B. Hayes won the disputed election in the electoral college, after a deal satisfied Democratic wishes for an end to Reconstruction.

Disputed Election of 1876 and Compromise of 1877

The results of the disputed presidential election of 1876 confirmed that economic issues predominated and that the North was no longer pursuing the goals of reconstruction. Samuel J. Tilden, the Democratic governor of New York, ran strongly in the South and needed one electoral vote to triumph over Rutherford B. Hayes, the Republican nominee. Nineteen electoral votes from Louisiana, South Carolina, and Florida (the only southern states not yet under Democratic rule) were disputed; both Democrats and Republicans claimed to have won those states despite fraud committed by their opponents (see Map 16.2).

To resolve this unprecedented situation, Congress established a fifteen-member electoral commission, balanced between Democrats and Republicans. Because Republicans held the majority in Congress, they prevailed, 8 to 7, on every attempt to count the returns. Hayes would become president if Congress accepted the commission's findings.

But Democrats controlled the House and could filibuster to block action on the vote. Many citizens worried about another civil war, as some southerners vowed "Tilden or Fight!" Finally, Democrats acquiesced in the election of Hayes based on a deal cut between Hayes's supporters and southerners who wanted federal aid to railroads, internal improvements, and removal of troops from southern states. Northern and southern Democrats simply decided not to contest the election of a Republican who was not going to continue Reconstruction.

Southern Democrats rejoiced that Reconstruction was over, but African Americans grieved over the betrayal of their hopes for equality. In a Fourth of July speech in Washington, D.C., in 1875, Frederick Douglass looked back on fifteen years of unparalleled change for his people and worried about the hold of white supremacy on America's historical memory: "If war among the whites brought peace and liberty to the blacks, what will peace among the whites bring?"

Summary

Reconstruction was an era of tragic aspirations and failures but also of unprecedented legal, political, and social change. The Union victory brought increased federal power, stronger nationalism, sweeping federal intervention in the southern states, and landmark constitutional amendments. But northern commitment to make these changes eroded, leaving the revolution unfinished. The early promise for new lives and liberties among freedpeople had fallen, at least temporarily, by the wayside.

The North had embraced emancipation, black suffrage, and constitutional alterations strengthening the central government, primarily to defeat the rebellion. As wartime pressures declined, Americans, especially northerners, retreated from Reconstruction. The American people and the courts maintained a preference for state authority and a distrust of federal power, while free-labor ideology stressed respect for property and individual self-reliance. Racism transformed into Klan terror and theories of black degeneration.

New challenges to American society gradually overwhelmed the aims of Reconstruction. Industrialization promised prosperity but also wrought increased exploitation of labor. Moreover, industry laid the foundation for an enlarged American role in international affairs.

In the wake of the Civil War, Americans faced two profound tasks—healing and dispensing justice. Making sectional reunion compatible with black freedom and equality overwhelmed American politics, and the nation faced much of this dilemma more than a century later.

The Lost Cause

All major wars compel a struggle over their memory. After the Civil War, white southerners and their northern allies constructed a Lost Cause tradition, a potent and racially exclusive version of the war and Reconstruction which persists today.

The Lost Cause emerged among ex-Confederates as a mourning ritual and a psychological response to the trauma of defeat. But it also took root in selective reinterpretations of the war's causes; southern resistance to Reconstruction; doctrines of white supremacy; and a mythic, nostalgic popular culture among northerners and southerners. Lost Cause advocates—from high-ranking officers to common soldiers—argued that the war had never been about slavery, that Confederates only lost to Yankee numbers and resources, and that the nation should reconcile by equally honoring southern and northern sacrifice. In the industrial, urban, multiethnic America of the emerging twentieth century, images of benevolent Southern masters and faithful slaves and of Robert E. Lee as America's truest Christian soldier provided a sentimentalized road to reunion. These images reverberated in Jim Crow America, and they endure in modern tastes for Civil War memorabilia and uses of the Confederate flag to oppose civil rights and affirmative action.

From 1865 to the 1880s, this Confederate legend was forged by wartime participants determined to vindicate the Confederacy. By the 1890s, however, Lost Cause culture emerged especially with the United Daughters of the Confederacy. Elite southern white women built monuments, lobbied congressmen, delivered lectures, ran contests for schoolchildren, and strove to control the content of history textbooks in the service of an exalted South. Above all, Lost Causers advocated what one historian has called a "victory narrative." This new victory was the nation's triumph over the racial revolution and constitutional transformations of Reconstruction.

In his 1881 memoir, Jefferson Davis declared the Lost Cause not lost: "Well may we rejoice in the regained possession of self-government. . . . This is the great victory . . . a total non-interference by the Federal government in the domestic affairs of the States."

Chapter Review

WARTIME RECONSTRUCTION

Which two political acts recognized the centrality of slavery to the war?

Passage of the Thirteenth Amendment and establishment of the Freedmen's Bureau in early 1865 sent a clear signal that slavery was a major cause for the Civil War. The Thirteenth Amendment first abolished slavery ("involuntary servitude") and second gave Congress the power to enforce it. Then, a few months later in March, Congress established the Bureau of Refugees, Freedmen and Abandoned Lands, known as the Freedmen's Bureau, to help former slaves. During its four years as a federal agency, it supplied food and medical services, built thousands of schools and colleges, negotiated job contracts between former slaves and masters, and managed confiscated lands.

THE MEANINGS OF FREEDOM

How did blacks exert their newfound freedom?

With emancipation, former slaves sought to reunite families broken apart through slave sales. Community also became important, as they built their own churches that ultimately served to unify racial ties. Seeking greater control over their work lives, African Americans wanted fairer employers and hoped to own land; when that was not possible, they rented land from former masters under the sharecropping system, in which they paid for supplies and rent by giving owners' half their crops on average. Former slaves also embraced the education that had been denied them under slavery and started schools, colleges, and universities throughout the South or attended those launched by the Freedman's Bureau.

JOHNSON'S RECONSTRUCTION PLAN

What was Johnson's vision for Reconstruction?

Johnson's approach to Reconstruction could be summed up in a single quote: "The Constitution as it is, and the Union as it was." As president, he controlled Reconstruction policy through 1865, pardoning former Confederates and reestablishing state governments in the South. Despising the planter class, he initially insisted that ex-Confederates with property worth more than $20,000 apply directly to him for pardons. Gradually, Johnson pardoned planters, too, which restored the former elite to power, possibly because he wanted to block Radical Republicans from implementing extensive and racial political changes in the South. Deeply racist, Johnson remained silent when southern states implemented black codes to restrict former slaves' freedom by requiring them to carry passes, obey curfew laws, and live in housing provided by a landowner. Nonetheless, after just eight months, Johnson declared Reconstruction was completed.

THE CONGRESSIONAL RECONSTRUCTION PLAN

What made Radical Reconstruction different from Johnson's plan?

Radical Republicans in Congress were upset at Johnson's moderate approach, which seemed to hold no one responsible for the war and re-established racial hierarchies and the southern elite. Initially a minority, the Radicals' popularity grew as Johnson increasingly dug in his heels. Radicals wanted to democratize the South through black suffrage, civil rights, and land confiscation and redistribution. They secured passage of the Fourteenth Amendment, which conferred citizenship on "all persons born or naturalized in the United States," and granted voting rights to males. They also passed four strident Reconstruction acts with strict and detailed plans for readmitting southern states to the Union. They barred ex-Confederates from voting until freedmen could and outlined the rules for voter registration boards and the adoption of state constitutions. Unpopular, land redistribution never materialized, but in 1869, Radicals pushed through their final measure, the Fifteenth Amendment, which prohibited states from denying the vote based on "race, color, or previous condition of servitude."

RECONSTRUCTION POLITICS AND ECONOMY IN THE SOUTH

How did black voters in the early days of Reconstruction transform the South?

With a large black voter turnout and prominent confederates barred from the polls and political positions, a new southern variant on the Republican Party came to power during the 1868 to 1870 state constitutional conventions. Their constitutions were highly democratic, eliminating property qualifications for voting and political office, shifting some appointed offices to elected ones, and establishing public schools. They also gave women greater rights in terms of property-holding and divorce. Blacks became state legislators for the first time in 1868. Angry whites charged they were being ruled by negroes, and some resorted to violent resistance. In truth, while blacks did play a greater role in government, they remained a minority.

RETREAT FROM RECONSTRUCTION

What led the North to lose interest in reconstructing the South?

First, northerners became disillusioned with Reconstruction, including some who thought federal expansion had cut too far into states rights. Second, economic and social changes in the North and West forced legislators to focus on their regional concerns. While immigration and industrialization made northern economies boom from 1865 to 1873, it also widened the gap between the richest and the poorest and created a powerful new class of industrialists. But when the Panic of 1873 brought hard times and job losses, interest in Reconstruction faded beside regional economic concerns. The Supreme Court also played a role, challenging congressional Reconstruction in several decisions. The Court ultimately narrowed the meaning of the Fourteenth Amendment by declaring state and national citizenship as separate issues and limited the amendment's ability to safeguard black citizens, as it was intended to do.

SUGGESTIONS FOR FURTHER READING

David W. Blight, *Race and Reunion: The Civil War in American Memory* (2001)

W. E. B. Du Bois, *Black Reconstruction in America* (1935)

Eric Foner, *Reconstruction: America's Unfinished Revolution, 1863–1877* (1988)

William Gillette, *Retreat from Reconstruction, 1869–1879* (1980)

Steven Hahn, *A Nation Under Our Feet: Black Political Struggles in the Rural South from Slavery to the Great Migration* (2003)

Gerald Jaynes, *Branches Without Roots: The Genesis of the Black Working Class in the American South, 1862–1882* (1986)

Michael Perman, *The Road to Redemption* (1984)

George Rable, *But There Was No Peace* (1984)

Heather Richardson, *The Death of Reconstruction* (2001)

Elliot West, "Reconstructing Race," *Western Historical Quarterly* (Spring 2003)

The Development of the West

In 1893 the young historian Frederick Jackson Turner delivered a stunning lecture at the Columbian Exposition in Chicago that shaped views of the American West for several generations. Titled "The Significance of the Frontier in American History," the paper argued that "free land, its continuous recession, and the advancement of American settlement westward" created a distinctively American spirit of democracy and egalitarianism. The settlement of several frontier Wests from colonial times onward explained American progress and character.

Across the street, the folk character Buffalo Bill Cody dramatized the conquest of frontiers in a stage extravaganza called "The Wild West." Whereas Turner described a peaceful settlement of empty western land, Cody portrayed violent conquest of territory occupied by savage Indians. Turner's heroes were farmers who tamed the wilderness with plows. Buffalo Bill's heroes were scouts who braved danger and vanquished Indians with firepower. Turner used log cabins, wagon trains, and wheat fields to argue that the frontier fashioned a new, progressive people. Cody depicted the West as a place of brutal aggression and heroic victory.

The American West inspired material progress, and it witnessed the forceful domination of one group over another and over the environment. Both Turner and Cody believed that by the 1890s the frontier era had ended. Over time, Turner's theory was abandoned (even by Turner himself) as too simplistic, and Buffalo Bill was relegated to the gallery of rogues and showmen. Yet both Wests persisted in the romance of American history, even while they obscured the complex story of western development in the late nineteenth century.

Much of the West was never empty, and its inhabitants utilized its resources differently. On the Plains, for example, the

This icon will direct you to interactive activities and study materials on A People And A Nation, Brief Edition website: **www.cengage.com/history/norton/ peoplenationbrief8e**

Chronology

1862	Homestead Act grants free land to citizens who live on and improve the land.
	Morrill Land Grant Act gives states public land to sell in order to finance agricultural and industrial colleges.
1864	Chivington's militia massacres Black Kettle's Cheyennes at Sand Creek.
1869	First transcontinental railroad is completed.
1872	Yellowstone becomes first national park.
1873	Barbed wire is invented, enabling western farmers to enclose and protect fields cheaply.
1876	Lakotas and Cheyennes ambush Custer's federal troops at Little Big Horn, Montana.
1877	Nez Percé Indians led by Young Joseph surrender to U.S. troops.
1878	Timber and Stone Act allows citizens to buy timberland cheaply but also enables large companies to acquire huge tracts of forest land.
1879	Carlisle School for Indians is established in Pennsylvania.
1880–81	Manypenny's *Our Indian Wards* and Jackson's *A Century of Dishonor* influence public conscience about poor government treatment of Indians.
1881–82	Chinese Exclusion Acts prohibit Chinese immigration to the United States.
1883	National time zones are established.
1884	U.S. Supreme Court defines Indians as wards under government protection.
1887	Dawes Severalty Act ends communal ownership of Indian lands and grants land allotments to individual native families.
	Hatch Act provides for agricultural experiment stations in every state.
	California passes law permitting farmers to organize into water districts.
1887–88	Devastating winter on Plains destroys countless livestock and forces farmers into economic hardship.
1890	Final suppression of Plains Indians by U.S. Army at Wounded Knee occurs.
	Census Bureau announces closing of the frontier.
	Yosemite National Park is established.
1892	Muir helps found Sierra Club.
1896	Rural Free Delivery is made available.
1902	Newlands Reclamation Act is passed.

Pawnee Indians planted crops in the spring, left their fields in summer to hunt buffalo, and then returned for harvesting. They sometimes battled with Cheyennes and Arapahos over access to hunting grounds and crops. Usually, Plains Indians developed and used natural resources in limited ways. In what now is the American Southwest, natives coexisted and sometimes integrated with Hispanic people, who were descendants of Spanish colonists and typically farmed small plots or worked for large landowners.

As white immigrants built new communities in the West in the late nineteenth century, they often exploited the environment for profit. They excavated the earth for minerals, felled forests for construction, built railroads, dammed rivers, and plowed soil with crop machines. Their goal included buying and selling in regional, national, and international markets. As they transformed the landscape, the triumph of their market economies transformed the nation.

The West, by 1870 spanned from the Mississippi River to the Pacific Ocean and consisted of several regions of varying economic potential. Abundant rainfall along the northern Pacific coast fed huge forests. South, California's woodlands and grasslands provided fertile valleys for vegetables and orange groves. Eastward, from the Cascades and the Sierra Nevada to the Rocky Mountains, gold, silver, and other minerals lay buried. East of the Rockies, the Great Plains divided into a semiarid western region of trees and buffalo grass and an eastern region of ample rainfall and tall grasses, which could support grain crops and livestock.

Before contact with whites, Indian peoples moved around the region, warring, trading, and negotiating with one another as they searched for food and shelter. In the Southwest, Hispanics moved north and south between Mexican and American territory, establishing towns, farms, and ranches. After the Civil War, white American migration overwhelmed the Indian and Hispanic people, swelling the population from 7 million to nearly 17 million between 1870 and 1890.

The West's abundance of exploitable land and raw materials made white Americans believe that anyone persistent enough could succeed. This confidence was based on the notion that white people were superior and asserted itself at the expense of people of color and the environment.

By 1890 farms, ranches, mines, towns, and cities existed in almost every corner of the present-day continental United States, but vast stretches of land remained un-settled. Although symbolically important to Frederick Jackson Turner, the fading frontier had little impact on people's behavior. Pioneers who failed in one locale tried again elsewhere. A surplus of seemingly uninhabited land led Americans to believe they would always have a second chance. This belief, more than Turner's theory of frontier democracy or Cody's "heroic" enactments left a deep imprint on the American character.

- **How did the interaction between people and the environment shape the physical landscape of the West and the lives of the region's inhabitants?**
- **How did the U.S. government's relations with Native Americans change over time throughout the late nineteenth century?**
- **Describe the societal and technological changes that revolutionized the lives of farmers and ranchers on the Great Plains.**

THE ECONOMIC ACTIVITIES OF NATIVE PEOPLES

Native Americans settled the West long before other Americans migrated there from the East. Neither passive nor powerless, Indians shaped their environment—for better and for worse—for centuries. Nevertheless, several factors contributed to the weakening of almost all native economic systems in the late nineteenth century.

Subsistence Cultures　Western Indian communities varied. Some natives inhabited permanent settlements, others temporary camps. Most Indians were both participants and recipients in a large-scale flow of goods, culture, language, and disease carried by migrating bands. Indian economies were based in differing degrees on four activities: crop growing; livestock raising; hunting, fishing, and gathering; and trading and raiding. Corn was the most common crop; sheep and horses, acquired from Spanish colonizers and other Indians, were the livestock; and buffalo (American bison) were the primary prey of hunts. Indians raided one another for food, tools, and hides. They subsisted on crops when a buffalo hunt failed, and hunted buffalo, traded livestock, or stole food and horses when crops failed.

For Indians on the Great Plains, daily life centered on the buffalo. They cooked and preserved buffalo meat; fashioned hides into clothing, shoes, and blankets; used sinew for thread and bowstrings; and carved tools from bones and horns. Buffalo were so valuable that the Pawnees and Lakotas often fought over access to herds. Plains Indians periodically set fire to tall-grass prairies, which burned away dead plants, facilitating the growth of new grasses so horses could feed all summer.

In the Southwest, Indians herded sheep, goats, and horses. Old Man Hat, a Navajo, explained, "The herd is money. . . . You know that you have some good clothing; the sheep gave you that. And you've just eaten different kinds of food; the sheep gave that food to you. Everything comes from the sheep." He was not speaking of money in a business sense but rather as status and security. Like many Indians, Navajos emphasized generosity and distrusted private property. Within the family, sharing was expected; outside the family, gifts and reciprocity governed relationships. Southwestern Indians, too, altered the environment, building elaborate irrigation systems to maximize the use of scarce water supplies.

What buffalo were to Plains Indians and sheep were to southwestern Indians, salmon were to northwestern Indians. Before the mid-nineteenth century, the Columbia River and its tributaries supported the densest native population in North America. The Clatsops, Klamathets, and S'Klallams developed technologies of stream diversion, platform construction, and special baskets to harvest fish. They traded salmon for horses, buffalo robes, beads, cloth, and knives.

Slaughter of Buffalo

On the Plains and parts of the Southwest, this native world gradually dissolved after 1850, when whites competed with Indians for natural resources. Perceiving buffalo and Indians as hindrances, whites endeavored to eliminate both. The U.S. Army refused to enforce treaties that reserved hunting grounds for exclusive Indian use, so railroads sponsored hunts in which eastern sportsmen shot at buffalo from slow-moving trains.

Neither Indians nor whites realized that a combination of circumstances doomed the buffalo before the slaughter of the late 1800s. Indians depleted herds by increasing their kills to trade with whites and other Indians. Also, in the generally dry years of the 1840s and 1850s Indians relocated to fertile river basins and forced bison out of this grazing territory to face starvation. Whites, too, settled in basin areas, further pushing buffalo out. At the same time, lethal animal diseases, such as anthrax and brucellosis, brought by white-owned livestock, decimated buffalo already weakened by malnutrition and drought. Increased numbers of horses, oxen, and sheep, owned by white newcomers and some Indians, devoured grasses that buffalo needed. The mass killing struck the final blow. By the 1880s only a few hundred remained of the 25 million buffalo estimated on the Plains in 1820.

Decline of Salmon

In the Northwest, salmon, suffered a similar fate. White commercial fishermen and canneries moved into the Columbia and Willamette River valleys during the 1860s and 1870s, and by the 1880s had greatly diminished the salmon runs. By the early

1900s, the construction of dams on the Columbia and its tributaries further impeded salmon reproduction. The U.S. government protected Indian fishing rights, and hatcheries restored some of this supply, but dams built to provide power, combined with overfishing and pollution, diminished salmon stocks.

THE TRANSFORMATION OF NATIVE CULTURES

Buffalo slaughter and salmon reduction undermined Indian subsistence, but demographic changes also contributed. Throughout the nineteenth century, white migrants were overwhelmingly single males in their twenties and thirties, the age when they were most prone to violent behavior. In 1870 white men outnumbered white women by three to two in California, two to one in Colorado, and two to one in the Dakota Territory. By 1900, the preponderance of men remained throughout these places. Indians were most likely to come into contact first with white explorers, traders, trappers, soldiers, prospectors, and cowboys, nearly all of whom had guns and no qualms about using them on animals and humans who got in their way.

Western Men

Moreover, these men subscribed to prevailing attitudes that Indians were primitive, lazy, devious, and cruel. Such contempt made exploiting and killing them easier, further "justified" by claims of preempting threats to life and property. When Indians raided white settlements, they sometimes mutilated bodies, burned buildings, and kidnapped women, acts that were embellished in campfire stories, pamphlets, and popular fiction—to reinforce images of Indians as savages. In saloons and cabins, men boasted about fighting Indians and showed off trophies of scalps and other body parts taken from victims.

Indian warriors, too, were young, armed, and prone to violence. Valuing bravery, they similarly boasted of fighting white interlopers. But Indian communities contained a large number of women and children, making native bands less mobile and more vulnerable. They also were susceptible to the bad habits of white bachelor society, copying their binges on whiskey and prostitution. The syphilis and gonorrhea that Indian men contracted from Indian women infected by whites killed many and hindered reproduction, which their populations, already dwindling from smallpox and other white diseases, could not afford. Thus the age and gender structure of the white frontier population, combined with an attitude of contempt toward Indians, threatened Indian existence in the West.

Lack of Native Unity

Government policy reinforced efforts to remove Indians. North American natives were organized not into tribes, as whites believed, but into bands, confederacies, and villages. Two hundred distinct languages and dialects separated these groups, making it difficult for Indians to unite against white invaders. Although a language group could be defined as a tribe, separate bands and clans had different leaders, and it was seldom that a tribal chief held widespread power. Moreover, bands often spent more time quarreling among themselves than with white settlers.

Territorial Treaties

After the Treaty of Greenville in 1795, American officials considered Indian tribes as nations with which they could make treaties, ensuring peace and definite land boundaries. But the government did not understand that a chief who agreed to a treaty did not speak for everyone and that the group might not abide by it. Moreover, whites seldom accepted treaties as guarantees of Indians' future land rights. In the Northwest, whites considered treaties protecting Indians' fishing rights on the Columbia River as nuisances and ousted Indians from the best locations. On the Plains, whites settled wherever they wished, often commandeering choice farmland.

Reservation Policy

Prior to the 1880s, the federal government tried to force western Indians onto reservations, where they might be "civilized." Reservations usually consisted of areas in a group's previous territory that were least desirable to whites. The government promised protection from white encroachment, along with food, clothing, and other necessities.

The reservation policy helped make way for the market economy. In the early years, trade benefited both Indians and whites equally. Indians acquired clothing, guns, and horses from whites in exchange for furs, jewelry, and, sometimes, military assistance against other Indians. Over time, Indians became more dependent, and whites increasingly dictated trade. For example, white traders persuaded Navajo weavers in the Southwest to produce heavy rugs suitable for eastern customers and to alter designs and colors to boost sales. Meanwhile, Navajos raised fewer crops and were forced to buy food. Soon they were selling land and labor to whites, and their dependency made it easier to force them onto reservations.

Indians had no say over their own affairs on reservations. Supreme Court decisions in 1884 and 1886 defined them as wards (falling, like helpless children, under government protection) and denied them U.S. citizenship. Thus they were unprotected by the Fourteenth and Fifteenth Amendments, which extended citizenship to African Americans. Second, pressure from white farmers, miners, and herders who sought Indian lands made it difficult for the government to preserve reservations intact. Third, the government ignored native history, even combining on the same reservation Indian bands that habitually warred against each other. Rather than serving as civilizing communities, reservations weakened Indian life.

Native Resistance

Not all Indians succumbed to market forces and reservation restrictions. Apaches in the Southwest battled whites even after being forced onto reservations. Pawnees in the Midwest resisted disadvantageous deals. In the Northwest, Nez Percé Indians escaped reservations by fleeing to Canada in 1877, until 1,800 miles later in Montana, their leader, Young Joseph, ended the flight. Sent to a reservation, Joseph unsuccessfully petitioned the government for a return of his ancestral lands.

Indian Wars

Whites responded to western Indian defiance with military aggression. In 1860, Navajos reacted to U.S. military pressure by raiding Fort Defiance in Arizona Territory.

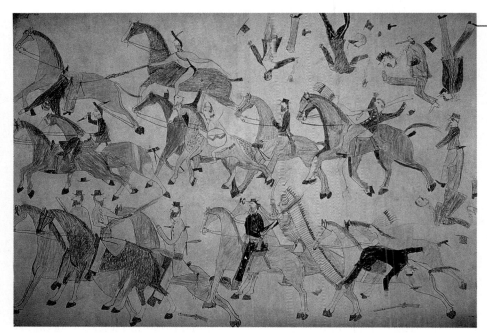

Plains Indians did not write books or letters as whites did, but they did tell stories and spread news through art. They painted scenes in notebooks and on hides, like this one which depicts the Indians' annihilation of General George A. Custer's soldiers at Little Big Horn in 1876.
(National Anthropological Archives, Smithsonian Institution NAA Ms. 2367A, 08583500)

The army attacked and starved the Navajo into submission, and in 1863–1864 forced them to a reservation at Bosque Redondo in New Mexico. In 1864, in the Sand Creek region of Colorado, a militia led by Methodist minister John Chivington attacked a Cheyenne band under Black Kettle, killing almost every Indian. In 1879, four thousand U.S. soldiers forced a surrender from Utes who were resisting further concessions after giving up most of their land.

The most publicized Indian battles occurred in June 1876, when 2,500 Lakotas and Cheyennes led by Chiefs Rain-in-the-Face, Sitting Bull, and Crazy Horse surrounded and annihilated 256 government troops led by Colonel George A. Custer near the Little Big Horn River in southern Montana. Although Indians demonstrated military skill, supply shortages and relentless pursuit by U.S. soldiers eventually overwhelmed armed Indian resistance. Native Americans were not so much conquered as they were harassed and starved into submission.

Reform of Indian Policy

In the 1870s and 1880s, officials and reformers sought more purposely to "civilize" and "uplift" natives through landholding and education. This meant outlawing customs deemed savage and barbarous and pressuring Indians to adopt American values of ambition, thrift, and materialism. In doing so, the United States copied other nations' imperialist policies, such as France, which banned native religious ceremonies in its Pacific island colonies. Other groups argued for sympathetic treatment. Reform treatises, such as George Manypenny's *Our Indian Wards* (1880) and Helen Hunt Jackson's *A Century of Dishonor* (1881), aroused the American conscience.

In the United States, the two most active Indian reform organizations were the Women's National Indian Association (WNIA) and the Indian Rights Association

(IRA). The WNIA, composed mainly of white women using domestic skills to help the needy, urged gradual Indian assimilation. The IRA, which had few Native American members, advocated citizenship and landholding. Most white reformers believed Indians were culturally inferior and could succeed economically only by embracing middle-class values of diligence and education.

Reformers particularly deplored Indians' sexual division of labor. Women seemed to do all the work—tending crops, raising children, cooking, curing hides, making tools and clothes—while being servile to men, who hunted but were otherwise idle. WNIA and IRA wanted Indian men to bear more responsibilities, treat Indian women respectfully, and resemble male heads of white middle-class households. But when Indian men and women adopted the model of white society, Indian women lost much of the economic independence and power over daily life that they once had.

Zitkala-Sa

Indians like Zitkala-Sa ("Red Bird") used white-controlled education to their advantage. Born on South Dakota's Pine Ridge reservation in 1876, at age twelve this Yankton Sioux girl attended an Indiana Quaker boarding school and later Earlham College and the Boston Conservatory of Music. Her major contribution was writing on behalf of her people's needs and advocating cultural preservation. In 1901 Zitkala-Sa published *Old Indian Legends,* translating Sioux oral tradition into written stories. Zitkala-Sa became known as Gertrude Bonnin when she married a Sioux who had taken the name Ray Bonnin. Subsequently, she was elected the first Indian secretary of the Society of American Indians.

Dawes Severalty Act

In 1887 Congress reversed its reservation policy and passed the Dawes Severalty Act, which authorized the dissolution of community-owned Indian property and granted land to individual Indian families. The government held that land in trust for twenty-five years, so families could not sell their allotments. The law also awarded citizenship to those accepting allotments (a 1906 act of Congress delayed citizenship for those Indians who had not yet taken their allotment). It also entitled the government to sell unallocated land to whites.

Indian policy, under the Interior Department, now pursed two main tactics to assimilate Indians into white American culture. First, the government distributed reservation land to individual families in the belief that the American institution of private property would integrate Indians into the larger society as productive citizens. Second, officials believed that Indians would abandon their "barbaric" habits more quickly if their children were educated in boarding schools.

The Dawes Act reflected a Euro-American and Christian world-view that a society of families headed by men was ideal. Government agents, reformers, and educators used schools to create a patriotic, industrious citizenry. Following Virginia's Hampton Institute, founded in Virginia in 1869 to educate newly freed slaves, teachers established the Carlisle School in Pennsylvania in 1879 as the flagship of the government's Indian school system. Boarding schools imposed white-defined sex roles: boys learned farming and carpentry, while girls were taught sewing, cleaning, and cooking.

Ghost Dance

With active resistance suppressed, Lakotas and others turned to the Ghost Dance as a spiritual means of preserving native culture. The Ghost Dance involved movement in a circle until the dancers reached a trancelike state and envisioned dead ancestors. As they engaged in days of dancing and meditation, Ghost Dancers embraced a messianic vision of the future when buffalo would return to the Plains and all elements of white civilization, including guns and whiskey, would be buried.

Ghost Dancers forswore violence, but as the religion spread, government agents worried about possible new Indian uprisings. Charging that the cult was anti-Christian, they arrested Ghost Dancers. Late in 1890, the government sent Custer's old regiment, the Seventh Cavalry, to detain Lakotas moving toward Pine Ridge, South Dakota. Although the Indians were starving, the army assumed they were armed for revolt. Overtaking the band at Wounded Knee Creek, the troops massacred an estimated three hundred men, women, and children in the snow.

The Losing of the West

The Indian wars and the Dawes Act effectively accomplished what whites wanted and Indians feared: it reduced native land control. Between 1887 and the 1930s, Indian landholdings dwindled from 138 million acres to 52 million. Land-grabbing whites were particularly cruel to the Ojibwas of the northern plains. In 1906 Senator Moses E. Clapp of Minnesota attached a rider to an Indian appropriations bill declaring that mixed-blood adults on the White Earth reservation were competent (meaning educated in white ways) enough to sell their property without the Dawes Act's twenty-five-year waiting period. When the bill became law, speculators duped many Ojibwas into signing away their land in return for counterfeit money and worthless merchandise. The Ojibwas lost more than half their original holdings and were ruined economically.

Ultimately, political and ecological crises overwhelmed most western Indians. Buffalo extinction, enemy raids, and disease, along with white military force, hobbled subsistence culture until Native Americans could only yield their lands to market-oriented whites. Believing themselves superior, whites determined to transform Indians by teaching them about private property and American ideals and eradicating their "backward" languages, lifestyles, and religions. Indians tried to retain their culture, but by the century's end, they lost control of their land and faced increasing pressure to shed their group identity.

THE EXTRACTION OF NATURAL RESOURCES

Unlike Indians, who used natural resources to meet subsistence needs and small-scale trading, most whites who migrated to the West and the Great Plains saw a vast territory as an untapped source of wealth (see Map 17.1). Extracting its resources advanced settlement and created new markets at home and abroad and fueled revolutions in transportation, agriculture, and industry across the United States in the late nineteenth century. This same extraction of nature's wealth led to environmental wastefulness and fed racial and sexual oppression.

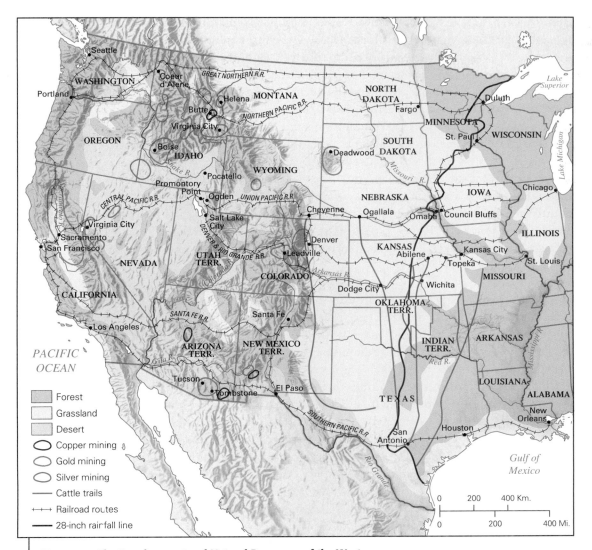

Map 17.1 The Development and Natural Resources of the West

By 1890, mining, lumbering, and cattle ranching had penetrated many areas west of the Mississippi River and railroad construction had linked together the western economy. These activities, along with the spread of mechanized agriculture, altered both the economy and the people who were involved in them.

Mining and Lumbering In the mid-1800s, the mining frontier drew thousands of people to Nevada, Idaho, Montana, Utah, and Colorado seeking gold, silver, copper, and other treasures. California's gold rush helped the thriving state by 1850 and furnished many of the miners traveling to nearby states. Others followed traditional routes from the East to the West.

Prospectors climbed mountains and trekked across deserts seeking precious metals. They shot game for food and financed their explorations by convincing merchants to advance credit for equipment in return for a share of the as-yet-undiscovered lode. Unlucky prospectors whose credit ran out took jobs and saved up to try again.

Digging for and transporting minerals was expensive, so prospectors who made discovereries sold their claims to large mining syndicates, such as the Anaconda Copper

Company. Financed by eastern capital, these companies brought in engineers, heavy machinery, railroad lines, and work crews, making western mining as corporate as eastern manufacturing. Although discoveries of gold and silver first drew attention to the West and its resources, mining companies usually exploited equally lead, zinc, tin, quartz, and copper.

Unlike mining, cutting trees for lumber to satisfy demand for construction and heating materials required vast tracts of forest land to be profitable. As tree supplies in the upper Midwest and South became depleted, lumber corporations moved into northwestern forests. The 1878 Timber and Stone Act sought to stimulate settlement in California, Nevada, Oregon, and Washington by allowing private citizens to buy inexpensive 160-acre plots "valuable chiefly for timber." Lumber companies grabbed millions of acres by hiring seamen from waterfront boarding houses to register claims to timberland and then transfer them to the companies. By 1900 private citizens had purchased more than 3.5 million acres, but most of it belonged to corporations.

Around the same time, oil companies began drilling in the Southwest. In 1900 petroleum came from the Appalachians and the Midwest, but rich oil reserves were discovered in southern California and eastern Texas, turning Los Angeles and Houston into boom cities. Although oil and kerosene were used primarily for lubrication and lighting, Southwest oil later became a vital new fuel source.

Complex Communities   The West became a multiracial society, including Native Americans, native-born white migrants, Mexicans, African Americans, and Asians. A crescent borderland from western Texas through New Mexico and Arizona to northern California supported Mexicano ranchers and sheepherders, descendants of early Spanish settlers. In New Mexico, Spaniards mixed with Indians to form a *mestizo* population. Across the Southwest, Mexican immigrants moved into American territory to find work. Some returned to Mexico seasonally. Although the Treaty of Guadalupe Hidalgo (1848) guaranteed property rights to Hispanics, Anglo (the Mexican name for a white American) miners, speculators, and railroads used fraud to steal Hispanic landholdings. Consequently, Mexicanos relocated to cities like San Antonio and Tucson and became wage laborers.

Before the Chinese Exclusion Act of 1882 prohibited them from immigrating, some 200,000 Chinese—mostly young, single males—came to the United States, building communities in California, Oregon, and Washington. Many came with five-year labor contracts for railroad construction; others worked in the fields. By the 1870s, the Chinese composed half of California's agricultural work force, often working in citrus groves. In cities like San Francisco, they labored in textile and cigar factories.

Japanese and European immigrants also toiled in mining and agricultural communities. The region consequently developed its own migrant economy, with workers relocating to take short-term jobs.

Many African Americans were "exodusters" who built all-black western towns. Nicodemus, Kansas, for example, was founded in 1877 by black migrants from Lexington, Kentucky. Despite challenges, the town developed newspapers, shops, churches, a hotel, and a bank, but declined when businesses left after it failed to obtain railroad connections. The major exodus occurred in 1879, when six thousand blacks, including many former slaves, moved from the South to Kansas, aided by the Kansas Freedmen's Relief Association. Other migrants, encouraged by newspaper editors and land speculators, went to the Oklahoma Territory, where they founded thirty-two all-black communities in the 1890s and early 1900s.

Western Women

Unmarried men dominated the frontier, but many white women headed west to similarly find fortune. They usually accompanied a husband or father, however. Using their labor as a resource, women earned money cooking, laundering, and sometimes as sex workers in houses of prostitution. In the Northwest, they worked in canneries, cleaning and salting fish.

Many white women helped bolster family and community life by participating in the home mission movement. They broke from traditional male-dominated Protestant missions and, in the mid-nineteenth century, sought to help women wherever polygamy and female infanticide existed. Using the slogan "Woman's work for women," they established missionary societies aiding women—unmarried mothers, Mormons, Indians, and Chinese—who they believed had fallen prey to men or had not yet adopted Christian virtue.

Significance of Race

For white settlers, race became an important means to control labor and social relations. They classified people into five races: Caucasians (themselves), Indians, Mexicans (both Mexican Americans, who had originally inhabited western lands, and Mexican immigrants), *Mongolians* (a term applied to the Chinese), and Negroes. In doing so, whites imposed racial distinctions on people who, with the possible exception of African Americans, never before considered themselves a race, and then deemed them permanently inferior. In 1878, for example, a federal judge in California ruled that Chinese could not become U.S. citizens because they were not "white persons."

Racial minorities occupied the bottom half of a two-tiered labor system and experienced prejudice as whites tried to reserve for themselves the West's riches. Whites dominated the top tier of managerial and skilled labor positions, while Irish, Chinese, Mexican, and African American laborers held unskilled positions. Anti-Chinese violence erupted during hard times. When the Union Pacific Railroad tried to replace white workers with lower-waged Chinese in Rock Springs, Wyoming, in 1885, whites burned down the Chinese part of town, killing twenty-eight. Mexicans, many of whom were the original landowners in California and elsewhere, saw their property claims ignored or their land stolen by whites.

Because so many white male migrants were single, intermarriage with Mexican and Indian women was common. Such intermarriage was acceptable for white men, but not for white women, especially with Asian immigrants. Most miscegenation laws passed by western legislatures were intended to prevent Chinese and Japanese men from marrying white women.

Conservation Movement

Questions about natural resources caught Americans between a desire for progress and a fear of spoiling nature. After the Civil War, people eager to protect the natural landscape organized a conservation movement. Sport hunters, concerned about loss of wildlife for them to kill for recreation, lobbied state legislatures to pass hunting regulations. Artists and tourists in 1864 persuaded Congress to preserve the Yosemite Valley by granting it to California for public use. In 1872, Congress designated the Yellowstone River region in Wyoming as the first national park. And in 1891 conservationists, led by naturalist John Muir, pressured Congress to authorize President Benjamin Harrison to create forest reserves—public lands protected from private-interest cutting.

Despite Muir's activism and efforts by the Sierra Club (which Muir helped found in 1892) and corporations supporting resource development, opposition was loudest in the West, where people remained eager to exploit nature. By prohibiting trespass in areas such as Yosemite and Yellowstone, conservation policy deprived Indians and white settlers of wildlife, water, and firewood previously available on federal lands.

Admission of New States

The development of mining and forest regions, along with farms and cities, brought western territories to the threshold of statehood. In 1889 Republicans seeking to solidify control of Congress passed an omnibus bill granting statehood to North Dakota, South Dakota, Washington, and Montana. Wyoming and Idaho, which allowed women to vote, were admitted the following year. Congress denied statehood to Utah until 1896, wanting assurances from the Mormons, a majority of the territory's population and leaders, that they would give up polygamy.

Western states' varied communities spiced American folk culture and fostered a go-getter optimism that distinguished the American spirit. The lawlessness of places like Deadwood, in the Dakota Territory, and Tombstone, in the Arizona Territory, gave the West notoriety and romance. Legends grew about characters whose lives magnified the western experience, and promoters like Buffalo Bill enhanced western folklore's appeal.

Arizona's mining towns, with their free-flowing cash and loose law enforcement, attracted gamblers, thieves, and opportunists who came to represent the Wild West. Near Tombstone, the infamous Clanton family and their partner John Ringgold (known as Johnny Ringo) were smugglers and cattle rustlers. The Earp brothers—Wyatt, Jim, Morgan, Virgil, and Warren—and their friends William ("Bat") Masterson and John Henry ("Doc") Holliday operated on both sides of the law as gunmen, gamblers, and politicians. A feud between the Clantons and the Earps climaxed on October 26, 1881, in a shootout at the OK Corral, where three Clantons were killed and Holliday and Morgan Earp were wounded.

Writers Mark Twain, Bret Harte, and others captured the flavor of western life, and characters like Buffalo Bill, Annie Oakley, Wild Bill Hickok, and Poker Alice became folk heroes. But in reality, miners and lumbermen worked long hours, often for corporations, and had little time, energy, or money for gambling, carousing, or gunfights. Women worked hard, too, as teachers, laundresses, storekeepers, and

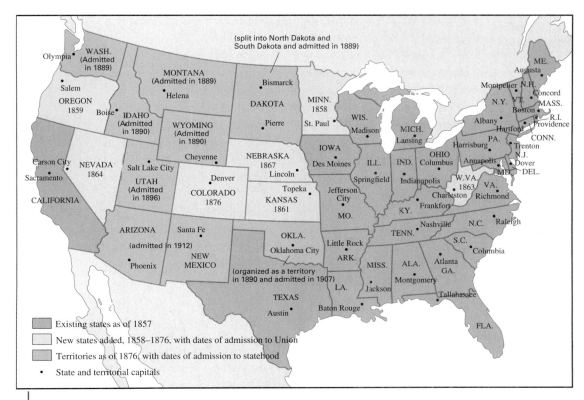

Map 17.2   The United States, 1876–1912

A wave of admissions between 1889 and 1912 brought remaining territories to statehood and marked the final creation of new states until Alaska and Hawai'i were admitted in the 1950s.

housewives. Only a few were sharpshooters or dance-hall queens. For most, western life was a struggle for survival.

IRRIGATION AND TRANSPORTATION

Western economic development is the story of how public and private interests used technology and organization to develop the region's river basins and make the arid land agriculturally productive.

For centuries, Indians irrigated southwestern lands for subsistence farming. When the Spanish arrived, they irrigated farms in southwest Texas and New Mexico. Later they channeled water to San Diego and Los Angeles, California. The Mormons were the first Americans of northern European ancestry to practice extensive irrigation. Arriving in Utah in 1847, they diverted streams and rivers into canals, enabling them to farm the hard-baked soil. By 1890 Utah boasted over 263,000 irrigated acres supporting more than 200,000 people.

Rights to Water

Efforts at land reclamation through irrigation in Colorado and California sparked conflict over rights to the precious streams that flowed through the West. Americans inherited the English common-law principle of riparian rights, which held that the stream

Water, aided by human resolve, coaxed crops from the dry soil and helped make the West habitable for whites. On this Colorado farm, a windmill pumps water for irrigation.
(Longmont Museum, Longmont, Colorado)

belonged to God; those who lived nearby could take water as needed but should not diminish the river. Intended to protect nature, this principle discouraged economic development by prohibiting property owners from damming or diverting water at the expense of others who lived downstream.

Western settlers rejected riparianism and embraced prior appropriation, which awarded a river's water to the first person claiming it. Westerners, taking cues from eastern Americans who diverted waterways to power mills and factories, asserted that water existed to serve human needs and advance profits. Anyone intending a reasonable (economically productive) use of river water should have the right to appropriation. The courts generally agreed.

Under appropriation, those who dammed and diverted water often reduced its flow downstream. People disadvantaged by such action could either sue or establish a public authority to regulate water usage. Thus, in 1879 Colorado created several water divisions. In 1890 Wyoming inserted a constitutional provision declaring that the state's rivers were public property subject to state supervision.

Destined to become the most productive agricultural state, California maintained a mixed legal system that upheld riparianism while allowing for some appropriation. This system disadvantaged irrigators, who sought to change state law. In 1887 the legislature passed a bill permitting farmers to organize into districts that would construct and operate irrigation projects. An irrigation district could use its public authority to purchase water rights, seize private property for irrigation canals, and finance projects through taxation or by issuing bonds. As a result, California became the nation's leader in irrigated acreage, with more than 1 million irrigated acres by 1890, making it the nation's most profitable agricultural state.

Newlands Reclamation Act

Even so, the federal government owned most western land in the 1890s. Prodded by land-hungry developers, states wanted part of the public domain lands, claiming they could make them profitable through reclamation and irrigation. Congress generally

The Australian Frontier

Australia, founded like the United States as a European colony, had a frontier society that resembled the American West in its mining development, folk society, and treatment of indigenous people. Australia experienced a gold rush in 1851, two years after the United States, and large-scale mining companies quickly moved into its western regions to extract lucrative mineral deposits.

A promise of mineral wealth lured thousands of mostly male immigrants to Australia in the late nineteenth century, many from China. As in the United States, anti-Chinese riots erupted, and beginning in 1854, Australia passed laws restricting Chinese immigration. When the country became an independent British federation in 1901, it implemented a literacy test that terminated Chinese immigration for over fifty years.

While Australians celebrate folk heroes symbolizing white masculinity, they also considered indigenous peoples, whom they called Aborigines, savages. Christian missionaries viewed aborigines as pagans and tried to convert them. In 1869 the government of Victoria Province passed an Aborigine Protection Act, encouraging the removal of native children from their families to learn European customs in white schools. Aborigines adapted in their own ways, or, if they had light skin, sometimes told census takers they were white. In the end, Australians resorted to reservations. Like the Americans, white Australians could not find a place for indigenous people in their land of opportunity.

Native Encampment River Murray.

Much like the American counterpart, the Australian frontier was populated by natives before Anglo colonists arrived. The Aborigines, as the Australian natives were called, lived in villages and utilized their own culture to adapt to the environment. This photo shows a native camp in the Maloga Reserve. (National Library of Australia)

refused such assignments because of potential controversies. If one state sponsored irrigation, who would regulate waterways that flowed through more than one state? If, for example, California controlled the Truckee River, which flowed westward over the California-Nevada border, how would Nevadans ensure that California would give them sufficient water? Only the federal government had the power to regulate regional water development.

In 1902, after years of debate, Congress passed the Newlands Reclamation Act. It allowed the federal government to sell western public lands to individuals in parcels less than 160 acres and to use the proceeds to finance irrigation. Often identified as sensitive to natural-resource conservation, the Newlands Reclamation Act in fact represented a decision by the federal government to aid the agricultural and general economic development of the West.

Railroad Construction

Between 1865 and 1890, railroad track grew from 35,000 to 200,000 miles, mostly west of the Mississippi River (see Map 17.1). By 1900 the United States contained one-third of all railroad track in the world. The Central Pacific employed thousands of Chinese to build its tracks; the Union Pacific used mainly the Irish. Workers lived in shacks and tents that were dismantled, loaded on flatcars, and relocated each day.

After 1880, when steel replaced iron rails, railroads helped push the nation's steel industry to international leadership. Railroad expansion also spawned related industries—coal production, passenger- and freight-car manufacture, and depot construction. Railroads also gave important impetus to western urbanization. Transporting people and freight, lines like the Union Pacific and the Southern Pacific accelerated the growth of hubs, such as Chicago, Omaha, Kansas City, Cheyenne, Los Angeles, Portland, and Seattle.

Railroad Subsidies

Railroads received some of the largest government subsidies in American history. Promoters argued that, because railroads were a public benefit, the government should give them land from the public domain, which they could then sell to finance construction. During the Civil War, Congress, dominated by business-minded Republicans, granted railroad corporations over 180 million acres, mostly for interstate routes. Railroads funded construction by using the land as security for bonds or by selling it. State legislators, many of whom had financial interests in railroads, granted some 50 million acres. Cities and towns also assisted, usually through loans or by purchasing railroad bonds or stocks.

Without public help, few railroads could have prospered sufficiently to attract private investment. Railroads sometimes pressured governments into offering it. The Southern Pacific, for example, threatened to bypass Los Angeles unless the city paid a bonus and built a depot. Some laborers and farmers fought subsidies, arguing that companies like the Southern Pacific would become too powerful. Many communities boomed, however, as railroads attracted investment into the West and drew farmers into the market economy.

Standard Gauge, Standard Time

Railroad construction triggered important technological and organizational reforms. By the late 1880s, almost all lines had adopted standard-gauge rails allowing their tracks to connect. Air brakes, automatic car couplers, standardized handholds on freight cars, and other devices made rail transportation safer and efficient. The need for gradings, tunnels, and bridges spurred the growth of the American engineering profession. Organizational advances included systems for coordinating passenger and freight schedules, and the adoption of uniform freight-classification systems.

Railroads also reinforced racism by segregating black and white passengers on cars and in stations.

Railroads altered conceptions of time and space. First, instead of expressing distance in miles, people referred to the time it took to travel from place to place. Second, railroad scheduling required the nationwide standardization of time. Before railroads, local church bells and clocks struck noon when the sun was directly overhead, and people set clocks accordingly. But because the sun was not overhead at the same moment everywhere, time varied from place to place. Boston's clocks differed from those in New York by almost twelve minutes. In 1883, without authority from Congress, the railroads established four standard time zones for the country. Railroad time became national time.

FARMING THE PLAINS

Western agriculture in the late nineteenth century exemplified two important achievements: the transformation of arid prairies into crop-producing land and the transformation of agriculture into big business via mechanization, long-distance transportation, and scientific cultivation. The climate and terrain of the Great Plains presented formidable challenges. Irrigation and the mechanization of agriculture enabled farmers to feed the nation's burgeoning population and turned the United States into the world's breadbasket.

Settlement of the Plains

During the 1870s and 1880s, more acres were farmed in states such as Kansas, Nebraska, and Texas than in the entire country during the previous 250 years. The number of farms tripled from 2 million to over 6 million between 1860 and 1910, as hundreds of thousands of hopeful farmers headed to the Plains. The Homestead Act of 1862 and other measures drew settlers with cheap or free plots for those who would live there and improve their property. Land-rich railroads advertised cheap land, arranged credit terms, and offered reduced fares to would-be settlers, while company agents—often former immigrants—traveled to Denmark, Sweden, Germany, and other European nations to recruit settlers.

To most migrating families, the West seemed to promise a chance at a better life. Railroad expansion enabled remote farmers to ship produce to market, and the construction of grain elevators eased storage problems. Worldwide and national population growth sparked the demand for farm products, and the prospects for commercial agriculture became increasingly favorable.

Hardship on the Plains

Farm life was harder than advertisements and railroad agents insinuated. Migrants often encountered scarcities of essentials they once enjoyed. Open prairies contained insufficient lumber, so pioneer families built houses of sod and burned buffalo dung for heat. Water was sometimes scarce also. Machinery for drilling wells was expensive, as were windmills for drawing water to the surface.

The weather posed a formidable challenge. The climate between the Missouri River and the Rocky Mountains divides along a line running from Minnesota

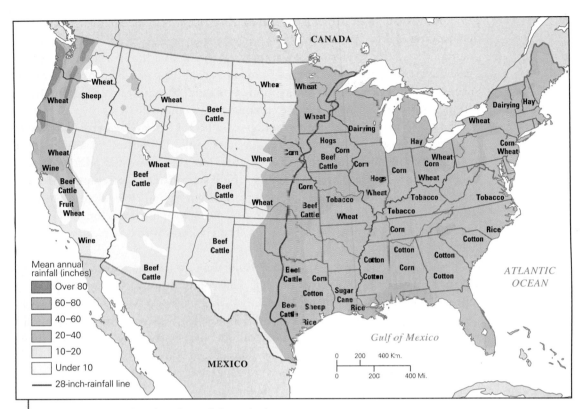

Map 17.3   Agricultural Regions of the United States, 1890
In the Pacific Northwest and east of the twenty-eight-inch-rainfall line, farmers could grow a greater variety of crops. Territory west of the line was either too mountainous or too arid to support agriculture without irrigation. The grasslands that once fed buffalo herds could now feed beef cattle.

southwest through Oklahoma, then south, bisecting Texas. West of this line, annual rainfall averages less than twenty-eight inches, not enough for most crops and even that rain was unreliable.

Weather was unpredictable. Weeks of torrid summer heat and parching winds suddenly gave way to violent storms that washed away crops and property. Winter blizzards piled up snowdrifts that halted outdoor movement. Melting snow swelled streams, and floods threatened millions of acres. In fall, a rainless week turned dry grasslands into tinder, and the slightest spark could ignite a prairie fire. A severe Texas drought between 1884 and 1886 drove many farmers off the land.

Nature could be cruel even under good conditions. Weather that was favorable for crops also bred insects. In the 1870s and 1880s, grasshopper swarms devoured everything: plants, tree bark, and clothing. One farmer lamented, the "hoppers left behind nothing but the mortgage."

Social Isolation

Settlers also faced isolation. New England and European farmers lived in villages, traveling daily to nearby fields. In the Plains, the Far West, and the South, peculiarities of land division compelled rural dwellers to live far apart. Because most plots were rectangular—usually encompassing 160 acres—at most four families could live near by, but only if they congregated around their shared four-corner intersection. In practice, farm families lived away from boundary lines with a half-mile separating farmhouses. Men might find escape from occasional trips to sell crops or buy supplies. Women were more isolated, confined by domestic chores to the household, with rare trips to exchange food and services with neighbors.

Letters that the young Nebraska homesteader Ed Donnell wrote to his family in Missouri reveal how time and circumstances could dull optimism. In fall 1885, Donnell rejoiced to his mother, "I like Nebr first rate. . . . I have saw a pretty tuff time a part of the time since I have been out here, but I started out to get a home and I was determined to win or die in the attempt. . . . Have got a good crop of corn, a floor in my house and got it ceiled overhead." Already, though, Donnell was lonely. "There is lots of other bachelors here but I am the only one I know who doesn't have kinfolks living handy."

A year and a half later, Donnell's dreams were dissolving, and still a bachelor, he was beginning to look elsewhere. By fall, conditions had worsened. Donnell lamented, "We have been having wet weather for 3 weeks. . . . My health has been so poor this summer and the wind and the sun hurts my head so. I think if I can sell I will . . . move to town for I can get $40 a month working in a grist mill and I would not be exposed to the weather." Thousands shared Donnell's hardships, and their cityward migration fueled late-nineteenth-century urban growth (see Chapter 19).

Mail-Order Companies and Rural Free Delivery

Farm families organized churches and clubs to ease isolation. By 1900 two developments brought rural settlers into closer contact with modern consumer society.

First, mail-order companies, such as Montgomery Ward and Sears, Roebuck, made new products widely attainable by the 1870s and 1880s. Letters to Ward and Sears reported family news and sought advice on needs from gifts to childcare. A Washington man wrote, "As you advertise everything for sale that a person wants, I thought I would write you, as I am in need of a wife, and see what you could do for me."

Second, after farmers petitioned Congress for extension of the postal service, in 1896 the government made Rural Free Delivery (RFD) widely available. Farmers who previously picked up mail in town, could receive letters, newspapers, and catalogues in a roadside mailbox almost daily. In 1913 the postal service inaugurated parcel post, making shipping costs much cheaper.

Mechanization of Agriculture

Machinery drove the agricultural revolution. When the Civil War drew men away from farms in the upper Mississippi River valley, women and older men who remained behind began using reapers and other mechanical implements. After the war, continued demand encouraged farmers to utilize machines, and inventors developed new implements. Seeders, combines, binders, mowers, and rotary plows improved grain production on the Plains and in California, while the centrifugal cream separator, patented in 1879, sped the skimming of cream from milk.

TABLE 17.1   Summary: Government Land Policy

Railroad land grants (1850–1871)	Granted 181 million acres to railroads to encourage construction and development
Homestead Act (1862)	Gave 80 million acres to settlers to encourage settlement
Morrill Act (1862)	Granted 11 million acres to states to sell to fund public agricultural colleges
Other grants	Granted 129 million acres to states to sell for other educational and related purposes
Dawes Act (1887)	Allotted some reservation lands to individual Indians to promote private property and weaken tribal values among Indians and offered remaining reservation lands for sale to whites (By 1906, some 75 million acres had been acquired by whites.)
Various laws	Permitted direct sales of 100 million acres by the Land Office

Source: Goldfield, David, et al., *The American Journey,* 3d ed. (Upper Saddle River. NJ: Prentice Hall, 2004).

For centuries, farmers planted only what they could harvest by hand. Machines—driven first by animals, then by steam—significantly increased productivity. Before mechanization, a farmer working alone could harvest about 7.5 acres of wheat. Using an automatic binder that cut and bundled the grain, he could harvest 135 acres. Machines made other crops more profitable as well (see Table 17.1).

Legislative and Scientific Aids

Congress and scientists worked to improve existing crops and develop new ones. The 1862 Morrill Land Grant Act gave states federal lands to sell for financing agricultural research. Consequently, new public universities were established in Wisconsin, Illinois, Minnesota, California, and other states. A second Morrill Act in 1890 aided more schools, including several all-black colleges. The Hatch Act of 1887 provided for agricultural experiment stations in every state, further encouraging farming science and technology.

Science enabled farmers to use the soil more efficiently. Researchers developed dry farming, a plowing and harrowing technique that minimized evaporation. Botanists perfected varieties of hard wheat whose seeds could withstand northern winters. Agriculturists also adapted new varieties of alfalfa from Mongolia, corn from North Africa, and rice from Asia. The horticulturist George Washington Carver, a son of slaves who became a chemist and taught at Alabama's Tuskegee Institute, created hundreds of products from peanuts, soybeans, and sweet potatoes. Other scientists combated plant and animal diseases. Technology helped American farmers expand productivity in the market economy.

THE RANCHING FRONTIER

Western commercial farming ran headlong into one of the region's most romantic industries—ranching. Beginning in the sixteenth century, Spanish landholders raised cattle in Mexico and what would become the American Southwest. They employed Indian and Mexican cowboys, known as *vaqueros,* to tend herds and round up cattle. Anglo ranchers moving into Texas and California in the early nineteenth century hired *vaqueros* to teach them roping, branding, horse training, and saddle making. About one-fourth of all cowboys were black. While they probably experienced less discrimination than other African American laborers, after work, they had to sit in separate sections in saloons and endured name-calling and mistreatment.

By the 1860s, cattle raising became increasingly profitable, as population growth boosted the demand for beef and railroads simplified food transportation. By 1870 drovers were herding thousands of Texas cattle northward to Kansas, Missouri, and Wyoming (see Map 17.1). At the northern terminus, the cattle were sold or loaded onto trains bound for Chicago and St. Louis slaughterhouses.

The long drive gave rise to romantic lore of bellowing cattle, buckskin-clad cowboys, and smoky campfires. But trekking 1,000 miles for months made cattle sinewy and tough. Herds that trespassed on Indian lands and farmers' fields were sometimes shot at. When ranchers discovered that crossing Texas longhorns with heavier Hereford and Angus breeds produced animals that were better able to survive harsh winters and were highly profitable, cattle raising expanded northward, and proliferating herds in Kansas, Nebraska, Colorado, Wyoming, Montana, and the Dakotas crowded out declining buffalo.

The Open Range

Cattle raisers minimized costs by buying a few acres bordering a stream and turning their herds loose on adjacent public domain that no one wanted because it lacked water access. Called open-range ranching, a cattle raiser could utilize thousands of acres by owning much less. Neighboring ranchers often formed associations and allowed herds to graze together, burning an identifying brand into each animal's hide. But as cattle production rose, cattle began to overrun the range, and other groups challenged ranchers over use of the land.

Sheepherders from California and New Mexico were also using the public domain, sparking territorial clashes. Ranchers complained that sheep ruined grassland by eating to the roots and that cattle refused to graze where sheep had been. Occasionally ranchers and sheepherders resorted to violence rather than settle disagreements in court, where a judge might discover that both were using public land illegally.

More important, the farming frontier generated new land demands. Lacking sufficient timber and stone for traditional fencing, western settlers could not easily define their property. Tensions flared when farmers accused cattle raisers of letting herds trespass on cropland and when herders charged that farmers should fence their property.

Barbed Wire

The solution was barbed wire. Invented in 1873 by Joseph F. Glidden, a DeKalb, Illinois, farmer, this inexpensive and mass-produced fencing consisted of wires held in place by sharp spurs twisted around them. It enabled Plains homesteaders to protect their farms from grazing cattle. It also ended open-range ranching and made roundups unnecessary, as large-scale ranchers enclosed herds within private property. Similarly, the development of the round silo for storing and making feed (silage) enabled cattle raisers to feed herds without grazing.

A group of cowboys prepare for a roundup. Note the presence of African Americans, who, along with Mexicans, made up one-fourth of all cowboys. Though they rarely became trail bosses or ranch owners, black cowboys enjoyed an independence on the trails that was unavailable to them on tenant farms and city streets. (Nebraska State Historical Society, RG 2608-PH-O-2167-a. Copy and reuse restrictions apply.)

Ranching as Big Business

By 1890 big businesses were taking over the cattle industry and applying scientific methods of breeding and feeding. Corporations also used technology to squeeze larger returns from meatpacking. Every part of a cow had uses: half was meat, but larger profits came from hides for leather, blood for fertilizer, hooves for glue, fat for candles and soap, and the rest for sausages. Cattle processing harmed the environment, as meatpackers and leather tanners dumped unsold goods into waterways. By the late nineteenth century, the Chicago River created a powerful stench that made nearby residents ill.

Open-range ranching made beef a staple of the American diet and created a few fortunes, but it could not survive the rush of history. Overgrazing destroyed Plains grass supplies, and the brutal winter of 1886–1887 destroyed 90 percent of some herds and drove small ranchers out of business. By 1890, large-scale ranchers owned or leased the land they used. Cowboys formed labor organizations and struck for higher pay. The myth of the cowboy's freedom and individualism lived on, but ranching became a corporate business.

Summary

The landscape of the American West exerted a lasting influence on the complex mix of people there. Living mostly in small groups, Indians, the original inhabitants, hunted, farmed, and depended on delicate resources, such as buffalo herds and salmon runs. When they came into contact with commerce-minded European Americans, their resistance to the market economy, diseases, and violence that whites brought failed.

Mexicans, Chinese, African Americans, and Anglos discovered a reciprocal relationship between human activities and the environment, too. Miners, timber cutters, farmers, and builders extracted raw minerals for eastern factories, used irrigation and mechanization to yield agricultural abundance, filled pastures with cattle and

The Myth of the Cowboy

The cowboy has been a distinctive American icon, yet actual American cowboys, whose heyday lasted only from about 1865 to 1890, were poorly paid, poorly fed, illiterate young men who sometimes stole employers' cattle. Of about thirty-five thousand cowboys, 25 percent were black and another 15 percent were Mexican, Indian, and Chinese, all of whom were treated worse by employers than their white counterparts. Often unemployed, some white and nonwhite cowboys joined unions and went on strike for job security and better wages. Mostly, cowboys got drunk more often than they engaged in gunfights, enforced the law, or defended a woman's honor.

Still, the apparently independent, masculine, outdoor existence that cowboys led fueled romantic notions that they symbolized the true American. Buffalo Bill Cody was one of the first to create this image in his Wild West shows through a cattle herder named Buck Taylor, whom Cody glamorized as King of the Cowboys. Writers and artists began depicting cowboys as valiant characters. Owen Wister's bestselling novel, *The Virginian* (1902), helped reinforce the image of a rugged, self-reliant individualist who took the law into his own hands. Myriad films, radio and television programs, and music similarly turned this common laborer into a hero. Roy Rogers, who acted in hundreds of movies and TV shows between 1938 and 1964, was one of many who enlarged the myth Gone were the ill-fitting, makeshift clothing, now replaced by fancy boots, Stetson hats, and blue jeans.

Equally important, the low-life reality was replaced by a lawman battling evil. President Ronald Reagan embellished his image by wearing western clothing and being photographed on horseback. And President George W. Bush, a Texan, assumed the role of "good cowboy" after September 11, 2001, while opponents of his Iraq invasion criticized America's "bad cowboy" tactics of reckless violence. The cowboy myth has consequently left a legacy of images and actions.

---

sheep to expand food sources, and constructed railroads to tie the nation together. But the environment exerted power through climate, insects and predators, undesirable plant growth, and impenetrable barriers to agriculture.

The West's settlers employed force, violence, and greed that sustained discrimination within a multiracial society, left many farmers feeling cheated, provoked contests over water and pastures, and sacrificed environmental balance for market profits. The region's raw materials and agricultural products improved living standards and hastened the industrial progress of the Machine Age, but not without costs.

Chapter Review

THE ECONOMIC ACTIVITIES OF NATIVE PEOPLES

What contributed to the weakening of Native Americans' economic systems in the late nineteenth century?

The Native American economic system was increasingly eroded after 1850 by a number of factors, some natural and some resulting from increasing interaction with, and encroachment by, whites. Southwestern Indian economies were devastated by the declining buffalo herd due to drought, diseases brought by white-owned livestock, excessive Native American hunting and trade, white settlement on Indian lands used for grazing, and whites' efforts to eliminate the buffalo to make way for railroads. Northwestern Indian economies, which relied on salmon fishing, similarly suffered when white commercial fisheries diminished salmon supplies and dammed up rivers and tributaries that were vital for fishing stocks.

THE TRANSFORMATION OF NATIVE CULTURES

How did the U.S. government's reservation policy make way for the market economy in the West?

U.S. reservation policy before the 1880s forced Indians onto western reservations, promising to protect this territory from white encroachment. Once on reservations, Indians' dependency on whites for trade goods such as clothing, guns, horses, and food made it easier for whites to control Indian affairs. The 1887 Dawes Severalty Act dissolved community-owned Indian land, granting it instead to qualifying individual Indian families. The land was held in trust for twenty-five years and allowed the U.S. government to sell unassigned allotments (typically to whites). The goal of this was to assimilate Indians into white culture via private property, but in truth it reduced their land holdings by more than half and made way for land sales and further white settlement of the West.

THE EXTRACTION OF NATURAL RESOURCES

What sparked the rise of the conservation movement?

Mining for precious metals, cutting trees for lumber, and drilling for oil drew thousands of people to the West seeking fortune and a better life. It also transformed the natural landscape, contributed to environmental wastefulness and sparked a debate over the desire for progress and the need to preserve nature. This gave rise to a conservation movement after the Civil War. Hunters lobbied legislatures for hunting regulations; artists and tourists pressured Congress to protect Yosemite Valley by granting it to California for public use; and in 1862, the Yellowstone River region in Wyoming became the first national park. Congress also authorized President Benjamin Harrison to create forest reserves, at the urging of a group led by activist John Muir, who founded the environmental group the Sierra Club in 1892.

IRRIGATION AND TRANSPORTATION

How did government policies aid the development of the West?

Two ways: first, during the Civil War era, government subsidies for railroad construction—among the largest in U.S. history—included massive land grants, which companies could use for interstate routes or sell to finance construction. Federal land grants topped 180 million acres, while states handed over another 50 million acres, and cities and towns helped by offering loans or buying railroad stocks. Second, through the Newlands Reclamation Act (1902), Congress supported the sale of western lands in parcels smaller than 160 acres to individuals, with the funds being used to finance irrigation projects in the region. That, in turn, facilitated the agricultural and economic development

FARMING THE PLAINS

What helped ease the hardships farmers faced when settling the West?

Migrant families hoped to find a better life in the West, but often experienced loneliness, isolation, the lack of essential products and services they previously knew, and even shortages of lumber needed to build homes. But the arrival of the railroad, the extension of the postal service into the West, and the advent of the mail order business ended some of their problems by bringing products and people to the region. New technology and mechanization also made farming easier, and the creation of social clubs and other organizations helped ease the isolation.

THE RANCHING FRONTIER

How did ranching shift from small, individual-owned endeavors to big business?

With the increasing demand for beef and expansion of herds, ranchers overgrazed the land, which destroyed grass supplies that fed Plains herds. A brutal winter in 1886 to 1887 killed off 90 percent of some ranchers' herds and drove many out of business. By 1890, big business took over the cattle industry and used scientific methods for breeding and feeding to eliminate dependency on grass and grazing lands.

SUGGESTIONS FOR FURTHER READING

William Cronon, *Nature's Metropolis: Chicago and the Great West* (1991)

Albert L. Hurtado and Peter Iverson, *Major Problems in American Indian History: Documents and Essays,* 2d ed. (2001)

Karl Jacoby, *Crimes Against Nature: Squatters, Poachers, Thieves and the Hidden History of American Conservation* (2001)

Patricia Nelson Limerick, *The Legacy of Conquest: The Unbroken Past of the American West* (1987)

Eugene P. Moehring, *Urbanism and Empire in the Far West, 1840–1890* (2004)

Alan Trachtenberg, *The Incorporation of America: Culture and Society in the Gilded Age* (1982)

Robert M. Utley, *The Indian Frontier of the American West, 1846–1890* (1984)

Richard White, *"It's Your Misfortune and None of My Own": A New History of the American* (1991)

The Machine Age | 1877–1920

In 1911 iron molders at the Watertown Arsenal, a government weapons factory near Boston, went on strike after a fellow worker was fired. Joseph Cooney objected to having an efficiency expert time his work with a stopwatch, and the molders feared management would impose new labor standards. The iron molders' union president John Frey explained, "The workman believes when he goes on strike that he is defending his job." The molders felt a property right to their labor, that jobs could not be changed or taken away without their consent.

The army officers who ran the factory thought they owned the molders' labor and that output was "one-half what it should be." To increase production, they hired Dwight Merrick, an expert in a new field called scientific management, to time workers and speed performance.

The day Merrick began his study, a molder named Perkins secretly timed the same task. Merrick reported that the job should take twenty-four minutes and that the workers were wasting time and materials; Perkins found that the job required fifty minutes and that there was no waste. That evening, the molders discussed how to respond to the discrepancy between Merrick's report and theirs. Cooney argued for resisting scientific management; the workers drew up a petition and were ready to walk out.

Eventually, the molders and their bosses compromised, but this incident reveals an important consequence of the industrialization that made countless new products available in the late 1800s, as a new consumer society emerged. To increase production, factory owners harnessed technology and divided work routines into minute, repetitive tasks organized by the clock. Workers who had long felt valued for their skills, now struggled to avoid becoming slaves to machines. Defenders of the new

This icon will direct you to interactive activities and study materials on A People And A Nation, Brief Edition
website: **www.cengage.com/history/norton/ peoplenationbrief8e**

Chronology

1869	Knights of Labor is founded.	**1894**	Workers of Pullman Palace Car Company strike.
1873–78	Economy declines.	**1895**	*U.S. v. E. C. Knight Co.* limits Congress's power to regulate manufacturing.
1876	Bonsack invents machine for rolling cigarettes.		
1877	Widespread railroad strikes protest wage cuts.	**1896**	*Holden v. Harcy* upholds law regulating miners' working hours.
1878	Edison Electric Light Company is founded.		
1879	George's *Poverty and Progress* argues for taxing unearned wealth.	**1898**	Taylor promotes scientific management as efficiency measure in industry.
1881	First federal trademark law begins spread of brand names.	**1901–03**	U.S. Steel Corporation is founded. E. I. du Pont de Nemours and Company is reorganized. Ford Motor Company is founded.
1882	Standard Oil Trust is founded.		
1884–85	Economy declines.	**1903**	Women's Trade Union League (WTUL) is founded.
1886	Haymarket riot in Chicago protests police brutality against labor demonstrations. American Federation of Labor (AFL) is founded.	**1905**	*Lochner v. New York* overturns law limiting bakery workers' working hours and limits labor protection laws. Industrial Workers of the World (IWW) is founded.
1888	Bellamy's *Looking Backward* depicts utopian world free of monopoly and class divisions.		
1890	Sherman Anti-Trust Act outlaws "combinations in restraint of trade."	**1908**	*Muller v. Oregon* upholds law limiting women to ten-hour workday. First Ford Model T is built.
1892	Homestead (Pennsylvania) steelworkers strike against Carnegie Steel Company.	**1911**	Triangle Shirtwaist Company fire in New York City leaves 146 workers dead.
1893–97	Economic depression causes high unemployment and business failures.	**1913**	Ford begins moving–assembly-line production.
		1919	Telephone operators strike in New England.

system devised theories to justify it, while laborers tried to combat what they thought were abuses of power.

In the mid-nineteenth century, an industrial revolution swept through parts of the United States, and its mechanization powered a second round in the late 1800s and early 1900s. Three technological developments characterized this new stage: electricity, the internal-combustion engine, and new applications in the use of chemicals. Electricity provided a needed alternative to less efficient steam engines. The demand for transportation beyond railroads spurred progress in automobile manufacture. And the textile industry's experiments with dyes, bleaches, and cleaning agents advanced chemical research.

In 1860 one-fourth of the American labor force worked in manufacturing and transportation; by 1900 over half did. As the twentieth century dawned, the United States was the world's largest producer of raw materials and food, and the most productive industrial nation (see Map 18.1). Between 1877 and 1920 (see Chapter 19), labor-saving machines boosted productivity. Innovations in business organization and marketing also fueled the drive for profits.

These developments had momentous effects on living standards and everyday life, as goods that had once been accessible to a few became available to many.

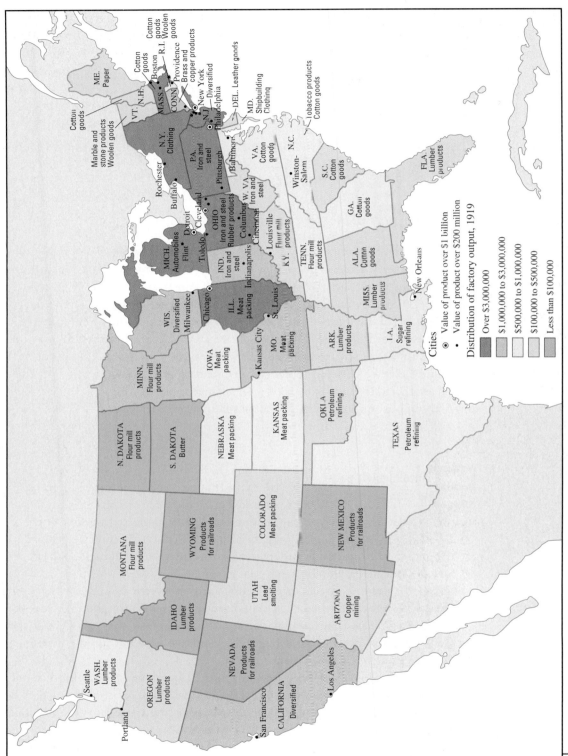

Map 18.1 Industrial Production, 1919

By the early twentieth century, each state could boast at least one kind of industrial production. Although the value of goods produced was still highest in the Northeast, states like Minnesota and California had impressive dollar values of outputs.

(*Source:* Data from U.S. Bureau of the Census, *Fourteenth Census of the United States, 1920, Vol. 9, Manufacturing* [Washington, DC: U.S. Government Printing Office, 1921].)

Industrialization furthered the extraction of natural resources and the expansion of agriculture (see Chapter 17). These processes combined people, the environment, and technology in ways that were both constructive and destructive.

- How did mechanization affect the lives of average workers and the makeup of the labor force?
- In what ways did technological innovation alter the American standard of living?
- What ideas did some Americans use to justify industrialization, and how did others criticize it?

TECHNOLOGY AND THE TRIUMPH OF INDUSTRIALIZATION

In 1876 Thomas Edison and his associates opened an invention factory in Menlo Park, New Jersey, where Edison said he hoped to create "a minor invention every ten days and a big thing every six months or so." If Americans wanted new products, Edison believed, they had to organize and work purposefully toward progress. His attitude reflected the spirit that propelled inventiveness and industrialization in the late nineteenth century. The U.S. Patent Office, created by the Constitution to "promote the Progress of science and useful Arts," reveals how innovative Americans were becoming. Between 1790 and 1860 the government granted 36,000 patents, and registered another 1.5 million from 1860 to 1930. Inventions in areas such as electricity, internal combustion, and chemistry often sprang from a marriage between technology and business organization.

Birth of the Electrical Industry Most of Edison's more than one thousand inventions used electricity to transmit light, sound, and images. In 1878 he embarked on a search for a cheap, efficient means of indoor lighting. After tedious experiments, Edison perfected the incandescent bulb. His Edison Electric Light Company also devised a system of power generation and distribution to widely provide electricity. To market his ideas, at Christmas 1880, he illuminated Menlo Park.

Edison's system of direct current could transmit electric power only a mile or two, losing voltage the farther it traveled. Inventor George Westinghouse solved the problem. He purchased European patent rights to generators that used alternating current and transformers that reduced high-voltage power, thus making long-distance transmission more efficient.

Other entrepreneurs utilized new business practices to market Edison's and Westinghouse's technological breakthroughs. Samuel Insull, Edison's private secretary, organized Edison power plants nationwide, amassing an electric utility empire. In the late 1880s and early 1890s, financiers Henry Villard and J. P. Morgan bought up patents in electric lighting and merged small equipment-manufacturing companies into the General Electric Company. General Electric and Westinghouse Electric established research laboratories to create electrical products for everyday use.

Individual inventors continued to work independently and sell their handiwork and patents to manufacturers. Granville T. Woods, an engineer sometimes called the

The Atlantic Cable

During the late nineteenth century, as American manufacturers expanded their markets overseas, their ability to communicate with customers and investors improved immeasurably as a result of telegraph cable beneath the Atlantic Ocean. The telegraph was an American invention, and Cyrus Field, who thought up the idea of laying cable across the ocean, was an American. Yet most of the engineers and capitalists involved were British. In 1851 a British company laid the first successful undersea telegraph cable from Dover, England, to Calais, France, proving that an insulated wire could carry signals underwater. Its effectiveness inspired British and American businessmen to attempt a larger project across the Atlantic.

The first attempts failed, but in 1866 a British ship, funded by British investors, successfully laid a telegraph wire that operated without interruption. Thereafter, England and the United States grew more closely linked in diplomatic relations, and citizens of both nations developed greater concern for each other. When American president James Garfield was assassinated in 1881, the news traveled almost instantly to Great Britain, and Britons mourned the death profusely.

Some people lamented the stresses that near-instant international communications now created. But financially savvy individuals experienced welcome benefits. Rapid availability of stock quotes helped the New York and London stock exchanges boom. Newspaper readers enjoyed learning about events on the other side of the ocean the next day, instead of a week later. By 1902 underwater cables circled the globe. The age of global telecommunications had begun.

Laid by British ships across the ocean in 1866, the Atlantic cable linked the United States with England and continental Europe so that telegraph communications could be sent and received much more swiftly than ever before. Now Europeans and Americans could exchange news about politics, business, and military movements almost instantly, whereas previously such information could take a week or more to travel from one country to another.
(Library of Congress)

469

black Edison, patented thirty-five devices vital to electronics and communications. Most were sold to companies like General Electric, including an automatic circuit breaker, an electromagnetic brake, and instruments to aid communications between railroad trains.

Henry Ford and the Automobile Industry

European inventors made early innovations in the technology of the internal-combustion engine. In 1885 a German engineer, Gottlieb Daimler, built a lightweight engine driven by vaporized gasoline. In the 1890s, Henry Ford, an electrical engineer in Detroit's Edison Company, experimented with Daimler's engine to power a vehicle. Applying organizational genius to this invention, Ford spawned a massive industry.

Ford had a scheme as well as a product, declaring in 1909, "I am going to democratize the automobile. When I'm through, everybody will be able to afford one." Ford planned to mass-produce thousands of identical cars, and engineers set up assembly lines that drastically reduced the time and production costs. Instead of performing numerous tasks, each worker did just one, repeatedly, assembling the entire car along a conveyor belt.

In 1913 the Ford Motor Company's first assembly line opened in Highland Park inside Detroit, Michigan, and the next year, Ford sold 248,000 cars. Soon, other manufacturers entered the field. Rising automobile output created jobs, higher earnings, and greater profits for related industries, such as oil, paint, rubber, and glass, as well; this in turn necessitated increased resources from the West and abroad. Moreover, assembly-line production would not have been possible without precision machine tools to create standardized and finely tuned parts.

The assembly line broke the production process down into simple tasks that individual workers could efficiently repeat hour after hour. Here, around 1914 assembly-line workers at the Ford plant in Highland Park, Michigan, outside Detroit, are installing pistons in engines of the Model T. (From the Collections of The Henry Ford Museum and Greenfield Village)

By 1914 a Ford car cost $490, one-fourth of the price a decade earlier. But that was too expensive for many workers, who earned at best $2 a day. That year, Ford tried to spur productivity, reduce labor turnover, head off unionization, and better enable his workers to buy the cars they produced through his Five-Dollar-Day plan—a combination of wages and profit sharing.

The du Ponts and the Chemical Industry

The du Pont family similarly transformed the chemical industry. In 1902, fearing antitrust prosecution for the company's near monopoly of the explosives industry, three cousins, Alfred, Coleman, and Pierre, took over E. I. du Pont de Nemours and Company and broadened production into fertilizers, dyes, and other chemical products. In 1911 du Pont scientists and engineers in the nation's first corporate research laboratory adapted cellulose to produce such consumer goods as photographic film, lacquer, textile fibers, and plastics. In 1914 Pierre du Pont invested $25 million in General Motors, helping that company compete with Ford. The du Pont company also pioneered methods of management, accounting, and reinvestment of earnings, which contributed to efficient production, better recordkeeping, and higher profits.

Technology and Southern Industry

The South's major staple crops, tobacco and cotton, helped industrialize the region after the Civil War. Before the 1870s, Americans used tobacco mainly for snuff, cigars, and chewing. But in 1876 James Bonsack, an eighteen-year-old Virginian, invented a cigarette-rolling machine. Sales soared after 1885 when the North Carolinian James B. Duke mass-produced cigarettes with Bonsack's machine and enticed consumers with free samples, trading cards, and billboard ads. By 1900 his American Tobacco Company was a global business, employing black and white workers (including women), though in separate workrooms.

New technology helped relocate the textile industry to the South. Factories with electric looms were more efficient than New England's water-powered mills, required fewer skilled workers, and expanded production hours. Investors built new plants in southern communities, where cheap labor was plentiful. By 1900 the South had more than four hundred textile mills, with 4 million spindles. Women and children earned 50 cents a day for twelve or more hours—about half the wages of northern workers. Most mills hired black workers only as janitors. Companies built villages around their mills, where they controlled housing, stores, schools, and churches and banned company criticism and union organization.

Northern and European investors financed other southern industries. During the 1880s, northern capitalists developed southern iron and steel manufacturing, much of it in Birmingham, Alabama. Between 1890 and 1900, northern lumber syndicates moved into the pine forests of the Gulf states, boosting production 500 percent. Southern wood production advanced the construction industry and relocated furniture and paper production from the North to the South. Challenging the power of the planter class, a business class of manufacturers, merchants, and financiers heralded the emergence of a New South with southern cities as the nerve centers of a new economic order (see Chapter 19).

Consequences of Technology

Machines broadly altered everyday life. Telephones and typewriters made face-to-face communication less important and facilitated correspondence and recordkeeping in growing insurance, banking, and advertising firms. Electric sewing machines made mass-produced clothing. Refrigeration enabled the preservation and shipment of meat, fruit, vegetables, and dairy products. Cash registers and adding machines revamped accounting and created new clerical jobs. At the same time, American universities established programs in engineering.

Profits resulted from higher production at lower costs. As technological innovations made large-scale production more economical, owners replaced small factories with larger ones. Between 1850 and 1900, average capital investment in a manufacturing firm increased by 250 percent. Only large companies could afford to buy complex machines. And large companies received discounts for buying raw materials and shipping in bulk—advantages economists call economies of scale.

Profitability also depended on how production was organized. Where once workers controlled the methods and timing of production, by the 1890s engineers and managers with scientific knowledge planned every task to increase output. Through standardization, they reduced the need for workers' skills, boosting profits at the expense of worker independence.

Frederick W. Taylor and Efficiency

The most influential advocate of efficient production was Frederick W. Taylor. As foreman and engineer for the Midvale Steel Company in the 1880s, Taylor concluded companies could best reduce costs and increase profits by applying studies of "how quickly the various kinds of work . . . ought to be done." This meant producing more for lower cost per unit, usually by eliminating unnecessary workers.

In 1898 Taylor took his stopwatch to the Bethlehem Steel Company to illustrate his principles of scientific management. His experiments required studying workers and devising "a series of motions which can be made quickest and best." For shoveling ore, Taylor designed fifteen kinds of shovels and prescribed the proper motions for each, thereby reducing a crew of 600 men to 140. Soon other companies, including the Watertown Arsenal, applied Taylor's theories.

Consequently, time, as much as quality, became the measure of acceptable work, and management dictated how things were done. As elements of the assembly line, employees feared they were becoming another interchangeable part.

MECHANIZATION AND THE CHANGING STATUS OF LABOR

By 1900, the status of labor shifted dramatically. Technological innovation and assembly-line production created new jobs, but because most machines were labor saving, fewer workers could produce more in less time. Instead of producers, the working class now consisted mainly of employees who worked for hire. Producers were paid on the basis of the quality of what they produced; employees received wages for time spent on the job.

Mass Production

Manufacturing being subdivided into small tasks, workers repeated the same standardized operation all day every day. One investigator found that a worker became "a mere machine." Workers no longer decided when to begin and end the workday or what tools and techniques to use. The clock regulated them. As a Massachusetts factory laborer testified in 1879, "During working hours the men are not allowed to speak to each other . . . on pain of instant discharge. Men are hired to watch and patrol the shop."

Workers such as the Watertown iron molders struggled to retain autonomy. Artisans—glass workers and coopers (barrel makers)—caught in the transition from hand labor to machine production, fought to preserve their work customs, for example, by appointing a fellow worker to read a newspaper aloud while they worked. Immigrant factory workers tried to persuade foremen to hire their relatives and friends. After work, workers enjoyed drinking and holiday celebrations, ignoring employers' attempts to control their social lives.

Concerned with efficiency, employers wanted behavior standards upheld. Ford Motor Company required workers to meet the company's behavior code before becoming eligible for the Five-Dollar-Day plan. To increase worker incentives, some employers established piecework rates, paying per item produced rather than per hour worked. Efforts to increase productivity tried to make workers perform like the machines they operated.

Restructuring of the Work Force

As machines reduced the need for skilled workers, employers cut labor costs by hiring women and children and paying them low wages. Between 1880 and 1900, the numbers of employed women soared from 2.6 million to 8.6 million (see Figure 18.1). The proportion of women in domestic service (maids, cooks, laundresses)—the most common and lowest-paid female employment—dropped as jobs opened in other sectors. In manufacturing, women usually held menial positions in textile mills and food-processing plants that paid $1.56 for a seventy-hour week. (Unskilled men received $7 to $10.) Although the number of female factory hands tripled between 1880 and 1900, the proportion of women workers remained the same.

Expansion of the clerical and retail sectors boosted the numbers and percentages of women who were typists, bookkeepers, and sales clerks—previously male jobs. Inventions, such as the typewriter, cash register, and adding machine, simplified these tasks. By 1920, women filled nearly half of all clerical jobs; in 1880 only 4 percent were women. Although poorly paid, women were attracted to sales jobs because of the respectability, pleasant surroundings, and contact with affluent customers these positions offered. Nevertheless, sex discrimination persisted. In department stores, only male cashiers took in cash and made change. Women held some low-level supervisory positions, but males dominated the managerial ranks.

Meanwhile, the number of children in nonagricultural occupations tripled between 1870 and 1900. In 1890 over 18 percent of children between ages ten and

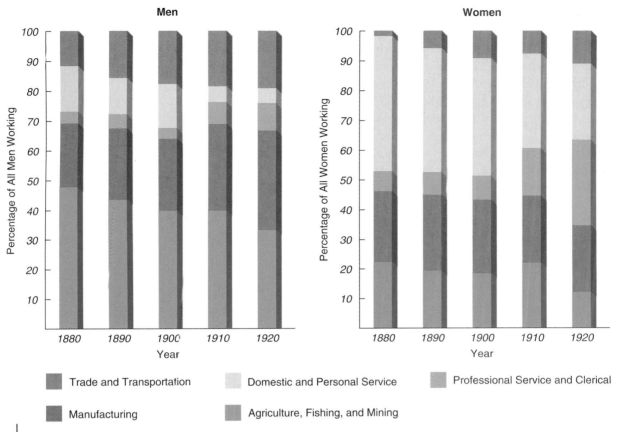

Figure 18.1   Distribution of Occupational Categories Among Employed Men and Women, 1880–1920
The changing lengths of the bar segments of each part of this graph represent trends in male and female employment. Over the forty years covered by this graph, the agriculture, fishing, and mining segment for men and the domestic service segment for women declined the most, whereas notable increases occurred in manufacturing for men and professional services (especially store clerks and teachers) for women.   (*Source:* U.S. Bureau of the Census, *Census of the United States, 1880, 1890, 1900, 1910, 1920* [Washington, DC: U.S. Government Printing Office].)

fifteen were gainfully employed (see Figure 18.2), particularly in textile and shoe factories. Mechanization created numerous light tasks, such as running errands, which children could handle cheaply. Conditions were especially hard for child laborers in the South, where mill owners induced desperate white sharecroppers and tenant farmers to bind their children to factories at miserably low wages.

Several states, especially in the Northeast, passed laws specifying minimum ages and maximum hours for child labor. But statutes regulated only firms operating within state borders, not those engaged in interstate commerce. Enforcing age requirements proved difficult because many parents, needing income, lied about their children's ages. After 1900, state laws and automation, along with compulsory school attendance laws, reduced the number of children employed in manufacturing, and Progressive era reformers sought federal legislation restricting child labor (see Chapter 21). Still, many children continued to work at street trades—shining shoes and peddling—while poor children scavenged the streets for coal and wood and discarded clothing and furniture.

Industrial Accidents

Repetitive tasks using high-speed machinery dulled concentration, and the slightest mistake could cause serious injury. Industrial accidents rose steadily before 1920, killing or maiming hundreds of thousands of people annually. In 1913, after factories installed safety devices, 25,000 people died in industrial mishaps and 1 million were injured. There was no disability insurance to replace lost income, and families suffered acutely.

The most notorious tragedy was a fire at New York City's Triangle Shirtwaist Company in 1911, which killed 146 workers, mostly teenage immigrant women trapped in locked workrooms. Despite public clamor, prevailing free-market views hampered the passage of legislation regulating working conditions, and employers denied responsibility for employees' well-being.

Freedom of Contract

To justify their treatment of workers, employers asserted the principle of freedom of contract, claiming wages and working conditions resulted from supply and demand. Employers asserted that since workers entered into a contract with bosses, workers could seek another job if they did not like the wages or hours. Employers used supply and demand to set wages as low as laborers would accept. Employees felt trapped. A factory worker told Congress in 1879, "The market is glutted, and . . . the pay is cut down; our tasks are increased, and if we remonstrate, we are told our places can be filled."

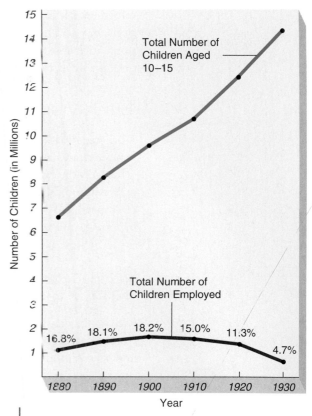

Figure 18.2   Children in the Labor Force, 1880–1930

The percentage of children in the labor force peaked around the turn of the century. Thereafter, the passage of state laws requiring children to attend school until age fourteen and limiting the ages at which children could be employed caused child labor to decline. (*Source:* Data from *The Statistical History of the United States from Colonial Times to the Present* [Stamford, CT: Fairfield Publishers, 1965].)

Court Rulings on Labor Reform

Reformers and union leaders lobbied for laws regulating working conditions, but the Supreme Court limited such legislation by narrowly defining which jobs were dangerous and which workers needed protection. In *Holden v. Hardy* (1896), the Court upheld a law regulating miners' working hours because overly long workdays increased potential injuries. In *Lochner v. New York* (1905), however, the Court voided a law that limited bakery workers to a sixty-hour week and ten-hour day. It ruled that baking was not a dangerous enough occupation to justify restricting workers' right to sell their labor freely. Such restriction, according to the Court, violated the Fourteenth Amendment's guarantee that no state could "deprive any person of life, liberty, or property without due process of law."

In *Muller v. Oregon* (1908), the Court used a different rationale to uphold limiting laundry women to a ten-hour workday. It set aside its *Lochner* argument to assert that a woman's well-being "becomes an object of public interest and care in order to preserve the strength and vigor of the race." The case represented a victory for labor reformers seeking government regulation of women's hours and working conditions. But on the basis of the *Muller* decision, later laws barred women from occupations, such as in printing and transportation, that required heavy lifting, long hours, or night work, further confining women to low-paying, dead-end jobs.

LABOR VIOLENCE AND THE UNION MOVEMENT

Workers adjusted to mechanization as best they could, but anxiety over lost independence and a desire for better wages, hours, and working conditions drew disgruntled workers into unions. Trade unions for skilled workers in crafts like printing and iron molding dated from the early 1800s, but their influence was limited. The National Labor Union, founded in 1866, claimed 640,000 members from various industries, but it collapsed in 1873 after legislative failures.

Railroad Strikes of 1877

In the economic slump that followed the Panic of 1873, railroad managers cut wages, increased workloads, and laid off workers, especially union members. Workers responded with strikes and riots. The year 1877 marked a crisis. In July, unionized railroad workers organized strikes to protest wage cuts. Violence spread from Pennsylvania and West Virginia to the Midwest, Texas, and California, derailing trains and burning rail yards. State militia, organized and commanded by employers, broke up picket lines and fired into crowds. Factory workers, wives, and merchants aided the strikers, while railroads enlisted strikebreakers to replace union men.

Pittsburgh experienced the worst violence. On July 21 state troopers bayoneted and fired on rock-throwing demonstrators, killing ten and wounding many more. Infuriated, the mob drove the troopers into a roundhouse and set fires that destroyed 39 buildings, 104 engines, and 1,245 freight and passenger cars. The next day, the troopers shot their way out and killed twenty more citizens before fleeing. After a month, President Rutherford B. Hayes sent in federal soldiers—the first significant use of the army to quell labor unrest.

Knights of Labor

About the same time as the railroad strike, the Knights of Labor tried to attract a broad base of laborers. Founded in 1869 by Philadelphia garment cutters, the Knights began recruiting other workers in the 1870s. In 1879 Terence V. Powderly, a machinist and the mayor of Scranton, Pennsylvania, was elected grand master. Under his guidance, Knights' membership grew, peaking at 730,000 in 1886. In contrast to most craft unions, Knights welcomed unskilled and semiskilled workers, including women, immigrants, and African Americans (but not Chinese).

The Knights sought a workers' alliance offering an alternative to profit-oriented industrial capitalism. They intended to eliminate conflict between labor and management by establishing a cooperative society in which laborers, not capitalists, owned factories, mines, and railroads. The goal, argued Powderly, was to "eventually make every man his own master—every man his own employer."

The cooperative idea, attractive in the abstract, was unattainable because employers could out-compete laborers who might try to establish businesses. Strikes might achieve immediate goals, but Powderly and other Knights leaders argued that strikes diverted attention from the long-term goal of a cooperative society and that workers lost more by striking.

Some Knights, however, supported militant action. In 1886 the railroad magnate Jay Gould refused to negotiate when Knights demanded higher wages and union recognition from Southwest Railroad. A strike began in Texas and spread to Kansas, Missouri, and Arkansas. As violence increased, Powderly met with Gould and called off the strike, hoping for a settlement. But Gould rejected concessions, and the Knights gave in. Militant craft unions deserted the Knights, upset by Powderly's compromise.

After the Haymarket riot (see below), Knights' membership dwindled, although the union made a brief attempt to unite with Populists in the 1890s (see Chapter 20). Craft unions replaced the Knights' broad-based but often vague appeal, and labor unity faded.

Haymarket Riot

While the Knights were striking, other groups calling for an eight-hour workday generated the largest labor demonstration in the country's history. On May 1, 1886, in Chicago, some 100,000 workers turned out, including anarchists who believed in using violence. Chicago police, fearing that European radicals were transplanting their tradition of violence to the United States, mobilized. The day passed calmly, but two days later, police stormed an area near the McCormick reaper plant and broke up a battle between striking unionists and nonunion strikebreakers, killing two unionists and wounding others.

The next evening, laborers protested police brutality at Haymarket Square near downtown Chicago. As police approached, a bomb exploded, killing seven policemen and injuring sixty-seven. Authorities made mass arrests, and a court convicted eight anarchists of the bombing, despite questionable evidence. Four were executed, and one committed suicide in prison. The remaining three were pardoned in 1893 by Illinois governor John P. Altgeld.

The Haymarket bombing, like the 1877 railroad strikes, drew attention to labor's growing discontent and heightened the fear of radicalism. The participation of anarchists and socialists, many of them foreign-born, heightened the urgency that law and order act swiftly to prevent social turmoil. Private Chicago donors helped establish a military base outside the city. Elsewhere, governments strengthened police forces and armories. Employer associations countered labor militancy by circulating blacklists of union activists whom they would not employ and by hiring private detectives to suppress strikes.

American Federation of Labor

Founded in 1886, the American Federation of Labor (AFL) emerged from that year's upheavals as the major workers' organization. An alliance of national craft unions, the AFL had about 140,000 members, mostly skilled workers. Led by Samuel Gompers, former head of the Cigar Makers' Union, the AFL pressed for higher wages, shorter hours, and the right to bargain collectively. Unlike the Knights, the AFL accepted capitalism and worked to improve conditions within it. The AFL avoided party politics, adhering instead to Gompers's dictum to support labor's friends and oppose its enemies, regardless of party.

AFL membership grew to 1 million by 1901 and 2.5 million by 1917, when it consisted of 111 national unions and 27,000 locals. Member unions organized by craft and had little interest in recruiting unskilled workers or women. Of 6.3 million employed women in 1910, fewer than 2 percent belonged to unions. Male unionists rationalized women's exclusion by insisting that women should not be employed. According to one labor leader, "The mental and physical makeup of woman is in revolt against wage service. She is competing with the man who is her father or husband or is to become her husband." Mostly, unionists worried that, because women were paid less, men's wages would be lowered or their jobs given to cheaper female laborers.

Influenced by nativism and racism, organized labor excluded most immigrant and African American workers, fearing they, too, would depress wages. A few trade unions welcomed skilled immigrants. Blacks were prominent in the coal miners' union and were partially unionized in such trades as construction, barbering, and dock work, where large numbers of African American worked. But they could belong only to segregated local unions in the South, and most northern AFL unions had exclusion policies. Long-held prejudices were reinforced when blacks and immigrants, eager for work, replaced striking whites.

Homestead Strike

The AFL and the labor movement suffered setbacks in the early 1890s, when labor violence stirred public fears. In July 1892 the AFL-affiliated Amalgamated Association of Iron and Steelworkers went on strike against pay cuts in Homestead, Pennsylvania. Henry C. Frick, president of Carnegie Steel Company, closed the plant. Shortly thereafter, Frick hired three hundred guards from the Pinkerton Detective Agency to protect the factory and snuck them in by barge at night. Lying in wait, angry workers attacked and routed the Pinkertons. State troops intervened, and after five months the strikers gave in. By then public opinion turned against the union.

Pullman Strike

In 1894 workers at the Pullman Palace (railroad passenger) Car Company walked out over exploitative policies at the company town near Chicago. The paternalistic owner, George Pullman, provided everything for the twelve thousand residents of the so-called model town named after him. His company controlled all land and buildings, the school, the bank, and the water and gas systems. It paid wages, fixed rents, and spied on disgruntled employees.

One thing Pullman would not do was negotiate with workers. When hard times hit in 1893, Pullman protected profits by cutting wages 25 to 40 percent while holding firm on rents and prices. Hard-pressed workers sent a committee to Pullman to protest. He reacted by firing three committee members. Enraged workers called a strike; Pullman closed the factory. The union, led by Eugene V. Debs, refused to handle Pullman cars attached to any trains. Pullman rejected arbitration, and the railroad owners' association enlisted aid from U.S. Attorney General Richard Olney, a former railroad lawyer, who obtained a court injunction to prevent the union from "obstructing the railways and holding up the mails." President Grover Cleveland ordered federal troops to Chicago. Within a month strikers gave in, and Debs was jailed for defying the injunction. The Supreme Court upheld Debs's six-month sentence, arguing that the federal government could legally remove obstacles to interstate commerce.

IWW

Colorado miners engaged in several bitter struggles. In 1905 they helped form a new, radical labor organization, the Industrial Workers of the World (IWW). Like the Knights, it strove to unite all laborers of all races. Its motto was "An injury to one is an injury to all." But the Wobblies, as IWW members were known, exceeded the Knights by espousing violence and sabotage.

Embracing the rhetoric of class conflict and socialism, Wobblies believed workers should seize and run the nation's industries. Mary "Mother" Jones, an Illinois coalfield union organizer; Elizabeth Gurley Flynn, a fiery orator known as the "Joan of Arc of the labor movement"; Italian radical Carlo Tresca; and William D. ("Big Bill") Haywood, the brawny, one-eyed founder of the Western Federation of Miners, headed a series of strikes. Although the Wobblies' anticapitalist goals and aggressive tactics attracted publicity, IWW membership probably never exceeded 150,000. The organization collapsed during World War I when federal prosecution sent many of its leaders to jail and local police violently harassed IWW members.

Women Unionists

Despite exclusion from unions, some women organized and fought employers as strenuously as men. The Uprising of the 20,000 in New York City, a 1909 strike by male and female immigrant members of the International Ladies' Garment Workers' Union (ILGWU), was one of the country's largest strikes. Female trade-union membership swelled during the 1910s, but men monopolized national leadership.

Women did dominate the Telephone Operators' Department of the International Brotherhood of Electrical Workers. Organized in Montana and San Francisco early in the twentieth century, the union spread throughout the Bell system, the nation's monopolistic telephone company and single largest employer of women. To promote solidarity among their mostly young members, union leaders organized dances, excursions, bazaars, and educational programs. The union resisted scientific management and rigid supervision. In 1919 several militant union branches paralyzed the phone service in five New England states, but the union collapsed after a failed strike there in 1923.

A key organization promoting laboring women's interests was the Women's Trade Union League (WTUL), founded in 1903 and patterned after a similar organization in England. The WTUL sought workplace protection legislation and reduced hours for female workers, sponsored educational activities, and campaigned for woman suffrage. It helped telephone operators organize, and in 1909 it supported the ILGWU's massive strike against New York City sweatshops. Initially the union's highest officers were middle-class women, but control shifted in the 1910s to forceful working-class leaders, notably Agnes Nestor, a glove maker, and Rose Schneiderman, a cap maker. The WTUL advocated opening apprenticeship programs to women and training female workers for leadership. It served as a vital link between the labor and women's movements into the 1920s.

The Experience of Wage Work

Dramatic strikes aside, only a small fraction of American wage workers belonged to unions. In 1900 about 1 million out of a total of 27.6 million workers were unionized. By 1920 union membership had grown to 5 million, only 13 percent of the work force. Unionization was strong in construction trades, transportation, communications, and, to a lesser extent, manufacturing. For many workers, getting and keeping a job took priority over higher wages and shorter hours. Job instability and the seasonal nature of work seriously hindered union organizing. Few companies employed workers year-round; most hired during peak seasons and laid workers off during slack periods.

The millions of men, women, and children who were not unionized tried to cope with machine age pressures. Many native-born and immigrant workers joined fraternal societies, such as the Polish Roman Catholic Union, the African American Colored Brotherhood and Sisterhood of Honor, and the Jewish B'nai B'rith. For small contributions, these organizations provided members with life insurance, sickness benefits, and burial costs.

During the machine age, industrial wages rose between 1877 and 1914, boosting purchasing power and creating a mass market for standardized goods. Yet in 1900 most employees worked sixty hours a week at wages averaging 20 cents an hour for skilled work and 10 cents an hour for unskilled. Even as wages rose, living costs increased faster.

STANDARDS OF LIVING

American ingenuity combined with mass production and mass marketing to make available myriad goods that previously had not existed or had been the province of the wealthy. The new material well-being, symbolized by canned foods, ready-made clothing, and appliances, blended Americans of differing status into consumer communities and accentuated differences between those who could afford goods and services and those who could not.

Commonplace Luxuries

If a society's affluence is measured by how it converts luxuries into commonplace articles, the United States was becoming affluent between 1880 and 1920. By 1899 manufactured goods and perishable foodstuffs had become increasingly available. That year Americans bought 2 billion machine-produced cigarettes and 151,000 pairs of silk stockings, consumed 100 crates of oranges for every 1,000 people, and spent an average of 63 cents per person on soap. By 1921 Americans smoked 43 billion cigarettes (403 per person), bought 217 million pairs of silk stockings, ate 248 crates of oranges per 1,000 people, and spent $1.40 on soap per year.

Data for the period show that incomes rose broadly, spawning massive fortunes and creating a new industrial elite. By 1920 the richest 5 percent of the population received almost one-fourth of all earned income. Incomes also rose among the middle

TABLE 18.1   American Living Standards, 1890–1910

	1890	1910
Income and Earnings		
Annual income		
Clerical worker	$843	$1,156
Public school teacher	256	492
Industrial worker	486	630
Farm laborer	233	336
Hourly wage		
Soft-coal miner	0.18	0.21
Iron worker	0.17*	0.23
Shoe worker	0.14*	0.19
Paper worker	0.12*	0.17
Labor Statistics		
Number of people in labor force	28.5 million	41.7 million†
Average workweek in manufacturing	60 h	51 h

*1892.
†1920.

class. Average pay for clerical workers rose 36 percent between 1890 and 1910 (see Table 18.1). At the turn of the century, federal employees averaged $1,072 a year (around $25,000 in modern dollars). The middle class could afford comfortable housing. A six- or seven-room house cost around $3,000 to buy (about $65,000 in current dollars) and from $15 to $20 per month ($400 to $500 in current dollars) to rent.

Although hourly wages for industrial employees increased, workers had to expend a disproportionate amount on necessities. Average, annual wages of factory laborers rose about 30 percent, from $486 in 1890 (about $12,000 in modern dollars) to $630 in 1910 (about $15,500 in current dollars). In industries with large female work forces, hourly pay rates remained lower than in male-dominated industries. Nevertheless, as Table 18.1 shows, most wages moved upward.

Cost of Living

Wage increases mean little, however, if living costs rise as fast or faster. The weekly cost of living for a typical family of four rose over 47 percent between 1889 and 1913. Goods that cost $68 in 1889 increased, after a slight dip in the mid-1890s, to $100 by 1913 (about $2,157 in current dollars).

How, then, could working-class Americans afford goods and services? Many could not. The daughter of a textile worker, recalling her school days, described how "some of the kids would bring bars of chocolate, others an orange. . . . I suppose they were richer than a family like ours. My father used to buy a bag of candy and a bag of peanuts every payday. . . . And that's all we'd have until the next payday."

Supplements to Family Income

Still, a family could raise its income and partake modestly in consumer society by sending children and women into the labor market. Where a father alone might earn $600 a year, wages of other family members could lift total household income to $900. Many families also rented rooms to boarders, yielding up to $200 annually. Between 1889 and 1901, working-class families markedly increased expenditures for life insurance and new leisure activities (see Chapter 19), improving their living standard.

More than ever, working Americans lived within a money economy. Between 1890 and 1920, the labor force increased by 50 percent, from 28 million workers to 42 million. These figures represent a change in the nature of work as much as increases in available jobs. In the rural households of the nineteenth century, women and children performed crucial tasks of cooking, cleaning, planting, and harvesting—labor absent from employment figures because they earned no wages. As the nation industrialized and the agricultural sector declined, paid employment became more common. The proportion of Americans who worked probably did not increase markedly. What was new was the increase in paid employment, making consumer goods and services more affordable.

Higher Life Expectancy Medical advances, better diets, and improved housing sharply reduced death rates and extended life. Between 1900 and 1920, life expectancy rose by six years, and the death rate dropped by 24 percent. Notable declines occurred in deaths from typhoid, diphtheria, influenza (except for a harsh pandemic in 1918 and 1919), tuberculosis, and intestinal ailments. There were, however, significantly more deaths from cancer, diabetes, and heart disease, afflictions of an aging population and of new environmental factors, such as smoke and chemical pollution. Homicides and automobile-related deaths also increased dramatically.

Not only were luxuries more attainable, but upward mobility seemed more accessible, too. Public education, aided by the construction of new schools and laws requiring children to stay in school to age fourteen, equipped young people to achieve a higher living standard than their parents. The creation of managerial and sales jobs in service industries helped counter downward mobility when mechanization pushed skilled workers from their crafts. And mass production added greater convenience to workers' lives.

Flush Toilets and Other Innovations At the vanguard of a revolution in lifestyles stood the toilet. The chain-pull, washdown water closet, invented in England around 1870, reached the United States in the 1880s. Shortly after 1900, the flush toilet appeared. Before 1880 only luxury hotels and wealthy families had private indoor bathrooms. By the 1890s the germ theory of disease was raising fears about carelessly disposed human waste as a source of infection and water contamination. Americans combined cleanliness with convenience, installing modern toilets in middle-class urban houses. By the 1920s, they were prevalent in working-class homes, too. Edward and Clarence Scott, who manufactured white tissue in perforated rolls, provided Americans a more convenient form of toilet tissue than the rough paper they previously used. Bodily functions took on an unpleasant image, and the home bathroom became a place of utmost privacy.

Before the mid-nineteenth century, Americans typically ate only foods in season. Drying, smoking, and salting could preserve meat for a short time, but the availability of fresh meat and milk was limited due to spoilage. A French inventor developed the cooking-and-sealing process of canning around 1810, and in the 1850s an American man named Gail Borden devised a means of condensing and preserving milk. Sales of canned goods and condensed milk increased during the 1860s, but there were production problems. In the 1880s, inventors fashioned machines to peel fruits and vegetables, process salmon, and mass-produce cans from tin plate. Now, people everywhere could consume tomatoes, milk, oysters, and other alternatives to previously monotonous diets.

Other inventions broadened Americans' diets. Growing urban populations created demands for more produce. Railroad refrigerator cars enabled growers and meatpackers to ship perishables farther and preserve them longer. By the 1890s, northern city dwellers could enjoy southern and western strawberries, grapes, and tomatoes for several months. Home iceboxes enabled middle-class families to store perishables, and by 1900 the nation had two thousand ice plants, many making home deliveries.

Dietary Reform

The availability of new foods also inspired health advocates to reform American diets. In the 1870s, John H. Kellogg, nutritionist and manager of the Western Health Reform Institute in Battle Creek, Michigan, began serving patients health foods, including peanut butter and wheat flakes. Years later, his brother, William K. Kellogg, invented corn flakes, and another nutritionist, Charles W. Post, introduced Grape-Nuts, replacing breakfast eggs, potatoes, and meat with supposedly healthier cereal. Growing numbers of published cookbooks and cooking schools reflected the heightened interest in food and its possibilities for health and enjoyment.

As in the past, the poorest people still consumed cheap foods, heavy in starches and carbohydrates, and little meat. Now, though, many could purchase previously unavailable fruits, vegetables, and dairy products. Workers spent almost half of a breadwinner's wages on food, but they never suffered the malnutrition that plagued other developing nations

Ready-Made Clothing

The sewing machine and standardized sizes sparked a revolution in clothing. Invented in Europe but refined in the mid-nineteenth century by Americans Elias Howe Jr. and Isaac M. Singer, the sewing machine was used in clothing and shoe manufacture. Demand for uniforms during the Civil War boosted the ready-made clothing industry, and by 1890 annual retail sales reached $1.5 billion. Mass

Using color, large-scale scenes, and fanciful images, manufacturers of consumer goods advertised their products to a public eager to buy. This ad from the W. K. Kellogg Company, maker of breakfast foods, shows the increasingly common practice of using an attractive young woman to capture attention.   (Picture Research Consultants and Archives)

production enabled manufacturers to turn out quality apparel at low cost and to standardize sizes. By 1900 only the poorest families could not afford ready-to-wear clothes. Tailors and seamstresses were relegated to repair work. Many women continued to make clothing at home, but commercial dress patterns simplified the process and injected another form of standardization into everyday life.

Mass-produced garments altered clothing styles and tastes. As women's participation in work and leisure activities increased, dress designers shifted from burdensome Victorian designs to more comfortable styles. In the 1890s, hemlines raised and high-boned collars disappeared. By the 1920s a dress required three yards of material instead of ten.

Men's clothes, too, became lightweight. Before 1900, men in the middle and well-off working classes would have owned two suits: one for Sundays and special occasions and one for everyday. After 1900, however, manufacturers produced inexpensive garments from seasonal fabrics. Men replaced derbies with felt hats, and stiff collars and cuffs with soft ones; somber, dark-blue serge gave way to lighter shades and more intricate weaves.

Department and Chain Stores

Department stores and chain stores helped create and serve this new consumerism. Between 1865 and 1900, Macy's Department Store in New York, Wanamaker's in Philadelphia, Marshall Field in Chicago, and Rich's in Atlanta became urban landmarks. Previously, working classes bought goods in stores with limited inventories, and wealthier people patronized fancy shops; prices, quality of goods, and social custom discouraged each from shopping at the other's shops. Now, department stores, with their open displays, caused a merchandising revolution, offering home deliveries, exchange policies, and charge accounts.

Meanwhile, the Great Atlantic Tea Company, founded in 1859, became the first grocery chain. Renamed the Great Atlantic & Pacific Tea Company in 1869 (known as A&P), the stores bought in volume and sold to the public at low prices. By 1915 there were eighteen hundred A&P stores, and twelve thousand more over the next ten years.

Advertising

In the late nineteenth century, companies that mass-produced consumer goods hired advertisers to create brand loyalty. In 1881 Congress passed a trademark law enabling producers to protect brand names. Thousands of companies registered products as varied as Hires Root Beer, Uneeda Biscuits, and Carter's Little Liver Pills. Advertising agencies—a service pioneered by N. W. Ayer and Son of Philadelphia—offered expert advice on cultivating consumer loyalty. In 1865 retailers spent about $9.5 million on advertising, $95 million by 1900, and nearly $500 million by 1919. Newspapers served as the prime instrument for advertising, as people read them to find out what was for sale as well as what was happening.

Outdoor billboards and electric signs were also important selling devices. Billboards on city buildings, in railroad stations, and alongside roads promoted such products as Gillette razors, Kodak cameras, Wrigley chewing gum, and Budweiser beer. In the mid-1890s, electric lights made billboards exciting. The flashing electric signs on New York City's Broadway gave the street its label: the Great White Way.

THE CORPORATE CONSOLIDATION MOVEMENT

Neither new products nor new marketing techniques could mask unsettling economic factors. The huge capital investment for new technology meant that factories had to operate near capacity to recover costs. But the more manufacturers produced, the more they had to sell, which meant spending more on advertising and cutting prices. To compensate, they further expanded production and often reduced wages. To expand, they borrowed money. And to repay loans, they had to produce and sell even more. This spiraling process strangled small firms and thrust workers into constant uncertainty.

In this environment, optimism could dissolve at the hint that debtors could not meet their obligations. Economic downturns occurred regularly—1873, 1884, and 1893. Some business leaders blamed overproduction, others, underconsumption; still others blamed lax credit and investment practices. Still, businesspeople wanted to combat the uncertainty of boom-and-bust business cycles. Many adopted centralized forms of business organization, notably corporations, pools, trusts, and holding companies.

Rise of Corporations

Industrialists never questioned the capitalist system. They sought new ways to build on the base of state laws of the early 1800s, encouraging commerce and industry. Under such laws, anyone could start a company and raise money by selling stock to investors. Stockholders shared in profits without personal risk, because laws limited their liability for company debts to the amount of their own investment. Responsibility for company administration rested with its managers.

By 1900 two-thirds of all U.S. manufactured goods were produced by corporations like General Electric and the American Tobacco Company. In the 1880s and 1890s, the Supreme Court ruled that corporations, like individuals, are protected by the Fourteenth Amendment. States could not deny corporations equal protection under the law and could not deprive them of rights or property without due process of law. Such rulings shielded corporations from government interference.

Pools

To combat downward business cycles, corporations sought larger economic concentration. Between the late 1880s and early 1900s, business consolidation produced massive conglomerates that have since dominated the nation's economy. At first such alliances were informal, consisting of cooperative agreements among firms making the same product or offering the same service. Through these arrangements, called pools, competing companies tried to control the market by agreeing how much each should produce and sharing profits. Used by railroads, steel producers, and whiskey distillers, pools depended on their members' honesty. During slow periods, however, pool members secretly reduced prices or sold more than the agreed quota to boost profits. Pools' usefulness was fading when the Interstate Commerce Act of 1887 outlawed them among railroads.

Trusts and Holding Companies

John D. Rockefeller, founder of Standard Oil, considered pools weak. In 1879 his lawyer, Samuel Dodd, devised another means of dominating the market. Because state laws prohibited one corporation from holding stock in another, Dodd utilized an old device called a trust, a legal arrangement whereby a responsible individual would manage the financial affairs of another person who was unwilling or unable to do so. Dodd reasoned that one company could control an industry by luring stockholders of smaller companies to yield control of their stock "in trust" to the larger company's board of trustees. This allowed Rockefeller to achieve horizontal integration—the acquisition of similar companies—of the profitable petroleum industry in 1882 by combining his corporation with other refineries.

In 1888 New Jersey adopted laws allowing corporations chartered there to own property in other states and stock in other corporations. (This facilitated the creation of the holding company, which owned a partial or complete interest in other companies.) Holding companies could merge their assets (buildings, equipment, inventory, and cash) as well as their management. Rockefeller's holding company, Standard Oil, merged forty independents. By 1898 Standard Oil refined 84 percent of all oil produced in the nation, controlled most pipelines, and engaged in natural-gas production and ownership of oil-producing properties.

To dominate their markets, many holding companies sought control over all aspects of the industry, including raw materials, manufacturing, and distribution. A model of such vertical integration, which fused related businesses under unified management, was Gustavus Swift's Chicago meat-processing operation. During the 1880s, Swift invested in livestock, slaughterhouses, refrigerator cars, and marketing to ensure profits from beef sales at prices he could control.

Mergers provided order and profits. Between 1889 and 1903, three hundred combinations were formed, mostly trusts and holding companies. The most spectacular was U.S. Steel Corporation, financed by J. P. Morgan in 1901. Made up of iron-ore properties, freight carriers, wire mills, and other firms, it was capitalized at over $1.4 billion (more than $35 billion in current dollars). In 1896 fewer than a dozen corporations were worth over $10 million; by 1903 three hundred were worth that, and seventeen had assets exceeding $100 million. These huge companies ruthlessly put thousands of small firms out of business.

Financiers

The merger movement created a new species of businessman, whose vocation was financial organizing. Shrewd investors sought opportunities for combination, formed a holding company, then persuaded producers to sell their firms to the new company. These financiers raised money by selling stock and borrowing from banks. Investment bankers like J. P. Morgan and Jacob Schiff piloted the merger movement, inspiring awe with their financial power.

Corporate growth turned stock and bond exchanges into hubs of activity. In 1886 trading on the New York Stock Exchange passed 1 million shares daily. By 1914 the number of industrial stocks traded reached 511, compared with 145 in 1869. Between 1870 and 1900, foreign investment in American companies rose from $1.5 billion to $3.5 billion. Assets of savings banks, concentrated in the Northeast and on the West Coast, rose by 700 percent between 1875 and 1897. States loosened regulations to enable banks to invest in railroads and industrial enterprises.

THE GOSPEL OF WEALTH AND ITS CRITICS

Business leaders used corporate consolidation to minimize competition and justified their tactics with the doctrine of Social Darwinism. This theory loosely grafted Charles Darwin's theory of survival of the fittest onto laissez faire, the doctrine that government should not interfere in private economic matters. Social Darwinists reasoned that in a free-market economy, wealth would flow naturally to those most capable of handling it. In this view, large corporations represented the natural accumulation of economic power by those best suited for it.

Social Darwinists reasoned, too, that wealth carried moral responsibilities. Steel baron Andrew Carnegie asserted the Gospel of Wealth—that as guardians of society's wealth, he and other industrialists had a duty to serve society. Carnegie donated more than $350 million to libraries, schools, peace initiatives, and the arts. Such philanthropy, however, enabled benefactors to define what was good for society; it did not translate into paying workers decent wages.

Government Assistance to Business

Leaders in the corporate consolidation movement extolled initiative but also pressed for government assistance. Denouncing efforts to legislate maximum working hours or factory conditions as interference, they nonetheless lobbied for public subsidies, loans, and tax relief to encourage business growth. Grants to railroads (see Chapter 17) were one form of such assistance. Tariffs, which benefited American products by placing import taxes on imported products, were another. Industrialists argued that tariff protection encouraged the development of new products and new enterprises. But tariffs also forced consumers to pay artificially high prices.

Dissenting Voices

Critics charged that trusts and other big businesses stifled opportunity and originated from greed. Such charges by farmers, workers, and intellectuals reflected an ardent fear of monopoly—the domination of an economic activity (such as oil refining) by one powerful company (such as Standard Oil). Those who feared monopoly believed that large corporations fixed prices, exploited workers by cutting wages, destroyed opportunity by crushing small businesses, and threatened democracy by corrupting politicians.

By the mid-1880s, some intellectuals increasingly challenged Social Darwinism and laissez-faire economics. In *Dynamic Sociology* (1883), the sociologist Lester Ward argued that a system guaranteeing survival only to the fittest was wasteful and brutal. Instead, Ward reasoned, cooperative activity fostered by government intervention was fairer. The economists Richard Ely, John R. Commons, and Edward Bemis denounced laissez faire and praised the assistance government could offer ordinary people.

Others questioned why the United States had to have so many poor people while a few became wealthy. Henry George was a struggling San Francisco printer with a seventh-grade education but an avid reader of economic theory. He believed that economic inequality stemmed from the ability of a few to profit from rising land values, which made landowners rich from ever-higher rents as demand for living and working space especially in cities, skyrocketed. To prevent profiteering, George proposed replacing all taxes with a single tax on the unearned increment—the rise in property values caused by increased demand rather than owners' improvements. Argued in *Progress and Poverty* (1879), George's popular plan almost won him the mayoralty of New York City in 1886.

Novelist Edward Bellamy believed that competitive capitalism promoted waste and proposed that government own the means of production. In his popular novel, *Locking Backward* (1888), he depicted Boston in the year 2000 as a peaceful community run by benevolent elders managing the economy with scientific principles that assured everyone a job. Bellamy hoped that a "principle of fraternal cooperation" would replace vicious competition and wasteful monopoly. Dubbed Nationalism, his vision sparked Nationalist clubs across the country and kindled popular appeals for political reform, social welfare measures, and government ownership of railroads and utilities.

Antitrust Legislation   Several states took steps to prohibit monopolies and regulate business. By 1900 twenty-seven states banned pools, and fifteen had constitutional provisions outlawing trusts (see Chapter 20). But state governments lacked the staff and judicial support for an effective attack on big business, and corporations found ways to evade restrictions.

Congress moved hesitantly toward such legislation but in 1890 passed the Sherman Anti-Trust Act. Introduced by Senator John Sherman of Ohio, the law made illegal "every contract, combination in the form of trust or otherwise, or conspiracy in the restraint of trade." Those found guilty of violating the law faced fines and jail terms, and those wronged by illegal combinations could sue for triple damages. However, the law was watered down when rewritten by pro-business eastern senators. It did not clearly define restraint of trade and consigned the interpretation of its provisions to the often business-friendly courts.

Judges used the law's vagueness to blur distinctions between reasonable and unreasonable restraints of trade. When in 1895 the federal government prosecuted the so-called Sugar Trust for owning 98 percent of sugar-refining capacity, eight of nine Supreme Court justices ruled in *U.S. v. E. C. Knight Co.* that control of manufacturing did not necessarily mean control of trade. According to the Court, the Constitution empowered Congress to regulate interstate commerce but not manufacturing.

Between 1890 and 1900, the federal government prosecuted only eighteen cases under the Sherman Anti-Trust Act. The most successful involved railroads directly involved in interstate commerce. Ironically, the act equipped the government to break up labor unions: courts that did not consider monopolistic production a restraint on trade willingly applied antitrust provisions to boycotts encouraged by striking unions.

Summary

Mechanization and new inventions thrust the United States into the vanguard of industrial nations and immeasurably altered daily life. By the early twentieth century, American industrial output surpassed that of Great Britain, France, and Germany

Technology of Recorded Sound

Today's iPods and digital recorders derive from technology, chemistry, and human resourcefulness that first united in the late nineteenth century. In 1877, Thomas Edison devised a way to preserve and reproduce his voice by storing it on indentations in tin foil. Edison intended his "speaking machine" to help businesses store dictation. But in 1878, a rivalry with the telephone inventor Alexander Graham Bell, who was working on a similar device, drew Edison to invent a phonograph for recorded music. By the 1890s, audiences paid to hear recorded sounds from these machines.

By 1901, companies like the Columbia Phonograph Company produced machines that played music recorded on cylinders molded from a durable wax compound. Over the next ten years, various inventors improved the phonograph so sound played from a stylus (needle) vibrating in grooves of a shellac disc. Records' playing time increased from two minutes to four.

Phonograph records now replaced sheet music as the most popular music medium, but soon radio emerged and boosted record sales. Radio's popularity was only possible via another electronic acoustic technology: the microphone. This new device achieved vastly improved sound quality over megaphones. As phonograph prices declined and sound quality rose, more records became available.

The 1938 invention of the idler wheel, which enabled a turntable to spin a phonograph at speeds at which the stylus could accurately pick up sound, brought an important advance. Shortly thereafter, significant improvements in recording, such as the magnetic tape recorder, allowed for greater manipulation of sound in the recording studio. In 1963 Philips, a Dutch electronics firm, introduced the compact audio cassette. Two decades later, Philips joined with the Japanese corporation Sony to adapt the digital laser discs, invented by an American for video storage, to hold music. The compact disc (CD) was born, and from there it was a short step for the Apple Computer Company to create the iPod, storing music on an internal hard drive.

combined. By 1900, factories, stores, and banks converted America from a debtor agricultural nation into an industrial, financial, and exporting power.

But aggressive industrial consolidation changed the nature of work from individual activity by skilled producers to mass production by wage earners. Laborers fought to retain control of their work and struggled to organize unions. The outpouring of products created a mass society based on consumerism and dominated by technology and the communications media.

The problems of enforcing the Sherman Anti-Trust Act reflected the uneven distribution of power. Corporations consolidated to control resources, production, and politics. Laborers and reformers benefited from new and less expensive mass-produced goods, but they accused businesses of acquiring influence and profits at their expense. Some people celebrated the economic transformation; others struggled with the dilemma of industrialism: whether the new accumulations of wealth would undermine the republican ideal of democracy and equality.

Industrial expansion proved impossible to stop because so many people were benefiting from it. Moreover, the waves of newcomers pouring into the nation's cities increasingly furnished workers and consumers for America's expanding productive capacity.

Chapter Review

TECHNOLOGY AND THE TRIUMPH OF INDUSTRIALIZATION

How did technological innovations transform American industry?

New inventions and technological advances made production of goods and services faster and cheaper, which in turn fueled the rise of mass production and consumption. Thomas Edison's system for inexpensively distributing electricity facilitated the emergence of countless other inventions in the late nineteenth and early twentieth centuries. Henry Ford built on a European invention for engines to create his assembly-line process that would mass produce thousands of identical cars, making them affordable to many Americans by the early twentieth century. The du Pont family similarly revolutionized the chemical industry; electric looms advanced textile production and relocated it from North to South; while North Carolinian James B. Duke mass-produced cigarettes and remade the tobacco industry.

MECHANIZATION AND THE CHANGING STATUS OF LABOR

How did mechanization and new systems of management change the nature and status of work?

Innovation created new jobs, but labor-saving machines also meant that fewer workers could produce more in less time. Instead of doing many different tasks, workers now did only one task repeatedly. As workers rather than producers, they lost control over their work days and were regulated by the time clock and the production mandates of bosses. Skill became less important, and as the need for skilled workers declined, manufacturers turned to women and children, whom they could pay much less. The advent of typewriters and other office machines opened clerical and white collar jobs to women, as well. But in manufacturing, long days and harsh and often hazardous working conditions led to increasing number of accidents as well as labor unrest.

LABOR VIOLENCE AND THE UNION MOVEMENT

How did employers and others respond to increasing strikes and labor unrest in the late nineteenth century?

After the Haymarket bombing and other strikes, labor violence and the increasing participation of socialists and anarchists in the labor movement heightened public fear and demands for the government to get involved. Governments strengthened police forces and armories; employer associations circulated blacklists of union activists, whom they agreed not to employ, and hired private detectives to suppress strikes. State and federal governments also sent in troops, as in the case of the Homestead and Pullman strikes, to break the strikes.

STANDARDS OF LIVING

How did the rise of consumer culture widen the gap between the haves and have-nots?

While items once deemed luxuries became affordable to mainstream Americans, workers' wages did not always keep pace with the cost of goods. To afford these increasingly expensive necessities, working families often began to rely on additional sources of income from wives and children, either via factory work or taking in borders. Even while advances in nutrition and medical science helped Americans to live longer and healthier lives, those at the lowest rungs of society still ate diets high in carbohydrates and starches with little meat, and often spent half of the breadwinner's wages even on this meager diet.

THE CORPORATE CONSOLIDATION MOVEMENT

What led corporations to increasingly consolidate in the late nineteenth century?

Big companies saw consolidation as a way to control downward economic cycles—they believed the more they pooled resources to set prices and influence profits by determining how much to supply the market, the more they could manage a downturn. Until the 1880s, however, laws made it illegal for companies to own stock in another firm. Instead, businessmen such as John D. Rockefeller turned to trusts, luring stockholders of smaller companies to yield control of their stock "in trust" to the larger company's board of trustees. Once states allowed companies within their borders to own stock in corporations in other states, holding companies emerged, where one firm would own partial or complete interest in another and merge their assets and resources. Holding companies also found it easier to dominate their markets by controlling all aspects of an industry from raw materials to manufacturing to distribution.

THE GOSPEL OF WEALTH AND ITS CRITICS

How did business leaders use Social Darwinism to justify their mergers and consolidations?

Social Darwinism applied Charles Darwin's theory of survival of the fittest to laissez-faire economics, which stressed that government should let the economy manage itself. Social Darwinists argued that in a free-market economy, wealth would flow to those most capable of handling it, and that corporations represented that accumulation of power in the best hands. On the flip side, they also believed those with wealth had a moral obligation to use it to improve society; hence, they donated to the arts, education, and other worthy causes. It did not, however, translate into better wages or working conditions for their employees.

SUGGESTIONS FOR FURTHER READING

Edward L. Ayers, *The Promise of the New South: Life After Reconstruction* (1992)

Ileen A. DeVault, *United Apart: Gender and the Rise of Craft Unionism* (2004)

Steven J. Diner, *A Very Different Age: Americans of the Progressive Era* (1998)

John F. Kasson, *Civilizing the Machine: Technology and Republican Values in America, 1776–1900* (1976)

Alice Kessler-Harris, *Out to Work: A History of Wage-Earning Women in the United States* (2003)

T. J. Jackson Lears and Richard W. Fox, eds., *The Culture of Consumption: Critical Essays in American History, 1880–1980* (1983)

David Montgomery, *The Fall of the House of Labor: The Workplace, the State and American Labor Activism, 1865–1925* (1987)

Jeffrey Sklansky, *The Soul's Economy: Market Society and Selfhood in American Thought, 1820–1920* (2002)

CHAPTER 19

The Vitality and Turmoil of Urban Life

1877–1920

Crowds on the street gasped as they looked up. A man bound in a straitjacket was hanging by his heels high above New York's Times Square. Suddenly, he wriggled wildly, and in seconds Harry Houdini, the early twentieth century's most celebrated showman, had escaped. As he had done many times, Houdini fed the public's taste for suspense, courage, and entertainment with a death-defying feat.

Born as Erich Weiss in Hungary in 1874, Houdini and his family emigrated to the United States in 1878. After Erich's father lost his job as a rabbi in Wisconsin, the family moved to New York City, where father and son worked in a necktie factory. Erich's father died in 1892, and the young man became an entertainer. He spent a few years as a magician, before discovering his true talent as an illusionist and escape artist. He changed his name to Harry Houdini and became one of America's most enthralling performers.

By the early 1900s, the Great Houdini was a feature in vaudeville, a new form of urban entertainment. His specialty was escaping from elaborate and dangerous confinements: ropes, manacles, padlocked crates, and jail cells. Houdini was a skillful self-publicist, promoting his act with posters and leaflets. Around 1913 Houdini introduced his famous Chinese water torture cell escape, in which he extracted himself from being bound and suspended upside down in a water-filled, locked glass-and-steel cabinet. Houdini escaped by manipulating his five-foot-five frame in unusual ways and also by concealing picks and keys, which he sometimes regurgitated. Although he constantly defied death on stage, Houdini could not escape the abdominal infection that took his life in 1926.

Like many people in the late nineteenth and early twentieth centuries, the Weiss family were immigrants who fled poverty

This icon will direct you to interactive activities and study materials on *A People And A Nation, Brief Edition* website: **www.cengage.com/history/norton/peoplenationbrief8e**

493

Chronology

1867	First law regulating tenements passes in New York State.	**1895**	Hearst buys the *New York Journal,* which becomes another popular yellow-journalism newspaper.
1870	One-fourth of Americans live in cities.	**1898**	Race riot erupts in Wilmington, North Carolina.
1876	National League of Professional Baseball Clubs is founded.	**1900–10**	Immigration reaches its peak. Vaudeville rises to popularity.
1880s	"New" immigrants from eastern and southern Europe begin to arrive in large numbers.	**1903**	Boston beats Pittsburgh in baseball's first World Series.
1883	Brooklyn Bridge is completed.	**1905**	Intercollegiate Athletic Association, forerunner of National Intercollegiate Athletic Association (NCAA), is formed, restructuring the rules of football.
	Pulitzer buys *New York World,* creating a major publication for yellow journalism.		
1885	Safety bicycle is invented.	**1915**	Griffith directs *The Birth of a Nation,* one of first major technically sophisticated movies.
1886	First settlement house opens in New York City.		
1889	Edison invents the motion picture and a viewing device.	**1919**	Race riot erupts in East St. Louis, Illinois.
1890s	Electric trolleys replace horse-drawn mass transit.	**1920**	Majority (51.4 percent) of Americans live in cities.
1893	Columbian Exposition opens in Chicago.		

and tried to remake themselves in a burgeoning American city. They faced daunting challenges of where to live and work, how to deal with a cash-based economy, how to preserve their ethnic consciousness amid bigotry, and how to achieve independence and respectability. These challenges made cities places of hope, frustration, achievement, and conflict.

Not until the 1880s did the United States begin to become an urban nation. The technological innovations and industrialization of the late nineteenth century sparked widespread economic and geographical expansion, funneling millions of people into cities. By 1920, the census showed for the first time that a majority of Americans (51.4 percent) lived in cities (settlements with more than 2,500 people).

Urban dwellers patronized dance halls, theatrical performances, vaudeville, movies, and sporting events in record numbers. By idolizing Houdini, sports heroes, and movie celebrities or by benefiting from the largesse of a political boss, ordinary working- and middle-class people could believe in the potential for individuals to free themselves from the constraints of an emerging technological and urban society. At the same time, poverty and discrimination haunted the lives of countless urban dwellers, combining the era's opportunities with persistent inequality and prejudice. How people built cities and adjusted to the urban environment shaped modern American society.

- **What were the most important factors contributing to the urban growth of the period 1877–1920?**
- **How did immigrants adjust to and reshape their adopted homeland?**
- **How did industrialization and urbanization affect patterns of family life and leisure time?**

GROWTH OF THE MODERN CITY

Initially commercial centers, cities became the main arenas for industrial growth in the late nineteenth century. As labor, transportation, and communication hubs, cities supplied everything factories needed. Capital accumulated by urban mercantile enterprises fed industrial investment. Residents also acted as consumers for new products. The further industrialization advanced, the more opportunities it created for jobs and investment, which, in turn, drew more people to cities. As workers and consumers, they fueled yet more industrialization.

Industrial Development

While industrial enterprises varied, cities increasingly specialized. Mass production of clothing concentrated in New York City, the shoe industry in Philadelphia, and textiles in New England cities. Other cities created goods derived from surrounding agricultural regions: flour in Minneapolis, cottonseed oil in Memphis, and beef and pork in Chicago. Still others processed natural resources: gold and copper in Denver, fish and lumber in Seattle, coal and iron in Pittsburgh and Birmingham, and oil in Houston and Los Angeles. Such activities increased cities' magnetic attraction for people seeking steady employment.

At the same time, the compact city of the early nineteenth century, where residences mingled among shops, factories, and warehouses, expanded past the original settlement. No longer did different social groups live close together. Instead, cities subdivided into distinct districts: working-class neighborhoods, downtown, and a ring of suburbs. Two forces were responsible for this: mass transportation, which propelled people and enterprises outward, and, economic change, which drew human and material resources inward.

Mechanization of Mass Transportation

Mass transportation moved people faster and farther. By the 1870s, horse-drawn vehicles shared city streets with motor-driven conveyances. At first, commuter railroads carried passengers to and from outlying communities; then in the 1880s, cable cars were introduced. In the 1890s, electric-powered streetcars began replacing horse cars and cable cars in nearly every large city. In a few cities, companies raised track onto trestles, enabling elevated vehicles (trains, called els) to travel above jammed downtown streets. In Boston, New York, and Philadelphia, transit firms solved the traffic problem by digging underground subway tunnels. Because el and subway construction was costly, they appeared only in cities with enough riders to ensure profits.

Urban Sprawl

Mass transit launched urban dwellers into remote neighborhoods and created a commuting public. Streetcar lines serviced districts that promised the most riders and would increase company revenues. Working-class families, who needed every cent, found streetcars unaffordable. But the growing middle class who could pay the fare—usually 5 cents a ride—could escape to quiet, tree-lined neighborhoods on the outskirts and commute to the inner city for work, shopping, and entertainment.

When consumers moved outward, businesses followed, locating near mass transit. Department stores and banks joined groceries, theaters, taverns, and shops to create neighborhood shopping centers. Meanwhile, the urban core became a work zone, where tall buildings loomed over streets clogged with people, horses, and, increasingly, vehicles.

Population Growth

Between 1870 and 1920, the number of Americans living in cities increased from 10 million to 54 million. During this period, the number of cities with more than 100,000 people swelled from fifteen to sixty-eight; the number with more than 500,000 rose from two to twelve (see Map 19.1).

American urban growth derived from the annexation of bordering land and people and net migration (excess of in-migrants over out-migrants). The most notable enlargement occurred in 1898, when New York City, previously only Manhattan and the Bronx, merged with Brooklyn, Staten Island, and part of Queens and doubled to 3 million people. Suburbs often desired annexation for the schools, water, fire protection, and sewer systems that cities provided.

Urban In-Migration

In-migration from the countryside and immigration from abroad made the greatest contribution to urban population growth. Urban newcomers arrived from two major sources: the American countryside and Europe. Asia, Canada, and Latin America also supplied smaller numbers of immigrants.

Rural populations declined as urban populations burgeoned. Low crop prices and high debts drove white farmers toward opportunities that cities seemly offered. These migrations filled major cities, such as Detroit, Chicago, and San Francisco but also secondary cities, such as Indianapolis, Salt Lake City, Nashville, and San Diego. Farm boys escaped economic hardship, but for every four men who migrated city-ward, five women did the same, often to escape unhappy homes and enjoy the independence that urban employment offered.

In the 1880s and 1890s, thousands of rural African Americans also moved city-ward, seeking better employment and fleeing crop liens, ravages of the boll weevil on cotton crops, racial violence, and political oppression. Although black migration accelerated after 1915, thirty-two cities already had more than ten thousand black residents by 1900. Because few factories would employ African Americans, most found jobs in the service sector—cleaning, cooking, and driving. Since these were traditionally female jobs, black women outnumbered black men in cities like New York, Baltimore, and New Orleans. In the South, blacks migrating from the countryside became an important source of unskilled labor in the region's growing cities. By 1900, almost 40 percent of the total population of Atlanta, Georgia, and Charlotte, North Carolina, was black.

In the West, many Hispanics also moved into cities. They took unskilled construction jobs previously held by Chinese laborers who had been driven from Southern California cities. In some Texas cities, native Mexicans (called *Tejanos*) held most of the unskilled jobs. In Los Angeles and other cities, males often left home to take temporary agricultural jobs, leaving behind female heads of household.

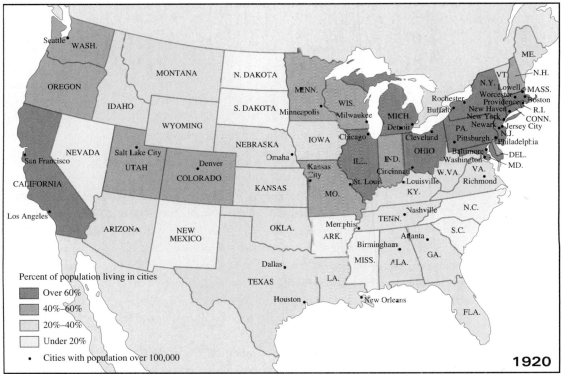

Map 19.1   Urbanization, 1880 and 1920

In 1880 the vast majority of states were still heavily rural. By 1920 only a few had less than 20 percent of their population living in cities.

Foreign Immigration

Foreign immigrants fleeing villages and cities in Europe, Asia, Canada, and Latin America flooded into the United States. Many wanted only to make enough money to return home and live in greater comfort. For every hundred foreigners who entered the country, thirty ultimately left. Still, like Houdini's family, most of the 26 million immigrants arriving between 1870 and 1920 remained, settling largely in cities.

The New Immigration

Population pressures, land redistribution, and industrialization induced millions of peasants, small landowners, and craftsmen to leave Europe and Asia for Canada, Australia, Brazil, and Argentina, as well as the United States. Religious persecution, too, particularly the merciless pogroms and military conscription that Jews suffered in eastern Europe, forced people to escape across the Atlantic. Late-nineteenth-century advances in communications and transportation spread the news of overseas opportunities and made travel cheaper.

Immigrants from northern and western Europe had long made the United States their destination, but after 1880 economic and demographic changes propelled immigrants from other regions. Increased numbers came from eastern and southern Europe, plus smaller bands from Canada, Mexico, and Japan. Between 1900 and 1909, two-thirds of the immigrants came from Italy, Austria-Hungary, and Russia. By 1910 arrivals from Mexico outnumbered arrivals from Ireland, and numerous Japanese moved to the West Coast and Hawai'i. Foreign-born blacks, chiefly from the West Indies, also came. (See the web site www.census.gov to search for population and immigration information.)

Many long-settled Americans feared these so-called new immigrants, whose customs, Catholic and Jewish faiths, and poverty made them seem particularly alien. Unlike earlier groups from Great Britain and Ireland, the new immigrants did not speak English and often worked in low-skill occupations. Yet old and new immigrants both made family the focus of all undertakings. New arrivals usually knew where to go and how to get there from relatives who had already immigrated. Workers often helped kin obtain jobs, and family members pooled resources to improve their standard of living.

Geographic and Social Mobility

Once they arrived, in-migrants and immigrants rarely stayed put. Each year millions of families moved elsewhere. The Weiss family stayed in Appleton, Wisconsin, only a few years before moving to New York City. More than half the families residing in a city were gone ten years later. Even within a city, it was not uncommon for a family to live at three or more different addresses over a ten- or fifteen-year period. One in every three or four families moved each year (today the rate is one in five).

Migration offered an escape to improved opportunity; occupational shifts offered another. An advance up the social scale through better jobs was available mostly to white males. Thousands of businesses were needed to supply goods and services to burgeoning urban populations, and as corporations grew and centralized operations, they required new managerial personnel. An aspiring merchant could open a saloon or shop for a few hundred dollars. Knowledge of accounting could qualify workers for white-collar jobs with higher incomes than manual labor.

Such advancement occurred often, but very few could accumulate large fortunes. Most of the era's wealthiest businessmen began their careers with distinct advantages: American birth, Protestant religion, education, and relatively affluent parents. Yet considerable movement occurred along the road from poverty to moderate success, from manual to nonmanual work.

Rates of upward occupational mobility were slow but steady between 1870 and 1920. In fast-growing cities like Atlanta, Los Angeles, and Omaha, approximately one in five white manual workers rose to white-collar or owner's positions within ten years. In older cities like Boston and Philadelphia, upward mobility averaged closer to one in six workers in ten years. Some men slipped from a higher to a lower rung, but rates of upward movement usually were double those of downward movement. Immigrants generally experienced less upward and more downward mobility than the native-born, yet the odds of a white male holding a higher-status job than his father were good.

The definition of a better job, however, depended on one's perspective. People who took pride in working with their hands neither desired nonmanual jobs nor encouraged their children to seek them. As one Italian tailor explained, "I learned the tailoring business in the old country. Over here, in America, I never have trouble finding a job. . . . I want that my oldest boy learn my trade because I tell him that you could always make at least enough for the family."

Failure rates were high among saloon owners and other small proprietors in working-class neighborhoods because customers' low incomes made profits uncertain. Many manual workers sought security rather than mobility, preferring a steady wage to the risks of ownership.

Many women held paying jobs, but since their standing was defined by the men in their lives, their chief means of upward mobility came from marrying men with wealth or potential. Laws limited what women could inherit; educational institutions blocked their training in such professions as medicine and law; and prevailing assumptions attributed higher aptitude for manual skills and business to men. Assigned to the lowest-paying occupations by prejudice, African Americans, American Indians, Mexican Americans, and Asian Americans could make fewer gains.

A person might achieve social mobility by acquiring property, which was not easily accomplished. Banks and savings-and-loan institutions had strict lending practices, and mortgage loans carried high interest rates and short repayment periods. Nevertheless, many families were able to amass a down payment on property. Ownership rates varied regionally—higher in western cities, lower in eastern cities—but 36 percent of all urban American families owned their homes in 1900, the highest homeownership rate of any western nation except Denmark, Norway, and Sweden.

Many who migrated, particularly unskilled workers, did not improve their status; they simply floated from one low-paying job to another. Others found greener pastures. The possibilities for upward mobility tempered people's dissatisfaction with the tensions and frustrations of city life. For every story of rags to riches, there were a multitude of small triumphs mixed with dashed hopes and discrimination. Although the gap between the very rich and the very poor widened, for those in between, the expanding economies of American cities created room.

URBAN NEIGHBORHOODS

American cities were characterized by collections of subcommunities where people, most of whom had migrated from somewhere else, coped with daily challenges to their cultures. Rather than yield completely to assimilation, migrants and immigrants interacted with the urban environment to retain their identity while altering their outlook and the social structure of cities.

Cultural Retention and Change

In their new surroundings, immigrants first anchored their lives to what they knew best: their culture. Old World customs persisted in immigrant districts of Italians from the same province, Japanese from the same island district, and Russian Jews from the same *shtetl*. Newcomers re-created mutual aid societies they knew in their homeland. For example, the Japanese transferred *ken* societies, which organized social celebrations and relief services. The Chinese used loan associations, called *whey*, which raised money to help members acquire businesses, and village associations called *fongs*, which rented apartments to homeless members. Southern Italians transplanted the system whereby a *padrone* (boss) found jobs for unskilled workers by negotiating with—and receiving a payoff from—an employer.

Urban Borderlands

In large cities, such as Chicago, Philadelphia, and Detroit, European immigrants initially clustered in inner-city neighborhoods where low-skill jobs and cheap housing were most available. These districts often were multiethnic, urban borderlands, where diverse people coexisted. Even within districts identified with a certain group, such as Little Italy, Jewtown, Polonia, or Greektown, rapid mobility constantly undermined homogeneity, as newcomers moved in and former inhabitants left. Even as population diversified, businesses and institutions, such as bakeries, churches, and club headquarters—operated by and for one ethnic group—gave a neighborhood its identity.

For first- and second-generation immigrants, their neighborhoods acted as havens until individuals were ready to move into the majority society. But borderland experiences often dissolved. The expansion of mass transportation and factories enabled people to move to other neighborhoods, where they interspersed with families of their own socioeconomic class but not necessarily their ethnicity. European immigrants encountered prejudice, such as the exclusion of Jews from certain neighborhoods, professions, and clubs, but discrimination rarely was systematic. For people of color, however—African Americans, Asians, and Mexicans—discrimination kept the borderlands from becoming multiethnic.

Racial Segregation and Violence

Although small numbers of African Americans may have lived near or interspersed with urban whites in the eighteenth and early nineteenth centuries, by the late nineteenth century racial discrimination forced them into highly segregated ghettos. By 1920 in Chicago, Detroit, Cleveland, and other cities, two-thirds or more of the total

African American population inhabited only 10 percent of the residential area. Within their neighborhoods, African Americans nurtured cultural institutions to cope with city life: shops, schools, clubs, theaters, dance halls, newspapers, and saloons. Churches, particularly the Baptist and African Methodist Episcopal (A.M.E.) branches of Protestantism, were especially influential. Membership in Cincinnati's black Baptist churches doubled between 1870 and 1900. In Louisville, blacks built their own theological institute. Black religious activity dominated urban local life and represented cooperation across class lines.

The only way blacks could relieve overcrowding from increased migration was to expand residential borders into surrounding, previously white neighborhoods, a process often resulting in harassment and attacks by white residents who feared that blacks would reduce property values. Moreover, blacks increased presence in cities, as well as their competition with whites for housing, jobs, and political influence, sparked race riots. In 1898 white citizens of Wilmington, North Carolina, resenting African Americans' involvement in local government and incensed by an African American newspaper editorial accusing white women of loose sexual behavior, rioted and killed dozens of blacks. White supremacists then overthrew the city government, expelling black and white officeholders, and instituted restrictions to prevent blacks from voting. An influx of unskilled black strikebreakers into East St. Louis, Illinois, heightened racial tensions in 1917, triggering a riot in which nine whites and thirty-nine blacks were killed and over three hundred buildings were destroyed.

Asians also encountered discrimination and isolation. Although Chinese immigrants often preferred to live apart from Anglos in Chinatowns of San Francisco, Los Angeles, and New York City, creating their own business, government, and social institutions, Anglos also tried to keep them separated. Using the slogan "The Chinese must go," Irish immigrant Denis Kearney and his followers intimidated San Francisco employers into refusing to hire Chinese and drove hundreds of Asians out of the city. San Francisco's government prohibited Chinese laundries from locating in white neighborhoods and banned the wearing of queues, the traditional Chinese hair braid. In 1882 Congress passed the Chinese Exclusion Act, which suspended Chinese immigration and prohibited naturalization of Chinese already residing in the United States. And in 1892 Congress approved the Geary Act, which extended immigration restriction and required Chinese Americans to carry certificates of residence issued by the Treasury Department. The U.S. Supreme Court upheld the Geary Act in 1893 in *Fong Yue Ting v. United States*. Similarly prevented from becoming American citizens, Japanese immigrants, called Issei, also developed separate communities.

Mexican Barrios

Mexicans in southwestern cities experienced more complex residential patterns. In places like Los Angeles, Santa Barbara, and Tucson, Mexicans had been the original inhabitants, and Anglos were migrants who pushed Mexicans out, so they became increasingly isolated in districts called barrios. Frequently, real-estate covenants kept Mexican families isolated as they pledged whites not to sell homes to Mexicans (or to African Americans or Jews). Instead, they were confined in areas away from central-city multiethnic borderlands housing European immigrants.

Although Chinese immigrants, like other immigrants, struggled to succeed in American society, they often faced severe discrimination because of their different lifestyle. As this photo of a San Francisco grocery shows, Chinese looked, dressed, and ate differently than white Americans did. Occasionally, they suffered from racist violence that caused them to fear not only for their personal safety but also for the safety of establishments like this one that might suffer damage from resentful mobs.   (The Bancroft Library, University of California)

Cultural Adaptation

Virtually everywhere immigrants lived, Old World culture mingled with New World realities. Although many foreigners identified themselves by their village or region of birth, native-born Americans categorized them simply by nationality. People from County Cork and County Limerick, for example, were merged into Irish, those from Calabria and Campobasso into Italians. Immigrant institutions, such as newspapers and churches, ultimately had to appeal to the entire nationality to survive.

Moreover, the diversity of American cities prompted foreigners to modify their habits and old ways of life. Although many immigrants tried to preserve their language, English, taught in schools and needed on the job, soon penetrated nearly every community. Foreigners fashioned homeland styled garments, but used American rather than traditional fabrics. Italians went to American doctors but still carried amulets to ward off evil spirits. Music especially revealed adaptations. Polka bands blended American and Polish folk music. Mexican ballads now described border crossing and hardships in the United States.

The influx of so many immigrants between 1870 and 1920 transformed the United States from a basically Protestant nation into a diverse collection of Protestants, Catholics, Orthodox Christians, Jews, Buddhists and Muslims. Newcomers from Italy, Hungary, Polish lands, and Slovakia joined Irish and Germans to boost the proportion of Catholics in many cities. German and Russian immigrants gave New York City one of the largest Jewish populations in the world.

Many Catholics and Jews tried to accommodate their faiths to the new environment. Catholic and Jewish leaders from earlier immigrant groups supported liberalizing trends—use of English in services, the phasing out of such Old World rituals as saints' feasts, and a preference for public over religious schools. As long as new immigrants continued to arrive, however, these trends met stiff resistance.

Newcomers usually held onto familiar practices, whether the folk Catholicism of southern Italy or the Orthodox Judaism of eastern Europe. Despite church attempts to make American Catholicism more uniform, bishops acceded to pressures from predominantly Polish congregations for Polish priests. Eastern European Jews, convinced that Reform Judaism sacrificed too much to American ways, established the Conservative branch, which retained traditional ritual but abolished the segregation of women in synagogues and allowed English prayers. But second-generation Catholics and Jews marrying coreligionists of other ethnic groups—an Italian Catholic wedding a Polish Catholic—kept religious identity strong while undercutting ethnic identity.

The cities nurtured rich cultural variety: American folk music and literature, Italian and Mexican cuisine, Irish comedy, Yiddish theater, African American jazz and dance, and much more. Newcomers changed their environment as much as they were changed by it.

LIVING CONDITIONS IN THE INNER CITY

The central sections of American cities were plagued by poverty, disease, crime, and the tensions resulting when large numbers of people live close together. City dwellers coped, and technology, private enterprise, and public authority achieved some remarkable successes.

Inner-City Housing In spite of massive construction in the 1880s and early 1900s, population growth outpaced housing supplies. Lack of inexpensive housing especially afflicted working-class families who, because of low wages, had to rent homes. Landlords took advantage of shortages by splitting up existing buildings to house more people, constructing multiple-unit tenements, and hiking rents. Low-income families adapted to high costs and short supply by sharing space and expenses. A one-family apartment was typically occupied by two or three families, or by a single family plus several boarders.

The result was unprecedented crowding. In 1890 New York City's immigrant-packed Lower East Side averaged 702 people per acre, one of the highest population densities in the world. Conditions were harsh. The largest rooms were barely ten feet wide, and interior rooms either lacked windows or opened onto narrow shafts that bred vermin and rotten odors. Few buildings had indoor plumbing; residents used privies (outdoor toilets) in the yard or basement. Often, the only heat source was dangerous, polluting coal-burning stoves.

Housing Reform

Housing problems sparked widespread reform campaigns. New York State led with laws in 1867, 1879, and 1901 that established light, ventilation, and safety codes for new tenement buildings. Reformers, such as journalist Jacob Riis and humanitarian Lawrence Veiller, advocated model tenements, with spacious rooms and better facilities for low-income families. Model tenements meant lower profits, a sacrifice few landlords would make. Reformers and public officials opposed government financing, fearing it would undermine private enterprise. Still, housing codes and regulatory commissions strengthened local government's power to oversee construction.

New Home Technology

Technology revolutionized home life. Advanced systems of central heating (furnaces), artificial lighting, and indoor plumbing created more comfort, first for middle-class households and later for most others. Whereas formerly families bought coal or chopped wood for cooking and heating, made candles for light, and hauled bath water, their homes were increasingly connected to outside pipes and wires for gas, electricity, and water. Moreover, these utilities helped create new attitudes about privacy. Middle-class bedrooms and bathrooms became private retreats.

Scientific and technological advances eventually enabled city dwellers and the nation to live healthier. By the 1880s, doctors began to accept the theory that microorganisms (germs) cause disease. Cities established more efficient water purification and sewage disposal, which helped control such dread diseases as cholera, typhoid fever, and diphtheria.

Meanwhile, street paving, modernized firefighting equipment, and electric street lighting spread rapidly across urban America. Steel-frame construction, which uses a metal skeleton rather than masonry walls for building support, made possible the erection of skyscrapers, and thus more efficient vertical use of scarce urban land. Steel-cable suspension bridges, developed by John A. Roebling and epitomized by his Brooklyn Bridge (completed in 1883), linked metropolitan sections more closely.

Poverty Relief

None of these improvements, however, lightened the burden of poverty. Since colonial days Americans have disagreed about public responsibility for poor relief. According to traditional beliefs, still widespread in the early twentieth century, anyone could escape poverty through hard work and clean living; moral weakness caused indigence. Such reasoning bred fear that aiding the poor encouraged them to rely on public support rather than their own efforts. As business cycles fluctuated and poverty increased, this attitude hardened, and city governments discontinued grants of food, fuel, and clothing to needy families. Instead, cities provided relief in return for work on public projects and sent special cases to state-run almshouses, orphanages, and homes for the blind, deaf, and mentally ill.

Between 1877 and 1892, philanthropists in ninety-two cities formed Charity Organization Societies to make social welfare (like business) more efficient by merging disparate charities into coordinated units. Believing poverty to be caused by personal defects, such as alcoholism and laziness, these organizations visited poor families to determine if they were deserving and encouraged them to be thriftier and more virtuous. Close observation of the poor, however, prompted some humanitarians to conclude that people's environments, not their shortcomings, caused poverty and that society should help improve social conditions. They believed they could reduce poverty through better housing, education, sanitation, and job opportunities. This fueled campaigns for building codes, factory regulations, and public health measures in the Progressive era of the early twentieth century (see Chapter 21). Still, most middle- and upper-class Americans embraced the creed that only the unfit were poor and that poverty relief should be tolerated but never encouraged.

Crime and Violence

Crime and disorder, as much as crowding and poverty, nurtured fears that cities, especially their slums, threatened the nation. While homicide rates declined in other industrialized nations, America's rose from: 25 murders per million people in 1881 to 107 per million in 1898. Domestic violence, muggings, and gang fights made cities turbulent, as did pickpockets, swindlers, and burglars. Urban outlaws, such as Rufus Minor, acquired as much notoriety as western desperadoes. Short and bald, Minor resembled a shy clerk, but a police chief labeled him "one of the smartest bank sneaks in America." Minor was implicated in bank heists in New York City, Cleveland, Detroit, Providence, Philadelphia, Albany, Boston, and Baltimore between 1878 and 1882.

Urban crime may simply have become more conspicuous rather than more prevalent. Certainly concentrations of wealth and the mingling of different peoples provided opportunities for larceny, vice, and assault. But urban lawlessness probably did not exceed that of backwoods mining camps and southern plantations. Nativists were quick to blame immigrants for crime, but the law-breaker population included native-born Americans and foreigners.

MANAGING THE CITY

Burgeoning populations, business expansion, and technological change created urgent needs for sewers, police and fire protection, schools, parks, and other services. Such needs strained municipal resources and city governments beyond their capacities. In addition to a mayor and a city council, independent boards administered health regulations, public works, poverty relief, and other functions. Philadelphia at one time had thirty such boards. State governments also interfered in local matters, appointing board members and limiting cities' abilities to levy taxes and borrow money.

Water Supply and Sewage Disposal

Finding sources of clean water and a way to dispose of waste became increasingly pressing challenges. In the early nineteenth century, urban households used privies to dispose of human excrement, and factories dumped untreated sewage into rivers, lakes, and bays. By the late nineteenth century, the installation of sewer systems and flush toilets, plus the use of water as a coolant in factories, overwhelmed waterways and contaminated drinking-water sources. The stench of rivers was often unbearable, and pollution bred disease. Memphis and New York experienced severe yellow-fever epidemics in the 1870s and 1880s, and typhoid fever threatened many cities.

Acceptance in the 1880s of the germ theory of disease prompted cities to reduce chances that human waste and other pollutants would endanger water supplies. Some states legally prohibited discharging raw sewage into rivers and streams, and a few cities began the expensive process of chemically treating sewage. Gradually, water managers installed mechanical filters, and cities, led by Jersey City, began purifying water supplies by adding chlorine. These efforts dramatically reduced deaths from typhoid fever.

But waste disposal remained a thorny problem. Experts in 1900 estimated that every New Yorker generated annually 160 pounds of garbage (food and bones), 1,200 pounds of ashes (from stoves and furnaces), and 100 pounds of rubbish. Solid waste from factories and businesses included tons of scrap metal and wood. Each of the estimated 3.5 million horses in American cities in 1900 daily dropped about 20 pounds of manure and a gallon of urine that rain washed into nearby water sources. By the twentieth century this refuse was a health and safety hazard.

Urban Engineers

Citizens' groups, led by women's organizations, began discussing these dilemmas in the 1880s, and by the turn of the century urban governments began to hire sanitary engineers to design garbage collection systems, disposing of it in incinerators and landfills. The American engineering profession developed new systems and standards of worldwide significance that made cities more livable, such as street lighting, bridge and street construction, and fire protection. Elected officials depended on engineers' expertise in aiding urban expansion. Insulated within bureaucratic agencies from tumultuous party politics, engineers made lasting contributions to urban management.

This scene, captured by a Philadelphia photographer sent to record the extent of trash that was littering city streets and sidewalks, illustrates the problems of disposal confronting inner-city, immigrant neighborhoods and the necessity for some form of public service to remove the refuse. Seemingly oblivious to the debris, the residents pose for the photographer.   (Philadelphia City Archives, Department of Records, Photo Negative #10716)

Law Enforcement After the mid-nineteenth century, urban dwellers increasingly depended on professional police to protect life and property, but law enforcement became complicated and controversial, as various groups differed about how laws should be enforced. Ethnic and racial minorities were more likely to be arrested, and police officers applied the law less harshly to members of their own ethnic groups and to people in power or offering bribes.

Often poorly trained and prone to corruption, police were caught between demands for swift and severe action on the one hand and leniency on the other. Some people clamored for police crackdowns on saloons, gambling halls, and houses of prostitution, while those who profited from and patronized such establishments favored loose law enforcement. Achieving a balance between criminal law and individual freedom grew increasingly difficult.

Political Machines Out of the apparent confusion surrounding urban management arose political machines, organizations whose main goals were the rewards—money, influence, and prestige—of getting and keeping power. Machine politicians routinely used fraud and bribery to further their ends. But they also provided relief, security, and services to voters.

Machines bred leaders, called bosses, who built power bases among urban working classes, especially new immigrants. Most bosses had immigrant backgrounds and grew up in the inner city. They knew their constituents' needs firsthand and gained power by tending to the problems of everyday life. In return for votes, bosses provided jobs, built parks and bathhouses, distributed food and clothing to the needy, and helped when someone ran afoul of the law. New York's Big Tim Sullivan, for example, gave out free shoes and sponsored annual picnics. Bosses, moreover, made politics a full-time profession; they attended weddings and wakes, joined clubs, and held open houses in saloons where neighborhood folk could speak to them personally. According to George Washington Plunkitt, a neighborhood boss in New York City, "As a rule [the boss] . . . plays politics every day and night in the year and his headquarters bears the inscription, 'Never closed.'"

To finance their activities and election campaigns, bosses exchanged favors for votes and money. Power over local government enabled machines to control who received public contracts, utility and streetcar franchises, and city jobs. Recipients were expected to repay the machine with a portion of their profits or salaries and to cast supporting votes. Critics called this process graft; bosses called it gratitude.

Bosses like Philadelphia's Duke Vare, Kansas City's Tom Pendergast, and New York's Richard Croker lived like kings, though their official incomes were slim. Yet machines were rarely as dictatorial or corrupt as critics charged. Rather, several machines evolved into tightly structured operations, such as New York's Tammany Hall organization (named after a society that began as a patriotic fraternal club), which wedded public accomplishments with personal gain. The system rested on a popular base and was held together by loyalty and service. Most machines were coalitions of smaller organizations that derived power directly from inner-city neighborhoods. Machine-led governments constructed urban infrastructure—public buildings, sewer systems, schools, bridges, and mass-transit lines—and expanded urban services—police, firefighting, and health departments.

Machine politics, however, was rarely neutral. Racial minorities and new immigrant groups, such as Italians and Poles, received only token jobs and nominal favors, if any. And bribes and kickbacks made machine projects and services costly to taxpayers. Cities could not ordinarily raise enough revenue for construction projects from taxes and fees, so they financed expansion with loans from the public in the form of municipal bonds, which caused public debts, and then taxes, to soar. And payoffs from gambling, prostitution, and illicit liquor traffic became important sources of machine revenue. But bosses were no guiltier of discrimination and self-interest than were business leaders who exploited workers, spoiled the environment, and manipulated government in pursuit of profits.

Civic Reform

Many middle- and upper-class Americans feared that immigrant-based political machines menaced democracy and wasted municipal finances. Anxious over the poverty, crowding, and disorder that accompanied city growth and convinced that urban services were making taxes too high, civic reformers organized to install more responsible leaders who would run government efficiently like a business.

To implement business principles in government, civic reformers supported structural changes, such as city-manager and commission forms of government, which would place administration in the hands of experts rather than politicians, and nonpartisan citywide rather than neighborhood-based election of officials. Reformers believed they could cleanse city government of party politics and weaken bosses' power bases.

A few reform mayors also addressed social problems. Hazen S. Pingree of Detroit, Samuel "Golden Rule" Jones of Toledo, and Tom Johnson of Cleveland worked to provide jobs to poor people, reduce charges by transit and utility companies, and promote government responsibility for citizens' welfare. They also supported public ownership of gas, electric, and telephone companies, quasi-socialist reforms that alienated their business allies. But Pingree, Jones, and Johnson were exceptions; civic reformers achieved some successes but rarely held office for very long.

Social Reform

Social reformers—mostly young and middle class—also wanted to solve urban problems. Housing reformers pressed local governments for building codes ensuring safety in tenements. Educational reformers sought to use public schools to prepare immigrant children for citizenship by teaching them American values.

Perhaps the most ambitious urban reform movement was the settlement house, a place located in inner-city neighborhoods and established mostly by young, middle-class women who lived and worked among the poor. The first American settlement, patterned after London's Toynbee Hall, opened in New York City in 1886, and others quickly followed, including Hull House, founded in Chicago in 1889. To help immigrants adjust, settlements offered vocational classes, English lessons, childcare, and programs to improve nutrition and housing.

Settlement-house workers like Jane Addams and Florence Kelley of Chicago and Lillian Wald of New York broadened their scope to fight for school nurses, factory safety codes, and public playgrounds. Their efforts to involve national and local governments in the solution of social problems made them key contributors to the Progressive era, when a reform spirit swept the nation (see Chapter 21). Moreover, settlement-house programs created new professional opportunities for women in social work, public health, and child welfare. These professions enabled female reformers to influence social policy and make valuable contributions to national and inner-city life.

But settlement houses were segregated. White female reformers lobbied for government programs to aid mostly white immigrant and native-born working classes. Black women reformers, excluded from white settlements, raised funds and aided their race by founding schools, old-age homes, and hospitals, as well as protecting black women from sexual exploitation. Their ranks included Jane Hunter, who founded a home for unmarried black working women in Cleveland in 1911 and inspired the establishment of similar homes in other cities.

The City Beautiful Movement

Male reformers similarly worked to improve cities by organizing the City Beautiful movement. Inspired by the Columbian Exposition of 1893, a dazzling world's fair held in Chicago, architects and planners urged the construction of civic centers, parks, and boulevards that would make cities economically efficient and beautiful. Projects were underway in Chicago, San Francisco, and Washington, D.C., in the early 1900s. Yet neither government nor private businesses could finance large-scale projects, and planners disagreed among themselves and with social reformers over whether beautification would solve urban problems.

Urban reformers wanted to save cities, but they often failed to understand cities' diverse populations and people's varying visions of reform. To civic reformers, appointing government workers on the basis of civil service exams rather than party loyalty meant progress, but to working-class men, civil service signified reduced employment opportunities. Moral reformers believed that restricting alcoholic beverages would prevent working-class breadwinners from squandering wages, but immigrants saw it as interference. Planners saw new streets and buildings as modern necessities, but such structures often displaced the poor. Well-meaning humanitarians criticized immigrant mothers for the way they dressed, did housework, and raised children, without regard for their income limitations. Thus urban reform merged idealism with naiveté and insensitivity.

FAMILY LIFE

Urbanization and industrialization strained family life. New institutions—schools, social clubs, political organizations, unions—increasingly competed with the family to provide nurture and education. Clergy and journalists warned that the growing separation between home and work, rising divorce rates, the entrance of women into the work force, and the loss of parental control over children spelled peril for home and family. Yet the family remained a cushion in an uncertain world.

Family and Household Structures

In previous eras, most American households (75 to 80 percent) consisted of nuclear families—usually a married couple, with or without children. About 15 to 20 percent of households consisted of extended families—usually a married couple, their children, and one or more relatives. About 5 percent of households had people living alone. Despite slight variations, this pattern held constant among ethnic, racial, and socioeconomic groups.

Several factors explain this pattern. Because immigrants tended to be young, the American population as a whole was young. In 1880 the median age was under twenty-one, and by 1920 it was still only twenty-five. (Median age at present is above thirty-five.) Moreover, in 1900 the death rate among people aged forty-five to sixty-four was double what it is today. Only 4 percent of the population was sixty-five or older, versus almost 13 percent today. Thus few families could form extended three-generation households, and fewer children than today had living grandparents. Migration split up many families, and the ideal of a home ownership encouraged nuclear household organization.

Declining Birth Rates

Most of Europe and North America experienced falling birth rates in the nineteenth century. In 1880 the birth rate was forty live births per one thousand people; by 1900 it had dropped to thirty-two; by 1920, to twenty-eight. Although birth rates were higher among black, immigrant, and rural women, birth rates of all groups fell.

Several factors explain this decline. First, as the United States became more urbanized, the economic value of children lessened. On farms, each child born represented an addition to the family labor force. In the wage-based urban economy, children could not contribute significantly to the family income for years, and a new child represented a draw on family income. Second, infant mortality fell as diet and medical care improved, and families did not have to bear as many children to ensure that some would survive.

Perhaps most importantly, as American society industrialized and urbanized, the idea of a child as an innocent being who needed shelter from society's corruptions spread, first among the middle class and gradually to the working class. A mother's care and attention could be more effective if she had fewer children. That seems to have stimulated decisions to limit family size, either by abstaining from sex or using contraception. Families with six or eight children became rare; three or four became more usual. Birth-control technology—diaphragms and condoms—had been utilized for centuries, but in this era new materials made these devices more convenient and dependable.

Stages of Life

Before the late nineteenth century, stages of life were less distinct than they are today. Childhood, for instance, was regarded as a period during which young people prepared for adulthood by gradually assuming more responsibilities. Subdivisions of youth—toddlers, schoolchildren, teenagers, and the like—were not defined. Because married couples had more children over a longer time span, active parenthood occupied most of adult life. Older children might begin parenting before reaching adulthood by caring for younger siblings. And older people were not isolated from other age groups. By the late nineteenth century, however, decreasing birth rates shortened the period of parental responsibility, so more middle-aged couples experienced an empty nest when children grew up and left home. Longer life expectancy and a tendency by employers to force aged workers to retire separated the old from the young.

New patterns of childhood also emerged. To be sure, youngsters in working-class families still helped out—working in factories, scavenging streets for scraps of wood and coal, and peddling newspapers. But as states passed compulsory school attendance laws in the 1870s and 1880s, education occupied more of children's daily time than ever, filling nine months of the year until they were teenagers. Schools strengthened peer rather than family influence over behavior. Researchers like G. Stanley Hall and Luther H. Gulick advocated that teachers and parents should match education and play activities to children's changing developmental stages.

The Unmarried   Although marriage rates were high, large numbers of city dwellers were unmarried. In 1890 almost 42 percent of adult American men and 37 percent of women were single, nearly twice as high as in 1960 but slightly lower than today. About half still lived with parents, but others inhabited boarding houses. Mostly young, these men and women constituted a separate subculture that supported institutions like dance halls, saloons, cafés, and the Young Men's Christian Association (YMCA) and Young Women's Christian Association (YWCA).

Some unmarried people were part of the homosexual populations that thrived in large cities like New York, San Francisco, and Boston. Although numbers are difficult to estimate, gay men had their own subculture of clubs, restaurants, coffee-houses, theaters, and support networks. A number of same-sex couples, especially women, formed lasting marital-type relationships, sometimes called Boston marriages. People in this subculture were categorized more by how they acted—men acting like women, women acting like men—than by who their sexual partners were. The term *homosexual* was not used. Men who dressed and acted like women were called fairies. Gay women remained mostly hidden, and a lesbian subculture did not develop until the 1920s.

Boarding and Lodging   In every city, boarding houses and lodging hotels were common, but families also took in boarders for rooms vacated by grown children and for additional income. By 1900 as many as 50 percent of city residents, including Erich Weiss's family, lived either as, or with, boarders at some point. Housing reformers charged that boarding and lodging caused overcrowding and loss of privacy. For people on the move, boarding or lodging was a transitional stage, providing a quasi-family environment until they set up their own households. Especially in communities where housing was expensive or scarce, newlyweds sometimes lived temporarily with one spouse's parents. Families also took in widowed parents or unmarried siblings.

Functions of Kinship   At a time when welfare agencies were scarce, the family was the institution to which people turned when in need. Relatives often resided nearby and helped with childcare, meals, advice, and consolation. They also obtained jobs for each other. According to one new arrival, "After two days my brother took me to the shop he was working in and his boss saw me and he gave me the job."

But kinship obligations were not always welcome. Immigrant families pressured last-born daughters to stay home to care for aging parents, a practice that stifled opportunities for education, marriage, and independence. Generational tensions also developed, such as when immigrant parents and American-born children clashed over the abandonment of Old World ways or the amount of wages employed children should contribute. Nevertheless, kinship helped people cope with the stresses of urban-industrial society.

Thus, by 1900, family life and functions were both changing and holding firm. New institutions were assuming tasks formerly performed by the family. Schools made education a community responsibility. Employment agencies, personnel offices, and labor unions took responsibility for employee recruitment and job security. Age-based peer groups exerted greater influence over people's values and activities. Migration and divorce seemed to be splitting families apart. Yet, kinship remained a dependable though not always appreciated institution.

Holiday Celebrations   An emphasis on family togetherness became especially visible at holiday celebrations. Middle-class moralists helped make Thanksgiving, Christmas, and Easter special times for family reunion and child-centered activities. Birthdays, too, took on an increasingly festive quality as a milestone for measuring the age-related norms that accompanied life stages. In 1914 President Woodrow Wilson signed a proclamation designating the second Sunday in May as Mother's Day, capping a six-year campaign by the schoolteacher Anna Jarvis, who believed grown children neglected their mothers. Ethnic and racial groups adapted national celebrations to their cultures, preparing special ethnic foods and engaging in special ceremonies.

THE NEW LEISURE AND MASS CULTURE

On December 2, 1889, as workers paraded through Worcester, Massachusetts, seeking shorter working hours, carpenters hoisted a banner proclaiming "Eight Hours for Work, Eight Hours for Rest, Eight Hours for What We Will." That last

SHOOTING THE CHUTES, CONEY ISLAND, N. Y.

Amusement centers like Luna Park, at Coney Island in New York City, became common and appealing features of the new leisure culture. One of the most popular Coney Island attractions was a ride called Shooting the Chutes, which resembled modern-day giant water slides. In 1904 Luna Park staged an outrageous stunt of an elephant sliding down the chute. The creature survived, apparently unfazed. (Picture Research Consultants and Archives) phrase laid claim to a segment of daily life by the individual. Increasingly, leisure activities filled this time.

Increase in Leisure Time

Mechanization and labor-saving assembly-line production cut the average manufacturing workweek from sixty-six hours in 1860 to sixty in 1890 and forty-seven in 1920. This meant shorter workdays and freer weekends. White-collar employees spent eight to ten hours a day on the job and often worked only half a day or not at all on weekends. As the economy shifted from production to consumption, more Americans engaged in recreation, and a substantial segment of the economy provided for—and profited from—leisure.

Amusement became a commercial activity, as games, toys, and musical instruments were sold for indoor family entertainment. Improvements in printing and paper production and the rise of manufacturers like Milton Bradley and Parker Brothers increased the popularity of board games. Significantly, board games shifted from moral lessons to topics involving transportation, finance, and sports. Middle-class families were buying mass-produced pianos and sheet music which made singing popular songs a common form of home entertainment. The vanguard of new leisure pursuits, however, was sports. Formerly a fashionable indulgence of elites, organized sports became a favored pastime of all classes.

Baseball

The most popular sport was baseball. Derived from older bat, ball, and base-circling games, in 1845 the Knickerbocker Club of New York standardized the rules of play. By 1860 at least fifty baseball clubs existed, and youths played informal games in fields and city lots nationwide. The National League of Professional Baseball Clubs, founded in 1876, gave the sport a businesslike structure, but as early as 1867 a color line excluded blacks from professional teams. By the 1880s professional baseball was big business. In 1903 the National League and the competing American League (formed in 1901) began a World Series between their championship teams. The Boston Red Sox beat the Pittsburgh Pirates in that first series.

Croquet and Cycling

Baseball appealed mostly to men. But croquet, also nationally popular, attracted both sexes. Middle- and upper-class people held croquet parties and night contests that increased opportunities for social contact between the sexes.

Meanwhile, cycling achieved a popularity rivaling baseball, especially after 1885, when the cumbersome velocipede, with its huge front wheel and tall seat, gave way to safety bicycles with pneumatic tires and identical-size wheels. By 1900 Americans owned 10 million bicycles, and clubs petitioned state governments to build more paved roads. African American cyclists were allowed to compete, and one rider, Major Taylor became famous in Europe and the United States between 1892 and 1910. Moreover, the bicycle helped free women from the constraints of Victorian fashions. To ride the dropped-frame female models, women had to wear divided skirts and simple undergarments. As the 1900 census declared, "Few articles . . . have created so great a revolution in social conditions as the bicycle."

Japanese Baseball

Baseball, the American pastime, was one of the new leisure-time pursuits that Americans brought to different parts of the world. The Shanghai Base Ball Club was founded by Americans in China in 1863, but was denounced by the Imperial Court as spiritually corrupting. However, when Horace Wilson, an American teacher, taught the rules of baseball to Japanese students around 1870, the game received an enthusiastic reception as a reinforcement of traditional virtues and became a part of Japanese culture.

During the 1870s, scores of Japanese high schools and colleges sponsored baseball, and in 1883 Hiroshi Hiraoka, a railroad engineer who had studied in Boston, founded the first official local team, the Shimbashi Athletic Club Athletics.

Before baseball, the Japanese had no team sports or recreational athletics. Once they learned about baseball, they found that the idea of a team sport fit their culture well. But to them, baseball was serious business, involving often brutal training. Practices at Ichiko, one of Japan's great high school baseball teams in the late nineteenth century, were dubbed "Bloody Urine" because many players passed blood after a day of drilling. There was a spiritual quality as well, linked to Buddhist values. According to one Japanese coach, "Student baseball must be the baseball of self-discipline, or trying to attain the truth, just as in Zen Buddhism." This attitude prompted the Japanese to consider baseball as a new method to pursue the spirit of Bushido, the way of the samurai.

When Americans played baseball in Japan, the Japanese admired their talent but found them lacking in discipline and respect. Americans insulted the Japanese by refusing to remove their hats and bow when they stepped up to bat. An international dispute occurred in 1891 when William Imbrie, an American professor at Tokyo's Meijo University, arrived late for a game and climbed over a locked fence. Japanese fans considered this sacrilege and attacked Imbrie, who suffered facial injuries. The American embassy lodged a formal complaint. Americans assumed that their game would encourage the Japanese to become like westerners, but the Japanese transformed baseball into a uniquely Japanese expression of team spirit, discipline, and nationalism.

Replete with bats, gloves, and uniforms, this Japanese baseball team of 1890 very much resembles its American counterpart of that era. The Japanese adopted baseball soon after Americans became involved in their country but also added their cultural qualities to the game.
(Japanese Baseball Hall of Fame and Museum)

Football

American football, as an intercollegiate competition, initially attracted mostly players and spectators wealthy enough to have access to higher education. By the late nineteenth century, however, the game appealed to a broader audience. The 1893 Princeton-Yale game drew fifty thousand spectators, and informal games were played throughout the country. Soon, however, football became a national scandal because of its violence and use of "tramp athletes," nonstudents hired to help teams win. Critics accused football of mirroring undesirable features of American society. An editor of *The Nation* charged in 1890 that "the lack of moral scruple which pervades the struggles of the business world meets with temptations equally irresistible in the miniature contests of the football field."

The scandals climaxed in 1905, when 18 players died from game-related injuries and 159 were seriously injured. President Theodore Roosevelt, a strong advocate of athletics, convened a White House conference to discuss ways to eliminate brutality. The gathering founded the Intercollegiate Athletic Association (renamed the National College Athletic Association in 1910) to police college sports. In 1906 the association altered the game to make it less violent and more open.

As more women enrolled in college, they participated in such sports as rowing, track, and swimming. Invented in 1891 as a winter sport for men, basketball—soon women's most popular sport—received women's rules (which limited dribbling and running and encouraged passing) from Senda Berenson of Smith College.

Show Business

Three branches of American show business—popular drama, musical comedy, and vaudeville—matured with the growth of cities. Theatrical performances offered audiences escape into melodrama, adventure, and comedy. For urban people unfamiliar with the frontier, popular plays made the mythical Wild West and Old South come alive through stories of Davy Crockett, Buffalo Bill, and the Civil War. Virtue and honor triumphed in melodramas like *Uncle Tom's Cabin* and *The Old Homestead*, reinforcing faith that in an uncertain world goodness would prevail.

The American musical derived from Europe's lavishly costumed operettas. George M. Cohan, a singer, dancer, and songwriter born into an Irish family of entertainers, became the master of American musical comedy after the turn of the century. Drawing on patriotism and traditional values in songs like "Yankee Doodle Boy" and "You're a Grand Old Flag," Cohan bolstered morale during World War I. Initially, American comic operas imitated European musicals, but by the early 1900s composers like Victor Herbert were writing for American audiences.

Probably the most popular mass entertainment in early-twentieth-century America, vaudeville offered something for everyone. Shows included jugglers, magicians, puppeteers, acrobats, comedians, singers, dancers, and specialty acts like Houdini's escapes. Around 1900, the number of vaudeville theaters and troupes skyrocketed, and operators like Tony Pastor and the partnership of Benjamin Keith and Edward Albee consolidated theaters and acts under their management. Producer Florenz Ziegfeld brilliantly packaged stylish shows—the Ziegfeld Follies—and gave the nation a new model of femininity, the Ziegfeld Girl, whose graceful dancing and alluring costumes suggested a haunting sensuality.

Opportunities for Women and Minorities
Show business provided social mobility to female, African American, and immigrant performers, but it also encouraged stereotyping and exploitation. The comic opera diva Lillian Russell, the vaudeville singer-comedienne Fanny Brice, and the burlesque queen Eva Tanguay attracted loyal fans and handsome fees. In contrast to the demure Victorian female, they conveyed pluck and independence. There was something both shocking and confident about Eva Tanguay singing, "It's All Been Done Before but Not the Way I Do It." But lesser female performers and showgirls (called soubrettes) were often exploited by male promoters and theater owners, who wanted to profit by titillating the public with scantily clad women.

Before the 1890s, the chief form of commercial entertainment employing African Americans was the minstrel show, but vaudeville opened new opportunities. Pandering to the prejudices of white audiences, composers ridiculed blacks, and black performers were forced to portray demeaning characters. In songs like "He's Just a Little Nigger, But He's Mine All Mine" blacks were degraded on stage as they were in society. Burt Williams, a talented black comedian and dancer, achieved success by wearing blackface (black makeup) and playing stereotypical roles of a smiling fool, but the humiliation tormented him.

Like Houdini, many performers were immigrants, and their acts reflected the everyday difficulties they faced. Vaudeville utilized ethnic humor and exaggerated dialects. Skits and songs were fast paced, replicating the tempo of factories, offices, and the streets. Performances reinforced ethnic stereotypes, but such distortions were more sympathetic than those directed at blacks. A typical scene involving Italians, for example, highlighted a character's uncertain grasp of English, which caused him to confuse *diploma* with *the plumber* and *pallbearer* with *polar bear*. Such scenes allowed audiences to laugh with, rather than at, foibles of the human condition.

Movies
Shortly after 1900 live entertainment gave way to the more accessible motion pictures. Perfected by Thomas Edison in the 1880s, movies began as slot-machine peepshows in arcades and billiard parlors. Eventually, images were projected onto a screen for large audiences. Producers, many of them from Jewish immigrant backgrounds, soon discovered that a film could tell a story in exciting ways. Using themes of patriotism and working-class experience, early filmmakers helped shift American culture away from its straitlaced Victorian values.

Movies presented controversial social messages as well as innovative technology and styles of expression. The film *The Birth of a Nation* (1915), by the director D. W. Griffith, a stunning epic about the Civil War and Reconstruction, fanned racial prejudice by depicting African Americans as threats to white moral values. The National Association for the Advancement of Colored People (NAACP), formed in 1909, led protests against it. But the film's ground-breaking techniques—close-ups, fade-outs, and battle scenes—heightened its drama.

Technology and entrepreneurship also made news a mass consumer product. Using high-speed printing presses, cheaply produced paper, and profits from growing advertisement revenues, shrewd publishers created an in-demand medium. Increased leisure time seemed to nurture a fascination with the sensational, and from the 1880s onward popular urban newspapers increasingly whetted that appetite.

Yellow Journalism

Joseph Pulitzer, a Hungarian immigrant who bought the *New York World* in 1883, pioneered journalism by making news a mass commodity. Pulitzer filled the *World* with stories of disasters, crimes, and scandals and featured screaming headlines set in large, bold type. *World* reporter Nellie Bly (real name, Elizabeth Cochrane) faked her way into a mental asylum and wrote a brazen exposé of the sordid conditions she found. Other reporters staged stunts and wrote heart-rending human-interest stories. Pulitzer also popularized comics, and the yellow ink in which they were printed gave rise to the term *yellow journalism* as a synonym for *sensationalism*.

In one year the *World*'s circulation increased from 20,000 to 100,000, and by the late 1890s it reached 1 million. Other publishers, such as William Randolph Hearst, who bought the *New York Journal* in 1895 and started a newspaper empire, adopted Pulitzer's techniques. Pulitzer, Hearst, and their rivals boosted circulation further by featuring sports and women's news. Newspapers previously reported sporting events, but yellow-journalism papers gave such stories greater prominence with separate, expanded sports pages. For women, newspapers added special sections devoted to household tips, fashion, etiquette, and club news.

Other Mass-Market Publications

By the early twentieth century, mass-circulation magazines overshadowed expensive elitist journals of earlier eras. Publications like *McClure's, Saturday Evening Post,* and *Ladies' Home Journal* offered human-interest stories, muckraking exposés, fiction, photographs, colorful covers, and eye-catching ads. Meanwhile, the total number of published books more than quadrupled between 1880 and 1917, reflecting the growing literacy. Between 1870 and 1920, the proportion of Americans over age ten who could not read or write fell from 20 to 6 percent.

Other forms of communication also expanded. In 1891 there was fewer than 1 telephone for every 100 people in the United States; by 1901 the number reached 2.1, and by 1921 it swelled to 12.6. In 1900 Americans used 4 billion postage stamps; in 1922 they bought 14.3 billion. More than ever before, people in different parts of the country knew about and discussed the same news event. America was becoming a mass society where the same products, the same technology, and the same information dominated everyday life.

To some extent, cities' new amusements and media had a homogenizing influence, allowing ethnic and social groups to share common experiences. Yet different groups adapted parks, ball fields, vaudeville shows, movies, and the feature sections of newspapers and magazines to their own cultural needs. To the dismay of reformers who hoped that public recreation and holidays would assimilate newcomers, immigrants used parks for ethnic gatherings and converted picnics and Fourth of July celebrations into occasions for boisterous drinking and sometimes violent behavior. Young working-class men and women resisted parents' and moralists' warnings and frequented urban dance halls, where they explored forms of courtship and sexual behavior. Thus, leisure—like work and politics—was shaped by the pluralistic forces that thrived in urban life.

Ethnic Food

Today, an American might eat a bagel for breakfast, a gyro sandwich for lunch, and wonton soup, shrimp creole, and rice pilaf for dinner. These items, each identified with a different ethnic group, serve as tasty reminders that immigrants have made influential and lasting contributions to the nation's culinary culture.

The American taste for ethnic food has a complicated history. Since the nineteenth century, the food business has offered immigrant entrepreneurs lucrative opportunities, many involving products unrelated to their own ethnic background. The industry is replete with success stories such as Hector Boiardi (Chef Boyardee), William Gebhardt (Eagle Brand chili and tamales), Jeno Paulucci (Chun King), and Alphonse Biardot (Franco-American), all of whom immigrated to the United States in the late nineteenth or early twentieth century. But Americans have also supported unheralded local immigrant merchants and restaurateurs offering regional fare—German, Chinese, Italian, Tex-Mex, Thai, or soul food—in every era.

The evolution of American eating habits has been peaceful. Occasionally criticisms developed, such as when dietitians and reformers in the early twentieth century charged that the rich foods of eastern European Jews made them overly emotional and less capable of assimilating. But relatively conflict-free sharing has characterized American food ways far more than intolerance. And mass marketers have been quick to capitalize.

As each wave of immigrants entered the nation—and especially as these newcomers occupied cities, where cross-cultural contact has been inevitable—food has given them ways of becoming American, of finding group acceptance, while confirming their identity. And those who already thought of themselves as Americans have made the newcomers' gastronomic legacy their own.

Summary

People and technology made the late nineteenth and early twentieth century the age of the city. Flocking cityward, migrants already in America and those from foreign lands remade themselves, like Houdini, and remade the urban environment as well. They brought cultures that in turn enriched American culture. They found escape in new forms of mass leisure and entertainment.

American cities experienced unheralded triumph by the early 1900s. Amid corruption and political conflict, engineers modernized sewer, water, and lighting services, and urban governments made cities safer by expanding professional police and fire departments. When native inventiveness met the traditions of European, African, and Asian cultures, a new society emerged. The jumble of social classes, ethnic and racial groups, and political and professional organizations sometimes lived in harmony, sometimes not.

Optimists envisioned the American nation as a melting pot, where various nationalities would fuse into a unified people. Instead, many ethnic groups proved unmeltable, and racial minorities got burned on the bottom of the pot. Instead, the United States became a pluralistic society in which cultural influences moved in both directions: imposed from above by people with power and influence and adopted from below through the traditions brought to cities by disparate peoples.

By 1920, immigrants and their offspring outnumbered the native-born in many cities, and the national economy depended on these new workers and consumers.

Migrants and immigrants transformed the United States into an urban nation. They gave American culture a varied texture and, like Harry Houdini, helped change the course of entertainment and consumerism. Together, they laid the foundations for the liberalism that would characterize American politics in the twentieth century.

Chapter Review

GROWTH OF THE MODERN CITY

What fueled urban growth in the late nineteenth century?

Cities grew two ways: by annexing areas that bordered them, as New York City did when it merged with Brooklyn, Staten Island, and parts of Queens, doubling its population to 3 million. Cities also expanded via in-migration from rural areas and immigration from abroad. Within the United States, low crop prices and heavy debts pushed some people from the country to the city; in other cases, young men sought to escape economic hardship for the excitement of cities while young women left unhappy homes for greater independence. Similarly, African Americans headed to cities for better jobs and to escape crop liens and racial violence. Population pressures, land redistribution, industrialization, and religious persecution pushed many immigrants to leave Europe, Asia, Canada, and Latin America for the United States, with most hoping to make enough money to return to their native countries and live more comfortably.

URBAN NEIGHBORHOODS

How did immigrants adapt to their new lives in U.S. cities?

While most immigrants sought to hang on to old world traditions, once in the United States, those former folkways were changed by, and also helped change, American cities. Traditions held on longer in neighborhoods with immigrants from the same region or district. Immigrants recreated the mutual aid societies, newspapers, and churches that existed in their homelands. While immigrants tried to hold fast to their native languages, English—which children learned in schools—soon dominated ethnic neighborhoods. Foreigners adapted their traditional garments to American fabrics, and their music evolved as well to include American influences or tales of their adjustment to life here. Catholics and Jews sought to merge their faiths with their new surroundings by liberalizing or eliminating some old world rituals.

LIVING CONDITIONS IN THE INNER CITY

What made cities seem particularly threatening/dangerous?

Overcrowding and housing shortages in inner cities, along with poverty and crime led to fears that cities were dangerous places filled with violence, muggings, gang fights, and even murder. While murder rates did increase fourfold from 1881 to 1898, crime in cities was not greater than that in backwoods mining camps or southern plantations. The high concentrations of people, particularly those of different classes and ethnic/racial backgrounds, mingling in cities simply made urban crime more visible, which in turn made cities seem scarier.

MANAGING THE CITY

What facilitated the rise of political machines in cities?

Political machines emerged in typically working class and immigrant neighborhoods to provide relief, security, and services to voters in exchange for votes, money, influence, and prestige. Each machine had a leader, or boss, who helped his constituents obtain jobs, clothing, or legal assistance. The power they exerted over local government meant machines could control which firms or individuals got public contracts and city jobs, and insist that those receiving these awards repay the machine with a share of their profits or salaries. Machine-led governments did build sewer systems, schools, bridges, and transportation lines and expand police and fire, but the bribes and kickbacks they commanded made their projects expensive to taxpayers.

FAMILY LIFE

What factors led to declining birth rates in the late nineteenth century United States?

As more people left farms for city life, the need for big families where children could help with heavy farm work diminished. Improvements in health, medicine, and diet meant that more babies lived past infancy into childhood so that families didn't need to bear more children in the hopes that some might survive. And as the United States became increasingly urbanized, the notion of children needing protection from the city's harsh realities meant that mothers could be more effective caregivers if they had fewer children to raise. New technology led to better materials for condoms, diaphragms, and other birth control devices, which made them more convenient and reliable.

THE NEW LEISURE AND MASS CULTURE

What fueled the rise of commercial leisure?

Mechanization and new, more efficient means of production, along with labor activism, led to shorter work weeks and hours—which, in turn, gave workers more time to use as they saw fit. New mass entertainment arose to fill this need, and included baseball and football leagues, bicycling, and other outdoor activities, as well as theater, vaudeville, and later film. Vaudeville was among the most popular entertainment because its shows tried to appeal to the broadest audiences with jugglers, magicians, comedians, singers, and dancers. Vaudeville, like other forms of show business, also provided new work opportunities for blacks, immigrants, and women.

SUGGESTIONS FOR FURTHER READING

John Bodnar, *The Transplanted: A History of Immigrants in Urban America* (1985)

Howard P. Chudacoff and Judith E. Smith, *The Evolution of American Urban Society*, 6th ed. (2005)

John D'Emilio and Estelle Freedman, *Intimate Matters: A History of Sexuality in America* (1988)

Nancy Foner and George M. Frederickson, eds., *Not Just Black and White: Historical and Contemporary Perspectives on Immigration, Race, and Ethnicity in the United States* (2004)

Kenneth T. Jackson, *The Crabgrass Frontier: The Suburbanization of the United States* (1985)

Matthew Frye Jacobson, *Whiteness of a Different Color: European Immigrants and the Alchemy of Race* (1998)

Erika Lee, *At America's Gates: Chinese Immigration During the Exclusion Era, 1882–1943* (2003)

Martin V. Melosi, *The Sanitary City: Urban Infrastructure in America from Colonial Times to the Present* (2000)

Robyn Muncy, *Creating a Female Dominion in American Reform, 1890–1935* (1991)

Kathy Peiss, *Cheap Amusements: Working Women and Leisure in Turn-of-the-Century New York* (1986)

Gilded Age Politics | 1877–1900

Known to friends as the People's Joan of Arc and to enemies as the Kansas Pythoness, sharp-tongued Mary Elizabeth Lease was an electrifying orator, who, noted one observer, could "set a crowd hooting and harrahing at her will." Born in 1853 in Pennsylvania, she lived most of her adult life in Kansas. Married at age twenty, she bore five children and studied law while she took in washing, pinning her notes above her washtub.

In 1885 Lease became the first woman admitted to the Kansas bar and became an activist. Joining the Woman's Christian Temperance Union and the Farmers' Alliance, she served as spokesperson for the new Populist Party, making over 160 speeches in 1890 on behalf of downtrodden rural folk and laborers. She later ran for the U.S. Senate. Lease also spoke out for prohibition, woman suffrage, and birth control. She proclaimed, "This is a nation of inconsistencies. . . . We fought England for our liberty and put chains on four million blacks. We wiped out slavery and [then] by our tariff laws and national banks began a system of white wage slavery worse than the first." Although she denied making the oft-quoted suggestion that Kansas farmers should "raise less corn and more hell," she thought it was good advice.

Lease's turbulent career paralleled an eventful era characterized by three themes: special interest ascendancy, legislative accomplishment, and political exclusion. Her fiery speeches voiced the growing dissatisfaction with greed and the abuses of power exerted by wealthy individuals and corporations. The era's wealth obsession seemed so widespread that, when Mark Twain and Charles Dudley Warner satirized America as a land of shallow money grubbers in their novel *The Gilded Age* (1874), the name stuck as a historical characterization of the late nineteenth century.

This icon will direct you to interactive activities and study materials on *A People And A Nation*, Brief Edition website: **www.cengage.com/history/norton/ peoplenationbrief8e**

Chronology

Year	Event
1873	Congress ends coinage of silver dollars.
1873–78	Economic hard times hit.
1876	Hayes is elected president.
1877	Georgia passes poll tax, disfranchising most African Americans.
1878	Bland-Allison Act requires Treasury to buy between $2 and $4 million in silver each month.
1880	Garfield becomes president.
1881	Garfield is assassinated; Arthur assumes presidency.
1883	Pendleton Civil Service Act introduces merit system.
	Supreme Court strikes down 1883 Civil Rights Act.
1884	Cleveland is elected president.
1886	*Wabash* case declares that only Congress can limit interstate commerce rates.
1887	Farmers' Alliances are formed.
	Interstate Commerce Commission begins regulating rates and practices of interstate shipping.
1888	B. Harrison is elected president.
1890	McKinley Tariff raises tariff rates.
	Sherman Silver Purchase Act commits Treasury to buying 4.5 million ounces of silver each month.
	Mississippi Plan uses poll taxes and literacy tests to prevent African Americans from voting.
	National Woman Suffrage Association is formed.
1890s	Jim Crow laws, discriminating against African Americans in legal treatment and public accommodations, are passed by southern states.
1892	Populist convention in Omaha draws up a reform platform.
	Cleveland is elected president for the second time.
1893	Sherman Silver Purchase Act is repealed.
1893–97	Major economic depression hits the United States.
1894	Wilson-Gorman Tariff passes.
	Coxey's Army marches on Washington, D.C.
1895	Cleveland makes a deal with bankers to save gold reserves.
1896	McKinley is elected president.
	Plessy v. Ferguson establishes separate-but-equal doctrine.
1898	Louisiana implements "grandfather clause," restricting voting by African Americans.
1899	*Cummings v. County Board of Education* applies the separate-but-equal doctrine to schools.
1900	Gold Standard Act requires all paper money to be backed by gold.
	McKinley is reelected president.

At the same time, Lease's rhetoric obscured economic and political accomplishments at national and state levels. Between 1877 and 1900, large corporations and business allies influenced politics and government, yet Congress achieved legislative landmarks in railroad regulation, tariff and currency reform, and civil service despite partisan and regional rivalries. Meanwhile, the judiciary countered reform by supporting big business and defending property rights against state and federal regulation. The presidency was occupied by respectable men who attempted to assert their authority. Still, exclusion prevented the majority of Americans—women, southern blacks, Indians, uneducated whites, and unnaturalized immigrants—from voting.

Until the 1890s, a stable party system and a balance of power among geographic sections kept politics in a delicate equilibrium. Then, in the 1890s, rural discontent rumbled through the West and South, and a deep economic depression revealed flaws in the industrial system. Mary Lease and others like her helped awaken the rural masses, and the 1896 presidential campaign further stirred Americans. A new party arose, old parties split, sectional unity dissolved, and fundamental disputes about the nation's future climaxed.

- **What were the functions of government in the Gilded Age, and how did they change?**

- **How did policies of exclusion and discrimination make their mark on the political culture of the age?**

- **How did the economic climate give rise to the Populist movement?**

THE NATURE OF PARTY POLITICS

Public interest in elections reached an all-time high between 1870 and 1896. Around 80 percent of eligible voters (white and black males in the North, somewhat lower rates among mostly white males in the South) consistently voted. (Fewer than 50 percent typically vote today.) Featuring parades, picnics, and speeches, politics became recreation, more popular than baseball or circuses.

Cultural-Political Alignments

In the Gilded Age, party loyalty was fierce. With some exceptions, people who opposed government interference in personal liberty identified with the Democratic Party; those who believed government could be an agent of reform identified with the Republicans. Democrats included immigrant and second-generation Catholics and Jews; Republicans consisted mostly of native-born Protestants. Democrats would restrict government power. Republicans believed in direct government action.

There was also a geographic dimension to these divisions. Well into the 1880s, northern Republicans capitalized on bitter memories of the Civil War by "waving the bloody shirt" at Democrats. Northern Democrats focused more on urban and economic issues, but southern Democratic candidates waved their own bloody shirt and called Republicans traitors to white supremacy and states' rights.

Adherents battled over how much government should control people's lives. The most contentious issues were over leisure time and the celebration of Sunday, the Lord's day. Protestant Republicans tried to keep the Sabbath holy through legislation that closed bars, stores, and commercial amusements on Sundays. Immigrant Democrats, accustomed to feasting after church, fought saloon closings and other restrictions.

Allegiances to national parties and candidates were so evenly divided that no faction gained control for long. Between 1877 and 1897, Republicans held the presidency for three terms, Democrats for two. Rarely did one party control the presidency and Congress simultaneously. From 1876 through 1892, presidential elections were close. The outcome often hinged on a few populous northern states—Connecticut, New York, New Jersey, Ohio, Indiana, and Illinois. Both parties tried to gain advantages by nominating candidates from these states (and also by committing vote fraud).

Party Factions

Factional quarrels split both the Republican and the Democratic Parties. Among Republicans, New York's pompous senator Roscoe Conkling led the faction known as Stalwarts and worked the spoils system to win government jobs for supporters.

Their rivals were the Half Breeds, led by James G. Blaine, who also blatantly pursued influence. On the sidelines stood more idealistic Republicans, or Mugwumps (supposedly an Indian term meaning "mug on one side of the fence, wump on the other"). Mugwumps, such as Senator Carl Schurz of Missouri, believed that only righteous men should govern. Meanwhile, Democrats subdivided into white-supremacist southerners, immigrant-stock, and working-class supporters of urban political machines, business-oriented advocates of low tariffs and the gold standard, and debtor-oriented advocates of free silver.

In each state, one party usually dominated, and often the state boss was a senator who parlayed his state power into national influence. Until the Seventeenth Amendment to the Constitution was ratified in 1913, state legislatures elected U.S. senators. As such, senators had enormous power, which they exercised brazenly.

ISSUES OF LEGISLATION

In Congress, sectional controversies, patronage abuses, railroad regulation, tariffs, and currency provoked heated debates. From the end of the Civil War into the 1880s, Congress struggled with soldiers' pensions. The Grand Army of the Republic, an organization of 400,000 Union Army veterans, allied with the Republican Party and cajoled Congress into generous pensions for former Union soldiers and their widows. Many were deserved: Union troops were poorly paid. The Union Army spent $2 billion fighting the Civil War, but veterans' pensions cost $8 billion, one of the largest welfare commitments the federal government ever made. By 1900 soldiers' pensions accounted for roughly 40 percent of the federal budget. Confederate veterans were excluded, though some southern states funded small pensions and built old-age homes for ex-soldiers.

Civil Service Reform   Few politicians dared oppose war pensions, but some attempted to dismantle the spoils system, the practice of awarding government jobs to party devotees (regardless of their qualifications). During the Civil War, the federal government expanded considerably, and the spoils system increasingly flourished, particularly after the war. As the postal service, diplomatic corps, and other government agencies grew, the number of federal jobs tripled, from 53,000 in 1865 to 166,000 in 1891. Elected officials scrambled to control these jobs to benefit themselves and their party. In return for short hours and high pay, appointees to federal positions pledged votes and part of their earnings to their patrons.

Shocked by such corruption, especially after the scandals in the Grant administration, some reformers began advocating appointments based on merit—civil service. Support for change accelerated in 1881 with the formation of the National Civil Service Reform League. The assassination of President James Garfield that year by a distraught job seeker hastened the drive for reform. The Pendleton Civil Service Act, passed by Congress in 1882, created the Civil Service Commission to oversee competitive examinations for government positions. The act gave the commission jurisdiction over only 10 percent of federal jobs, though the president could expand the list. Because the Constitution barred Congress from interfering in state affairs, civil service at state and local levels developed more haphazardly.

Economic policy was the Gilded Age's main issue. Railroads particularly provoked controversy. In their quest for customers, railroads launched rate wars and angered shippers with inconsistent freight charges. On noncompetitive routes, railroads often boosted charges to compensate for unprofitably low rates on competitive routes. Railroads also played favorites, reducing rates to large shippers, and offering free passenger passes to preferred customers and politicians.

Railroad Regulation

Such favoritism stirred farmers, small merchants, and reform politicians to demand rate regulation. By 1880 fourteen states established commissions to limit freight and storage charges of state-chartered lines. Railroads fought back, arguing that the Fourteenth Amendment to the Constitution guaranteed them freedom to acquire and use property without government restraint. But in 1877, in *Munn v. Illinois,* the Supreme Court upheld state regulation, declaring that grain warehouses owned by railroads acted in the public interest and therefore must submit to regulation for "the common good."

Only the federal government could regulate interstate lines, as affirmed by the Supreme Court in the *Wabash* case of 1886. In 1887, Congress passed the Interstate Commerce Act, which prohibited pools, rebates, and long-haul/short-haul rate discrimination. It also created the Interstate Commerce Commission (ICC), the nation's first regulatory agency, to investigate railroad rate making and issue cease-and-desist orders against illegal practices. The legislation's weak provisions for enforcement, however, left railroads room for evasion, and federal judges chipped away at ICC powers. In the *Maximum Freight Rate* case (1897), the Supreme Court ruled that the ICC lacked power to set rates, and in the *Alabama Midlands* case (1897), it overturned prohibitions against long-haul/short-haul discrimination. Still, regulation, though weakened, remained in force.

Tariff Policy

From 1789 onward, Congress created tariffs, which levied duties (taxes) on imported goods, to protect American products from European competition. But tariffs quickly became a tool special interests used to enhance profits. By the 1880s these interests succeeded in obtaining tariffs on more than four thousand items. A few economists and farmers argued for free trade, but most politicians insisted that tariffs were necessary to support industry and preserve jobs.

The Republican Party put protective tariffs at the core of its agenda. Democrats complained that tariffs made prices artificially high by keeping out less expensive foreign goods, thereby benefiting domestic manufacturers while hurting consumers and farmers whose crops were not protected. During the Gilded Age, revenues from tariffs and other levies created a federal budget surplus. Most Republicans liked that the government was earning more than it spent and hoped to keep the extra money as a Treasury reserve or use it for projects that would aid commerce. Democrats acknowledged a need for protection of some manufactured goods and raw materials, but they favored lower tariff duties to encourage foreign trade and reduce the Treasury surplus.

Manufacturers and their congressional allies firmly controlled tariff policy. The McKinley Tariff of 1890 boosted already-high rates another 4 percent. When House Democrats passed a bill to trim tariffs in 1894, Senate Republicans, aided by southern Democrats, added six hundred amendments restoring most cuts (Wilson-Gorman Tariff). In 1897 the Dingley Tariff raised rates further. Attacks on duties made tariffs a symbol of privileged business in the public mind.

Monetary Policy

Monetary policy inflamed stronger emotions than tariffs. When increased industrial and agricultural production caused prices to fall after the Civil War, debtors and creditors had opposing reactions. Farmers suffered because their incomes dropped and because high demand for a limited supply of available money raised interest rates on loans, making it costly to borrow to repay mortgages and other debts. They favored coinage of silver to increase the amount of currency in circulation. This, they reasoned, would reduce interest rates. Small businessmen, also in need of loans, agreed. Large businesses and bankers favored a stable, limited money supply backed by gold, fearing currency fluctuations that would threaten investors' confidence in the U.S. economy.

Creditor-debtor tension translated into class divisions between haves and have-nots. The debate also reflected sectional cleavages: western silver-mining areas and agricultural regions of the South and West against the industrial Northeast.

Taking advantage of the new fad of bicycling (see Chapter 19), a cartoonist in an 1886 issue of the humor magazine *Puck* illustrated the controversy over silver coinage. Depicting two uncoordinated wheels, one a silver coin and the other a gold coin, the illustration conveys the message of how hard it was to proceed with conflicting kinds of currency. (Picture Research Consultants and Archives)

By the 1870s, the currency controversy boiled down to whether gold or silver should back national paper money. Previously, the government bought both, setting a ratio that made a gold dollar worth sixteen times more than a silver dollar. The gold rush of 1848, however, increased gold supply and lowered its market price relative to silver. Consequently, silver dollars disappeared from circulation as owners hoarded them. In 1873 Congress officially stopped coining them. The United States and many of its trading partners unofficially adopted the gold standard.

But within a few years, new mines in the American West began flooding the market with silver, and its price dropped. Gold now was relatively less plentiful, worth more than sixteen times the value of silver (the ratio reached twenty to one by 1890). Silver producers wanted the government to resume buying silver at the old sixteen-to-one ratio, which amounted to a subsidy. Congress tried to compromise. The Bland-Allison Act (1878) authorized the Treasury to buy $2 million to $4 million worth of silver monthly, and the Sherman Silver Purchase Act (1890) increased the government's silver purchase by specifying weight (4.5 million ounces) rather than dollars. Neither measure satisfied the different interest groups. Creditors wanted the government to stop buying silver, whereas for debtors, the legislation failed to expand the money supply satisfactorily. The issue would intensify during the 1896 presidential election.

Legislative Accomplishments

Members of Congress worked under difficult conditions. They earned small salaries yet had to maintain two residences: in their home district and in Washington. Weather was sweltering in summer, and most Congressmen had no private offices, worked long hours, wrote their own speeches, and paid their staff themselves. Still, they managed to pass significant legislation.

TENTATIVE PRESIDENTS

Operating under the cloud of Andrew Johnson's impeachment, Grant's scandals, and doubts about the legitimacy of the 1876 election (see Chapter 16), American presidents between 1877 and 1900 moved to restore authority to their office. Proper and honest, Presidents Rutherford Hayes (1877–1881), James Garfield (1881), Chester Arthur (1881–1885), Grover Cleveland (1885–1889 and 1893–1897), Benjamin Harrison (1889–1893), and William McKinley (1897–1901) tried to act as legislative and administrative leaders. Each president initiated legislation and used vetoes to guide national policy.

Hayes, Garfield, and Arthur

Rutherford B. Hayes had been a Union general and an Ohio congressman and governor before his disputed presidential election, which prompted opponents to label him Rutherfraud. Hayes served as conciliator, emphasizing national harmony over sectional rivalry and opposing racial violence. He tried to overhaul the spoils system by appointing the civil service reformer Carl Schurz to his cabinet and battling New York's patronage king, Senator Conkling.

When Hayes declined to run for reelection in 1880, Republicans nominated another Ohio congressman and Civil War hero, James A. Garfield, who won by just 40,000 votes out of 9 million cast. By winning the pivotal states of New York and Indiana, however, Garfield carried the electoral college by 214 to 155. Garfield hoped to reduce the tariff and develop economic relations with Latin America, and he rebuffed Conkling's patronage demands. But his chance to make lasting contributions ended in July 1881 when Charles Guiteau shot him in a Washington railroad station. Garfield lingered for seventy-nine days before dying September 19.

Garfield's successor was Vice President Chester A. Arthur, the New York spoilsman whom Hayes fired in 1878. Arthur became a temperate executive. He signed the Pendleton Civil Service Act, urged Congress to modify outdated tariff rates, and supported federal regulation of railroads. But congressional partisans frustrated his plans for reducing the tariff and strengthening the navy. Arthur lost the 1884 Republican presidential nomination to James G. Blaine.

Democrats named New York governor Grover Cleveland, a bachelor who fathered an out-of-wedlock son—which he admitted during the campaign. Cleveland beat Blaine by only 29,000 popular votes; his tiny margin of 1,149 votes in New York secured that state's 36 electoral votes for a 219-to-182 victory in the electoral college. Cleveland may have won New York thanks to remarks of a Protestant minister, who equated Democrats with "rum, Romanism, and rebellion." Democrats publicized the slur among New York's large Irish-Catholic population, urging voters to support Cleveland.

Cleveland and Harrison

Cleveland, the first Democratic president since James Buchanan (1857–1861), expanded the civil service, vetoed hundreds of private pension bills, and urged Congress to cut tariff duties. When advisers worried about his chances for reelection, the president retorted, "What is the use of being elected or reelected, unless you stand for something?" When Democrats renominated Cleveland in 1888, businessmen convinced him to moderate his attacks on high tariffs.

Republicans in 1888 nominated Benjamin Harrison, a former Indiana senator and grandson of President William Henry Harrison (1841). Bribery and multiple voting helped him win Indiana by 2,300 votes and New York by 14,000. (Democrats also indulged in such cheating, but Republicans proved more successful at it.) Although Cleveland outpolled Harrison by 90,000 popular votes, Harrison carried the electoral college by 233 to 168.

The first president since 1875 whose party had majorities in both Congressional houses, Harrison influenced legislation with everything from threats of vetoes to informal dinners and consultations with politicians. Partly in response, the Congress of 1889–1891 passed 517 bills, 200 more than the average passed by Congresses between 1875 and 1889. Harrison showed support for the civil service by appointing the reformer Theodore Roosevelt as civil service commissioner. But pressured by special interests, Harrison signed the Dependents' Pension Act, which provided pensions for disabled Union veterans, and widows and children—doubling the number of welfare recipients from 490,000 to 966,000.

The Pension Act and other appropriations in 1890 pushed the federal budget past $1 billion for the first time. Democrats blamed the Billion-Dollar Congress on spendthrift Republicans, and in 1890, voters unseated seventy-eight Republican congressmen. Capitalizing on voter unrest, Democrats nominated Grover Cleveland to run against Harrison in 1892. With large business contributions, Cleveland beat Harrison by 370,000 popular votes (3 percent of the total), easily winning the electoral vote.

In office again, Cleveland addressed currency, tariffs, and labor unrest, but his actions reflected political weakness and a narrow orientation toward business. Cleveland promised sweeping tariff reform, but Senate protectionists undercut his efforts. And when 120,000 boycotting railroad workers paralyzed commerce in the 1894 Pullman strike, Cleveland bowed to requests from railroad managers and Attorney General Richard Olney (a former railroad lawyer) to send in troops.

DISCRIMINATION, DISFRANCHISEMENT, AND RESPONSES

Despite speeches about freedom during the Gilded Age, policies of discrimination haunted more than half the nation's population. Racial issues shaped politics in the South, home to the majority of African Americans. Southern white farmers and workers feared that newly enfranchised African American men would challenge their political and social superiority (real and imagined). Wealthy landowners and merchants fanned these fears, keeping blacks and whites from uniting to protest their economic subjugation.

Violence Against African Americans

In 1880, 90 percent of southern blacks farmed or worked in personal and domestic service, just as they had as slaves. The New South, moreover, proved as violent for blacks as the Old South had been. Between 1889 and 1909, more than seventeen hundred African Americans were lynched in the South, often in sparsely populated districts where whites felt threatened by an influx of migrant blacks. Most lynching victims were accused of assault—rarely proved—on a white woman.

Blacks did not suffer such violence silently, however. The most notable activist was Ida B. Wells, a Memphis schoolteacher, who was removed from a railroad car in 1884 when she refused to give up her seat to a white man. In 1889 Wells became a partner of a Memphis newspaper, the *Free Speech and Headlight*, in which she published attacks against white injustice, especially in the case of three black grocers lynched in 1892 after defending themselves against whites. She herself fled to England to escape death threats, but soon returned and wrote *A Red Record* (1895), which tabulated statistics on racial lynchings and served as a foundation for further protest campaigns.

Disfranchisement

Southern leaders, eager to reassert authority and racial superiority, instituted measures to prevent blacks from voting and keep them legally segregated. Despite threats and intimidation, blacks still formed the backbone of the southern Republican Party and won numerous elective positions. In North Carolina, for example, eleven African Americans served in the state Senate and forty-three in the House between 1877 and 1890. In response, beginning with Tennessee in 1889 and Arkansas in 1892, southern states levied $1 to $2 on all voters—prohibitive to most blacks, who were poor and in debt. Other schemes disfranchised—or deprived voting rights to—blacks who could not read.

The Supreme Court determined in *U.S. v. Reese* (1876) that Congress had no control over local and state elections other than upholding the Fifteenth Amendment, which prohibits states from denying the vote "on account of race, color, or previous condition of servitude." State legislatures found ways to exclude black voters, however. An 1890 state constitutional convention established the Mississippi Plan, requiring voters to pay a poll tax eight months before each election, present the tax receipt at election time, and prove that they could read and interpret the state constitution. Registration officials applied stiffer standards to blacks than to whites, even declaring black college graduates ineligible due to illiteracy.

Such restrictions proved highly effective. In South Carolina, 70 percent of eligible blacks voted in the 1880 presidential election; by 1896 the rate dropped to 11 percent. By the 1900s African Americans effectively lost political rights in the South. Disfranchisement also affected poor whites, few of whom could meet poll tax, property, and literacy requirements. Thus the total number of eligible voters in Mississippi shrank from 257,000 in 1876 to 77,000 in 1892.

Legal Segregation

In a series of cases during the 1870s, the Supreme Court opened the door to racial discrimination by ruling that the Fourteenth Amendment protected citizens' rights only against infringement by state governments—but not from individuals or organizations. If blacks wanted legal protection from private sector discrimination, the Court said, they must seek it from state laws because under the Tenth Amendment states retained all powers not specifically assigned to Congress. These rulings climaxed in 1883 when the Court struck down the 1875 Civil Rights Act, which prohibited segregation in public facilities, such as streetcars, theaters, and parks.

States could legally segregate on a "separate-but-equal" basis, as upheld by the Supreme Court in the case of *Plessy v. Ferguson* (1896). This case began in 1892 when a New Orleans organization of prominent African Americans chose Homer Plessy, a dark-skinned Creole who was only one-eighth black (but considered black by Louisiana law), to sit in a whites-only railroad car. Plessy was arrested, and the appeal of his conviction reached the U.S. Supreme Court in 1896. The Court, however, affirmed that a state law providing for separate facilities for blacks and whites was reasonable because it preserved "public peace and good order." To the court, a law separating the races did not necessarily "destroy the legal equality of the races." Although the ruling did not use the phrase "separate but equal," it made legal separate facilities for black and white people as long as they were equal. In 1899 the Court legitimated school segregation in *Cummins v. County Board of Education,* until it was overturned by *Brown v. Board of Education* in 1954.

Segregation laws—known as Jim Crow laws—multiplied throughout the South, reminding African Americans of their inferior status. State and local statutes passed in the 1890s restricted blacks to the rear of streetcars, separate public drinking fountains and toilets, and separate sections of hospitals and cemeteries. A Birmingham, Alabama, ordinance required that the races be "distinctly separated . . . by well defined physical barriers" in "any room, hall, theatre, picture house, auditorium, yard, court, ballpark, or other indoor or outdoor place."

African American Activism

African American women and men challenged prejudice. Some boycotted discriminatory businesses; others considered moving to Africa. Still others promoted Negro enterprise. In 1898, the Atlanta University professor John Hope urged blacks to become their own employers and support Negro Business Men's Leagues. In the optimistic days following Reconstruction, many blacks saw higher education as a means to elevate their status. In all-black teachers' colleges, men and women sought opportunities for themselves and their race.

While disfranchisement pushed African American men out of public life, African American women used traditional roles as mothers, educators, and moral guardians to uplift the race and seek better services. They successfully lobbied southern governments for cleaner city streets, improved public health, expanded charity services, and vocational education. While black and white women sometimes united to achieve their goals, white women often sympathized with men in white-supremacist campaigns.

Woman Suffrage

In the North, white women pursued the vote with limited success. Prior to 1870, each state determined voting qualifications. That year, the Fifteenth Amendment forbade states from denying the vote "on account of race, color or previous condition" but omitted reference to sex. For the next twenty years, two organizations, the National Woman Suffrage Association (NWSA) and the American Woman Suffrage Association (AWSA), crusaded for female suffrage. The NWSA, led by Elizabeth Cady Stanton and Susan B. Anthony, advocated women's rights in courts, workplaces, and the ballot box. The AWSA, led by the former abolitionists Lucy Stone and Thomas Wentworth Higginson, focused narrowly on suffrage. Anthony's effort to get a constitutional amendment for woman suffrage never received support, with senators claiming suffrage would interfere with women's family obligations.

While the NWSA fought for suffrage on the national level, the AWSA worked to amend state constitutions. (The groups merged in 1890, forming the National American Woman Suffrage Association.) Between 1870 and 1910, eleven states (mostly in the West) legalized limited woman suffrage. By 1890 nineteen states allowed women to vote on school issues, and three granted suffrage on tax and bond issues. The right to vote in national elections awaited a later generation, but women like Mary Lease, Ida B. Wells, Susan B. Anthony, and Lucy Stone proved that women could be politically active even without the vote.

Agrarian Unrest and Populism

Economic inequities sparked a mass movement. Despite rapid industrialization and urbanization in the late nineteenth century, the United States remained an agrarian society, with 64 percent of the population living in rural areas in 1890. The expression of farmers' discontent—a mixture of strident rhetoric, nostalgic dreams, and hard-headed egalitarianism—began in Grange organizations in the early 1870s and accelerated when Farmers' Alliances formed in Texas later in the decade and across the Cotton Belt and Great Plains in the 1880s. The movement flourished where tenancy, debt, weather, and insects endangered struggling farmers.

Sharecropping and Tenant Farming in the South

Southern agriculture did not benefit much from mechanization (see Chapter 17). Tobacco and cotton, the principal southern crops, required constant hoeing and weeding by hand. Tobacco leaves matured at different rates and stems were too fragile for machines. Also, mechanical devices were not precise enough to pick cotton. Thus, after the Civil War, southern agriculture remained labor-intensive, and landlords replaced slaves with sharecroppers and tenant farmers.

Sharecropping and tenant farming—where farmers rented rather than owned land—entangled millions of black and white southerners in webs of debt and humiliation, at whose center loomed the crop lien. Too poor to have ready cash, most farmers borrowed to buy necessities, offering future crops as collateral. To get supplies, a farmer dealt with a furnishing merchant, who would exchange them for a lien, or legal claim, on the farmer's forthcoming crop. After the crop was harvested and brought to market, the merchant collected the portion of the crop that would repay the loan. Often, however, the debt exceeded the crop's value. The farmer could pay off only part of the debt, but borrowed more for food and supplies for the coming year, sinking deeper into debt.

Merchants frequently took advantage by inflating prices and charging excessive interest on advances farmers received. Suppose, for example, that a farmer needed a 20-cent bag of seed. The furnishing merchant would sell it to him on credit but for 28 cents; by year's end, that loan would have accumulated interest of 50 percent or more. The farmer, pledging more than his crop's worth against such debts, fell behind and never recovered. In the southern backcountry, after the Civil War, farmers shifted from diversified agriculture to commercial farming, namely cotton production. Consequently, yeoman began purchasing supplies such as flour, potatoes, and corn that they previously grew themselves. This move to the market economy came about for two reasons: constant debt forced farmers to grow crops that would net cash, and railroads enabled them to transport cotton to market more easily than before. As backcountry yeomen devoted more acres to cotton and less to subsistence crops, they found themselves more frequently at the mercy of merchants.

Hardship in the Midwest and West

In the Midwest, as growers cultivated more land, as mechanization boosted productivity, and as foreign competition increased, supplies of agricultural products exceeded national and worldwide demand, leading to steady price drops for staple crops. A bushel of wheat that sold for $1.45 in 1866 brought only 80 cents in the mid-1880s and 49 cents by the mid-1890s. Meanwhile, transportation and storage fees remained high relative to other prices. To buy necessities and pay bills, farmers had to produce more, but the more they produced, the lower crop prices dropped (see Figure 20.1).

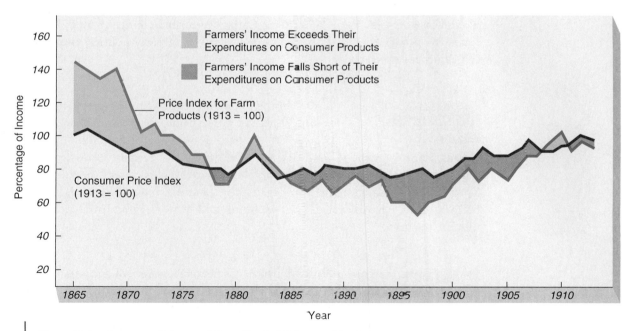

Figure 20.1   Consumer Prices and Farm Product Prices, 1865–1913

Until the late 1870s, in spite of falling farm prices, farmers were able to receive from their crops more income than they spent on consumer goods. But beginning in the mid-1880s, consumer prices leveled off and then rose, while prices for farm products continued to drop. As a result, farmers found it increasingly difficult to afford consumer goods, a problem that plagued them well into the twentieth century.

The West suffered from special hardships. In Colorado, absentee capitalists seized control of the access to transportation and water, and the concentration of technology by large mining companies pushed out small firms. Charges of monopolistic behavior by railroads echoed among farmers, miners, and stockmen in Wyoming and Montana. In California, Washington, and Oregon, wheat and fruit growers found their opportunities blocked by railroads' control of transportation and storage rates.

Grange Movement

With aid from Oliver H. Kelley, a clerk in the Department of Agriculture, farmers in almost every state during the 1860s and 1870s founded local organizations called Granges, dedicated to improving economic conditions. By 1875 the Grange had twenty thousand branches and a million members. Strongest in the Midwest and South, Granges sponsored meetings and educational events to relieve the loneliness of farm life. Family-oriented local Granges welcomed women's participation.

As membership flourished, Granges turned to economic and political action. Local Grange branches formed cooperative associations to buy supplies and to market crops and livestock. A few Grangers operated farm-implement factories and insurance companies. Most enterprises failed, however, because farmers lacked capital for large-scale buying and because large manufacturers and dealers undercut them. Granges declined in the late 1870s, after convincing states to establish agricultural colleges, electing sympathetic legislators, and pressing state legislatures for so-called Granger laws to regulate transportation and storage rates. But in the *Wabash* case of 1886, the U.S. Supreme Court overturned Granger laws by denying states the power to regulate railroad rates. Disavowing party politics, Granges became farmers' social clubs.

The White Hats

In the Southwest, migrations of English-speaking ranchers into Mexican pastureland sparked another agrarian protest. In the late 1880s, a group calling itself Las Gorras Blancas, or the White Hats, struggled to control formerly ancestral lands, harassing Anglo ranchers and destroying fences that Anglos erected on public land. They could not halt Anglos from legally buying and using public land, however; by 1900 many Hispanics had given up farming to work as agricultural laborers or migrate to cities.

Farmers' Alliances

By 1890, two networks of Farmers' Alliances—one in the Great Plains and one in the South—became the center of rural activism. The first Farmers' Alliances arose in Texas, where hard-pressed farmers rallied against crop liens, merchants, railroads, and money power. Using traveling lecturers to recruit members, Alliance leaders extended the movement into other southern states, boasting 2 million southern Alliance members by 1889. A separate Colored Farmers' National Alliance claimed 1 million black members. In the late 1880s, the Plains movement similarly organized 2 million members in Kansas, Nebraska, and the Dakotas.

To bypass corporate power and to control markets, Alliances, like the Grange, proposed that farmers form cooperatives, joining together to sell crops and livestock and buy supplies and manufactured goods. By pooling resources, Alliances reasoned, farmers could exert greater economic pressure and share the benefits of their work rather than competing with each other. They also encouraged women's participation and invited the Knights of Labor to join their "struggle against monopolistic oppression."

To relieve the most serious rural problem, shortages of cash and credit, Alliances proposed a government aid system called a subtreasury. The plan first called for the federal government to construct warehouses where farmers could store nonperishable crops while awaiting higher market prices the government would then loan farmers Treasury notes amounting to 80 percent of the market price of the stored crops. Farmers could use these notes for debts and purchases. Once the crops were sold, farmers would repay the loans plus small interest and storage fees, thereby avoiding the exploitative crop-lien system.

The subtreasury plan's second part would provide low-interest government loans to farmers to buy land. These loans, along with the Treasury notes for stored crops, would inject cash into the economy and encourage the kind of inflation that advocates hoped would raise crop prices without raising other prices.

Problems in Achieving Alliance Unity

If Farmers' Alliances had been able to unite politically, they could have been a formidable force; but racial and sectional differences and personality clashes thwarted their merger efforts. Racial voting restrictions weakened Alliance voter strength, and racism impeded acceptance of blacks by white Alliances. Some southern leaders, such as Georgia's Senator Tom Watson, tried to unite distressed black and white farmers, but whites held fast to prejudices. Many came from families that had previously owned slaves; they considered African Americans inferior and took comfort that there would always be people worse off than they were. Regional politics also predominated. Northern farmers favored protective tariffs to keep out foreign grain, whereas white southerners wanted low tariffs to hold down costs of imports. However, both northern and southern alliances favored government regulation of railroads, equitable taxation, currency reform, an end to alleged election frauds that perpetuated special interests in office, and prohibition of landownership by foreign investors.

Rise of Populism

Expanding membership drew Alliances into politics. By 1890, farmers elected several sympathetic officeholders, especially in the South, where Alliances controlled four governorships, eight state legislatures, and forty-seven seats in Congress (forty-four in the House, three in the Senate). In the Midwest, Alliance candidates often ran on third-party tickets, such as the Greenback Party, with some success in Kansas, Nebraska, and the Dakotas. Leaders crisscrossed the country to recruit support for a new party. In summer 1890, the Kansas Alliance held a convention of the people and nominated candidates who swept the state's fall elections. Formation of this People's, or Populist, Party gave a title to Alliance political activism. (Populism is the

Russian Populism

Before American Populism, a different form of populism emerged in another largely rural country: Russia. Whereas American Populism came from the Alliance farm organizations, Russian populism was created by intellectuals seeking to educate peasants to agitate for social and economic freedom.

Russian society began to modernize in the mid-nineteenth century. Town governments were given control of local taxation and education became more widespread. Perhaps most importantly, in 1861 Czar Alexander II signed an Edict of Emancipation, freeing Russian serfs (slaves attached to specific lands) and granting them compensation to buy land. The reforms progressed slowly, prompting some educated Russians to press for more radical solutions, including socialism. The reformers became known as *narodniki*, or populists, from *narod*, the Russian term for "peasant."

Narodniki envisioned a society of self-governing village communes, somewhat like the cooperatives proposed by American Farmers' Alliances. One of their leaders, Peter Lavrov, believed that intellectuals must get closer to the people and help the masses improve their lives. Russian populists believed that only an uprising against the czar could realize their goals. When Alexander instituted repressive policies against the *narodniki* in the late 1870s, many turned to terrorism, culminating in Alexander II's assassination in 1881.

Russian peasants remained tied to tradition and could not abandon their loyalty to the czar. Government arrests and imprisonments after Alexander's assassination discouraged populists' efforts, and the movement declined. Nevertheless, the ideas of Russian populism became the cornerstone of the 1917 Russian Revolution and of Soviet social and political ideology that followed.

Russian peasants, like American tenant farmers and owners of small landholdings, suffered from poverty and pressures of the expanded market economy. The plight of struggling Russian farm families stirred up empathy from young populist intellectuals, who adopted radical solutions, but did not stir up as much political fervor among farmers as American Populism did.

(© Bettmann/Corbis)

political doctrine that asserts the rights and powers of common people versus elites.) By 1892, southern Alliance members joined their northern counterparts in summoning a People's Party convention in Omaha, Nebraska, on July 4 to draft a platform and nominate a presidential candidate.

Charging that inequality (between white classes) threatened to splinter society, the new party's platform declared, "The fruits of the toil of millions are boldly stolen to build up colossal fortunes for a few" and that "wealth belongs to him that creates it." The document addressed three sources of rural unrest: transportation, land, and money. Frustrated with weak regulation, Populists demanded government ownership of railroad and telegraph lines. The monetary plank called for the government to make more money available for farm loans and restore free and unlimited coinage of silver. Other planks advocated a graduated income tax, postal savings banks, direct election of U.S. senators, and a shorter workday. As its presidential candidate, the party nominated James B. Weaver of Iowa, a former Union general and supporter of an expanded money supply.

Populist Spokespeople

The Populist campaign featured dynamic personalities such as Mary Lease and Sockless Jerry Simpson, an unschooled but canny rural reformer who got his nickname after he ridiculed silk-stockinged wealthy people causing a reporter to muse that Simpson probably wore no stockings. The South produced leaders such as Texas's Charles W. Macune, Georgia's Tom Watson, and North Carolina's Leonidas Polk. Minnesota's Ignatius Donnelly, a pseudoscientist and writer of apocalyptic novels, became chief visionary of the northern plains and penned the Omaha platform's thunderous language. Not since 1856 had a third party done so well in its first national effort. In 1892 Weaver garnered 8 percent of the popular vote, majorities in four states, and twenty-two electoral votes. Nevertheless, the party faced a dilemma of whether to stand by its principles or compromise to gain power. Populist candidates were successful only in the West. The vote-rich Northeast ignored Weaver, and Alabama was the only southern state that gave Populists as much as one-third of its votes.

Still, Populism gave southern and western rural dwellers faith in a future based on American ideals, as they looked toward the 1896 presidential election. Amid hardship and desperation, millions came to believe that a cooperative democracy in which government would ensure equal opportunity could overcome corporate power.

THE DEPRESSION AND PROTESTS OF THE 1890S

In 1893, shortly before Grover Cleveland's second presidency began, the Philadelphia and Reading Railroad, once a thriving and profitable line, went bankrupt. Like other railroads, it borrowed heavily to lay track and build stations and bridges. Overexpansion cut into profits, and ultimately the company could not pay its debts.

Similar problems beset manufacturers. Output at McCormick farm machinery factories was nine times greater in 1893 than in 1879, but revenues had only tripled. The company bought more equipment and squeezed more work out of fewer laborers, but it only increased debt and unemployment. Jobless workers also could not pay their bills. Banks suffered when customers defaulted. The failure of the National Cordage Company in May 1893 sparked a chain reaction of business and bank closings. Between 1893 and 1897, the nation suffered a devastating economic depression.

Nearly 20 percent of the labor force was jobless during the depression. Falling demand caused prices to drop between 1892 and 1895, but layoffs and wage cuts more than offset declining living costs. Many people could not afford basic necessities. The New York police estimated that twenty thousand homeless and jobless people roamed the city's streets.

Continuing Currency Problems

As the depression deepened, the currency dilemma reached a crisis. The Sherman Silver Purchase Act of 1890 committed the government to use Treasury notes (silver certificates) to buy 4.5 million ounces of silver each month. Recipients could redeem these certificates for gold, at the ratio of one ounce of gold for every sixteen ounces of silver. But a western mining boom increased silver supplies, causing its market value to fall and prompting holders of Sherman silver notes and Civil War greenbacks to exchange their notes for more valuable gold. As a result, the nation's gold reserve dwindled, falling below $100 million in early 1893.

If investors believed that the country's gold reserve was disappearing, they would lose confidence in America's economic stability and refrain from investing. British capitalists, for example, owned some $4 billion in American stocks and bonds and were likely to stop investing if dollars were to depreciate. The lower the gold reserve dropped, the more people rushed to redeem their money. Panic spread, causing more bankruptcies and unemployment.

To protect the gold reserve, President Cleveland called a special session of Congress to repeal the Sherman Silver Purchase Act. Repeal passed in late 1893, but the run on gold continued through 1894. In early 1895, reserves fell to $41 million, and Cleveland desperately accepted an offer of 3.5 million ounces of gold for $65 million in federal bonds from a banking syndicate led by financier J. P. Morgan. When the bankers resold the bonds, they made a $2 million profit. Cleveland claimed that he had saved the reserves, but discontented farmers, workers, silver miners, and some of Cleveland's Democratic allies saw only humiliation in the president's deal with big businessmen.

The deal between Cleveland and Morgan did not end the depression. After improving slightly in 1895, the economy plunged again. Farm income, declining since 1887, continued to slide; factories closed; banks restricted withdrawals. The tight money supply depressed housing construction and dried up jobs. Cities like Detroit encouraged citizens to cultivate potato patches on vacant land to alleviate food shortages. Urban police stations filled up nightly with homeless persons who had no place to stay.

Consequences of the Depression

In the final years of the century, gold discoveries in Alaska, good harvests, and industrial growth brought relief. But the downturn hastened the crumbling of the old economic system and emergence of a new one. The American economy expanded beyond sectional bases; when farmers in the West fell into debt, they affected the economic health of railroads, farm-implement manufacturers, and banks in other sections. Moreover, the corporate consolidation that characterized the new business system tempted many companies to expand too rapidly. When contraction occurred, their reckless debts dragged them down, and they pulled other industries down with them.

A new global marketplace was emerging, forcing American farmers to contend with discriminatory transportation rates and falling crop prices at home, along with Canadian and Russian wheat growers, Argentine cattle ranchers, Indian and Egyptian cotton manufacturers, and Australian wool producers. Consequently, one country's economy affected that of other countries. With the glutted domestic market, American businessmen sought new markets abroad (see Chapter 22).

Depression-Era Protests

The depression exposed fundamental tensions in the industrial system. Technological and organizational changes had been widening the gap between employees and employers for half a century. Labor protest began with the railroad strikes of 1877. Their vehemence and support from working-class people raised fears that the United States would experience a popular uprising like one in France in 1871, which had briefly overturned the government and introduced communist principles. The Haymarket riot of 1886, a general strike in New Orleans in 1891, and a prolonged strike at the Carnegie Homestead Steel plant in 1892 heightened anxieties. In 1892 violence erupted at a silver mine in Coeur d'Alene, Idaho, when striking miners, angered by wage cuts and a lockout, seized the mine and battled federal troops.

In 1894, there were over thirteen hundred strikes and countless riots. Contrary to accusations by businessmen, few protesters were anarchists or communists. Rather, they were men and women who believed that in a democracy their voices should be heard.

Socialists

Small numbers of socialists participated in these and other confrontations. Some socialists believed workers should control factories and businesses; others supported government ownership. All, however, opposed the private enterprise of capitalism. Their ideas derived from Karl Marx (1818–1883), a German philosopher and the father of communism, who contended that whoever controls the means of production determines how well people live. Marx wrote that industrial capitalism generates profits by paying workers less than the value of their labor and that mechanization and mass production alienate workers from their labor. According to Marx, only by abolishing the return on capital—profits—could labor receive its true value, possible only if workers owned the means of production. Marx predicted that workers worldwide would revolt and seize factories, farms, banks, and transportation lines. This revolution would establish a socialist order of justice and equality. Marx's vision appealed to some workers because it promised independence and to some intellectuals because it promised to end class conflict and crass materialism.

In America, socialism suffered from disagreement over how to achieve Marx's vision. Much of the movement consisted of ideas brought by immigrants—first Germans, later Russian Jews, Italians, Hungarians, and Poles. It splintered into small groups, such as the Socialist Labor Party, which failed to attract the mass of laborers because it often focused on doctrine rather than workers' everyday needs. Social mobility and the philosophy of individualism also undermined socialist aims. Workers hoped that they would benefit through education and the acquisition of property; most American workers sought individual betterment rather than the betterment of all.

Eugene V. Debs

In 1894, a new and inspiring Socialist leader emerged. The Indiana-born Eugene V. Debs headed the newly formed American Railway Union which carried out that year's strike against the Pullman Company. Jailed for defying an injunction against the strike, Debs read Karl Marx's works in prison. Once released, he became the leading spokesman for American socialism, combining visionary Marxism with Jeffersonian and Populist antimonopolism. Debs captivated audiences with attacks on the free-enterprise system. "Many of you think you are competing," he would lecture. "Against whom? Against Rockefeller? About as I would if I had a wheelbarrow and competed with the Santa Fe [railroad] from here to Kansas City." By 1900 the group soon to be called the Socialist Party of America was uniting around Debs.

Coxey's Army

In 1894, however, a quiet businessman named Jacob Coxey from Massillon, Ohio, captured public attention. Coxey believed that, to aid debtors, the government should issue $500 million of legal tender paper money and make low-interest loans to local governments, which would use the funds to pay the unemployed to build roads and other public works. He planned to publicize his scheme by leading a march from Massillon to Washington, D.C., gathering unemployed workers along the way. Coxey's army, about two hundred strong, left in March 1894. Moving across Ohio into Pennsylvania, the marchers received food and housing in depressed industrial towns and rural villages and added new recruits. A dozen similar processions from places such as Seattle, San Francisco, and Los Angeles also headed eastward. Sore feet prompted some marchers to commandeer trains, but most marches were law-abiding.

Coxey's band of five hundred, including women and children, entered Washington on April 30. The next day (May Day, the anniversary of the Haymarket violence), the group, armed with "war clubs of peace," advanced to the Capitol. When Coxey and a few others vaulted the wall surrounding the Capitol grounds, mounted police routed the demonstrators. Police dragged Coxey away. As arrests and clubbings continued, Coxey's dream of a demonstration of 400,000 jobless workers dissolved.

Unlike socialists, who wished to replace the capitalist system, Coxey's troops merely wanted more jobs and better living standards. The brutal reactions of officials, however, reveal how threatening dissenters like Coxey and Debs seemed to the existing social order.

THE SILVER CRUSADE AND THE ELECTION OF 1896

Social protest and economic depression made the 1896 presidential election seem pivotal. Debates over money and power were climaxing, Democrats and Republicans battled to control Congress and the presidency. The key question, however, was whether voters would abandon old party loyalties for the Populist Party.

Free Silver

The Populist crusade against money power settled on the issue of silver, which many believed would solve the nation's complex ills. To them, free coinage of silver symbolized an end to special privileges for the rich and the return of government to the people by lifting common people out of debt, increasing the cash in circulation, and reducing interest rates.

As the election of 1896 approached, Populists had to decide whether to join with sympathetic factions of the major parties, thus risking a loss of identity, or remain an independent third party. Except in mining areas of the Rocky Mountain states, where free coinage of silver had strong support, Republicans were unlikely allies because their support for the gold standard and big business represented what Populists opposed.

Alliance with northern and western Democrats was more plausible since the party there retained vestiges of antimonopoly ideology and sympathy for a looser currency system, despite the influence of "gold Democrats," such as President Cleveland and Senator David Hill of New York. Linking with Southern Democrats seemed less viable since candidates' failure to have carried out their promises left southern farmers feeling betrayed. Whichever they chose, Populists ensured that the 1896 election would be the most issue oriented since 1860.

Republican Nomination of McKinley

Both major parties were divided. For a year, the Ohio industrialist Marcus A. Hanna maneuvered to win the Republican nomination for Ohio's governor, William McKinley, and had corralled enough delegates to succeed. The Republicans' only distress occurred when they adopted a moderate platform supporting the gold standard, rejecting a prosilver stance proposed by Colorado senator Henry M. Teller. Teller, a party founder forty years earlier, left in tears, taking a small group of silver Republicans with him.

At the Democratic convention, prosilver delegates wearing silver badges and waving silver banners paraded through the Chicago Amphitheatre. A *New York World* reporter remarked that "all the silverites need is a Moses." They found one in William Jennings Bryan.

William Jennings Bryan

Bryan, age thirty-six, arrived at the Democratic convention as a member of a contested Nebraska delegation. A former congressman whose support for the coinage of silver annoyed President Cleveland, Bryan found the depression's impact on midwestern farmers distressing. Shortly after the convention seated Bryan, he joined

THE LOCKOUT IS ENDED; HE HOLDS THE KEY.

During the 1896 presidential campaign, Republicans depicted their candidate, William McKinley, as holding the key to prosperity for both the working man and the white-collar laborer, shown here raising their hats to the candidate. Republicans successfully made this economic theme, rather than the silver crusade of McKinley's unsuccessful opponent, William Jennings Bryan, the difference in the election's outcome.
(Collection of David J. and Lanice L. Frent)

the resolutions committee and helped write a platform calling for unlimited coinage of silver. Bryan's now-famous closing words ignited the delegates.

> Having behind us the producing masses of this nation and the world, supported by the commercial interests, the laboring interests, and the toilers everywhere, we will answer [the wealthy classes'] demand for a gold standard by saying to them: You shall not press down upon the brow of labor this crown of thorns, you shall not crucify mankind upon a cross of gold.

After that speech, it took five ballots to win Bryan the nomination, but the magnetic Boy Orator proved irresistible. In accepting the silverite goals of southerners and westerners and repudiating Cleveland's policies, the Democratic Party became more attractive to discontented farmers. But it, too, alienated a minority wing, who withdrew and nominated their own candidate.

Bryan's nomination presented the Populist Party convention with a dilemma. Should Populists join Democrats in support of Bryan or nominate their own candidate? Some reasoned that supporting a separate candidate would split the anti-McKinley vote and guarantee a Republican victory. The convention compromised, first naming Tom Watson as its vice-presidential nominee to preserve party identity (Democrats had nominated the Maine shipping magnate Arthur Sewall) and then nominating Bryan for president.

The campaign, as the Kansas journalist William Allen White observed, "took the form of religious frenzy." Bryan preached that "every great economic question is in reality a great moral question." Republicans countered Bryan's attacks on privilege by predicting chaos if he won. Hanna invited thousands of people to McKinley's home in Canton, Ohio, where the candidate plied them with homilies on moderation and prosperity, promising something for everyone. In an appeal to working-class voters, Republicans stressed the new jobs that a protective tariff would create.

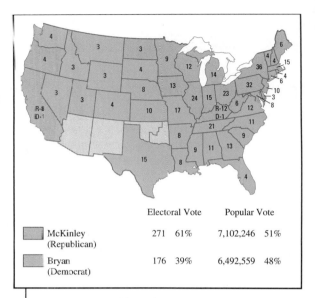

	Electoral Vote		Popular Vote	
McKinley (Republican)	271	61%	7,102,246	51%
Bryan (Democrat)	176	39%	6,492,559	48%

Map 20.1 Presidential Election, 1896
William Jennings Bryan had strong voter support in the South and West, but the numerically superior industrial states, plus California, created majorities for William McKinley.

Election Results

The election revealed that the political standoff had finally ended. McKinley, symbol of urban and corporate ascendancy, beat Bryan by 600,000 popular votes and won in the electoral college by 271 to 176 (see Map 20.1).

Bryan worked hard to rally the nation, but their obsession with silver prevented Populists from building the urban-rural coalition that would have expanded their political appeal. Urban workers, who might have benefited from Populist goals, feared that silver coinage would shrink the value of their wages. Labor leaders, such as the AFL's Samuel Gompers, though partly sympathetic, would not commit fully because they viewed farmers as businessmen, not workers. And socialists denounced Populists as retrograde because they believed in free enterprise. Thus the Populist crusade collapsed. Although Populists and fusion candidates won a few state and congressional elections, the Bryan-Watson ticket of the Populist Party polled only 222,600 votes nationwide.

The McKinley Presidency

As president, McKinley reinforced his support of business by signing the Gold Standard Act (1900), requiring that all paper money be backed by gold. A seasoned politician, McKinley had guided passage of record-high tariff rates as a congressman in 1890. He accordingly supported the Dingley Tariff of 1897, which raised duties even higher. A believer in opening new markets abroad to sustain profits at home, McKinley encouraged imperialistic ventures in Latin America and the Pacific. Good times and victory in the Spanish-American War enabled him to beat Bryan again in 1900.

Summary

Politicians during the Gilded Age prepared the nation for the twentieth century. Laws encouraging economic growth with some principles of regulation, measures expanding government agencies while reducing patronage, and federal intervention in trade and currency issues evolved during the 1870s and 1880s.

True to Mary Lease's characterization, the United States remained a "nation of inconsistencies." Those who supported disfranchisement of African Americans and

Interpreting a Fairy Tale

The *Wizard of Oz*, one of the most popular movies of all time, began as a work of juvenile literature penned by the journalist L. Frank Baum in 1900. Originally titled *The Wonderful Wizard of Oz*, the story used memorable characters to create an adventurous quest.

Adults, however, have searched for hidden meanings. In 1964 one scholar, Henry M. Littlefield, asserted that Baum really intended to write a Populist parable about the conditions of overburdened farmers and laborers. Dorothy, he theorized, symbolized the well-intentioned common person; the Scarecrow, the struggling farmer; the Tin Man, the industrial worker. Hoping for a better life, these friends, along with the Cowardly Lion (William Jennings Bryan), followed a yellow brick road (the gold standard) that led nowhere. The Emerald City was presided over by a wizard, who tried to be all things to all people, but Dorothy revealed him as a fraud. Dorothy was able to leave this muddled society and return to her simple Kansas farm family of Aunt Em and Uncle Henry by using her magical silver slippers (representing coinage of silver, though the movie made them red).

Subsequent theorists identified additional symbols, such as Oz being the abbreviation for ounces (oz.), the chief measurement of gold. The Wicked Witch of the East—who, Baum wrote, kept the little people (Munchkins) "in bondage"—could represent industrial capitalism.

But in 1983 the historian William R. Leach asserted that Baum's tale actually was a celebration of urban consumer culture. Its language exalted the opulence of Emerald City, which to Leach resembled the "White City" of the Chicago World's Fair of 1893. Baum's career supported this new interpretation. Before he was a writer, he designed display windows and was involved in theater—activities that gave him an appreciation of modern urban life.

The real legacy of *The Wonderful Wizard of Oz* has been its ability to provoke differing interpretations. Baum's fairy tale, the first truly American work of this sort, has bequeathed many fascinating images about the diversity and contradictions of American culture.

continued discrimination against both blacks and women still dominated politics. People in power could not tolerate radical views like socialism or Populism, but many of those ideas continued to find supporters in the new century.

The 1896 election realigned national politics. The Republican Party, founded in the 1850s amid a crusade against slavery, became the majority party by emphasizing government aid to business, drawing the urban middle class, and playing down moralism. The Democratic Party miscalculated on the silver issue but held its traditional support in the South and in urban political machines. At the national level, however, loyalties lacked their former potency, as suspicion of party politics increased and voter participation declined. The Populists tried to energize a third-party movement, but their success was fleeting.

Still, by 1920 many Populist goals had been incorporated by the major parties, including regulation of railroads, banks, and utilities; shorter workdays; a variant of the subtreasury plan; a graduated income tax; and direct election of senators. These reforms succeeded because various groups supported them. Immigration, urbanization, and industrialization had transformed the United States into a pluralistic society in which compromise had become a political fact of life. As the Gilded Age ended, business was still in the ascendancy, and large segments of the population remained excluded from political and economic opportunity. But the winds of dissent and reform had begun to blow more strongly.

Chapter Review

THE NATURE OF PARTY POLITICS

How did regional and factional disputes complicate party politics in the Gilded Age?

Most Democrats sought to restrict government power and included immigrants and Catholics, while most Republicans were native-born Protestants who believed government should play a bigger role in reforming society. Both parties were ultimately divided by factional rifts that kept them from simultaneously controlling the presidency and Congress or holding power in either for very long. Republican factions included Stalwarts and Half Breeds, who each sought to wield influence and jobs toward supporters; and Mugwumps who thought only the most upstanding men should be allowed in government. Democrats split into white-supremacist southerners, immigrant and working-class advocates of urban political machines, businessmen who sought lower tariffs and the gold standard, and those who embraced free silver. Such divisions within parties made unity difficult.

ISSUES OF LEGISLATION

What was at issue in the debate over the gold standard versus free silver?

The debate over gold versus free silver was in many ways a struggle between debtors and creditors in the late nineteenth century. Farmers and small businessmen (debtors) pushed for silver coinage, which they believed would put more money in circulation and lower interest rates, thereby making it easier for them to repay mortgages and other debts. Large businesses (creditors) preferred money backed by gold, because they considered it more stable, and therefore likely to maintain foreign investors' confidence in the U.S. economy. In effect, the debate became a class struggle, as well as a sectional one: those in the West and South where mining and agriculture dominated, favored silver; those in the industrial Northeast, gold.

TENTATIVE PRESIDENTS

What actions did American presidents between 1877 and 1900 take to restore authority to their office?

After Andrew Johnson's impeachment and the scandals plaguing both the Grant administration and the 1876 election, the presidency was tarnished. Presidents Rutherford Hayes (1877–1881), James Garfield (1881), Chester Arthur (1881–1885), Grover Cleveland (1885–1889 and 1893–1897), Benjamin Harrison (1889–1893), and William McKinley (1897–1901) sought to bring integrity back to federal government through various legislative initiatives. They all supported Civil Service (and its expansion) as a means to end the corruption of the spoils system. With varying success, they addressed currency, tariffs, railroad regulation, and labor unrest.

DISCRIMINATION, DISFRANCHISEMENT, AND RESPONSES

How did southerners find legal means to discriminate against newly enfranchised African Americans in the decades following the Civil War?

First, southern leaders instituted measures such as poll taxes, which most blacks could not afford, and literacy tests to keep them from voting. These measures were upheld in the Supreme Court, which noted that the Fifteenth Amendment could only prohibit states from denying the vote based on "race, color, or previous condition of servitude," but could not control the local election process. Similarly, Jim Crow, or segregation laws, confined African Americans to separate areas in public places such as streetcars, hospitals, and parks, thereby deliberately reminding them of their inferior status. These laws were upheld by the Supreme Court in *Plessey v. Ferguson*, which allowed that states could legally segregate on a "separate-but-equal" basis.

AGRARIAN UNREST AND POPULISM

How did farmers' discontent crystallize in the Grange movement and Farmers' Alliances?

As farm prices dropped, farmers found it increasingly difficult to earn a living from their land. Those conditions were made worse by the fact that as smallholders, most could not compete with large firms, which could negotiate lower costs for transportation and supplies by virtue of their size. In response, farmers founded local organizations called Granges in the 1860s and 1870s partly as social clubs and partly to enable them to join forces in cooperatives where they could get the same competitive advantage as larger firms. Granges declined in the late 1870s, replaced a decade later by Farmers' Alliances, which rallied against crop liens, merchants, railroads, and money power. Along with cooperatives, Alliances sought a government aid system called a subtreasury which they hoped would provide low-interest loans to farmers seeking to buy land and would assist farmers in warehousing crops until market prices increased.

THE DEPRESSION AND PROTESTS OF THE 1890S

Why did socialism fail to take hold amid the labor activism of the late nineteenth century?

The depression and thousands of strikes beginning with the 1877 railroad strike revealed general worker dissatisfaction that certainly created the conditions ripe for socialism to flourish, particularly once its charismatic leader Eugene V. Debs came to the fore in the 1890s. But American socialists could not agree on how best to implement Marxist strategies for worker control of the means of production and the end of capitalism's inequities. Socialism was also thwarted by that distinctly American celebration of social mobility and individual achievement. While workers found some aspects of socialism attractive, their ultimate aim was individual advancement, which they were unwilling to sacrifice for the greater good of all workers.

THE SILVER CRUSADE AND THE ELECTION OF 1896

How did Bryan's focus on free silver undermine his presidential campaign and the Populist Party?

Populists embraced the issue of silver because they believed it would end special privileges for the rich by lifting mainstream Americans from debt, increasing the money in circulation and lowering interest rates. Populists fused these ideas to the Democratic Party by joining forces with them behind William Jennings Bryan for president in 1896. Bryan was singularly focused on silver, but this cost him votes from urban workers, who feared silver coinage would cut their wages. Labor leaders equated farmers with businessmen and as such, could not join forces with Populists on this issue. Bryan received only 222,600 votes nationwide, and while Populists continued to influence elections, the party itself collapsed.

SUGGESTIONS FOR FURTHER READING

Edward L. Ayers, *The Promise of the New South: Life After Reconstruction* (1992)

Nancy Cohen, *The Reconstruction of American Liberalism, 1865–1914* (2002)

Glenda Elizabeth Gilmore, *Gender and Jim Crow: Women and the Politics of White Supremacy in North Carolina, 1896–1920* (1996)

Steven Hahn, *A Nation Under Our Feet: Black Political Struggles in the Rural South, from Slavery to the Great Migration* (2003)

Michael Kazin, *The Populist Persuasion: An American History* (1995)

Jean V. Matthews, *The Rise of the New Woman: The Women's Movement in America, 1875–1930* (2003)

Nick Salvatore, *Eugene V. Debs: Citizen and Socialist* (1992)

The Progressive Era | 1895–1920

What Ben Lindsey saw made him furious. As a young Colorado lawyer in the 1890s, a judge asked him to defend two boys, about twelve years old, arrested on burglary charges. The boys had been imprisoned for sixty days without a trial and did not understand what *burglary* meant or how the justice system worked. Visiting them in jail, Lindsey found the youngsters playing poker with two older cellmates—a safe cracker and a horse thief. Outraged that children were housed with hardened criminals, Lindsey later wrote, "Here were two boys, neither of them serious enemies of society, who were about to be convicted of burglary and have felony records. . . . I had made up my mind to smash the system that meant so much injustice to youth."

In 1901 Lindsey ran for county judge and began fighting for juvenile protection from criminal prosecution, exploitative labor practices, and the burdens of poverty. He and his wife, Henrietta, spread the ideas of a separate juvenile court system and of aiding families with children at risk of becoming criminals. They wrote reform laws, adopted by many states and foreign countries. The Lindseys' efforts to abolish injustice showed compassion and middle-class bias as part of a broader movement seeking solutions to modern America's social and economic problems.

During the 1890s, economic depression, labor violence, political upheaval, and foreign entanglements shook the nation. Great numbers of Americans continued to suffer from poverty and disease. Business and politics seemed out of control. Tensions created by urbanization and industrialization fragmented society into conflicting interest groups.

By 1900, the previous decade's political tumult had calmed, and economic depression seemed to be over. The nation emerged victorious from a war against Spain (see Chapter 22), and a new

This icon will direct you to interactive activities and study materials on A People And A Nation, Brief Edition website: **www.cengage.com/history/norton/ peoplenationbrief8e**

Chronology

1895	Booker T. Washington gives Atlanta Compromise speech.
	National Association of Colored Women is founded.
1898	*Holden v. Hardy* upholds limits on miners' working hours.
1900	McKinley is reelected.
1901	McKinley is assassinated; T. Roosevelt assumes the presidency.
1904	T. Roosevelt is elected president.
	Northern Securities case dissolves railroad trust.
1905	*Lochner v. New York* removes limits on bakers' working hours.
	NCAA is founded.
1906	Hepburn Act tightens ICC control over railroads.
	Meat Inspection Act is passed.
	Pure Food and Drug Act is passed.
1908	Taft is elected president.
	Muller v. Oregon upholds limits on women's working hours.
1909	NAACP is founded.
1910	Mann-Elkins Act reinforces ICC powers.
	White Slave Traffic Act (Mann Act) prohibits transportation of women for "immoral purposes."
	Taft fires Pinchot.
1911	Society of American Indians is founded.
1912	Wilson is elected president.
1913	Sixteenth Amendment, legalizing income tax, is ratified.
	Seventeenth Amendment, providing for direct election of senators, is ratified.
	Underwood Tariff institutes income tax.
	Federal Reserve Act establishes central banking system.
1914	Federal Trade Commission is created to investigate unfair trade practices.
	Clayton Anti-Trust Act outlaws monopolistic business practices.
1916	Wilson is reelected.
	Adamson Act mandates eight-hour workday for railroad workers.
1919	Eighteenth Amendment, establishing prohibition of alcoholic beverages, is ratified.
1920	Nineteenth Amendment, giving women the vote in federal elections, is ratified.

era of dynamic political leaders, such as Theodore Roosevelt and Woodrow Wilson, was dawning. A sense of renewal both intensified anxiety over continuing problems and raised hopes that democracy could be reconciled with capitalism.

Between 1895 and 1920, a complex reform movement emerged, aiming to renovate or restore American society, values, and institutions. By the 1910s, reformers from Republican and Democratic Parties were calling themselves Progressives; in 1912 Progressives formed their own party. Historians have used the term *Progressivism* to refer to the era's spirit, while disagreeing over its meaning and over which groups and individuals actually were Progressive.

The reform impulse had many sources. Industrial capitalism created awesome technology, unprecedented productivity, and copious consumer goods. But it also brought overproduction, domineering monopolies, labor strife, and the destruction of natural resources. Burgeoning cities facilitated the distribution of goods and services but also bred poverty, disease, and crime. Rising immigration and a new professional class reconfigured the social order. And the depression of the 1890s forced leading citizens to realize what working people already knew: America's central promise, equality of opportunity, was elusive.

Reformers organized around three goals. First, they sought to end abuses of power. Progressives broadened the offensive to make trustbusting, consumers' rights, and good government compelling issues.

Second, Progressives like Ben Lindsey wished to supplant corrupt power with humane institutions, such as schools, courts, and medical clinics. They abandoned conceptions that hard work and good character guaranteed success and that the poor were to blame for their plight. Instead, Progressives acknowledged that society had a responsibility to improve individual lives, and they believed that government must protect the common good and elevate public interest above self-interest. They challenged entrenched views on women's roles, race relations, education, legal and scientific thought, and morality.

Third, Progressives wanted to establish bureaus of experts who would end wasteful competition and promote social and economic order. Just as corporations applied scientific management to achieve economic efficiency, Progressives advocated expertise and planning to achieve social and political efficiency.

Progressives had faith in humankind's ability to create a better world. Rising incomes, new educational opportunities, and increased availability of goods and services inspired confidence that social improvement would follow. Judge Ben Lindsey expressed the Progressive creed when he wrote, "In the end the people are bound to do the right thing, no matter how much they fail at times."

- **What were the major characteristics of Progressivism?**
- **In what ways did Progressive reform succeed, and in what ways did it fail?**
- **How did women and racial minorities challenge previous ways of thinking about American society?**

THE VARIED PROGRESSIVE IMPULSE

After the heated election of 1896, party loyalties eroded and voter turnout declined. In northern states, voter participation in presidential elections dropped from the 1880s' levels of 80 percent to less than 60 percent. In southern states, where poll taxes and literacy tests excluded most African Americans and many poor whites from voting, it fell below 30 percent. At the same time, new interest groups, which championed their own special causes, gained influence.

National Associations and Foreign Influences Many formerly local organizations spread nationwide after 1890. These included professional associations, such as the American Bar Association; women's organizations, such as the National American Woman Suffrage Association; issue-oriented groups, such as the National Consumers League; civic-minded clubs, such as the National Municipal League; and minority-group associations, such as the National Negro Business League and the Society of American Indians. Because they were usually independent from political parties, these groups made politics more fragmented and issue focused than in earlier eras.

Reformers adapted foreign models. Some were introduced by Americans who were exposed to reforms while studying in England, France, and Germany; others, by foreigners visiting the United States. Americans copied from England the settlement house, in which reformers live among and aid the urban poor, and workers' compensation for victims of industrial accidents. Other European reforms, such as old-age insurance, subsidized workers' housing, city planning, and rural reconstruction, were modified in America. Although Populist rural-based goals of moral regeneration, political democracy, and antimonopolism continued, the Progressive quest for social justice, labor laws, educational and legal reform, and government streamlining had a largely urban bent.

The New Middle Class and Muckrakers

Progressive goals—ending abuse of power, protecting the welfare of all classes, reforming social institutions, and promoting bureaucratic and scientific efficiency—existed across society. But a new middle class—men and women in law, medicine, engineering, social service, religion, teaching, and business—formed the reform vanguard. Offended by inefficiency and immorality in business, government, and human relations, they determined to apply the rational techniques of their professions to social problems. They also believed that they could create a unified society by Americanizing immigrants and Indians through education and programs stressing middle-class customs.

Progressive views were voiced by journalists whom Theodore Roosevelt dubbed muckrakers (after a character in the Puritan allegory *Pilgrim's Progress,* who, rather than looking heavenward at beauty, looked downward and raked the muck). Muckrakers fed public tastes for scandal by exposing social, economic, and political wrongs. Investigative articles in popular magazines attacked adulterated foods, fraudulent insurance, prostitution, and political corruption. Lincoln Steffens hoped his exposés of bosses' misrule in *McClure's* (later published as *The Shame of the Cities* in 1904) would inspire mass outrage and reform. Other well-known muckraking works included Upton Sinclair's *The Jungle* (1906), exposing outrages of the meatpacking industry; and Ida M. Tarbell's disparaging history of Standard Oil (first published in *McClure's,* 1902–1904).

Progressives advocated nonpartisan elections to prevent fraud and bribery bred by party loyalties, and promoted direct primaries instead of party caucuses. To make officeholders more responsible, they urged adoption of the initiative, which permitted voters to propose laws; the referendum, which enabled voters to accept or reject a law; and the recall, which allowed voters to remove offending officials from office.

Upper-Class Reformers

The Progressive spirit also stirred some businessmen and wealthy women. Executives like Alexander Cassatt of the Pennsylvania Railroad supported some government regulation and political reforms to protect their interests from more radical reformers. Others, like E. A. Filene, founder of a Boston department store, were humanitarians who worked for social justice. Business-dominated organizations like the Municipal Voters League and the U.S. Chamber of Commerce thought that running schools, hospitals, and local government like businesses would stabilize society. Elite women led organizations like the Young Women's Christian Association (YWCA), which aided unmarried working women, and they joined middle- and working-class women in the Woman's Christian Temperance Union (WCTU), the largest women's organization of its time.

Working-Class Reformers

But also vital elements of what became modern American liberalism derived from working-class urban experiences. By 1900 many urban workers were pressing for bread-and-butter reforms, such as safe factories, shorter workdays, workers' compensation, and better housing. Politicians who embraced such causes trained in machine politics, and their constituents supported political bosses. Yet bossism was not necessarily at odds with humanitarianism. Big Tim Sullivan, an influential boss in New York City's Tammany Hall political machine, said he supported shorter workdays for women because "I had seen me sister go out to work when she was only fourteen and I know we ought to help these gals by giving 'em a law which will prevent 'em from being broken down while they're still young." Working-class advocates opposed prohibition, Sunday closing laws, civil service, and nonpartisan elections, but joined with other reformers to pass laws aiding labor and promoting social welfare.

The Social Gospel

Much of Progressive reform rested on religious values. A movement known as the Social Gospel, led by the Protestant ministers Walter Rauschenbusch, Washington Gladden, and Charles Sheldon countered competitive capitalism by interjecting Christian churches into worldly matters, such as arbitrating industrial harmony and improving the environment of the poor. Believing that helping others provided the way to individual salvation, Social Gospelers governed their lives by asking, "What would Jesus do?"

Those who believed in service to others tried to Americanize immigrants and Indians by expanding educational, economic, and cultural opportunities. But imposing their values on people of different cultures undermined their efforts to help. Catholic and Jewish immigrants sometimes rejected the Americanization efforts of Social Gospelers, settlement-house workers, and other reformers. Working-class families, too, resented reformers' interference in child rearing.

Socialists

Disillusioned immigrant intellectuals, industrial workers, Populists, miners, and women's rights activists desired a different society altogether and turned to socialism. They wanted the United States to follow the example of Germany, England, and France, where the government sponsored low-cost housing, workers' compensation, old-age pensions, public ownership of municipal services, and labor reform. By 1912, the Socialist Party of America, a merger of several groups and founded in 1901, claimed 150,000 members, and 700,000 subscribers to its newspaper. But American socialism had difficulty sustaining widespread acceptance.

Politically, many socialists united behind Eugene V. Debs, the American Railway Union organizer who drew nearly 100,000 votes as the Socialist presidential candidate in 1900. A spellbinding orator who appealed to urban immigrants and western farmers alike, Debs won 400,000 votes in 1904 and 900,000 in 1912, at the pinnacle of his and his party's career. Some Progressives joined the Socialist Party, but most had too much at stake in capitalism to want it overthrown. Municipal ownership of public utilities represented their limit of drastic change.

Workers' Compensation

At the dawn of the twentieth century, accident rates on American railroads and in mines and factories far exceeded those in Great Britain and Germany, the other two major industrial nations, and muckraking journalists wrote about them extensively. In 1911 one study concluded that the accident rate in the nation's industries "equals the average yearly casualties of the American Civil War, plus all of those of the Philippine War, plus all of those of the Russo-Japanese War." American legal theory protected employers from liability and prevented workers from recovering medical costs and lost income from job-related injuries. Progressives argued that employers, guided by government, should shoulder the obligation.

The principle that employers should be legally responsible for compensating victims of industrial accidents emerged most strongly in Germany and Britain in the late nineteenth century. Germany required employers and wage earners to contribute to quasi-public funds to cover those injured at work, while England compelled employers to pay them through insurance company contributions or their own funds. Variations later appeared in Denmark, France, and Italy. But not until 1907 did President Theodore Roosevelt advocate for employers' liability legislation. The next year, two different Progressive organizations, the social reform–minded Russell Sage Foundation and the business-oriented National Civic Foundation, took up the cause.

Most American Progressives favored the German system because it operated more under government administration than the British method. But states, not the federal government, assumed responsibility for the form of a program. By 1911, Ohio and Washington had state-administered insurance funds into which employers made contributions, and between 1911 and 1913, twenty other states enacted some form of workers' compensation laws. By 1919, the majority of workers' compensation funds were handled by private insurance firms. American legislators, propelled by Progressive arguments, had borrowed an insurance system from abroad, but applied their imprint of private enterprise.

A SUCCESSFUL WORKMAN

This man who lost an arm in an industrial accident in Cleveland, invented a good substitute arm, wears it at work, and uses it in earning his living. He has made good by his own unaided efforts. The average man, however, needs a lift in the way of training.

In the early twentieth century, industrial accidents continued to kill and maim thousands of workers. Without insurance to support them when they were disabled, some employees created aids to enable them to continue on the job. This man, who lost an arm in a factory mishap, invented his own artificial limb. Other victims of misfortune, however, were not so handy and could receive compensation only if their state or their employer adopted the European model and instituted a workers' insurance program. (Library of Congress)

Southern and Western Progressivism

Progressive reform in the South focused on railroad and utility regulation, factory safety, pure food and drug legislation, and moral reform. The South pioneered some political reforms: the direct primary originated in North Carolina; the city-commission plan arose in Galveston, Texas; and the city-manager plan began in Staunton, Virginia. Like their northern counterparts, Progressive governors introduced business regulation, educational expansion, and other reforms.

In the West, several politicians championed humanitarianism and regulation, putting the region at the forefront of efforts to expand federal and state government functions. Nevada's Progressive senator Francis Newlands advocated federal control of water resources. California governor Hiram Johnson fought for regulation of children's and women's labor, workers' compensation, a pure food and drug act, and education reform.

Southern and western women, white and black, made notable contributions to Progressive causes. In western states, women could vote on state and local matters, but the more effective women's reform occurred outside politics in racially distinctive ways. White women crusaded against child labor, founded social service organizations, and challenged unfair wages, African American women, using a guise as homemakers and religious leaders—which whites found more acceptable than political activism—advocated for street cleaning, better education, and health reforms.

Opponents of Progressivism

It would be incorrect to assume that all of America was captivated by the Progressive spirit between 1895 and 1920. Defenders of free enterprise opposed regulatory measures, believing government programs undermined the initiative and competition basic to a free-market system. "Old-guard" Republicans, such as Senator Nelson W. Aldrich of Rhode Island and House Speaker Joseph Cannon of Illinois, championed this ideology.

Moreover, prominent Progressives were not always progressive. Governor Hiram Johnson promoted discrimination against Japanese Americans, and most southern governors rested their power on appeals to white supremacy. Settlement houses in northern cities kept blacks and whites apart in separate programs and buildings.

Progressive reformers generally occupied the center of the ideological spectrum, believing on the one hand that laissez faire was obsolete and on the other that a radical departure from free enterprise was dangerous. Like Thomas Jefferson, they expressed faith in the will of the people; like Alexander Hamilton, they desired a strong central government to act in the interest of conscience.

GOVERNMENT AND LEGISLATIVE REFORM

Mistrust of tyranny traditionally prompted Americans to believe that democratic government should be small, interfere in private affairs only in unique circumstances, and withdraw quickly. In the late 1800s this viewpoint weakened when economic problems led corporations to pursue government aid and protection. Discontented farmers sought government regulation of railroads and other monopolistic businesses. City dwellers, accustomed to favors from political machines, expected government to act on their behalf. Before 1900, state governments had been concerned largely with railroads and economic growth; the federal government had focused primarily on tariffs and the currency.

Restructuring Government

Middle-class Progressive reformers rejected the laissez-faire principle of government, reasoning that in a complex age, public authority needed to counteract inefficiency and exploitation. But to tap this power, activists would have to reclaim government from politicians whose greed they believed soiled the democratic system.

Prior to the Progressive era, reformers attacked corruption in cities by trying to regulate government through such structural reforms as civil service, nonpartisan elections, and close scrutiny of public expenditures. After 1900, campaigns to make cities more efficient resulted in city-manager and commission forms of government, in which urban officials were chosen for professional expertise rather than for political connections.

At the state level, Progressives supported several skillful governors. In the West, California governor Hiram Johnson attacked business and political corruption and inspired state laws regulating utilities and child labor and initiating workers' compensation for state employees. In the South, Georgia's Hoke Smith achieved railroad regulation, juvenile courts, and better-funded public education, though he also supported voting restrictions that disfranchised blacks.

Wisconsin's Robert M. La Follette was one of the most dynamic Progressive governors. A small-town lawyer, La Follette rose through the state Republican Party to become governor in 1900. There, he initiated direct primaries, more equitable taxes, and railroad regulation. After three terms as governor, La Follette became a U.S. senator. Battling Bob displayed a rare ability to approach reform scientifically, proclaiming that his goal was "not to 'smash' corporations, but to drive them out of politics."

Crusades against corrupt politics made the system more democratic. Political reformers achieved a major goal in 1913 with the adoption of the Seventeenth Amendment to the Constitution, which provided for the direct election of U.S. senators, replacing election by state legislatures. But party bosses were still able to control elections, and special-interest groups spent large sums to influence voting.

Labor Reform

At the instigation of middle-class–working-class coalitions, many states enacted factory inspection laws, and by 1916 nearly two-thirds of the states required compensation for victims of industrial accidents. Some legislatures granted aid to mothers with dependent children. Under pressure from the National Child Labor Committee, nearly every state set a minimum age for employment (varying from twelve to sixteen) and limited the hours that children could work. Labor laws were imperfect, however. They seldom provided for the close inspection of factories that enforcement required. And families needing extra income falsified their children's ages to employers.

Several groups also united to achieve restricted working hours for women and aided retirees. After the Supreme Court, in *Muller v. Oregon*, upheld Oregon's ten-hour limit in 1908, more states passed laws protecting female workers. In 1914 the American Association for Old Age Security secured old-age pensions in Arizona. Judges struck down the law, but the demand for pensions continued and in the 1920s many states enacted such laws.

Prohibition

Reformers did not always agree about whether laws should regulate drinking habits and sexual conduct. The Anti-Saloon League (formed in 1893) allied with the Woman's Christian Temperance Union (founded in 1874) to publicize alcoholism's role in health problems like liver disease. The league successfully shifted attention from the immorality of drunkenness to the alleged link between drinking and accidents, poverty, and poor productivity.

The war on saloons prompted many states and localities to restrict liquor consumption. By 1900 almost one-fourth of the nation's population lived in dry communities, prohibiting liquor sales. But alcohol consumption increased after 1900, convincing prohibitionists that a nationwide ban was needed. In 1918 Congress passed the Eighteenth Amendment (ratified in 1919 and implemented in 1920), outlawing the manufacture, sale, and transportation of intoxicating liquors. Not all prohibitionists were Progressive reformers, and vice versa. Nevertheless, the Eighteenth Amendment embodied the Progressive goal to protect family and workplace through reform legislation.

Controlling Prostitution

Moral outrage erupted when muckraking journalists charged that international gangs were kidnapping young women and forcing them into prostitution, a practice called white slavery. Accusations were exaggerated, but they alarmed moralists who falsely perceived a link between immigration and prostitution. Reformers prodded governments to investigate and pass corrective legislation. The Chicago Vice Commission undertook a "scientific" survey of dance halls and illicit sex and published its findings as *The Social Evil in Chicago* in 1911. The report concluded that poverty, gullibility, and desperation drove women into prostitution.

Such investigations found rising numbers of prostitutes but failed to prove that criminal organizations lured women into the trade. Reformers nonetheless believed they could attack prostitution by punishing those who promoted and practiced it. In 1910 Congress passed the White Slave Traffic Act (Mann Act), prohibiting interstate and international transportation of a woman for immoral purposes. By 1915 nearly every state outlawed brothels and solicitation of sex.

Like prohibition, the Mann Act reflected growing sentiment that government could improve behavior by restricting it. Middle-class reformers believed that the source of evil was not human nature but the social environment. The working classes, however, resented such unwarranted attempts to control them. Thus, when Chicagoans voted on a referendum to make their city dry before the Eighteenth Amendment was passed, three-fourths of the city's immigrant voters opposed it, and the measure was defeated.

NEW IDEAS IN SOCIAL INSTITUTIONS

Preoccupation with efficiency and scientific management infiltrated education, law, religion, and the social sciences. Darwin's theory of evolution challenged belief in a God-created world; immigration created complex social diversity; and technology made old production habits obsolete. Professionals grappled with how to embrace progress yet preserve the best from the past.

John Dewey and Progressive Education

As late as 1870, when families needed children to do farm work, Americans attended school only a few months a year for four years on average. By 1900, however, the urban-industrial economy and its expanding middle class advanced the goal of sheltering youngsters from society's dangers by protecting their physical and emotional growth. That meant ensuring that youngsters were exposed to age-appropriate educational materials and activities. ▷ *figures*

Thus schools shared with, and even replaced the home as the best environment for promoting children's development and producing adult citizens and workers. In the 1870s and 1880s, laws required children to attend school to age fourteen. The number of public high schools grew from five hundred in 1870 to ten thousand in 1910. By 1900 educational reformers, such as the psychologist G. Stanley Hall and the philosopher John Dewey, asserted that schools needed to prepare children for a modern world by making personal development the focus of the curriculum.

Progressive education, based on Dewey's *The School and Society* (1899) and *Democracy and Education* (1916), stressed that learning should involve real-life problems and that children should be taught to use ingenuity to control their environments. Dewey and his wife, Alice, tested their theories that children should learn by experience not rote memorization in their Laboratory School at the University of Chicago. △ *they don ot really do either these days.* ▽

Growth of Colleges and Universities

A more practical curriculum similarly drove higher education reform. Previously, American colleges resembled their European counterparts in training a select few for careers in law, medicine, and religion. But in the late 1800s, institutions of higher learning multiplied via state and federal grants. Between 1870 and 1910, American colleges and universities grew from 563 to nearly 1,000. Curricula expanded to make learning more appealing and to keep pace with technological and social changes. Harvard University, under President Charles W. Eliot, pioneered new teaching methods and substituted electives for required courses. Many schools considered athletics vital to a student's growth, and men's intercollegiate sports became a permanent feature.

Southern states created segregated land-grant colleges for blacks and whites. Although African Americans continued to suffer from inferior educational opportunities, they found intellectual stimulation in all-black colleges and used their education to help uplift their race.

Between 1890 and 1910, the number of women in colleges swelled from 56,000 to 140,000. Roughly 106,000 attended coeducational institutions (mostly state universities); the rest enrolled in women's colleges. By 1920, 283,000 women attended college, accounting for 47 percent of total enrollment. But women were encouraged (and usually sought) to take home economics and education courses, and most medical schools refused to admit women. Separate women's medical schools, such as the Women's Medical College of Philadelphia, trained numerous female physicians, but most of these schools were absorbed or put out of business by larger, male-dominated institutions.

By 1920, 78 percent of children ages five to seventeen were enrolled in public schools; another 8 percent attended private and parochial schools. There were 600,000 college and graduate students in 1920, compared with only 52,000 in 1870. Yet critical analysis seldom tested the faith that schools could promote equality as well as personal growth and responsible citizenship.

Progressive Legal Thought

The Harvard law professor Roscoe Pound and Oliver Wendell Holmes Jr., associate justice of the Supreme Court between 1902 and 1932, led the attack on the traditional view of law as universal and unchanging. Their argument that law should reflect society's needs challenged the practice of invoking inflexible legal precedents. Louis D. Brandeis, a lawyer who later joined Holmes on the Supreme Court, insisted that judges' opinions be based on scientifically gathered information about social realities. Brandeis collected extensive data on the harmful effects of long working hours to convince the Supreme Court, in *Muller v. Oregon* (1908), to uphold Oregon's ten-hour limit to women's workday.

Judges raised on laissez-faire economics and a strict interpretation of the Constitution overturned laws that Progressives thought necessary for reform. Thus, in 1905 the Supreme Court, in *Lochner v. New York,* revoked a New York law limiting bakers' working hours. The Court's majority argued that the Fourteenth Amendment protected an individual's right to make contracts without government interference.

Several decisions, beginning with *Holden v. Hardy* (1898), in which the Supreme Court sustained a Utah law regulating miners' working hours, confirmed the use of state police power to protect health, safety, and morals. Judges also affirmed federal police power and Congress's authority over interstate commerce by upholding federal legislation, such as the Pure Food and Drug Act, the Meat Inspection Act, and the Mann Act.

But even if one agreed that laws should address society's needs, whose needs should prevail in a mixed nation? In many localities a native-born Protestant majority imposed Bible reading in public schools (offending Catholics and Jews), required businesses to close on Sundays, limited women's rights, restricted religious practices of Mormons and others, prohibited interracial marriage, and enforced racial segregation. Justice Holmes asserted that laws should be made for "people of fundamentally differing views," but how to accomplish that continues to spark debate today.

Social Science

Social science—the study of society and its institutions—underwent changes. Economics scholars used statistics to argue that laws governing economic relationships were not timeless but should reflect prevailing social conditions. A new breed of sociologists led by Lester Ward, Albion Small, and Edward A. Ross agreed, adding that citizens should work to cure social ills.

Meanwhile, the historians Frederick Jackson Turner, Charles A. Beard, and Vernon L. Parrington examined the past to explain present American society. Beard, like other Progressives, believed that the Constitution was a flexible document. His *Economic Interpretation of the Constitution* (1913) argued that a group of merchants and business-oriented lawyers created the Constitution to defend private property. If the Constitution served special interests in one age, he believed, it could be changed to serve broader interests in another.

In public health, organizations such as the National Consumers League (NCL), founded in 1899 by Florence Kelley, joined physicians and social scientists to secure far-reaching Progressive reforms. NCL activities included the protection of female and child laborers and the elimination of potential health hazards. Local branches united with women's clubs to advance consumer protection measures, such as the licensing of food vendors and the inspection of dairies. They urged city governments to fund neighborhood clinics providing medical care to the poor.

Eugenics

The Social Gospel was a response to Social Darwinism, the application of biological natural selection and survival of the fittest to human interactions. But another movement, eugenics, sought to apply Darwinian principles more intrusively. The brainchild of Francis Galton, an English statistician and cousin of Charles Darwin, eugenics rested on the belief that human character and habits could be inherited, specifically bad traits, such as criminality, insanity, and feeblemindedness. Eugenicists believed society had an obligation to prevent the reproduction of the mentally defective and the criminally inclined, by prohibiting such people from marrying and, in extreme cases, by sterilizing them. Inevitably such ideas targeted immigrants and people of color. Supported by such American notables as Alexander Graham Bell, Margaret Sanger, and W. E. B. Du Bois, eugenics was discredited, especially after it became a linchpin of Nazi racial policies.

Some reformers endorsed eugenics; others embraced immigration restriction to control the composition of American society. Madison Grant's *The Passing of the Great Race* (1916) bolstered theories that immigrants from southern and eastern Europe threatened to weaken American society because they were inferior mentally and morally to earlier Nordic immigrants. Thus, many people, including some Progressives, sought new laws to curtail the influx of Poles, Italians, Jews, and other eastern and southern Europeans, and Asians. In the 1920s, restrictive legislation closed the door to "new" immigrants.

CHALLENGES TO RACIAL AND SEXUAL DISCRIMINATION

The white male reformers of the Progressive era dealt primarily with politics and institutions and ignored issues affecting former slaves, nonwhite immigrants, Native Americans, and women. Yet these groups caught the Progressive spirit and made strides toward advancement themselves. Their efforts, however, posed a dilemma. Should women and nonwhites aim to be on a par with white men? Or was there something unique about racial and sexual cultures worth preserving at the risk of broader gains?

Continued Discrimination for African Americans

In 1900 nine-tenths of African Americans lived in the South, where repressive Jim Crow laws multiplied in the 1880s and 1890s. In 1910 only 8,000 out of 970,000 high-school-age blacks in the South were enrolled in high schools. And blacks met with violence from lynching and acts of intimidation. Consequently, many African Americans moved northward in the 1880s, accelerating their migration after 1900. Although conditions in places like Chicago and Detroit represented improvement, job discrimination, inferior schools, and segregated housing prevailed.

African American leaders differed over how—and whether—to assimilate. After emancipation, ex-slave Frederick Douglass urged "ultimate assimilation through self-assertion." Others supported emigration to Africa or the establishment of all-black communities in the Oklahoma Territory and Kansas. Still others advocated militancy.

Booker T. Washington and Self-Help

Most blacks could neither escape nor conquer white society. Self-help, a strategy articulated by educator Booker T. Washington, offered one popular alternative. Born into slavery in Virginia in 1856, Washington obtained an education and in 1881 founded the Tuskegee Institute, an all-black vocational school, in Alabama. There he developed a philosophy that blacks' best hopes lay in at least temporarily accommodating to whites. Rather than fighting for rights, Washington counseled African Americans to work hard, acquire property, and prove they were worthy of respect. "Dignify and glorify common labor," he urged in a speech at the 1895 Atlanta Exposition that

Booker T. Washington's Tuskegee Institute helped train young African Americans in useful crafts, such as shoemaking and shoe repair, as illustrated here. At the same time, however, Washington's intentions and the Tuskegee curriculum reinforced what many whites wanted to believe: that blacks were unfit for anything except manual labor.

(Tuskegee University Library)

became known as the Atlanta Compromise. Washington observed that "in all things that are purely social we can be as separate as the fingers, yet one as the hand in all matters essential to mutual progress."

Because he said what they wanted to hear, white businesspeople, reformers, and politicians regarded Washington as representing all African Americans. Washington never argued that blacks were inferior to whites; rather, he asserted that they could enhance their dignity through self-improvement.

Some blacks, however, concluded that Washington endorsed second-class citizenship. In 1905 a group of anti-Bookerites convened near Niagara Falls and pledged militant pursuit of unrestricted voting, economic opportunity, integration, and equality before the law. Representing the Niagara movement was W. E. B. Du Bois, an outspoken critic of the Atlanta Compromise.

W. E. B. Du Bois and the Talented Tenth

A New Englander and the first black to receive a Ph.D. degree from Harvard, Du Bois was both a Progressive and a member of the black elite. While a faculty member at Atlanta University, Du Bois compiled sociological studies of black urban life and wrote in support of civil rights. He treated Washington politely but could not accept accommodation. Du Bois believed that an intellectual vanguard of cultured blacks, the Talented Tenth, could use their skills to pursue racial equality. In 1909 he joined with white liberals similarly discontented with Washington's accommodationism to form the National Association for the Advancement of Colored People (NAACP). The organization aimed to end racial discrimination, prevent lynching, and obtain voting rights through legal redress in the courts. By 1914 the NAACP had fifty branch offices and six thousand members.

African Americans struggled with questions about their place in white society. Du Bois voiced this dilemma, observing that "one ever feels his twoness—an American, a Negro, two souls, two thoughts, two unreconciled strivings, two warring ideals in one dark body." As Du Bois wrote in 1903, a black "would not bleach his Negro soul in a flood of white Americanism, for he knows that Negro blood has a message for the world. He simply wishes to make it possible for a man to be both a Negro and an American."

Society of American Indians

In 1911, however, middle-class Indians broke with white-led organizations and formed their own association, the Society of American Indians (SAI), to work for better education, civil rights, and healthcare. It also sponsored American Indian Days to cultivate pride and offset the images of savage peoples promulgated in Wild West shows.

SAI's emphasis on racial pride, however, was squeezed between pressures for assimilation and tribal allegiance. Its small membership did not fully represent the diverse and unconnected Indian nations. Individual hard work was not enough to overcome white prejudice, and attempts to redress grievances through legal action faltered for lack of funds. Ultimately, SAI had little effect on poverty-stricken Indians who seldom knew that the organization existed. Torn by internal disputes, the association folded in the early 1920s.

The Woman Movement

Women's groups faced similar quandaries about the tactics they should use to achieve rights. Should they try to achieve equality within a male-dominated society or use female qualities to create new roles for themselves within society?

The answers that women found involved a subtle but important shift in their politics. Before 1910, women's rights activists called themselves the woman movement. Often middle-class, these women strived to move beyond the household into higher education and paid professions. They claimed that women's special, even superior, traits as guardians of family and morality would humanize the broader society. Settlement-house founder Jane Addams, for example, endorsed woman suffrage by asking, "If women have in any sense been responsible for the gentler side of life which softens and blurs some of its harsher conditions, may not they have a duty to perform in our American cities?"

Women's Clubs

Originating as literary and educational organizations, women's clubs began taking stands on public affairs in the late nineteenth century. They asserted traditional female responsibilities for home and family as the rationale for reforming society through an enterprise that historians have called social housekeeping. These female reformers worked for factory inspection, regulation of children's and women's labor, improved housing and education, and consumer protection.

African American women had their own club movement, including the Colored Women's Federation, which sought to establish a training school for "colored girls." Founded in 1895, the National Association of Colored Women was the nation's first African American social service organization; it concentrated on establishing nurseries, kindergartens, and retirement homes. Black women also developed reform organizations within Black Baptist and African Methodist Episcopal churches.

Feminism

Around 1910 some of those concerned with women's place in society began using the term *feminism* to represent their ideas. Whereas the woman movement spoke of moral purity and duty to society, feminists emphasized women's rights and self-development. Charlotte Perkins Gilman, a major figure in the movement, declared in her book *Women and Economics* (1898) that domesticity was obsolete, and attacked men's monopoly on economic opportunity. Arguing that paid employees should handle domestic chores, Gilman asserted that modern women must take jobs in industry and the professions to be independent.

Margaret Sanger's Crusade

Several feminists joined the birth-control movement led by Margaret Sanger. A former visiting nurse who believed in women's rights, Sanger helped reverse state and federal Comstock laws—named after a nineteenth-century New York moral reformer—which had banned the distribution of information about sex and contraception. Although Sanger later gained acceptance, she initially aroused opposition from those who saw birth control as a threat to family and morality. In 1921 she formed the American Birth Control League, enlisting physicians and social workers to convince judges to allow the distribution of birth-control information. Most states still prohibited the sale of contraceptives, but Sanger provoked public debate.

Woman Suffrage

During the Progressive era, a generation of feminists, represented by Harriot Stanton Blatch, daughter of the nineteenth-century suffragist Elizabeth Cady Stanton, carried on women's battle for the vote. Blatch's chief goal was the improvement of women's working conditions. Declaring that every woman worked, for wages or unpaid housework, Blatch believed that all women's efforts contributed to society's betterment. Thus women should exercise the vote to promote and protect their economic roles.

Nine states, all in the West, allowed women to vote in state and local elections by 1912 (see Map 21.1). Their tactics ranged from moderate but persistent letter-writing and publications of the National American Woman Suffrage Association, led by Carrie Chapman Catt, to spirited meetings and militant marches of the National Woman's Party, led by Alice Paul and Harriot Stanton Blatch. More decisive, however, was women's service during World War I as factory laborers, medical volunteers, and municipal workers. Legislators could no longer deny women's ability to shoulder public responsibilities and passed the national suffrage amendment (the Nineteenth) in 1920.

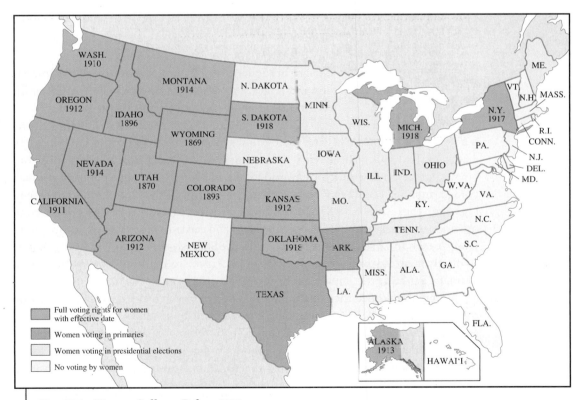

Map 21.1 Woman Suffrage Before 1920

Before Congress passed and the states ratified the Nineteenth Amendment, woman suffrage already existed, but mainly in the West. Several midwestern states allowed women to vote only in presidential elections, but legislatures in the South and Northeast generally refused such rights until forced to do so by constitutional amendment.

During the Progressive era, leaders like Blatch, Paul, and Catt helped clarify issues that concerned women, but winning the vote was a step, not a conclusion. Discrimination in employment, education, and the law continued to shadow women for decades to come, and feminists, women's clubs, and suffragists failed to unite to overcome men's political, social, and economic control. As the feminist Crystal Eastman observed after the suffrage crusade: "Men are saying perhaps, 'Thank God, this everlasting women's fight is over!' But women, if I know them, are saying, 'Now at last we can begin.' . . . Now they can say what they are really after, in common with all the rest of the struggling world, is freedom."

THEODORE ROOSEVELT AND THE REVIVAL OF THE PRESIDENCY

The Progressive era's reform spirit focused on the federal government as the foremost agent of change. Although the federal government had notable accomplishments during the Gilded Age, its role was mainly to support rather than control economic expansion. Then, in September 1901, the assassination of President William McKinley by the anarchist Leon Czolgosz vaulted Theodore Roosevelt, the young vice president, into the White House. As governor of New York, Roosevelt angered state Republican bosses by showing sympathy for regulatory legislation. He would become the nation's most forceful president since Lincoln, one who bestowed the office with much of its twentieth-century character.

Theodore Roosevelt

Driven throughout his life by an obsession to overcome the physical limitations of asthma and nearsightedness of his youth, Roosevelt exerted a zest for action and display of courage that contemporaries called manliness. In his teens he became an expert marksman and horseman, and later competed on Harvard's boxing and wrestling teams. In the 1880s he lived on a Dakota ranch, roping cattle and brawling with cowboys. Roosevelt had wealth, but he also inherited a sense of civic responsibility which guided him into public service. He served three terms in the New York State Assembly, sat on the federal Civil Service Commission served as New York City's police commissioner, was assistant secretary of the navy, and earned a reputation as a combative, crafty leader. In 1898 he thrust himself into the Spanish-American War by organizing a volunteer cavalry brigade, called the Rough Riders, to fight in Cuba. Although his dramatic act had little impact on the war's outcome, it made him a media hero.

When he assumed the presidency, Roosevelt carried his youthful exuberance into the White House. A Progressive, he concurred with allies that a small, uninvolved government would not suffice in the industrial era. Instead, economic progress necessitated a government powerful enough to guide national affairs broadly. Especially in economic matters, he wanted the government to decide when big business was good and when it was bad.

Regulation of Trusts

The federal regulation of business that characterized twentieth-century America began with Roosevelt's presidency. Although labeled a trustbuster, Roosevelt actually considered business consolidation an efficient means to material progress. He believed in distinguishing between good and bad trusts and preventing bad ones from manipulating markets. Thus he instructed the Justice Department to use antitrust laws to prosecute railroad, meatpacking, and oil trusts, which he believed unscrupulously exploited the public. Roosevelt's policy triumphed in 1904 when the Supreme Court ordered the breakup of the Northern Securities Company, the huge railroad combination created by J. P. Morgan and his business allies. Roosevelt did not attack other trusts, such as U.S. Steel, another of Morgan's creations.

When prosecution of Northern Securities began, Morgan reportedly asked Roosevelt, "If we have done anything wrong, send your man to my man and they can fix it up." The president refused but was more sympathetic to cooperation between business and government than it might seem. He urged the Bureau of Corporations (part of the newly created Department of Labor and Commerce) to assist companies in merging and expanding. Through investigation and consultation, the administration cajoled businesses to regulate themselves.

Roosevelt also supported regulatory legislation. After a year of wrangling, Roosevelt persuaded Congress to pass the Hepburn Act (1906) which gave the Interstate Commerce Commission (ICC) greater authority to set railroad freight rates and extend that authority over ferries, express companies, storage facilities, and oil pipelines. The Hepburn Act still allowed courts to overturn ICC decisions, but it now required shippers to prove they had not violated regulations, rather than making the government demonstrate violations.

Pure Food and Drug Laws

Roosevelt was willing to compromise to secure pure food and drug legislation. For decades reformers urged government regulation of processed meat and patent medicines. Public outrage flared in 1906 when Upton Sinclair published *The Jungle,* a fictionalized exposé of Chicago meatpacking plants. Sinclair, a socialist who sought to improve working conditions, shocked the public with his vivid descriptions.

> There would be meat stored in great piles in rooms; and the water from the leaky roofs would drip over it, and thousands of rats would race about on it. It was too dark in these storage places to see well, but a man could run his hand over these piles of meat and sweep off handfuls of dried dung of rats . . . the packers would put poisoned bread out for them; they would die, and then rats, bread, and meat would go into the hoppers together.

Roosevelt ordered an investigation, and finding Sinclair's descriptions accurate, he supported the Meat Inspection Act (1906). This law required government agents to monitor the quality of processed meat. But as part of a compromise with meatpackers and their congressional allies, the government had to finance inspections, and meatpackers could appeal adverse decisions. Nor were companies required to provide date-of-processing information on canned meats. Most large meatpackers benefited because the legislation helped them force out smaller competitors and restore foreign confidence in American meat products.

The Pure Food and Drug Act (1906) also addressed abuses in the patent medicine industry. Makers of tonics and pills had long been making undue claims about their products' effects and liberally using alcohol and narcotics as ingredients. The law required that labels list the ingredients—a goal consistent with Progressive confidence that with the truth, people would make wiser purchases.

GET FAT on LORINGS FAT-TEN-U AND CORPULA FOODS.

Makers of unregulated patent medicines advertised that their products had exorbitant abilities to cure almost any ailment and remedy any unwanted physical condition. Loring's Fat-Ten-U tablets and Loring's Corpula were two such products. The Pure Food and Drug Act of 1906 did not ban these items but tried to prevent manufacturers from making unsubstantiated claims. (© Bettmann/Corbis)

Roosevelt's approach to labor resembled his compromises with business. When the United Mine Workers struck against Pennsylvania coal-mine owners in 1902 over their demand for an eight-hour workday and higher pay, the president employed investigation and arbitration. Owners refused to recognize the union or arbitrate grievances. As winter approached and fuel shortages loomed, Roosevelt threatened to use federal troops to reopen the mines, thus forcing management to accept arbitration. The arbitration commission supported higher wages and reduced hours and required management to deal with miners' grievance committees, but it did not mandate recognition of the union. The settlement embodied Roosevelt's belief that the president or his representatives should determine which labor demands were legitimate and which were not.

Race Relations

Although he invited Booker T. Washington to the White House to discuss racial matters, Roosevelt believed in white superiority and was neutral toward blacks only when it helped him politically. Case in point: in 1906 the army transferred African American soldiers from Nebraska to Brownsville, Texas. Anglo and Mexican residents resented their presence and banned them from parks and businesses. On August 14, a battle between blacks and whites broke out, and a white man was killed. Brownsville residents blamed soldiers, but soldiers refused to help investigators or name names. Consequently, Roosevelt discharged 167 black soldiers without a hearing and prevented them from receiving pay and pensions. Black leaders were outraged. To gain black support for Republican candidates in the 1906 elections, Roosevelt waited until after the elections to sign discharge papers.

Conservation

Roosevelt's Progressive impulse for efficiency and love for the outdoors inspired lasting contributions to resource conservation. Government establishment of national parks began in the late nineteenth century. Roosevelt advanced the movement by favoring *conservation* over *preservation*. Thus he not only exercised presidential power to protect such natural wonders as the Grand Canyon in Arizona by declaring them national monuments, but also backed a policy of wise use of forests, waterways, and other resources. Previously, the government transferred ownership of natural resources on federal land to the states and private interests. Roosevelt, however, believed effective resource conservation demanded that the federal government manage the lands that remained in the public domain.

Roosevelt exerted federal authority over resources by protecting waterpower sites from sale to private interests and charging permit fees for users who wanted to produce hydroelectricity. He also supported the Newlands Reclamation Act of 1902, which controlled the sale of irrigated federal land in the West. Roosevelt tripled the number of national forests and supported conservationist Gifford Pinchot in creating the U.S. Forest Service.

Gifford Pinchot

As principal advocate of the wise use policy, Pinchot promoted scientific management of the nation's woodlands. He obtained Roosevelt's support for transferring management of the national forests from the Interior Department to his bureau in the Agriculture Department. The Forest Service charged fees for grazing livestock within the national forests, supervised bidding for the cutting of timber, and hired university-trained foresters as federal employees.

Pinchot and Roosevelt did not seek to preserve resources permanently; rather, they wanted to conserve their efficient use and make companies profiting from using public lands pay the government. Many involved in natural-resource exploitation welcomed such a policy because it enabled them to better control products, such as when Roosevelt and Pinchot encouraged large lumber companies to engage in reforestation.

Panic of 1907

In 1907 a financial panic caused by reckless speculation forced some New York banks to close to prevent frightened depositors from withdrawing money. J. P. Morgan helped stem the panic by persuading financiers to stop dumping their stocks. In return for Morgan's aid, Roosevelt approved a deal allowing U.S. Steel to absorb the Tennessee Iron and Coal Company—a deal at odds with Roosevelt's trustbusting aims.

During his last year in office, Roosevelt retreated from the Republican Party's friendliness to big business. He supported stronger business regulation and heavier taxation of the rich. Promising he would not seek reelection, Roosevelt backed Secretary of War William Howard Taft in 1908. Taft easily defeated three-time Democratic nominee William Jennings Bryan by 1.25 million popular votes and a 2-to-1 margin in the electoral college.

Taft Administration

Taft faced political problems that Roosevelt had postponed, foremost, extremely high tariffs. Honoring Taft's pledge to cut rates, the House passed a bill providing numerous reductions. Protectionists in the Senate prepared to amend the bill and revise rates upward. But Senate Progressives attacked the tariff for benefiting special interests, trapping Taft between reformers who claimed to be preserving Roosevelt's antitrust campaign and protectionists who dominated the Republican Party. In the end, Senator Nelson Aldrich of Rhode Island restored many of the cuts, and Taft signed what became known as the Payne-Aldrich Tariff (1909). To Progressives, Taft failed to fill Roosevelt's shoes.

In reality Taft was as sympathetic to reform as Roosevelt was. He prosecuted more trusts than Roosevelt; expanded national forest reserves; signed the Mann-Elkins Act (1910), which bolstered regulatory powers of the ICC; and supported such labor reforms as shorter work hours and mine safety legislation. The Sixteenth

Amendment, which legalized the federal income tax, and the Seventeenth Amendment, which provided for direct election of U.S. senators, were initiated during Taft's presidency (and ratified in 1913). Like Roosevelt, Taft compromised with big business, but unlike Roosevelt, he lacked the ability to manipulate the public with spirited rhetoric. Roosevelt expanded presidential power; Taft, by contrast, believed in the strict restraint of law. He had been a successful lawyer and judge, and returned to the bench as chief justice of the United States between 1921 and 1930.

Candidates in 1912

In 1910, when Roosevelt returned from a trip to Africa, he found his party torn and tormented. Reformers formed the National Progressive Republican League and rallied behind Robert La Follette for president in 1912, though many hoped Roosevelt would run. Another wing of the party remained loyal to Taft. Disappointed by Taft, Roosevelt spoke out for the welfare of the people and stronger regulation of business. When La Follette became ill early in 1912, Roosevelt, proclaiming himself fit as a bull moose, sought the Republican presidential nomination.

Taft's supporters controlled the Republican convention and nominated him for a second term. In protest, Roosevelt's supporters formed a third party—the Progressive, or Bull Moose, Party—and nominated the former president. Meanwhile, Democrats took forty-six ballots to select their candidate, New Jersey's Progressive governor Woodrow Wilson. Socialists, by now a growing party, again nominated Eugene V. Debs.

New Nationalism Versus New Freedom

Central to Theodore Roosevelt's campaign was a scheme called the New Nationalism, which envisioned an era of national unity in which government would coordinate and regulate economic activity. Roosevelt asserted that he would establish regulatory commissions to protect citizens' interests and ensure wise use of economic power.

Wilson offered a more idealistic proposal, the New Freedom. He argued that concentrated economic power threatened individual liberty and that monopolies should be broken up to ensure a free marketplace. But he would not restore laissez faire. Like Roosevelt, Wilson would enhance government authority to protect and regulate. "Without the watchful . . . resolute interference of the government, there can be no fair play between individuals and such powerful institutions as the trust," he declared. Wilson stopped short, however, of advocating the cooperation between business and government inherent in Roosevelt's New Nationalism.

Roosevelt and Wilson stood closer together than their rhetoric implied. Both believed in individual freedom. Both supported equality of opportunity (chiefly for white males), conservation of natural resources, fair wages, and social betterment for all. Neither would hesitate to expand government activity through strong leadership and bureaucratic reform.

In the election, the popular vote was inconclusive. The victorious Wilson won just 42 percent, though he did capture 435 out of 531 electoral votes. Roosevelt received 27 percent of the popular vote. Taft polled 23 percent of the popular vote and only 8 electoral votes. Debs won 6 percent of the total but no electoral votes. Three-quarters of the electorate supported alternatives to Taft's view of restrained government.

WOODROW WILSON AND THE EXTENSION OF PROGRESSIVE REFORM

Woodrow Wilson

Born in Virginia in 1856 and raised in the South, Wilson was the son of a Presbyterian minister. He earned a B.A. degree at Princeton University, studied law at the University of Virginia, received a Ph.D. degree from Johns Hopkins University, and became a professor of history, jurisprudence, and political economy at Princeton University. Between 1885 and 1908, he published several respected books on American history and government.

Wilson was a superb orator who could inspire loyalty with religious imagery and eloquent expressions of American ideals. In 1902 he became president of Princeton and initiated curricular reforms and battles against aristocratic elements. But his racism kept him from admitting blacks to the college. In 1910 New Jersey's Democrats nominated Wilson for governor. Once elected, Wilson repudiated party bosses and promoted Progressive legislation. A poor administrator, he often lost his temper and was uncooperative, but his accomplishments nevertheless won him the Democratic presidential nomination in 1912.

Wilson's Policy on Business Regulation

As president, Wilson blended New Freedom competition with New Nationalism regulation, setting the direction of future federal economic policy. The corporate merger movement made restoration of open competition impossible. Hence, Wilson sought to prevent abuses by expanding government regulation. He supported congressional passage in 1914 of the Clayton Anti-Trust Act and a bill creating the Federal Trade Commission (FTC). The Clayton Act corrected deficiencies of the Sherman Anti-Trust Act of 1890 by outlawing such practices as price discrimination (lowering prices in some regions but not others) and interlocking directorates (management of two or more competing companies by the same executives). The act also aided labor by exempting unions from its anticombination provision, thereby making peaceful strikes, boycotts, and picketing less vulnerable to government interference. The FTC could investigate companies and issue cease-and-desist orders against unfair practices to protect consumers.

Wilson expanded banking regulation with the Federal Reserve Act (1913), which established the nation's first central banking system since 1836. To break the power of banking syndicates, like the power that J. P. Morgan's syndicate held over the money supply, the act created twelve district banks to hold reserves of member banks nationwide. The district banks, supervised by the Federal Reserve Board, would lend money to member banks at a low interest rate called the discount rate. By adjusting this rate (and thus the amount a bank could afford to borrow), district banks could increase or decrease the amount of money in circulation, enabling the Federal Reserve Board to loosen or tighten credit, thereby making interest rates fairer.

Tariff and Tax Reform

Wilson and Congress attempted to restore competition with the Underwood Tariff of 1913. By the 1910s, prices for some consumer goods had become unnaturally high because tariffs discouraged the importation of cheaper foreign goods. By reducing or eliminating certain tariff rates, the Underwood Tariff encouraged imports. To replace revenues lost because of tariff reductions, the act levied a graduated income tax on U.S. residents. Incomes under $4,000 were exempt; thus almost all factory workers and farmers escaped taxation. Individuals and corporations earning between $4,000 and $20,000 had to pay a 1 percent tax; thereafter rates rose gradually to a maximum of 6 percent on earnings over $500,000.

The outbreak of World War I (see Chapter 23) and the approaching 1916 presidential election prompted Wilson to support stronger reforms. He backed the Federal Farm Loan Act, which created twelve federally supported banks that could lend money at moderate interest to farmers who belonged to credit institutions—a watered-down version of the Populists' subtreasury plan proposed a generation earlier.

To forestall railroad strikes, Wilson in 1916 pushed passage of the Adamson Act, which mandated eight-hour workdays and time-and-a-half overtime pay for railroad laborers. He pleased Progressives by appointing Brandeis, the people's advocate, to the Supreme Court, though an anti-Semitic backlash almost blocked Senate approval of the Court's first Jewish justice. Wilson also backed laws regulating child labor and providing workers' compensation for federal employees who suffered work-related injuries or illness.

But Wilson never overcame his racism. Although in 1918 he tried to appoint W. E. B. Du Bois as an army officer to keep race relations calm (Du Bois, age fifty, failed the physical), Wilson fired several black federal officials. His administration also preserved racial separation in restrooms, restaurants, and government office buildings. When the pathbreaking but inflammatory film about the Civil War and Reconstruction, *The Birth of a Nation,* was released in 1915, Wilson allowed a showing at the White House.

Election of 1916

Republicans snubbed Theodore Roosevelt as their candidate in 1916, choosing Charles Evans Hughes, Supreme Court justice and former reform governor of New York. Aware of public anxiety over the world war raging in Europe since 1914, Wilson ran on a platform of neutrality and Progressivism, using the slogan "He Kept Us Out of War." The election was close. Wilson received 9.1 million votes to Hughes's 8.5 million and barely won in the electoral college, 277 to 254. The Socialist candidate drew only 600,000 votes, largely because Wilson's reforms won over some Socialists and because the ailing Eugene Debs was no longer the party's standard-bearer.

During Wilson's second term, U.S. involvement in World War I increased government regulation of the economy. Mobilization and war, he came to believe, required greater coordination of production and cooperation between the public and private sectors. The War Industries Board exemplified this cooperation: private businesses submitted to the board's control on condition that their profit motives would be satisfied. After the war, Wilson's administration dropped these measures, including farm price supports, guarantees of collective bargaining, and high taxes. This retreat from regulation, prompted in part by the election of a Republican Congress in 1918, stimulated a new era of business ascendancy in the 1920s.

Margaret Sanger, Planned Parenthood, and the Birth-Control Controversy

Some reforms of the Progressive era illustrate how earnest intentions to help can become tangled in divisive issues of morality. Such is the legacy of the birth-control advocate Margaret Sanger. In 1912 Sanger produced a column on sex education in the New York Call entitled "What Every Girl Should Know." Moralists accused her of writing obscene literature because she publicly discussed venereal disease and contraception. She counseled poor women on New York's Lower East Side about how to avoid the pain of frequent childbirth, miscarriage, and bungled abortion. In 1914 Sanger launched The Woman Rebel, a monthly newspaper advocating a woman's right to birth control. Indicted for distributing obscenity through the mails, she fled to England, where she gave speeches promoting family planning and enjoying sexuality without fear of pregnancy.

Returning to the United States, Sanger opened the country's first birth-control clinic in Brooklyn in 1916. She was arrested, but when a court exempted physicians from a law prohibiting distribution of contraceptive information, she set up a doctor-run clinic in 1923. Staffed by female doctors and social workers, the Birth Control Clinical Research Bureau became a model for other clinics. Sanger organized the American Birth Control League (1921) and tried to win support from medical and social reformers, even from the eugenics movement, for legalized birth control. After a falling out with some allies, she resigned from the American Birth Control League in 1928.

The movement continued, however, and in 1938 the American Birth Control League and the Birth Control Clinical Research Bureau merged to form the Birth Control Federation of America, renamed the Planned Parenthood Federation of America (PPFA) in 1942. The organization's name defined its mission to strengthen the family and stabilize society rather than focus on the right to voluntary motherhood. Throughout the 1940s, the PPFA emphasized family planning through making contraceptives more accessible. In 1970 it began receiving federal funds.

In the 1960s, the emergence of new feminist agitation for women's rights and rising concerns about overpopulation moved birth control and abortion into an arena of passionate controversy. Although the PPFA had initially dissociated itself from abortion, the debate between a woman's choice and a fetus's right to life drew the organization into the fray, especially after 1973, when the Supreme Court validated women's right to abortion in Roe v. Wade. PPFA fought legislative and court attempts to make abortions illegal and helped organize a women's march on Washington in 1989. Some Latino and African American groups attacked the PPFA's stance, charging that abortion was a kind of eugenics program meant to reduce births among nonwhite races.

Because of the PPFA's involvement in abortion politics, several of its clinics have been targets of picketing and even violence by those who believe abortion is immoral. The PPFA now operates nearly nine hundred health centers providing medical services and education. But birth control's legacy to a people and a nation includes disagreement over whose rights and whose morality should prevail.

Summary

By 1920 a quarter-century of reform had wrought momentous changes. Progressives established the principle of public intervention to ensure fairness, health, and safety. Concern over poverty and injustice reached new heights, but reformers could not sustain their efforts indefinitely. Although Progressive values lingered after World War I, a mass-consumer society refocused people's attention from reform to materialism.

Multiple and sometimes contradictory goals characterized the Progressive era because there was no single Progressive movement. Programs on the national level ranged from Roosevelt's faith in big government as a coordinator of big business to Wilson's promise to dissolve economic concentrations and legislate open competition. At state and local levels, reformers pursued causes as varied as neighborhood improvement, government reorganization, public ownership of utilities, and better working conditions. A new consciousness about identity confronted women and African Americans, and although women made some inroads into public life, both groups still found themselves in confined social roles.

Successes aside, the failure of many Progressive initiatives indicates the strength of the opposition, as well as weaknesses within the reform movements. As issues such as Americanization, eugenics, prohibition, education, and general moral uplift illustrate, social reform often merged into social control—attempts to impose white values on all of society. Courts asserted constitutional and liberty-of-contract doctrines in striking down key Progressive legislation, notably the federal law prohibiting child labor. Federal regulatory agencies rarely had enough resources for thorough investigations; they had to depend on information from the very companies they policed. In 1920, as in 1900, government remained under the influence of business.

Yet Progressive era reforms reshaped the national outlook. Trustbusting, however faulty, made industrialists more sensitive to public opinion. Progressive legislation equipped government with tools to protect consumers against price fixing and dangerous products. Social reformers relieved some ills of urban and industrial life. Although the questions they raised about American life remained unresolved, Progressives made the nation acutely aware of its principles and promises.

Chapter Review

THE VARIED PROGRESSIVE IMPULSE

How did Progressive reform cut across class lines?

The impulse to improve society at the turn of the twentieth century had variants in the working, middle, and wealthier classes. An emerging class of educated male and female professionals stood at the vanguard of Progressivism and sought to apply the techniques of professions such as law, engineering, medicine, social service, and teaching to end the abuse of power and inefficiency in business and government, and protect the welfare of all classes. They also believed they could unify disparate factions of society, particularly new immigrants, through education and Americanization programs. Wealthy businessmen and elite women also embraced humanitarian causes. Workers, too, pressed for reforms to improve safety and housing and to include workers' compensation for injuries on the job. There was even a religious component as Protestant ministers sought to counter the negative impact of competitive capitalism and industrialization with a message of Christian salvation known as the "Social Gospel."

GOVERNMENT AND LEGISLATIVE REFORM

According to Progressives, what was the government's role in improving society?

Unlike earlier generations of Americans who believed in a limited role for government, Progressives felt the government not only had an obligation to improve society but could protect people and families by restricting behavior. Progressives pushed officials to adopt regulations that would end labor abuses (notably, factory inspection laws), compensation for injured workers, minimum age and wage laws, child labor laws, and protective legislation regulating the hours women could work. Next, Progressives focused on ending vice, pushing for the passage of state laws and later a constitutional amendment (the Eighteenth Amendment, implemented in 1920) banning the manufacture and sale of alcohol—which they believed contributed to accidents, poverty, and poor productivity. Inspired by muckraking articles about gangs forcing women into prostitution (dubbed "white slavery"), Progressives called for government investigations and laws. Congress passed the Mann Act in 1910, prohibiting the interstate and international transportation of women for immoral purposes. By 1915 nearly every state outlawed brothels and solicitation of sex.

NEW IDEAS IN SOCIAL INSTITUTIONS

What was the impact of Progressive education reforms?

Increasing concerns about the social impact of industrialization, along with a penchant for scientific management and efficiency, drove Progressive approaches to education. Reformers such as John Dewey not only wanted to ensure that children were exposed to age appropriate materials, but they also focused on preparing children for the modern world by teaching them to use their ingenuity to solve real-life problems. College curricula shifted from its previous nearly exclusive focus on preparing primarily white men for a few professions such as medicine, religion, and law, to a focus on learning that kept pace with technological and social changes. Regarded as vital to a student's growth, athletics became a permanent feature. The number of colleges expanded, including all-black land grant colleges and women's colleges.

CHALLENGES TO RACIAL AND SEXUAL DISCRIMINATION

What strategies did women use in their quest for equality in the early twentieth century?

Women's organizations had long struggled over whether to focus on their shared humanity with men—their "samenesss"—or accentuate their unique female qualities—their "difference"—in pursuit of equality and new social roles for women. Calling themselves "the woman movement" before 1910, they played up women's special, even superior, traits as guardians of the family and morality. After that date, activists adopted the term *feminism,* emphasizing women's right to citizenship. Activist styles ranged from moderate to radical, but all saw the vote as a first and vital step to influencing the laws affecting them, be it improving women's working conditions or assuring their economic roles. Women's participation in the war effort also showed their ability and willingness to serve their country and made it impossible for legislators to continue to justify denying them the vote (which women finally received in 1920).

THEODORE ROOSEVELT AND THE REVIVAL OF THE PRESIDENCY

Theodore Roosevelt was known as a trustbuster, but was he?

Yes and no. As a Progressive, Roosevelt believed government should guide national affairs and economic development and determine when business was a positive or negative force. But he also thought there were times when business consolidation and mergers could aid economic progress and urged the Bureau of Consolidation to assist them in these efforts. At the same time, he was willing to step in when business consolidation led to corruption and market manipulation, as he did when he had the Justice Department use antitrust laws to prosecute railroad, meatpacking, and oil trusts, which he believed exploited the public. Roosevelt similarly supported regulatory legislation over interstate commerce and the quality of food and drugs. While Roosevelt supported the breakup of J. P. Morgan's Northern Securities Company, he did not break up the huge U.S. Steel Corp., and actually allowed it to acquire additional companies during the economic panic of 1907.

WOODROW WILSON AND THE EXTENSION OF PROGRESSIVE REFORM

How did participation in World War I alter Wilson's position on business?

In his first term as president, Wilson was disheartened by the corporate merger movement that seemed to weaken the prospects of fair business competition. To restore that, he increased government regulation of the business sector, supporting the Clayton Antitrust Act and the establishment of the Federal Trade Commission to ensure fair business practices and protect labor. He also established banking regulation with the Federal Reserve Act of 1913 and similarly supported tariff reform and farm loans. With war mobilization a priority in his second term, Wilson sought greater cooperation between the private and public sector. Businesses agreed to submit to the federal War Industry Board's directives in exchange for the promise of profits. After the war, Wilson retreated from the regulation that had been his pre-war policy, dropping farm supports, collective bargaining guarantees for labor, and high taxes, thereby inaugurating a new era of big business in the 1920s.

SUGGESTIONS FOR FURTHER READING

Francis L. Broderick, *Progressivism at Risk: Electing a President in 1912* (1989)

Nancy F. Cott, *The Grounding of Modern Feminism* (1987)

Steven J. Diner, *A Very Different Age: Americans of the Progressive Era* (1998)

Glenda Gilmore, *Who Were the Progressives?* (2002)

Hugh D. Hindman, *Child Labor: An American History* (2002)

Alice Kessler-Harris, *Out to Work: A History of Wage-Earning Women in the United States*, 20th anniversary ed. (2003)

Michael McGerr, *A Fierce Discontent: The Rise and Fall of the Progressive Movement in America, 1870–1920* (2003)

Patricia A. Schecter, *Ida B. Wells and American Reform, 1880–1930* (2001)

David Tyack, *Seeking Common Ground: Public Schools in a Diverse* (2003)

The Quest for Empire

1865–1914

"Foreign devil!" they shouted at Lottie Moon. The Southern Baptist missionary, half a world away from home, braced herself against the cries of the Chinese crowd she sought to convert to Christianity in the 1880s. She walked steadily and persistently through the hecklers, silently vowing to win their acceptance and their souls.

Born in 1840 in Virginia and educated at what is now Hollins College, Charlotte Diggs Moon volunteered in 1873 for woman's work in northern China. There she taught and proselytized, largely among women and children, until her death in 1912.

In the 1870s and 1880s, Lottie Moon (Mu Ladi or 慕拉第) made sometimes dangerous evangelizing trips to isolated Chinese hamlets. Curious peasant women pinched her, pulled on her skirts, purring, "How white her hand is!" They asked: "How old are you?" "Where do you get money to live on?" Speaking in Chinese, Lottie held a picture book about Jesus Christ, drawing attention to the foreign doctrine that she hoped would displace Confucianism, Buddhism, and Taoism.

In the 1890s, a storm of persecution against foreigners swept China, and missionaries became targets. One missionary conceded that, in believing in Jesus, girls and women alarmed men who worried that "disobedient wives and daughters" would no longer "worship the idols when told." In the Shaling village in early 1890, Lottie Moon's Christian converts were beaten. Fearing for her life, she left China for several months in 1900, during the violent Boxer Rebellion.

Lottie Moon and thousands of missionaries converted to Christianity only a small minority of Chinese people. Although she, like other missionaries, probably never shed the view that western religion and culture was superior, she felt affection for the Chinese. In letters and articles for a U.S. audience, she lobbied

This icon will direct you to interactive activities and study materials on A People And A Nation, Brief Edition website: **www.cengage.com/history/norton/ peoplenationbrief8e**

Chronology

1861–69	Seward sets expansionist course.		**1899**	Treaty of Paris enlarges U.S. empire.
1867	United States acquires Alaska and Midway.			United Fruit Company is formed and becomes influential in Central America.
1876	Pro-U.S. Díaz begins thirty-four-year rule in Mexico.			Philippine insurrection breaks out, led by Emilio Aguinaldo.
1878	United States gains naval rights in Samoa.		**1901**	McKinley is assassinated; Theodore Roosevelt becomes president.
1885	Strong's *Our Country* celebrates Anglo-Saxon destiny of dominance.		**1903**	Panama grants canal rights to United States. Platt Amendment subjugates Cuba.
1887	United States gains naval rights to Pearl Harbor, Hawai'i.		**1904**	Roosevelt Corollary declares United States a hemispheric police power.
1890	Mahan publishes *The Influence of Sea Power upon History*. McKinley Tariff hurts Hawaiian sugar exports.		**1905**	Portsmouth Conference ends Russo-Japanese War.
1893	Economic crisis leads to business failures and mass unemployment. Pro-U.S. interests stage successful coup against Queen Lili'uokalani of Hawai'i.		**1906**	San Francisco School Board segregates Asian schoolchildren. United States invades Cuba to quell revolt.
1895	Cuban revolution against Spain begins. Japan defeats China in war, annexes Korea and Formosa (Taiwan).		**1907**	Great White Fleet makes world tour.
			1910	Mexican revolution threatens U.S. interests.
1898	United States formally annexes Hawai'i. U.S. battleship *Maine* blows up in Havana harbor. United States defeats Spain in Spanish-American War.		**1914**	U.S. troops invade Mexico. World War I begins. Panama Canal opens.

to recruit Christian women to stir up "a mighty wave of enthusiasm for Woman's Work for Woman."

Like many Americans who went overseas in the late nineteenth and early twentieth centuries, Lottie Moon helped spread American culture abroad. Other peoples sometimes adopted and sometimes rejected American ways. American participants likewise were transformed. Lottie Moon, for example, strove to understand the Chinese and learn their language. She assumed their dress and abandoned such derogatory phrases as "heathen Chinese." She reminded less sensitive missionaries that the Chinese rightfully took pride in their ancient history.

Lottie Moon also changed—in her own words—from "a timid self-distrustful girl into a brave self-reliant woman." As she questioned the Chinese confinement of women, most conspicuous in arranged marriages, foot binding, and sexual segregation, she advanced women's rights. She understood that she could not convert Chinese women unless they had the freedom to listen to her appeals. She also challenged the male domination of America's religious missions. When the Southern Baptist Foreign Mission Board denied woman missionaries the right to vote in meetings, she resigned. The board soon reversed itself.

Decades later, critics labeled missionaries' activities as cultural imperialism, accusing the missionaries of subverting indigenous traditions and sparking cultural clashes. Defenders of missionary work have celebrated their efforts to break down cultural barriers. Either way, Lottie Moon's story illustrates how Americans in the late nineteenth century interacted with the world, how the categories domestic and foreign intersected, and how Americans expanded abroad not only to seek land, trade, investments, and strategic bases but also to promote American culture.

Between the Civil War and World War I, an expansionist United States joined the great world powers. Before the Civil War, Americans repeatedly extended the frontier: they bought and annexed territories, pushed Indians out of the path of white migration, seized California and other western areas from Mexico, and acquired southern parts of present-day Arizona and New Mexico from Mexico (the Gadsden Purchase). Americans also developed a lucrative foreign trade with most of the world and promoted American culture everywhere.

By the 1870s, most of Europe's powers were carving up Africa and large parts of Asia and Oceania for themselves. By 1900 they had conquered more than 10 million square miles and 150 million people. As the century turned, France, Russia, and Germany were spending heavily on modern steel navies, challenging an overextended Great Britain. In Asia, a rapidly modernizing Japan was expanding at the expense of China and Russia.

Engineering advances altered the world's political geography through the Suez Canal (1869), the British Trans-Indian railroad (1870), and the Russian Trans-Siberian Railway (1904), while steamships, machine guns, telegraphs, and malaria drugs facilitated the imperialists' task. Simultaneously, Europe's optimism in the 1850s and 1860s gave way to a pessimistic sense of impending warfare informed by notions of racial conflict and survival of the fittest.

Observant Americans argued that the United States risked being left behind if it failed to join the scramble for territory and markets. Republican senator Henry Cabot Lodge of Massachusetts argued that "civilization and the advancement of the [Anglo-Saxon] race" were at stake. Such thinking enticed Americans to reach beyond the continental United States for land, markets, cultural penetration, and power.

By 1900 the United States emerged as a great power with particular clout in Latin America, especially as Spain declined and Britain disengaged from the Western Hemisphere. In the Pacific, the new U.S. empire included Hawai'i, American Samoa, and the Philippines. In the decade that followed, President Theodore Roosevelt would seek to consolidate this power.

Most Americans applauded expansionism—the outward movement of goods, ships, dollars, people, and ideas. But many became uneasy whenever expansionism gave way to imperialism—the imposition of control over other peoples, undermining their sovereignty. Abroad, native nationalists, commercial competitors, and other imperial nations tried to block the spread of U.S. influence.

- **What accounts for the increased importance of foreign policy concerns in American politics in the closing years of the nineteenth century?**
- **What key arguments were made by American anti-imperialists?**
- **How did late-nineteenth-century imperialism transform the United States?**

IMPERIAL DREAMS

Foreign policy assumed a new importance for Americans at the end of the nineteenth century. Internal matters such as industrialization, the construction of the railroads, and the settlement of the West still preoccupied many, but political and business leaders now began to advocate an activist approach to world affairs. Their motives were complex, but all emphasized the supposed benefits to the country's domestic health.

Leaders who guided America's expansionist foreign relations also guided the economic development of the machine age, forged the transcontinental railroad, built America's bustling cities and giant corporations, and shaped a mass culture. They unabashedly believed the United States was an exceptional nation, different from and superior to others because of its Anglo-Saxon heritage and its God-favored and prosperous history.

Along with exceptionalism, American leaders were influenced by nationalism, capitalism, Social Darwinism, and a paternalistic attitude toward foreigners. "They are children and we are men in these deep matters of government," future president Woodrow Wilson announced in 1898. His words reveal the gender and age bias of American attitudes. Where these attitudes intersected with foreign cultures, the result was a mix of adoption, imitation, and rejection.

Foreign Policy Elite

Foreign policy is usually dominated by what scholars have labeled the foreign policy elite—opinion leaders in politics, journalism, business, agriculture, religion, education, and the military. Better read and traveled than most Americans and more politically active in the post-Civil War era, they believed that U.S. prosperity and security depended on the exertion of U.S. influence abroad. Increasingly in the late nineteenth century, the expansionist-minded elite urged formal and informal imperialism. They often met in Washington, D.C., at the homes of the historian Henry Adams and the writer and diplomat John Hay (who became secretary of state in 1898) or at the Metropolitan Club. They talked about building a bigger navy and digging a canal across Panama, Central America, or Mexico; establishing colonies; and selling surpluses abroad. Among them was Theodore Roosevelt, appointed assistant secretary of the navy in 1897; Senator Henry Cabot Lodge, who joined the Foreign Relations Committee in 1896; and the corporate lawyer Elihu Root, who later served as secretary of war and secretary of state.

These American leaders believed that selling, buying, and investing in foreign marketplaces were important to the United States. Why? One reason was profits from foreign sales. Another was the belief that foreign markets might offset American overproduction and unemployment since the nation's farms and factories produced more than Americans could consume. This was especially true during the depression of the 1890s. Economic ties also enabled Americans to exert political influence abroad and helped spread the American way of life, especially capitalism.

Foreign Trade Expansion

Foreign trade figured prominently in the United States' tremendous economic growth after the Civil War. Foreign commerce stimulated the building of a larger navy, the

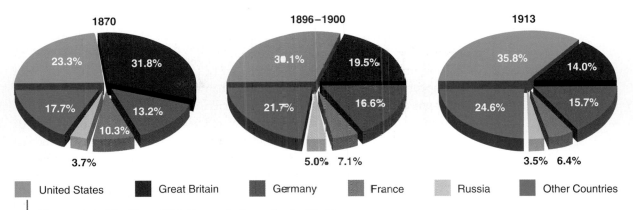

Figure 22.1   The Rise of U.S. Economic Power in the World

These pie charts showing percentage shares of world manufacturing production for the major nations of the world demonstrate that the United States came to surpass Great Britain in this significant economic measurement of power.   (*Source:* League of Nations data presented in Aaron L. Friedberg, *The Weary Titan: Britain and the Experience of Relative Decline, 1895–1905* [Princeton, NJ: Princeton University Press, 1988], 26.)

professionalization of the foreign service, calls for more colonies, and a more interventionist foreign policy. In 1865 U.S. exports totaled $234 million; by 1900 they reached $1.5 billion (see Figure 22.1). By 1914, exports hit $2.5 billion. In 1874 the United States reversed its historically unfavorable balance of trade (importing more than it exported) and began to enjoy a long-term favorable balance. Most of America's products went to Britain, continental Europe, and Canada, but increasing amounts flowed to new markets in Latin America and Asia. Meanwhile, American investments abroad reached $3.5 billion by 1914, placing the United States among the top four investor countries.

Agricultural goods accounted for about three-fourths of total exports in 1870 and about two-thirds in 1900, with grain, cotton, meat, and dairy products topping the list. Farmers' livelihoods thus became tied to world-market conditions and foreign wars. Wisconsin cheesemakers shipped to Britain; the Swift and Armour meat companies exported refrigerated beef to Europe.

In 1913, manufactured goods led U.S. exports for the first time (see Figure 22.1). Much of America's steel, copper, and petroleum were sold abroad, making many workers in those industries dependent on American exports.

Race Thinking and the Male Ethos

In expanding U.S. influence overseas, officials championed a nationalism based on notions of American supremacy. Some found justification for expansionism in racist theories then permeating western thought. For decades, the western scientific establishment classified humankind by race, and students of physical anthropology drew on phrenology and physiognomy—the analysis of skull size and facial features—to produce a hierarchy of superior and inferior races. One French researcher claimed that blacks represented a female race and "like the woman, the black is deprived of political and scientific intelligence."

The language of U.S. leaders was also weighted with words like *manliness* and *weakling*. Theodore Roosevelt viewed people of color (or "darkeys," as he called them) as effeminate weaklings who were unable to govern themselves and could not cope with world politics. Americans debased Latin Americans by referring to them as half-breeds needing supervision or distressed damsels begging for manly rescue. The gendered imagery prevalent in U.S. foreign relations joined racial thinking to place women, people of color, and nations weaker than the United States low in the hierarchy of power and, hence, in a dependent status justifying U.S. dominance.

"As America goes, so goes the world," declared Reverend Josiah Strong, author of the influential *Our Country* (1885), which celebrated an Anglo-Saxon race destined to lead others. Social Darwinists saw Americans as a superior people certain to overcome competition. Secretary of State Thomas F. Bayard (1885–1889) applauded the "overflow of our population and capital" into Mexico to "saturate those regions with Americanism."

Racial thinking—popularized in magazine photos and cartoons, world's fairs, postcards, school textbooks, museums, and political orations—reinforced notions of American greatness, influenced the way U.S. leaders dealt with other peoples, and obviated the need to think about the subtle textures of other societies. *National Geographic,* which began publication in 1888, pictorially chronicled America's new overseas involvements in Asia and the Pacific, regularly featuring images of exotic, premodern peoples who had not become western. Fairs also put so-called uncivilized people of color on display in the freak or midway section. Dog-eating Filipinos aroused comment at the 1904 St. Louis World's Fair. Such racism downgraded diplomacy and justified domination and war.

Similar thinking permeated attitudes toward immigrants, whose entry into the United States was first restricted in these years. Although the Burlingame Treaty (1868) provided for free immigration between the United States and China, riots against Chinese immigrants continuously erupted in the American West. An 1880 treaty permitted Congress to suspend Chinese immigration to the United States. Tensions continued: in 1885, white coal miners and railway workers in Rock Springs, Wyoming, massacred at least twenty-five Chinese.

In 1906 the San Francisco School Board ordered Chinese, Koreans, and Japanese segregated in special schools. Tokyo protested, and President Roosevelt quieted the crisis by striking a gentleman's agreement with Tokyo restricting Japanese immigration. Relations with Tokyo worsened again in 1913 when the California legislature denied Japanese residents the right to own property.

The "Civilizing" Impulse

Expansionists believed that empire benefited Americans and those who came under their control. When the United States intervened in weaker states, Americans claimed they were extending liberty and prosperity to less fortunate people. William Howard Taft, as civil governor of the Philippines (1901–1904), described the United States' mission in its new colony as lifting Filipinos up "to a point of civilization" that will make them "call the name of the United States blessed." Later, Taft said about the Chinese that "the more civilized they become . . . the wealthier they become, and the better market they become for us."

Missionaries dispatched to Africa and Asia, like Lottie Moon, helped spur the transfer of American culture and power abroad—"the peaceful conquest of the world,"

National Geographic

In early 1888, thirty-three members of Washington, D.C.'s elite Cosmos Club considered "organizing a society for the increase and diffusion of geographical knowledge." The result was the National Geographic Society, the world's largest nonprofit scientific and educational institution.

At the heart of the enterprise was *National Geographic Magazine*, which debuted in October 1888. Early issues were brief and visually bland, and sales lagged. When Alexander Graham Bell became the society's president in 1898, he shifted emphasis from newsstand sales to society membership, reasoning correctly that the notion of a distinguished fellowship would draw members. He also appointed a talented new editor, Gilbert H. Grosvenor, age twenty-three, who commissioned general interest articles and filled eleven pages with photographs.

Early photos showed people posed in their native costumes, displayed as anthropological specimens. By 1908 pictures occupied 50 percent of the magazine. In 1910 the first color photographs appeared in a twenty-four-page spread on Korea and China—then, the largest collection of color photographs published in a single magazine. *National Geographic*'s other photographic firsts included the first natural-color photos of Arctic life, the stratosphere, and the undersea world.

The society also sponsored expeditions, such as Robert Peary's and Matthew Henson's 1909 journey to the North Pole and, later, Jacques Cousteau's oceanic explorations and Jane Goodall's observations of wild chimpanzees. These adventures then appeared in the magazine's pages. By the end of Grosvenor's tenure as editor, in 1954, circulation topped 2 million.

Less admirably, Grosvenor's editors pressured photographers for pictures of pretty girls. One photographer recalled, "Hundreds of bare-breasted women, all from poorer countries, were published at a time of booming subscription rates." Editors also developed a well-earned reputation for presenting a rosy world-view. An article about Berlin published before the start of World War II, for example, contained no criticism of the Nazi regime and no mention of its persecution of Jews. Recently, the magazine has featured more newsworthy topics—AIDS, stem cell research, Hurricane Katrina, global warming—but in measured tones.

Throughout, the society expanded its reach, producing books, atlases, globes, and television documentaries. Targeting overseas readers, the society in 1995 launched a Japanese-language edition and later twenty-five other foreign editions. *National Geographic*, after a century linking Americans to faraway places, now connected readers around the globe to the United States.

National Geographic had already gone through five different cover formats when Robert Weir Crouch, an English-born Canadian decorative artist, came up with a design that cemented the magazine's visual identity. Singular and immediately recognizable, the oak-and-laurel frame on the cover of the February 1910 issue would remain largely unchanged for nearly half a century, though the buff-colored border would be replaced with a golden one. Even today, the gold border and the crown of laurels remain.

(National Geographic Society Image Collection)

as Reverend Frederick Gates put it. In 1915, 10,000 American missionaries worked overseas. In China by 1915, more than 2,500 mostly female American Protestant missionaries taught, preached the gospel, and administered medical care.

AMBITIONS AND STRATEGIES

The U.S. empire grew gradually, as American leaders defined guiding principles and built institutions to support overseas ambitions. William H. Seward, one of its chief architects, argued for extension of the American frontier as a senator from New York (1849–1861) and secretary of state (1861–1869). Seward envisioned a large U.S. empire encompassing Canada, the Caribbean, Cuba, Central America, Mexico, Hawai'i, Iceland, Greenland, and the Pacific islands. This empire would result from a natural process of gravitation toward the United States. Commerce would hurry the process, as would a canal across Central America, a transcontinental American railroad, and a telegraph system to speed communications.

Seward's Quest for Empire

Most of Seward's grandiose plans did not reach fruition in his lifetime. In 1867, his efforts for a treaty with Denmark to buy the Danish West Indies (Virgin Islands), was scuttled by Senate foes and a hurricane that wrecked St. Thomas. The Virgin Islanders, who voted for annexation, would wait until 1917 for official U.S. status. Seward's scheme with unscrupulous Dominican Republic leaders to gain a Caribbean naval base at Samaná Bay also failed. The corruption surrounding this deal foiled President Ulysses S. Grant's initiative in 1870 to buy the island nation.

Anti-imperialism blocked Seward. Senator Carl Schurz and E. L. Godkin, editor of the magazine *The Nation,* argued that creating a showcase of democracy and prosperity on unsettled land at home would best persuade other peoples to adopt American ways. Some anti-imperialists, sharing the era's racism, opposed the annexation of territory populated by dark-skinned people.

Seward enjoyed some successes. In 1866, citing the Monroe Doctrine, he sent troops to the Mexico border and demanded that France abandon its puppet regime there. Also facing angry Mexican nationalists, Napoleon III abandoned the Maximilian monarchy that he forcibly installed three years earlier. In 1867 Seward paid Russia $7.2 million for the 591,000 square miles of Alaska—land twice the size of Texas. That same year, Seward claimed the Midway Islands (two small islands and a coral atoll northwest of Hawai'i).

International Communications

In 1866, through the efforts of financier Cyrus Field, an underwater transatlantic cable linked European and American telegraph networks. Backed by J. P. Morgan, the communications pioneer James A. Scrymser strung telegraph lines to Latin America, entering Chile in 1890. In 1903 a submarine cable spanned the Pacific to the Philippines; three years later, it reached Japan and China. Wire telegraphy—like radio (wireless telegraphy) later—shrank the globe. Nellie Bly, a reporter for the *New York World,* accented the impact of the new technology in 1890 when she completed a well-publicized trip around the world in seventy-two days. Drawn closer through improved communications and transportation, nations found that faraway events had greater impact on their prosperity and security.

Increasingly, American diplomats negotiated with their European counterparts as equals, signaling the United States' arrival on the international stage. Seward's successor, Hamilton Fish (1869–1887), for example, achieved a diplomatic victory in resolving the knotty problem of the *Alabama* claims. Great Britain built the ship and other vessels for the Confederacy during the Civil War to prey on Union shipping. Senator Charles Sumner demanded that Britain pay $2 billion in damages or cede Canada to the United States. But in 1871 Fish negotiated the Washington Treaty, whereby the British apologized and agreed to the creation of a tribunal which later awarded the United States $15.5 million.

Washington officials also confronted European powers over Samoa, South Pacific islands 4,000 miles from San Francisco on the trade route to Australia. In 1878 the United States gained the exclusive right to a coaling station at Samoa's coveted port of Pago Pago. Eyeing the same prize, Britain and Germany began cultivating ties with Samoan leaders. Tensions grew, and war seemed possible. Britain, Germany, and the United States met in Berlin in 1889 and, without consulting the Samoans, devised a three-part protectorate that limited Samoa's independence. Ten years later, the three powers partitioned Samoa: the United States received Pago Pago through annexation of part of the islands (now called American Samoa), Germany took what is today independent Western Samoa, and Britain obtained the Gilbert Islands and Solomon Islands.

Alfred T. Mahan and Navalism Calling attention to the naval buildup by European powers, notably Germany, U.S. expansionists argued for a bigger, modernized navy, adding the "blue water" command of the seas to its traditional role of "brown water" coastline defense. Captain Alfred Thayer Mahan, a popularizer of this New Navy, argued that because foreign trade was essential, the nation required an efficient navy to protect its shipping; in turn, a navy required colonies for bases. Mahan's ideas were published as *The Influence of Sea Power upon History* (1890). Theodore Roosevelt and Henry Cabot Lodge consulted Mahan, sharing his belief in the links between trade, navy, and colonies and his alarm over Germany's aggressive military spirit.

Moving toward naval modernization, Congress in 1883 authorized construction of the first steel-hulled warships. American factories produced steam engines, high-velocity shells, powerful guns, and precision instruments. The navy shifted from sail power to steam and from wood construction to steel. New Navy ships, such as the *Maine, Oregon,* and *Boston,* earned the United States naval prominence.

CRISES IN THE 1890S: HAWAI'I, VENEZUELA, AND CUBA

In the depression-plagued 1890s, crises in Hawai'i and Cuba—and the belief that the frontier at home had closed—reinforced the expansionist argument. In 1893 the historian Frederick Jackson Turner postulated that the ever-expanding continental frontier, which shaped the American character, was gone. He did not say that a new *why?* frontier had to be found overseas, but he did claim that "American energy will continually demand a wider field for its exercise."

annex-controlling without being part of US.

Annexation of Hawai'i

Hawai'i, the Pacific Ocean archipelago of eight major islands located 2,000 miles from the U.S. West Coast, emerged as America's new frontier. The Hawaiian Islands had long commanded American attention—commercial, missionary religious, naval, and diplomatic. By 1881 Secretary of State James Blaine already declared the Hawaiian Islands "essentially a part of the American system." By 1890 Americans owned about three-quarters of Hawai'i's wealth and subordinated its economy to that of the United States through sugar exports that entered the U.S. marketplace duty-free.

In Hawai'i's multiracial society, Chinese and Japanese nationals far outnumbered Americans, who represented a mere 2.1 percent of the population. Prominent Americans on the islands organized secret clubs and military units to contest the royal government. In 1887 they forced the king to accept a constitution that allowed foreigners to vote and shifted decision making from the monarchy to the legislature. The same year, Hawai'i granted the United States naval rights to Pearl Harbor. Many native Hawaiians believed that the *haole* ("foreigners")—especially Americans—were taking their country from them.

greedy america

they did!

The native government was further undermined when the McKinley Tariff of 1890 eliminated the duty-free status of Hawaiian sugar exports in the United States. Suffering declining sugar prices and profits, the American island elite pressed for annexation by the United States, thereby classifying their sugar as domestic. When Princess Lili'uokalani assumed the throne in 1891, she sought to roll back the political power of the *haole*. The next year, the white oligarchy formed the subversive Annexation Club.

The annexationists struck in January 1893 in collusion with John L. Stevens, America's chief diplomat in Hawai'i, who dispatched troops from the USS *Boston* to occupy Honolulu. The queen, arrested and confined, surrendered. Rather than yield to the new provisional regime, headed by Sanford B. Dole, son of missionaries and a prominent attorney, she relinquished authority to the U.S. government. President Benjamin Harrison hurriedly sent an annexation treaty to the Senate.

Sensing foul play, incoming President Grover Cleveland ordered an investigation, which confirmed a conspiracy and noted that most Hawaiians opposed annexation. But when Hawai'i proved a strategic and commercial way station to Asia and the Philippines during the Spanish-American War, President William McKinley maneuvered annexation through Congress on July 7, 1898. Under the Organic Act of June 1900, the people of Hawai'i became U.S. citizens. Statehood came in 1959.

Venezuelan Boundary Dispute

The Venezuelan crisis of 1895 also saw the United States in an expansive mood. For decades Venezuela and Great Britain had quarreled over the border between Venezuela and British Guiana, a territory containing rich gold deposits and a commercial gateway to northern South America via the Orinoco River. Venezuela sought U.S. help, and in July 1895, Secretary of State Richard Olney brashly lectured the British that the Monroe Doctrine prohibited European powers from denying self-government to nations in the Western Hemisphere. With almost no Venezuelan input, in 1896 an Anglo-American arbitration board divided the disputed territory between Britain

rude!

and Venezuela. Thus the United States displayed a typical imperialist trait: disregard for the rights of small nations.

In 1895 Cuba was the site of another crisis. From 1868 to 1878 the Cubans battled Spain for their independence, winning only the end of slavery. While the Cuban economy suffered, repressive Spanish rule continued. Insurgents committed to *Cuba libre* waited for another chance, and José Martí, one of the heroes of Cuban history, collected money, arms, and men in the United States.

Revolution in Cuba   Cuban and U.S. culture intersected as Cubans settled in Baltimore, New York, Boston, and Philadelphia. Prominent Cubans on the island sent their children to schools in the United States. When Cuban expatriates returned home, many spoke English, had American names, played baseball, and jettisoned Catholicism for Protestant denominations.

The Cuban and U.S. economies were also intertwined. American investments of $50 million, mostly in sugar, dominated the island. Over 90 percent of Cuba's sugar was exported to the United States, and most island imports came from the United States. Havana's famed cigar factories relocated to Key West and Tampa to evade U.S. tariff laws. Martí, however, feared that "economic union means political union," for "the nation that buys, commands" and "the nation that sells, serves."

Martí's fears of a conquering U.S. policy were prophetic. In 1894 the Wilson-Gorman Tariff imposed a duty on Cuban sugar. The Cuban economy, highly dependent on exports, plunged into crisis, hastening the island's revolution against Spain and its further incorporation into the American system.

From American soil, Martí launched a revolution against Spain in 1895. Rebels burned sugar-cane fields and razed mills. U.S. investments evaporated, and Cuban-American trade dwindled. To separate insurgents from supporters, Spanish general Valeriano Weyler instituted a policy of reconcentration. Some 300,000 Cubans were herded into fortified towns and camps, where starvation and disease caused tens of thousands of deaths. As reports of atrocity and destruction became headline news in the United States, Americans sympathized with the insurrectionists. In late 1897, a new government in Madrid modified reconcentration and promised some autonomy for Cuba, but the insurgents continued to gain ground.

Sinking of the *Maine*   President William McKinley took office as an imperialist who advocated foreign bases for the New Navy, the export of surplus production, and U.S. supremacy in the Western Hemisphere. Vexed by Cuba's turmoil, he explored purchasing Cuba from Spain for $300 million. In January 1898, when antireform pro-Spanish loyalists and army rioted in Havana, Washington ordered the battleship *Maine* to Havana harbor to demonstrate U.S. concern and to protect American citizens.

On February 15 an explosion ripped the *Maine*, killing 266 of 354 American officers and crew. A week earlier, William Randolph Hearst's inflammatory *New York Journal* published a stolen private letter written by the Spanish minister in Washington, Enrique Dupuy de Lôme, belittling McKinley and suggesting that Spain would fight on. Congress complied unanimously with McKinley's request for $50 million in

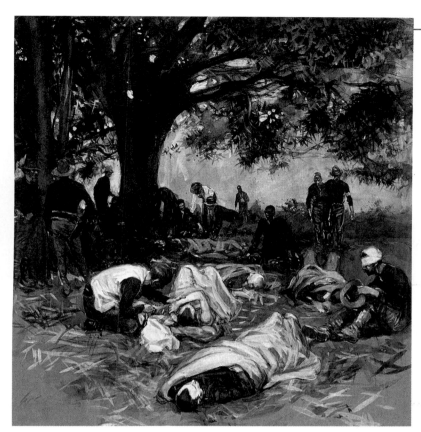

On July 1, 1898, U.S. troops stormed Spanish positions on San Juan Hill near Santiago, Cuba. Both sides suffered heavy casualties. A *Harper's* magazine correspondent reported a "ghastly" scene of hundreds killed and thousands wounded. The American painter William Glackens (1870–1938) put to canvas what he saw. Because Santiago surrendered on July 17, propelling the United States to victory in the war, and because the Rough Rider Theodore Roosevelt fought at San Juan Hill and later gave a self-congratulatory account of the experience, the human toll has often gone unnoticed.   (Wadsworth Atheneum Museum of Art, Hartford, Connecticut. Gift of Henry Schnakenberg)

defense funds. Vengeful Americans blamed Spain. (Later, official and unofficial studies attributed the sinking to an accidental internal explosion.)

McKinley's Ultimatum and War Decision

Though reluctant to go to war, McKinley sent Spain an ultimatum: accept an armistice, end reconcentration, and designate McKinley as arbiter. Madrid made concessions. It abolished reconcentration and rejected, then accepted, an armistice. The president would no longer tolerate chronic disorder 90 miles off the U.S. coast. On April 11, McKinley asked Congress for authorization to use force "to secure a full and final termination of hostilities between . . . Spain and . . . Cuba, and to secure in the island the establishment of a stable government, capable of maintaining order."

McKinley listed the reasons for war: the "cause of humanity"; the protection of American life and property; the "very serious injury to the commerce, trade, and business of our people"; and, referring to the destruction of the *Maine,* the "constant menace to our peace." On April 19, Congress declared Cuba free and independent and directed the president to use force to remove Spanish authority. The legislators also passed the Teller Amendment, which disclaimed U.S. intention to annex Cuba or control the island except to ensure its "pacification." McKinley blocked a congressional amendment to recognize the rebel government, arguing they were not ready for self-government.

THE SPANISH-AMERICAN WAR AND THE DEBATE OVER EMPIRE

By the time the Spanish concessions were on the table, prospects for compromise appeared dim. Cuban insurgents wanted full independence, and no Spanish government could have given up and remained in office. Nor did the United States welcome a truly independent Cuban government that might attempt to reduce U.S. interests.

Motives for War

McKinley's April message expressed a humanitarian impulse to stop the bloodletting and a concern for commerce and property. Republican politicians wanted the Cuba question solved to secure their party's victory in the upcoming congressional elections. Many businesspeople and farmers believed that ejecting Spain would open new markets for surplus production.

Imperialists saw the war as an opportunity to fulfill expansionist dreams, while conservatives, alarmed by Populism and labor strikes, welcomed war as a national unifier. One senator commented that "internal discord" was disappearing in the "fervent heat of patriotism." Theodore Roosevelt and others too young to remember the Civil War looked on war as adventure.

More than 263,000 regulars and volunteers served in the army, and another 25,000 in the navy during the war. Most, however, never left the United States. The typical volunteer was young (early twenties), white, unmarried, native-born, and working class. Deaths numbered 5,462, mostly from a typhoid epidemic in Tennessee, Virginia, and Florida. Only 379 died in combat. About 10,000 African American troops in segregated regiments found no relief from racism, even though black troops were central to the victorious battle for Santiago de Cuba. For all, food, sanitary conditions, and medical care were bad. Still, Roosevelt could hardly contain himself. Although Roosevelt's Rough Riders, a motley unit of Ivy Leaguers and cowboys, proved undisciplined and ineffective, Roosevelt's self-serving publicity efforts ensured they received good press.

Dewey in the Philippines

The first war news came from faraway Asia, from the Spanish colony of the Philippine Islands, where Filipinos were also seeking independence. On May 1, 1898, Commodore George Dewey's New Navy ship *Olympia* led an American squadron into Manila Bay and wrecked the Spanish fleet. Dewey received orders from Washington to attack the islands if war broke out. Manila was a choice harbor, and the Philippines sat en route to China's potentially huge market.

Facing Americans and rebels in Cuba and the Philippines, Spanish resistance collapsed rapidly. U.S. ships blockaded Cuban ports and insurgents cut off supplies from the countryside, causing starvation and illness for Spanish soldiers. American troops landed near Santiago de Cuba on June 22 and laid siege to the city. On July 3, U.S. warships sank the Spanish Caribbean squadron in Santiago harbor. American forces then assaulted the Spanish colony of Puerto Rico, winning another Caribbean naval base and pushing Madrid to defeat.

armistice- peace treaty

Treaty of Paris

On August 12, 1898, Spain and the United States signed an armistice ending the war, and in December they agreed on peace terms: independence for Cuba and cession of the Philippines, Puerto Rico, and the Pacific island of Guam to the United States for $20 million. The U.S. empire now stretched deep into Asia, and the annexation of Wake Island (1898), Hawai'i (1898), and Samoa (1899) gave American traders, missionaries, and naval promoters other steppingstones to China.

part of us but not state? confusing?

During the war, the *Washington Post* detected that "The taste of empire is in the mouth of the people." But anti-imperialists such as the author Mark Twain, Nebraska politician William Jennings Bryan, reformer Jane Addams, and industrialist Andrew Carnegie argued against annexation of the Philippines. Their concern that a war to free Cuba had led to empire, stimulated debate over American foreign policy.

Anti-Imperialist Arguments

Imperial control could be imposed either formally (by military occupation, annexation, or colonialism) or informally (by economic domination, political manipulation, or the threat of intervention). Anti-imperialist ire focused mostly on formal imperial control. Some critics cited the Declaration of Independence and the Constitution, arguing that the conquest of people against their will violated the right of self-determination.

Other anti-imperialists feared that the American character was being corrupted by imperialist zeal. Jane Addams, seeing children playing war games on Chicago streets, noted that they were not freeing Cubans but slaying Spaniards. Hoping to build a distinct foreign policy constituency from women's organizations, prominent women championed peace and an end to imperial conquest.

Some anti-imperialists protested that the United States was practicing a double standard—"offering liberty to the Cubans with one hand, cramming liberty down the throats of the Filipinos with the other, but with both feet planted upon the neck of the negro," as an African American politician from Massachusetts put it. Still other anti-imperialists warned that annexing people of color would undermine Anglo-Saxon purity and supremacy at home.

For Samuel Gompers and other anti-imperialist labor leaders, the issue was jobs. Might not the new colonials be imported as cheap contract labor to drive down American wages? Would not exploitation of the weak abroad become contagious and lead to further exploitation at home? The anti-imperialists, however, never launched an effective campaign. Although they organized the Anti-Imperialist League in November 1898, they differed so profoundly on domestic issues that they found it difficult to speak with one voice on a foreign question.

Imperialist Arguments

The imperialists appealed to patriotism, destiny, and commerce. They envisioned American merchant ships plying the waters to boundless Asian markets, naval vessels protecting America's Pacific interests, and missionaries uplifting inferior peoples. It was America's duty, they insisted, quoting a then-popular Rudyard Kipling poem, to "take up the white man's burden." Furthermore, Filipino insurgents were beginning to resist U.S. rule, and it seemed cowardly to pull out under fire, especially with Germany and Japan ready to seize the islands.

In February 1899, by a 57-to-27 vote , the Senate passed the Treaty of Paris, ending the war with Spain. Most Republicans voted yes and most Democrats no. An amendment promising independence once the Filipinos formed a stable government lost by only the tie-breaking ballot of the vice president.

ASIAN ENCOUNTERS: WAR IN THE PHILIPPINES, DIPLOMACY IN CHINA

The Philippine crisis was far from over. Emilio Aguinaldo, the Philippine nationalist leader who battled the Spanish for years, believed that American officials promised independence for his country. But after the victory, U.S. officers ordered Aguinaldo out of Manila. In early 1899, he proclaimed an independent Philippine Republic and took up arms.

Philippine Insurrection and Pacification

Both sides fought viciously; American soldiers burned villages and tortured captives, while Filipino forces staged brutal hit-and-run guerilla ambushes. U.S. troops introduced a variant of the Spanish reconcentration policy; in the province of Batangas, for instance, U.S. troops forced residents to live in designated zones to separate insurgents from local supporters. Poor sanitation, starvation, and malaria and cholera killed thousands. Outside secure areas, Americans destroyed food supplies to starve out the rebels. At least one-quarter of the population of Batangas died or fled.

Before the Philippine insurrection was suppressed in 1902, some 20,000 Filipinos died in combat, and 600,000 succumbed to starvation and disease. More than 4,000 Americans lay dead. Resistance to U.S. rule, however, continued. When the fiercely independent, often violent Muslim Filipinos of Moro Province refused to knuckle under, the U.S. military threatened extermination. In 1906, 600 Moros, including women and children, were slaughtered at the Battle of Bud Dajo.

U.S. officials soon tried to Americanize the Philippines, instituting a new education system with English as the main language. The architect Daniel Burnham, leader of the City Beautiful movement, planned modern Manila. The Philippine economy grew as an American satellite, and a sedition act sent U.S. critics to prison. In 1916 the Jones Act vaguely promised independence once the Philippines established a "stable government." But the United States did not end its rule until 1946.

China and the Open Door Policy

In China, McKinley successfully focused on a policy emphasizing negotiation. Outsiders had pecked away at China since the 1840s. Taking advantage of the Qing (Manchu) dynasty's weakness, the major imperial powers carved out spheres of influence (regions over which they claimed political control and exclusive commercial privileges): Germany in Shandong, Russia in Manchuria, France in Yunnan and Hainan, and Britain in Kowloon and Hong Kong. Then, in 1895, Japan claimed victory over China in a short war and assumed control of Formosa and Korea and parts of China proper (see Map 22.1). American religious and business leaders petitioned Washington to halt the dismemberment of China before they were closed out.

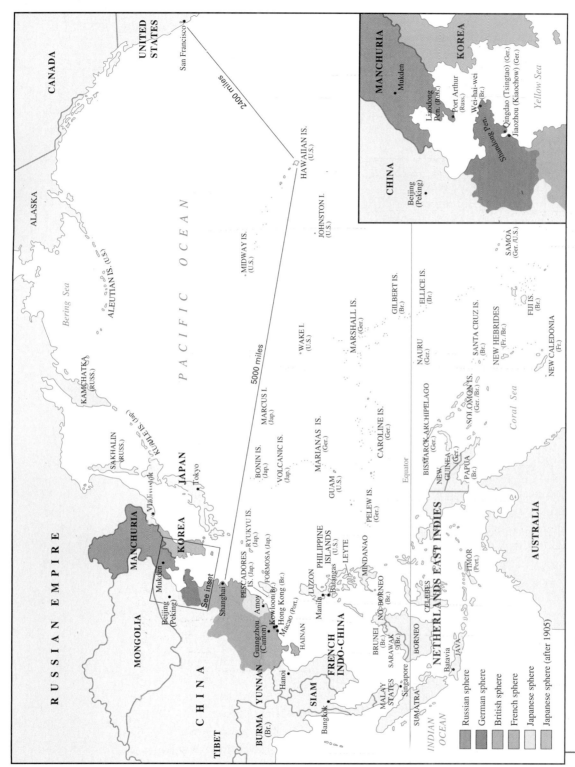

Map 22.1 Imperialism in Asia: Turn of the Century

China and the Pacific region had become imperialist hunting grounds by the turn of the century. The European powers and Japan controlled more areas than the United States, which nonetheless participated in the imperial race by annexing the Philippines, Wake, Guam, Hawai'i, and Samoa; announcing the Open Door policy; and expanding trade. As the spheres of influence in China demonstrate, that besieged nation succumbed to outsiders despite the Open Door policy.

Secretary of State John Hay knew that missionaries like Lottie Moon had become targets of Chinese nationalist anger and that American oil and textile companies had been disappointed with their investments there. Thus, in September 1899, Hay sent nations with spheres of influence in China a note seeking their respect for the principle of equal trade opportunity—an Open Door. The recipients sent evasive replies, privately complaining that the United States was seeking, for free, the trade rights in China that they had gained at considerable cost.

The next year, the Boxers, a Chinese secret society, (so named in the western press because some members were martial artists) sought to expel foreigners. They rioted, killing many outsiders and laying siege to the foreign legations in Beijing. The United States joined the other imperial powers in sending troops. Hay also sent a second Open Door note instructing other nations to preserve China's territorial integrity and honor "equal and impartial trade." China continued for years to be fertile soil for foreign exploitation, especially by the Japanese.

The Open Door policy became a cornerstone of U.S. diplomacy. While the United States had long opposed barriers to international commerce, after 1900, when the U.S. emerged emerge as the premier world trader the Open Door policy became an instrument first to pry open markets and then to dominate them. The Open Door also developed as an ideology with several tenets: first, that America's domestic well-being required exports; second, that foreign trade would suffer interruption unless the United States intervened abroad; and third that the closing of any area to American products, citizens, or ideas threatened the survival of the United States.

TR's World

Theodore Roosevelt played an important role in shaping U.S. foreign policy in the McKinley administration. As assistant secretary of the navy (1897–1898), as a Spanish-American War hero, and then as vice president in McKinley's second term, Roosevelt worked to make the United States a great power. Long fascinated by power, he also relished hunting and killing. After an argument with a girlfriend in his youth, he vented his anger by shooting a neighbor's dog. Roosevelt justified the slaughtering of American Indians, if necessary, and took his Rough Riders to Cuba, desperate to get in on the fighting.

Like many Americans of his day, Roosevelt took for granted the superiority of Protestant Anglo-American culture and believed in using American power to shape world affairs. In Roosevelt's view, there were civilized and uncivilized nations; the former, primarily white and Anglo-Saxon or Teutonic, had a right and a duty to intervene in the affairs of the latter (generally nonwhite, Latin, or Slavic, and therefore "backward") to preserve order, even if that meant using violence.

Presidential Authority   Roosevelt's love of the good fight caused many to rue his ascension to the presidency after McKinley's assassination in September 1901. But the cowboy was also an astute analyst of foreign policy. Roosevelt understood that American power, though growing, remained limited and that in many parts of the world the United States would have to rely on diplomacy to achieve satisfactory outcomes.

Roosevelt sought to centralize foreign policy in the White House, believing the president should lead foreign relations as he did domestic affairs. Congress was too large and unwieldy, and he saw public opinion as "the voice of the devil, or what is still worse, the voice of the fool." Most presidents after Roosevelt shared the notion that foreign policy belonged primarily in the executive branch.

Roosevelt's first efforts were focused on Latin America, where U.S. economic and power towered (see Map 22.2). He also focused on Europe, where repeated disputes persuaded Americans to develop friendlier relations with Great Britain while avoiding the continent's troubles, which Americans blamed on Germany.

As U.S. economic interests expanded in Latin America, so did U.S. political influence. Exports to Latin America rose from over $50 million in the 1870s to more than $120 million in 1901 and $300 million in 1914. Investments by U.S. citizens in Latin America climbed to $1.26 billion in 1914. In 1899 two large banana importers merged to form the United Fruit Company, owning much of the land in Central America (more than a million acres in 1913) and the railroad and steamship lines.

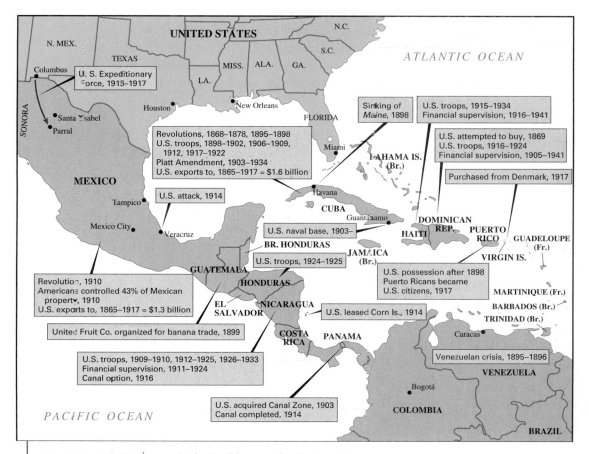

Map 22.2   U.S. Hegemony in the Caribbean and Latin America

Through many interventions, territorial acquisitions, and robust economic expansion, the United States became the predominant power in Latin America in the early twentieth century. The United States often backed up the Roosevelt Corollary's declaration of a police power by dispatching troops to Caribbean nations, where they met nationalist opposition.

Cuba and the Platt Amendment

After the war in Cuba, U.S. business interests continued to dominate the island's economy, controlling the sugar, mining, tobacco, and utilities industries, and most of the rural lands. Private U.S. investments grew from $50 million before the revolution to $220 million by 1913, and U.S. exports to the island rose from $26 million in 1900 to $196 million in 1917. The Teller Amendment outlawed the annexation of Cuba, but Washington officials used its call for pacification to justify U.S. control and maintenance of American troops there until 1902.

U.S. authorities restricted voting rights to propertied Cuban males, excluding two-thirds of adult men and all women. American officials also forced Cubans to add the Platt Amendment to their constitution. This prohibited Cuba from making treaties that might impair its independence; in practice, this meant all treaties required U.S. approval. Most important, the Platt Amendment granted the United States "the right to intervene" to preserve the island's independence and maintain domestic order. Finally, it required Cuba to lease a naval base to the United States (at Guantánamo Bay, still under U.S. jurisdiction today). Formalized in a 1903 treaty, the amendment governed Cuban-American relations until 1934.

Cubans widely protested the Platt Amendment, and a rebellion in 1906 prompted another U.S. invasion. The marines stayed until 1909, returned briefly in 1912 and again from 1917 to 1922. U.S. officials helped develop a transportation system, expand the public school system, found a national army, and increase sugar production. When Dr. Walter Reed's experiments, based on the theory of the Cuban physician Carlos Juan Finlay, proved that mosquitoes transmitted yellow fever, sanitary engineers eradicated the disease.

Puerto Rico, the Caribbean island taken as a spoil of war in the Treaty of Paris, first welcomed the United States as an improvement over Spain. But the U.S. military governor, General Guy V. Henry, regarded Puerto Ricans as children who needed "kindergarten instruction in controlling themselves without allowing them too much liberty." Some residents warned against the "Yankee peril"; others applauded the "Yankee model" and futilely anticipated statehood.

Panama Canal

Panama, meanwhile, became the site of a bold U.S. expansionist venture. In 1869 the world marveled when the newly completed Suez Canal facilitated travel between the Indian Ocean and Mediterranean Sea and enhanced the British Empire's power. Surely that feat could be duplicated in the Western Hemisphere, possibly in Panama, a province of Colombia. Business interests joined politicians, diplomats, and navy officers in insisting that the United States control such an interoceanic canal.

But the Clayton-Bulwer Treaty with Britain (1850) provided for joint control of a canal. The British, recognizing their diminishing influence in the region and cultivating friendship with the United States as a counterweight to Germany, permitted a solely U.S.-run canal in the Hay-Pauncefote Treaty (1901). When Colombia resisted Washington's terms, Roosevelt encouraged Panamanian rebels to declare independence and ordered American warships to back them.

In 1903 the new Panama awarded the United States a canal zone and long-term rights to its control. The treaty guaranteed Panama its independence. In 1922 the

In a suit and hat, President Theodore Roosevelt occupies the controls of a ninety-five-ton power shovel at a Panama Canal worksite. Roosevelt's November 1906 trip to inspect the massive project was the first time a sitting president left the United States.   (AP Images)

United States paid Colombia $25 million in conscience money but did not apologize.) A technological achievement, the Panama Canal was completed in 1914.

Roosevelt Corollary

Worried that Latin American nations' defaults on debts owed to European banks were provoking European intervention, Theodore Roosevelt in 1904 issued the Roosevelt Corollary to the Monroe Doctrine. He warned Latin Americans to stabilize their politics and finances or risk "intervention by some civilized nation." Roosevelt's declaration provided the rationale for frequent U.S. interventions in Latin America.

From 1900 to 1917, U.S. presidents ordered American troops to Cuba, Panama, Nicaragua, the Dominican Republic, Mexico, and Haiti to quell civil wars, thwart challenges to U.S. influence, gain ports and bases, and forestall European meddling (see Map 22.2). U.S. authorities ran elections, trained national guards, and shifted foreign debts to U.S. banks. They also controlled tariff revenues and government budgets (as in the Dominican Republic, from 1905 to 1941).

U.S.-Mexican Relations

U.S. officials focused particular attention on Mexico, where long-time dictator Porfirio Díaz (1876–1910) aggressively recruited foreign investors through tax incentives and land grants. American capitalists came to own Mexico's railroads and mines and invested heavily in petroleum and banking, thereby dominating Mexico's foreign trade in the early 1890s. By 1910 Americans controlled 43 percent of Mexican property and produced more than half of the country's oil. The Mexican revolutionaries who ousted Díaz in 1910 wanted to end their economic dependence on the United States.

The revolution descended into a bloody civil war with strong anti-Yankee overtones, and the Mexican government intended to nationalize American-owned properties. President Woodrow Wilson twice ordered troops onto Mexican soil: once in 1914, at Veracruz, to overthrow President Victoriano Huerta, and again in 1916, in northern Mexico, where General John J. "Black Jack" Pershing spent months pursuing Mexican rebel Pancho Villa for raiding an American border town. Failing to capture Villa and facing another nationalistic government, U.S. forces departed in January 1917.

As the United States demonstrated its power to enforce the Monroe Doctrine, European nations reluctantly honored U.S. hegemony in Latin America. In turn, the

United States continued to stand outside European embroilments. Theodore Roosevelt did help settle a Franco-German clash over Morocco by mediating a settlement at Algeciras, Spain (1906), but he drew American criticism for this involvement. Americans endorsed the Hague peace conferences (1899 and 1907) and negotiated arbitration treaties, but generally remained outside the European arena, except for trade.

Peacemaking in East Asia

In East Asia, Roosevelt and his successor, William Howard Taft, sought to preserve the Open Door and to contain Japan's rising power. The United States gradually made concessions to Japan to protect the Philippines and sustain the Open Door policy. Japan continued to plant interests in China and then smashed the Russians in the Russo-Japanese War (1904–1905). President Roosevelt mediated the negotiations at the Portsmouth Conference in New Hampshire and won the Nobel Peace Prize for helping to preserve a balance of power in Asia.

In 1905, in the Taft-Katsura Agreement, the United States conceded Japanese hegemony over Korea in return for Japan's respect for the U.S. position in the Philippines. Three years later, in the Root-Takahira Agreement, Washington recognized Japan's interests in Manchuria, and Japan again pledged the security of U.S. Pacific possessions and endorsed the Open Door in China. Roosevelt deterred the Japanese with reinforced naval power; in late 1907 he sent the navy's Great White Fleet on a world tour. Impressed, the Japanese expanded their navy.

Dollar Diplomacy

President Taft hoped to counter Japanese advances in Asia through dollar diplomacy—the use of private funds to serve American diplomatic goals while garnering profits for American financiers and bringing reform to developing countries. Taft induced American bankers to join an international consortium to build a railway in China. But it seemed only to embolden Japan to solidify its holdings in China.

In 1914, when World War I broke out in Europe, Japan seized Shandong and some Pacific islands from the Germans. In 1915 Japan issued its Twenty-One Demands, insisting on hegemony over China. The United States lacked power in Asia to block Japan's imperialism. A new president, Woodrow Wilson, worried about how the "white race" could blunt the rise of "the yellow race."

Anglo-American Rapprochement

British officials shared this concern, though their attention was focused on rising tensions in Europe. Anglo-American cooperation blossomed during the Roosevelt-Taft years. The intense German-British rivalry and the rise of the United States to world power furthered London's quest for friendship with Washington. The two nations shared a common language and respect for private property rights, and Americans appreciated British support in the 1898 war and the Hay-Pauncefote Treaty, London's virtual endorsement of the Roosevelt Corollary, and the withdrawal of British warships from the Caribbean.

British-American trade and U.S. investment in Britain also secured ties. By 1914 more than 140 American companies operated in Britain, including H. J. Heinz's

Guantánamo Bay

Four hundred miles from Miami, near the southeastern corner of Cuba, sits the U.S. naval base Guantánamo Bay (Gitmo). The oldest American base outside the United States, it is the only one in a country with which Washington does not have an open political relationship. The United States has occupied Guantánamo since the aftermath of the Spanish-American War, leasing it from Cuba for $4,085 annually (originally $2,000 in gold coins).

Cuban leaders were dissatisfied with the deal early on, and after Fidel Castro's communist takeover in 1959, Guantánamo fueled tensions between the two countries. Castro called it "a dagger pointed at Cuba's heart" and refused to cash the rent checks. That he cashed the very first check, however, enabled Washington to argue that Castro's government accepts the lease.

Since late 2001 Gitmo has contained a detainment camp for alleged combatants captured in Afghanistan and, later, Iraq and elsewhere. By late 2005, there were over five hundred detainees from more than forty countries. The George W. Bush administration called the detainees "unlawful enemy combatants" but promised to follow the Geneva accords governing prisoners of war. Soon there were allegations of abuse and complaints that holding detainees without trial, charges, or prospect of release was unlawful. Some detainees committed suicide. For critics the camp became an international symbol of American heavy-handedness and harmful to America's image abroad.

In June 2006, the U.S. Supreme Court ruled that President Bush overstepped his power in establishing procedures for the Guantánamo detainees without congressional authority—and that the procedures violated the Uniform Code of Military Justice and the Geneva accords. Bush said he would like to close the Guantánamo camp but some prisoners were too "darned dangerous" to release or deport. The question for a people and a nation remained: how would the United States balance security with due process and the rule of law?

processed foods and F. W. Woolworth's "penny markets." Many decried an Americanization of British culture. Such exaggerated fears, however, gave way to cooperation, especially in 1917 when the United States entered World War I supporting Britain against Germany.

Summary

By 1914 Americans held extensive economic, strategic, and political interests worldwide. The outward reach of U.S. foreign policy from Seward to Wilson sparked opposition from domestic critics, other imperialist nations, and foreign nationalists, but expansionists prevailed, and the trend toward empire endured.

Economic and strategic needs motivated and justified expansion. The belief that the United States needed foreign markets to absorb surplus production joined missionary zeal in reforming other societies through American products and culture. Notions of racial and male supremacy and appeals to national greatness also fed the appetite for foreign adventure. The greatly augmented navy became a primary means for satisfying America's expansionist desires.

Revealing the diversity of America's intersection with the world, missionaries like Moon, generals, companies, and politicians carried American ideas, guns, and goods abroad to a mixed reception. When world war broke out in August 1914, the United States' self-proclaimed greatness and political isolation from Europe were tested.

Chapter Review

IMPERIAL DREAMS

What drove U.S. expansion overseas in the late nineteenth century?

A new group of elite leaders and intellectuals believed the nation's future prosperity and security depended on greater U.S. influence over world affairs. They believed foreign trade could prevent future downturns by shipping surplus products overseas. Leaders also embraced the notion of American "exceptionalism"— that the United States was unique and superior to other regions because of its heritage and God-favored prosperity. Nationalism, capitalism, Social Darwinism, and a paternalistic racism also provided rationales for U.S. expansion and imperialism in the late nineteenth and early twentieth centuries. Together, these theories depicted Latin Americans, Filipinos, and others as less advanced and less human than their U.S. counterparts; hence, expansionists argued that when they intervened in these regions, they were helping to bring prosperity and liberty to weaker, less fortunate peoples.

AMBITIONS AND STRATEGIES

What happened to Seward's vision of an American empire?

Secretary of State William Seward longed for a U.S. empire that would extend the frontier to include Canada, the Caribbean, Cuba, Central America, Mexico, Hawai'i, Iceland, Greenland, and the Pacific islands. He anticipated these areas would naturally gravitate to—and easily become enveloped by—the United States, and that foreign trade and certain infrastructure developments—such as a transcontinental U.S. railroad, a canal across Central America, and a telegraph system—would speed things along. Most of his vision never came to pass, blocked by anti-imperialists, political foes, and failed schemes. He had a few successes, however, including chasing the French puppet government from Mexico in 1866, purchasing Alaska from the Russians in 1867, and claiming the Midway Islands for the United States that year.

CRISES IN THE 1890S: HAWAI'I, VENEZUELA, AND CUBA

What typically imperialist actions did the United States take in its dealings with Hawai'i and Venezuela?

In both cases, the United States showed disregard for the rights of small nations. Hawai'i was annexed despite the objections of its queen and most Hawaiians because it proved strategically and commercially important to the United States—particularly during the Spanish-American War, when it served as a way station to Asia and the Philippines. Venezuela, also a small nation, sought U.S. assistance in its border dispute with Great Britain over where its boundary with British Guiana should lie. The Anglo-American arbitration board divided up the territory, which was rich with gold and provided a commercial gateway to South America, between Britain and Venezuela, with almost no input from the latter.

THE SPANISH-AMERICAN WAR AND THE DEBATE OVER EMPIRE

What were the U.S. justifications for entering a war with Spain?

Among his reasons for the war, President McKinley listed protecting "American life and property," particularly in the wake of the destruction of the *Maine*. Many American business people and farmers believed opening up the regions held by Spain—initially Cuba and later the Philippines—would open up new markets for US surplus production. Imperialists looked to the war to fulfill expansionist dreams by adding new U.S. territories, while conservatives, alarmed by Populism and labor strikes, hoped the war could unify the nation behind a single cause.

What were the anti-imperialist arguments against U.S. annexation of the Philippines after the Spanish-American War?

Anti-imperialists expressed a wide range of concerns about the potential annexation of the Philippines. For many it seemed hypocritical for Americans to fight a war for Cuban liberation, only to acquire another small nation in the process. Some argued that it violated the fundamental right of a people to self-determination that Americans themselves embraced in the Declaration of Independence and Constitution. Prominent women felt imperialist zeal corrupted the American character. Racists saw the annexation of non white nation as a potential threat to Anglo-Saxon purity and supremacy, while labor leaders feared the new colonists might become a cheap labor force to drive down American wages.

ASIAN ENCOUNTERS: WAR IN THE PHILIPPINES, DIPLOMACY IN CHINA

What made the Open Door policy a key component of U.S. diplomacy?

The Open Door Policy originated in the late nineteenth century as a solution to U.S. trade difficulties in China. The concept called for nations with spheres of influence in turbulent China to respect the principle of equal trade opportunity. After 1900, when the United States became the world's preeminent trader, the Open Door became the tool by which it could first enter new markets and then dominate them. As it developed, the Open Door included the following tenets: that America's economy required exports to remain strong; that trade abroad could be interrupted unless the United States intervened; and that keeping U.S. citizens, products, or ideas from other regions threatened U.S. survival.

TR's WORLD

What solidified U.S.-British ties heading into World War I?

Aside from their shared language and respect for private property rights, England and the United States were united by several other factors. Both were concerned about growing Japanese influence in Asia. U.S. investment in Britain, along with increased trade, further strengthened their bonds. British support for the Roosevelt Corollary to Monroe doctrine (granting the United States hegemony in the Western Hemisphere) and the withdrawal of British ships from the

Caribbean made relations easier, as did England's respect for the United States's growing status as a world power. Increased tensions between Germany and England, along with British support for the 1898 war, increased cooperation between the two countries and ensured the United States would take England's side in the impending global conflict.

SUGGESTIONS FOR FURTHER READING

Robert L. Beisner, *Twelve Against Empire: The Anti-Imperialists, 1898–1900* (1968)

Kristin L. Hoganson, *Fighting for American Manhood: How Gender Politics Provoked the Spanish-American and Philippine-American Wars* (1998)

Michael H. Hunt, *Ideology and U.S. Foreign Policy* (1987)

Paul A. Kramer, *The Blood of Government: Race, Empire, the United States, and the Philippines* (2006)

Walter LaFeber, *The American Search for Opportunity, 1865–1913* (1993)

Brian M. Linn, *The Philippine War, 1899–1902* (2000)

Eric T. Love, *Race over Empire: Racism and U.S. Imperialism, 1865–1900* (2004)

Stuart Creighton Miller, *"Benevolent Assimilation": The American Conquest of the Philippines, 1899–1903* (1982)

John Offner, *An Unwanted War: The Diplomacy of the United States and Spain over Cuba, 1895–1898* (1992)

Louis A. Perez Jr., *The War of 1898: The United States and Cuba in History and Historiography* (1998)

Americans in the Great War

On May 7, 1915, Secretary of State William Jennings Bryan was lunching with cabinet members in Washington when he received a bulletin: the luxurious British ocean liner *Lusitania* had been sunk, apparently by a German submarine. He rushed to his office, and at 3:06 P.M. received confirmation from London: "THE LUSITANIA WAS TORPEDOED OFF THE IRISH COAST AND SANK IN HALF AN HOUR." In fact, the giant vessel sank in eighteen minutes; 1,198 people perished, including 128 Americans. With Europe at war, Bryan feared such a calamity. Britain imposed a naval blockade on Germany, and the Germans responded with submarine warfare against Allied shipping, proclaiming the North Atlantic a danger zone, then sinking British and Allied ships. As a passenger liner, the *Lusitania* was supposed to be spared, but German officials warned Americans in newspaper notices that they traveled on British or Allied ships at their own risk; passenger liners suspected of carrying munitions or contraband were subject to attack. For weeks Bryan urged President Woodrow Wilson to stop Americans from booking passage on British ships; Wilson refused.

The *Lusitania,* it soon emerged, *was* carrying munitions. Desperate to keep the United States out of the war, Bryan urged Wilson to condemn Germany and Britain and ban Americans from traveling on belligerent ships. Others, including former president Theodore Roosevelt, called the sinking "an act of piracy" and pressed for war. Wilson did not want war, but disagreed with Bryan. He sent a strong note to Berlin, insisting Germany end its submarine warfare.

As Bryan pressed his case, he became increasingly isolated within the administration. When in early June Wilson refused to ban Americans from travel on belligerent ships and sent a second protest note to Germany, Bryan resigned.

This icon will direct you to interactive activities and study materials on A People And A Nation, Brief Edition
website: **www.cengage.com/history/norton/ peoplenationbrief8e**

Chronology

1914	World War I begins in Europe.
1915	Germans sink the *Lusitania* off the coast of Ireland.
1916	After torpedoing the *Sussex,* Germany pledges not to attack merchant ships without warning.
	National Defense Act expands the U.S. military.
1917	Germany declares unrestricted submarine warfare.
	Russian Revolution ousts the tsar; Bolsheviks take power later.
	United States enters World War I.
	Selective Service Act creates the draft.
	Espionage Act limits First Amendment rights.
	Race riot breaks out in East St. Louis, Illinois.
1918	Wilson announces Fourteen Points for a new world order.
	Sedition Act further limits free speech.

	U.S. troops at Château-Thierry help blunt the German offensive.
	U.S. troops intervene in Russia against Bolsheviks.
	Spanish flu pandemic kills 20 million people worldwide.
	Armistice ends World War I.
1919	Paris Peace Conference punishes Germany and launches the League of Nations.
	May Day bombings help instigate the Red Scare.
	American Legion organizes for veterans' benefits and antiradicalism.
	Wilson suffers a stroke after a speaking tour.
	Senate rejects the Treaty of Versailles and U.S. membership in the League of Nations.
	Schenck v. U.S. upholds the Espionage Act.
1920	Palmer Raids round up suspected radicals.

Americans were similarly divided over Europe's war. Eastern newspapers charged Bryan with stabbing the country in the back. In the Midwest and South, Bryan won praise from pacifists and German American groups. A few weeks later, speaking to fifteen thousand people at Madison Square Garden, Bryan was applauded when he warned against "war with any of the belligerent nations." Although many Americans agreed with Wilson that honor ranked above peace, others shared Bryan's position that some sacrifice of neutral rights was reasonable to keep the country out of war.

To many, full-scale war seemed unthinkable. The new machine guns, howitzers, submarines, and dreadnoughts were awesome death engines; one social reformer lamented that using them would mean "civilization is all gone, and barbarism come."

For almost three years President Wilson kept America out of the war, while protecting U.S. trade interests and improving the nation's military posture. But American property, lives, and neutrality fell victim to British and German naval warfare. When, two years after the *Lusitania* went down, the president asked Congress for a declaration of war, he insisted America would not just win but "make the world safe for democracy."

A year and a half later, the Great War would be over. Some 10 million soldiers perished. Europeans experienced the destruction of ideals, confidence, and goodwill. Economically, too, the damage was immense. The Great War toppled four empires of the Old World—the German, Austro-Hungarian, Russian, and Ottoman Turkish—and left two others, the British and French, drastically weakened.

Losses for the United States were comparatively small, yet American involvement tipped the scales in favor of the Allies by contributing troops, supplies, and loans. The war years also witnessed a massive international transfer of wealth from Europe across the Atlantic, as the United States went from the world's largest debtor nation to its largest creditor. The conflict marked the United States as a world power.

At home, World War I intensified social divisions. Racial tensions accompanied the northward migration of southern blacks, and pacifists and German Americans were harassed. The federal government trampled on civil liberties to promote patriotism and silence critics. After Russia's communist revolution, a Red Scare in America repressed radicals and tarnished America's democratic image. Although reformers continued to address issues like prohibition and woman suffrage, the war splintered the Progressive movement.

Abroad, Americans who marched to battle grew disillusioned with the peace process. They recoiled from victors squabbling over the spoils, and they chided Wilson for failing to deliver his promised "peace without victory." Americans again debated about foreign policy. After negotiating the Treaty of Versailles at Paris following World War I, the president urged U.S. membership in the new League of Nations, which he believed would reform world politics. The Senate rejected his appeal (the League nonetheless organized without U.S. membership), because many Americans feared that the League might threaten the U.S. empire and entangle Americans in Europe's problems.

- **Why did the United States try to remain neutral and then enter the European war in 1917?**
- **How was American society changed by the war?**
- **What were the main elements of Woodrow Wilson's postwar vision, and why did he fail to realize them?**

PRECARIOUS NEUTRALITY

The war that erupted in August 1914 grew from years of European competition over trade, colonies, allies, and armaments. Two powerful alliance systems had formed: the Triple Alliance of Germany, Austria-Hungary, and Italy and the Triple Entente of Britain, France, and Russia. All had imperial holdings and wanted more. But as Germany challenged Great Britain for world leadership, many Americans saw Germany as an excessively militaristic nation that threatened U.S. interests in the Western Hemisphere.

Outbreak of the First World War

Crises in the Balkans triggered a chain of events that shattered Europe's delicate balance of power. Slavic nationalists sought to enlarge independent Serbia by annexing regions such as Bosnia, then a province of the Austro-Hungarian Empire. On June 28, 1914, Archduke Franz Ferdinand, heir to the Austro-Hungarian throne, was assassinated by a Serbian nationalist while visiting Sarajevo, the capital of Bosnia. Austria-Hungary consulted its Triple Alliance partner Germany, which urged toughness. When Serbia called on its Slavic friend Russia for help, Russia enlisted France and began mobilizing its armies.

Germany struck first, declaring war against Russia on August 1 and against France two days later. When German forces slashed into neutral Belgium to get to France, London declared war against Germany on August 4. Eventually Turkey (the

Ottoman Empire) joined Germany and Austria-Hungary as the Central Powers, and Italy (switching sides) and Japan teamed up with Britain, France, and Russia as the Allies. Japan seized Shandong, Germany's area of influence in China.

President Wilson at first distanced America by proclaiming neutrality—the traditional U.S. policy toward European wars. Privately, the president worried that without neutrality, "our mixed populations would wage war on each other."

Taking Sides

Despite Wilson's appeal for unity at home, ethnic groups did take sides. Many German Americans and anti-British Irish Americans (Ireland was then trying to break free from British rule) cheered for the Central Powers. Americans with roots in Allied nations, championed the Allied cause. Germany's attack on Belgium confirmed for many that Germany was the archetype of unbridled militarism.

The pro-Allied sympathies of Wilson's administration also weakened the U.S. neutrality proclamation. Wilson shared the conviction with British leaders that a German victory would destroy free enterprise and government by law. If Germany won the war, he prophesied, "it would change the course of our civilization and make the United States a military nation."

U.S. economic links with the Allies also rendered neutrality difficult, if not impossible. England, a long-time customer, flooded America with new orders, especially for arms. Sales to the Allies helped end an American recession. Between 1914 and 1916, American exports to England and France grew 365 percent, from $753 million to $2.75 billion. Largely because of Britain's naval blockade, exports to Germany dropped by more than 90 percent, from $345 million to only $29 million. Loans to Britain and France from private American banks—totaling $2.3 billion during neutrality—financed much of U.S. trade with the Allies. Germany received only $27 million in the same period.

To Germans, the links between the U.S. economy and the Allies meant that the United States had become the Allied arsenal and bank. Americans, however, worried that cutting their economic ties with Britain would constitute a nonneutral act in favor of Germany. Under international law, Britain—which controlled the seas—could buy contraband (war-related goods) and noncontraband from neutrals. It was Germany's responsibility, not America's, to stop such trade as international law prescribed by blockading the enemy's territory, seizing contraband from neutral (U.S.) ships, or confiscating goods from belligerent (British) ships.

Wilsonianism

Wilsonianism, the cluster of ideas that Wilson espoused, consisted of traditional American principles (such as democracy and the Open Door) and a vision of the United States as a beacon of freedom. Only the United States could lead the convulsed world into a peaceful era of unobstructed commerce free-market capitalism, democratic politics, and open diplomacy. "America had the infinite privilege of fulfilling her destiny and saving the world," Wilson claimed. Critics, however, charged that Wilson often violated his own credos while forcing them on others—as his military interventions in Mexico in 1914, Haiti in 1915, and the Dominican Republic in 1916 testified. Nonetheless, his ideals served U.S. commercial purposes.

To say that U.S. neutrality was never a real possibility given ethnic loyalties, economic ties, and Wilsonian preferences is not to say that Wilson sought to enter the war. In early 1917, the president remarked that "we are the only one of the great white nations that is free from war today, and it would be a crime against civilization for us to go in." But go in the United States finally did. Why?

Violations of Neutral Rights

The short answer is that Americans got caught in the Allied–Central Power crossfire. The British sought to cripple the German economy by severing neutral trade. They declared a blockade of water entrances to Germany and mined the North Sea. They seized cargoes and defined a broad list of contraband (including foodstuffs) that they prohibited neutrals from shipping to Germany. Furthermore, to counter German submarines, the British flouted international law by arming their merchant ships and flying neutral (sometimes U.S.) flags. Wilson frequently protested British violations of neutral rights, but London deflected Washington's criticism by paying for confiscated cargoes, while German provocations made British behavior appear less offensive in comparison.

Germany looked for victory at sea by using submarines. In February 1915, Berlin declared a war zone around the British Isles, warned neutral vessels to stay out so as not to be mistakenly attacked, and advised passengers to stay off Allied ships. Wilson informed Germany it would be held accountable for any losses of American life and property.

Wilson held to a strict interpretation of international law and expected Germans to warn passenger or merchant ships before attacking, so that passengers and crew could disembark safely into lifeboats. The Germans thought that surfacing

Initially underestimated as a weapon, the German U-boat proved to be frighteningly effective against Allied ships. At the beginning of the war, Germany had about twenty operational submarines in its High Seas Fleet, but officials moved swiftly to speed up production. This photograph shows a German U-boat under construction in 1914. (Bibliothek fuer Zeitgeschichte, Stuttgart, Germany)

its slender and sluggish *Unterseebooten* (U-boats) would risk their advantage and leave them vulnerable to attack. Berlin protested that Wilson was denying it the one weapon that could break the British economic stranglehold, disrupt the Allies' substantial connection with U.S. producers and bankers, and win the war. To British, Germans, and Americans, naval warfare became a matter of life and death.

THE DECISION FOR WAR

In early 1915, German U-boats sank ship after ship, notably the *Lusitania* on May 7. Germany's subsequent brief promise to refrain from attacking passenger liners ended in mid August when another British vessel, the *Arabic,* was sunk off Ireland. Three Americans died. The Germans quickly pledged that an unarmed passenger ship would never again be attacked without warning. But the *Arabic* incident led critics to ask: why not require Americans to sail on American craft? From August 1914 to March 1917, after all, only 3 Americans died on an American ship (the tanker *Gulflight,* sunk by a German U-boat in May 1915), versus 190 killed on belligerent ships.

Peace Advocates

In March 1916, a U-boat attack on the *Sussex,* a French vessel crossing the English Channel, injured four Americans and brought the United States closer to war. Wilson threatened Berlin that the United States would sever diplomatic relations if the attacks continued. Again the Germans retreated. At the same time, U.S.-British relations soured after Britain's crushing response to the Easter Rebellion in Ireland and further British restriction of U.S. trade with the Central Powers.

As the United States became more entangled in the Great War, many Americans urged Wilson to keep the nation out. In early 1915 Jane Addams, Carrie Chapman Catt, and other suffragists helped found the Woman's Peace Party, the U.S. section of the Women's International League for Peace and Freedom. Later that year, some pacifist Progressives organized an antiwar coalition, the American Union Against Militarism. The businessmen Andrew Carnegie and Henry Ford financed peace efforts, standing alongside the socialist Eugene Debs.

Antiwar advocates emphasized that war drained a nation of its youth, resources, and reform impulse; that it fostered repression at home; that it violated Christian morality; and that wartime business barons reaped huge profits at the expense of the people. Militarism and conscription, Addams pointed out, were what millions of immigrants left behind in Europe. Although the peace movement was splintered, it articulated several ideas that Wilson, who campaigned on a peace platform in the 1916 election, shared. Wilson futilely labored once again to bring the belligerents to the conference table, urging them in early 1917 to temper their acquisitive war aims and embrace "peace without victory."

Unrestricted Submarine Warfare

In Germany, Wilson's overture went unheeded. Since August 1916, German leaders debated whether to resume the unrestricted U-boat campaign. Opponents feared a break with the United States, but proponents claimed that only through an all-out attack on Britain's supply shipping could Germany win the war. True, the United States might enter the war, but victory might be achieved before U.S. troops crossed the Atlantic. Consequently, in early February 1917, Germany launched unrestricted submarine warfare, attacking all warships and merchant vessels—belligerent or neutral—in the declared war zone. Wilson quickly broke diplomatic relations with Berlin.

In late February, British intelligence intercepted and passed to U.S. officials a telegram addressed to the German minister in Mexico from German foreign secretary Arthur Zimmermann. Its message: If Mexico joined an alliance against the United States, Germany would help Mexico recover the territories it lost in 1848. Zimmermann hoped to "set new enemies on America's neck—enemies which give them plenty to take care of over there."

Although Mexico rejected Germany's offer, Wilson judged Zimmermann's telegram "a conspiracy against this country." The prospect of a German-Mexican collaboration helped turn the tide of opinion in the American Southwest, where antiwar sentiment had been strong.

Soon afterward, Wilson asked Congress for "armed neutrality" to defend U.S. lives and commerce, seeking authority to arm U.S. merchant ships, for example. In the midst of the debate, Wilson released Zimmermann's telegram to the press. Americans were outraged. The antiwar senators Robert M. La Follette and George Norris, among others, saw the armed-ship bill as a blank check for the president to move the country to war, and they filibustered it to death. Wilson armed U.S. commercial vessels anyway, but acted too late to prevent the sinking of several U.S. ships. War cries escalated. In late March, Wilson called Congress into special session.

War Message and War Declaration

On April 2, 1917, the president stepped before a hushed Congress and enumerated U.S. grievances: Germany's violation of freedom of the seas, disruption of commerce, interference with Mexico, and breach of human rights by killing innocent Americans. Congress declared war against Germany on April 6 by a vote of 373 to 50 in the House and 82 to 6 in the Senate. (This vote was for war against Germany only; a declaration of war against Austria-Hungary came months later, on December 7.) Montana's Jeannette Rankin, the first woman in Congress, cast a ringing no vote.

For principle, for morality, for honor, for commerce, for security, for reform—for all of these reasons, Wilson took the United States into the Great War. The submarine was certainly the culprit that drew a reluctant president and nation into the maelstrom. Critics blamed Wilson's rigid definition of international law and his contention that Americans should be entitled to travel anywhere, even on a belligerent ship loaded with contraband. Most Americans came to accept Wilson's view that the Germans had to be checked to ensure an open, orderly world in which U.S. principles and interests would be safe.

The United States went to war to reform world politics, not to destroy Germany. By early 1917 the president concluded that the United States would not be able to claim a seat at the postwar peace conference unless it became a combatant. At the peace conference, Wilson intended to promote the principles he thought essential to a stable world order, to advance democracy and the Open Door, and to outlaw revolution and aggression. In designating the United States an "Associated" rather than an Allied nation, Wilson tried to preserve part of his country's neutrality, but to no avail.

WINNING THE WAR

Even before the U.S. declaration of war, the Wilson administration strengthened the military under the banner of "preparedness." The National Defense Act of 1916 provided for increases in the army and National Guard, and for summer training camps modeled on the one in Plattsburgh, New York, where some of America's social and economic elite trained in 1915 as "citizen-soldiers." The Navy Act of 1916 started the largest naval expansion in American history.

The Draft and the Soldier

To raise an army, Congress in May 1917 passed the Selective Service Act, requiring all males between the ages of twenty-one and thirty (later changed to eighteen and forty-five) to register. National service, proponents believed, would prepare the nation for battle and instill patriotism and respect for democracy and personal sacrifice. Critics feared it would lead to the militarization of American life.

On June 5, 1917, more than 9.5 million men signed up for the "great national lottery." By war's end, 24 million men had been registered by local draft boards. The typical soldier was in his early to mid-twenties, white, single, American-born, and poorly educated (most had not attended high school, and perhaps 30 percent could not read or write). Tens of thousands of women enlisted in the army Nurse Corps, served as "hello girls" (volunteer bilingual telephone operators) in the army Signal Corps, and became clerks in the navy and Marine Corps.

Some 400,000 African Americans also served in the military. Many southern politicians feared arming African Americans, but the army drafted them into segregated units and assigned them to menial labor. They endured miserable conditions. Ultimately more than 40,000 blacks would see combat in Europe, and several black units served with distinction in the French army. The all-black 369th Infantry Regiment spent more time in the trenches—191 days—and received more medals than any other American outfit.

Although French officers had their share of racial prejudice and often treated the soldiers from their own African colonies poorly, black Americans serving with the French reported a degree of respect lacking in the American army. The irony was not lost on African American leaders, such as W. E. B. Du Bois, who endorsed the National Association for the Advancement of Colored People's (NAACP) support for the war and urged blacks to volunteer to help make the world safe for democracy.

Approximately 3 million men evaded draft registration. Some were arrested, others fled to Mexico or Canada, but most stayed home and were never discovered. Another 338,000 men who registered never showed up for induction. Nearly 65,000 draftees applied for conscientious-objector (CO) status (refusing to bear arms for religious or pacifist reasons), but some changed their minds or failed preinduction examinations. Quakers and Mennonites were numerous among the 4,000 inductees classified as COs. COs who refused noncombat service, such as in the medical corps, faced imprisonment.

Trench Warfare

U.S. general John J. Pershing, head of the American Expeditionary Forces (AEF), insisted that his "sturdy rookies" remain a separate army. He refused to turn over his "doughboys" (so termed, apparently, because the large buttons on American uniforms in the 1860s resembled a deep-fried bread of that name) to Allied commanders, who favored deadly trench warfare. Since fall 1914, zigzag trenches fronted by barbed wire and mines stretched across France. Between the muddy, stinking trenches lay "no man's land," denuded by artillery fire. When ordered out, soldiers would charge enemy trenches, only to face machine gun fire and poison gas.

First used by the Germans in April 1915, chlorine gas stimulated overproduction of fluid in the lungs, leading to death by drowning. Gas in a variety of forms (mustard and phosgene, in addition to chlorine) would be used throughout the war, sometimes blistering, sometimes incapacitating, often killing.

The death toll in trench warfare was overwhelming. At the Battle of the Somme in 1916, the British and French suffered 600,000 dead or wounded to earn only 125 square miles; the Germans lost 400,000 men. At Verdun that year, 336,000 Germans perished, and at Passchendaele in 1917 more than 370,000 British men died to gain about 40 miles of mud and barbed wire.

| **Shell Shock** | Not long after arriving on the French front, U.S. units faced the horrors caused by advanced weaponry. Some |

suffered shell shock, a mental illness also known as war psychosis. Symptoms included a fixed, empty stare; violent tremors; paralyzed limbs; listlessness; jabbering; screaming; and haunting dreams. The illness could strike anyone; even soldiers who appeared courageous cracked after days of incessant shelling and inescapable human carnage. Providing some relief were Red Cross canteens, staffed by women volunteers, which offered haircuts, food, and recreation.

In Paris, where forty large houses of prostitution thrived, venereal disease became such a problem that French prime minister Georges Clemenceau offered licensed, inspected prostitutes in special houses to the U.S. army. Still, by war's end, about 15 percent of America's soldiers contracted venereal disease, costing the army $50 million and 7 million days of active duty. Periodic inspections, chemical prophylactic treatments, and the threat of court-martial for infected soldiers kept the problem from being greater.

| **American Units in France** | In France, soldiers filled their diaries and letters with descriptions of local customs and "ancient" architecture and noted how the war-torn French countryside bore little |

resemblance to the groomed landscapes in paintings. "Life in France for the American soldier meant marching in the dirt and mud, living in cellars in filth, being wet and cold and fighting," the chief of staff of the Fourth Division remarked. "He had come to help . . . but these French people did not seem to appreciate him at all."

With both sides exhausted, the Americans tipped the balance toward the Allies. But not right away. Initially, the U.S. Navy battled submarines and escorted troop carriers, and pilots in the U.S. Air Service, flying mostly British and French aircraft, saw limited action. American flying aces like Eddie Rickenbacker defeated their German counterparts in aerial dogfights and became heroes in France and their own country. But only ground troops could make a decisive difference, and U.S. units did not engage in much combat until after the harsh winter of 1917–1918.

The Bolshevik Revolution

The military and diplomatic situation changed dramatically as a result of the Bolshevik Revolution in Russia. In November 1917, the liberal-democratic government of Aleksander Kerensky, which had led the country since the tsar's abdication early in the year, was overthrown by V. I. Lenin's radical socialists. Lenin vowed to change world politics and end imperial rivalries on terms that challenged Wilson's. To Lenin, the war signaled the impending end of capitalism and the rise of a global revolution of workers. For western leaders, the prospect of Bolshevik-style revolutions worldwide was too frightening to contemplate.

In the weeks following their takeover, the Bolsheviks attempted to embarrass the capitalist governments and incite world revolution by publishing several Allied secret agreements for dividing up the colonies and other territories of the Central Powers if Allies were victorious. Wilson confided to Colonel House that he really wanted to tell the Bolsheviks to "go to hell," but he accepted the colonel's argument that he would have to address Lenin's claims that there was little to distinguish the two warring sides and that socialism represented the future.

Fourteen Points

In the Fourteen Points, unveiled in January 1918, Wilson reaffirmed America's commitment to an international system governed by laws and renounced territorial gains as a legitimate war aim. The first five points called for diplomacy "in the public view," freedom of the seas, lower tariffs, armament reductions, and the decolonization of empires. The next eight points specified the evacuation of foreign troops from Russia, Belgium, and France and appealed for self-determination for nationalities in Europe, such as the Poles. For Wilson, the fourteenth point was the mechanism for achieving the others: "a general association of nations," or League of Nations.

Lenin was unimpressed and called for an immediate end to the fighting, the eradication of colonialism, and self-determination for all peoples. Lenin also made a separate peace with Germany—the Treaty of Brest-Litovsk, signed on March 3, 1918. The deal erased centuries of Russian expansion, as Poland, Finland, and the Baltic states were taken from Russia and Ukraine was granted independence. One of Lenin's motives was to allow Russian troops loyal to the Bolsheviks to return home to fight anti-Bolshevik forces attempting to oust his government.

Americans in Battle

In March 1918, the Germans launched a major offensive, and by May they were within 50 miles of Paris. U.S. First Division troops helped blunt the German advance at Cantigny (see Map 23.1). In June the Third Division and French forces held positions along the Marne River at Château-Thierry, and the Second Division attacked the Germans in the Belleau Wood. U.S. soldiers won the battle after three weeks, but thousands died or were wounded in sacrificial frontal assaults against German machine guns.

Allied victory in the Second Battle of the Marne in July 1918 stemmed German advances. In September, French and American forces took St. Mihiel in a ferocious battle. Then, in the Meuse-Argonne offensive, over 1 million Americans joined British and French troops in weeks of combat; some 25,000 Americans died before

Map 23.1   American Troops at the Western Front, 1918

America's 2 million troops in France met German forces head-on, ensuring the defeat of the Central Powers in 1918.

the Allies claimed the Argonne Forest on October 10. For Germany—its ground and submarine war stymied, its troops and cities mutinous, its allies Turkey and Austria dropping out, its Kaiser abdicating—peace became imperative. The Germans accepted a punishing armistice effective November 11, 1918.

Casualties

The cost of the war is impossible to compute: the belligerents counted 10 million soldiers and 6.6 million civilians dead and 21.3 million people wounded. Fifty-three thousand American soldiers died in battle and another 62,000 from disease, mainly a virulent strain of influenza that ravaged the world in late 1918. Economic damage was colossal, and output dwindled, contributing to widespread starvation in Europe in the winter of 1918–1919.

The German, Austro-Hungarian, Ottoman, and Russian empires were gone. For a time it appeared the Bolshevik Revolution might spread westward, as communist

The Influenza Pandemic of 1918

In summer and fall 1918, a terrible influenza outbreak swept the earth. It claimed more than twice as many lives as the Great War, between 25 and 40 million people. In the United States, 675,000 people died.

The first cases were identified in midwestern military camps in early March. At Fort Riley, Kansas, forty-eight men died. Soldiers shipped out to Europe in large numbers (84,000 in March), some unknowingly carrying the virus. The illness appeared on the western front in April. By June, an estimated 8 million Spaniards were infected, giving the disease its name, the Spanish flu.

In August, a second, deadlier form of the influenza erupted simultaneously in three cities on three continents: Freetown, Sierra Leone; Brest, France; and Boston, Massachusetts. In September, the disease swept down the East Coast, killing twelve thousand Americans.

People could be healthy at the start of the weekend and dead by the end of it. Some experienced a rapid accumulation of fluid in the lungs and literally drowned. Others died slowly. Mortality rates were highest for twenty- to twenty-nine-year-olds—the same group as those dying in the trenches.

In October, the epidemic hit full force, spreading to Japan, India, Africa, and Latin America. In the United States, 200,000 perished. There was a nationwide shortage of caskets and gravediggers, and funerals were limited to fifteen minutes. Bodies were left in gutters or on front porches, to be picked up by trucks that drove the streets.

Suddenly, in November, for reasons still unclear, the epidemic eased, though the dying continued into 1919. In England and Wales, the final toll was 200,000, while in India the epidemic may have claimed 20 million. It was, in the historian Roy Porter's words, "the greatest single demographic shock mankind has ever experienced." World War I had helped spread the disease. Americans, accustomed to thinking that two great oceans isolated them, were reminded that they were immutably linked to the rest of humankind.

The influenza pandemic of 1918 perhaps started in earnest here, at Camp Funston, Kansas, in the spring of that year. Soldiers were struck with a debilitating illness they called "knock me down fever."

(National Museum of Health and Medicine, Armed Forces Institute of Pathology) uprisings shook Germany and parts of central Europe. Before the armistice, revolutionaries temporarily took power in the German cities of Bremen, Hamburg, and Lübeck. In Moscow, meanwhile, the new Soviet state sought to consolidate its power.

MOBILIZING THE HOME FRONT

The war had a tremendous impact on America. The federal government expanded its power over the economy to meet war needs and intervened in American life as never before. The enlarged Washington bureaucracy managed the economy, labor force, military, and public opinion. The government spent more than $760 million a month from April 1917 to August 1919. As tax revenues lagged, the administration resorted to deficit spending (see Figure 23.1). To Progressives of the New Nationalist persuasion, the wartime expansion and centralization of government power were welcome, but others worried about the dangers of concentrated federal power.

Business-Government Cooperation

The federal government and private business became partners during the war. Early on, the government relied on industrial committees for advice on purchases and prices. But evidence of self-interested businesspeople cashing in on the national interest aroused public protest. The head of the aluminum advisory committee, for example, was also president of the largest aluminum company. Consequently, the committees were replaced in July 1917 with a single manager, the War Industries Board. The

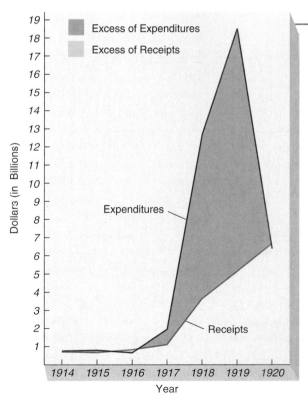

Figure 23.1   The Federal Budget, 1914–1920

During World War I, the federal government spent more money than it received from increased taxes. It borrowed from banks or sold bonds through Liberty Loan drives. To meet the mounting costs of the war, in other words, the federal government had to resort to deficit spending. Expenditures topped receipts by more than $13 billion in 1919. Given this wartime fiscal pattern, moreover, the U.S. federal debt rose from $1 billion in 1914 to $25 billion in 1919. (*Source:* U.S. Department of Commerce, *Historical Statistics of the United States: Colonial Times to 1957* [Washington, DC: Bureau of the Census, 1960], 711.)

government also suspended antitrust laws and signed cost-plus contracts, guaranteeing companies healthy profits and a means to head off labor strikes with higher wages. Competitive bidding was virtually abandoned, and big business grew bigger.

Hundreds of new government agencies, staffed primarily by businesspeople, used economic controls to shift the nation's resources to the Allies, the AEF, and war-related production. The Food Administration, led by the engineer and investor Herbert Hoover, urged Americans to grow victory gardens and eat meatless meals on Mondays and wheatless meals on Wednesdays. It also regulated prices and distribution. The Railroad Administration took over the railway industry. The Fuel Administration controlled coal supplies and rationed gasoline. When strikes threatened the telephone and telegraph companies, the federal government seized and ran them.

The largest of the superagencies was the War Industries Board (WIB), headed by the financier Bernard Baruch. This Wall Streeter told Henry Ford that he would dispatch the military to seize his plants unless the automaker accepted WIB limits on car production. Designed as a clearing-house to coordinate the national economy, the WIB made purchases, allocated supplies, and fixed prices at levels that business requested. The WIB also ordered the standardization of goods to streamline production. The varieties of automobile tires, for example, were reduced from 287 to 3.

Economic Performance   About one-quarter of American production was diverted to war needs. As farmers enjoyed boom years, they put more acreage into production and mechanized. Gross farm income from 1914 to 1919 increased more than 230 percent. Although manufacturing output leveled off in 1918, wartime demand fueled substantial growth for industries such as steel, which reached peak production of 45 million tons in 1917, twice the prewar figure. Overall, the gross national product in 1920 stood 237 percent higher than in 1914.

Mistakes happened in the rush to production. Weapons deliveries fell short, and the bloated bureaucracy of the War Shipping Board failed to build enough ships. In the severe winter of 1917–1918, coal companies reduced production to raise prices; railroads did not have enough coal cars; and harbors froze, closing out coal barges. People died from pneumonia and freezing. To pay its wartime bills, the government hiked taxes. The Revenue Act in 1916 started by raising the surtax on high incomes and corporate profits, imposing a federal tax on large estates, and significantly increasing the tax on munitions manufacturers. Still, taxation financed only one-third of the war. The other two-thirds came from loans, including Liberty bonds sold to the American people. The War Revenue Act of 1917 provided a steeply graduated personal income tax, a corporate income tax, an excess-profits tax, and increased excise taxes on alcoholic beverages, tobacco, and luxury items.

Although taxes curbed excessive corporate profiteering, there were loopholes. Sometimes companies inflated costs to conceal profits. Corporate net earnings for 1913 totaled $4 billion; in 1917 they reached $7 billion; and in 1918, after the tax bite and the war's end, they still stood at $4.5 billion. The abrupt cancellation of billions of dollars' worth of contracts at war's end, however, caused a brief downturn, a short boom, and then an intense decline (see Chapter 24).

Labor Shortage

For American workers, the full-employment wartime economy increased earnings. With the higher cost of living, however, workers saw minimal improvement. Turnover rates escalated as workers switched jobs for better pay and conditions. Some employers sought to overcome labor shortages by expanding welfare and social programs and establishing personnel departments.

To meet the labor crisis, the Department of Labor's U.S. Employment Service matched laborers with job vacancies, attracting workers from the South and Midwest to war industries in the East. The department also temporarily relaxed the literacy-test and head-tax provisions of immigration law to attract farm labor, miners, and railroad workers from Mexico. As workers crammed into cities, the U.S. Housing Corporation and Emergency Fleet Corporation built row houses in Newport News, Virginia, and Eddystone, Pennsylvania.

The tight wartime labor market meant new job opportunities for women. In Connecticut, a special motion picture, *Mr. and Mrs. Hines of Stamford Do Their Bit,* appealed to housewives' patriotism, urging them to take factory jobs. Although the total number of women in the work force increased slightly, the real story was that many moved into formerly male jobs. Some white women left domestic service for factories, shifted from clerking in department stores to stenography and typing, or departed textile mills for firearms plants. At least 20 percent of employees in the wartime electrical-machinery, airplane, and food industries were women. For the first time, department stores employed African American women as elevator operators and cafeteria waitresses. But most working women were single and remained in the sex-segregated occupations of typists, nurses, teachers, and domestic servants.

Women also participated in the war effort as volunteers, making clothing for refugees and soldiers, serving at Red Cross facilities, and teaching French to nurses assigned to the war zone. Many worked for the Women's Committee of the Council of National Defense, a network of state and local organizations publicizing government mobilization programs, encouraging home gardens, sponsoring drives to sell Liberty bonds, and promoting social welfare reforms. This patriotic work improved prospects for passing the Nineteenth Amendment granting woman suffrage. "We have made partners of women in this war," Wilson said as he endorsed woman suffrage in 1918. "Shall we admit them only to a partnership of suffering and sacrifice . . . and not to a partnership of privilege and right?"

War mobilization encouraged a great migration of southern African Americans to northern cities to work in railroad yards, packing houses, steel mills, shipyards, and coal mines. Between 1910 and 1920, Cleveland's African American population swelled by more than 300 percent, Detroit's by more than 600 percent, and Chicago's by 150 percent. All told, about a half-million African Americans moved to the North, with families pooling savings or selling household goods to fund the journey. Most migrants were unmarried and skilled or semiskilled males in their early twenties. Northern wartime jobs provided an escape from low wages, sharecropping, tenancy, crop liens, debt peonage, lynching, and political disfranchisement. One African American wrote to a friend in Mississippi: "I just begin to feel like a man. . . . I don't have to humble to no one. . . . Will vote the next election."

National War Labor Board

To keep factories running smoothly, Wilson instituted the National War Labor Board (NWLB) in early 1918. The NWLB discouraged strikes and lockouts and urged management to negotiate with existing unions. In July, after the Western Union Company fired eight hundred union members for trying to organize the firm's workers, the president nationalized the telegraph lines and put the laborers back to work. But in September the NWLB ordered striking Bridgeport, Connecticut, machinists back to munitions factories, threatening to revoke the draft exemptions they received for working in an essential industry.

Labor leaders hoped the war would lead to recognition and better pay through partnership with government. Samuel Gompers threw the AFL's loyalty to Wilson, promising to deter strikes. He and other moderate labor leaders accepted appointments to federal agencies. The antiwar Socialist Party blasted the AFL for becoming a "fifth wheel on [the] capitalist war chariot," but union membership climbed from roughly 2.5 million in 1916 to more than 4 million in 1919.

The AFL, however, could not curb strikes by the radical Industrial Workers of the World (IWW, also known as Wobblies) or rebellious AFL locals, especially those controlled by socialists. In the nineteen war months, more than six thousand strikes expressed workers' demands for a living wage and improved working conditions. Unions sought to create industrial democracy, a more representative workplace with labor helping to determine job categories and content. Defying the AFL, labor parties had sprung up in twenty-three states by 1920.

CIVIL LIBERTIES UNDER CHALLENGE

Wilson and his advisers enjoyed the support of newspapers, religious leaders, and public officials. They were less certain, however, about ordinary Americans. An official and unofficial campaign soon began to silence dissenters who questioned Wilson's decision for war or who protested the draft. The Wilson administration compiled one of the worst civil liberties records in American history.

The targets of government and quasi-vigilante repression included hundreds of thousands of Americans and aliens; pacifists, conscientious objectors, socialists, radical labor groups, the debt-ridden Oklahoma tenant farmers who staged the Green Corn Rebellion against the draft, the Non-Partisan League, reformers like Robert La Follette and Jane Addams, and others. In the wartime debate over democratic free speech, the concept of civil liberties emerged for the first time as a major public policy issue (see Legacy for a People and a Nation, page 623).

The Committee on Public Information

Spearheading the administration's war campaign was the Committee on Public Information (CPI), formed in April 1917 and headed by the Progressive journalist George Creel. Employing talented writers and scholars, the CPI used propaganda to mobilize public opinion. Pamphlets and films demonized the Germans, and CPI *rude!* "Four-Minute Men" spoke at movie theaters, schools, and churches to pump up patriotism. Encouraged by the CPI, film companies and the National Association of the Motion Picture Industry produced documentaries, newsreels, and anti-German movies, such as The Kaiser, the Beast of Berlin (1918).

The committee also urged the press to practice self-censorship and encouraged people to spy on neighbors. Ultrapatriotic groups, such as the Sedition Slammers and the American Defense Society, used vigilantism. In Hilger, Montana, citizens burned history texts mentioning Germany. To avoid trouble, the Kaiser-Kuhn grocery in St. Louis changed its name to Pioneer Grocery. The townspeople in Berlin, Iowa, henceforth hailed from Lincoln. The German shepherd became the Alsatian shepherd.

what ?!

Towns had Liberty Loan quotas and sometimes bullied slackers into purchasing bonds. Nativist advocates of "100% Americanism" exploited the atmosphere to exhort immigrants to throw off their Old World cultures. Companies offered English language and naturalization classes and refused jobs and promotions to those who did not learn English. Even institutions that had long prided themselves on tolerance became contaminated. Wellesley College economics professor Emily Greene Balch was fired for her pacifist views (she won the Nobel Peace Prize in 1946). Three Columbia University students were apprehended in mid-1917 for circulating an antiwar petition. Columbia fired Professor J. M. Cattell, a distinguished psychologist, for his antiwar stand. His colleague Charles Beard, a historian with a prowar perspective, resigned in protest. Local school boards also dismissed teachers who questioned the war.

that is just wrong!

Espionage and Sedition Acts

The Wilson administration guided through an obliging Congress the Espionage Act (1917) and the Sedition Act (1918), giving the government wide latitude to crack down on critics. The first statute forbade "false statements" designed to impede the draft or promote military insubordination, and it banned from the mails materials considered treasonous. The Sedition Act made it unlawful to obstruct the sale of war bonds and to use "disloyal, profane, scurrilous, or abusive" language to describe the government, the Constitution, the flag, or the military uniform. More than two thousand people were prosecuted under the acts, with many others intimidated into silence.

that is against freedom of speech!

Progressives and conservatives used the war emergency to throttle the Industrial Workers of the World and the Socialist Party. Government agents raided IWW meetings, and the army put down IWW strikes. By war's end, most of the union's leaders were in jail. In summer 1918, the Socialist Party leader Eugene V. Debs was arrested by federal agents for an oration extolling socialism and freedom of speech—including the freedom to criticize Wilson on the war. Debs told the court what many thought of the Espionage Act: it was "a despotic enactment in flagrant conflict with democratic principles and with the spirit of free institutions." Handed a ten-year sentence, Debs remained in prison until he was pardoned in late 1921.

Yes!

good

The Supreme Court endorsed such convictions. In *Schenck v. U.S.* (1919), the Court upheld the conviction of a Socialist Party member who mailed pamphlets urging draft resistance. In wartime, Justice Oliver Wendell Holmes wrote, the First Amendment could be restricted when words "are of such a nature as to create a clear and present danger that they will bring about the substantial evils that Congress has a right to prevent."

what!

RED SCARE, RED SUMMER

The line between wartime suppression of dissent and the postwar Red Scare is not easily drawn. Together they stabbed at the Bill of Rights and wounded radicalism in America. But while wartime fears focused on subversion, after the armistice it was revolution; and while the prewar target was often German Americans, in 1919 it was frequently organized labor. Alarmed by the Russian Revolution and the communist uprisings in Europe, American fears grew in 1919 when the Soviet leadership formed the Communist International (or Comintern) to export revolution worldwide. Terrified conservatives sought out pro-Bolshevik sympathizers (or Reds, from the red flag used by communists) in the United States, especially in immigrant groups and labor unions.

Labor Strikes

Labor union leaders emerged out of the war determined to secure higher wages and retain wartime bargaining rights. Employers instead rescinded benefits they were forced to grant during the war, including recognition of unions. The result was more than 3,300 strikes involving 4 million laborers in 1919. On May 1, a day of celebration for workers worldwide, bombs were sent to prominent Americans, though most were intercepted and dismantled. Police never captured the conspirators, but many blamed anarchists and others bent on destroying the American way of life. When the Boston police went on strike in September, some claimed a Bolshevik conspiracy, but others thought it ridiculous to label Boston's Irish American, Catholic cops radicals.

Unrest in the steel industry in September stirred more ominous fears. Many steelworkers worked twelve hours a day, seven days a week, and lived in squalid housing, counting on the National Committee for Organizing Iron and Steel Workers to improve their lives. When postwar unemployment in the industry climbed and the U.S. Steel Corporation refused to meet with committee representatives, some 350,000 workers walked off the job, demanding the right to collective bargaining, a shorter workday, and a living wage. The steel barons hired strikebreakers and sent agents to club strikers. The strike collapsed in early 1920.

Political and business leaders dismissed the steel strike as a foreign threat orchestrated by American radicals. There was no conspiracy, and the American left was badly splintered. Two defectors from the Socialist Party, John Reed and Benjamin Gitlow, founded the Communist Labor Party in 1919. The rival Communist Party of the United States of America, composed largely of aliens, was launched the same year. But their combined membership did not exceed seventy thousand, and in 1919 the harassed Socialist Party could muster barely thirty thousand members.

American Legion

Although divisiveness signified radicals' weakness, Progressives and conservatives interpreted the rise of new parties as strengthening the radical menace. Organized in May 1919 to lobby for veterans' benefits, the American Legion soon preached an antiradicalism that fueled the Red Scare. By 1920, 843,000 Legion members, mostly middle- and upper-class, embraced an impassioned Americanism demanding conformity.

Wilson's attorney general, A. Mitchell Palmer, also insisted that Americans think alike. A Progressive reformer, Quaker, and ambitious politician, Palmer appointed J. Edgar Hoover to head the Radical Division of the Department of Justice. Hoover compiled index cards naming allegedly radical individuals and organizations. During 1919, agents jailed IWW members; Palmer made sure that 249 alien radicals, including anarchist Emma Goldman, were deported to Russia.

States passed peacetime sedition acts and arrested hundreds of people. Vigilante groups and mobs flourished once again, their numbers swelled by returning veterans. In November 1919, in Centralia, Washington, American Legionnaires broke from a parade to storm the IWW hall. Several were wounded, others were arrested, and one ex-soldier was taken from jail by a mob, then beaten, castrated, and shot. The New York State legislature expelled five elected Socialist Party members in early 1920.

Palmer Raids

The Red Scare reached a climax in January 1920 in the Palmer Raids. Planned and directed by J. Edgar Hoover, government agents in thirty-three cities broke into meeting halls and homes without search warrants, jailing four thousand people without counsel. In Boston some four hundred people were detained on bitterly cold Deer Island; two died of pneumonia, one leaped to his death, and another went insane. Because of court rulings and the courageous efforts of Assistant Secretary of Labor Louis Post, most of the arrestees were released, although in 1920–1921 nearly six hundred were deported.

Palmer's disregard for elementary civil liberties drew criticism, with many charging that his tactics violated the Constitution. When Palmer called for a peacetime sedition act, he alarmed both liberal and conservative leaders. His dire prediction that pro-Soviet radicals would incite violence on May Day 1920 proved mistaken; no disturbances occurred anywhere. Palmer, who called himself the Fighting Quaker, was jeered as the Quaking Fighter.

Racial Unrest

Palmer also blamed communists for the racial violence that gripped the nation, though the charge was equally baseless. African Americans realized well before the war ended that their participation did little to change discriminatory white attitudes. The Ku Klux Klan was reviving, and racist films like D. W. Griffith's *The Birth of a Nation* (1915) fed prejudice with its celebration of the Klan and its demeaning depiction of blacks. Despite wartime declarations of humanity, between 1914 and 1920, 382 blacks were lynched, some of them in military uniform.

Northern whites who resented "the Negro invasion" rioted, as in East St. Louis, Illinois, in July 1917 and a month later in Houston. During the bloody Red Summer of 1919 (so named by African American author James Weldon Johnson for the blood that was spilled), race riots rocked two dozen cities and towns. The worst violence occurred in Chicago, a favorite destination for migrating African Americans. In the very hot days of July 1919, an African American youth swimming at a segregated white beach was hit by a thrown rock and drowned. Soon African Americans and whites were battling each other. Stabbings, burnings, and shootings continued for days until state police restored some calm. Thirty-eight people died, twenty-three African Americans and fifteen whites.

A disillusioned W. E. B. Du Bois vowed a struggle: "We return from fighting. We return fighting." Or, as the poet Claude McKay put it after the Chicago riot in his poem "If We Must Die,"

> Like men we'll face the murderous cowardly pack.
> Pressed to the wall, dying, but fighting back.

African American Militancy

Du Bois and McKay reflected a newfound militancy among African American veterans and northern African American communities. Editorials in African American newspapers subjected white politicians to increasingly harsh criticism and implored readers to embrace their own prowess and beauty. The NAACP stepped up its campaign for civil rights and equality, vowing in 1919 to publicize the terrors of lynching and seek legislation against it. Other blacks, doubting the potential for equality, turned instead to the charismatic Jamaican immigrant Marcus Garvey, who called on African Americans to seek a separate black nation.

The crackdown on laborers and radicals and the resurgence of racism in 1919 dashed wartime hopes. Although the passage of the Nineteenth Amendment in 1920, guaranteeing women the right to vote, showed that reform could happen, it was the exception. Unemployment, inflation, racial conflict, labor upheaval, and a campaign against free speech inspired disillusionment in the immediate postwar years.

THE DEFEAT OF PEACE

President Wilson seemed focused on confronting the threat of radicalism more abroad than at home. In mid-1918, Wilson revealed his ardent anti-Bolshevism when he ordered five thousand American troops to northern Russia and ten thousand more to Siberia, where they joined other Allied contingents in fighting what was now a Russian civil war. Wilson did not consult Congress. He said the military expeditions would guard Allied supplies and Russian railroads from German seizure, and would also rescue Czechs who wished to fight the Germans.

Seeking to smash the infant Bolshevik government, Wilson backed an economic blockade of Russia, sent arms to anti-Bolshevik forces, and refused to recognize Lenin's government. The United States also secretly passed military information to anti-Bolshevik forces and used food relief to shore up Soviet opponents in the Baltic region. Later, at the Paris Peace Conference, Soviets were denied a seat. U.S. troops did not leave Russia until spring 1920, after the Bolsheviks demonstrated their staying power.

Wilson faced a monumental task in securing a postwar settlement, though some observers suggested that he underestimated his task. During the 1918 congressional elections, Wilson misstepped in suggesting that patriotism required the election of a Democratic Congress; Republicans blasted the president for questioning their love of country and gained control of both houses. This created problems because a peace treaty would require approval from a potentially hostile Senate and because the election results at home diminished Wilson's stature before foreign leaders. Wilson aggravated his political problems by not naming a senator to his advisory

American Peace Commission and refusing to take any prominent Republicans with him to, or to consult with the Senate Foreign Relations Committee before, the Paris Peace Conference.

Wilson was greeted by adoring crowds in Paris, London, and Rome, but their leaders—Georges Clemenceau of France, David Lloyd George of Britain, and Vittorio Orlando of Italy (with Wilson, the Big Four)—became formidable adversaries. After four years of horrible war, the Allies were not going to be cheated out of the fruits of victory. The late-arriving Americans had not suffered the way the peoples of France and Great Britain had. Germany would have to pay big for the calamity it caused.

Paris Peace Conference

The Big Four tried to work out an agreement, mostly behind closed doors. The victors demanded that Germany (which had been excluded from the proceedings) pay a huge reparations bill. Wilson instead called for a small indemnity, fearing that an economically hobbled Germany might turn to Bolshevism. Unable to moderate the Allied position, the president reluctantly agreed to a clause blaming the war on Germany and to the creation of a commission to determine reparations (later set at $33 billion). Wilson acknowledged that the peace terms were hard, but he also came to believe that "the German people must be made to hate war."

As for dismantling empires and the principle of self-determination, Wilson could only achieve some of his goals. Creating a League-administered mandate system, Japan gained authority over Germany's Pacific colonies, while the French obtained what became Lebanon and Syria and the British received the three former Ottoman provinces that became Iraq. Britain also secured Palestine, on the condition that it promote "the establishment in Palestine of a national home for the Jewish people" without prejudice to "the civil and religious rights of existing non-Jewish communities"—the so-called Balfour Declaration of 1917.

Elsewhere in Europe, Wilson's prescriptions fared better. Out of Austria-Hungary and Russia came the newly independent states of Austria, Hungary, Yugoslavia, Czechoslovakia, and Poland. Wilson and his colleagues also built a *cordon sanitaire* (buffer zone) of new westward-looking nations (Finland, Estonia, Latvia, and Lithuania) around Russia, to quarantine the Bolshevik contagion.

League of Nations and Article 10

Wilson worked hardest on the charter for the League of Nations, the centerpiece of his plans for the postwar world. He envisioned the League as having power over all disputes among states; as such, it could transform international relations. Even so, the great powers would have preponderant say: the organization would have an influential council of five permanent members and elected delegates from smaller states, an assembly of all members, and a World Court.

Wilson identified Article 10 as the "kingpin" of the League covenant: "The Members of the League undertake to respect and preserve as against external aggression the territorial integrity and existing political independence of all Members of the League." Wilson insisted that there could be no future peace with Germany without a league to oversee it.

German representatives at first refused to sign the punitive treaty but submitted in June 1919. They gave up 13 percent of Germany's territory, 10 percent of its population, all of its colonies, and a huge portion of its national wealth. Many people wondered how the League could function in the poisoned postwar atmosphere of humiliation and revenge.

Critics of the Treaty

In March 1919, thirty-nine senators (enough to deny the treaty the necessary two-thirds vote) signed a petition stating that the League's structure did not adequately protect U.S. interests. Wilson denounced his critics as having pygmy minds, but persuaded the peace conference to exempt the Monroe Doctrine and domestic matters from League jurisdiction. Wilson would budge no more. Could his critics not see that League membership would give the United States leadership in the world?

By summer, criticism intensified: Wilson had bastardized his own principles. He conceded Shandong to Japan and killed a provision affirming the racial equality of all peoples. The treaty ignored freedom of the seas, and tariffs were not reduced. Reparations promised to be punishing on Germany. Critics on the left protested that the League would perpetuate empire. Conservative critics feared that the League would limit American freedom of action in world affairs, stymie U.S. expansion, and intrude on domestic questions. And Article 10 raised serious questions: Would the United States be *obligated* to use armed force to ensure collective security? And would the League feel compelled to crush colonial rebellions, such as in Ireland or India?

Henry Cabot Lodge of Massachusetts led the Senate opposition. A Harvard-educated Ph.D. and partisan Republican who intensely disliked Wilson, Lodge packed the Foreign Relations Committee with critics and introduced several reservations to the treaty, most importantly that Congress had to approve any obligation under Article 10.

In September 1919 Wilson embarked on a speaking tour of the United States. Growing more exhausted, he dismissed antagonists as "contemptible quitters." While doubts about Article 10 multiplied, Wilson highlighted neglected features of the League charter—such as the arbitration of disputes and an international conference to abolish child labor. In Colorado, the president awoke to nausea and uncontrollable facial twitching. A few days later, he suffered a massive stroke that paralyzed his left side. He became peevish and more stubborn, increasingly unable to conduct presidential business. Advised to placate Lodge and other senatorial critics so the Versailles treaty might receive Congressional approval, Wilson rejected "dishonorable compromise."

Senate Rejection of the Treaty and League

Twice in November the Senate rejected the Treaty of Versailles and thus U.S. membership in the League. In March 1920 the Senate again voted; this time, a majority (49 for and 35 against) favored the treaty with reservations, but the tally fell short of the two-thirds needed. Had Wilson permitted Democrats to compromise—to accept reservations—he could have achieved his goal of membership in the League, which, despite the U.S. absence, came into being.

At the core of the debate lay a basic foreign policy issue: whether the United States would endorse collective security or continue the more solitary path articulated in George Washington's Farewell Address and the Monroe Doctrine. In a world dominated by imperialist states unwilling to subordinate their strategic ambitions to an international organization, Americans preferred their traditional nonalignment and freedom of choice over binding commitments to collective action. Wilson countered that the League promised something better than the status quo for the United States and the world: collective security in place of the frail protection of alliances and the instability of a balance of power.

An Unsafe World

World War I did not make the world safe for democracy, but it did make the United States an even greater world power. By 1920 the United States was the world's leading economic power, producing 40 percent of its coal, 70 percent of its petroleum, and half of its pig iron. It also ranked first in world trade. American companies used the war to nudge Germans and British out of foreign markets, especially in Latin America. Meanwhile, the United States shifted from a debtor to a creditor nation, becoming the world's leading banker.

After the disappointment of Versailles, the peace movement revitalized, and the military became more professional. The Reserve Officers Training Corps (ROTC) became permanent; military colleges provided upper-echelon training; and the Army Industrial College, founded in 1924, pursued business-military cooperation in logistics and planning. The National Research Council, created in 1916 with government money and Carnegie and Rockefeller funds, continued a defense research alliance. Tanks, quick-firing guns, armor-piercing explosives, and oxygen masks for high-altitude-flying pilots were among the technological advances emerging from World War I.

The international system born in these years was unstable. Nationalist leaders active during World War I, such as Ho Chi Minh of Indochina and Mohandas K. Gandhi of India, vowed independence for their people. Communism became a disruptive force in world politics, and the Soviets bore a grudge against those who tried to thwart their revolution. The new states in central and eastern Europe proved weak. Germans bitterly resented the harsh peace settlement, and German war debts and reparations problems dogged international order for years.

Summary

The war years marked the emergence of the United States as a world power, and Americans could take justifiable pride in their contribution to the Allied victory. But the war exposed deep divisions among Americans: white versus African American, nativist versus immigrant, capital versus labor, men versus women, radical versus Progressive and conservative, pacifist versus interventionist, and nationalist versus internationalist.

During the war, the federal government intervened in the economy and influenced people's everyday lives as never before. Although the Wilson administration shunned reconversion plans (war housing projects, for example, were sold to private

Freedom of Speech and the ACLU

Before World War I, those with radical views often received harsh treatment for exercising their freedom of speech. During the war, however, the Wilson administration's suppression of dissidents led some Americans to reformulate the traditional definition of allowable speech. Roger Baldwin, a conscientious objector, and Crystal Eastman, a woman suffrage activist, were among the first to advance the idea that the content of political speech could be separated from the identity of the speaker and that patriotic Americans could—indeed should—defend the right of others to express political beliefs abhorrent to their own. After defending conscientious objectors, Baldwin and Eastman—joined by activists such as Jane Addams, Helen Keller, and Norman Thomas—formed the American Civil Liberties Union (ACLU).

Since 1920 the ACLU, which today has some 300,000 members, has aimed to protect the basic civil liberties of all Americans. It has been involved in almost every major civil liberties case in U.S. courts, among them the landmark Brown v. Board of Education case (1954) which ended federal tolerance of racial segregation. More recently, the ACLU was involved in the 1997 Supreme Court case, ruling that the 1996 Communications Act banning "indecent speech" violated First Amendment rights.

Conservatives have criticized the ACLU for its opposition to official prayers in public schools and its support of legal abortion, as well as its decisions on whose free speech to defend. ACLU proponents countered that it had also defended those on the right, such as Oliver North, a key figure in the 1980s Iran-contra scandal.

Either way, the principle of free speech is today broadly accepted by Americans, so that even ACLU bashers take it for granted. Membership in the ACLU has skyrocketed since the September 11, 2001, terrorist attacks, due to concern about government policies eroding privacy and legal protections for Americans and foreign detainees at Guantánamo Bay. Ironically, the Wilson administration's crackdown on dissent produced an expanded commitment to freedom of speech for a people and a nation.

investors) and quickly dismantled the many government agencies, the World War I experience of the activist state served as guidance for 1930s reformers battling the Great Depression (see Chapter 25). The partnership of government and business in managing the wartime economy advanced the development of a mass society through the standardization of products and the promotion of efficiency. Wilsonian wartime policies also nourished the concentration of corporate ownership by suspending antitrust laws. Business power dominated the next decade, while labor entered lean years.

Although the disillusionment evident after Versailles did not cause the United States to adopt isolationism (see Chapter 26), skepticism about America's ability to right wrongs abroad marked the postwar American mood. People recoiled from photographs of shell-shocked faces and bodies dangling from barbed wire. American soldiers, tired of idealism, craved regular jobs. Many Progressives lost their enthusiasm for crusades, disgusted by the bickering of the victors.

By 1920 idealism faded at home and abroad. Americans were unsure what their country's newfound status as a leading world power meant for the nation. With uneasiness and a mixed legacy from the Great War, the country entered the new era of the 1920s.

Chapter Review

PRECARIOUS NEUTRALITY

How viable was U.S. neutrality during World War I?

President Woodrow Wilson, like most Americans, not only embraced neutrality, he took pride in being one of the few western nations to be free from the war for its first three years. Still, U.S. economic links with Allied nations and Wilson's shared belief with the British that a German victory would spell the end of free enterprise, made pure neutrality less believable to the outside world and less possible. The United States relied on sales to Allied nations to end a recession. It was also difficult to claim U.S. neutrality while banks here made extensive loans to Britain and France. Indirectly, or at least via commerce, the United States had taken sides.

THE DECISION FOR WAR

How did the Zimmerman telegram lead Americans to abandon neutrality?

For months in early 1917, Germany had launched a submarine attack on both warships and commercial vessels regardless of stated neutrality. Americans were already outraged by this when British intelligence passed on to the United States an intercepted telegram in which the German minister in Mexico, Arthur Zimmerman, promised to help Mexico regain the territories it lost to the United States in 1848 if it united with Germany against the United States. Wilson released the telegram to the press, which led many Americans to shed their antiwar position. When several American ships were sunk shortly thereafter, war cries heightened, and Wilson asked Congress to declare war against Germany.

WINNING THE WAR

What was the impact of modern, trench warfare on soldiers?

Aside from an increased risk of casualty or fatality, trench warfare was mentally debilitating. Battles would be fought in zigzag, muddy, vile-smelling trenches fronted by barbed wire and mines across France. Soldiers would charge enemy trenches, often facing machine gun fire or poison gas. Many surviving soldiers suffered a mental illness dubbed "shell shock." Though not labeled as such, its victims faced a kind of post-traumatic stress disorder, with symptoms including a fixed stare, violent tremors, paralyzed limbs, listlessness, jabbering, screaming, and nightmares.

MOBILIZING THE HOME FRONT

How did wartime labor shortages create new opportunities for American workers?

A full employment economy during the war not only meant that workers saw salaries increase (albeit sometimes only slightly ahead of inflation), but they also could easily leave jobs with low salaries or harsh conditions for something better.

Worker shortages also enabled women to move into higher-paying, formerly male jobs, trading domestic service for factories, shifting from clerking in department stores to stenography and typing, or leaving textile mills for firearms plants. Blacks made gains, too, as war mobilization pushed a half million African Americans to migrate to northern cities, leaving behind low-paid sharecropping and tenant farming for better wages in railroad yards, packing houses, steel mills, shipyards, and coal mines.

CIVIL LIBERTIES UNDER CHALLENGE

How did free speech come under fire during World War I and the years that followed?

President Wilson worried about mainstream Americans' feelings regarding the war and the draft and launched a campaign to silence those who disagreed with him. His Committee on Public Information launched propaganda films and pamphlets to mobilize support for the war. Ultrapatriotic groups employed vigilantism, burning textbooks that mentioned Germany or bullying people to buy war bonds. Professors who articulated pacifist views found themselves fired or forced to resign. Labor unions were similarly quashed. Passage of the Espionage Act (1917) and the Sedition Act (1918) empowered the federal government to legally prosecute its critics (nearly 20,000 were prosecuted), while others were intimidated into silence. Federal agents arrested Socialist Party leader Eugene V. Debs when he spoke out about socialism and freedom of speech, including the freedom to criticize Wilson's move to war.

RED SCARE, RED SUMMER

How did the postwar Red Scare dash wartime hopes?

Fears of a communist invasion began shortly after the Bolshevik Revolution and heightened when the Communist Party promised to spread its message worldwide. As membership in both the Socialist and Communist Parties in the United States grew, nationwide crackdowns began against radicals, with labor a particular target. The passage of the nineteenth amendment granting women the right to vote in 1920 provided a glimmer of hope for postwar social improvement, but it was the rare exception. Instead, violations of the Bill of Rights and freedom of speech combined with unemployment, inflation, resurgent racism, and a revitalized Ku Klux Klan to dampen hopes for a more promising postwar America.

THE DEFEAT OF PEACE

What kept the United States out of the League of Nations?

While the League of Nations was Wilson's brainchild, the United States never joined. To Wilson, the League promised a balance of power and solid international allies. But the notion of the League's collectivity was problematic for Americans accustomed to being in world politics. Critics on the left feared that the League would perpetuate empire. Conservative critics worried that it might limit America's freedom to act as it saw fit in world affairs, block U.S. expansion, and intrude on domestic concerns. Worse, critics at home worried about being compelled to participate in collective action deemed necessary by the League.

SUGGESTIONS FOR FURTHER READING

John Milton Cooper Jr., *Breaking the Heart of the World: Woodrow Wilson and the Fight for the League of Nations* (2001)

David S. Foglesong, *America's Secret War Against Bolshevism* (1995)

James B. Grossman, *Land of Hope: Chicago, Black Southerners, and the Great Migration* (1989)

Michael Kazin, *A Godly Hero: The Life of William Jennings Bryan* (2006)

Jennifer D. Keene, *Doughboys, the Great War, and the Remaking of America* (2001)

David M. Kennedy, *Over Here: The Home Front in the First World War* (1980)

Thomas J. Knock, *To End All Wars: Woodrow Wilson and the Quest for a New World Order* (1992)

Margaret Macmillan, *Paris 1919: Six Months That Changed the World* (2002)

John A. Thompson, *Woodrow Wilson* (2002)

Robert H. Zieger, *America's Great War: World War I and the American Experience* (2000)

The New Era | 1920–1929

Beth and Robert Gordon were not compatible marriage partners. Beth was frumpy and demanding; Robert liked to party. One evening at a nightclub, he met Sally Clark, who liked to party, too. When Robert came home smelling of perfume, he and Beth argued, and then subsequently divorced. Soon, however, Robert missed Beth's intellect. Meanwhile, Beth bought new clothes and makeup, becoming a glamorous beauty. The couple coincidentally visited the same summer resort and rekindled their romance. When Robert was injured in an accident, Beth nursed him back to health, much to Sally's disappointment, and in the end, Beth and Robert remarried.

This story is the plot of the 1920 motion picture *Why Change Your Wife?*—one of dozens of films directed by Cecil B. DeMille. DeMille gave audiences what they wanted to see and fantasized about doing. Beth, Robert, and Sally dressed stylishly, went out dancing, listened to phonograph records, rode in cars, and visited resorts. Although DeMille's films and others of the 1920s usually ended by reinforcing marriage, ruling out premarital sex, and supporting the work ethic, they also exuded a new morality. Both male and female characters shed old-style values for the pursuit of luxury, fun, and the trappings of sexual freedom, just as actors such as the stars of *Why Change Your Wife?*—Gloria Swanson and Thomas Meighan—were doing in their off-screen lives. In this way, the film was a harbinger of a new era.

During the 1920s, consumerism flourished. Although poverty beset small farmers, workers in declining industries, and nonwhites in inner cities, most other people enjoyed a high standard of living relative to previous generations. Spurred by advertising and installment buying, Americans acquired radios, automobiles, real estate, and stocks. As in the Gilded Age, the federal government maintained a favorable climate for business.

This icon will direct you to interactive activities and study materials on A People And A Nation, Brief Edition website: **www.cengage.com/history/norton/ peoplenationbrief8e**

Chronology

1920	Volstead Act implements prohibition (Eighteenth Amendment).
	Nineteenth Amendment, legalizing the vote for women in federal elections, is ratified.
	Harding is elected president.
	KDKA transmits the first commercial radio broadcast.
1920–21	Postwar deflation and depression occur.
1921	Federal Highway Act funds the national highway system.
	Emergency Quota Act establishes immigration quotas.
	Sacco and Vanzetti are convicted.
	Sheppard-Towner Act allots funds to states to set up maternity and pediatric clinics.
1922	Economic recovery raises the standards of living.
	Coronado Coal Company v. United Mine Workers rules that strikes could be illegal actions in restraint of trade.
	Bailey v. Drexel Furniture Company voids restrictions on child labor.

	Federal government ends strikes by railroad shop workers and miners.
	Fordney-McCumber Tariff raises rates on imports.
1923	Harding dies; Coolidge assumes the presidency.
	Adkins v. Children's Hospital overturns a minimum wage law affecting women.
1923–24	Government scandals (Teapot Dome) are exposed.
1924	Snyder Act grants citizenship to all Indians not previously citizens.
	National Origins Act revises immigration quotas.
	Coolidge is elected president.
1925	Scopes trial highlights the battle between religious fundamentalists and modernists.
1927	Lindbergh pilots the first solo transatlantic flight.
	Ruth hits sixty home runs.
	The Jazz Singer, the first movie with sound, is released.
1928	Stock market soars.
	Hoover is elected president.
1929	Stock market crashes; the Great Depression begins.

In contrast to the Progressive era, few people worried about abuses of power. Still, state and local governments undertook important reforms.

It was an era in which people embraced new technology while trying to preserve long-held values. New forms of leisure coincided with creativity in the arts and advances in science and technology. Changes in work habits, family responsibilities, and healthcare fostered new uses of time and new attitudes about behavior, including encouragements to "think young." While many people experienced material bounty, others continued to endure hardship. The decade's modernism and materialism were appealing to many but unsettling to those who held tightly to traditional beliefs.

The glitter of consumer culture that dominated DeMille's films blinded Americans to rising debt and uneven prosperity. A devastating depression would bring the era to a close.

- **How did developments in technology and the workplace stimulate social change during the 1920s?**
- **What were the benefits and costs of consumerism, and how did people deal with challenges to old-time values?**
- **What caused the stock market crash and the ensuing deep depression that signaled the end of the era?**

BIG BUSINESS TRIUMPHANT

The 1920s began with economic decline. After World War I, industrial output dropped as wartime orders dried up. In the West, railroads and the mining industry suffered, and layoffs spread through New England as textile companies abandoned outdated factories for the South's convenient raw materials and cheap labor. When demobilized soldiers flooded the work force, unemployment, around 2 percent in 1919, passed 12 percent in 1921. Consumer spending dwindled, causing more contraction and joblessness.

New Economic Expansion

Electric energy prompted a recovery in 1922 that continued unevenly until 1929. Electric motors replaced steam engines, producing goods more cheaply and efficiently. Most urban households now had electric service, enabling them to utilize the new appliances, such as refrigerators and vacuum cleaners. The growing economy gave Americans more spending money for new services, too, such as restaurants, beauty salons, and movie theaters. Installment, or time-payment, plans drove the new consumerism. Of 3.5 million automobiles sold in 1923, 80 percent were bought on credit.

Although Progressive era trustbusting had reined in big business, it had not eliminated oligopoly, the control of an entire industry by one or a few large firms. By the 1920s, a few sprawling companies, such as U.S. Steel and General Electric, dominated basic industries, and oligopolies controlled marketing, distribution, and finance.

Associations and "New Lobbying"

Business and professional organizations also expanded in the 1920s. Retailers and manufacturers formed trade associations to swap information. Farm bureaus promoted scientific agriculture and tried to stabilize markets. These special-interest groups participated in what is called the "new lobbying." With government playing an increasingly influential role, hundreds of organizations sought to convince legislators to support their interests. Government policies helped business thrive, and legislators depended on lobbyists' expertise. Prodded by lobbyists, Congress cut taxes on corporations and wealthy individuals in 1921 and passed the Fordney-McCumber Tariff Act in 1922. Presidents Warren G. Harding, Calvin Coolidge, and Herbert Hoover appointed cabinet officers who were favorable toward business. Regulatory agencies, such as the Federal Trade Commission and the Interstate Commerce Commission, cooperated with corporations more than they regulated them.

Key Supreme Court decisions sheltered business from government regulation and hindered organized labor. In *Coronado Coal Company v. United Mine Workers* (1922), Chief Justice and former president William Howard Taft ruled that a striking union, like a trust, could be prosecuted for illegal restraint of trade. Yet in *Maple Floor Association v. U.S.* (1929), the Court decided that trade associations that distributed anti-union information were not acting in restraint of trade. The Court also voided restrictions on child labor (*Bailey v. Drexel Furniture Company*, 1922), and overturned a minimum wage law affecting women because it infringed on liberty of contract (*Adkins v. Children's Hospital*, 1923).

Setbacks for Organized Labor

Public opinion turned against organized labor in the 1920s, linking it with communism brought to America by radical immigrants. Using Red Scare tactics, the Harding administration in 1922 obtained a sweeping court injunction to quash a strike by 400,000 railroad workers. State and federal courts issued injunctions to prevent other strikes and permitted businesses to sue unions for damages suffered from labor actions.

Some companies imposed yellow dog contracts which made refusal to join a union a condition of employment. Companies also countered the appeal of unions by offering pensions, profit sharing, and company-sponsored picnics and sporting events—a policy known as welfare capitalism. State legislators aided employers by prohibiting closed shops (workplaces where union membership was mandatory) and permitting open shops (where employers could hire nonunion employees). As a result of court action, welfare capitalism, and ineffective leadership, union membership fell from 5.1 million in 1920 to 3.6 million in 1929.

Languishing Agriculture

Agriculture languished during the 1920s, as farmers faced international competition and and went into debt when they tried to increase productivity by investing in new machines, such as harvesters and tractors. Irrigation and mechanization made large-scale farming so efficient that fewer farmers could produce more crops. As a result, crop prices plunged, big agribusinesses took over, and small landholders and tenants struggled when incomes plummeted and debts rose.

POLITICS AND GOVERNMENT

A series of Republican presidents extended Theodore Roosevelt's government-business cooperation, but they made government a compliant coordinator rather than the active manager Roosevelt advocated. President Warren G. Harding, elected in 1920, was a symbol of government's good will toward business. He captured 16 million popular votes to 9 million for the Democratic nominee, Ohio governor James M. Cox. (The total vote in the 1920 presidential election was 36 percent higher than in 1916, reflecting the first-time participation of women voters.)

A small-town newspaperman and senator from Ohio, Harding appointed assistants who promoted business growth, notably Secretary of State Charles Evans Hughes, Secretary of Commerce Herbert Hoover, Secretary of the Treasury Andrew Mellon, and Secretary of Agriculture Henry C. Wallace. Harding also backed reforms such as the Budget and Accounting Act of 1921 to streamline federal spending, and he supported antilynching legislation (rejected by Congress) and bills assisting farm cooperatives and liberalizing farm credit.

Scandals of the Harding Administration

Harding, however, had personal weaknesses, among them his extramarital affairs. In 1917 he began a relationship with Nan Britton, thirty-one years his junior, that resulted in a daughter in 1919. Britton reputedly visited Harding in the White House, although Harding never acknowledged his illegitimate offspring.

Of greater consequence, Harding appointed cronies who used office holding for personal gain. Charles Forbes, head of the Veterans Bureau, went to federal prison, convicted of fraud and bribery in government contracts. Most notoriously, a congressional inquiry in 1923 and 1924 revealed that Secretary of the Interior Albert Fall accepted bribes to lease government property to oil companies. Fall was fined $100,000 and spent a year in jail for his role in the so-called Teapot Dome scandal, named for the Wyoming oil reserve he handed to the Mammoth Oil Company.

By mid-1923, Harding had become disillusioned. On a speaking tour, he became ill and died in San Francisco on August 2. Although his death preceded revelation of the Teapot Dome scandal, some speculated that Harding committed suicide to avoid impeachment or was poisoned by his wife. Most evidence, however, points to death from natural causes, probably heart disease.

Vice President Calvin Coolidge, who became president, was less outgoing than Harding. As governor of Massachusetts, Coolidge had attracted national attention in 1919 with his stand against striking Boston policemen and won business support and the vice-presidential nomination in 1920.

Coolidge Prosperity

Respectful of private enterprise and aided by Andrew Mellon, who was retained as treasury secretary, Coolidge's administration reduced federal debt, lowered income-tax rates (especially for the wealthy), and began construction of a national highway system. With farm prices falling, Congress twice passed bills to establish government-backed price supports for staple crops (the McNary-Haugen bills of 1927 and 1928). Resembling the 1890s Farmers' Alliances subtreasury scheme, these bills would have established a system whereby the government would buy surplus farm products and either hold them until prices rose or sell them abroad. Coolidge, however, vetoed the measures as improper government interference in the market economy.

"Coolidge prosperity" was the decisive issue in the 1924 presidential election. Both major parties ran candidates who favored private initiative over government intervention. At their convention, Democrats voted 542 to 541 against condemning the revived Ku Klux Klan and deadlocked for 103 ballots between southern prohibitionists, who supported former treasury secretary William G. McAdoo, and antiprohibition easterners, who backed New York's governor Alfred E. Smith. They compromised on John W. Davis, a New York corporate lawyer.

Remnants of the Progressive movement, along with farm, labor, and socialist groups, formed a new Progressive Party and nominated Robert M. La Follette, the aging Wisconsin reformer. The new party stressed public ownership of railroads and power plants, conservation of natural resources, aid to farmers, rights for organized labor, and regulation of business. Coolidge beat Davis by 15.7 million to 8.4 million popular votes and 382 to 136 electoral votes. La Follette received 4.8 million popular votes and 13 electoral votes.

Extensions of Progressive Reform

The urgency for political and economic reform that inspired the previous Progressive generation faded in the 1920s. Much reform, however, occurred at state and local levels. Following pre–World War I initiatives, thirty-four states instituted or expanded workers' compensation laws and public welfare programs in the 1920s. By

1926 every major city and many smaller ones had planning and zoning commissions to harness physical growth to the common good. A new generation of reformers who later influenced national affairs acquired valuable experience in statehouses, city halls, and universities.

Indian Affairs and Politics   Organizations such as the Indian Rights Association, the Indian Defense Association, and the General Federation of Women's Clubs worked to obtain justice and social services for Native Americans, including better education and the return of tribal lands. But like other minorities, Indians generally met discrimination and pressure to assimilate. Severalty, the policy created by the Dawes Act of 1887 of allotting land to individuals rather than to tribes, failed to make Indians self-supporting. Deeply attached to their land, they showed little inclination to move to cities. Whites still hoped to convert native peoples into "productive" citizens, typically ignoring indigenous cultures. Reformers were especially critical of Indian women, who refused to adopt middle-class homemaking habits and balked at sending their children to boarding schools.

Citizenship remained unclear. The Dawes Act had conferred citizenship on Indians who accepted land allotments, but not those who remained on reservations. After several court challenges, Congress passed an Indian Citizenship Act (Snyder Act) in 1924, granting citizenship to all Indians. President Hoover reinforced this measure's intent by stating that citizenship was the best means for Indians to assimilate.

Women and Politics   Ratification of the Nineteenth Amendment in 1920 gave women the vote, but they remained excluded from local and national power structures. Instead, they worked through voluntary organizations to lobby legislators on issues such as birth control, peace, education, Indian affairs, or opposition to lynching.

In 1921 women's groups persuaded Congress to pass the Sheppard-Towner Act, allotting funds to states to create maternity and pediatric clinics to reduce infant mortality. (The measure ended in 1929, when Congress, pressured by physicians, canceled funding.) The Cable Act of 1922 reversed the law under which an American woman who married a foreigner assumed her husband's citizenship, allowing her to retain U.S. citizenship. At the state level, women achieved some rights, such as the ability to serve on juries.

As new voters, however, women pursued diverging goals. Women in the National Association of Colored Women, for example, fought for the rights of minorities. Other groups, such as the National Woman's Party, pressed for an equal rights amendment to ensure women's equality under the law. But such activity alienated the National Consumers League, the Women's Trade Union League, the League of Women Voters, and other organizations that supported special protective legislation to limit hours and improve conditions for employed women.

A CONSUMER SOCIETY

The consumerism depicted in *Why Change Your Wife?* reflected important economic changes affecting the nation. Between 1919 and 1929, the gross national product—the total value of all goods and services produced in the United States—swelled by

TABLE 24.1   Consumerism in the 1920s

1900	
2 bicycles	$ 70.00
Wringer and washboard	5.00
Brushes and brooms	5.00
Sewing machine (mechanical)	25.00
Total	$ 05.00
1928	
Automobile	$ 700.00
Radio	75.00
Phonograph	50.00
Washing machine	150.00
Vacuum cleaner	50.00
Sewing machine (electric)	50.00
Other electrical equipment	25.00
Telephone (per year)	35.00
Total	$1,115.00

Source: From an article in *Survey Magazine* in 1928 reprinted in *Another Part of the Twenties,* by Paul Carter. Copyright 1977 by Columbia University Press. Reprinted with permission of the publisher.

40 percent. Wages and salaries also grew (though not as drastically), while the cost of living remained relatively stable. People had more purchasing power (see Table 24.1). By 1929, two-thirds of all Americans had electricity, compared to one-sixth in 1912. In 1929 one-fourth of all families owned vacuum cleaners. Many could afford such goods as radios, beauty products, and movie tickets, because several family members worked or because the breadwinner took a second job. Nevertheless, new products and services were available to more than just the rich.

Effects of the Automobile

During the 1920s, automobile registrations soared from 8 million to 23 million, and by 1929 there was one car for every five Americans. Mass production and competition made cars affordable. A Ford Model T cost less than $300, and a Chevrolet sold for $700 by 1926—when factory workers earned about $1,300 a year and clerical workers about $2,300. At those prices, people could consider the car a necessity rather than a luxury.

Cars altered American life. Streets became cleaner as autos replaced the horses that daily dumped tons of manure. Women who learned to drive achieved newfound independence. By 1927 most autos were enclosed (they previously had open tops), creating new private space for courtship and sex. Most important, the car was the ultimate social equalizer. As one writer observed in 1924, "It is hard to convince Steve Popovich, or Antonio Branca, or plain John Smith that he is being ground into the dust by Capital when at will he may drive the same highways . . . and get as much enjoyment from his trip as the modern Midas."

After World War I, motorists joined farmers and bicyclists in their decades-old campaign for improved roads. In 1921 Congress passed the Federal Highway Act, providing funds for state roads, and in 1923 the Bureau of Public Roads planned a national highway system. Road building inspired such technological developments as mechanized road graders and concrete mixers. The oil-refining industry, which produced gasoline, became vast and powerful. In 1920 the United States produced about 65 percent of the world's oil. Public officials paid more attention to traffic control, with General Electric Company producing the first timed stop-and-go traffic light in 1924.

Advertising

By 1929 more money was spent on advertising than on formal education. Blending psychological theory with practical cynicism, advertising theorists asserted that people's tastes could be manipulated. For example, cosmetics manufacturers like Max Factor, Helena Rubenstein, and African American entrepreneur Madame C. J. Walker used movie stars and beauty advice in magazines to entice female customers. The baseball star Babe Ruth was hired to endorse food and sporting goods.

Radio

Radio became an influential advertising medium. By 1929 over 10 million Americans owned radios, spending $850 million annually on radio equipment. In the early 1920s, Congress decided that broadcasting should be a private enterprise, not a tax-supported public service as in Great Britain. American programming focused on entertainment rather than educational content, because entertainment attracted larger audiences and therefore higher advertising profits. Station KDKA in Pittsburgh, owned by Westinghouse Electric Company, pioneered commercial radio in 1920. In 1922, an AT&T-run station in New York City broadcast advertisements—commercials. Other stations followed; by late 1922 there were 508 commercial stations.

advertisement base newsb business

Radio transformed American society. In 1924, both political parties broadcast their presidential nominating conventions, enabling candidates to reach more Americans. And radio's mass marketing and standardized programming blurred ethnic boundaries and created—at least in one way—a homogeneous American culture, which television and other mass media expanded throughout the twentieth century.

CITIES, MIGRANTS, AND SUBURBS

The 1920 federal census revealed that, for the first time, a majority of Americans lived in urban areas (defined as places with 2,500 or more people). Growth in manufacturing and services helped propel urbanization. Industries like steel, oil, and auto production energized Birmingham, Houston, and Detroit; services and retail trades boosted expansion in Seattle, Atlanta, and Minneapolis.

During the 1920s, 6 million Americans left their farms for the city. Young farm people traded seemingly staid rural life for the flashy openness of cities, relocating to regional centers like Kansas City and Indianapolis or to the West. Between 1920 and 1930, California's population increased 67 percent, and California became a highly urbanized state while retaining its status as a leading agricultural producer.

African American Migration

African Americans, in what is called the Great Migration, made up a sizable portion of people on the move during the 1920s. Pushed from cotton farming by a boll weevil plague and lured by industrial jobs, 1.5 million African Americans moved, doubling the African American populations of New York, Chicago, Detroit, and Houston.

Forced by low wages and discrimination to seek cheap housing, African American newcomers squeezed into low-rent ghettos like Chicago's South Side. The only way to expand their housing opportunities was to spill into nearby white neighborhoods, which sparked resistance and violence. Fears of such invasion prompted neighborhood associations to adopt restrictive covenants, whereby white homeowners pledged not to sell or rent property to African Americans

that is wrong!

Marcus Garvey

In response to discrimination and violence, thousands of urban African Americans joined movements that glorified racial independence. The most influential of these black nationalist groups was the Universal Negro Improvement Association (UNIA), led by Marcus Garvey, a Jamaican immigrant who believed blacks should separate from corrupt white society. His newspaper, *Negro World,* preached black independence, and Garvey promoted black-owned businesses that would manufacture and sell products to black consumers, establishing the Negro Factories Corporation to fund such enterprises. He also founded the Black Star steamship line to transport products among black businesses in North America, the Caribbean and Africa.

promoting segregation

The UNIA declined in the mid-1920s after mismanagement forced dissolution of the Negro Factories Corporation, and Garvey was deported for mail fraud involving the bankrupt Black Star line. His prosecution, however, was politically motivated. Middle-class African American leaders, such as W. E. B. Du Bois, opposed the UNIA, fearing that its extremism would undermine their efforts. The U.S. Bureau of Investigation monitored Garvey's radical activities since 1919, and in 1923 eight prominent African Americans petitioned the attorney general to deport Garvey. Nevertheless, for years the UNIA attracted a large following (contemporaries estimated 500,000; Garvey claimed 6 million), and Garvey's speeches instilled in many African Americans a heightened sense of racial pride.

Newcomers from Mexico and Puerto Rico

The newest immigrants to U.S. cities came from Mexico and Puerto Rico, where declining fortunes pushed people off the land. During the 1910s, Anglo farmers' associations encouraged Mexican immigration to provide cheap agricultural labor, and by the 1920s Mexican migrants constituted three-fourths of farm labor in the U.S. West. Growers treated Mexican laborers as slaves, paying them extremely low wages. Although some achieved middle-class status, most crowded into low-rent districts plagued by poor sanitation, poor police protection, and poor schools. Mexicans moved back and forth across the border, creating a way of life that Mexicans called *sin fronteras*—without borders.

The 1920s also witnessed an influx of Puerto Ricans to the mainland, as a shift in the island's economy from sugar to coffee production created a labor surplus. Attracted by contracts from employers seeking cheap labor, they created *barrios* (communities) and found jobs in factories, hotels, restaurants, and domestic service. Like Mexicans, Puerto Ricans maintained traditional customs and developed businesses—*bodegas* (grocery stores), cafés, boarding houses—and social organizations to help them adapt to American society. Educated elites—doctors, lawyers, and business owners—became community leaders.

Pan American Airways

Air transportation and airmail service between the United States and Latin America began in the 1920s, but anti-American hostility in the region made establishing connections difficult. In 1926 the U.S. government, fearful that German aircraft might bomb the Panama Canal in future conflicts, signed a treaty with Panama giving American airplanes exclusive rights to Panamanian airports. Charles Lindbergh and a formerly obscure pilot, Juan Trippe, played key roles in expanding American air service throughout Latin America

With help from his father-in-law, a banking partner of J. P. Morgan, Trippe established Pan American Airways (informally known as Pan Am) in 1927 and won a contract to carry mail between Florida and Cuba. In December of that year, Lindbergh charmed the Mexicans into accepting airline links to the United States. The next year, Lindbergh joined Pan Am and began flying company planes to Central and South America, helping Trippe initiate mail and passenger service to Panama, Mexico, and other Latin American countries. By 1929 Trippe advertised to wealthy Americans the opportunity to escape prohibition and enjoy Caribbean beaches on Pan Am.

Pan Am built airports that became essential connections between Latin America and the rest of the world. Trippe's employees created aerial maps that provided navigational aids. Pan Am not only linked Latin America with the United States but also helped unite parts of Latin America that were previously divided by impenetrable mountain ranges. Yet Pan Am would resort to almost any tactic to build an airport: it cooperated with unsavory dictators, engaged in bribery, and violated human rights, in one case helping Bolivian police corral local Indians behind barbed wire for days in order to clear a new airport.

Still, Pan Am enabled Americans (mostly the wealthy) to travel abroad and brought more foreigners to the United States. In 1942 its aircraft became the first to fly around the world. In the 1940s, the company began offering flights to Europe and Africa. Until its demise in 1991, Pan Am provided a leading link between the United States and the rest of the world.

Providing air transport connections to the Caribbean, Central America, and South America, Pan American Airways established the first major passenger and cargo links between the United States and other nations. By the early 1930s, flights were so numerous that the timetable announced in this illustration consisted of twelve pages. (The Pan American Heritage Web Site)

Over half a million Mexicans immigrated to the United States during the 1920s. Many of them traveled in families and worked together in the fields and orchards of California and other western states. This family is shown pitting apricots in Los Angeles County in 1924.   (Seaver Center for Western History Research, Natural History Museum of Los Angeles County)

Growth of Suburbs

Prosperity and automobile transportation in the 1920s made suburbs more accessible to those wishing to flee congested urban neighborhoods. Between 1920 and 1930, suburbs of Chicago (such as Oak Park and Evanston), Cleveland (Shaker Heights), and Los Angeles (Burbank and Inglewood) grew five to ten times faster than nearby central cities. Los Angeles builders alone erected 250,000 suburban homes. Most suburbs were middle- and upper-class bedroom communities; some, like Highland Park (near Detroit) were industrial satellites.

Suburbanites wanted to escape big-city crime, grime, and taxes, and they fought to preserve control over their own police, schools, and water and gas services. Particularly in the Northeast and Midwest, the suburbs' independence prevented central cities from accessing the resources and tax bases of wealthier suburban residents. Population dispersal spread the environmental problems of city life—trash, pollution, noise—across the metropolitan area.

Most of the consumers who jammed shops, movie houses, and sporting arenas and who embraced fads like crossword puzzles and miniature golf, lived in or around cities. People defied morals by patronizing speakeasies (illegal saloons during prohibition), wearing outlandish clothes, and dancing to jazz, while others reminisced about the simplicity of a world gone by.

NEW RHYTHMS OF EVERYDAY LIFE

Amid changes, people increasingly split their day into distinct time compartments: work, family, and leisure. For many, mechanization and higher productivity enabled employers to shorten the workweek for many industrial laborers from six days to five and a half. White-collar employees often worked a forty-hour week, enjoyed the weekend off, and received annual vacations.

Family size decreased between 1920 and 1930 as birth control became more widely practiced. Over half the women married in the 1870s and 1880s had five or more children; only 20 percent of their counterparts marrying in the 1920s had that birth pattern. The divorce rate jumped from 1 divorce for every 7.5 marriages in 1920 to 1 in 6 by 1929.

Household Management

Although housework remained time-consuming, machines now lightened some household tasks. Especially in middle-class households, electric irons and washing machines simplified wives' chores. Gas- and oil-powered central heating and hot-water heaters eliminated the hauling of wood, coal, and water; maintaining a kitchen fire; and removing ashes.

But technology and economic change also created new demands on women's time. Daughters of working-class families stayed in school longer, making them less available for housework. The availability of washing machines, hot water, vacuum cleaners, and commercial soap put greater pressure on housewives to keep everything clean. No longer a producer of food and clothing as her ancestors were, a housewife instead became the chief shopper. And the automobile also made her the family's chauffeur. One survey found that urban housewives spent seven and one-half hours per week driving to shop and transport children.

Health and Life Expectancy

Nutrition added a scientific dimension to housewives' responsibilities. With the discovery of vitamins between 1915 and 1930, nutritionists advocated certain foods to prevent illness, and giant companies advertised their products as filled with vitamins and minerals. Producers of milk, canned fruits and vegetables, and other foods made claims that were hard to dispute because little was known about these invisible, tasteless ingredients. Welch's Grape Juice, for example, avoided mentioning its excess sugars when it advertised that it was "Rich in Health Values."

Better diets and improved hygiene made Americans healthier. Life expectancy at birth increased from fifty-four to sixty years between 1920 and 1930, and infant mortality decreased by two-thirds. Public sanitation and research in bacteriology reduced life-threatening diseases such as tuberculosis and diphtheria. But infant mortality rates were 50 to 100 percent higher among nonwhites, and tuberculosis in inner-city slums remained alarmingly common. Nevertheless, the total population over age sixty-five grew 35 percent between 1920 and 1930.

Older Americans and Retirement

Industrialism put premiums on youth and agility, pushing older people into poverty from forced retirement and reduced income. Most European countries established state-supported pension systems in the early 1900s. Many Americans, however, believed that pensions smacked of socialism and that individuals should prepare for old age by saving in their youth.

Most inmates in state poorhouses were older people, and almost one-third of Americans age sixty-five and older depended financially on someone else. Few employers, including the federal government, provided for retired employees. Resistance to pension plans finally broke at the state level in the 1920s. Led by the physician Isaac Max Rubinow and the journalist Abraham Epstein, reformers persuaded voluntary associations, labor unions, and legislators to endorse old-age assistance. By 1933 almost every state provided at least minimal support to the needy elderly, opening the door to a national program of old-age insurance.

Social Values

New influences altered habits and values. Women and men wore more casual and gaily colored styles than their parents' generation. The line between acceptable and inappropriate behavior blurred as smoking, drinking, and frankness about sex became fashionable. Birth control gained a large following in respectable circles. Newspapers, magazines, motion pictures, and popular songs (such as "Hot Lips" and "Burning Kisses") made certain that Americans did not suffer from sex starvation.

Because state child-labor laws and compulsory-attendance rules kept children in school longer, peer groups played a more influential role in socializing youngsters. Graded school classes, sports, and clubs constantly brought together children of the same age, separating them from the company and influence of adults. Meanwhile, parents relied less on traditions of childcare and more on experts who wrote manuals on successful child rearing.

Between 1890 and the mid-1920s, ritualized middle- and upper-class courtship, consisting of men's formally calling on women and chaperoned social engagements, faded in favor of dating without supervision. Employed unmarried young people, living away from family restraints, were eager to go on dates to new commercial amusements, such as movies and nightclubs. Automobiles made dating even more extensive. A woman's job, however, seldom provided sufficient income for entertainments, but she could enjoy them if a man treated her. Companionship, romance, and, at times, sexual exploitation accompanied the practice, especially when a woman was expected to trade sexual favors for being treated. Under the courtship system, a woman controlled who could call on her, but reliance on a man's money for entertainment presented difficult moral choices.

Women in the Work Force

After World War I, women continued to stream into the labor force. By 1930, 10.8 million women held paying jobs, an increase of 2 million since war's end. Although the proportion of women working in agriculture shrank, their proportion in categories of urban jobs grew or held steady (see Figure 24.1). Sex segregation persisted; most women took jobs that men seldom sought. Thus, over 1 million women worked as

Figure 24.1   Changing Dimensions of Paid Female Labor, 1910–1930

These charts reveal the extraordinary growth in clerical and professional occupations among employed women and the accompanying decline in agricultural labor in the early twentieth century. Notice that manufacturing employment peaked in 1920 and that domestic service fluctuated as white immigrant women began to move out of these jobs and were replaced by women of color.

teachers and nurses. Some 2.2 million women were typists, bookkeepers, and filing clerks, a tenfold increase since 1920. Another 736,000 were store clerks, and growing numbers were personal service workers, such as waitresses and hairdressers. Although almost 2 million women worked in manufacturing, their numbers grew little over the decade. Women's wages seldom exceeded half of those paid to men.

Family economic needs were paramount among women's reasons for working. Consumerism tempted working- and middle-class families to live beyond their means or expand their incomes with women's wages. Although the majority of married women did not hold paying jobs (only 12 percent were employed in 1930), married women as a proportion of the work force rose by 30 percent during the 1920s, and the number of employed married women swelled from 1.9 million to 3.1 million.

Employment of Minority Women

The proportion of nonwhite women in paid labor was double that of white women. Often they entered the work force because their husbands were unemployed or underemployed. The majority of employed African American women held domestic jobs doing cooking, cleaning, and laundry. The few who held factory jobs performed the least desirable, lowest-paying tasks. Some opportunities opened for educated African American women in social work, teaching, and nursing, but these women also faced discrimination and low incomes.

Next to African American women, Japanese American women were the most likely to hold paying jobs, similarly working as field hands and domestics, facing racial bias and low pay. Economic necessity also drew thousands of Mexican American women into the labor force, although their tradition resisted female employment. Most worked as domestic servants, operatives in garment factories, and agricultural laborers.

Alternative Images of Femininity

Women remade the image of femininity, casting aside the heavy, floor-length dresses and long hair of previous generations. Instead, many opted for the independence and sexual freedom of the 1920s flapper with her short skirts and bobbed hair. Although few women lived the flapper life, office workers, store clerks, and college coeds adopted the look. As Cecil B. DeMille's movies showed, new female icons included movie temptresses, such as Clara Bow, known as the It Girl, and Gloria Swanson, notorious for torrid love affairs on and off the screen. Many women were asserting a new social equality with men. One observer described the new woman as intriguingly independent.

> She takes a man's point of view as her mother never could. . . . She'll drive you from the station . . . in her own little sports car. . . . She'll dive as well as you, perhaps better, she'll dance as long as you care to, and she'll take everything you say the way you mean it.

Gay and Lesbian Culture

The era's sexual openness enabled the underground homosexual culture to surface somewhat. In nontraditional city neighborhoods, such as New York's Greenwich Village, cheap rents and a relative tolerance attracted gay men and lesbians, who patronized dance halls, speakeasies, and cafés. Still, gay establishments remained targets for police raids, demonstrating that there was little acceptance from the rest of society.

These trends represented a break with the nineteenth century's more restrained culture. But social change rarely proceeds smoothly. As the decade advanced, groups mobilized to defend older values.

LINES OF DEFENSE

Early in 1920, the leader of a newly formed organization hired two public relations experts, Edward Clarke and Elizabeth Tyler. They canvassed the South, Southwest, and Midwest, where they found countless people eager to pay a $10 membership fee and $6 for a white uniform. Clarke and Tyler pocketed $2.50 from each membership and secured 5 million members by 1923.

Ku Klux Klan

This was the Ku Klux Klan, a revived version of the hooded order that terrorized southern communities after the Civil War. The new KKK vowed to protect female, racial, and ethnic purity. As one pamphlet declared, "Every criminal, every gambler, every thug, every libertine, every girl ruiner, every home wrecker, every wife beater, every dope peddler, every moonshiner, every white slaver, every Rome-controlled newspaper, every black spider—is fighting the Klan. . . . Which side are you on?"

Reconstituted in 1915 by William J. Simmons, an Atlanta, Georgia, evangelist and insurance salesman, the Klan adopted the hoods, intimidating tactics, and mystical terminology of its forerunner (its leader was the Imperial Wizard; its book of rituals, the Kloran). But the new Klan fanned outward from the Deep South, wielding power in places as diverse as Oregon, where Portland's mayor was a Klan member, and Indiana, where Klansmen held the governorship and several legislative seats. Members included many from the urban middle class who feared losing social and economic gains and were nervous about a new youth culture that eluded family control.

One phrase summed up Klan goals: "Native, white, Protestant supremacy." *Native* meant no immigration, no mongrelization of American culture. According to Imperial Wizard Hiram Wesley Evans, "The world has been so made so that each race must fight for its life, must conquer, accept slavery, or die." Evans accused the Catholic Church of discouraging assimilation and enslaving people to priests and a foreign pope.

Using threatening assemblies, violence, and political and economic pressure, the Klan meted out vigilante justice to suspected bootleggers, wife beaters, and adulterers; forced schools to stop teaching evolution; campaigned against Catholic and Jewish political candidates; and fueled racial tensions against Mexicans in Texas border cities. Klan women promoted native white Protestantism but also worked for moral reform and prohibition. Because the KKK vowed to protect women's virtue, housewives sometimes appealed to the Klan to punish abusive or irresponsible husbands when legal authorities would not intervene. The Klan's method of justice was flogging.

By 1925, however, scandal undermined the Klan's moral base. Indiana grand dragon David Stephenson was convicted of second-degree murder after he kidnapped and raped a woman who later died. Eventually, the Klan's negative, exclusive brand of patriotism and purity could not compete in a pluralistic society.

Intolerance pervaded American society in the 1920s. Nativists charged that Catholic and Jewish immigrants clogged city slums, flouted community norms, and stubbornly embraced alien religious and political beliefs. Fear of immigrant radicals also fueled the dramatic 1921 trial of two Italian anarchists, Nicola Sacco and Bartolomeo Vanzetti, convicted of murdering a paymaster and guard in Braintree, Massachusetts, though the evidence was flimsy.

Immigration Quotas

Efforts to restrict immigration gathered support. Labor leaders warned that aliens would depress wages and raise unemployment. Business executives, who formerly desired cheap immigrant laborers, now realized that mechanization would keep wages low. Drawing support from such groups, Congress set yearly immigration allocations for each nationality in the Emergency Quota Act of 1921. By restricting annual immigration of a given nationality to 3 percent of the number of immigrants from that nation residing in the United States in 1910, the Act favored Anglo-Saxon Protestant immigrants. It discriminated against Catholics and Jews from southern and eastern Europe, whose numbers were comparatively small in 1910.

In 1924 Congress replaced the Quota Act with the National Origins Act. This law limited annual immigration to 150,000 people and set quotas at 2 percent of each nationality residing in the United States in 1890, except for Asians, who were banned completely. The act further restricted southern and eastern Europeans, since fewer of those groups lived in the United States in 1890 than in 1910, although it allowed wives and children of U.S. citizens to enter as nonquota immigrants. In 1927 a revised National Origins Act redefined quotas to be distributed among European countries in proportion to the national origins (country of birth or descent) of

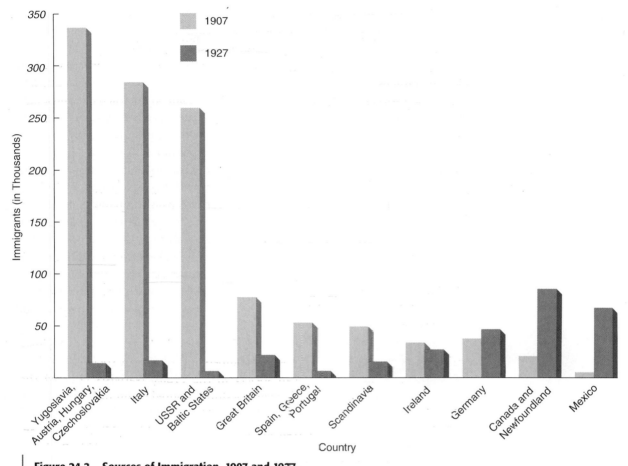

Figure 24.2 Sources of Immigration, 1907 and 1927

Immigration peaked in 1907 and 1908, when newcomers from southern and eastern Europe poured into the United States. After immigration restriction laws were passed in the 1920s, the greatest number of immigrants came from the Western Hemisphere (Canada and Mexico), which was exempted from the quotas, and the number coming from eastern and southern Europe shrank.

American inhabitants in 1920. People from the Western Hemisphere did not fall under the quotas (except for those whom the Labor Department defined as potential paupers) and became the largest immigrant groups (see Figure 24.2).

Fundamentalism The pursuit of spiritual purity stirred religious fundamentalists, as millions sought salvation from what they perceived as the irreverence of a materialistic, hedonistic society. Resolutely believing that God's miracles created the world, they condemned the theory of evolution as heresy. Wherever fundamentalists constituted a majority of a community, they sought to determine what schools taught. Their enemies were modernists, who used social sciences, such as psychology, to interpret behavior. To modernists, God was important to the study of culture and history, but science advanced knowledge.

Scopes Trial

In 1925 Christian fundamentalism clashed with modernism in Dayton, Tennessee. The Tennessee legislature had banned public schools from teaching the theory that humans evolved from lower forms of life rather than descending from Adam and Eve. The high school teacher John Thomas Scopes volunteered to serve as a test case and was arrested for violating the law. William Jennings Bryan, former secretary of state and three-time presidential candidate, argued for the prosecution, and civil liberties lawyers headed by Clarence Darrow represented Scopes. News correspondents crowded into town, and radio stations broadcast the trial.

Although Scopes was convicted—clearly he had broken the law—modernists claimed victory. The testimony, they believed, showed fundamentalism to be illogical. The trial's climax was when Bryan testified as an expert on the Bible. He asserted that Eve really had been created from Adam's rib, that the Tower of Babel was responsible for the diversity of languages, and that Jonah had been swallowed by a big fish. Spectators in Dayton cheered Bryan, but the liberal press mocked him. Nevertheless, fundamentalists continued to pressure schools to stop teaching evolution and created an independent subculture of schools, camps, radio ministries, and missionary societies.

Religious Revivalism

Urban Pentecostal churches attracted African Americans and whites struggling with economic insecurity, nervous about modernism's attack on old-time religion, and swayed by their depiction of a personal Savior. Using modern advertising and elaborately staged radio broadcasts, magnetic preachers, such as Aimee Semple McPherson of Los Angeles, the former baseball player Billy Sunday, and Father Divine (an African American who amassed an interracial following) stirred revivalist fervor.

Clergy and teachers of all faiths condemned dancing, new dress styles, and sex in movies. Many urban dwellers supported prohibition, believing that it would win the battle against poverty, vice, and corruption. Yet most Americans sincerely sought balance as they tried to adjust to the modern order. Few refrained from the radio and movies like *Why Change Your Wife?*—activities that proved less corrupting than critics feared. Americans sought fellowship in civic organizations, such as Rotary, Elks, and women's clubs. Perhaps most important, people were finding release in recreation and leisure time.

THE AGE OF PLAY

Americans in the 1920s embraced commercial entertainment, spending $2.5 billion on leisure in 1919; by 1929 spending topped $4.3 billion. Spectator amusements—movies, music, and sports—accounted for 21 percent of the 1929 total; the rest involved participatory recreation, such as games, hobbies, and travel. Entrepreneurs fed an appetite for fads and spectacles. Early in the 1920s, mahjong, a Chinese tile game, was the craze. In the mid-1920s, devotees popularized crossword puzzles, printed in mass-circulation newspapers and magazines. By 1930 the nation boasted thirty thousand miniature golf courses. Dance crazes like the Charleston and recorded music on radio boosted the growing popularity of jazz.

Movies and Sports

Americans also enjoyed watching movies and sports. In total capital investment, motion pictures became one of the nation's leading industries. In 1922 movies attracted 40 million viewers weekly; by decade's end, nearly 100 million—at a time when the nation's population was 120 million and total weekly church attendance was 60 million. Between 1922 and 1927, the Technicolor Corporation developed a means of producing movies in color. That, along with the introduction of sound in 1927's *The Jazz Singer*, made movies more exciting.

Although DeMille's romantic comedies like *Why Change Your Wife?* were entertaining, his most popular films—*The Ten Commandments* (1923) and *The King of Kings* (1927)—were biblical. Lurid dramas like *Souls for Sale* (1923) and *A Woman Who Sinned* (1924) also drew big audiences, as did slapstick comedies starring Harold Lloyd and Charlie Chaplin. In 1927 producers, bowing to pressure from legislators and religious leaders, instituted self-censorship, forbidding nudity, rough language, and plots that did not end with justice and morality triumphant.

Spectator sports drew millions every year. In an age when technology and mass production robbed experiences of their uniqueness, sports provided the unpredictability that people craved. Newspapers and radio magnified this tension, glorifying events with such dramatic narrative that promoters did not need advertising.

Baseball's drawn-out suspense, variety of plays, and potential for keeping statistics attracted a huge following. After the 1919 Black Sox scandal, when eight members of the Chicago White Sox were banned for allegedly throwing the World Series to the Cincinnati Reds (even though a jury acquitted them), baseball transformed itself. Discovering that home runs excited fans, the leagues redesigned the ball. A record 300,000 people attended the six-game 1921 World Series between the New York Giants and New York Yankees. Millions enjoyed professional games on the radio. Although African American ballplayers were prohibited from the major leagues, they formed their own teams, and in 1920 the first successful Negro League was founded in Kansas City, Missouri.

Sports Heroes

As technology and mass society made the individual less significant, people clung to heroic athletes as a means of identifying with the unique. Bill Tilden in tennis, Gertrude Ederle in swimming (in 1926 she became the first woman to swim across the English Channel), and Bobby Jones in golf were famous. But boxing, football, and baseball produced the most popular sports heroes. Heavyweight champion Jack Dempsey, the Manassa (Colorado) Mauler, attracted the first of several-million-dollar gates in his fight with Georges Carpentier in 1921.

Baseball's foremost hero was George Herman "Babe" Ruth, who began his career as a pitcher but broke records hitting home runs. Ruth hit twenty-nine homers in 1919, fifty-four in 1920 (the year the Boston Red Sox traded him to the New York Yankees), fifty-nine in 1921, and sixty in 1927—each year a record. His talent and boyish grin endeared him to millions. Known for overindulgence in food, drink, and sex, he charmed fans with public appearances and visiting hospitalized children.

Movie Stars and Public Heroes

Americans fulfilled their yearning for romance and adventure through movie idols. One of the decade's most adored movie personalities was Rudolph Valentino, whose image exploited the era's sexual liberalism. In his most famous film, Valentino played a passionate sheik who carried away beautiful women to his tent, combining the roles of abductor and seducer. When he died at thirty-one of complications from ulcers and appendicitis, the press turned his funeral into a public extravaganza.

The era's most celebrated hero was Charles A. Lindbergh, who in May 1927 flew a plane solo from New York to Paris. The flight riveted America, as newspaper and telegraph reports followed Lindbergh's progress. After the pilot landed successfully, President Coolidge dispatched a warship to bring Lucky Lindy home, where he was greeted with a triumphant parade. Among countless prizes, Lindbergh received the Distinguished Flying Cross and the Congressional Medal of Honor. Promoters offered him millions of dollars to tour the world and $700,000 for a movie contract. Although his flight symbolized the merger of technology and mass culture in the 1920s, Lindbergh epitomized individual achievement and courage—old-fashioned values that attracted public allegiance.

Prohibition

The Eighteenth Amendment (1919) and subsequent federal law (the Volstead Act of 1920) prohibited the manufacture, sale, and transportation of alcoholic beverages. It worked well at first. Per capita consumption of liquor dropped, as did arrests for drunkenness. But it was barely enforced: in 1922 Congress gave the Prohibition Bureau less than $7 million for nationwide enforcement, and by 1927 most state budgets omitted funds to enforce prohibition.

After 1925, prohibition broke down as thousands made their own wine and gin illegally and bootleg importers evaded the few patrols that existed. Moreover, drinking was a business with willing customers, and criminal organizations capitalized on public demand. The most notorious of such mobs belonged to Al Capone, who seized control of illegal liquor and vice in Chicago, maintaining power over politicians and the vice business through intimidation, bribery, and violence. Americans wanted liquor, and until 1931, when a federal court convicted and imprisoned Capone for income-tax evasion (the only charge for which authorities could obtain hard evidence), he supplied them.

CULTURAL CURRENTS

Intellectuals were quick to expose the era's hypocrisies. Writers and artists felt at odds with society, and their rejection of materialism and conformity was biting and bitter.

Literature of Alienation

Several writers from the so-called Lost Generation, including the novelist Ernest Hemingway and the poets Ezra Pound and T. S. Eliot, abandoned the United States for Europe. Others, like the novelists William Faulkner and Sinclair Lewis, remained in America but expressed disillusionment with the materialism that they witnessed.

F. Scott Fitzgerald's novels *This Side of Paradise* (1920) and *The Great Gatsby* (1925) and Eugene O'Neill's plays scorned Americans' preoccupation with money. Edith Wharton explored the clash of old and new moralities in novels such as *The Age of Innocence* (1920). Hemingway's *A Farewell to Arms* (1929) interwove antiwar sentiment with critiques of the emptiness in modern relationships.

Harlem Renaissance

Discontent inspired a new generation of African American artists. Middle-class, educated, and proud of their African heritage, African American writers rejected white culture and exalted the militantly assertive New Negro. In the Negro Mecca of New York's Harlem, African American intellectuals and artists, aided by a few white patrons, celebrated African American culture during what became known as the Harlem Renaissance.

The popular 1921 musical comedy *Shuffle Along* is often credited with launching the Harlem Renaissance and showcased talented African American artists, such as the composer Eubie Blake and the singer Josephine Baker. Harlem in the 1920s also fostered gifted writers, including Langston Hughes, Countee Cullen, Zora Neale Hurston, Jessie Fauset, and Alain Locke.

Though cherishing their African heritage and black folk culture of the slave South, these artists and intellectuals realized that African Americans had to come to terms with being free Americans. Langston Hughes wrote, "We younger Negro artists who create now intend to express our individual dark-skinned selves without fear or shame. If white people are pleased, we are glad. If they are not, it doesn't matter. We know we are beautiful."

Jazz

The Jazz Age, as the 1920s is sometimes called, owes its name to the music of the African American culture. Evolving from African and African American folk music, early jazz communicated exuberance, humor, and autonomy that African Americans seldom experienced in their public and political lives. Jazz's emotional rhythms and improvisation blurred the distinction between composer and performer. Urban dance halls and nightclubs, some of which included interracial audiences, featured performers like the trumpeter Louis Armstrong and the blues singer Bessie Smith. Music recorded by African American artists and aimed at African American consumers (sometimes called "race records") gave African Americans a place in commercial culture. More important, jazz endowed America with its own distinctive art form.

In many ways the 1920s were the nation's most creative years. Painters such as Georgia O'Keeffe, Aaron Douglas, and John Marin forged a uniquely American style of visual art. Composer Henry Cowell pioneered electronic music, and Aaron Copland built orchestral works around native folk motifs. George Gershwin blended jazz rhythms, classical forms, and folk melodies in serious works (*Rhapsody in Blue*, 1924, and *Piano Concerto in F*, 1925) and hit tunes, such as "The Man I Love." In architecture, skyscrapers drew worldwide attention to American forms. The "emotional and aesthetic starvation" that essayist Harold Stearns lamented early in the decade were gone by 1929.

THE ELECTION OF 1928 AND THE END OF THE NEW ERA

Intellectuals' uneasiness about materialism seldom affected the confident rhetoric of politics. Herbert Hoover voiced that confidence when he accepted the Republican nomination for president in 1928. "We in America today," Hoover boasted, "are nearer to the final triumph over poverty than ever before in the history of any land."

Herbert Hoover

As the Republican candidate in 1928 (Coolidge chose not to seek reelection) Hoover fused the tradition of individual hard work with the modern emphasis on corporate action. A Quaker from Iowa, orphaned at age ten, Hoover put himself through Stanford University and became a wealthy mining engineer. During and after World War I, he distinguished himself as a U.S. food administrator.

As secretary of commerce under Harding and Coolidge, Hoover promoted associationalism. Recognizing that nationwide associations dominated commerce and industry, Hoover sought business and government cooperation. He made the Commerce Department a center for the promotion of business, encouraging trade associations, holding conferences, and issuing reports, all aimed at improving productivity and profits.

Al Smith

In sharp contrast, Democrats in 1928 chose New York's governor Alfred E. Smith. Hoover had rural, native-born, Protestant, and business roots but had never run for public office. Smith was an urbane politician of Irish stock with a career embedded in New York City's Tammany Hall political machine. He relished the give-and-take of city streets.

Smith was the first Roman Catholic to run for president on a major party ticket. His religion enhanced his appeal among urban ethnics, who increasingly voted, but intense anti-Catholic sentiments lost him southern and rural votes. Smith had a strong record on Progressive reform and civil rights, but his campaign stressed issues unlikely to unite these groups, particularly his opposition to prohibition.

Hoover, who emphasized national prosperity under Republican administrations, won the popular vote by 21 million to 15 million and the electoral vote by 444 to 87. Smith carried the nation's twelve largest cities, formerly Republican strongholds, and he lured millions of foreign-stock voters to the polls for the first time. For the next forty years, the Democratic Party solidified this urban base, which when combined with its traditional strength in the South, made the party a formidable force in national elections.

Hoover's Administration

At his inaugural, Hoover proclaimed a New Day, "bright with hope." His cabinet featured mostly businessmen, including six millionaires. To lower ranking posts, Hoover appointed young professionals who agreed that a scientific approach could solve national problems. Like Hoover, Americans widely believed that individual effort led to success and that poverty suggested personal weakness. Prevailing opinion also held that fluctuations of the business cycle were natural and therefore not to be tampered with by government.

Stock Market Crash

This trust dissolved on October 24, 1929, later known as Black Thursday, when stock market prices suddenly plunged, wiping out $10 billion in value (worth around $100 billion today). Panic set in. Prices of many stocks hit record lows; some sellers could find no buyers. At noon, leading bankers put up $20 million and ceremoniously began buying stocks. The mood brightened and some stocks rallied.

But as news spread, frightened investors sold off stocks to avoid further losses. On Black Tuesday, October 29, prices plummeted again. Hoover assured Americans that "the crisis will be over in sixty days." He shared the popular assumption that the economy was strong enough to endure until the market righted itself. Instead, the crash unleashed a devastating worldwide depression.

In hindsight, the depression began long before the stock market crash. Prosperity in the 1920s was not as widespread as optimists believed. Agriculture had languished for decades, and many areas, especially in the South, were outside the new bounty of consumer society. Industries such as mining and textiles failed to sustain profits throughout the decade, and even the automotive and household goods industries had been stagnant since 1926. The fever of speculation included rash investment in California and Florida real estate, as well as in the stock market, and masked what was unhealthy in the national economy.

Declining Demand

The economic weakness that underlay the Great Depression had several interrelated causes. Since mid-1928, demand for new housing faltered, reducing sales of building materials and increasing unemployment. Growth industries, such as automobiles and electric appliances, saw demand level off, so factory owners cut back production and workers. Retailers had amassed large inventories that were going unsold and started ordering less. Farm prices continued to sag, leaving farmers with less income for new machinery and goods. As wages and employment fell, families could not afford to buy consumer goods. Thus by 1929 a sizable population of underconsumers was causing serious repercussions.

As the rich grew richer, middle- and lower-income Americans barely made modest gains. Although average per capita disposable income (income after taxes) rose about 9 percent between 1920 and 1929, income of the wealthiest 1 percent rose 75 percent. Much of this increase was put into stock market investments, not consumer goods.

Corporate Debt and Stock Market Speculation

Furthermore, many businesses overloaded themselves with debt. To obtain loans, they misrepresented their assets in ways that hid their inability to repay. Such practices, overlooked by lending agencies, put the nation's banking system on a precarious footing.

Risky stock market speculation also precipitated the depression. Individuals and corporations bought millions of stocks on margin, meaning that they invested with a down payment of only a fraction of a stock's price and then used these partially paid-for stocks as collateral for more stock purchases. When stock prices stopped rising, people tried to unload what they bought on margin. But with numerous investors selling simultaneously, prices dropped. Brokers then demanded full payment for stocks bought on margin. Bankers pressured businesses to pay back their loans, tightening the vise further. The more obligations went unmet, the more the system tottered. Inevitably, banks and investment companies collapsed.

International Economic Troubles

International economic conditions also contributed to the Depression. During and after World War I, Americans loaned billions to European nations. By the late 1920s, however, American investors instead kept their money in the lucrative U.S. stock market. Europeans, unable to borrow more or sell goods in the American market because of high tariffs, bought less from the United States. Moreover, the Allied nations depended on German war reparations to pay their debts to the United States, and the German government depended on American bank loans to pay those reparations. When the crash choked off American loans, the western economy ground to a halt.

Failure of Federal Policies

The government refrained from regulating speculation. In supporting business expansion, the Federal Reserve Board pursued easy credit policies, charging low discount rates (interest rates on its loans to member banks) even though such loans were financing the speculative mania.

Neither experts nor people on the street realized what really happened in 1929. Conventional wisdom, based on previous depressions, held that economic problems had to run their course. So in 1929 people waited for the tailspin to ease, never realizing that the new era had ended and that the economy, politics, and society would have to be rebuilt.

Summary

Two critical events, the end of World War I and the beginning of the Great Depression, marked the boundaries of the 1920s. After the war, traditional customs weakened as women and men sought new forms of self-expression and gratification. Modern science and technology touched rich and poor alike through mass media, movies, sports, automobiles, and electric appliances. Moreover, the decade's freewheeling consumerism enabled ordinary Americans to emulate wealthier people by purchasing more and engaging in stock market speculation.

Beneath the new era's materialism, prejudice and ethnic tensions tainted the American dream. Prohibitionists, Klansmen, and immigration restrictionists encouraged discrimination against racial minorities and ethnic groups. Meanwhile, the distinguishing forces of twentieth-century life—technological change, bureaucratization, mass culture, and growth of the middle class—accelerated, making the decade truly new.

Intercollegiate Athletics

In 1924 brutality, academic fraud, and illegal payments to recruits prompted the Carnegie Foundation for the Advancement of Higher Education to undertake a five-year investigation of college sports. Its 1929 report recommended the abolition of football and condemned coaches and alumni but had minimal effect. Football was immensely popular, and colleges and universities built stadiums to attract spectators, bolster alumni allegiance, and enhance revenues.

For most of the twentieth century and into the twenty-first, intercollegiate athletics ranked as a major commercial entertainment. Still, American institutions have struggled to reconcile conflicts between the commercialism of athletic competition and the ideals of scholarship and amateurism. The economic potential of college sports coupled with expanding athletic departments—elaborate facilities as well as staffs—has created programs that compete with and sometimes overshadow an institution's academic mission.

Since the 1920s, recruiting scandals, academic fraud, and felonious behavior sparked controversy in college sports. In 1952, after revelations of point-shaving (fixing the outcome) of basketball games at several colleges, the American Council on Education undertook its own study. Its recommendations, including the elimination of football bowl games, went largely unheeded. In 1991 further abuses prompted the Knight Foundation Commission on Intercollegiate Athletics to urge college presidents to reform intercollegiate athletics. Few significant changes resulted, even after a follow-up study in 2001.

The most sweeping reforms followed court rulings in the 1990s, mandating that women's sports be treated equally with men's under Title IX of the Educational Amendments Act of 1972. Enforcement, however, provoked a backlash that resulted in efforts to prevent men's teams from being cut to satisfy Title IX. In recent years, the National College Athletic Association (NCAA) has attempted to regulate academic standards in college athletics, but its success depends on cooperation from member institutions. With millions of dollars involved, the system established in the 1920s has withstood most pressures for change.

Chapter Review

BIG BUSINESS TRIUMPHANT

What triggered the post–World War I economic recovery?

Two factors helped turn the initial postwar recession into recovery: the advent of electric energy in 1922 and new government pro-business initiatives. Electricity enabled goods to be produced more inexpensively, thereby driving consumer demand and stimulating the economy across the board. New installment or credit plans for purchasing big items such as cars also drove consumption. As business organizations used lobbying to influence government, new federal policies emerged to aid business growth and development. Congress cut taxes on corporations and wealthy individuals in 1921, and passed the Fordney-McCumber Tariff Act (1922). The Federal Trade Commission and the Interstate Commerce Commission tended to cooperate with corporations rather than regulate them. And several Supreme Court decisions sheltered business from government regulation and hindered organized labor.

Politics and Government

What happened to Progressive reform in the 1920s?

While Progressivism faded or a national level, its reform spirit continued to inspire local and state initiatives, as well as those by women and ethnic groups. After the war, many states adopted or expanded workers' compensation laws and public welfare programs. Native American groups worked for better education and return of tribal lands, while white reformers held out hope of getting Indians to adopt white middle-class standards of work, family, and citizenship. Although women got the right to vote in 1920, their voluntary organizations became the tools for lobbying for various issues from birth control to protective labor legislation to questions of citizenship and equality.

A Consumer Society

How did the emergence of a consumer society change American life?

In the 1920s, incomes increased, while new mass production methods kept the price of goods stable or made them more affordable. Consequently, greater numbers of Americans could afford products such as automobiles that once were the province of the wealthy. Car ownership led consumers to join with farmers in seeking improved roadways. At the same time, the emergence of advertising as a tool helped manipulate purchases and increasingly erased ethnic differences to create a more homogenous consumer society. And the growth of the radio, with its mass marketing and standardized programs, further blurred differences and heightened "Americanization."

Cities, Migrants, and Suburbs

What fueled the growth of cities in the 1920s?

In 1920, for the first time in U.S. history, more people lived in urban areas than rural areas. In part, the shift was driven by young people, who left farms for the more exciting and varied life of cities. The demographic change was also driven by the migration of African Americans from poverty on southern farms to seek better paying factory jobs in the North. Immigrants from Mexico and Puerto Rico were similarly pushed off their land due to agricultural changes to find better opportunities in America. Many Mexicans became underpaid and exploited farm laborers in the West, while Puerto Ricans found jobs in factories and restaurants or as domestic servants.

New Rhythms of Everyday Life

How did technological advances impact social life in America in the 1920s?

First, improved productivity and mechanization led to shorter workweeks, permitting the expansion of leisure activities and greater freedom, especially for young people. Industrialism privileged youth and agility over experience and forced older people to retire, which often meant economic hardship or poverty. Second, new appliances made housework less arduous and time-consuming and shifted women's roles from producer within the home to consumer for the family. Third, advances in nutrition helped people live longer and healthier lives. Birth control also enabled families to separate sexuality from reproduction, and family size decreased. Finally, as products and services became more widely available, an increasing number of married women moved into the work force to expand their families' purchasing power.

LINES OF DEFENSE

How did various groups defend an older version of America against the tide of change in the 1920s?

Troubled by the liberal social influences of the era, several groups emerged seeking to restore what they considered to be traditional American values. The Ku Klux Klan was reconstituted in 1915 to re-establish native white American supremacy in the face of increasing immigration and back migration and to protect white women's virtue against so-called corrupting influences. They were joined in their anti-immigration sentiment by other nativist groups, who pressed Congress to establish immigration quotas. Similarly, fundamentalist Christian groups sought to replace the modern emphasis on science with a renewed centrality of God's role in creation and daily life. Hence the Tennessee legislature banned the teaching of the theory of evolution, resulting in the pivotal Scopes trial in 1925. Religious revivalism likewise condemned the new social practices of dating, dancing, and fashion and the hint of sex in movies.

THE AGE OF PLAY

Why did movie and sports heroes become so pivotally important during the 1920s?

As mechanization and mass consumption took hold, Americans felt robbed of a sense of individual distinctiveness and sense of purpose. Prohibition added to their sense of restricted personal freedom. To recover that lost sensibility, Americans gravitated toward leisure activities that celebrated individual achievement or that inspired a sense of adventure or romance. Sports provided drama, unpredictability, and a chance to celebrate a particular player's talent. Motion pictures not only let viewers live vicariously through the exciting lives of characters, but also inspired the hope for adventure in their own lives. Finally, national heroes such as aviator Charles Lindbergh made the possibility of greatness seem real and attainable, even if most Americans would never personally experience it for themselves.

CULTURAL CURRENTS

How did discontent with 1920s conformity give rise to important creative cultural movements?

Many artists and writers felt disillusioned with the materialism and preoccupation with money they witnessed in America during this age of mass consumption and innovation. While some, like Ernest Hemingway, left for Europe, others remained in the United States and transformed these feelings into novels and other creative works that explored the problems of modern society or proffered a particular political view. Middle-class, educated African Americans rejected white culture and celebrated their heritage in novels, poems, plays, and art, creating the literary and artistic movement known as the Harlem Renaissance. Black culture also produced the Jazz Age, creating a distinctly American musical form.

THE ELECTION OF 1928 AND THE END OF THE NEW ERA

What were the early signs that the prosperity of the 1920s was coming to an end?

While the 1929 stock market crash put a definitive ending on the era's seeming prosperity, in truth, the seeds of recession were sown many years before. First, so-called prosperity had never reached farmers; agriculture had lagged for decades. Mining, textiles, and other industries did not remain profitable the entire decade, and even the automobile industry was stagnant after 1926. As demand faltered, factories cut back on production and workers, which in turn meant less disposable income to purchase consumer goods, triggering further cutbacks in retail orders and production. Housing demand dropped off after mid-1928, and at the same time, businesses were overloaded with debt. Together, this made for a perfect economic storm when the market crashed in 1929.

SUGGESTIONS FOR FURTHER READING

Lynn Dumenil, *The Modern Temper: American Culture and Society in the 1920s* (1995)

James R. Grossman, *Land of Hope: Chicago, Black Southerners, and the Great Migration* (1989)

Maury Klein, *Rainbow's End: The Crash of 1929* (2003)

Roland Marchand, *Advertising the American Dream: Making Way for Modernity, 1920–1940* (1985)

David Montgomery, *The Fall of the House of Labor: The Workplace, the State, and American Activism, 1865–1925* (1987)

Mae M. Ngai, *Impossible Subjects: Illegal Aliens and the Making of Modern America* (2004)

George Sanchez, *Becoming Mexican American: Ethnicity, Culture and Identity in Chicano Los Angeles, 1900–1945* (1993)

Susan Thistle, *From Marriage to the Market: The Transformation of Women's Lives and Work* (2006)

Michael Miller Topp, *The Sacco and Vanzetti Case: A Brief History With Documents* (2005)

The Great Depression and the New Deal

CHAPTER 25

1929–1941

I n 1931 the rain stopped in the Great Plains. Montana and North Dakota became as arid as the Sonora Desert, and temperatures reached 115 degrees in Iowa. Farmers watched rich black dirt turn to gray dust.

Then the winds began to blow. In the 1920s farmers stripped the Plains of native grasses to put millions of acres into production. Now, with nothing to hold the earth, it began to blow away. The dust storms began in 1934 and worsened in 1935. Cattle, blinded by blowing grit, ran in circles until they died. Boiling clouds of dust filled the skies in Kansas, Colorado, Oklahoma, Texas, and New Mexico—the Dust Bowl.

In late 1937, on a farm near Stigler, Oklahoma, Marvin Montgomery counted his assets: $53 and a 1929 Hudson automobile he had just bought. On December 29, 1937, Montgomery, his wife, and four children—along with their furniture, bedding, pots, and pans—squeezed into the Hudson. Traveling west on Route 66, the Montgomerys headed for California.

At least a third of the farms in the Dust Bowl were abandoned in the 1930s, and many families headed west, lured by advertisements promising work in California fields. Some 300,000 people migrated to California in the 1930s; many were white-collar workers seeking opportunity in California's cities. But the plight of families like the Montgomerys, captured in federal government–sponsored Farm Security Administration (FSA) photographs, came to represent the human suffering of the Great Depression.

The Montgomerys ran out of money in Arizona and worked the cotton fields there for five weeks before they moved on. In California, wages were low, and migrant families found little welcome. Because they took over the agricultural labor formerly done by Mexicans and Mexican Americans, they forfeited their

This icon will direct you to interactive activities and study materials on A People And A Nation, Brief Edition website: **www.cengage.com/history/norton/peoplenationbrief8e**

Chronology

1929	Stock market crashes (October); Great Depression begins.
1930	Hawley-Smoot Tariff raises rates on imports.
1931	Scottsboro Boys are arrested in Alabama.
1932	Banks fail throughout the nation.
	Bonus Army marches on Washington.
	Hoover's Reconstruction Finance Corporation tries to stabilize banks, insurance companies, and railroads.
	F. D. Roosevelt is elected president.
1933	13 million Americans are unemployed.
	During its First Hundred Days, the Roosevelt administration offers major legislation for economic recovery and poor relief.
	National bank holiday halts run on banks.
	Agricultural Adjustment Act (AAA) encourages decreased farm production.
	National Industrial Recovery Act (NIRA) attempts to spur industrial growth.
	Tennessee Valley Authority (TVA) is established.
1934	Long starts Share Our Wealth Society.
	Townsend proposes old-age pension plan.

	Indian Reorganization (Wheeler-Howard) Act restores lands to tribal ownership.
1935	National Labor Relations (Wagner) Act guarantees workers' right to unionize.
	Social Security Act establishes insurance for the aged, the unemployed, and needy children.
	Works Progress Administration (WPA) creates jobs in public works projects.
	Revenue (Wealth Tax) Act raises taxes on business and the wealthy.
1936	9 million Americans are unemployed.
	United Auto Workers win sit-down strike against General Motors.
1937	Roosevelt's "Court-packing" plan fails.
	Memorial Day massacre of striking steelworkers occurs.
	"Roosevelt recession" begins.
1938	10.4 million Americans are unemployed.
	80 million movie tickets are sold each week.
1939	Marian Anderson performs at the Lincoln Memorial.
	Social Security amendments add benefits for spouses and widows.

"whiteness" in the eyes of many Californians. "Negroes and 'Okies' upstairs," read a sign in a San Joaquin valley movie theater.

Most migrants to rural California lived in squalid makeshift camps, but the Montgomerys secured housing provided by the Farm Security Administration. The FSA camp had 240 tents and 40 small houses. For nine months the Montgomery family lived in a fourteen-by-sixteen-foot tent, which rented for 10 cents a day plus four hours of volunteer labor a month. Then they proudly moved into an FSA house, "with water, lights, and everything, yes sir; and a little garden spot furnished." Soon many employment opportunities emerged in California in aircraft factories and shipyards mobilizing for World War II.

Between 1929 and 1933, the U.S. gross national product was cut in half. Corporate profits fell from $10 billion to $1 billion; 100,000 businesses closed. Four million workers were unemployed in January 1930; by November the number jumped to 6 million. When President Herbert Hoover left office in 1933, 13 million workers—about one-fourth of the labor force—were idle, and millions had only part-time work. There was no national safety net: no welfare system, no unemployment compensation, no Social Security. And, as thousands of banks failed, with no federally guaranteed deposit insurance, families' savings disappeared.

Herbert Hoover, who was elected president in the prosperous late 1920s, looked first to private enterprise for solutions. By the end of his term, he extended the federal government's role in managing an economic crisis further than his predecessors had. Still, the depression deepened, and Americans felt increasingly desperate. The economic catastrophe exacerbated existing racial and class tensions in the United States, while in Germany, the international economic crisis propelled Adolf Hitler to power. By late 1932 many feared the depression was a crisis of capitalism, even of democracy itself.

In 1932 voters replaced Hoover with a man who promised a New Deal. Franklin Delano Roosevelt's programs did not end the depression (only the massive mobilization for World War II did that), but they did alleviate suffering. For the first time, the federal government assumed responsibility for the nation's economy and its citizens' welfare, thus strengthening its power in relation to states.

As it transformed the role of the federal government, however, the New Deal maintained America's existing economic and social systems. Although some Americans saw the depression as an opportunity for major economic change—even revolution—Roosevelt's goal was to save capitalism. New Deal programs increased federal government regulation without altering the existing capitalist system or the distribution of wealth. And, despite pressure to attack racial discrimination, Roosevelt never directly challenged legal segregation in the South—in part because he relied on southern white Democrats to pass New Deal legislation.

Despite its limits, the New Deal preserved America's democratic experiment through uncertainty and crisis. By decade's end, a world war shifted America's focus from domestic to foreign policy. But the changes set in motion by the New Deal continued to transform the United States for decades to come.

- How did economic hard times during the 1930s affect Americans, and what differences were there in the experiences of specific groups and regions?

- How and why did the power of the federal government expand during the Great Depression?

- What were the successes and the failures of the New Deal?

HOOVER AND HARD TIMES, 1929-1933

As the depression deepened in the early 1930s, tens of millions of Americans were desperately poor. In the cities, the hungry ate at soup kitchens or scratched through garbage cans for food. In West Virginia and Kentucky, widespread hunger and limited resources led the American Friends Service Committee to distribute food only to those weighing 10 percent less than the normal weight for their height. In November 1932, *The Nation* told readers that one-sixth of the American population risked starvation over the coming winter.

Families, unable to pay rent, were evicted. The new homeless poured into shantytowns, called Hoovervilles in ironic tribute to the formerly popular president. Over a million men took to the road or rails in search of work. The average marriage age rose by more than two years during the 1930s. People delayed having children, and in 1933 the birth rate sank below the replacement rate.

Farmers and Industrial Workers

The agricultural sector, which employed almost one-quarter of American workers and missed the good times of the 1920s, was hit hard by the depression. As urbanites cut spending and foreign competitors dumped agricultural surpluses into the global market, farm prices hit bottom. Farmers tried to compensate for lower prices by producing more, thus adding to the surplus and further depressing prices. By 1932, a bushel of wheat that cost North Dakota farmers 77 cents to produce brought only 33 cents. Cash-strapped farmers could not pay property taxes or mortgages. Banks, facing their own ruin, foreclosed. In Mississippi, on a single day in April 1932, approximately one-fourth of all farmland was auctioned off to meet debts. By the middle of the decade, the ecological crisis of the Dust Bowl would drive thousands of farmers from their land.

America's industrial workers had seen their standard of living improve during the 1920s, and their consumer spending bolstered the nation's growth. But as incomes declined, sales of manufactured goods plummeted and factories closed—more than seventy thousand were out of business by 1933. As car sales dropped from 4.5 million in 1929 to 1 million in 1933, Ford laid off more than two-thirds of its Detroit workers. Almost one-quarter of industrial workers were unemployed, and those with jobs saw the average wage fall by almost one-third.

Marginal Workers

For workers on the lowest rungs of the employment ladder, the depression was a crushing blow. In the South, jobs that many white men had considered below their dignity—bellhop, garbage collector—now seemed desirable. In 1930 a short-lived fascist-style organization, the Black Shirts, recruited forty thousand members with the slogan "No Jobs for Niggers Until Every White Man Has a Job!" Northern African Americans did not fare much better. An Urban League survey of 106 cities found African American unemployment rates averaged 30 to 60 percent higher than rates for whites. By 1932, African American unemployment reached almost 50 percent.

Mexican Americans and Mexican nationals in the Southwest also felt the twin impacts of depression and racism. Their wages on California farms fell from a miserable 35 cents an hour in 1929 to 14 cents an hour by 1932. Throughout the Southwest, campaigns against foreigners hurt not only Mexican immigrants but also American citizens of Hispanic background whose families lived in the Southwest for centuries, long before the land belonged to the United States. In 1931 the Labor Department announced plans to deport illegal immigrants to free jobs for American citizens. This policy fell hardest on people of Mexican origin. Even those who immigrated legally often lacked full documentation. Officials often ignored that children born in the United States were U.S. citizens. The U.S. government deported 82,000 Mexicans between 1929 and 1935, but a half a million people repatriated to Mexico during the 1930s. Some left voluntarily, but many were tricked into believing they had no choice.

Even before the depression, women were barred from many jobs and paid significantly less than men. With widespread male unemployment, many believed that women who worked took jobs from men. In fact, men laid off from U.S. Steel would not have been hired as elementary school teachers, secretaries, "salesgirls," or

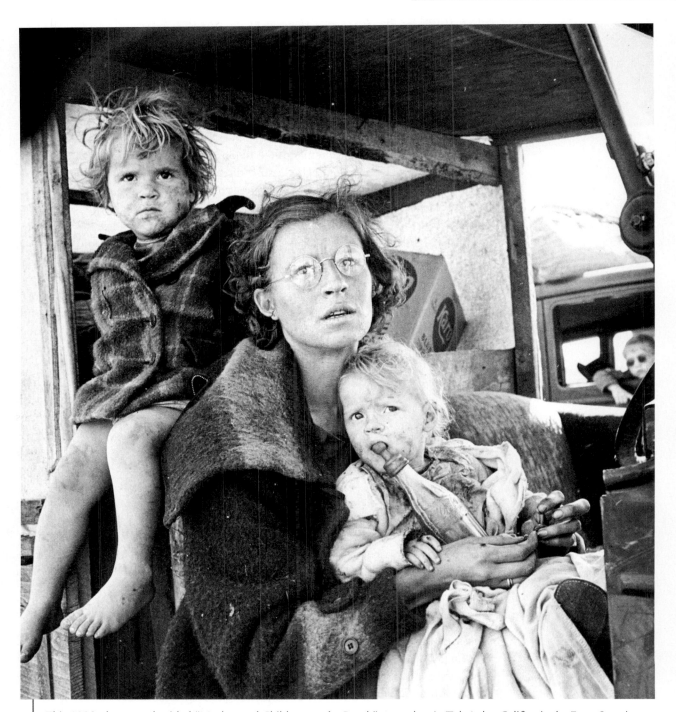

This 1939 photograph, titled "Mother and Children on the Road," was taken in Tule Lake, California, by Farm Security Administration photographer Dorothea Lange. The FSA used photos like this one to build public support for New Deal programs to assist migrant workers and the rural poor.   (Library of Congress)

maids. Nonetheless, when a 1936 Gallup poll asked whether wives should work if their husbands had jobs, 82 percent of respondents (including 75 percent of the women) answered no. Such beliefs became policy. In 1930 and 1931, 77 percent of urban school systems refused to hire married women as teachers, and 63 percent fired female teachers who married.

At first, women lost jobs faster than men. Women in low-wage manufacturing jobs were laid off before male employees. Almost one-quarter of women in domestic service—many of them African American—lost jobs as middle-class families economized by dispensing with household help. Despite discrimination and a poor economy, the number of women working outside the home rose during the 1930s. Women's jobs, such as teaching and clerical work were not hit as hard as men's jobs in heavy industry, and women increasingly sought employment to keep their families afloat during hard times. Still, by 1940 only 15.2 percent of married women were employed.

Middle-Class Workers and Families

Although unemployment climbed to 25 percent, most Americans did not lose their homes or jobs during the depression. Professional and white-collar workers did not fare as badly as industrial workers and farmers. Many middle-class families, however, made do with less. Housewives economized, using cheap ingredients to make food go further (cracker-stuffed cabbage). Although most families' income fell, the impact was cushioned by the decreasing cost of consumer goods. Even for the relatively affluent, the psychological impact of the depression was inescapable. The human toll of the depression was visible everywhere, and no one took economic security for granted any more.

Hoover's Limited Solutions

Although Herbert Hoover, the Great Engineer, had a reputation as a problem solver, no one knew what to do about the crisis. Experts disagreed about the depression's causes and the proper course of action. Many business leaders believed that financial panics and depressions, no matter how painful, were part of a natural and ultimately beneficial business cycle. Economic depressions, according to this theory, brought down inflated prices and cleared the way for economic growth.

Herbert Hoover disagreed. "The economic fatalist," he said, "believes that these crises are inevitable. . . . I would remind these pessimists that exactly the same thing was once said of typhoid, cholera, and smallpox." Hoover had faith in associationalism: business and professional organizations, coordinated by the federal government, working together to solve the nation's problems. The federal government's role was limited to a clearing-house for ideas that state and local governments, along with private industry, could voluntarily implement.

While many Americans thought Hoover was doing nothing to fight the downturn, in truth he stretched his beliefs about the role of government to their limit. He tried voluntarism, exhortation, and limited government intervention. First, he sought voluntary pledges from hundreds of business groups to keep wages stable and renew economic investment. But when businessmen looked at their own bottom lines, few could live up to those promises.

As unemployment climbed, Hoover continued to encourage voluntary responses, creating the President's Organization on Unemployment Relief (POUR) to generate private contributions to aid the destitute. Although 1932 saw record charitable contributions, they were inadequate. By mid-1932 one-quarter of New York's private charities, funds exhausted, closed their doors. State and city officials found their treasuries drying up, too.

Hoover feared that government relief would destroy self-reliance in the poor. Thus he authorized federal funds to feed the drought-stricken livestock of Arkansas farmers but rejected a smaller grant providing food for impoverished farm families. Many Americans became angry at Hoover's seeming insensitivity. Two years after his election, Hoover was the most hated man in America.

Hoover eventually endorsed limited federal action to combat the crisis, but it was too little. Federal public works projects, such as the Grand Coulee Dam in Washington, created some jobs. The Federal Farm Board, established in 1929, supported crop prices by lending money to cooperatives to buy crops and keep them off the market. But the board soon ran short of money, and unsold surpluses jammed warehouses.

Hoover also signed the Hawley-Smoot Tariff (1930) to support American farmers and manufacturers by raising import duties to a staggering 40 percent. Instead it hampered international trade as other nations created their own protective tariffs. And, as other nations sold less to the United States, they had less money to repay their U.S. debts or buy U.S. products. Fearing the collapse of the international monetary system, Hoover in 1931 announced a moratorium on the payment of World War I debts and reparations.

In January 1932, the administration took its most forceful action. The Reconstruction Finance Corporation (RFC) provided federal loans to banks, insurance companies, and railroads, which Hoover hoped would shore up those industries and halt disinvestment in the U.S. economy. Here, Hoover compromised his principles: this was direct government intervention, not voluntarism. If he would support direct assistance to private industries, why not relief to the millions of unemployed?

Protest and Social Unrest

Increasingly, Americans asked that same question. As the depression worsened, social unrest and violence surfaced. Increasing violence raised the specter of popular revolt, and Chicago mayor Anton Cermak told Congress that, if the federal government did not send his citizens aid, it would have to send troops instead.

Tens of thousands of farmers nationwide took the law into their own hands. Angry crowds forced auctioneers to accept just a few dollars for foreclosed property, and then returned it to the original owners. In August 1932, a new group, the Farmers' Holiday Association, encouraged farmers to withhold agricultural products to limit supply and drive prices up. In the Midwest, farmers barricaded roads to stop other farmers' trucks, and then dumped the contents in roadside ditches.

In the cities, the most militant actions came from Unemployed Councils, local groups for unemployed workers that were created and led by Communist Party members. Communist leaders believed that the depression demonstrated capitalism's failure and offered an opportunity for revolution. Few of the quarter-million Americans joining the local Unemployed Councils sought revolution, but they did demand action. "Fight, Don't Starve," read banners in a Chicago demonstration.

As social unrest spread, so did racial violence. Vigilante committees offered bounties to force African Americans off the Illinois Central Railroad's payroll: $25 for maiming and $100 for killing African American workers. Ten men were murdered and at least seven wounded. The Ku Klux Klan reemerged, and at least 140 attempted lynchings were recorded between January 1930 and February 1933. In most cases local authorities were able to prevent the lynchings, but white mobs tortured, hanged, and mutilated thirty-eight African American men during the depression's early years. Outside the South, lynchings also took place in Pennsylvania, Minnesota, Colorado, and Ohio.

Bonus Army   The worst public confrontation happened in summer 1932. More than fifteen thousand unemployed World War I veterans and their families converged on the nation's capital as Congress debated a bill authorizing immediate payment of cash bonuses that veterans were scheduled to receive in 1945. Calling themselves the Bonus Army, they set up a sprawling Hooverville shantytown across the river from the Capitol. Concerned about the impact on the federal budget, President Hoover opposed the bonus bill, and the Senate voted it down.

Most of the Bonus Marchers left Washington, but several thousand stayed. Calling them insurrectionists—though many were simply destitute—the president set a deadline for their departure. On July 28, Hoover sent in General Douglas MacArthur and four infantry companies, four troops of cavalry, a machine gun squadron, and six tanks. What followed shocked the nation: men and women chased by horsemen, children tear-gassed, shacks set afire. The next day, newspapers carried photographs of U.S. troops attacking their own citizens.

Many Americans worried about the growing disillusionment with democracy, for as the depression worsened the appeal of a strong leader—someone who would take decisive action, unencumbered by constitutionally mandated checks and balances—grew. In February 1933 the U.S. Senate passed a resolution calling for newly elected president Franklin D. Roosevelt to assume "unlimited power." The rise of Hitler and his National Socialist Party in depression-ravaged Germany is an obvious parallel.

FRANKLIN D. ROOSEVELT AND THE LAUNCHING OF THE NEW DEAL

In the presidential campaign of 1932, Democratic challenger Franklin Delano Roosevelt insisted that the federal government had to play a much greater role than Hoover's limited intervention. Roosevelt supported direct relief payments for the unemployed, declaring that such governmental aid was "a matter of social duty." During the campaign, he was never very explicit about the outlines of his New Deal. His most concrete proposals, in fact, were sometimes contradictory. But he had committed to use the power of the federal government to combat the paralyzing economic crisis. Roosevelt's 22.8 million popular votes outdistanced Hoover's

15.8 million. Third-party Socialist candidate Norman Thomas drew nearly 1 million votes.

Franklin Roosevelt, the twentieth-century president most beloved by America's common people, was born into upper-class privilege. After graduating from Harvard College and Columbia Law School, he married Eleanor Roosevelt, Theodore Roosevelt's niece and his own fifth cousin, once removed. He served in the New York State legislature, was appointed assistant secretary of the navy by Woodrow Wilson, and at the age of thirty-eight, ran for vice president in 1920 on the Democratic Party's losing ticket.

In 1921, Roosevelt was stricken with polio and was bedridden for two years. He lost the use of his legs but gained, according to his wife Eleanor, a new strength of character. By 1928 Roosevelt was sufficiently recovered to run for—and win—the governorship of New York, and then to accept the Democratic Party's presidential nomination in 1932.

Elected president in November 1932, Roosevelt would not take office until March 4, 1933. (The Twentieth Amendment to the Constitution shifted future inaugurations to January 20.) In this long interregnum, the American banking system reached the verge of collapse.

Banking Crisis

The origins of the banking crisis lay in the flush years of World War I and the 1920s, when American banks made risky loans. After real-estate and stock market bubbles burst in 1929 and agriculture prices collapsed, many of these loans soured, leaving many banks without sufficient funds to cover customers' deposits. Fearful of losing their savings, depositors pulled money out of banks and put it into gold or under mattresses. Bank runs, in which crowds of frightened customers demanded their money, became common.

By the 1932 election, the bank crisis was escalating rapidly. Hoover, the lame-duck president, refused to take action without Roosevelt's support, while Roosevelt refused to endorse actions he could not control. By Roosevelt's March 4 inauguration, every state had either suspended banking operations or restricted depositors' access to their money. The new president understood that the total collapse of the U.S. banking system would threaten the nation's survival.

Standing in a cold rain on the Capitol steps, Roosevelt vowed in his inaugural address to face the crisis "frankly and boldly." The lines best remembered from his speech are words of comfort: "The only thing we have to fear is fear itself—nameless, unreasoning, unjustified terror." But the only loud cheers came when Roosevelt asserted that, if need be, "I shall ask the Congress for the one remaining instrument to meet the crisis—broad Executive power to wage a war against the emergency, as great as the power that would be given to me if we were in fact invaded by a foreign foe."

The next day Roosevelt, using powers legally granted by the World War I Trading with the Enemy Act, closed the nation's banks for a four-day "holiday" and summoned Congress to an emergency session. He immediately introduced the Emergency Banking Relief Bill, which was passed sight unseen by a unanimous House vote, approved 73 to 7 in the Senate, and signed into law the same day. It provided federal authority to reopen solvent banks and reorganize the rest and authorized federal money to shore up private banks. Roosevelt attacked "unscrupulous money changers," and many critics of the failed banking system hoped he planned to remove the banks from private hands. Instead, Roosevelt's banking policy was much like Hoover's—a fundamentally conservative approach that upheld the status quo.

The banking bill could save the U.S. banking system only if Americans were confident enough to deposit money in the reopened banks. In the first of his radio Fireside Chats, Roosevelt asked Americans for support. "We have provided the machinery to restore our financial system," he said. "It is up to you to support and make it work." The next morning, when the banks opened, people lined up—this time, most waited to deposit money.

First Hundred Days

During the ninety-nine-day-long special session of Congress, dubbed by journalists the First Hundred Days, the federal government took on dramatically new roles. Roosevelt , aided by advisers—lawyers, university professors, and social workers collectively nicknamed the Brain Trust—and by the enormously capable First Lady, sought to revive the American economy. These New Dealers had no single plan, and Roosevelt fluctuated between attempts to balance the budget and massive deficit spending (spending more than is taken in in taxes and borrowing the difference). But with a strong mandate for action and the support of a Democrat-controlled Congress, the administration produced a flood of legislation. Two basic strategies emerged during the First Hundred Days. New Dealers experimented with national economic planning, and they created a range of relief programs for the needy.

National Industrial Recovery Act

At the heart of the New Deal experiment were the National Industrial Recovery Act (NIRA) and the Agricultural Adjustment Act (AAA). The NIRA was based on the belief that destructive competition worsened industry's economic woes. Skirting antitrust regulation, the NIRA authorized competing businesses to cooperate in crafting industrywide codes. Thus automobile manufacturers, for example, would cooperate to limit production and establish industrywide prices and wages. With wages and prices stabilized, the theory went, consumer spending would increase, thus allowing industries to rehire workers. Participation in this National Recovery Administration (NRA) program was voluntary, so though it was larger than previous government-private sector cooperation, it was not very different from Hoover-era associationalism.

As small-business owners feared, big business easily dominated the NRA-mandated cartels. Often NRA staff were unable to stand up to corporate representatives. The twenty-six-year-old NRA staffer who oversaw the creation of the petroleum industry code was "helped" by twenty highly paid oil industry lawyers. The majority of the 541 codes approved by the NRA reflected the interests of major corporations, not small-business owners, labor, or consumers. Most fundamentally, the NRA did not deliver economic recovery. In 1935 the Supreme Court put an end to the fragile, floundering system when it found that the NRA extended federal power past its constitutional bounds.

Agricultural Adjustment Act

The Agricultural Adjustment Act (AAA) had a more enduring effect. Establishing a national system of crop controls, it offered subsidies to farmers who agreed to limit production of specific crops. (Overproduction drove crop prices down.) In 1933, the nation's farmers destroyed 8.5 million piglets and plowed under crops in the fields. Millions of hungry Americans found it difficult to understand this waste of food.

Government crop subsidies proved a disaster for tenant farmers and sharecroppers, who were turned off the land as landlords cut production. In the South the number of sharecropper farms dropped by almost one-third between 1930 and 1940. The result was a homeless population of dispossessed Americans—many of them African American—heading to cities and towns. But subsidies did help many. In the Dakotas, government payments accounted for almost three-quarters of the total farm income for 1934.

In 1936 the Supreme Court found that the AAA, like the NRA, was unconstitutional. But the AAA (unlike the NRA) was too popular with its constituency, American farmers, to disappear. The legislation was rewritten to meet the Supreme Court's objections, and farm subsidies continued into the twenty-first century.

Relief Programs

Roosevelt moved quickly to implement poor relief: $3 billion in federal dollars was allocated in 1935. New Dealers, like many other Americans, disapproved of direct relief payments. Thus New Deal programs emphasized work relief. By January 1934, the Civil Works Administration hired 4 million people, most earning $15 a week. And the Civilian Conservation Corps (CCC) paid unmarried young men, segregated by race, $1 a day to do hard outdoor labor: building dams and reservoirs, creating trails in national parks. By 1942 the CCC employed 2.5 million men, including 80,000 Native Americans working on western Indian reservations.

Work relief programs rarely included poor women. Mothers of young children were usually classified as unemployable and offered mother's-aid grants, which historian Linda Gordon explains, were miniscule compared to wages in federal works program jobs. And while federal relief programs rejected the poor-law tradition that distinguished between the "deserving" and the "undeserving" poor, local officials often did not. "The investigators, they were like detectives," complained one woman who had requested relief.

The Public Works Administration (PWA), created by Title II of the National Industrial Recovery Act, appropriated $3.3 billion in 1933. PWA workers built the Grand Coulee Dam (begun during Hoover's administration) and the Triborough Bridge in New York City, as well as hundreds of public buildings. But the PWA's main purpose was to pump federal money into the economy. This huge appropriation shows the Roosevelt administration's willingness to use controversial deficit spending to stimulate the economy.

In the three months until Congress adjourned on June 16, 1933, Roosevelt delivered fifteen messages to Congress proposing major legislation, and Congress passed fifteen significant laws (see Table 25.1). The United States rebounded from near collapse. As New Deal programs were implemented, unemployment fell from

TABLE 25.1   New Deal Achievements

Year	Labor	Agriculture and Environment	Business and Industrial Recovery	Relief	Reform
1933	Section 7(a) of NIRA	Agricultural Adjustment Act Farm Credit Act	Emergency Banking Relief Act Economy Act Beer-Wine Revenue Act Banking Act of 1933 (guaranteed deposits) National Industrial Recovery Act	Civilian Conservation Corps Federal Emergency Relief Act Home Owners Refinancing Act Public Works Administration Civil Works Administration	TVA Federal Securities Act
1934	National Labor Relations Board	Taylor Grazing Act			Securities Exchange Act
1935	National Labor Relations (Wagner) Act	Resettlement Administration Rural Electrification Administration		Works Progress Administration National Youth Administration	Social Security Act Public Utility Holding Company Act Revenue Act (wealth tax)
1937		Farm Security Administration		National Housing Act	
1938	Fair Labor Standards Act	Agricultural Adjustment Act of 1938			

Source: Adapted from Charles Sellers, Henry May, and Neil R. McMillen, *A Synopsis of American History*, 6th ed. Copyright © 1985 by Houghton Mifflin Company. Reprinted by permission.

13 million in 1933 to 9 million in 1936. Farm prices rose, along with wages and salaries, and business failures abated (see Figure 25.1).

POLITICAL PRESSURE AND THE SECOND NEW DEAL

The unprecedented popular and congressional support for Roosevelt's New Deal did not last. The seeming unity of the First Hundred Days masked deep divides within the nation, and once the immediate crisis was averted, the struggle over solutions began in earnest. Some tried to stop the expansion of government power; others pushed for increased governmental action to combat continuing poverty and inequality.

Business Opposition

As the economy partially recovered, many wealthy business leaders criticized the New Deal. They condemned government regulation and taxation, along with the use of deficit financing. In 1934 several corporate leaders joined former presidential candidate

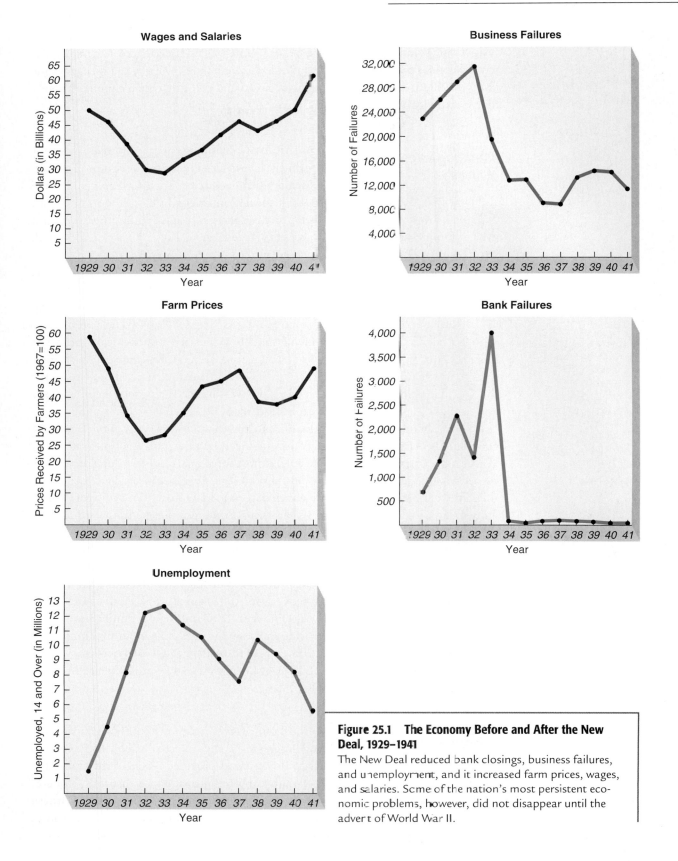

Figure 25.1 The Economy Before and After the New Deal, 1929–1941

The New Deal reduced bank closings, business failures, and unemployment, and it increased farm prices, wages, and salaries. Some of the nation's most persistent economic problems, however, did not disappear until the advent of World War II.

Al Smith and disaffected conservative Democrats to establish the American Liberty League and campaign against New Deal "radicalism." Hoping to turn southern whites against the New Deal and splinter the Democratic Party, the Liberty League also secretly channeled funds to a racist group in the South, which circulated incendiary pictures of the First Lady with African Americans.

Demagogues and Populists

Other Americans (sometimes called populists) thought the government favored business over the common people. Unemployment had decreased—but 9 million people were still jobless. In 1934 a wave of strikes hit the nation, affecting 1.5 million workers. In 1935 enormous dust storms enveloped the southern plains, killing livestock and driving families like the Montgomerys from their land. As dissatisfaction mounted, so did the appeal of demagogues, who played to people's prejudices.

Father Charles Coughlin, a Roman Catholic priest whose weekly radio sermons reached 30 million listeners, spoke to those who felt they had lost control of their lives to distant elites. Increasingly anti–New Deal, he was also anti-Semitic, telling listeners that an international conspiracy of Jewish bankers caused their problems.

Another challenge came from Dr. Francis E. Townsend, a public health officer in Long Beach, California, who lost his job at age sixty-seven with only $100 in savings. His situation was common. With social welfare left to the states, only about 400,000 of the 6.6 million elderly Americans received any state-supplied pensions. As employment and savings disappeared with the depression, many older people fell into poverty.

Townsend proposed that Americans over the age of sixty should receive a government pension of $200 a month, financed by a new transaction (sales) tax. Townsend's plan was fiscally impossible (almost three-quarters of working Americans earned $200 a month or less) and profoundly regressive (because sales tax rates are the same for everyone, they take a larger share of income from those who earn least). Nonetheless, 20 million Americans, or 1 in 5 adults, signed petitions supporting this plan.

Then, there was Huey Long, perhaps the most successful populist demagogue in American history. As a U.S. senator, Long initially supported the New Deal but soon decided that Roosevelt had fallen captive to big business. Long countered in 1934 with the Share Our Wealth Society, advocating the seizure (by taxation) of all income exceeding $1 million a year and wealth in excess of $5 million per family. From these funds, the government would provide each American family an annual income of $2,000 and a one-time homestead allowance of $5,000. By mid-1935 Long's movement claimed 7 million members. But Long was killed by a bodyguard's bullet during an assassination attempt in September 1935.

Left-Wing Critics

The political left also gained ground. In Wisconsin, the left-wing Progressive Party reelected Robert La Follette to the Senate in 1934 and provided seven of the state's ten representatives to Congress. Disclaiming any intention of overthrowing the U.S. government, the Communist Party proclaimed that "Communism Is Twentieth Century Americanism" and cooperated with left-wing labor unions, student groups, and writers' organizations in a Popular Front against fascism abroad and racism at home. In the late 1920s, the Communist Party established the League of Struggle for Negro Rights to fight lynching and, from 1931 on, provided legal and financial support to the Scottsboro Boys, who were falsely accused of raping two white women in Alabama. In 1938, the party had 55,000 members.

Shaping the Second New Deal

It was not only external critics who pushed Roosevelt to focus on social justice. Due to Eleanor Roosevelt's influence, the president's administration included many progressive activists. Frances Perkins, America's first woman cabinet member, came from a social work background, as did Roosevelt's close adviser Harold Ickes. Women social reformers who coalesced around the First Lady played important roles, and African Americans had an unprecedented voice in this White House. By 1936 at least fifty African Americans held relatively important positions in New Deal agencies and cabinet-level departments. Journalists called these officials—who met on Friday evenings at the home of Mary McLeod Bethune, Director of Negro Affairs for the National Youth Administration—the black cabinet.

As Roosevelt faced the 1936 election, he knew he had to appeal to seemingly contradictory desires. Americans hit hard by the depression looked to the New Deal for help. Those with a tenuous hold on the middle class feared continued chaos and disorder. They wanted security and stability. Still others, frightened by the populist promises of people like Long and Coughlin, wanted the New Deal to preserve American capitalism. With this in mind, Roosevelt took the initiative once more.

During the period historians call the Second New Deal, Roosevelt introduced progressive programs aimed at providing "greater security for the average man than he has ever known before in the history of America." The first triumph of the Second New Deal was a law that Roosevelt called the Big Bill. The Emergency Relief Appropriation Act provided $4 billion in new deficit spending, primarily for massive public works programs for the jobless. It also established the Resettlement Administration, which resettled destitute families and organized rural homestead communities and suburban greenbelt towns for low-income workers; the Rural Electrification Administration, which brought electricity to isolated rural areas; and the National Youth Administration, which sponsored work-relief programs for young adults.

Works Progress Administration

The largest and best-known program was the Works Progress Administration (WPA), later renamed the Work Projects Administration. The WPA employed more than 8.5 million people who built 650,000 miles of highways and roads and 125,000 public buildings, as well as bridges, reservoirs, irrigation systems, sewage treatment plants, parks, playgrounds, and swimming pools nationwide.

The WPA also employed artists, musicians, writers, and actors in cultural programs. The WPA's Federal Theater Project brought vaudeville, circuses, and theater, including African American plays and Yiddish plays to cities and towns. Its Arts Project hired painters and sculptors to teach in rural schools and commissioned artists to decorate post office walls with murals depicting life in America. Perhaps the most ambitious program, the WPA's Federal Writers' Project (FWP) hired authors such as John Steinbeck and Richard Wright to create guidebooks for every state and write about the people of the United States. More than two thousand elderly former slaves told their stories to FWP writers as slave narratives. Life stories of sharecroppers and textile workers were published as *These Are Our Lives* (1939). WPA arts projects were controversial, for many of the artists, performers, and writers sympathized with the political struggles of workers and farmers and some were communists.

Social Security Act

Big Bill programs were part of a short-term emergency strategy, but Roosevelt's long-term strategy centered on the Social Security Act. This measure created, for the first time, a federal system to provide for the social welfare of American citizens. Its key provision was a pension system in which eligible workers paid mandatory Social Security taxes on their wages and their employers contributed an equivalent amount; these workers then received federal retirement benefits. The Social Security Act also created several welfare programs, including a cooperative federal-state system of unemployment compensation and Aid to Dependent Children (later renamed Aid to Families with Dependent Children, AFDC) for needy children in families without fathers present.

Compared with the national systems of social security in most western European nations, the U.S. system was fairly conservative. First, the government did not pay for old-age benefits; workers and their bosses did. Second, the tax was regressive in that the more workers earned, the less they were taxed proportionally. Finally, the law did not cover agricultural labor, domestic service, and "casual labor not in the course of the employer's trade or business" (for example, janitorial work at a hospital). Thus a disproportionately high number of people of color, who worked as farm laborers or domestic servants or in service jobs, received no benefits. The act also excluded public-sector employees, so many teachers, nurses, librarians, and social workers (mostly women) went uncovered. (Although the original Social Security Act provided no retirement benefits for spouses or widows of covered workers, Congress added these benefits in 1939.) Despite these limitations, the federal government took some responsibility for the economic security of the aged, the temporarily unemployed, dependent children, and people with disabilities.

Roosevelt's Populist Strategies

As the 1936 election approached, Roosevelt adopted the populist language of his critics. Denouncing the "unjust concentration of wealth and power," he proposed that government should "cut the giants down to size" through antitrust suits and heavy corporate taxes. He also supported the Wealth Tax Act, which helped slightly redistribute income by raising the wealthy's income taxes (see Figure 25.2). It imposed a new tax on business profits and increased taxes on inheritances, large gifts, and profits from the sale of property.

Roosevelt won by a landslide, defeating Republican nominee Governor Alf Landon of Kansas by 27.8 to 16.7 million votes. The Democrats also won majorities in the House and Senate. The Democrats forged a powerful New Deal coalition, consisting of the urban working class (especially immigrants from southern and eastern Europe), organized labor, the eleven states of the Confederacy (the Solid South), and northern African Americans. African Americans in northern cities now constituted

Figure 25.2   Distribution of Total Family Income Among the American People, 1929–1944 (percentage)

Although the New Deal provided economic relief to the American people, it did not, as its critics so often charged, significantly redistribute income downward from the rich to the poor.   *Source:* Adapted from U.S. Bureau of the Census, *Historical Statistics of the United States, Colonial Times to 1970,* 2 parts [Washington, DC: U.S. Government Printing Office, 1975], Part 1, p. 301.)

voting blocks, and New Deal benefits drew them away from the Republican Party, which they had long supported as the party of Lincoln. This New Deal coalition ensured Democrats would occupy the White House for most of the next thirty years.

LABOR

During the worst years of the depression, American workers continued to struggle for the rights of labor. Management, however, resisted unionization vigorously, with some employers refusing to recognize unions, and others hiring armed thugs to intimidate workers. When workers walked off the job, employers replaced them with strikebreakers. Workers tried to keep strikebreakers from crossing picket lines, and the situation often turned violent. Local police or National Guard troops frequently intervened for management. As strikes spread, violence erupted in the steel, automobile, and textile industries, among lumber workers in the Pacific Northwest, and among teamsters in the Midwest.

The Roosevelt administration provided support for labor with the 1935 National Labor Relations (Wagner) Act. It guaranteed workers the right to organize unions and bargain collectively. It outlawed "unfair labor practices," such as firing workers who joined unions, prohibited management from sponsoring company unions, and required employers to bargain with labor's elected union representatives on wages, hours, and working conditions. Critically important, the Wagner Act created an enforcement mechanism: the National Labor Relations Board (NLRB). By decade's end, the NLRB played a key role in mediating disputes. With federal protection, union membership grew from 3.6 million in 1929 to more than 7 million in 1938. The business-sponsored Liberty League insisted—incorrectly—that the Supreme Court would find the Wagner Act unconstitutional.

Rivalry Between Craft and Industrial Unions

The rapid growth and increasing militancy of the labor movement exacerbated an existing division between craft and industrial unions. Craft unions represented labor's elite—skilled workers in a particular trade, such as carpentry. Industrial unions represented all workers, skilled and unskilled, in a given industry. In the 1930s, industrial unions grew dramatically.

Craft unions dominated the American Federation of Labor, the powerful umbrella organization for specific unions. Most AFL leaders offered little support for industrial organizing. Many looked down on the industrial workers, disproportionately immigrants from southern and eastern Europe—"the rubbish at labor's door," in the words of the Teamsters' president. Skilled workers had economic interests different from those of the great mass of unskilled workers, and more conservative craft unionists were alarmed by what they saw as the radicalism of industrial unions.

In 1935 John L. Lewis, head of the United Mine Workers and the nation's most prominent labor leader, resigned as vice president of the AFL. He and other industrial unionists created the Committee for Industrial Organization (CIO); the AFL then suspended all CIO unions. In 1938 the slightly renamed Congress of Industrial Organizations had 3.7 million members, slightly more than the AFL's 3.4 million. Unlike the AFL, the CIO included women and people of color, giving these marginal workers greater employment security and the benefits of collective bargaining.

Sit-Down Strikes

The most decisive labor conflict came when the United Auto Workers (UAW) demanded recognition from General Motors (GM), Chrysler, and Ford. When GM refused, workers at the Fisher Body plant in Flint, Michigan, responded on December 30, 1936 with a sit-down strike, *inside* the factory. Refusing to leave, they immobilized a key part of the GM production system. GM tried to force them out by turning off the heat. The police used tear gas; strikers turned the plant's water hoses on the police.

As the sit-down strike spread to adjacent plants, auto production plummeted. General Motors obtained a court order to evacuate the plant, but strikers stood firm, risking imprisonment and fines. Michigan's governor refused to send in the National Guard. After forty-four days, GM agreed to recognize the union, and Chrysler followed. Ford held out until 1941.

Memorial Day Massacre

On the heels of this triumph, however, came a grim reminder of the costs of labor's struggle. On Memorial Day 1937, picnicking workers and their families marched toward the Republic Steel plant in Chicago, intending to support strikers there. Police ordered them to disperse. One marcher threw something, and the police attacked. Ten men were killed, seven shot in the back. Thirty marchers were wounded, including a woman and three children. Many Americans, fed up with labor strife and violence, showed little sympathy for the workers. Gradually violence receded, as the National Labor Relations Board successfully mediated disputes. Unionized workers—about 23 percent of the nonagricultural work force—saw their standard of living rise. By 1941 the average steelworker could afford to buy a pair of shoes for each of his children every other year.

FEDERAL POWER AND THE NATIONALIZATION OF CULTURE

In the 1930s, both national media and the federal government played an increasingly important role in the lives of Americans from different regions, classes, and ethnic backgrounds. In 1930, with the single exception of the post office, Americans had little direct contact with the federal government. By the end of the 1930s, almost 35 percent of the population received some federal benefit, whether crop subsidies through the federal AAA or a WPA job. Americans now expected the federal government to play a major role in the life of the nation.

New Deal in the West

The New Deal changed the American West more than any other region, as the federally sponsored construction of dams and other public works projects reshaped the region's economy and environment. During the 1930s, the federal Bureau of Reclamation, an obscure agency created by the Newlands Reclamation Act of 1902, expanded its mandate dramatically to build large multipurpose dams that controlled river systems. The Boulder Dam (later renamed for Herbert Hoover) harnessed the Colorado River, providing water to southern California municipalities and using hydroelectric power to produce electricity for Los Angeles and southern Arizona.

The water from these dams opened new areas to agriculture and allowed western cities to expand; the cheap electricity they produced attracted industry. After the completion of Washington State's Grand Coulee Dam in 1941, the federal government controlled a great deal of water and hydroelectric power in the region, which effectively meant control over the region's future.

The federal government also brought millions of acres of western land under its control in the 1930s. To combat the environmental disaster of the Dust Bowl and keep agriculture prices from falling further, federal programs worked to limit production. In 1934 the Taylor Grazing Act imposed new restrictions on ranchers' use of public lands for grazing stock. Federal livestock reduction programs probably saved the western cattle industry, but they destroyed the traditional economy of the Navajos by forcing them to reduce the size of their sheep herds on federal reservation lands. The large farms and ranches of the West benefited from federal subsidies and crop supports through the AAA, but such programs also increased federal control in the region.

New Deal for Native Americans

New federal activism also extended to the West's people. Previous federal policies toward Native Americans, especially those on western Indian reservations, were disastrous. The

Bureau of Indian Affairs (BIA) was riddled with corruption; in its attempts to assimilate Native Americans, it separated children from parents, suppressed native languages, and outlawed tribal religious practices. The division of tribal lands, however, failed to promote individual land ownership. In the early 1930s, Native Americans were the poorest group in the nation, with an infant mortality rate twice that of white Americans.

In 1933 Roosevelt named one of the BIA's most vocal critics to head the agency. John Collier, founder of the American Indian Defense Agency, meant to completely reverse the course of America's Indian policy. The Indian Reorganization Act (1934) worked toward ending forced assimilation and restoring Indian lands to tribal ownership. Indian tribes regained their status as semisovereign nations, guaranteed "internal sovereignty" in all matters not limited by acts of Congress.

Some Indians denounced the IRA as a "back-to-the-blanket" measure based on romantic notions of "authentic" Indian culture. The tribal government structure specified by the IRA was culturally alien to tribes such as the Papagos, whose language had no word for "representative." The Navajo nation also refused to ratify the IRA, especially since the vote was timed during the federally mandated destruction of Navajo sheep herds. Eventually, however, 181 tribes organized under the IRA, which laid the groundwork for future economic development and limited political autonomy among native peoples.

New Deal in the South

New Dealers did not set out to transform the American West, but they did intend to transform the American South. Well before the Great Depression, the South was mired in debilitating poverty. In 1929 the South's per capita income of $365 per year was less than half of the West's $921. More than half of southern farm families were tenants or sharecroppers with no land of their own. Almost 15 percent of South Carolina's people could not read or write.

The largest federal intervention in the South was the Tennessee Valley Authority (TVA), authorized by Congress during Roosevelt's First Hundred Days. The TVA was created to develop a water and hydroelectric power project similar to the multipurpose dams of the West. However, confronted with the poverty of the Tennessee River Valley region (which included parts of Virginia, North Carolina, Tennessee, Georgia, Alabama, Mississippi, and Kentucky), the TVA expanded to promote economic development, bring electricity to rural areas, restore fields worn out from overuse, and fight malaria.

Although it benefited many southerners, the TVA proved to be a monumental environmental disaster. TVA strip mining caused soil erosion. Its coal-burning generators released sulfur oxides, which combined with water vapor to produce acid rain. Above all, the TVA degraded the water by dumping untreated sewage, toxic chemicals, and metal pollutants from strip mining into streams and rivers.

Southern senators benefited from the flow of federal dollars to their states, but they were suspicious of federal intervention. When federal action threatened the South's racial hierarchy, they resisted passionately. As the nation's poorest and least educated region, the South would not easily be integrated into the national culture and economy. But New Deal programs began that process and improved the lives of at least some of the region's people.

Mass Media and Popular Culture

America's national popular culture helped break down regional boundaries and foster national connections. Radio filled the days and nights of the depression era. As cheaper models became available, by 1937 Americans were buying radios at the rate of twenty-eight a minute. By decade's end, 27.5 million households owned radios, and families listened on average five hours a day. Roosevelt used radio to speak directly to the American people with Fireside Chats.

In a time of uncertainty, radio gave citizens immediate access to the political news and the actual voices of their elected leaders. During hard times, radio offered escape: for children, the adventures of *Flash Gordon* and *Jack Armstrong, The All-American Boy;* for housewives, new soap operas, such as *The Romance of Helen Trent* and *Young Widder Brown*. Families gathered to listen to the comedy of the ex-vaudevillians George Burns and Gracie Allen, and Jack Benny.

Listeners were carried to New York City for performances of the Metropolitan Opera on Saturday afternoons, to the Moana Hotel on the beach at Waikiki through the live broadcast of *Hawaii Calls,* and to major league baseball games (begun by the St. Louis Cardinals in 1935) in distant cities. Millions shared the horror of the kidnapping of aviator Charles Lindbergh's son in 1932; African Americans in the urban North and rural South shared the triumphs of African American boxer Joe Louis (the Brown Bomber). Radio lessened the isolation of individuals and helped create a more homogeneous mass culture across class and regional lines.

The shared popular culture of 1930s America also centered on Hollywood movies. The film industry suffered in the initial years of the depression, but it rebounded after 1933. In a nation of fewer than 130 million people, 80 to 90 million tickets were sold weekly by the mid-1930s, as Americans sought escape at the movies. Comedies were especially popular, from the slapstick of the Marx Brothers to the sophisticated banter of *My Man Godfrey*.

Yet as gangster movies (including *Little Caesar* and *Scarface*) drew crowds in the early 1930s, many Americans worried about their glamorization of crime. Faced with a boycott organized by the Roman Catholic Legion of Decency, in 1934 the film industry established a production code that would determine what American film audiences saw—and did not see—for decades.

Finally, in an unintended consequence, federal policies intended to channel jobs to male heads of households strengthened the power of national popular culture. During Roosevelt's first two years in office, 1.5 million youths lost jobs; many young people who would have gone to work at the age of fourteen in better times decided to stay in school. By the end of the decade, three-quarters of

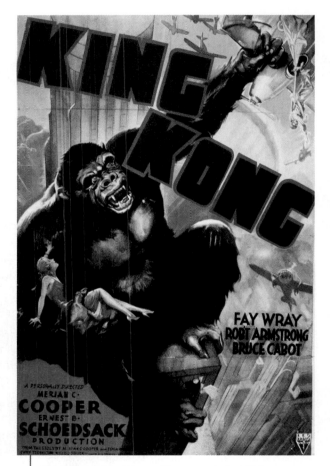

King Kong broke all box-office records in 1933, as Americans flocked to see the giant ape fighting off airplanes from the top of New York's new Empire State Building—the tallest building in the world. (The Granger Collection, New York)

The 1936 Olympic Games

The 1936 Olympic Games scheduled in Berlin, under the Nazi regime, created a dilemma for the United States and other nations. Would participation in the Nazi-orchestrated spectacle lend credence to Hitler? Or would victories by other nations undermine Hitler's claims about the superiority of Germany's "Aryan race"?

From the first modern Olympic Games in 1896, international politics were always near the surface. Germany was excluded in 1920 and 1924 following its World War I defeat. The International Olympic Committee's choice (in 1931) of Berlin for the XI Olympiad was intended to welcome Germany back into the world community. However, with Hitler's rise to power in 1933, Germany determined to use the games as propaganda for the Nazi state. Soon thereafter, campaigns to boycott the Berlin Olympics emerged in several nations, including the United States.

Americans were divided over the boycott. Some U.S. Jewish groups led campaigns against U.S. participation in Berlin, and Jewish athletes decided individually whether to attend. But the debate over the Berlin Olympics revealed pockets of American anti-Semitism. The president of the American Olympic Committee, Avery Brundage, attributed the boycott movement to a "conspiracy of Jews and communists." African Americans opposed the

boycott and looked forward to demonstrating in Berlin how wrong Hitler's notions of Aryan superiority were.

The United States sent 312 athletes to Berlin; 18 were African Americans, who won 14 medals, almost one-quarter of the U.S. total of 56. Track and field star Jesse Owens earned 4 gold medals. Jewish athletes won 13 medals.

Despite the controversy, the XI Olympiad was a public relations triumph for Germany. The New York Times, impressed by the games and Germans' hospitality, proclaimed that the XI Olympiad put Germany "back in the fold of nations." Still, the idealistic vision of nations linked in peaceful athletic competition hit a low point at the 1936 Olympics. The 1940 Olympic Games, scheduled for Tokyo, were cancelled because of the escalating world war.

The eleventh summer Olympic Games in Berlin were carefully crafted as propaganda for the Nazi state. And the spectacle of the 1936 games, as represented in this poster, was impressive. But on the athletic fields, Nazi claims of Aryan superiority were challenged by athletes such as African American Jesse Owens, who is shown breaking the Olympic record in the 200-meter race.

(Above: © Leonard de Selva/Corbis; left: © Bettmann/ Corbis)

American youth went to high school—up from one-half in 1920—and graduation rates doubled. As more young people went to high school, more participated in that national youth culture, increasingly listening to the same music and adopting similar clothing, dance, and speech. Paradoxically, the hard times of the depression caused youth culture to spread more widely among America's young.

THE LIMITS OF THE NEW DEAL

Roosevelt began his second term with a strong mandate for reform. Almost immediately, however, the president's own actions undermined his New Deal agenda. Labor strife and racial issues divided America. As the world inched toward war, domestic initiatives lost ground to foreign affairs and defense. By late 1938, New Deal reform ground to a halt.

Court-Packing Plan

Following his landslide in 1936, Roosevelt set out to safeguard his progressive agenda. He saw the Supreme Court as its greatest threat. In ruling both the National Industrial Recovery Act (in 1935) and the Agricultural Adjustment Act (in 1936) unconstitutional, the Court not only rejected specific legislative provisions but also the expansion of presidential and federal power this legislation entailed. Only three of the nine justices were consistently sympathetic to New Deal emergency measures, and Roosevelt was convinced the Court would invalidate most of the Second New Deal legislation. Citing the advanced age and heavy workload of the nine justices, he asked Congress for authority to appoint up to six new justices. But in an era that had seen the rise of Hitler, Mussolini, and Stalin, many Americans saw Roosevelt's plan as an attack on constitutional government. Congress rebelled, and Roosevelt experienced his first major congressional defeat.

Ironically, during the long debate over court packing, key swing-vote justices began to vote for pro–New Deal rulings. The Court upheld both the Social Security Act and the Wagner Act (*NLRB v. Jones & Laughlin Steel Corp.*), extending Congress's power to regulate interstate commerce to production of goods for interstate commerce. Moreover, a new judicial pension program encouraged older judges to retire, and the president appointed seven new associate justices. In the end, Roosevelt got what he wanted from the Supreme Court, but the court-packing plan damaged his political credibility.

Roosevelt Recession

Another New Deal setback was the recession of 1937–1939, sometimes called the Roosevelt recession. In 1937, confident that the depression had ebbed, Roosevelt reduced government spending. At the same time, the Federal Reserve Board, concerned about a 3.6 percent inflation rate, tightened credit. These actions sent the economy into a tailspin: unemployment climbed from 7.7 million in 1937 to 10.4 million in 1938.

New Dealers struggled over the direction of liberal reform. Some urged trust-busting; others advocated the resurrection of national economic planning. But Roosevelt instead chose deficit financing to stimulate consumer demand and create jobs. And in 1939, with conflict over the world war in Europe commanding more of the nation's attention, the New Deal came to an end. Roosevelt sacrificed further domestic reforms in return for conservative support for his programs of military rearmament and preparedness.

Election of 1940

No president had ever served more than two terms, and Americans speculated about whether Franklin Roosevelt would seek a third term in 1940. Roosevelt seemed undecided until spring, when Adolf Hitler's military advances in Europe convinced him to stay on. In the 1940 campaign, Roosevelt promised Americans, "Your boys are not going to be sent into any foreign wars."

Roosevelt did not win this election in a landslide, but the New Deal coalition held. Roosevelt again won in the cities, supported by blue-collar workers, ethnic Americans, and African Americans. He also carried every southern state.

Race and the Limits of the New Deal

While the New Deal benefited many Americans, it fell short of equality for people of color. Implemented at the local level, national programs were subjected to local custom. In the South, that meant African Americans received lower relief payments than whites and were paid less for WPA jobs. In Tucson, Arizona, Federal Emergency Relief Agency officials divided applicants into four groups—Anglos, Mexican Americans, Mexican immigrants, and Indians—and allocated relief payments in descending order.

Such discriminatory practices were rooted not only in racism but also in the economic interests of whites, or Anglos. The majority of African American and Mexican American workers were paid so poorly that they *earned* less than impoverished whites got for relief. Why would these workers take low-paying private jobs if government relief or government work programs provided more income? Local communities understood that federal programs threatened a political, social, and economic system based on racial hierarchies.

The case of the Scottsboro Boys illustrates the power of racism in the conflict between local and national power in 1930s America. One night in March 1931, two white women riding the rails on a Southern Railroad freight train claimed that young black hobos on this train had raped them. Medical evidence later showed that the women were lying. But within two weeks, eight of the so-called Scottsboro Boys were convicted of rape by all-white juries and sentenced to death. The ninth, a boy of thirteen, was saved from the death penalty by one vote. The case—clearly a product of southern racism—became a cause célèbre, both nationally and, through the efforts of the Communist Party, around the world.

The Supreme Court intervened, ruling that Alabama deprived black defendants of equal protection under the law by systematically excluding African Americans from juries and denying the defendants counsel. Alabama, however, staged new trials, convicting five of the young men (four would be paroled by 1950, and one escaped from prison). On issues of race, the South would not yield easily to federal power.

Second, the gains made by people of color under the New Deal were limited by the political realities of southern resistance. For example, in 1938 southern Democrats blocked an antilynching bill with a six-week-long filibuster in the Senate. Roosevelt refused to use his political capital to break the filibuster and pass the bill. He knew African Americans would not desert the Democratic Party, but without southern senators, his legislative agenda was dead. Roosevelt wanted all Americans to enjoy the benefits of democracy, but he had no strong commitment to civil rights.

African American Support

Why, then, did African Americans support Roosevelt? Because, despite discriminatory policies, the New Deal helped African Americans. By 1939, almost one-third of African American households survived on income from a WPA job. African Americans held significant positions in the Roosevelt administration, and the First Lady publically showed her commitment to racial equality. When the Daughters of the American Revolution refused to allow acclaimed African American contralto Marian Anderson to perform in Washington's Constitution Hall, Eleanor Roosevelt arranged for Anderson to sing at the Lincoln Memorial instead. Nonetheless, given the limits of New Deal reform, some African Americans concluded that self-help and direct-action movements were a surer alternative. In 1934 African American tenant farmers and sharecroppers joined with poor whites to form the Southern Tenant Farmers' Union. In the North, African American consumers boycotted white merchants who refused to hire African Americans. Their slogan was "Don't Buy Where You Can't Work." And the Brotherhood of Sleeping Car Porters, under the astute leadership of A. Philip Randolph, fought for African American workers. Such actions helped improve the lives of African Americans during the 1930s.

An Assessment of the New Deal

Assessments of Roosevelt varied widely during his presidency: he was passionately hated and passionately loved. When he spoke to Americans in his Fireside Chats, hundreds of thousands wrote to him, asking for help and offering advice.

Eleanor Roosevelt played an unprecedented role in the Roosevelt administration. As First Lady, she worked for social justice, bringing reformers, trade unionists, and advocates for the rights of women and African Americans to the White House. Sometimes described as the conscience of the New Deal, she took public positions—especially on African American civil rights—far more progressive than those of her husband's administration. She served as a lightning rod, deflecting conservative criticism from her husband to herself. And she cemented the allegiance of groups such as African Americans to the New Deal.

Most historians consider Franklin Roosevelt a truly great president, citing his courage, his willingness to experiment, and his capacity to inspire the nation. Some, who see the New Deal as a squandered opportunity for "true" change, charge that Roosevelt lacked vision. They judge Roosevelt by goals that were not his own: Roosevelt was a pragmatist whose goal was to preserve the system. But even critics agree he transformed the presidency. Some find this transformation troubling, tracing the roots of the imperial presidency to the Roosevelt administration.

During his more than twelve years in office, Roosevelt strengthened the presidency and the federal government. Through New Deal programs, the government expanded its regulatory responsibilities, including overseeing the nation's financial systems. For the first time the federal government offered relief to the jobless and used deficit spending to stimulate the economy. Millions of Americans benefited from government programs that are still operating today, among them Social Security.

However, as late as 1939, more than 10 million men and women remained jobless, and the nation's unemployment rate stood at 19 percent. It was not until 1941, as the nation mobilized for war, that unemployment fell to 10 percent. By 1944, only 1 percent of the labor force was unemployed. World War II, not the New Deal, reinvigorated the American economy.

Summary

In the 1930s, a major economic crisis threatened the nation. By 1933 almost one-quarter of American workers were unemployed. Millions were homeless and hungry. Herbert Hoover, elected president in 1928, believed government should play only a limited role in managing the economy. He tried to solve the nation's economic problems through associationalism, a voluntary partnership of businesses and the federal government. In the 1932 presidential election, voters turned to the candidate who promised them a New Deal, Franklin Delano Roosevelt.

The New Deal was a liberal reform program that developed within the parameters of America's capitalist and democratic system. It expanded the power of the federal government. New Deal reforms forced banks, utilities, stock markets, farms, and most businesses to adhere to federal guidelines. The government guaranteed the workers' right to join unions, and federal law required employers to negotiate with workers' unions on wages, hours, and working conditions. Many unemployed workers, elderly and disabled Americans, and dependent children were protected by a national welfare system administered through the federal government.

The New Deal had its detractors. Business leaders attacked the New Deal for its new regulation and support of organized labor. As the federal government expanded its role, tensions between national and local authority sometimes flared, and differences in regional ways of life and in social and economic structures challenged national policymakers. Both the West and the South were transformed by federal government action, but citizens of both regions were suspicious of federal intervention, and white southerners resisted challenges to the racial system of Jim Crow. The political realities of a fragile New Deal coalition and strong opposition shaped—and limited—New Deal programs of the 1930s. But the New Deal fundamentally changed the way that the U.S. government would deal with future economic downturns and with the needs of its citizens in good times and in bad.

Social Security

The New Deal's Social Security system created a secure old age for millions of Americans. Although Social Security initially excluded some of America's neediest citizens, such as farm and domestic workers, amendments expanded eligibility. At present, almost 99 percent of American workers are covered by Social Security.

Today's Social Security system faces an uncertain future. Its troubles are partly due to decisions made during the 1930s. President Franklin Roosevelt did not want Social Security to be confused with poor relief. Instead he created a system financed by payments from workers and their employers. This system, however, presented a short-term problem. If benefits came from their own contributions, workers who began receiving Social Security payments in 1940 would have received less than $1 a month. Therefore, Social Security payments from current workers paid the benefits of those already retired.

Over time, this financing system has become increasingly unstable. In 1935, average life expectancy was under sixty-five years, the age one could collect benefits. Today, American men live almost sixteen years past retirement age, and women close to twenty years past retirement age. In 1935 there were 16 current workers paying into the system for each person receiving retirement benefits. In 2000 there were fewer than 3.5 workers per retiree. Unless the system is reformed, many argue, the retirement of 77 million baby boomers born in the 1940s, 1950s, and 1960s could bankrupt the system.

When the stock market rose dramatically during the 1990s, some proposed that, because Social Security paid only a fraction of what individuals might have earned by investing their Social Security tax payments in the stock market, let Americans do just that. Opponents declared this proposal too risky; others asked if current workers kept their money to invest, where would benefits for current retirees come from? With the stock market's huge decline in the first years of the twenty-first century (and the losses sustained by private pension funds), President George W. Bush's privatization initiative gained little congressional support. But, with the oldest baby boomers beginning to retire, questions about the future of Social Security will become increasingly important.

Chapter Review

HOOVER AND HARD TIMES, 1929–1933

Why was Hoover so reluctant to implement relief programs during the Great Depression?

Hoover was afraid that government hand-outs would create dependency among the struggling and poor. When he made federal funds available to feed livestock, but not people, he was reviled by Americans everywhere. By the time he finally initiated federal programs, it was too late to change public opinion or make much difference in the crisis. His public works projects, such as the Grand Coulee Dam, created some jobs, but nowhere near enough to have an impact. While the Federal Farm Board, established in 1929, supported farm prices and lent money to coops, it was poorly funded. Hoover's most direct government program—the Reconstruction Finance Corporation implemented at the end of his presidency in 1932—offered relief to businesses, but still provided nothing for the unemployed.

FRANKLIN D. ROOSEVELT AND THE LAUNCHING OF THE NEW DEAL

How did the government take on new roles during the period dubbed "The First Hundred Days"?

During this special session of Congress, Roosevelt sought to revive the flagging economy through two types of federal initiatives: national economic planning and relief programs. The planning portion of this "New Deal" focused on the National Industrial Recovery Act (NIRA) and the Agricultural Adjustment Act (AAA). The NIRA encouraged industries to adopt wage and price standards that could erase competition and increase consumer spending and, therefore, demand for workers. The AAA established crop controls and offered farm subsidies. Roosevelt also spent $3 billion on work relief programs, such as the Civilian Conservation Corps, which hired young men to help build dams, reservoirs, and trails in national parks; and the Public Works Administration, whose workers completed the Grand Coulee Dam and built New York City's Triborough Bridge and hundreds of other public facilities. All tolled, fifteen laws were passed, helping the United States to recover and unemployment to drop from 13 million in 1933 to 9 million in 1936.

POLITICAL PRESSURE AND THE SECOND NEW DEAL

What were the hallmarks of the Second New Deal?

Roosevelt's goal for the Second New Deal was more far-reaching than his initial efforts. First, the Emergency Relief Appropriation Act allocated $4 billion in deficit spending to provide public works jobs through the Works Progress Administration (WPA)—building roads, bridges, and parks and renovating schools and hospitals. It also implemented initiatives to teach illiterate Americans to read and write and employed artists, writers and actors to put on plays, create original artwork, produce guidebooks for every state, and collect stories about the American people, including those of former slaves. The Resettlement Administration relocated poor families and organized homestead communities, while the Rural Electrification Administration brought electricity to rural areas. But Roosevelt's long-term strategy was the Social Security Act, a federal pension system taxing workers' wages and providing retirement benefits. The SSA included an unemployment compensation program, as well as welfare for needy families without fathers present under Aid to Dependent Children.

LABOR

How did Roosevelt provide support for labor?

Labor unrest and dissatisfaction with dwindling wages and harsh working conditions increased throughout the 1930s. Public support for strikes waned as violence escalated throughout the decade. But Roosevelt bolstered labor with the 1935 National Labor Relations (Wagner) Act, which guaranteed workers the right to organize unions and bargain collectively. It made it illegal for businesses to fire workers who joined unions and banned management from sponsoring company unions. It also required firms to bargain with union representatives about wages, hours, and working conditions and created a National Labor Relations Board to mediate disputes. As the NLRB took hold, violence dissipated and workers' wages increased.

FEDERAL POWER AND THE NATIONALIZATION OF CULTURE

> **How did the Depression cause youth culture to spread?**

Government policies focused on channeling jobs to the male heads of household. That meant that young boys who, at age 14, under normal economic conditions would have gone to work, could not find jobs. Hence, they stayed in school longer, and high school graduation rates by the end of the decade doubled. As young people spent more time in school they were influenced more greatly by their peers than by parents as well as by a shared youth culture in music, clothing, and manner of speaking.

THE LIMITS OF THE NEW DEAL

> **How did Roosevelt undermine his New Deal agenda and, ultimately, his legacy?**

Roosevelt made two moves with serious consequences for the New Deal. First, since the Supreme Court had ruled unconstitutional both the NIRA and the AAA, Roosevelt considered the Court an adversary and sought to pack it with sympathetic justices. He asked Congress to give him the authority to appoint six new justices, arguing that the present nine were getting old and were overworked. Congress refused, and although he ultimately was able to name seven new associate justices when a new pension program encouraged older judges to retire, Roosevelt's political credibility was damaged by his court-packing scheme. Second, in 1937, Roosevelt reduced government spending, certain that the depression was winding down. That, combined with the Federal Reserve's move to tighten credit, triggered a two-year recession.

SUGGESTIONS FOR FURTHER READING

Anthony J. Badger, *The New Deal: The Depression Years, 1933–1940* (1989)

Alan Brinkley, *The End of Reform: New Deal Liberalism in Recession and War* (1995)

Alan Brinkley, *Voices of Protest: Huey Long, Father Coughlin, and the Great Depression* (1982)

Lizabeth Cohen, *Making a New Deal: Industrial Workers in Chicago* (1990)

Blanche Wiesen Cook, *Eleanor Roosevelt*, Vols. 1 and 2 (1992, 1999)

Sidney Fine, *Sitdown: The General Motors Strike of 1936–37* (1969)

James E. Goodman, *Stories of Scottsboro* (1994)

David M. Kennedy, *Freedom from Fear: The American People in Depression and War* (1999)

Robert McElvaine, The *Great Depression: America, 1929–1941* (1984)

Donald Worster, *Dust Bowl: The Southern Plains in the 1930s* (2004)

The United States in a Troubled World

In 1921 the Rockefeller Foundation dedicated several million dollars for projects to control yellow fever in Latin America, beginning in Mexico. Carried by mosquitoes, the virus caused severe headaches, vomiting, jaundice (yellow skin), and often death. Learning from the pioneering work of Carlos Juan Finlay of Cuba, Oswaldo Cruz of Brazil, and U.S. Army surgeon Walter Reed, scientists sought to destroy the mosquito in its larval stage, before it became an egg-laying adult.

U.S. diplomats, military officers, and business executives agreed that the disease threatened public health, and this in turn disturbed political and economic order. When outbreaks occurred, ports were closed and quarantined, disrupting trade and immigration. The infection struck U.S. officials, merchants, investors, and soldiers stationed abroad and incapacitated workers. Throughout Latin America, insufficient official attention to yellow-fever epidemics stirred public discontent against regimes the United States supported. When the Panama Canal opened in 1914, leaders feared that the disease would spread, even reinfecting the United States, which had suffered its last epidemic in 1905.

Gradually overcoming strong local anti-U.S. feelings, Rockefeller personnel inspected breeding places and deposited larvae-eating fish in public waterworks. In 1924 La Fundación Rockefeller declared yellow fever eradicated in Mexico. Elsewhere in Latin America, the foundation's antimosquito campaign proved successful in maritime and urban areas but less so in rural and jungle regions. Politically, Rockefeller Foundation efforts in the 1920s and 1930s strengthened central governments by providing a public health infrastructure and diminished anti-U.S. sentiment.

The Rockefeller Foundation's campaign offers insights into Americans' fervent but futile effort to build a stable international

This icon will direct you to interactive activities and study materials on *A People And A Nation*, Brief Edition website: **www.cengage.com/history/norton/peoplenationbrief8e**

Chronology

1921–22	Washington Conference limits naval arms. Rockefeller Foundation begins the battle against yellow fever in Latin America.
1922	Mussolini comes to power in Italy.
1924	Dawes Plan eases German reparations.
1928	Kellogg-Briand Pact outlaws war.
1929	Great Depression begins. Young Plan reduces German reparations.
1930	Hawley-Smoot Tariff raises duties.
1931	Japan seizes Manchuria.
1933	Adolf Hitler becomes chancellor of Germany. United States extends diplomatic recognition to the Soviet Union. United States announces the Good Neighbor policy for Latin America.
1934	Batista comes to power in Cuba.
1935	Italy invades Ethiopia. Congress passes the first Neutrality Act.
1936	Germany reoccupies the Rhineland. Spanish Civil War breaks out.
1937	Sino-Japanese War breaks out. Roosevelt makes Quarantine Speech against aggressors.
1938	Mexico nationalizes U.S.-owned oil companies. Munich Conference grants part of Czechoslovakia to Germany.
1939	Germany and the Soviet Union sign a nonaggression pact. Germany invades Poland; World War II begins.
1940	Germany invades Denmark, Norway, Belgium, the Netherlands, and France. Selective Training and Service Act starts the first U.S. peacetime draft.
1941	Lend-Lease Act gives aid to the Allies. Germany attacks the Soviet Union. United States freezes Japanese assets. Roosevelt and Churchill sign the Atlantic Charter. Japanese flotilla attacks Pearl Harbor, Hawai'i; United States enters World War II.

order after World War I. Despite the isolationist tag sometimes applied to U.S. foreign relations during the interwar decades, Americans remained active in world affairs in the 1920s and 1930s—from gunboats on Chinese rivers, to negotiations in European financial centers, to marine occupations in Haiti and Nicaragua, to oil wells in the Middle East, to campaigns against diseases in Africa and Latin America. President Wilson rightly said after World War I that the United States had "become a determining factor in the history of mankind."

The most apt description of interwar U.S. foreign policy is independent internationalism. Notwithstanding the nation's overseas projects—colonies, spheres of influence, naval bases, investments, trade, missionary activity, humanitarian projects—many Americans regarded themselves as isolationists, meaning that they wanted no part of Europe's political squabbles or military alliances or the League of Nations, which might drag them into war. Internationalist-minded Americans, including most senior officials, also wanted to stay out of future European wars but were more willing than isolationists to attempt to reshape the world.

A stable world would better facilitate American prosperity and security. In the interwar years, American diplomats increasingly sought to exercise U.S. power through conferences, humanitarian programs, cultural penetration (Americanization), moral lectures and calls for peace, nonrecognition of disapproved regimes, arms control, and economic and financial ties under the Open Door principle.

But a stable world order proved elusive. Public health projects saved lives but could not address staggering poverty around the globe. World War I debts and reparations bedeviled the 1920s. The Great Depression shattered world trade and threatened America's prominence in international markets. It also spawned political extremism, militarism, and war in Europe and Asia. As Nazi Germany marched to war, the United States adopted a neutrality policy. The United States sought to defend its interests in Asia against Japanese aggression by invoking the Open Door policy.

After the outbreak of European war in September 1939, many Americans came to agree with President Franklin D. Roosevelt that Germany and Japan imperiled U.S. interests because they were building self-sufficient spheres of influence on the basis of military and economic domination. Roosevelt first pushed for U.S. military preparedness and then favored aiding Britain and France. A German victory, he reasoned, would destroy traditional economic ties, threaten U.S. influence in the Western Hemisphere, and place at the pinnacle of European power Adolf Hitler, whose ambitions and barbarities seemed limitless.

Meanwhile, Japan seemed determined to dismember the United States' Asian friend China, destroy the Open Door principle, and endanger a U.S. colony—the Philippines. To deter the Japanese, the United States cut off supplies of vital U.S. products, such as oil. Japan's surprise attack on Pearl Harbor, Hawai'i, in December 1941 brought the United States into World War II.

- **Why and by what means did Americans try to facilitate a stable world order in the interwar period?**
- **How did the Roosevelt administration respond to the growing Nazi German threat in the second half of the 1930s?**
- **Why did the United States enter World War II?**

SEARCHING FOR PEACE AND ORDER IN THE 1920s

World War I left Europe in shambles. Between 1914 and 1921, Europe suffered tens of millions of casualties from world war, civil wars, massacres, epidemics, and famine. Germany and France lost 10 percent of their workers. The American Relief Administration and private charities delivered food to needy Europeans, including Russians wracked by famine in 1921 and 1922. Through food relief, Americans hoped to dampen any appeal political radicalism might have overseas. Secretary of State Charles Evans Hughes and other leaders expected U.S. economic expansion to promote international stability, believing prosperity would eliminate ideological extremes, revolution, arms races, aggression, and war.

Collective security, as envisioned by Woodrow Wilson, elicited little enthusiasm among Republican leaders. Senator Henry Cabot Lodge gloated in 1920 that "we have destroyed Mr. Wilson's League of Nations." The Geneva-headquartered League of Nations, envisioned as a peacemaker, proved feeble, not just because the United States did not join but also because members failed to utilize it to settle disputes. Still, starting in the mid-1920s, U.S. officials participated discreetly in League meetings on public health, prostitution, drug and arms trafficking, counterfeiting of currency, and other questions. The Rockefeller Foundation donated $100,000 a year to the League's public health ventures.

Peace Groups

During the interwar years, peace groups drew widespread support. Women gravitated to their own organizations because they lacked influence in the male-dominated groups and because of the popular assumption that women—as nurturing mothers—had a unique aversion to war. Carrie Chapman Catt's moderate National Conference on the Cure and Cause of War, formed in 1924, and the U.S. section of the Women's International League for Peace and Freedom (WILPF), organized in 1915 by Jane Addams and Emily Greene Balch, became the largest women's peace groups. When Addams won the Nobel Peace Prize in 1931, she transferred her award money to the League of Nations.

Peace groups differed over strategies to ensure world order. Some urged cooperation with the League of Nations and the World Court. Others championed arbitration, disarmament and arms reduction, the outlawing of war, and strict neutrality during wars. The WILPF called for an end to U.S. economic imperialism, which, it claimed, compelled the United States to intervene militarily in Latin America to protect U.S. business interests. The Women's Peace Union (organized in 1921) lobbied for a constitutional amendment requiring a national referendum on a declaration of war. Quakers, YMCA officials, and Social Gospel clergy in 1917 created the American Friends Service Committee to identify pacifist alternatives to warmaking.

Washington Naval Conference

Peace advocates influenced Warren G. Harding's administration to convene the Washington Naval Conference of November 1921–February 1922. Delegates from Britain, Japan, France, Italy, China, Portugal, Belgium, and the Netherlands joined a U.S. team led by Secretary of State Hughes to discuss limiting naval armaments. American leaders worried that huge military spending endangered economic rehabilitation and that an expansionist Japan, with the world's third largest navy, would overtake the United States's, ranked second behind Britain.

Secretary of State Hughes opened the conference with the stunning proposal to scrap thirty major U.S. ships, totaling 846,000 tons. He urged the British and Japanese delegations to do away with smaller amounts. The final limit was 500,000 tons each for the Americans and the British, 300,000 tons for the Japanese, and 175,000 tons each for the French and the Italians. These limits were agreed to in the Five-Power Treaty, which also set a ten-year moratorium on building capital ships (battleships and aircraft carriers). The governments further pledged not to build new fortifications in their Pacific possessions (such as the Philippines).

Next, the Nine-Power Treaty reaffirmed the Open Door in China, recognizing Chinese sovereignty. Finally, in the Four-Power Treaty, the United States, Britain, Japan, and France agreed to respect one another's Pacific possessions. These treaties did not limit submarines, destroyers, or cruisers and did not provide enforcement powers for the Open Door. Still, Hughes achieved arms limitation and improved America's strategic position vis-à-vis Japan in the Pacific.

Kellogg-Briand Pact

Peace advocates welcomed the Locarno Pact of 1925, several agreements among European nations that sought to reduce tensions between Germany and France, and the

Kellogg-Briand Pact of 1928. In the latter document, sixty-two nations agreed to "condemn recourse to war for the solution of international controversies, and renounce it as an instrument of national policy." The Kellogg-Briand Pact passed the U.S. Senate 85 to 1, but it lacked enforcement provisions. It did reflect popular opinion that war was barbaric. But arms limitations, peace pacts, and efforts by peace groups failed to muzzle the dogs of war, which fed on the economic troubles that upended world order.

THE WORLD ECONOMY, CULTURAL EXPANSION, AND GREAT DEPRESSION

While Europe struggled to recover after World War I, the international economy wobbled and collapsed. The Great Depression set off a political chain reaction that carried the world to war. Cordell Hull, U.S. secretary of state from 1933 to 1944, argued that political extremism and militarism sprang from maimed economies. Hull proved right.

Economic and Cultural Expansion

Due to World War I, the United States became a creditor nation and the financial capital of the world (see Figure 26.1). From 1914 to 1930, private investments abroad grew fivefold, to more than $17 billion. By the late 1920s, the United States produced nearly half of the world's industrial goods and ranked first among exporters ($5.2 billion worth of shipments in 1929). Britain and Germany lost ground to American businesses in Latin America, where Standard Oil operated in eight nations and the United Fruit Company became a huge landowner.

America's economic prominence facilitated the export of American culture. Hollywood movies saturated the global market and stimulated interest in all things American. Although some foreigners warned against Americanization, others aped American mass-production methods and emphasis on efficiency and modernization. Coca-Cola opened a bottling plant in Essen, Germany; Ford built an automobile assembly plant in Cologne.

Germans marveled at Henry Ford's industrial techniques (*Fordismus*). In the 1930s, Nazi leader Adolf Hitler sent German car designers to Detroit before launching the Volkswagen. The Phelps-Stokes Fund further advertised the American capitalist model, exporting to black Africa Booker T. Washington's Tuskegee philosophy of education, while the Rockefeller Foundation supported colleges to train doctors in Lebanon and China and funded medical research in Europe.

The U.S. government assisted this expansion. The Webb-Pomerene Act (1918) excluded from antitrust prosecution those combinations set up for export trade, the Edge Act (1919) permitted U.S. banks to open foreign-branch banks, and overseas offices of the Department of Commerce distributed market information. The federal government also stimulated foreign loans by American investors. U.S. government support for expansion of the telecommunications industry helped International Telegraph and Telephone (IT&T), Radio Corporation of America (RCA), and the Associated Press (AP) become international giants by 1930.

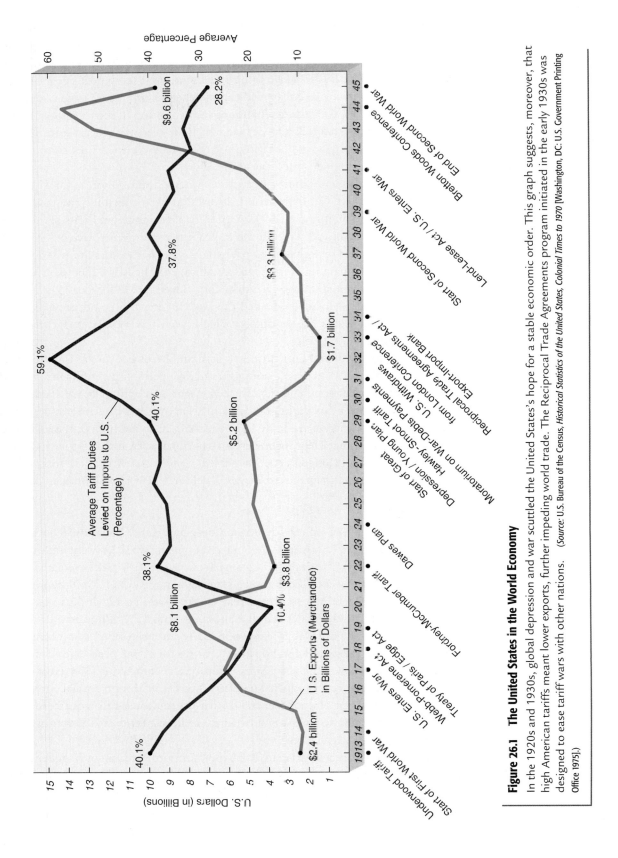

Figure 26.1   The United States in the World Economy

In the 1920s and 1930s, global depression and war scuttled the United States's hope for a stable economic order. This graph suggests, moreover, that high American tariffs meant lower exports, further impeding world trade. The Reciprocal Trade Agreements program initiated in the early 1930s was designed to ease tariff wars with other nations.   (*Source:* U.S. Bureau of the Census, *Historical Statistics of the United States, Colonial Times to 1970* [Washington, DC: U.S. Government Printing Office 1975].)

War Debts and German Reparations

Europeans branded the United States stingy for its handling of World War I debts and reparations. Twenty-eight nations became entangled in inter-Allied government debts totaling $26.5 billion ($9.6 billion of them owed to the U.S. government). Europeans owed private American creditors another $3 billion and urged Americans to erase government debts as a magnanimous contribution to the war effort. During the war, they angrily charged, Europe bled while America profited. American leaders insisted on repayment, some pointing out that the victorious European nations gained vast territory and resources as war spoils.

The debts question became linked to Germany's $33 billion reparations bill, which some believed Germany could afford but was unwilling to pay. When Germany defaulted on its payments, American bankers loaned millions of dollars to keep the nation afloat and forestall the radicalism that might thrive on economic troubles. A triangular relationship developed: American investors' money flowed to Germany, Germany paid reparations to the Allies, and the Allies then paid some of their debts to the United States. The American-crafted Dawes Plan of 1924 reduced Germany's annual payments, extended the repayment period, and provided more loans. The United States also gradually scaled down Allied obligations, cutting the debt by half during the 1920s.

But everything hinged on continued German borrowing in the United States, and in 1928 and 1929 American lending abroad dropped sharply in the face of more lucrative stock market opportunities. The U.S.-negotiated Young Plan of 1929, which reduced Germany's reparations, salvaged little as the world economy collapsed following the stock market crash. By 1931, the Allies had paid back only $2.6 billion. Staggered by the Great Depression—an international catastrophe—they defaulted on the rest. Annoyed, Congress in 1934 passed the Johnson Act, which forbade U.S. government loans to foreign governments in default to the United States.

Decline in Trade

As the depression deepened, tariff wars revealed a reinvigorated economic nationalism. By 1932 twenty-five nations retaliated against rising American tariffs (created in the Fordney-McCumber Act of 1922 and the Hawley-Smoot Act of 1930) by imposing higher rates on foreign imports. From 1929 to 1933, world trade declined by 40 percent. Exports of American merchandise slumped from $5.2 billion to $1.7 billion.

For Secretary of State Hull, the solution to the crisis depended on reviving world trade; this he insisted would also boost the chances for global peace. He successfully pressed Congress to pass the Reciprocal Trade Agreements Act in 1934, empowering the president to reduce U.S. tariffs by up to 50 percent through special agreements with foreign countries. The act's central feature was the most-favored-nation principle, whereby the United States was entitled to the lowest tariff rate set by any nation with which it had an agreement.

In 1934 Hull also helped create the Export-Import Bank, a government agency providing loans to foreigners purchasing American goods. The bank stimulated trade and became a diplomatic weapon, allowing the United States to exact concessions by approving or denying loans. In the short term, Hull's ambitious programs brought mixed results.

U.S. Recognition of the Soviet Union

The Roosevelt administration's move to extend diplomatic recognition to the Soviet Union was also economically inspired. Throughout the 1920s the Republicans refused diplomatic relations with the Soviet government, which failed to pay $600 million for confiscated American-owned property and repudiated preexisting Russian debts. Nonetheless, in the late 1920s American businesses, such as General Electric and International Harvester, entered the Soviet marketplace, and Henry Ford signed a contract to build an automobile plant there. By 1930 the Soviet Union was the largest buyer of American farm and industrial equipment.

Roosevelt speculated that closer Soviet-American relations might help the economy while deterring Japanese expansion. In 1933 Roosevelt granted U.S. diplomatic recognition to the Soviet Union in return for Soviet agreement to discuss its debts, forgo subversive activities in the United States, and grant Americans in the Soviet Union religious freedom and legal rights.

U.S. DOMINANCE IN LATIN AMERICA

Through the Platt Amendment, the Roosevelt Corollary, the Panama Canal, military intervention, and economic preeminence, the United States had thrown an imperial net over Latin America in the early twentieth century. U.S. dominance in the hemisphere grew after World War I. A prominent State Department officer patronizingly remarked that Latin Americans were of their "low racial quality" and "easy people to deal with if properly managed."

U.S.-made schools, roads, telephones, and irrigation systems dotted Caribbean and Central American nations. American "money doctors" in Colombia and Peru helped reform tariff and tax laws and invited U.S. companies to build public works. Washington forced private high-interest loans on the Dominican Republic and Haiti. Republican administrations curtailed U.S. military intervention in the hemisphere, withdrawing troops from the Dominican Republic (1924) and Nicaragua (1925). But marines returned to Nicaragua in 1926 to end fighting between conservative and liberal Nicaraguans and protect American property. In Haiti, the U.S. troop commitment lasted from 1915 until 1934, with soldiers there to keep pro-Washington governments in power.

U.S. Economic Muscle

By 1929 direct U.S. investments in Latin America (excluding bonds and securities) totaled $3.5 billion, and U.S. exports dominated the region's trade. Country after country experienced the repercussions of U.S. economic and political decisions. For example, the price that Americans set for Chilean copper determined the health of Chile's economy.

Latin American nationalists protested that their resources were being drained away by U.S. companies, leaving many nations in a disadvantageous position. Unapologetic Americans believed they were bringing material improvements and the blessings of liberty to Latin American neighbors.

Criticism of U.S. imperialism in the region mounted in the interwar years. In 1928, at the Havana Inter-American conference, U.S. officials unsuccessfully tried to kill a resolution stating that "no state has a right to intervene in the internal affairs of another." Two years later, a Chilean newspaper warned that the U.S. Colossus had "financial might" without "equal in history" and that its aim was "Americas for the Americans—of the North." In the United States, Senator William Borah of Idaho urged that Latin Americans be granted the right to decide their own futures. Business leaders feared that Latin American nationalists would direct their anti-Yankee feelings against U.S.-owned property.

Good Neighbor Policy

Renouncing unpopular military intervention, the United States tried new methods to maintain its influence in Latin America: Pan-Americanism (a fifty-year-old concept strengthening ties between North and South America), support for strong local leaders, the training of national guards, economic and cultural penetration, Export-Import Bank loans, financial supervision, and political subversion. Dubbed the Good Neighbor policy by Roosevelt in 1933, it meant that the United States would be less blatant in its domination—less willing to defend exploitative business practices and to launch military expeditions and less reluctant to consult with Latin Americans.

Most notably, Roosevelt ordered home the U.S. military forces stationed in Haiti (since 1915) and Nicaragua (since 1912, with a hiatus in 1925–1926), and he restored some sovereignty to Panama and increased that nation's income from the canal. Roosevelt's popularity in Latin America grew when, in a series of pan-American conferences, he joined in pledging that no nation in the hemisphere would intervene in the "internal or external affairs" of any other.

Roosevelt promised more than he could deliver. His administration continued to bolster dictators in the region, believing that they would preserve U.S. economic interests. When a revolution brought a radical government to power in Cuba in 1933, FDR instructed the American ambassador in Havana to work with conservative Cubans to replace the new government with one friendlier to U.S. interests. With Washington's support, army sergeant Fulgencio Batista took power in 1934.

During the Batista era, which lasted until Fidel Castro ousted Batista in 1959, Cuba protected U.S. investments and aligned itself with U.S. foreign policy. In return, the United States provided military aid and Export-Import Bank loans, abrogated the unpopular Platt Amendment, and gave Cuban sugar a favored position in the U.S. market. American tourists flocked to Havana's nightlife of rum, rhumba, prostitution, and gambling. Nationalistic Cubans protested that their nation had become a mere extension of the United States.

Clash with Mexican Nationalism

In Mexico, Roosevelt again showed the restraint his predecessors had lacked. Since Woodrow Wilson sent troops to Mexico in 1914 and 1916, U.S.-Mexican relations struggled as the two governments wrangled over U.S. economic interests. Still, by 1934, the United States accounted for 61 percent of Mexico's imports and received 52 percent of its exports. That year, however, a new government under Lázaro Cárdenas pledged "Mexico for the Mexicans" and strengthened trade unions to strike against foreign corporations.

In 1937 workers struck foreign oil companies for higher wages and recognition, but the companies, including Standard Oil, rejected union appeals, hoping to send a message across the hemisphere that economic nationalism could never succeed. The following year, the Cárdenas government expropriated the property of all foreign-owned petroleum companies, calculating that the approaching war in Europe would restrain the United States from attacking Mexico. The United States countered by reducing purchases of Mexican silver and promoting a multinational business boycott. But Roosevelt rejected appeals to intervene militarily, fearing that Mexicans would increase oil sales to Germany and Japan. Tense negotiations led to a 1942 agreement whereby the United States conceded that Mexico owned and controlled its raw materials, and Mexico compensated the companies for their lost property.

While the United States remained the dominant power in the hemisphere, the Good Neighbor policy filled Latin Americans with hope that a new era had dawned. The sober-minded nationalists in the region knew that deepening tensions in Europe and Asia might have influenced Washington's restraint. But these threats also created a sense that nations in the Western Hemisphere should stand together.

THE COURSE TO WAR IN EUROPE

On March 5, 1933, one day after Roosevelt's inauguration, Germany's parliament granted dictatorial powers to the new chancellor, Adolf Hitler, leader of the Nazi Party. It was a stunning rise to power for Hitler, whose Nazis probably would have remained a fringe party had the Great Depression not hit Germany so hard. Production plummeted 40 percent, and unemployment ballooned to 6 million, meaning that two out of five people were jobless. A disintegrating banking system, which robbed millions of their savings, and widespread German resentment over the Versailles peace settlement fueled mass discontent. While the communists preached a workers' revolution, German businessmen and property owners supported Hitler and the Nazis, believing they could manipulate him once he had thwarted the communists. They were wrong.

Like Benito Mussolini, who gained control of Italy in 1922, Hitler was a fascist. Fascism (called Nazism, or National Socialism, in Germany) celebrated supremacy of the state over the individual, dictatorship over democracy, authoritarianism over freedom of speech, a state-regulated economy over a free market, and militarism over peace. The Nazis vowed to revive Germany, cripple communism and "purify" the German "race" by destroying Jews and others, such as homosexuals and Gypsies, whom Hitler deemed inferior. The Nuremberg Laws of 1935 stripped Jews of citizenship and outlawed Jewish intermarriage with Germans. Half of all German Jews were without work.

German Aggression Under Hitler

Determined to get out from under the Versailles treaty, Hitler withdrew Germany from the League of Nations, ended reparations payments, and began to rearm. While secretly laying plans to conquer neighboring states, he watched admiringly as Mussolini's troops invaded Ethiopia in 1935. The next year Hitler ordered his troops into the Rhineland, an area demilitarized by the Versailles treaty.

In 1936 Italy and Germany formed an alliance called the Rome-Berlin Axis. Shortly thereafter, Germany and Japan united against the Soviet Union in the Anti-Comintern Pact. Britain and France responded with a policy of appeasement, hoping to curb Hitler's expansionism by permitting him a few territorial nibbles. Instead, the German leader continually raised his demands.

The Spanish Civil War in 1936 upped the ante for Hitler. Beginning in July, about three thousand American volunteers, known as the Abraham Lincoln Battalion of the International Brigades, joined Spanish Loyalists in defending Spain's elected republican government against Francisco Franco's fascist movement. The Soviet Union also aided the Loyalists. Hitler and Mussolini sent military aid to Franco, who won in 1939, tightening fascism's grip on the European continent.

Early in 1938, Hitler again tested European tolerance when he sent soldiers to annex his birth nation, Austria. In September, he seized the Sudeten region of Czechoslovakia. France and Britain, without consulting the Czechs, agreed to allow Hitler this territorial bite, in exchange for a pledge that he would not take more. British prime minister Neville Chamberlain returned home to proclaim "peace in our time." In March 1939 Hitler swallowed the rest of Czechoslovakia (see Map 26.2).

Isolationist Views in the United States

Many Americans sought to distance themselves from Europe's tumult by embracing isolationism, because they either hated war or opposed U.S. alliances with other nations. Americans learned powerful negative lessons from World War I: that war damages reform movements, undermines civil liberties, dangerously expands federal power, disrupts the economy, and accentuates racial and class tensions. In a 1937 Gallup poll nearly two-thirds thought U.S. participation in World War I was a mistake.

Conservative isolationists feared higher taxes and increased executive power if the nation went to war. Liberal isolationists worried that domestic problems might go unresolved with increased military spending. Many isolationists predicted that, in attempting to spread democracy, Americans would lose freedoms at home. The vast majority of isolationists opposed fascism, but they did not think the United States should do what Europeans refused to do: block Hitler.

Nye Committee Hearings

A congressional committee headed by Senator Gerald P. Nye held hearings from 1934 to 1936 on the role of business in the U.S. decision to enter World War I. The Nye committee did not prove that American munitions makers dragged the nation into war, but it uncovered evidence that corporations bribed foreign politicians to bolster arms sales in the 1920s and 1930s.

Isolationists grew suspicious of American business ties with Nazi Germany and fascist Italy. Twenty-six of the top American corporations, including DuPont, Standard Oil, and General Motors, had contracts in 1937 with German firms. After Italy attacked Ethiopia in 1935, American petroleum, copper, scrap iron, and steel exports to Italy increased substantially, despite Roosevelt's call for a moral embargo. Other businesses, such as the Wall Street law firm of Sullivan and Cromwell, severed lucrative ties with Germany to protest the Nazi persecution of Jews.

Roosevelt signed a series of neutrality acts. Congress meanwhile outlawed the kinds of contacts that had compromised U.S. neutrality during World War I. The Neutrality Act of 1935 prohibited arms shipments to either side in a war, once the president declared the existence of belligerency. The Neutrality Act of 1936 forbade loans to belligerents and introduced the cash-and-carry principle which required warring nations to pay cash for nonmilitary purchases and carry goods from U.S. ports in their own ships. The act also forbade Americans from traveling on the ships of belligerent nations.

Roosevelt's Evolving Views

President Roosevelt shared isolationist views in the early 1930s. Although prior to World War I he was an expansionist and interventionist, during the interwar period FDR talked more about the horrors of war. In a speech in August 1936 at Chautauqua, New York, Roosevelt appealed to pacifist voters in the upcoming election. The United States, he promised, would remain unentangled in the European conflict. During the crisis over Czechoslovakia in 1938, Roosevelt endorsed appeasement.

Meanwhile, Roosevelt grew troubled by the arrogance of Germany, Italy, and Japan—aggressors that he called the three bandit nations. He condemned Nazi persecution of the Jews and Japan's expansionist actions in East Asia. In November 1938, Hitler launched *Kristallnacht* ("Crystal Night," named for the shattered glass that littered the streets after the attack on Jewish synagogues, businesses, and homes) and sent tens of thousands of Jews to concentration camps. Shocked, Roosevelt recalled the U.S. ambassador to Germany and allowed fifteen thousand refugees on visitor permits to remain longer in the United States. But he would not break trade relations with Hitler or push Congress to loosen immigration laws. Congress rejected all measures, including a bill to admit twenty thousand children under age fourteen. Motivated by economic concerns and widespread anti-Semitism, more than 80 percent of Americans supported Congress's decision to uphold immigration restrictions.

Even the tragic voyage of the *St. Louis* did not change government policy. The vessel left Hamburg in mid-1939 carrying 930 desperate Jews. Denied entry to Havana, the *St. Louis* headed for Miami, where Coast Guard cutters prevented it from docking and forced its return to Europe. Some refugees took shelter in countries that later were overrun by Hitler's legions.

Quietly, Roosevelt began readying for war. In early 1938 he successfully pressured the House of Representatives to defeat a constitutional amendment that would require a majority vote in a national referendum before a congressional declaration of war could take effect (unless the United States were attacked). Later, in the wake of the Munich crisis, Roosevelt asked Congress for funds to fortify the air force, which he believed essential to deter aggression. In January 1939 the president secretly decided to sell bombers to France. Although these five hundred combat planes did not deter war, French orders spurred the growth of the U.S. aircraft industry.

Hitler's swallowing of Czechoslovakia in March 1939 proved a turning point for Western leaders. Until now, they could explain away Hitler's actions by saying he was only trying to reunite German-speaking peoples. They realized it would take force to stop him. When Hitler began eyeing Poland, London and Paris stood by the Poles.

Undaunted, Berlin signed a nonaggression pact with Moscow in August 1939, including a top-secret protocol that carved eastern Europe into German and Soviet zones and let the Soviets grab the eastern half of Poland and the Baltic states of Lithuania, Estonia, and Latvia, formerly part of the Russian Empire.

Poland and the Outbreak of World War II

Early on September 1, 1939, German tanks rolled into Poland. German fighter planes covered the advance, thereby launching a new type of warfare, the *blitzkrieg* ("lightning war")—highly mobile land forces and armor combined with tactical aircraft. Within forty-eight hours, Britain and France declared war on Germany.

When Europe descended into war in September 1939, Roosevelt declared neutrality and pressed for repeal of the arms embargo. After much debate, Congress in November lifted the embargo on contraband and approved cash-and-carry exports of arms. Using methods short of war, Roosevelt thus began to aid the Allies. Hitler sneered that a "half Judaized . . . half Negrified" United States was "incapable of conducting war."

JAPAN, CHINA, AND A NEW ORDER IN ASIA

Asia suffered the aggressive march of Japan. The United States had interests at stake in Asia: the Philippines and Pacific islands, religious missions, trade and investments, and the Open Door in China. In missionary fashion, Americans believed that they were China's friend and protector. Pearl Buck's bestselling novel and subsequent film, *The Good Earth* (1931), countered prevailing images of the "heathen Chinee" by representing the Chinese as noble, persevering peasants. By contrast, the aggressive Japan loomed as a threat to American interests. The Tokyo government seemed bent on subjugating China and unhinging the Open Door doctrine of equal trade and investment.

The Chinese were uneasy about the U.S. presence in Asia and shared Japan's desire to reduce Western influence. The Chinese Revolution of 1911 still rumbled in the 1920s, as antiforeign riots damaged American property and imperiled American missionaries. Chinese nationalists criticized the American imperialist practice of extraterritoriality (the exemption of foreigners from Chinese legal jurisdiction) and demanded an end to this affront.

Jiang Jieshi

In the late 1920s, civil war broke out in China when Jiang Jieshi (Chiang Kai-shek) ousted Mao Zedong from the ruling Guomindang Party. Americans applauded this anti-Bolshevism and Jiang's conversion to Christianity in 1930. Jiang's new wife, American-educated Soong Meiling, won their hearts with her flawless English and western fashion. Warming to Jiang, U.S. officials signed a treaty in 1928 restoring control of tariffs to the Chinese. U.S. gunboats and marines still remained in China to protect American citizens and property.

Japan grew suspicious of U.S. ties with China. In the early twentieth century, Japanese-American relations deteriorated as Japan gained influence in Manchuria,

Shandong, and Korea. The Japanese sought to dominate Asian territories that produced the raw materials that their import-dependent island nation required. The Japanese also resented the discriminatory immigration law of 1924, which excluded them from emigrating to the United States. Secretary Hughes called the law "a lasting injury" to Japanese-American relations. Despite the Washington Conference treaties, naval competition continued, as did commercial rivalry. In the United States the importation of inexpensive Japanese goods spawned Buy America campaigns.

Manchurian Crisis

Relations further soured in 1931 after the Japanese military seized Manchuria from China (see Map 26.1). Larger than Texas, Manchuria served Japan both as a buffer against the Soviets and as a vital source of coal, iron, timber, and food. More than half of Japan's foreign investments rested in Manchuria. Although the seizure of Manchuria violated the Nine-Power Treaty and the Kellogg-Briand Pact, the

Map 26.1 Japanese Expansion Before Pearl Harbor
The Japanese quest for predominance began at the turn of the century and intensified in the 1930s. China suffered the most at the hands of Tokyo's military. Vulnerable U.S. possessions in Asia and the Pacific proved no obstacle to Japan's ambitions for a Greater East Asia Co-Prosperity Sphere.

United States lacked the power to compel Japanese withdrawal, and the League of Nations merely condemned the Tokyo government. The American response came as a moral lecture known as the Stimson Doctrine: the United States would not recognize any impairment of China's sovereignty or of the Open Door policy, Secretary Stimson declared in 1932.

Japan continued to pressure China, triggering the Sino-Japanese War in mid-1937. Japanese forces seized Beijing and several coastal cities. The bombing of Shanghai intensified anti-Japanese sentiment in the United States. To help China by permitting it to buy American arms, Roosevelt refused to declare the existence of war, thus avoiding activation of the Neutrality Acts.

Roosevelt's Quarantine Speech

On October 5, 1937, the president called for a quarantine to curb the "epidemic of world lawlessness." People who thought Washington had been too gentle with Japan cheered. Isolationists warned that Roosevelt was edging toward war. On December 12, Japanese aircraft sank the American gunboat *Panay,* an escort for Standard Oil Company tankers on the Yangtze River, killing two American sailors. Roosevelt was relieved when Tokyo apologized and offered to pay for damages.

Japan's declaration of a New Order in Asia, in the words of one American official, "banged, barred, and bolted" the Open Door. Alarmed, the Roosevelt administration during the late 1930s gave loans and sold military equipment to Jiang's Chinese government. In mid-1939 the United States abrogated its trade treaty with Tokyo, yet Americans continued to ship oil, cotton, and machinery to Japan. The administration hesitated to initiate economic sanctions because it might spark a Japanese-American war at a time when Germany posed a more serious threat and the United States was unprepared for war. When war broke out in Europe in late summer 1939, Japanese-American relations were stalemated.

U.S. ENTRY INTO WORLD WAR II

A stalemate was fine with many Americans if it kept the United States out of war. Roosevelt remarked in 1939 that the United States could not "draw a line of defense around this country and live completely and solely to ourselves." Polls showed that Americans favored the Allies and supported aid to Britain and France, but the great majority emphatically wanted the United States to remain at peace. Troubled by this conflicting advice—oppose Hitler, aid the Allies, but stay out of the war—the president gradually moved the nation from neutrality to undeclared war against Germany and then, after the Japanese attack on Pearl Harbor, to full-scale war.

Unprecedented numbers of Americans spoke out on foreign affairs and joined organizations that addressed the issues. The widespread use of radio, the nation's chief news source, helped stimulate public interest. So did ethnic affiliations with the various belligerents and victims. The American Legion, the League of Women Voters, labor unions, and local chapters of the Committee to Defend America by Aiding the Allies and the isolationist America First Committee provided outlets for citizen participation in the national debate. African American churches organized anti-Italian boycotts to protest Mussolini's pummeling of Ethiopia.

Map 26.2   The German Advance

Hitler's drive to dominate Europe pushed German troops deep into France and the Soviet Union. Great Britain took a beating but held on with the help of American economic and military aid before the United States itself entered World War II in late 1941.

In March 1940, the Soviet Union invaded Finland. In April, Germany conquered Denmark and Norway (see Map 26.2). On May 10, 1940, Germany attacked Belgium, the Netherlands, and France, ultimately pushing French and British forces back to the English Channel. At Dunkirk, France, between May 26 and June 6, more than 300,000 Allied soldiers frantically escaped to Britain on a flotilla of small boats. The Germans occupied Paris a week later. A new French government in the town of Vichy collaborated with the Nazis and, on June 22, surrendered France to Berlin. The German Luftwaffe (air force) launched massive bombing raids against Great Britain.

Alarmed by the swift defeat of one European nation after another, Americans shed their isolationism. Insisting that New Deal reforms would not be sacrificed for military preparedness, the president aided the beleaguered Allies to prevent the fall of Britain. In May 1940 he ordered the sale of old surplus military equipment to Britain and France. In July he cultivated bipartisan support by naming the Republicans Henry L. Stimson and Frank Knox, backers of aid to the Allies, to be secretaries of war and the navy, respectively. In September, the president traded fifty over-age American destroyers for leases to eight British military bases, including Newfoundland, Bermuda, and Jamaica.

Radio News

In radio's early years, network executives believed their job was to entertain Americans, and that left current affairs to newspapers. Yet radio could report news events as they happened, something no previous medium could do.

Franklin Roosevelt was among the first to grasp radio's potential. As governor of New York, he occasionally went on the air, and after becoming president, he commenced his Fireside Chats, reassuring Americans during the depression that the government was working to help them. The broadcasts were so successful that one journalist remarked, "The President has only to look toward a radio to bring Congress to terms."

Across the Atlantic, Adolf Hitler also used the radio to carry speeches directly to the German people. His message: Germany had been wronged by enemies abroad and by Marxists and Jews at home. But under Hitler, the Nazis promised to restore the country's former greatness. As *Sieg Heil!* thundered over the airwaves, millions of Germans saw Hitler as their salvation.

In 1938, as events in Europe escalated, American radio networks increased news coverage. When Hitler annexed Austria in March, NBC and CBS broke into scheduled programs to deliver bulletins. Then, on March 13, CBS broadcast the first international news roundup, a half-hour show featuring live reports. A new era in American radio was born. In the words of author Joseph Persico, what made the broadcast revolutionary "was the listener's sensation of being on the scene" in far-off Europe. When leaders from France and Britain met with Hitler in Munich later that year, millions of Americans listened intently to live radio updates.

Correspondents became well known, none more than CBS's Edward R. Murrow. During the Nazi air blitz of London in 1940–1941, Murrow's understated, nicotine-scorched voice kept Americans spellbound, as he tried to "report suffering to people [Americans] who have not suffered."

Undoubtedly, Murrow's reports strengthened the interventionist voices in Washington by emphasizing Winston Churchill's greatness and England's bravery. And radio reports from Europe made Americans feel closely linked to people living an ocean away.

Edward R. Murrow at his typewriter in wartime London.
(Library of Congress)

First Peacetime Military Draft

Two weeks later, Roosevelt signed the hotly debated and narrowly passed Selective Training and Service Act, the first peacetime military draft in American history. The law called for the registration of all men between the ages of twenty-one and thirty-five; more than 16 million men signed up. Meanwhile, Roosevelt won reelection in November 1940 with promises of peace: "Your boys are not going to be sent into any foreign wars."

Roosevelt claimed that the United States could avoid war by enabling the British to win. In January 1941, Congress debated the president's Lend-Lease bill. Because Britain was broke, the president explained, the United States should lend rather than sell weapons. In March 1941, with pro-British sentiment running high, the House passed the Lend-Lease Act by 317 votes to 71; the Senate followed with a 60-to-31 tally. The initial appropriation was $7 billion, but by war's end, it reached $50 billion, more than $31 billion of it for Britain.

To ensure delivery of Lend-Lease goods, Roosevelt ordered the U.S. Navy to patrol halfway across the Atlantic, and he sent American troops to Greenland. In July, the president dispatched marines to Iceland, arguing that it was essential for safeguarding the Western Hemisphere. He also sent Lend-Lease aid to the Soviet Union, which Hitler attacked in June (thereby shattering the 1939 Nazi-Soviet nonaggression pact). If the Soviets could hold off two hundred German divisions in the east, Roosevelt calculated, Britain would gain some breathing time.

Atlantic Charter

In August 1941, Churchill and Roosevelt met for four days on a British battleship off the coast of Newfoundland. The two leaders issued the Atlantic Charter, a set of war aims reminiscent of Wilsonianism: collective security, disarmament, self-determination, economic cooperation, and freedom of the seas. Churchill later recalled that the president told him that he could not ask Congress to declare war against Germany, but "he would wage war" and "become more and more provocative."

On September 4, a German submarine launched torpedoes at (but did not hit) the American destroyer *Greer*. Henceforth, Roosevelt said, the U.S. Navy would fire first when under threat. He also made good on a promise to Churchill: American warships would convoy British merchant ships across the ocean. Thus the United States entered into an undeclared naval war with Germany. When in early October the destroyer *Reuben James* went down with the loss of more than one hundred American lives, Congress scrapped the cash-and-carry policy and further revised the Neutrality Acts to permit transport of munitions to Britain on armed American merchant ships. The United States was edging close to being a belligerent.

U.S. Demands on Japan

It seems ironic that World War II came to the United States by way of Asia. Roosevelt wanted to avoid war with Japan to concentrate on defeating Germany. In September 1940, after Germany, Italy, and Japan signed the Tripartite Pact (to form the Axis powers), Roosevelt slapped an embargo on shipments of aviation fuel and scrap metal to Japan. After Japanese troops occupied French Indochina in July 1941, Washington froze Japanese assets in the United States, virtually ending trade (including oil) with Japan. "The oil gauge and the clock stood side by side" for Japan, wrote one observer.

Tokyo recommended a summit meeting between President Roosevelt and Prime Minister Prince Konoye, but American officials insisted that the Japanese first agree to respect China's sovereignty and honor the Open Door policy. Roosevelt supported Secretary Hull's hard line against Japan's pursuit of the Greater East Asia Co-Prosperity Sphere—the name Tokyo gave to the vast Asian region it intended to dominate.

Roosevelt told his advisers to string out ongoing Japanese-American talks to gain time to fortify the Philippines and check the fascists in Europe. By deciphering intercepted messages through Operation MAGIC, American officials learned that Tokyo's patience with diplomacy was fast dissipating. In late November, the Japanese rejected American demands to withdraw from Indochina. An intercepted message on December 3 instructed the Japanese embassy in Washington to burn codes and destroy cipher machines—a step suggesting that war was coming.

Surprise Attack on Pearl Harbor

In a daring raid on Pearl Harbor in Hawai'i, an armada of sixty Japanese ships, including six carriers bearing 360 airplanes, crossed 3,000 miles of the Pacific Ocean. To avoid detection, they maintained radio silence. Early on December 7, some 230 miles northwest of Honolulu, the carriers unleashed their planes, dropping torpedoes and bombs on an unsuspecting American naval base and nearby airfields.

The battleship USS *Arizona* fell victim to a Japanese bomb that ignited explosives below deck, killing more than 1,000 sailors. The USS *Nevada* tried to escape by heading out to sea, but was hit in a second aerial attack. Altogether the invaders sank or damaged eight battleships, many smaller vessels, and more than 160 aircraft on the ground. A total of 2,403 died; 1,178 were wounded. The Pearl Harbor tragedy, from the perspective of the war's outcome, amounted to a military inconvenience more than a disaster.

Explaining Pearl Harbor

American cryptanalysts may have broken the Japanese diplomatic code, but the intercepted messages never revealed naval or military plans and never mentioned Pearl Harbor specifically. Roosevelt did not, as some critics charged, conspire to leave

The stricken USS *West Virginia* was one of eight battleships caught in the surprise Japanese attack at Pearl Harbor, Hawai'i, on December 7, 1941. In this photograph, sailors mount a launch attempt to rescue a crew member from the water as oil burns around the sinking ship.   (U.S. Army)

the fleet vulnerable to attack so that the United States could enter World War II through the back door of Asia. The base at Pearl Harbor was not on red alert because a message from Washington warning of the imminence of war was transmitted by a slow method and arrived too late. Base commanders believed Hawai'i too far from Japan to be a target. Like Roosevelt's advisers, they expected an assault on British Malaya, Thailand, or the Philippines (see Map 26.1). The Pearl Harbor calamity stemmed from mistakes and insufficient information, not from conspiracy.

On December 8, referring to the previous day as "a date which will live in infamy," Roosevelt asked Congress for a declaration of war against Japan. He noted that the Japanese had also attacked Malaya, Hong Kong, Guam, the Philippines, Wake, and Midway. A unanimous vote in the Senate and a 388-to-1 vote in the House thrust America into war. Representative Jeannette Rankin of Montana voted against war, as she had for World War I. Britain declared war on Japan, but the Soviet Union did not. Three days later, Germany and Italy, honoring the Tripartite Pact they had signed with Japan in September 1940, declared war against the United States.

A fundamental clash of systems explains why war came. Germany and Japan preferred a world divided into closed spheres of influence. The United States sought a liberal capitalist world. American principles manifested respect for human rights; fascists in Europe and militarists in Asia did not. The United States prided itself on democracy; Germany and Japan embraced authoritarian regimes. When the United States protested against German and Japanese expansion, Berlin and Tokyo charged that Washington conveniently ignored its sphere of influence in Latin America and its history of military and economic aggrandizement. Such incompatible objectives obstructed diplomacy and made war likely.

Summary

In the 1920s and 1930s, Americans could not create a peaceful and prosperous world order. The Washington Conference treaties failed to curb a naval arms race or protect China, and both the Dawes Plan and the Kellogg-Briand Pact proved ineffective. U.S. trade policies, shifting from protectionist tariffs to reciprocal trade agreements, only minimally improved U.S. or international commerce during the Great Depression. Recognition of the Soviet Union barely improved relations. Most ominous, the aggressors Germany and Japan ignored repeated U.S. protests. Even where U.S. policies seemed to satisfy Good Neighbor goals in Latin America, nationalist resentments simmered and Mexico challenged U.S. dominance.

During the late 1930s and early 1940s, President Roosevelt hesitantly but steadily moved the United States from neutrality to aiding the Allies, to belligerency, and finally to war after the attack on Pearl Harbor. Congress gradually revised and retired the Neutrality Acts in the face of growing danger.

World War II offered yet another opportunity for Americans to set things right in the world. As the publisher Henry Luce wrote in the *American Century* (1941), the United States must "exert upon the world the full impact of our influence." Isolationists joined the president's call for victory, when he said, "We are going to win the war, and we are going to win the peace that follows."

Presidential Deception of the Public

Before U-652 launched two torpedoes at the *Greer*, heading for Iceland on September 4, 1941, the U.S. destroyer had stalked the German submarine for hours. After the attack, which missed its mark, the *Greer* also released depth charges. But when President Roosevelt described the encounter in a radio Fireside Chat on September 11, he declared that the German submarine fired the first shot and accused Germany of violating freedom of the seas.

Roosevelt misled the American people about the events of September 4. The incident had little to do with freedom of the seas, which related to merchant ships, not U.S. warships in a war zone. Roosevelt's words were a call to arms, yet he never asked Congress for a declaration of war against Germany. The president believed that deceiving Americans would move them toward war as noble and necessary. The practice worked: polls showed that most Americans approved Roosevelt's shoot-on-sight policy following the *Greer* incident.

Over time, even those who agreed that Germany had to be stopped, questioned Roosevelt's methods as dangerous to the democratic process, which cannot work in an environment of dishonesty and a usurping of congressional powers. In the 1960s, during the Vietnam War, Senator J. William Fulbright of Arkansas recalled the *Greer* incident: "FDR's deviousness in a good cause made it easier for LBJ to practice the same kind of deviousness in a bad cause." In the mid-1980s, Reagan administration officials consciously lied about U.S. arms sales to Iran and covert aid to the Nicaraguan rebels. After the March 2003 U.S. invasion of Iraq, there were charges that President George W. Bush and his aides did the same in claiming that Iraq had weapons of mass destruction, which its leader, Saddam Hussein, intended to use. Bush, critics charged, had used "weapons of mass deception" to justify the invasion of Iraq.

Following Roosevelt, presidents have found it easier to distort, withhold, or lie about foreign relations to shape public opinion. One result: the growth of the imperial presidency—grabbing power from Congress and using questionable means to reach presidential objectives. The practice of deception, even for a noble end, was one of Roosevelt's legacies for a people and a nation.

Chapter Review

SEARCHING FOR PEACE AND ORDER IN THE 1920S

How did the peace movement influence U.S. foreign policy in the interwar years?

In the wake of World War I, several peace organizations—some formed by female activists—emerged to ensure world order and prevent another war. Their strategies varied: some embraced alliances with the League of Nations and the World Court; others looked to arbitration, disarmament, arms reduction, making wars illegal, and observing strict neutrality. Peace activism led President Warren Harding to convene the Washington Naval Conference from November 1921 to February 1922 in which delegates from Britain, Japan, France, Italy, China, Portugal, Belgium, and the Netherlands agreed to limit naval armaments and set a ten-year moratorium on ship-building. Other important policy developments included the Nine-Power Treaty, which reaffirmed the Open Door in

China and recognized Chinese sovereignty; the Locarno Pact of 1925, which sought to reduce tensions between Germany and France; and the Kellogg-Briand Pact of 1928, in which sixty-two nations agreed to condemn war as the solution to international disputes.

THE WORLD ECONOMY, CULTURAL EXPANSION, AND GREAT DEPRESSION

How did the Great Depression help push the world to the brink of war?

Economic tensions existed between the United States and Europe after World War I. The United States emerged as a creditor nation and Europeans—particularly Germany—largely as debtors. Europeans often accused the United States of stinginess and profiting from their hardships. While the United States did gradually scale down Allied debts and reduce Germany's payments, still, much depended on loan repayments. When the stock market crashed in 1929, Europeans defaulted on a large portion of what they owed. The Great Depression not only created an international economic crisis, it also inspired economic nationalism in countries that were already pushed financially to the edge. Secretary of State Charles Hull aptly predicted that maimed economies inspired militarism and extremism, and no country's economy was as hard-pressed as Germany's.

U.S. DOMINANCE IN LATIN AMERICA

How was Roosevelt's Good Neighbor policy different from past dealings in Latin America?

Prior to Roosevelt, the U.S. strategy for maintaining its influence in Latin America focused on military intervention. The Good Neighbor policy took a more subtle approach: it centered on building friendship ties through Pan-Americanism; supporting strong local leaders; training national guards; penetrating the region through economic and cultural means; providing financial supervision and loans; and relying on political subversion. Roosevelt withdrew troops from Haiti and Nicaragua and restored some sovereignty to Panama and increased that nation's income from the canal. While the administration-backed dictators who seemed supportive of U.S. economic interests, the Good Neighbor policy nonetheless convinced Latin Americans that a new era of friendship had begun.

THE COURSE TO WAR IN EUROPE

Why did most Americans support isolationism for much of World War II?

Americans had long embraced isolationism largely because of their aversion to war and because of a long legacy of political independence that did not allow for alliances with other nations. That was fortified by the experience of World War I, which damaged reform movements at home, disrupted the U.S. economy, and expanded federal power. In fact, two-thirds of Americans surveyed thought entry into World War I had been a mistake. Americans similarly feared tax increases, the loss of freedom at home, and the shift of federal funds away from domestic problems toward military spending. They also distrusted the role of business in pushing the nation toward war.

JAPAN, CHINA, AND A NEW ORDER IN ASIA

How did the United States perceive its interests to be threatened by Japanese expanisionism?

As Japan moved to lessen—and eliminate—western influence in the East and to dominate Asian territories producing beneficial raw materials, the United States worried about what this would mean to its interests in Asia, notably, the Philippines and Pacific islands, religious missions, trade and investments, and the Open Door doctrine in China of equal trade and investment. They feared it portended Japanese control of China. The Japanese resented the United States's discriminatory immigration law of 1924, which excluded them from emigrating to the United States. U.S. leaders acknowledged, and were sometimes frustrated that, its immigration policies thwarted efforts toward friendly relations with Japan, and the two nations remained locked in a stalemate as World War II loomed.

U.S. ENTRY INTO WORLD WAR II

In what way did Roosevelt gradually move Americans into World War II?

Like most Americans, Roosevelt remained an isolationist, but as one European nation after another was defeated, staying out of the conflict in Europe proved increasingly difficult. Concerned about events overseas, Americans slowly shed their isolationism. Roosevelt was horrified by Germany's treatment of Jews and Japan's expansionism in East Asia, but Hitler's 1939 takeover of Czechoslovakia proved the turning point. Roosevelt quietly began preparing for war, even while hoping that he could keep the United States out of it by ensuring that Britain did not fall. The president secretly sold bombers to France, and in May 1940 he ordered the sale of surplus military equipment to Britain and France. Because England had no money to pay for weapons, the president urged Congress to let them borrow the necessary arms. He also signed the Selective Training and Service Act, the first peacetime military draft.

SUGGESTIONS FOR FURTHER READING

Patrick Cohrs, *The Unfinished Peace After World War I: America, Britain and the Stabilization of Europe, 1919–1932* (2006)

Frank Costigliola, *Awkward Dominion: American Political, Economic, and Cultural Relations with Europe* (1984)

Robert Dallek, *Franklin D. Roosevelt and American Foreign Policy* (1995)

Justus D. Doenecke, *Storm on the Horizon: The Challenge to American Intervention, 1939–1941* (2000)

Akira Iriye, *The Origins of the Second World War in Asia and the Pacific* (1987)

David M. Kennedy, *Freedom from Fear: The American People in Depression and War, 1929–1945* (1999)

Walter LaFeber, *Inevitable Revolutions: The United States in Central America*, 2d and extended ed. (1993)

Fredrick B. Pike, *FDR's Good Neighbor Policy* (1995)

Emily S. Rosenberg, *Spreading the American Dream: American Economic and Cultural Expansion, 1890–1945* (1982)

Linda A. Schott, *Reconstructing Women's Thoughts: The Women's International League for Peace and Freedom Before World War II* (1997)

CHAPTER 27

The Second World War at Home and Abroad | 1941–1945

Willam Dean Wilson was sixteen in 1942 when U.S. Marine Corps recruiters came to Shiprock, New Mexico, where he attended the Navajo boarding school. Five years too young to be drafted and a year too young to volunteer, he lied about his age and removed the note reading, "Parents will not consent" from his recruiting file.

Wilson was recruited for one of the most important projects of the war. Battles were won or lost because nations broke the codes enemies used to transmit messages, and the Marines wanted a code based on Diné, the highly complex Navajo language. In 1942 there was no written form and fewer than thirty non-Navajos worldwide—none of them Japanese—understood it. This code promised to be unbreakable. Navajo words represented the first letter of their English translations; thus *wol-la-chee* ("ant") stood for the letter *A*. Each operator also memorized Navajo words that represented 413 basic military terms and concepts. *Dah-he-tih-hi* ("hummingbird") meant fighter plane, *ne-he-mah* ("our mother") was the United States, and *beh-na-ali-tsosie* ("slant-eye") stood for Japan.

Beginning with the Battle of Guadalcanal, Wilson and others of the 420 code talkers participated in every Marine assault in the Pacific. Usually, two code talkers were assigned to a battalion, one going ashore with assault forces and the other receiving messages on ship. Often under hostile fire, code talkers set up their equipment and transmitted enemy sightings or directed shelling by American detachments. "Were it not for the Navajos," declared Major Howard Conner, Fifth Marine Division signal officer, "the Marines would never have taken Iwo Jima. The entire operation was directed by Navajo code. They sent and received over eight hundred messages without an error."

Nice!

This icon will direct you to interactive activities and study materials on *A People And A Nation*, Brief Edition website: **www.cengage.com/history/norton/peoplenationbrief8e**

Chronology

1941	Government war-preparedness study concludes United States will not be ready for war before June 1943.
	Roosevelt issues Executive Order No. 8802, forbidding racial discrimination by the defense industry.
	Japan attacks Pearl Harbor.
	United States enters World War II.
1942	War Production Board is created to oversee the conversion to military production.
	Millions of Americans move to take jobs in war industries.
	Allies are losing the war in the Pacific to Japan; U.S. victory at Battle of Midway in June is the turning point.
	Office of Price Administration creates a rationing system for food and consumer goods.
	United States pursues Europe First war policy; Allies reject Stalin's demands for a second front in Europe and invade North Africa.
	West Coast Japanese Americans are relocated to internment camps.
	Manhattan Project is set up to create an atomic bomb.
	Congress of Racial Equality is established.

1943	Soviet army defeats German troops at Stalingrad.
	Congress passes War Labor Disputes (Smith-Connally) Act following coal miners' strike.
	"Zoot suit riots" occur in Los Angeles; race riots break out in Detroit, Harlem, and other cities.
	Allies invade Italy.
	Roosevelt, Churchill, and Stalin meet at the Teheran Conference.
1944	Allied troops land at Normandy on D-Day, June 6.
	Roosevelt is elected to fourth term as president.
	United States retakes the Philippines.
1945	Roosevelt, Stalin, and Churchill meet at the Yalta Conference.
	British and U.S. forces firebomb Dresden, Germany.
	Battles of Iwo Jima and Okinawa result in heavy Japanese and U.S. losses.
	Roosevelt dies; Truman becomes president.
	Germany surrenders; Allied forces liberate Nazi death camps.
	Potsdam Conference calls for Japan's unconditional surrender.
	United States uses atomic bombs on Hiroshima and Nagasaki.
	Japan surrenders.

Wartime service changed the Navajo code talkers' lives, broadening their horizons and often deepening their ambitions. William Dean Wilson later became a tribal judge. From "the service," recalled Raymond Nakai, a navy veteran who became chairman of the Navajo nation, "the Navajo got a glimpse of what the rest of the world is doing." But in 1945 most Navajo war veterans were happy to return to their homes and traditional culture. World War II marked a turning point in the lives of Americans and in the history of the United States.

Although the war began badly for the United States, by mid-1942 the Allies halted the Axis powers' advance. In June 1944, U.S. troops, together with Canadian, British, and Free French units, launched a massive invasion across the English Channel, landing at Normandy and pushing into Germany the following spring. Battered by bombing raids, leaderless after Adolf Hitler's suicide, and pressed by a Soviet advance, the Nazis capitulated in May 1945. In the Pacific, Americans drove Japanese forces back, island by island, toward Japan. America's devastating conventional bombing of Japanese cities, followed by the atomic bombs that demolished Hiroshima and Nagasaki in August 1945, led to Japan's surrender. Throughout the war, the Grand Alliance—Britain, the Soviet Union, and the United States—united to defeat Germany but disagreed about how best to fight and how to shape the postwar world. Prospects for postwar international cooperation seemed bleak, and the advent of the atomic age frightened everyone.

The war was fought far from the United States, but it had a major impact on American society. America's leaders committed the United States to become the arsenal of democracy, producing vast quantities of arms. All sectors of the economy were mobilized. America's big businesses got even bigger, as did its central government, labor unions, and farms. The federal government had the monumental task of coordinating these spheres and two new ones: higher education and science.

During the war, nearly one of every ten Americans moved to another state. Most headed for war-production centers, especially cities in the North and on the West Coast. Japanese Americans were rounded up by the army and placed in internment camps. And while the war encouraged African Americans to demand citizenship rights, competition for jobs and housing sparked race riots. For women, the war offered new job opportunities in the armed forces and war industries.

On the home front, Americans supported the war effort by collecting scrap iron, rubber, and newspapers for recycling, and planting "victory gardens." At war's end, although many Americans grieved for lost loved ones and worried about the postwar order, the United States had unprecedented power and prosperity.

- **What military, diplomatic, and social factors influenced decisions about how to fight World War II?**
- **Was the generation of Americans that fought World War II the greatest generation?**
- **How did World War II transform the United States?**

THE UNITED STATES AT WAR

As Japanese bombs fell on the U.S. territory of Hawai'i, American antiwar sentiment evaporated. Franklin Roosevelt declared war with Japan on December 8. When Germany declared war on the United States three days later, America joined British and Soviet Allied nations in battling the Axis powers of Japan, Germany, and Italy. The American public's shift from caution—even isolationism—to fervent support for war was dramatic. As the world went to war, the United States had not been idle. America's embargo of shipments to Japan and refusal to accept Japan's expansionist policies brought the two nations to the brink of war. The United States was also involved in an undeclared naval war with Germany well before Japan's attack on Pearl Harbor. By December 1941, Roosevelt had already instituted an unprecedented peacetime draft, created war mobilization agencies, and commissioned war plans for simultaneous struggle in Europe and the Pacific.

A Nation Unprepared   Still, the nation was not ready for war. Throughout the 1930s, military funding was a low priority. In September 1939 (when Hitler invaded Poland and began World War II), the U.S. Army ranked forty-fifth in size among the world's armies and could fully equip only one-third of its 227,000 men. A peacetime draft instituted in 1940 expanded the U.S. military to 2 million men, but Roosevelt's 1941 survey of war preparedness estimated that the United States could not be ready to fight before June 1943.

In December 1941, the Allies were losing the war (see Map 26.1). Hitler claimed Austria, Czechoslovakia, Poland, the Netherlands, Denmark, and Norway. Romania was lost, then Greece and Bulgaria. France fell in 1940. Britain fought on, but German planes rained bombs on London. More than 3 million German-led soldiers penetrated the Soviet Union and Africa. German U-boats controlled the Atlantic from the Arctic to the Caribbean. Within months of America's entry into the war, German submarines sank 216 vessels—some so close to American shores that people could see the glow of burning ships.

War in the Pacific   In the Pacific, the war was largely America's. The Soviets had not declared war on Japan, and there were too few British troops protecting England's Asian colonies to make much difference. By late spring 1942 Japan had captured most European colonial possessions in Southeast Asia. The Japanese attacked the Philippines hours after Pearl Harbor and destroyed U.S. air capability in the region. American and Filipino troops retreated to the Bataan Peninsula, hoping to hold the main island, Luzon, but Japanese forces were superior. In March 1942, General Douglas MacArthur, the commander of U.S. forces in the Far East, departed the Philippines, proclaiming, "I shall return."

Left behind were almost eighty thousand American and Filipino troops. Starving and weakened by disease, they held on for almost another month before surrendering. The Japanese troops, lacking supplies, were unprepared to deal with this large number of prisoners, and most believed the prisoners forfeited honorable treatment by surrendering. In what came to be known as the Bataan Death March, the Japanese force-marched their captives to prison camps 80 miles away, denying them food and water and bayoneting or beating to death those who fell behind. Ten thousand Filipinos and six hundred Americans died on the march.

The United States struck back. On April 18, sixteen American B-25s appeared over Japan. The Doolittle raid (named after the mission's leader) did little harm, but pushed Japanese commander Yamamoto to bold action. Japan moved to lure the weakened United States into a decisive battle. The target was Midway—two tiny islands about 1,000 miles northwest of Honolulu, where the U.S. Navy had a base. If Japan could take Midway—not implausible, given Japan's string of victories—it would secure a defensive perimeter far from the home islands (see Map 27.1). By using Guam, the Philippines, and even Australia as hostages, Japan believed it could negotiate a favorable peace agreement with the United States.

General Yamamoto did not know that America's MAGIC code-breaking machines could decipher Japanese messages. When the Japanese fleet arrived, it found the U.S. Navy lying in wait. The Battle of Midway in June 1942 was a turning point in the Pacific war. Japan's hope to force the United States to withdraw, leaving Japan to control the Pacific, vanished. Now Japan was on the defensive.

Europe First Strategy   Despite the importance of these early Pacific battles, America's war strategy was Europe First. American war planners believed that if Germany conquered the Soviet Union, it might directly threaten the United States. Roosevelt also feared that the

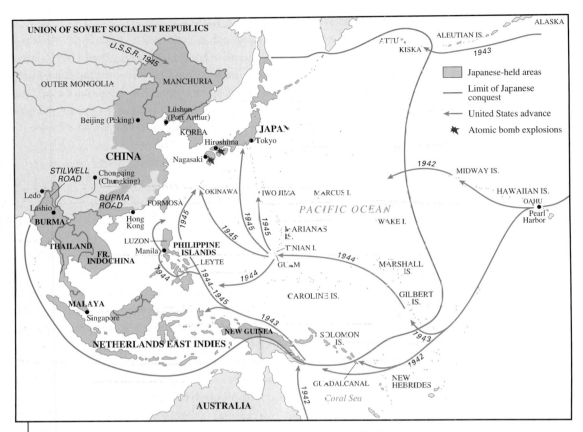

Map 27.1 The Pacific War

The strategy of the United States was to island-hop, from Hawai'i in 1942 to Iwo Jima and Okinawa in 1945. Naval battles were also decisive, notably the Battles of the Coral Sea and Midway in 1942. The war in the Pacific ended with Japan's surrender on August 15, 1945 (V-J Day). (*Source:* Thomas G. Paterson, J. Garry Clifford, Kenneth J. Hagan, *American Foreign Policy: A History,* Vol. 2, 3d ed. Copyright © 1991 by D. C. Heath Company. Used by permission of Houghton Mifflin Company.)

Soviet Union, suffering heavy losses against Hitler, might pursue a separate peace with Germany and so undo the Allied coalition. Therefore, the United States would work with Britain and the Soviet Union to defeat Germany, then deal with an isolated Japan.

British Prime Minister Winston Churchill and Soviet Premier Joseph Stalin disagreed over strategy. By late 1941, German troops nearly reached Moscow and Leningrad (present-day St. Petersburg) and slashed into Ukraine, taking Kiev and claiming the lives of over a million Soviet soldiers. Stalin pressed for British and American troops to attack Germany from the west to draw Germans away from the Soviet front. Roosevelt agreed and promised to open a second front before the end of 1942. Churchill, however, blocked this plan. Churchill wanted to win control of the North Atlantic shipping lanes first and promoted air attacks on Germany and a smaller, safer attack on Axis positions in North Africa. He believed halting the Germans there would protect British imperial possessions in the Mediterranean and the oil-rich Middle East.

Against his advisers' advice, Roosevelt accepted Churchill's plan. The U.S. military was not yet ready for a major campaign, and Roosevelt needed to show the American public some success in the European war. Thus, instead of rescuing the Soviet Union, the British and Americans made a joint landing in North Africa in November 1942, winning quick victories in Algeria and Morocco. In Egypt, the British confronted General Erwin Rommel and his Afrika Korps in a struggle over the Suez Canal and the Middle East oil fields, with Rommel's army surrendering after six months. Meanwhile, the Soviet army hung on. The Soviet Union lost 1.1 million men in the Battle of Stalingrad, but defeated the German Sixth Army there in early 1943. By spring 1943, Germany, like Japan, was on the defensive. But relations among the Allies remained precarious as the United States and Britain continued to resist Stalin's demand for a second front.

THE PRODUCTION FRONT AND AMERICAN WORKERS

Although the war would be fought on the battlefields of Europe and the Pacific, America's strategic advantage lay on the production front at home. By making the machines that would win the war for the Allies, the United States would prevail through a "crushing superiority of equipment," Roosevelt told Congress.

Goals for military production were staggering. In 1940, American factories built 3,807 airplanes. Following Pearl Harbor, Roosevelt wanted 60,000 aircraft in 1942 and twice that in 1943. Plans called for the manufacture of 16 million tons of shipping and 120,000 tanks. The military needed supplies for a force that would reach almost 16 million men. During the war, military production superseded the manufacture of civilian goods. Automobile plants built tanks and airplanes instead of cars; dress factories sewed military uniforms. The War Production Board, established in early 1942, allocated resources and coordinated production among thousands of independent factories.

Businesses, Universities, and the War Effort

During the war, American businesses overwhelmingly cooperated with government war-production plans. Patriotism was one reason, but generous incentives were another. In 1940, as the United States produced armaments for the Allies, the U.S. economy began to recover from the depression. Rising consumer spending built industrial confidence. Auto manufacturers, for example, expected to sell 25 percent more in 1941 than in 1939. The massive retooling necessary to produce planes or tanks instead of cars would be expensive and leave manufacturers dependent on a single client—the federal government.

The federal government, however, paid for retooling and factory expansions; it guaranteed profits by allowing corporations to charge it production costs plus a fixed profit. It created generous tax write-offs and exemptions from antitrust laws. Consequently, corporations doubled their net profits between 1939 and 1943. Most military contracts went to the United States's largest corporations, which had the facilities to guarantee rapid production. From mid-1940 through September 1944 the government awarded contracts totaling $175 billion, with about two-thirds going to the top hundred corporations. General Motors received 8 percent of the total. This approach made sense for a nation that wanted enormous quantities of war goods manufactured in the shortest possible time; most small businesses lacked the necessary capacity. However, wartime government contracts further consolidated U.S. manufacturing in the hands of a few giant corporations.

Manhattan Project

Wartime needs also created a new relationship between science and the U.S. military. Millions of dollars went to fund university research programs. Such federally sponsored research programs developed new technologies of warfare, such as vastly improved radar systems. The most important government-sponsored scientific research program was the Manhattan Project, a $2 billion secret effort to build an atomic bomb. Roosevelt was convinced by scientists fleeing the Nazis in 1939 that Germany was developing an atomic weapon, and he resolved to do it first. The Manhattan Project achieved the world's first sustained nuclear chain reaction in 1942 at the University of Chicago, and in 1943 the federal government established a secret community for atomic scientists and their families at Los Alamos, New Mexico, to develop the weapon that would change the world.

New Opportunities for Workers

The United States's new defense factories required millions of workers. At first workers were plentiful: 9 million Americans were still unemployed in 1940 when war mobilization began. But the armed forces took almost 16 million men, forcing industry to look elsewhere for workers. Women, African Americans, Mexican Americans, and poor whites from Appalachia and the Deep South streamed into defense plant jobs.

Still, many industries refused to hire African Americans. A. Philip Randolph, head of the Brotherhood of Sleeping Car Porters, proposed a march on Washington, D.C., to demand equal access to defense jobs. Roosevelt, fearing race riots, offered the March on Washington movement a deal. In exchange for canceling the march, he issued Executive Order No. 8802, which prohibited discrimination in war industries and government jobs. Although enforcement was uneven, hundreds of thousands of African Americans migrated from the South to northern and western industrial cities on the strength of this official guarantee of job equality.

Mexican workers also filled wartime jobs in the United States. About 200,000 Mexican farm workers, or *braceros,* were offered short-term agricultural contracts as Americans sought well-paid war work. Mexican and Mexican American workers faced discrimination and segregation, but they seized these new economic opportunities. In 1941 there were no Mexican Americans working in the Los Angeles shipyards; by 1944, 17,000 were employed there.

Women at Work

Initially, employers insisted that women were not suited for industrial jobs. But as labor shortages loomed, employers did an about-face. Posters and billboards urged women to "Do the Job HE Left Behind." The government's War Manpower Commission glorified the invented worker Rosie the Riveter, who was featured on posters, in magazines, and in recruitment jingles.

Rosie the Riveter was an inspiring, albeit inaccurate, image of working women. Only 16 percent of women workers had jobs in defense plants, and only 4.4 percent held skilled jobs (such as riveting). Nonetheless, during the war, more than 6 million women entered the labor force, and the number of working women increased by 57 percent. More than 400,000 African American women left domestic service for higher-paying industrial jobs, often with union benefits. Seven million women moved to war-production areas, such as southern California. Women workers in all fields kept the U.S. economy going.

Workers in defense plants were often expected to work ten days for every day off or to accept difficult night shifts. Businesses and the federal government provided workers new support to keep them on the job. The West Coast Kaiser shipyards offered high pay, but also childcare, subsidized housing, and healthcare: the Kaiser Permanente Medical Care Program, a forerunner of the health maintenance organization (HMO). The federal government also funded childcare centers and before- and after-school programs, with 130,000 preschoolers and 320,000 school-age children enrolled during peak years.

Organized Labor During Wartime

The federal government attempted to ensure that labor strikes, so common in the 1930s, would not interrupt production. Days after Pearl Harbor, a White House labor-management conference agreed to a no-strike/no-lockout pledge. In 1942 Roosevelt created the National War Labor Board (NWLB) to settle disputes. The NWLB forged a temporary compromise between union demands for a closed shop, in which only union members could work, and management's desire for an open shop, in which union and nonunion workers could work. Workers could not be required to join a union, but unions could enroll as many members as possible. Between 1940 and 1945, union membership ballooned from 8.5 million to 14.75 million.

The government did restrict union power if it threatened war production. When coal miners in the United Mine Workers union went on strike in 1943, following an NWLB attempt to limit wage increases to a cost-of-living adjustment, lack of coal halted railroads and shut down steel mills. Congress responded with the War Labor Disputes (Smith-Connally) Act, granting the president authority to seize and operate any strike-bound plant deemed necessary to national security.

Success on the Production Front

For nearly four years, U.S. factories operated twenty-four hours a day, seven days a week, turning out roughly 300,000 airplanes, 102,000 armored vehicles, 77,000 ships, 20 million small arms, 40 billion bullets, and 6 million tons of bombs. By war's end, the United States was producing 40 percent of the world's weaponry. This feat depended on transforming formerly skilled work into assembly-line mass production. Henry Ford, now seventy-eight years old, created a massive bomber plant outside Detroit with assembly lines almost a mile long producing one B-24 Liberator bomber every hour. On the West Coast, William Kaiser cut construction time for Liberty ships—the huge, 440-foot-long cargo ships transporting tanks, guns, and bullets overseas—from 355 to 56 days. The ships were not well made; welded hulls sometimes split in rough seas. However, as the United States struggled to produce cargo ships faster than German U-boats could sink them, production was more important than quality.

LIFE ON THE HOME FRONT

The United States was protected by two oceans from its enemies and spared the war that other nations experienced. Americans grieved the loss of loved ones abroad, but bombs did not fall on U.S. cities; invading armies did not burn and rape and kill. Instead, war mobilization ended the Great Depression and brought prosperity. American civilians experienced the paradox of good times amid global conflagration.

Supporting the War Effort

Still the war was a constant presence for Americans on the home front. Civilians supported the war efforts, though Americans were never as committed to shared sacrifice as images of the greatest generation—widely circulated in early twenty-first century popular history and culture—suggest. During the war, however, families planted 20 million victory gardens to free up food supplies for the military. Housewives saved cooking fat and returned it to butchers because it yielded glycerin to make black powder used in shells or bullets. Children collected scrap metal—the iron in one old shovel blade could make four hand grenades.

Many consumer goods were rationed or unavailable. To save wool for military use, the War Production Board redesigned men's suits, narrowing lapels, shortening jackets, and eliminating vests and pant cuffs. Bathing suits, the WPB specified, must shrink by 10 percent. When silk and nylon were diverted from stockings to parachutes, women used makeup on their legs. The Office of Price Administration (OPA), created by Congress in 1942, established a nationwide rationing system for such goods as sugar, coffee, and gasoline. By early 1943, every citizen—regardless of age—received two ration books each month. Sugar was tightly rationed, and people saved for months to make a birthday cake. A black market existed, but most Americans understood that sugar produced alcohol for weapons manufacture and meat fed our boys overseas.

Propaganda and Popular Culture

Despite near-unanimous support for the war, government leaders worried that, over time, public willingness to sacrifice might lag. In 1942 Roosevelt created the Office of War Information (OWI), which hired Hollywood filmmakers and New York copywriters to sell the war at home. OWI posters exhorted Americans to save and sacrifice and reminded them to watch what they said, for "loose lips sink ships."

Popular culture also reinforced wartime messages. A *Saturday Evening Post* advertisement for vacuum cleaners (unavailable for the duration) urged women war workers to fight "for freedom and all that means to women everywhere. You're fighting for a little house of your own, and . . . the right to bring up your children without the shadow of fear." Songs urged Americans to "Remember December 7th" or to "Accentuate the Positive." Others made fun of America's enemies ("You're a sap, Mr. Jap/Uncle Sam is gonna spanky").

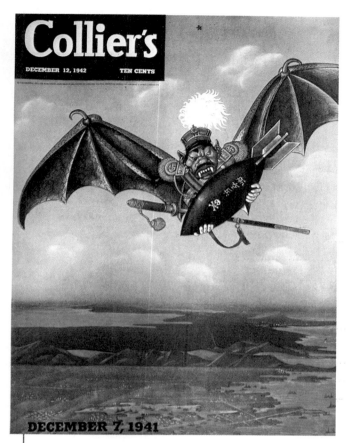

DECEMBER 7, 1941

In the days following the attack on Pearl Harbor, the Japanese were often pictured as subhuman—buck-toothed, nearsighted rodents and other vermin. Racial stereotyping would affect how both the Americans and the Japanese waged war. The Americans badly underestimated the Japanese, leaving themselves open for the surprise attack on Pearl Harbor and American forces in the Philippines. And the Japanese, believing Americans were barbarians who lacked a sense of honor, mistakenly expected that the United States would withdraw from East Asia once confronted with Japanese power and determination. (*Collier's*, December 12, 1942)

Movies drew 90 million viewers a week in 1944—out of a total population of 132 million. Hollywood sought to meet Eleanor Roosevelt's challenge to "Keep 'em laughing." *A WAVE, a WAC, and a Marine* promised "no battle scenes, no message, just barrels of fun." Others, such as *Bataan* or *Wake Island*, portrayed actual—if sanitized—events in the war. Even in comedies, the war was always present. Theaters held plasma premieres, offering free admission to those who donated a half-pint of blood to the Red Cross. Audiences rose to sing "The Star Spangled Banner," then watched newsreels with censored combat footage. In movie theaters Americans saw the horror of Nazi death camps in May 1945.

Wartime Prosperity

The war demanded sacrifices from Americans, but between 1939 and the end of the war, per capita income rose from $691 to $1,515. Price controls kept inflation down so that wage increases did not disappear to higher costs. With little to buy, savings rose.

World War II cost approximately $304 billion (more than $3 trillion in today's dollars), which the United States financed through deficit spending, borrowing money by selling war bonds. The national debt skyrocketed, from $49 billion in 1941 to $259 billion in 1945 (and was not paid off until 1970). However, wartime revenue acts increased the number of Americans paying personal income tax from 4 million to 42.6 million—at rates ranging from 6 to 94 percent—and introduced a new system where employers withheld taxes from employee paychecks. For the first time, individual Americans paid more in taxes than corporations.

A Nation in Motion

Despite hardships and fears, the war offered home-front Americans new opportunities. More than 15 million civilians moved during the war. Seven hundred thousand African Americans left the South during the war. People who never traveled farther than the next county found themselves on the other side of the country or of the world.

The rapid influx of war workers to cities and small towns strained community resources. Migrants crowded into substandard housing—even woodsheds, tents, or cellars—and into trailer parks without adequate sanitary facilities. Disease spread: scabies and ringworm, polio, tuberculosis. Many long-term residents found the newcomers, especially the unmarried male war workers, a rough bunch.

In and around Detroit, where car factories now produced tanks and planes, established residents called war workers freshly arrived from southern Appalachia hillbillies and white trash. Many migrants knew little about urban life. One man from rural Tennessee, unfamiliar with traffic lights and street signs, navigated by counting the trees between his home and the war plant where he worked. Some Appalachian trailerites appalled their neighbors by building outdoor privies or burying garbage in their yards.

Racial Conflicts

As people from different backgrounds confronted one another, tensions rose and racism flared. In 1943 almost 250 racial conflicts exploded in forty-seven cities. In Detroit in June, white mobs, undeterred by police, roamed the city attacking African Americans. African Americans hurled rocks at police and dragged white passengers off streetcars. After thirty hours of rioting, twenty-five African Amerians and nine whites lay dead.

In Los Angeles in 1943, young Mexican American gang members, or *pachucos*, wore zoot suits: long jackets with wide padded shoulders, loose pants pegged below the knee, wide-brimmed hats, and dangling watch chains. With cloth rationed, wearing pants requiring five yards of fabric was a purposeful rejection of wartime sacrifice. Although a high percentage of Mexican Americans served in the military, many white servicemen believed otherwise. Racial tensions fueled rumors that *pachucos* attacked white sailors, triggering violence. For four days, mobs of white men—mainly soldiers and sailors—attacked and stripped zoot suiters. Los Angeles outlawed zoot suits, but the riots only ended when naval personnel left.

Families in Wartime

War profoundly transformed families. Despite policies exempting married men and fathers from the draft, almost 3 million families were broken up. The divorce rate of 16 per 1,000 marriages in 1940 almost doubled to 27 per 1,000 in 1944. Still, the number of marriages rose from 73 per 1,000 unmarried women in 1939 to 93 in 1942. Some couples scrambled to marry before the man was sent overseas; others sought military deferments. Total births rose from 2.4 million in 1939 to 3.1 million in 1943. Many were goodbye babies, conceived to guarantee the family's continuation if the father died in the war.

On college campuses, women complained, along with the song lyrics, "There is no available male." But other young women found plenty of male company, sparking concern about wartime threats to sexual morality. *Youth in Crisis*, a 1943 newsreel, featured a girl with "experience far beyond her age" necking with a soldier on the street. These victory girls were said to support the war by giving their all to men in uniform. Many young men and women behaved as they never would in peacetime, which often meant hasty marriages to strangers, especially if a baby was on the way. Wartime mobility increased opportunities for young people to explore same-sex attraction, and gay communities grew in such cities as San Francisco.

In many ways, the war reinforced traditional gender roles weakened during the depression, when men often lost the breadwinner role. Now, while men defended their nation, women "kept the home fires burning," sometimes filling jobs vacated by soldiers. Women who worked were frequently blamed for neglecting their children and creating an epidemic of juvenile delinquency. Nonetheless, millions of women took on new responsibilities and enjoyed greater independence. Many husbands returned to find that their families' lives seemed complete without them.

THE LIMITS OF AMERICAN IDEALS

The U.S. government worked hard to explain to its citizens the reasons for their wartime sacrifices. In 1941 Roosevelt pledged the United States to defend four essential human freedoms—freedom of speech, freedom of religion, freedom from want, and freedom from fear—and government-sponsored films contrasted democracy and totalitarianism, freedom and fascism, equality and oppression.

[handwritten margin note: like everyone right in America has those freedoms...]

As the United States fought the totalitarian regimes of the Axis powers, the nation confronted tough questions. What limits on civil liberties were justified in the interest of national security? How freely could information flow without revealing military secrets and costing American lives? How could the United States protect itself against spies or saboteurs, especially from German, Italian, or Japanese citizens living in the United States? And what about the United States's ongoing race problem? The answers revealed tensions between the nation's democratic ideals and its wartime practices.

Regarding civil liberties, U.S. leaders embraced a strategy of truth, declaring that citizens required a truthful accounting of the war's progress. However, the government closely controlled military information, as even seemingly unimportant details might tip off enemies about troop movements. While government-created propaganda sometimes dehumanized the enemy, such hate mongering was used much less frequently than during World War I.

More complex was how to handle dissent and guard against the possibility that enemy agents were operating within the nation's borders. The 1940 Alien Registration (Smith) Act made it unlawful to advocate the overthrow of the U.S. government by force or violence. After Pearl Harbor, the government arrested thousands of Germans, Italians, and other Europeans as suspected spies and potential traitors. The government interned 14,426 Europeans in Enemy Alien Camps and prohibited ten thousand Italian Americans from living or working in restricted zones along the California coast.

Internment of Japanese Americans   In March 1942, Roosevelt ordered that all 112,000 foreign-born Japanese and Japanese Americans living in California, Oregon, and the state of Washington (the vast majority of the mainland population) be removed from the West Coast to relocation centers. There were no individual charges, as was the case with Italians and Germans; Japanese and Japanese Americans were imprisoned solely because they were of Japanese descent.

Anger at Japan's sneak attack on Pearl Harbor fueled calls for internment, as did fears that West Coast cities might come under attack. Long-standing racism also played a major role, as people in economic competition with Japanese Americans strongly supported internment. Although Japanese nationals were forbidden U.S. citizenship or property ownership, American-born Nissei (second generation) and

War Brides

During and immediately after World War II, more than sixty thousand U.S. servicemen married women from other nations. The U.S. government promised servicemen that it would deliver their wives and babies to the United States free of charge.

Beginning in Britain in 1946, the U.S. Army's Operation War Bride eventually transported more than seventy thousand women and children. The first group—455 British women and their 132 children—arrived in the United States on February 4, 1946. As the former World War II transport *Argentina* sailed into New York harbor in the predawn darkness, the Statue of Liberty was specially illuminated. Women who sang, "There'll Always Be an England" as they set sail from Southampton, England, gathered on deck to attempt "The Star-Spangled Banner."

These women, many of them teenagers, left their homes and families behind to join their new husbands in a strange land.

Women from war-destroyed cities were impressed by America's material abundance and the warm welcome they received. But America's racial prejudice shocked Shanghai native Helen Chia Wong, wife of Staff Sergeant Albert Wong, when she and her husband were refused rental of a house with the explanation "The neighbors wouldn't like it." It was not always easy, but most of the war brides settled into their new communities, becoming part of their new nation and helping to forge an intimate link between the United States and other nations of the world.

The army's Operation War Bride (sometimes called Operation Mother-in-Law or the Diaper Run) began in Britain in early 1946. Employing eleven former World War II troopships, including the *Queen Mary,* the U.S. government relocated the wives and babies of U.S. servicemen from dozens of nations to the United States. These English war brides, with babies their fathers had not yet seen, were waiting to be reunited with their husbands in Massachusetts, Missouri, and Iowa.

(© Bettmann/Corbis)

Sansei (third generation), all U.S. citizens, were increasingly successful in business and agriculture. The relocation order forced Japanese Americans to sell property valued at $500 million for a fraction of its worth.

The internees were sent to flood-damaged lands at Relocation, Arkansas, to the intermountain terrain of Wyoming and the desert of western Arizona, and to other desolate spots in the West. The camps were bleak: behind barbed wire, entire families lived in a single room furnished only with cots, blankets, and a bare light bulb. Toilets and dining and bathing facilities were communal. People nonetheless attempted to sustain community life, setting up schools and clubs.

Betrayed by their government, almost 6,000 internees renounced U.S. citizenship and demanded to be sent to Japan. Some sought legal remedy, but the Supreme Court upheld the government's action in *Korematsu v. U.S.* (1944). Others sought to demonstrate their loyalty. The all–Japanese American 442nd Regimental Combat Team, drawn heavily from internees, was the most decorated unit of its size, receiving a Congressional Medal of Honor, 47 Distinguished Service Crosses, 350 Silver Stars, and more than 3,600 Purple Hearts. In 1988 Congress publically apologized and paid $20,000 to each of the 60,000 surviving Japanese American internees.

African Americans and Double V

Meanwhile, African American leaders wanted the nation to confront the parallels between the Nazi racist doctrines and the persistence of Jim Crow segregation in the United States. Proclaiming a Double V campaign (victory at home and abroad), groups such as the National Association for the Advancement of Colored People (NAACP) hoped to "persuade, embarrass, compel and shame our government and our nation . . . into a more enlightened attitude toward a tenth of its people." The NAACP, 50,000 strong in 1940, had 450,000 members by 1946. In 1942 civil rights activists founded the Congress of Racial Equality (CORE), which stressed "nonviolent direct action" and staged sit-ins to desegregate restaurants and movie theaters in Chicago and Washington, D.C.

Military service was a key issue for African Americans, who understood the traditional link between the military service and citizenship. But the U.S. military remained segregated by race and strongly resisted using African American units as combat troops. As late as 1943, less than 6 percent of the armed forces were African American. The Marines initially refused to accept African Americans at all, and the navy approximated segregation by assigning African American men to service positions in which they would rarely interact with non–African Americans as equals or superiors.

A Segregated Military

The U.S. federal government and War Department decided that the world war was no time to integrate the armed forces. The majority of Americans (approximately 89 percent of Americans were white) opposed integration. Racism was so entrenched that the Red Cross segregated blood plasma during the war Integration of military installations, the majority of which were in the South, would have provoked a crisis as federal power contradicted state law. Pointing to outbreaks of racial violence in southern training camps, government and military officials argued that wartime integration would provoke more racial violence and hinder America's war effort. Hopes for racial justice, were another casualty of the war.

Despite such discrimination, African Americans stood up for their rights. Lt. Jackie Robinson refused to move to the back of the bus at the army's Camp Hood, Texas, in 1944 and faced court-martial, even though military regulations forbade racial discrimination on military vehicles. African American sailors disobeyed orders to return to work after an explosion that destroyed two ships and killed 320 men—an explosion caused by the navy practice of assigning untrained men to load bombs onto Liberty ships. When they were court-martialed for mutiny, future Supreme Court justice and chief counsel for the NAACP Thurgood Marshall asked why only African American sailors did this work. He proclaimed, "This is the Navy on trial for its whole vicious policy toward Negroes."

African American servicemen did eventually fight on the front lines. The Marine Corps commandant in the Pacific proclaimed that "Negro Marines are . . . Marines, period." The Tuskegee Airmen, trained at the Tuskegee Institute in Alabama, saw heroic service in all-black units, such as the Ninety-ninth Pursuit Squadron, which won eighty Distinguished Flying Crosses. After the war, African Americans called on their wartime service to claim full citizenship rights. African Americans shared fully in veterans' benefits under the GI Bill. The war marked a turning point for equal rights.

America and the Holocaust

America's inaction in what we now call the Holocaust is tragic, though the consequences are clearer in retrospect than at the time. When the United States turned away refugees on the *St. Louis* (page 695) in early 1939 and refused to relax immigration quotas to admit European Jews and others fleeing Hitler's Germany, almost no one foresaw death camps like Auschwitz. While American anti-Semitism played a significant role, it was not unusual to refuse those seeking refuge, especially during a major economic crisis.

In 1942, American newspapers reported the mass slaughter of Jews and other "undesirables" (Gypsies, homosexuals, the physically and mentally handicapped) under Hitler. Many Americans, having been duped by manufactured atrocity tales during World War I, wrongly discounted these stories. But Roosevelt knew about Nazi death camps capable of killing up to two thousand people an hour using the gas Zyklon-B.

In 1943 British and American representatives met in Bermuda but took no action. Appalled, Secretary of the Treasury Henry Morgenthau Jr. charged that the State Department's foot dragging made the United States an accessory to murder. In 1944, Roosevelt created the War Refugee Board, establishing refugee camps in Europe and helping to save 200,000 Jews. But it came too late. By war's end, the Nazis had systematically murdered almost 11 million people.

LIFE IN THE MILITARY

More than 15 million men and approximately 350,000 women served in the U.S. armed forces during World War II. Eighteen percent of American families had a father, son, or brother in the armed forces. Some men (and all of the women) volunteered. But more than 10 million were draftees. By presidential order, the military stopped accepting volunteers in December 1942. Instead, the Selective Service system and the new War Manpower Commission attempted to centralize control over filling military positions while maintaining war production. The draft extended mostly equitably across the population during World War II.

Selective Service

The Selective Service Act allowed deferments, but they did not disproportionately benefit the wealthy. Almost 10,000 Princeton students or alumni served—as did all 4 of Franklin and Eleanor Roosevelt's sons. The small number of college deferments was balanced by deferments for many critical occupations, including war workers and almost 2 million agricultural workers. Most exemptions were for men deemed physically or mentally unqualified to serve. Army physicians discovered the depression's impact as draftees arrived with rotted teeth and deteriorated eyesight—signs of malnutrition. Army dentists pulled 15 million teeth; optometrists prescribed 2.5 million pairs of glasses. Up to one-third of African American draftees were functionally illiterate, while forty-six percent were classified 4-F—unfit for service.

Nonetheless, almost 12 percent of America's population served in the military. Ethnic and regional differences were profound, and northerners and southerners often could not understand one another. Although African Americans and Japanese Americans served in separate units, Hispanics, Native Americans, and Chinese Americans served in "white" units. The result was often tension, but many Americans became less prejudiced as they served with men unlike themselves.

Fighting the War

Although military service was widespread, the burdens of combat were not equally shared. Women's roles in the U.S. military were much more restricted than in the British or Soviet militaries, where women served in combat-related positions. U.S. women served as nurses, in communications offices, and as typists or cooks. The recruiting slogan for the WACs (Women's Army Corps) was "Release a Man for Combat." However, most men never saw combat either; one-quarter never left the United States. One-third of U.S. military personnel served in clerical positions, with well-educated men most likely slotted into noncombat positions. African Americans, though assigned dirty and dangerous tasks, were largely kept from combat. In World War II, lower-class, less-educated white men bore the brunt of the fighting.

Combat in World War II was horrible. Hollywood war films depicted men dying bravely, shot cleanly and comforted by buddies in their last moments. In reality, less than 10 percent of casualties were caused by bullets; most men were killed or wounded by mortars, bombs, or grenades. Seventy-five thousand American men remained missing at war's end, blown into fragments too small to identify. Combat meant sliding down a mud-slicked hill into a pile of putrid corpses and using flamethrowers that burned at 2,000 degrees Fahrenheit on other human beings. It meant steering a landing craft through floating body parts of those who went ahead, knowing that if you made it ashore you could be blown apart by artillery. Service was for the duration of the war. Only death, serious injury, or victory offered release.

Close to 300,000 U.S. servicemen died in combat, and nearly 1 million were wounded, half of them seriously. Medical advances, such as the development of penicillin and the use of blood plasma to prevent shock, helped wounded men survive, but many never fully recovered. Between 20 and 30 percent of combat casualties were psychoneurotic. The federal government strictly censored images of American combat deaths, consigning them to a secret file known as the chamber of horrors. Many men never talked about their experiences in the war.

WINNING THE WAR

Axis hopes for victory depended on a short war. German and Japanese leaders knew that, if the United States had time to fully mobilize, the war was lost. Hitler, blinded by racial arrogance, stated, "I don't see much future for the Americans. . . . It's a decayed country. . . . American society [is] half Judaized, and the other half Negrified. How can one expect a State like that to hold together?" By mid-1942 the Axis powers understood that they had underestimated American resolve and the other Allies' willingness to sacrifice their citizens to stop the Axis advance (see Map 27.2). The chance of an Axis victory grew slim as months passed, but though the outcome was virtually certain after spring 1943, two years of bloody fighting lay ahead.

Tensions Among the Allies

The Allies' suspicions of one another undermined cooperation. The Soviets continued to press Britain and the United States to open a second front to draw German troops away from the Soviet Union. The United States and Britain, however, continued to delay. With the alliance badly strained, the three Allied leaders met in Teheran, Iran, in December 1943. Stalin dismissed Churchill's proposal for another peripheral attack, this time through the Balkans to Vienna. The three agreed to launch Operation Overlord—the cross-Channel invasion of France—in early 1944. And the Soviet Union promised to aid the Allies against Japan once Germany was defeated.

War in Europe

The second front opened in the dark morning hours of June 6, 1944: D-Day. In the largest amphibious landing in history, more than 140,000 Allied troops commanded by American general Dwight D. Eisenhower scrambled ashore at Normandy, France. Landing craft and soldiers immediately encountered the enemy; they triggered mines and were pinned down by fire from cliffside pillboxes. Although heavy aerial and naval bombardment and the clandestine work of saboteurs softened the German defenses, the fighting was ferocious.

Allied troops spread across the countryside, liberating France and Belgium by the end of August and entering Germany in September. Almost 54,000 Allied troops died in the struggle, and 20,000 French civilians were killed, most by Allied bombing. German armored divisions counterattacked in Belgium's Ardennes Forest in December, hoping to reach Antwerp to halt Allied supplies through that Belgian port. After weeks of heavy fighting in the Battle of the Bulge, the Allies gained control in late January 1945.

Map 27.2   The Allies on the Offensive in Europe, 1942–1945

The United States pursued a Europe First policy: first defeat Germany, then focus on Japan. U.S. military efforts began in North Africa in late 1942 and ended in Germany in 1945 on May 8 (V-E Day).

By that point, strategic bombing (not nearly as precise as was publicly claimed) destroyed Germany's war production and devastated its economy. In early 1945, the British and Americans began morale bombing, killing tens of thousands of civilians in aerial attacks on Berlin and then Dresden. Meanwhile, Soviet troops marched through Poland and cut a path to Berlin. American forces crossed the Rhine River in March 1945 and captured the industrial Ruhr valley. Several units entered Austria and Czechoslovakia, where they met Soviet soldiers.

Yalta Conference

Allied leaders began planning the peace in early 1945. Franklin Roosevelt, by this time very ill, called for a summit meeting. The three Allied leaders convened at Yalta, in the Russian Crimea, in February 1945, each with definite goals for the postwar world. Britain, its formerly powerful empire now vulnerable and shrinking, sought to protect its colonial possessions and to limit Soviet power. The Soviet Union, with 21 million dead, wanted German reparations for its massive rebuilding effort. The Soviets hoped to expand their sphere of influence throughout eastern Europe and guarantee their national security; Germany, Stalin insisted, must be permanently weakened.

The three Allied leaders—Winston Churchill, Franklin D. Roosevelt, and Joseph Stalin—met at Yalta in February 1945. Having been president for twelve years, Roosevelt showed signs of age and fatigue. Two months later, he died of a massive cerebral hemorrhage. (Franklin D. Roosevelt Library, Hyde Park, New York)

The United States also sought to expand its influence and control the peace. Roosevelt lobbied for the United Nations organization, approved in principle the previous year at Dumbarton Oaks in Washington, D.C., through which the United States hoped to exercise influence. The United States hoped to avoid the debts-reparations fiasco that plagued Europe after World War I. U.S. goals included self-determination for liberated peoples; gradual decolonization; and management of world affairs by the Soviet Union, Great Britain, the United States, and China. (Roosevelt hoped China might help stabilize Asia after the war. The United States abolished the Chinese Exclusion Act in 1943 to consolidate ties between the two nations.) The United States was also determined to limit Soviet influence in the postwar world.

Military positions during the Yalta conference helped shape the negotiations. Soviet troops occupied eastern European nations, including Poland, where Moscow had installed a pro-Soviet regime despite a British-supported Polish government-in-exile in London. With Soviet troops in place, Britain and the United States were limited in negotiating this region's future. The Big Three agreed that some eastern German territory would be transferred to Poland and the remainder divided into four zones, the fourth zone to be administered by France. Berlin, within the Soviet zone, would also be divided among the four victors. In exchange for U.S. promises to support Soviet claims on territory lost to Japan in the Russo-Japanese War of 1904–1905, Stalin agreed to a treaty of friendship with Jiang Jieshi (Chiang Kai-shek), America's ally, rather than with the communist Mao Zedong (Mao Tse-tung), and to declare war on Japan within three months of Hitler's defeat.

Harry Truman

Franklin D. Roosevelt, reelected to an unprecedented fourth term in November 1944, did not live to see the war's end. He died on April 12, and Vice President Harry S Truman became president. Truman, who replaced the former vice president Henry Wallace as Roosevelt's running mate in 1944, was inexperienced in foreign policy and was not informed about the top-secret atomic weapons project until after he became president. Eighteen days into Truman's presidency, Adolf Hitler killed himself in a bunker in bomb-ravaged Berlin. On May 8 Germany surrendered.

As the great powers jockeyed for influence after Germany's surrender, the Grand Alliance began to crumble. At the Potsdam Conference in mid-July, Truman—a novice at international diplomacy—was less patient with the Soviets than Roosevelt had been. And Truman learned during the conference that a test of the new atomic weapon had been successful. The United States no longer needed the Soviet Union's help in the Pacific war. The Allies did agree that Japan must surrender unconditionally. But with the end of the European war, the wartime bonds between the Allies were strained.

War in the Pacific

In the Pacific, the war continued. Since the Battle of Midway in June 1942, American strategy had been to island-hop toward Japan, skipping the most fortified islands whenever possible and taking the weaker ones, aiming to strand Japanese forces on their island outposts. To cut off supplies, Americans targeted the Japanese merchant marine. By 1944, Allied troops—from the United States, Britain, Australia, and New Zealand—secured the Solomon, Gilbert, Marshall, and Mariana Islands. General Douglas MacArthur landed at Leyte in the Philippines to retake them in October 1944.

In February 1945, U.S. and Japanese troops battled for Iwo Jima, a small island about 700 miles south of Tokyo. Twenty-one thousand Japanese defenders occupied the island's high ground. Hidden in caves, trenches, and underground tunnels, they were protected from U.S. aerial bombardment supporting its amphibious landing. The island offered no cover, and Marines were slaughtered as they came ashore. For twenty days, U.S. forces fought their way up Mount Suribachi, the highest and most heavily fortified point on Iwo Jima. Iwo Jima claimed 6,821 Americans and more than 20,000 Japanese lives.

A month later, U.S. troops landed on Okinawa, an island at the southern tip of Japan, from which Allied forces planned to invade the main Japanese islands. Fighting raged for two months. The monsoon rains began in May, turning battlefields into seas of mud filled with decaying corpses. The supporting fleet endured mass kamikaze ("suicide") attacks, as Japanese pilots intentionally crashed bomb-laden planes into American ships. On Okinawa, 7,374 Americans died in battle. Almost the entire Japanese garrison of 100,000 was killed. More than one-quarter of Okinawa's people, or approximately 80,000 civilians, perished.

Bombing of Japan

With American forces just 350 miles from Japan's main islands, a powerful Japanese military faction was determined to avoid the humiliation of an unconditional surrender and preserve the emperor's sovereignty. On March 9, 1945, 333 American B-29 Superfortresses dropped explosives and incendiary devices on a 4-by-3-mile area of Tokyo. They created a firestorm, a fierce blaze that sucked the oxygen from the air, creating hurricane-force winds and growing hot enough to melt concrete and steel. Almost 100,000 people were incinerated, suffocated, or boiled to death hiding in canals. Over the following five months, U.S. bombers attacked sixty-six Japanese cities, leaving 8 million people homeless, killing almost 900,000.

Japan, meanwhile, was attempting to bomb the U.S mainland. Thousands of bomb-bearing high-altitude balloons, constructed from rice paper and potato-flour paste by schoolgirls, were launched into the jet stream. Those that reached the United States fell on unpopulated areas, occasionally starting forest fires. The only mainland U.S. casualties in the war were five children and an adult on a Sunday school picnic in Oregon who accidentally detonated a balloon bomb that they found in the underbrush.

Early in summer 1945, Japan put out peace feelers through the Soviets. Japan was not, however, willing to accept the unconditional surrender terms that Allied leaders agreed to at Potsdam, and Truman chose not to pursue a negotiated peace. U.S. troops were mobilizing to invade the Japanese home islands, factoring in the experiences of Iwo Jima and Okinawa. The Manhattan Project's success offered another option, and Truman took it. Using atomic bombs on Japan, Truman believed, would end the war quickly and save American lives.

Historians still debate Truman's decision to use the atomic bomb rather than negotiate surrender terms. Was Japan on the verge of an unconditional surrender, as some argue? Or was the antisurrender faction of Japanese military leaders strong enough to prevail? Truman knew the bomb could give the United States real and psychological power in negotiating the peace. How much did his desire to demonstrate the bomb's power to the Soviet Union influence him? Did racism or a desire for retaliation play a role? Whatever the answers, bombing (whether conventional or atomic) fit the established U.S. strategy of using machines rather than men whenever possible.

The decision to use the bomb did not seem as momentous to Truman as it does in retrospect. The moral line had already been crossed with wholesale bombing of civilian populations: the Japanese bombed Shanghai in 1937; Germans terror-bombed Warsaw, Rotterdam, and London. British and American bombers purposely created firestorms in German cities, killing, for example, 225,000 people in Dresden. The U.S. bombing of Japanese cities with conventional weapons had already killed nearly a million people. What distinguished the atomic bombs from conventional bombs was their power and their efficiency, not that they killed huge numbers of civilians in unspeakable ways.

On July 26, 1945, the Allies delivered an ultimatum to Japan: promising that the Japanese people would not be enslaved, the Potsdam Declaration called for unconditional surrender or threatened "prompt and utter destruction." Tokyo radio announced that the government would respond with *mokusatsu* (literally, "kill with silence," or ignore the ultimatum). On August 6, 1945, a B-29 bomber *Enola Gay* dropped an atomic bomb above Hiroshima, igniting a firestorm and killing 130,000 people. Tens of thousands more would suffer from radiation poisoning.

On August 8, the Soviet Union declared war on Japan. On August 9, Americans dropped a second atomic bomb on Nagasaki, killing 60,000 people. Five days later, Japan surrendered. Recent histories argue that the Soviet declaration of war played a more significant role in Japan's surrender than America's use of atomic weapons. In the end, the Allies promised that the Japanese emperor could remain as the nation's titular head. World War II was over.

Summary

Hitler once prophesied, "We may be destroyed, but if we are, we shall drag a world with us." World War II devastated much of the globe. In Asia and in Europe, people pawed through rubble, searching for food. One out of nine people in the Soviet Union had perished: at least 21 million civilian and military war dead. The Chinese lost 10 million; the Germans and Austrians, 6 million; the Japanese, 2.5 million. Almost 11 million people were murdered in Nazi death camps. Across the globe, World War II killed at least 55 million people.

War required Allied nations with different goals to cooperate. Tensions remained high, as the United States and Britain resisted Stalin's demands for a second front to draw Germans away from the Soviet Union. The United States, meanwhile, was fighting the Japanese in the Pacific. When Japan surrendered in August 1945, the

Nuclear Proliferation

Virtually from the moment of the Hiroshima and Nagasaki atomic bombings, U.S. strategists grappled with the problem of others joining the nuclear club, particularly the Soviet Union. On September 23, 1949, President Truman informed shocked Americans that the Soviets had successfully tested an atomic device.

In the years thereafter, membership in the nuclear club grew, through a combination of national investments, espionage, and a black market selling raw materials and western technologies. There were successful detonations by Great Britain (1952), France (1960), China (1964), India (1974), and Pakistan (1998). Israel crossed the nuclear weapon threshold on the eve of the 1967 Six-Day War but to this day has refused to confirm that it has the bomb. Recently, credible reports indicate that North Korea has a small nuclear arsenal and that Iran is working to get one. But in June 2008, after much pressure by an American-led initiative to halt its nuclear weapons program, North Korea destroyed the cooling tower of its main nuclear power plant, possibly signaling an initial step in that direction.

Still, the number of nuclear states is fewer than experts predicted in the 1960s, when analysts thought thirty nations might be so armed by the 1990s. The main reason it did not happen is that the five existing nuclear powers committed themselves in the mid-1960s to promoting nonproliferation. Subsequently, twenty-two of thirty-one states that started down the nuclear path changed course and renounced the bomb. By late 2006, the Treaty on the Non-Proliferation of Nuclear Weapons (NPT), enacted on July 1, 1968, had 187 signatories and was hailed as one of the great international agreements of the post-1945 era.

Skeptics took a different view, noting that three states outside the NPT (Israel, India, and Pakistan) became nuclear powers. They charged the original five with preventing others from obtaining nuclear arms while keeping large stockpiles themselves. With the world in 2007 awash in some twenty-seven thousand nuclear weapons (97 percent belonging to the United States and Russia), critics feared terrorist groups or other nonstate actors getting one or more bombs. In that nightmare scenario, they warned, the post-Nagasaki international moratorium on the use of nuclear weapons would be literally blown away.

strains between the Soviet Union and its English-speaking Allies made postwar stability unlikely.

U.S. servicemen covered the globe, while at home, Americans worked around the clock to make the weapons. Despite wartime sacrifices, many Americans found the war improved their lives. Mobilization ended the Great Depression. Americans moved to war-production centers. The influx of workers strained the resources of existing communities and sometimes led to social friction and violence. But many Americans—African Americans, Mexican Americans, women, and poor whites from the South—found new opportunities in well-paid war jobs.

The federal government became a stronger presence regulating business and employment, overseeing military conscription, and even controlling what people could buy to eat or wear. At war's end, only the United States had the economic resources to spur international recovery; only the United States was more prosperous than when war began. In the coming international struggle to fashion a new world— the Cold War—the United States held a commanding position. For better or worse, World War II was a turning point in the nation's history.

Chapter Review

THE UNITED STATES AT WAR

Was the United States prepared for war when it finally entered World War II?

No. Aside from its long history of caution and isolationism, the United States had also made military spending a low priority, particularly as the nation struggled to pull itself out of the Great Depression. In 1939, the U.S. Army ranked forty-fifth among world armies, and there was only enough equipment for one-third of its troops. The army grew to 2 million men after the establishment of a peacetime draft in 1941, but President Roosevelt's study about U.S. preparedness determined that the country would not be up to fighting before 1943—a luxury it would not have after the December 7, 1941 attack on Pearl Harbor pulled America officially into the war.

What was America's strategy in World War II?

While the battle against Japan was a U.S.-only situation, it was not America's military priority. America's war strategy was Europe First because U.S. leaders feared that if Germany conquered the Soviet Union, it could threaten the United States. The Russians might also agree to a separate peace treaty with Germany, thereby unraveling the Allied unity. Hence, the United States made defeating Germany its first priority; once that was achieved, it would focus on Japan.

THE PRODUCTION FRONT AND AMERICAN WORKERS

How did wartime production needs create a new relationship between government and business, and government and science?

Mobilizing for war required that factories shift from producing consumer goods to wartime necessities such as uniforms, arms, tanks, and so forth. The federal government enticed businesses to cooperate by offering generous tax write-offs and exemptions from antitrust laws. It also paid to retool or expand factories and guaranteed the bottom line by allowing corporations to charge production costs plus a fixed profit, enabling companies to double their profits by 1944. The government ensured that labor strikes would not disrupt production by having the newly-formed National War Labor Board settle disputes. The government spent millions on university research programs developing new war technologies, most importantly, the $2 billion secret Manhattan Project to build an atomic bomb.

LIFE ON THE HOME FRONT

How did Roosevelt sell the war to Americans?

While Americans did not experience the ravages of war on their own soil, they felt it through loss of, or injury to, loved ones and everyday sacrifices of products and conveniences that might benefit soldiers. Housewives returned cooking fat to butchers because it could be used to make black powder for shells or bullets.

Men's suits were redesigned with narrower lapels and shorter jackets to save wool for uniforms. Items such as sugar, coffee, and gasoline were rationed, with families given ration books with points for in-demand items. While citizens considered such sacrifices part of their patriotic duty, government leaders wanted to keep that goodwill from waning, and developed, via the Office of War Information, a series of films and posters that would do the job. Even ads for everyday items reminded consumers that they were fighting for their right to live freely and without fear. Movie audiences were treated to newsreels with censored combat footage that would inspire their ongoing wartime support, and audiences rose to sing the national anthem.

THE LIMITS OF AMERICAN IDEALS

What drove the decision to intern Japanese nationals and Japanese Americans within the United States during World War II?

Within months of Japan's attack on Pearl Harbor, fears about potential enemies on U.S. shores led President Roosevelt to order that all 112,000 foreign-born Japanese and Japanese Americans in California, Oregon, and Washington state (where most resided) be moved to "relocation centers." Racism was also a factor, as those who competed with Japanese-owned businesses supported internment. Internees were forced to quickly sell their property—valued at $500 million total—which often meant huge financial losses. They were then transported to internment camps in Arkansas, Wyoming, and Arizona, which were enclosed in barbed wire and housed entire families in a single room. Almost 6,000 internees renounced U.S. citizenship and asked to return to Japan. In 1988 Congress issued a public apology, with included a $20,000 payment to each of the surviving 60,000 Japanese American internees.

LIFE IN THE MILITARY

How did racial and gender norms play out in the military during World War II?

Nearly 12 million Americans served in World War II, including women and racial minorities. The discrimination that existed throughout American society was replicated in the armed services: African Americans and Japanese Americans served in units segregated from whites (although Hispanics, Native Americans, and Chinese Americans were part of "white" units). African Americans were given the dirtiest and most dangerous assignments, although they were kept from combat for most of the war. Less-educated, lower class white men did most of the fighting. Women were similarly kept from combat and their military organizations, such as the Women's Army Corps, were treated as auxiliaries. Their primary positions were as nurses, communications officers, typists, and cooks, a military extension of their traditional helpmeet roles.

WINNING THE WAR

Why did Truman opt to use the atomic bomb to help end the war, rather than negotiate a peace with Japan?

Historians continue to debate this question. Certainly, some argue that racism was a factor. From a military standpoint, Truman had insisted on an unconditional surrender of the Japanese. Although Japan indicated to the Soviet Union its interest in negotiating peace, it was not about to accept Truman's terms. Truman believed that using the atomic bomb would end the war fast and save U.S. soldiers' lives. Because extensive bombing of Japanese civilian areas had already occurred, Truman did not see the use of the bomb as the historic turning-point it would later seem to have been. The only difference in his mind—and many leaders' minds at the time—between conventional and atomic bombs was in their power and efficiency, not their manner of killing or the huge numbers who would likely perish.

SUGGESTIONS FOR FURTHER READING

Michael C. C. Adams, *The Best War Ever: America and World War II* (1993)

Roger Daniels, *Prisoners Without Trial: Japanese Americans in World War II* (1993)

Tsuyoshi Hasegawa, *Racing the Enemy: Stalin, Truman, and the Surrender of Japan* (2005)

David M. Kennedy, *Freedom from Fear: The American People in Depression and War, 1929–1945* (1999)

Warren F. Kimball, *Forged in War: Roosevelt, Churchill, and the Second World War* (1997)

Nelson Lichtenstein, *Labor's War at Home: The CIO in World War II* (1983)

Gerald F. Linderman, *The World Within War: America's Combat Experience in World War II* (1997)

Leisa Meyers, *Creating G.I. Jane: Sexuality and Power in the Women's Army Corps During World War II* (1996)

George Roeder Jr., *The Censored War: American Visual Experience During World War II*

Ronald Takaki, *Double Victory: A Multicultural History of America in World War II* (2000)

The Cold War and American Globalism

On July 16, 1945, the Deer Team leader parachuted into northern Vietnam, near Kimlung, a village in a valley of rice paddies. Colonel Allison Thomas and five members of his Office of Strategic Services (OSS) unit could not know that the end of the Second World War was weeks away. Their mission: to work with the Vietminh, a nationalist Vietnamese organization, to sabotage Japanese forces that seized Vietnam from France in March. A banner proclaimed, "Welcome to Our American Friends." Ho Chi Minh, head of the Vietminh, offered supper to the OSS team. The next day Ho denounced the French but remarked, "We welcome 10 million Americans." "Forget the Communist Bogy," Thomas radioed OSS headquarters in China.

A communist dedicated to winning his nation's independence from France, Ho joined the French Communist Party after World War I. For the next two decades, living in China, the Soviet Union, and elsewhere, he planned and fought to free his nation from French colonialism. During World War II, Ho's Vietminh warriors harassed French and Japanese forces and rescued downed American pilots. In March 1945 Ho met with U.S. officials in China. Receiving no aid from ideological allies in the Soviet Union, Ho hoped the United States would favor his nation's quest for liberation.

Other OSS personnel soon parachuted into Kimlung, including a male nurse who diagnosed Ho's ailments as malaria and dysentery. Quinine and sulfa drugs restored his health, but Ho remained frail. Everywhere the Americans went, impoverished villagers thanked them with gifts of food and clothing, interpreting the foreigners' presence as a sign of U.S. anticolonial and anti-Japanese sentiments. In early August the Deer Team offered Vietminh soldiers weapons training. Ho hoped young

This icon will direct you to interactive activities and study materials on A People And A Nation, Brief Edition website: **www.cengage.com/history/norton/ peoplenationbrief8e**

Chronology

1945	Roosevelt dies; Truman becomes president.
	United States drops atomic bombs on Japan.
1946	Kennan's long telegram criticizes Soviet Union.
	Vietnamese war against France erupts.
1947	Truman Doctrine seeks aid for Greece and Turkey.
	Marshall offers Europe economic assistance.
	National Security Act reorganizes government.
1948	Communists take power in Czechoslovakia.
	Truman recognizes Israel.
	United States organizes Berlin airlift.
1949	NATO is founded as anti-Soviet alliance.
	Soviet Union explodes atomic bomb.
	Mao's communists win power in China.
1950	NSC-68 recommends major military buildup.
	Korean War starts in June; China enters in fall.
1951	United States signs Mutual Security Treaty with Japan.

1953	Eisenhower becomes president.
	Stalin dies.
	United States helps restore shah to power in Iran.
	Korean War ends.
1954	Geneva accords partition Vietnam.
	CIA-led coup overthrows Arbenz in Guatemala.
1955	Soviets create Warsaw Pact.
1956	Soviets crush uprising in Hungary.
	Suez crisis sparks war in Middle East.
1957	Soviets fire first ICBM and launch *Sputnik*.
1958	U.S. troops land in Lebanon.
	Berlin crisis occurs.
1959	Castro ousts Batista in Cuba
1960	Eighteen African colonies become independent.
	Vietcong are organized in South Vietnam.

Vietnamese could study in the United States and that U.S. technicians could help build an independent Vietnam.

A second OSS unit, the Mercy Team, headed by Captain Archimedes Patti, arrived in Hanoi on August 22. But, unbeknownst to these OSS members, who believed that President Franklin D. Roosevelt's sympathy for eventual Vietnamese independence remained U.S. policy, the new Truman administration wanted France to decide Vietnam's fate. That policy change explains why Ho never received answers to the letters and telegrams he sent to Washington beginning August 30, 1945.

On September 2, 1945, with OSS personnel present, an emotional Ho Chi Minh read his declaration of independence for the Democratic Republic of Vietnam: "All men are created equal; they are endowed by their Creator with certain unalienable Rights; among these are Life, Liberty, and the pursuit of Happiness." Having borrowed from the internationally renowned 1776 American document, Ho itemized Vietnamese grievances against France.

In a last meeting with Captain Patti, Ho expressed sadness that the United States armed the French to reestablish their colonial rule in Vietnam. Sure, Ho said, U.S. officials in Washington judged him a Moscow puppet because he was a communist. But Ho claimed that he drew inspiration from the American struggle for independence. Ho insisted the Vietnamese would go it alone. And they did—first against the French and eventually against more than half a million U.S. troops in what became the United States's longest war.

Because Ho Chi Minh and his nationalist followers declared themselves communists, U.S. leaders rejected their appeal. Endorsing the containment doctrine against communism, U.S. presidents from Truman to George H. W. Bush believed that a ruthless Soviet Union directed a worldwide communist conspiracy against peace, free-market capitalism, and democracy. Soviet leaders from Joseph Stalin to Mikhail Gorbachev protested that a militarized, economically aggressive United States sought world domination. This protracted contest between the United States and the Soviet Union acquired the name Cold War.

The primary feature of world affairs for more than four decades, the Cold War was fundamentally a contest between the United States and the Soviet Union over spheres of influence. The contest between the capitalist West and the communist East dominated international relations and eventually took the lives of millions, cost trillions of dollars, spawned doomsday fears, and destabilized several nations. Occasionally, the two superpowers negotiated and signed agreements to temper their dangerous arms race; at other times they went to the brink of war and armed allies to fight vicious Third World conflicts. Sometimes these allies had their own ambitions and resisted pressure from one or both superpowers.

Vietnam was part of the *Third World*, a term for nations that in the Cold War era wore neither the West (the First World) nor the East (the Second World) label. Sometimes called developing countries, Third World nations were generally nonwhite, nonindustrialized, and located in the southern half of the globe—in Asia, Africa, the Middle East, and Latin America. Many had been colonies of European nations or Japan and were vulnerable to the Cold War rivalry. U.S. leaders often interpreted their anticolonialism as Soviet inspired rather than as expressions of indigenous nationalism. Vietnam became one among many sites where Cold War fears and Third World aspirations intersected, prompting U.S. intervention and a globalist foreign policy that regarded the world as the appropriate sphere for America's influence.

Critics in the United States challenged Cold War exaggerations of threats from abroad, meddlesome interventions in the Third World, and militarization of foreign policy. But when leaders like Truman described the Cold War as a life-and-death struggle against a monstrous enemy, critics were drowned out by charges that dissenters were soft on communism, if not un-American. U.S. leaders successfully cultivated a Cold War consensus that stifled debate and shaped the mindset of generations of Americans.

- Why did relations between the Soviet Union and the United States turn hostile soon after their victory in World War II?
- When and why did the Cold War expand from a struggle over the future of Europe and central Asia to one encompassing virtually the entire globe?
- By what means did the Truman and Eisenhower administrations seek to expand the United States's global influence in the late 1940s and the 1950s?

FROM ALLIES TO ADVERSARIES

World War II unsettled the international system. Germany was in ruins. Great Britain was overstrained, France was rent by internal division, and Italy was weakened. Japan was decimated and occupied, and China was headed toward renewed civil war. Throughout Europe and Asia, factories, transportation, and communications links were reduced to rubble, and agricultural production plummeted. The United States and the Soviet Union offered different solutions. The collapse of Germany and

Japan, moreover, created power vacuums that drew the two major powers into collision as they sought influence where Axis aggressors had once held sway. For example, in Greece and China, where civil wars raged between leftists and conservative regimes, the two powers supported opposite sides.

Decolonization

With empires disintegrating, a new Third World came into being. Financial constraints and nationalist rebellions forced the imperial states to set their colonies free. Britain exited India (and Pakistan) in 1947 and Burma and Sri Lanka (Ceylon) in 1948. The Philippines gained independence from the United States in 1946. After four years of battling nationalists in Indonesia, the Dutch left in 1949. In the Middle East, Lebanon (1943), Syria (1946), and Jordan (1946) gained independence, while in Palestine, British officials faced pressure from Zionists intent on creating a Jewish homeland and from Arab leaders opposed to it. In Iraq, nationalist agitation increased against the British-installed government. Washington and Moscow saw these emerging Third World states as potential allies that might provide military bases, resources, and markets. Some new nations chose nonalignment in the Cold War.

Stalin's Aims

The United States and Soviet Union assessed their most pressing tasks differently. The Soviets, though committed to victory over capitalist countries, were most concerned about preventing another invasion of their homeland. Its land mass was three times that of the United States, but it had only 10,000 miles of seacoast, which was under ice for much of the year. Russian leaders before and after the revolution made increased maritime access a chief foreign policy aim.

Worse, the Soviet Union's geographical frontiers were hard to defend. Siberia, vital for its mineral resources, lay 6,000 miles east of Moscow and was vulnerable to encroachment by Japan and China. In the west, the border with Poland generated violent clashes since World War I, and in World War II 21 million Russians died and there was massive physical destruction. Henceforth, Soviet leaders wanted no dangers along their western borders.

Overall, however, Soviet territorial objectives were limited. Although Americans were quick to compare Stalin to Hitler, Stalin's aims were more limited and resembled those of tsars before him: he wanted to push the Soviet Union's borders to include the Baltic states of Estonia, Latvia, and Lithuania, along with the eastern part of prewar Poland. To the south, Stalin wanted a presence in northern Iran, and he pressed the Turks for naval bases and free access out of the Black Sea. Economically, the Soviets did not promote rapid rebuilding of the region's war-ravaged economies or expanded world trade.

U.S. Economic and Strategic Needs

The United States, by contrast, came out of the war secure in its borders. Separated from other world powers by two oceans, the U.S. home base was virtually immune from attack during the fighting. American casualties were fewer than any of the other major combatants. With its fixed capital intact, its resources more plentiful than ever, and in lone possession of the atomic bomb, the United States was the strongest power in the world at war's end.

But Washington officials worried about complacency. Some other power—almost certainly the Soviet Union—could take advantage of instability in war-torn Europe and Asia and seize control of these areas, with dire implications for the United States's security. Therefore, Washington sought bases overseas to keep an airborne enemy at bay. To enhance U.S. security, U.S. planners sought the quick reconstruction of nations—including former enemies Germany and Japan—and a world economy based on free trade.

The Soviets refused to join the new World Bank and International Monetary Fund (IMF), created at the July 1944 Bretton Woods Conference by forty-four nations to stabilize trade and finance. They held that the United States dominated both institutions and used them to promote private investment and open international commerce, which Moscow saw as capitalist tools. With the United States as its largest donor, the World Bank opened in 1945 and made loans to finance members' reconstruction projects; the IMF, also heavily U.S.-backed, helped members meet their balance of payments through currency loans.

Stalin and Truman

Joseph Stalin, though hostile to the western powers and capable of ruthlessness against his people (his periodic purges since the 1930s took the lives of millions), did not want war. He was aware of his country's weakness vis-à-vis the United States and believed he must try to achieve his aspirations through cooperation. Stalin believed that Germany and Japan would eventually threaten the Soviet Union, and his suspicion of capitalist powers was boundless. Many concluded that Stalin was clinically paranoid. As historian David Reynolds has noted, this alleged paranoia, coupled with Stalin's xenophobia (fear of anything foreign) and his Marxist-Leninist ideology, created in him a mental map of them versus us that influenced his approach to world affairs.

To a lesser degree, Harry Truman was also prone to a them versus us worldview. He often glossed over nuances, ambiguities, and counterevidence, preferring an either/or answer. Truman exaggerated, as when he declared in his undelivered farewell address that he "knocked the socks off the communists" in Korea. When Truman protested in 1945 during a meeting at the White House that the Soviets were not fulfilling the Yalta agreement on Poland, the Soviet commissar of foreign affairs, V. M. Molotov, stormed out. Truman self-consciously developed what he called his tough method, which became a trademark of U.S. Cold War diplomacy.

The Beginning of the Cold War

No precise start date for the Cold War can be given. It resulted from an ongoing process that arguably began in 1917 with the Bolshevik Revolution and the western powers' hostile response, but in a more meaningful sense began in mid-1945, as World War II ended. By the spring of 1947, certainly, the struggle had begun.

One of the first Soviet-American clashes came in Poland in 1945, when the Soviets blocked the Polish government-in-exile in London from becoming part of the communist government that Moscow sponsored. The Soviets also extinguished civil liberties in Romania, arguing that the United States similarly manipulated Italy. Moscow initially allowed free elections in Hungary and Czechoslovakia, but as the Cold War accelerated and U.S. influence in Europe expanded, the Soviets encouraged communist coups in Hungary (1947) and Czechoslovakia (1948). Yugoslavia was unique: its independent communist government, led by Josip Broz Tito, broke with Stalin in 1948.

To defend their actions, Moscow officials noted that the United States was reviving their traditional enemy, Germany, and was meddling in eastern Europe. The Soviets cited clandestine American meetings with anti-Soviet groups, repeated calls for elections likely to produce anti-Soviet regimes, and the use of loans to gain political influence (financial diplomacy). Moscow charged that the United States was pursuing a double standard—intervening in eastern Europe but demanding that the Soviet Union stay out of Latin America and Asia. The United States called for free elections in the Soviet sphere, Moscow noted, but not in the U.S. sphere in Latin America.

Atomic Diplomacy

The Soviets believed that the United States was practicing atomic diplomacy, maintaining a nuclear monopoly to scare the Soviets into diplomatic concessions. Secretary of State James F. Byrnes thought that the atomic bomb could deter Soviet expansion, but Secretary of War Henry L. Stimson disagreed in 1945. If Americans continued to have "this weapon rather ostentatiously on our hip," he warned Truman, the Soviets' "suspicions and their distrust of our purposes and motives will increase."

In this atmosphere, Truman refused to turn over the weapon to an international authority. In 1946 he backed the Baruch Plan, named after its author, financier Bernard Baruch, which provided for U.S. abandonment of its atomic monopoly only after the world's fissionable materials were controlled by an international agency. The Soviets retorted that it would require them to shut down their atomic-bomb development project while the United States continued its own. Washington and Moscow soon became locked in a frightening nuclear arms race.

By mid-1946, the Soviets and Americans clashed on every front. When the United States refused the Soviets a reconstruction loan but gave one to Britain, Moscow upbraided Washington for using its dollars to manipulate foreign governments. The two Cold War powers also backed different groups in Iran, where the United States helped bring the pro-West shah to the throne. Unable to agree on the unification of Germany, the former allies built up their zones independently.

Warnings from Kennan and Churchill

After Stalin gave a speech in February 1946 depicting the world as threatened by capitalist acquisitiveness, the U.S. chargé d'affaires in Moscow, George F. Kennan, sent a pessimistic long telegram to Washington. His widely circulated report fed a growing belief among U.S. officials that only toughness would work with the Soviets. The following month, in Fulton, Missouri, former British prime minister Winston Churchill warned that a Soviet-erected iron curtain cut off eastern European countries from the West. With an approving Truman nearby, Churchill called for Anglo-American partnership to resist the new menace.

The growing Soviet-American tensions had major implications for the United Nations. The delegates who gathered in San Francisco in April 1945 to sign the U.N. charter agreed on an organization that included a General Assembly of all member states and a smaller Security Council spearheading peace and security issues. Five great powers were given permanent seats on the council—the United States, the Soviet Union, Great Britain, China, and France—and each could exercise a veto against any proposed action. To be effective, therefore, the U.N. needed great-power cooperation. Of the fifty-one founding states, twenty-two came from the Americas and another fifteen from Europe, which effectively gave the United States a majority in the assembly. In retaliation, Moscow exercised its veto in the Security Council.

Some high-level U.S. officials were dismayed by the administration's harsh anti-Soviet posture. Secretary of Commerce Henry A. Wallace charged that Truman's get-tough policy substituted atomic and economic coercion for diplomacy. Wallace told a Madison Square Garden audience in September 1946 that "getting tough never brought anything real and lasting—whether for schoolyard bullies, or businessmen or world powers." Truman fired Wallace, blasting him privately as "a real Commy."

On March 5, 1946, former British prime minister Winston S. Churchill (1874–1965) delivered a speech, which he intended for a worldwide audience, at Westminster College in Fulton, Missouri. President Harry S Truman (right) had encouraged Churchill (seated) to speak on two themes: the need to block Soviet expansion and the need to form an Anglo-American partnership. Always eloquent and provocative, Churchill denounced the Soviets for drawing an iron curtain across eastern Europe. This speech became one of the landmark statements of the Cold War. (Terry Savage / Harry S. Truman Presidential Library, Independence, Missouri)

Truman Doctrine

East-West tensions escalated further in early 1947, when the British requested American help defending their conservative client-government (a government dependent on the economic or military support of a more powerful country) in Greece in a civil war against leftists. The Republican Eightieth Congress wanted less spending, and many members had little respect for the Democratic president who voters repudiated in the 1946 elections by giving the GOP ("Grand Old Party," the Republican Party) majorities in both congressional houses. Republican senator Arthur Vandenberg of Michigan, a bipartisan leader, told the president that he would have to "scare hell out of the American people" to gain congressional approval.

Thus, the president delivered a speech laced with alarmist language staking out the United States's role in the postwar world. Truman claimed that communism imperiled the world. "If Greece should fall under the control of an armed minority," he concluded in an early version of the domino theory, "the effect upon its neighbor, Turkey, would be immediate and serious. Confusion and disorder might well spread throughout the entire Middle East." Truman articulated what became known as the Truman Doctrine: "It must be the policy of the United States to support free peoples who are resisting attempted subjugation by armed minorities or by outside pressures."

Critics correctly pointed out that the Soviet Union was little involved in the Greek civil war, that the communists in Greece were more pro-Tito than pro-Stalin, and that the resistance movement had noncommunist as well as communist members. Truman countered that, should communists gain control of Greece, they might open the door to Soviet power in the Mediterranean. The Senate approved Truman's request by 67 to 23 votes. Using U.S. dollars and military advisers, the Greek government defeated the insurgents in 1949, and Turkey became a U.S. ally on the Soviets' border.

Inevitable Cold War? In the months after Truman's speech, the term *Cold War* slipped into the lexicon as a description of the Soviet-American relationship. Within two years of the victory over the Axis powers, the two Grand Alliance members were locked in a struggle for world dominance that would last almost half a century. Even before World War II ended, observers anticipated that the United States and the Soviet Union would seek to fill the power vacuum. The two countries had a history of hostility and were militarily powerful. Most of all, they were divided by sharply differing political economies with divergent needs and by a deep ideological chasm.

It is far less clear that the conflict had to result in a Cold War. The "cold peace" that prevailed from the revolution in 1917 through World War II could conceivably have continued into the postwar years. Neither side's leadership wanted war. Both hoped—at least initially—that cooperation could be maintained. The Cold War resulted from decisions by individuals who might have done more to maintain diplomatic dialogue and negotiate solutions to international problems. For decades, Americans would wonder if the high price they were paying for victory in the superpower confrontation was necessary.

CONTAINMENT IN ACTION

To counter Soviet and communist expansion, the Truman team chose a policy of containment. George Kennan, now at the State Department in Washington, published an influential statement of the containment doctrine. Writing as Mr. X in the July 1947 issue of *Foreign Affairs* magazine, Kennan advocated a "policy of firm containment, designed to confront the Russians with unalterable counterforce at every point where they show signs of encroaching upon the interests of a peaceful and stable world." Such counterforce, Kennan argued, would check Soviet expansion. Kennan's X article joined the Truman Doctrine as a key manifesto of Cold War policy.

Lippmann's Critique The veteran journalist Walter Lippmann took issue with the containment doctrine in his powerful book *The Cold War* (1947), calling it a "strategic monstrosity" that failed to distinguish between areas vital and peripheral to U.S. security. Nor did Lippmann share Truman's conviction that the Soviet Union was plotting to take over the world. Ironically, Kennan agreed with much of Lippmann's critique and soon distanced himself from the doctrine he helped create.

Invoking the containment doctrine, the United States in 1947 and 1948 began to build an international economic and defensive network to protect U.S. prosperity and security and advance U.S. hegemony. In western Europe, the region of primary concern, American diplomats pursued economic reconstruction, the ouster of communists from governments, as occurred in 1947 in France and Italy, and blockage of third force, or neutralist, tendencies. U.S. officials kept the decolonization of European empires orderly. Meanwhile, American culture—consumer goods, music, consumption ethic, and production techniques—permeated European societies. Some Europeans resisted Americanization, but transatlantic ties strengthened.

Marshall Plan

Americans, who already spent billions on European relief and recovery by 1947, remembered all too well the troubles of the 1930s: global depression, political extremism, and war born of economic discontent. Such cataclysms could not be allowed to happen again; communism must not replace fascism.

Hence, in June 1947, Secretary of State George C. Marshall announced that the United States would finance a massive European recovery program. Launched in 1948, the Marshall Plan sent $12.4 billion to western Europe until 1951 (see Map 28.1). To stimulate business at home, the legislation required that Europeans spend this aid on U.S.-made products. The Marshall Plan proved a mixed success; it caused inflation, failed to solve a balance-of-payments problem, took only tentative steps toward economic integration, and further divided Europe between East and West. But the program spurred impressive western European industrial production and investment, started the region toward self-sustaining economic growth, and—from the U.S. perspective—contained communism.

National Security Act

Truman streamlined U.S. defense by working with Congress on the National Security Act of July 1947. The act created the Office of Secretary of Defense (which became the Department of Defense two years later) to oversee the armed services, the National Security Council (NSC) of high-level officials to advise the president, and the Central Intelligence Agency (CIA) to conduct spy operations and information gathering overseas. By the early 1950s the CIA expanded to include covert (secret) operations aimed at overthrowing unfriendly foreign leaders. The National Security Act gave the president increased powers regarding foreign policy.

In response, Stalin forbade communist satellite governments in eastern Europe to accept Marshall Plan aid and ordered communist parties in western Europe to work to thwart it. He also created the Cominform, an organization designed to coordinate communist activities around the world. Whereas U.S. planners saw the Marshall Plan as protecting their European friends against a potential Soviet threat, to Stalin it raised anew the specter of capitalist penetration. He tightened his grip on eastern Europe—most notably, engineering a coup in Czechoslovakia in February 1948 that ensured full Soviet control, which heightened anxiety in the United States.

Map 28.1 Divided Europe

After World War II, Europe broke into two competing camps. When the United States launched the Marshall Plan in 1948, the Soviet Union countered with its own economic plan the following year. When the United States created NATO in 1949, the Soviet Union answered with the Warsaw Pact in 1955. On the whole, these two camps held firm until the late 1980s.

*North Atlantic Treaty Organization
**Council for Mutual Economic Assistance

Berlin Blockade and Airlift

In June 1948, the Americans, French, and British agreed to fuse their German zones and integrate West Germany (the Federal Republic of Germany) into the western European economy. Fearing a resurgent Germany tied to the U.S. Cold War camp, the Soviets cut off western land access to the jointly occupied city of Berlin, located inside the Soviet zone. President Truman then ordered a massive airlift of food, fuel, and other supplies to Berlin. The Soviets finally lifted the blockade in May 1949 and founded the German Democratic Republic, or East Germany.

The successful airlift may have saved Truman's political career; he narrowly defeated Republican Thomas E. Dewey in the November 1948 presidential election. Truman next formalized the military alliance among the United States, Canada, and western Europe. In April 1949, twelve nations signed a mutual defense treaty, agreeing that an attack on any one of them would be considered an attack on all, and establishing the North Atlantic Treaty Organization (NATO; see Map 28.1).

Not since 1778 had the United States entered a formal European military alliance, and some critics, such as Senator Robert A. Taft, Republican of Ohio, claimed that NATO would provoke rather than deter war. Administration officials responded that should the Soviets ever probe westward, NATO would bring the full force of the United States to bear on the Soviet Union. Truman officials also hoped that NATO would keep western Europeans from embracing communism or even neutralism in the Cold War. The Senate ratified the treaty by 82 votes to 13, and the United States began to spend billions of dollars under the Mutual Defense Assistance Act.

By the summer 1949, Truman and his advisers were basking in the successes of their foreign policy. Containment was working, West Germany was on the road to recovery, the Berlin blockade had been defeated, and NATO had been formed. True, there was trouble in China, where the communists under Mao Zedong were winning a civil war. But that struggle would likely wax and wane for years to come. Just possibly, some dared to think, Harry Truman was on his way to winning the Cold War.

Twin Shocks

Then, suddenly, in late September, came the twin shocks, two momentous developments that made Americans feel in even greater danger than ever before. First, a U.S. reconnaissance aircraft detected unusually high radioactivity in the atmosphere: the Soviets had exploded an atomic device. With the U.S. nuclear monopoly erased, western Europe seemed more vulnerable. Second, the communists in China completed their conquest sooner than many expected. Now the world's largest and most populous countries were ruled by communists, and one of them had the atomic bomb.

Rejecting calls for high-level negotiations, Truman in early 1950 gave the go-ahead for production of a hydrogen bomb, the "Super." Kennan bemoaned the militarization of the Cold War and was replaced at the State Department by Paul Nitze. The National Security Council delivered to the president in April 1950 a significant top-secret document tagged NSC-68. Predicting continued tension with expansionistic communists, the report, authored primarily by Nitze, urged a much enlarged military budget and the mobilization of public support. The Cold War was about to become vastly more expensive and far-reaching.

THE COLD WAR IN ASIA

Asia gradually became ensnared in the Cold War. Indeed, the consequences of an expansive containment doctrine would exact its heaviest price on the United States, in large scale in Korea and Vietnam. Though less important to both superpowers than Europe, Asia was where the Cold War turned hot.

From the start, Japan was crucial to U.S. strategy. The United States monopolized Japan's reconstruction through a military occupation directed by General Douglas MacArthur. Truman disliked "Mr. Prima Donna, Brass Hat" MacArthur, but MacArthur wrote a democratic constitution, gave women voting rights, revitalized the economy, and destroyed the nation's weapons. U.S. authorities Americanized Japan by censoring films critical of the United States (for the destruction of Hiroshima, for example) or depicting Japanese customs, such as suicide, arranged marriages, and swordplay. In 1951 the United States and Japan signed a separate peace that restored Japan's sovereignty and ended the occupation. A Mutual Security Treaty that year provided for the stationing of U.S. forces in Japan, including a U.S. base on Okinawa.

Chinese Civil War

The administration had less success in China. The United States had long backed the Nationalists of Jiang Jieshi (Chiang Kai-shek) against Mao Zedong's communists. But after World War II, Generalissimo Jiang's government had become corrupt, inefficient, and out of touch with discontented peasants, whom the communists enlisted with promises of land reform. Jiang also subverted U.S. efforts to negotiate a cease-fire and a coalition government.

U.S. officials divided on the question of whether Mao was an Asian Tito—communist but independent—or, as most believed, part of an international communist movement that might give the Soviets a springboard into Asia. Thus, when the Chinese communists made secret overtures to the United States for diplomatic talks in 1945 and again in 1949, U.S. officials rebuffed them. Mao leaned to the Soviet side in the Cold War. Because of China's fierce independence, a Sino-Soviet schism opened.

With his victory in September 1949, Mao proclaimed the People's Republic of China (PRC). Truman hesitated to extend diplomatic recognition to the new government. U.S. officials became alarmed by the 1950 Sino-Soviet treaty of friendship and the harassment of Americans in China. Truman also chose nonrecognition because vocal Republican critics, the so-called China lobby, pinned Jiang's defeat on Truman. The president argued that despite billions of dollars in American aid, Jiang proved a poor instrument of containment. Not until 1979 did official Sino-American relations resume.

Vietnam's Quest for Independence

Mao's victory in China drew urgent U.S. attention to Indochina, the southeast Asian peninsula held by France for more than half a century. The Japanese wrested control over Indochina during World War II, but still the Vietnamese nationalist movement grew. Their leader, Ho Chi Minh, hoped to use Japan's defeat to assert Vietnamese independence and sought U.S. support. American officials rejected Ho's appeals in favor of restoring French rule, mostly to ensure France's cooperation in the emerging Soviet-American confrontation. Paris warned that U.S. support of the Vietnamese would strengthen the French Communist Party. In addition, the Truman administration feared that Ho Chi Minh was an agent of international communism who would assist Soviet and, after 1949, Chinese expansionism. Overlooking the native roots of the nationalist rebellion against French colonialism, Washington officials interpreted events in Indochina through a Cold War lens.

When war between the Vietminh and France broke out in 1946, the United States initially took a hands-off approach. But when Jiang's regime collapsed in China three years later, the Truman administration in February 1950 recognized the French puppet government of Bao Dai, a playboy and former emperor. To many Vietnamese, the United States thus became in essence a colonial power, an ally of the hated French. Second, in May, the administration agreed to send weapons and assistance to sustain the French in Indochina. From 1945 to 1954, the United States gave $2 billion of the $5 billion that France spent to keep Vietnam within its empire—to no avail (see Chapters 30 and 31). How Vietnam became the site of the United States's longest war is one of the most tragic stories of modern history.

THE KOREAN WAR

Early on June 25, 1950, a large military force of the Democratic People's Republic of Korea (North Korea) moved into the Republic of Korea (South Korea). Colonized by Japan since 1910, Korea was divided in two after Japan's defeat in 1945. Although the Soviets armed the North and the Americans armed the South (U.S. aid had reached $100 million a year), the Korean War began as a civil war. Since its division, the two parts had been skirmishing while antigovernment (and anti-U.S.) guerrilla fighting flared in the South.

Both the North's communist leader, Kim Il Sung, and the South's president, Syngman Rhee, sought to reunify their nation. Kim's military gained strength when tens of thousands returned home in 1949 after serving in Mao's army. President Truman claimed that the Soviets masterminded the North Korean attack.

Actually, Stalin reluctantly approved the attack after Kim predicted an early victory and after Mao backed Kim. When the U.N. Security Council voted to defend South Korea, the Soviet representative was not present to veto because the Soviets were boycotting the United Nations for its refusal to admit the People's Republic of China. During the war, Moscow gave limited aid to North Korea and China, reneging on promised Soviet airpower. Aware of his strategic inferiority vis-à-vis the United States, Stalin did not want war.

U.S. Forces Intervene The president first ordered General Douglas MacArthur to send arms and troops to South Korea. He did not seek congressional approval—fearing lawmakers would initiate a lengthy debate—and thereby set the precedent of waging war on executive authority alone. After the Security Council voted to assist South Korea, MacArthur became commander of U.N. forces in Korea. Sixteen nations contributed troops, but 40 percent were South Korean and about 50 percent American. In the war's early weeks,

North Korean tanks and superior firepower sent the South Korean army into retreat. The first U.S. soldiers, taking heavy casualties, could not stop the North Korean advance. Within weeks, the South Koreans and Americans were pushed into the tiny Pusan perimeter at South Korea's tip.

General MacArthur planned a daring amphibious landing at heavily fortified Inchon, several hundred miles behind North Korean lines. After U.S. bombs pounded Inchon, marines sprinted ashore on September 15, 1950, liberating the South Korean capital of Seoul and pushing the North Koreans back. Truman meanwhile redefined the U.S. war goal from the containment of North Korea to the reunification of Korea by force.

Chinese Entry into the War

In September, U.N. forces drove deep into North Korea, and U.S. aircraft began strikes against bridges on the Yalu River, the border between North Korea and China. Mao publicly warned that China could not permit the bombing of its transportation links with Korea and would not accept the annihilation of North Korea. MacArthur shrugged off the warnings, and Washington officials agreed, confident that the Soviets were not preparing for war.

MacArthur was right about the Soviets, but wrong about the Chinese. On October 25, the Chinese sent soldiers into the war near the Yalu River. Perhaps to lure U.S. forces into a trap or to signal willingness to negotiate, they pulled back after a successful offensive against South Korean troops. Then, on November 26, tens of thousands of Chinese troops surprised U.S. forces and drove them southward. One U.S. officer described "the men of a whole United States Army fleeing from a battlefield, abandoning their wounded, running for their lives."

Truman's Firing of MacArthur

By 1951 the front had stabilized around the 38th parallel. Both Washington and Moscow welcomed negotiations, but MacArthur called for an attack on China and Jiang's return. Denouncing the concept of limited war (war without nuclear weapons, confined to one place), MacArthur hinted that the president was practicing appeasement. In April, backed by the Joint Chiefs of Staff (the heads of the various armed services), Truman fired MacArthur, who nonetheless returned home a hero. Truman's popularity sagged, but he weathered scattered demands for his impeachment.

Armistice talks began in July 1951, but the fighting continued for two years. Defying the Geneva Prisoners of War Convention (1949), U.S. officials announced that only those North Korean and Chinese prisoners of war (POWs) who wished to go home would be returned. While Americans resisted forced repatriation, the North Koreans denounced forced retention. Both sides undertook reeducation, or brainwashing, on POWs.

Peace Agreement

As the POW issue stalled negotiations, U.S. officials made deliberately vague statements about using atomic weapons in Korea. Not until July 1953 was an armistice signed. Stalin's death in March and new leaders in Moscow and Washington facilitated a settlement. The combatants agreed to hand over the POW question to a special panel of neutral nations, which later gave prisoners their choice of staying or leaving. The North Korean–South Korean borderline was set near the 38th parallel, the prewar boundary, and a demilitarized zone was created between them.

U.S. casualties totaled 54,246 dead and 103,284 wounded. Nearly 5 million Asians died: 2 million North Korean civilians and 500,000 soldiers; 1 million South Korean civilians and 100,000 soldiers; and at least 1 million Chinese soldiers—ranking Korea as one of the costliest wars of the twentieth century.

Consequences of the War

The Korean War carried major domestic political consequences. The failure to achieve victory and the public's impatience undoubtedly helped to elect Republican Dwight Eisenhower to the presidency in 1952, as the former general promised to end the war. The powers of the presidency grew as Congress repeatedly deferred to Truman. The president never asked Congress for a declaration of war, believing that, as commander-in-chief, he had the authority to send troops wherever he wished. He saw no need to consult Congress, except to get the $69.5 billion Korean War bill paid. In addition, Republican lawmakers, including Wisconsin senator Joseph McCarthy, accused Truman and Secretary of State Dean Acheson of being soft on communism; this pushed the administration into an uncompromising position in the negotiations.

The Sino-American hostility generated by the war made U.S. reconciliation with the Beijing government impossible and made South Korea and Formosa major recipients of American foreign aid. The alliance with Japan strengthened as its economy boomed after filling large U.S. procurement orders. Australia and New Zealand joined the United States in a mutual defense agreement, the ANZUS Treaty (1951). The U.S. Army sent four divisions to Europe and initiated plans to rearm West Germany. The military budget jumped from $14 billion in 1949 to $44 billion in 1953; it remained between $35 billion and $44 billion a year throughout the 1950s. The Soviet Union matched this military buildup, resulting in an arms race. Truman's legacy was a highly militarized U.S. foreign policy on a global scale.

UNRELENTING COLD WAR

President Eisenhower and Secretary of State John Foster Dulles largely sustained Truman's Cold War policies. As a World War II general, Eisenhower negotiated with world leaders. After the war, he served as army chief of staff and NATO supreme commander. Dulles had been closely involved with U.S. diplomacy since the first decade of the century.

Eisenhower and Dulles

Eisenhower and Dulles accepted the Cold War consensus about the threat of communism and the need for global vigilance. Although Democrats promoted an image of Eisenhower as a bumbling, aging hero, deferring most foreign policy matters to Dulles, the president in fact commanded the policymaking process and occasionally tamed the more hawkish proposals of Dulles and Vice President Richard Nixon. Even so, the secretary of state was influential. Few Cold Warriors rivaled Dulles's impassioned anticommunism, often expressed in biblical terms. A graduate of Princeton and George Washington Universities, Dulles assisted Woodrow Wilson at Versailles and later became a senior partner in a prestigious Wall Street law firm and an officer of the Federal Council of Churches. Dulles impressed people as arrogant and unwilling to compromise, a successful diplomatic strategy for getting others to back down. His assertion that neutrality was an "immoral and short-sighted conception" did not sit well with Third World leaders, who resented being forced to choose between East and West.

Dulles conceded much to the anticommunist McCarthyites, who claimed that the State Department was infested with communists. The State Department's chief security officer targeted homosexuals and other "incompatibles," making few distinctions between New Dealers and communists. Dulles thus forced many talented officers out of the Foreign Service, among them, Asia specialists. "The wrong done," the journalist Theodore A. White wrote, "was to poke out the eyes and ears of the State Department on Asian affairs, to blind American foreign policy."

Massive Retaliation

Considering containment too defensive, Dulles called instead for liberation, freeing eastern Europe from Soviet control. *Massive retaliation* was the administration's plan for the nuclear obliteration of the Soviet state or its assumed client, the People's Republic of China, if either one took aggressive action.

Militarily, Eisenhower and Dulles emphasized airpower and nuclear weaponry. The president's preference for heavy weapons stemmed partly from his desire to trim the federal budget (and get more bang for the buck, as the saying went). Galvanized by the successful test of the world's first hydrogen bomb in November 1952, Eisenhower oversaw a massive stockpiling of nuclear weapons—from 1,200 at the start of his presidency to 22,229 at the end. With this huge military arsenal, the United States could practice *brinkmanship*: not backing down, even if it meant taking the nation to the brink of war. Eisenhower also popularized the *domino theory*: that small, weak, neighboring nations would fall to communism like a row of dominoes unless they were supported by the United States.

CIA as Foreign Policy Instrument

Eisenhower increasingly utilized the Central Intelligence Agency as an instrument of foreign policy. The CIA put foreign leaders (such as King Hussein of Jordan) on its payroll; subsidized foreign labor unions, newspapers, and political parties; planted false stories in newspapers through disinformation projects; and trained foreign military officers in counterrevolution. It hired American journalists and professors, used business executives as fronts, and conducted experiments on unsuspecting Americans to determine the effects of mind control drugs (the MKULTRA program). The CIA also launched covert operations (including assassination schemes) to subvert Third World governments, helping to overthrow the governments of Iran (1953) and Guatemala (1954).

The U.S. intelligence community followed the principle of plausible deniability: covert operations should be conducted in such a way and the decisions that launched them concealed so well that the president could deny any knowledge of them. Thus President Eisenhower disavowed any U.S. role in Guatemala, even though he ordered the operation. He and his successor, John F. Kennedy, also denied instructing the CIA to assassinate Cuba's Fidel Castro, whose regime after 1959 became stridently anti-American.

Nuclear Buildup

Leaders in Moscow quickly became aware of Eisenhower's covert actions, as well as his stockpiling of nuclear weapons. They increased their intelligence and tested their first H-bomb in 1953. Four years later, they fired the world's first intercontinental ballistic missile (ICBM) and propelled the satellite *Sputnik* into outer space. Americans felt more vulnerable to air attack, even though in 1957 the United States had 2,460 strategic weapons and a nuclear stockpile of 5,543, compared with the Soviet Union's 102 and 650. The administration deployed intermediate-range missiles in Europe, targeted against the Soviet Union. At the end of 1960 the United States added Polaris missile–bearing submarines to its navy. To foster future technological advancement, the National Aeronautics and Space Administration (NASA) was created in 1958.

Overall, Eisenhower sought to avoid military confrontations with the Soviet Union and China, content to follow Truman's containment of communism. Eisenhower refused to use nuclear weapons and proved more reluctant than other Cold War presidents to send soldiers into battle. Convinced that the struggle against Moscow would be largely decided by international public opinion, he wanted to win the hearts and minds of people overseas. The People-to-People campaign, launched in 1956, used ordinary Americans and nongovernmental organizations to enhance the international image of the United States.

Sometimes the propaganda war was waged on the Soviets' turf. In 1959 Vice President Richard Nixon traveled to Moscow for a U.S. products fair. In the display of a modern American kitchen, Nixon extolled capitalist consumerism, while Soviet premier Nikita Khrushchev, Stalin's successor, touted the merits of communism. The encounter became famous as the kitchen debate.

Rebellion in Hungary

In February 1956, Khrushchev called for peaceful coexistence between capitalists and communists, denounced Stalin, and suggested that Moscow would tolerate different brands of communism. Testing Khrushchev's permissiveness, revolts erupted in Poland and Hungary. After a new Hungarian government in 1956 withdrew from the Warsaw Pact (the Soviet military alliance formed in 1955 with communist countries of eastern Europe), Soviet troops and tanks crushed the rebellion.

Although the Eisenhower administration's propaganda encouraged liberation efforts, U.S. officials could not aid the rebels without igniting a world war. Instead, they promised only to welcome more Hungarian immigrants than American quota laws allowed. The West could have reaped some propaganda advantage had not British, French, and Israeli troops—U.S. allies—invaded Egypt during the Suez crisis just before the Soviets smashed the Hungarian uprising.

The People-to-People Campaign

Just after the Cold War began, U.S. officials determined that the Soviet-American confrontation was as much psychological and ideological as military and economic. One result was the People-to-People campaign, a state-private venture initiated by the United States Information Agency in 1956, which aimed to win the hearts and minds of people around the world. In this program, U.S. propaganda experts used ordinary Americans, businesses, civic organizations, labor groups, and women's clubs to promote confidence abroad in American goodness. The People-to-People campaign, one USIA pamphlet said, made "every man an ambassador."

Campaign activities resembled the home-front mobilization efforts of World War II. Americans were told that $30 could send a ninety-nine-volume portable library of American books to schools and libraries overseas. Publishers donated magazines and books for free distribution to foreign countries. People-to-People committees organized sister-city affiliations and pen-pal letter exchanges, hosted exchange students, and organized traveling People-to-People delegations. The travelers were urged to behave like goodwill ambassadors and "help overcome any feeling that America is a land that thinks money can buy everything."

Camp Fire Girls in more than three thousand communities took photographs on the theme "This is our home. This is how we live. These are my People." The photographs were sent to girls in Latin America, Africa, Asia, and the Middle East. The Hobbies Committee connected people with interests in radio, photography, coins, stamps, and horticulture.

The persistence to this day of the widespread impression that Americans are a provincial, materialistic people prompts skepticism about the People-to-People campaign's success. But alongside this negative image is a positive one that sees Americans as admirably open, friendly, optimistic, and pragmatic. Whatever role the People-to-People campaign played in the larger Cold War struggle, it certainly linked ordinary Americans more closely to people around the world.

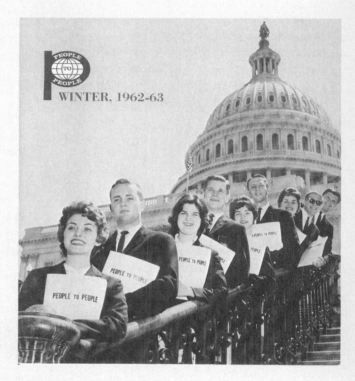

This Alice Nast painting of two girls—one from the United States and one from Taiwan—was commissioned by the Kansas City chapter of People to People and the Kansas City/Tainan Sister City Committee. The painting was presented to the mayor of Tainan in September 1994, prior to the 11th Worldwide Conference of the People-to-People International. (Courtesy of People to People International, Kansas City, Missouri, www.ptpi.org)

The turmoil barely subsided when the divided city of Berlin again became a Cold War flash point. The Soviets railed against U.S. bombers capable of carrying nuclear warheads in West Germany, and they complained that West Berlin had become an escape route for East Germans. In 1958 Khrushchev announced that the Soviet Union would recognize East German control of all of Berlin unless the United States and its allies began talks on German reunification and rearmament. The United States refused; Khrushchev backed down but promised to press the issue again.

U-2 Incident

Two weeks before a summit in Paris on May 1, 1960, a U-2 spy plane carrying high-powered cameras crashed 1,200 miles inside the Soviet Union. Moscow admitted shooting down the plane and promptly displayed captured CIA pilot Francis Gary Powers and the pictures he had snapped of Soviet military sites. Khrushchev demanded an apology for the U.S. violation of Soviet airspace. When Washington refused, the Soviets left the Paris summit.

Meanwhile, both sides kept a wary eye on the People's Republic of China. Despite evidence of a widening Sino-Soviet split, most U.S. officials treated communism as a monolithic movement. In 1954, in a dispute over Jinmen (Quemoy) and Mazu (Matsu), two tiny islands off the Chinese coast, the United States and the People's Republic of China lurched toward the brink. Taiwan's Jiang Jieshi used these islands to raid the mainland. Communist China bombarded the islands in 1954. Thinking that U.S. credibility was at stake, Eisenhower defended the outposts, hinting that he might use nuclear weapons. "Let's keep the Reds guessing," advised John Foster Dulles.

Formosa Resolution

In early 1955, Congress passed the Formosa Resolution, authorizing the president to deploy troops to defend Formosa and adjoining islands. In so doing, Congress formally surrendered to the president what it informally gave up in the 1950 Korea decision: the constitutional power to declare war. The crisis passed, but war loomed again in 1958 over Jinmen and Mazu. This time, as Jiang withdrew some troops, China relaxed its bombardments. But Eisenhower's nuclear threats persuaded the Chinese that they, too, needed nuclear arms. In 1964 China exploded its first nuclear bomb.

THE STRUGGLE FOR THE THIRD WORLD

In much of the Third World, the process of decolonization that began during World War I accelerated after World War II, when the economically wracked imperial countries proved incapable of resisting their colonies' demands for freedom. From 1943 to 1994, 125 countries became independent (including the former Soviet republics that departed the Soviet Union in 1991) (see Map 28.2). The emergence of so many new states after the 1940s shook the foundations of the international system. In the traditional U.S. sphere of influence, Latin America, nationalists once again challenged Washington's dominance.

Interests in the Third World

By the late 1940s, Soviet-American rivalry shifted increasingly to the Third World. The new nations could buy U.S. goods, supply strategic raw materials, and invite investments (more than one-third of the United States's private foreign investments were in Third World countries in 1959). Both great powers looked to these new states for votes in the United Nations and for military and intelligence bases. But many new nations sought to end the economic, military, and cultural hegemony of the West

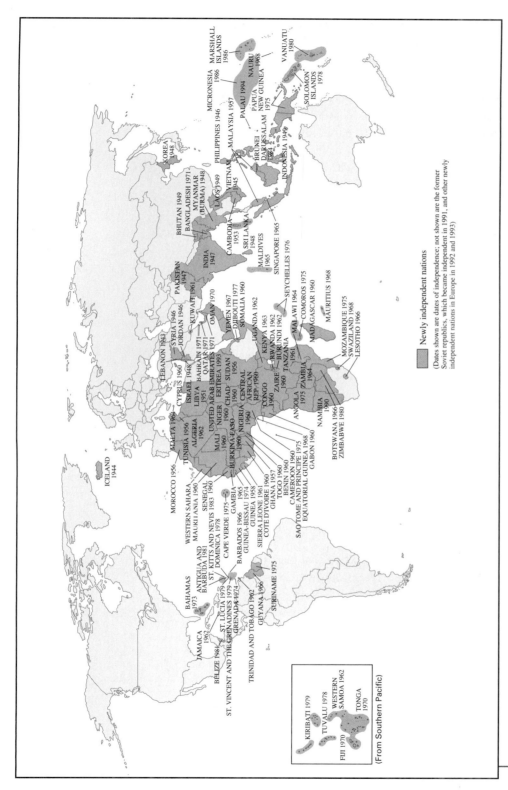

Map 28.2   The Rise of the Third World: Newly Independent Nations Since 1943

Accelerated by World War II, decolonization liberated many peoples from imperial rule. New nations emerged in the postwar international system dominated by the Cold War rivalry of the United States and the Soviet Union. Many newly independent states became targets of great-power intrigue but chose nonalignment in the Cold War.

and played the two superpowers against each other to garner more aid and arms. U.S. interventions—military and otherwise—in the Third World, American leaders believed, became necessary to impress Moscow with Washington's might and to counter other potential threats to U.S. interests.

To thwart nationalist, radical, and communist challenges, more than 90 percent of U.S. foreign aid was going to developing nations by 1961. Washington also allied with undemocratic but anticommunist regimes, meddled in civil wars, and unleashed CIA covert operations. When some of the larger Third World states—notably India, Ghana, Egypt, and Indonesia—refused to take sides in the Cold War, Secretary of State Dulles declared that neutralism was a step toward communism, insisting with Eisenhower that every nation should take sides.

American leaders argued that technologically "backward" Third World countries needed western-induced capitalist development to enjoy economic growth and political moderation. U.S. officials ascribed stereotyped race-, age-, and gender-based characteristics to Third World peoples, seeing them as emotional and irrational, and therefore dependent on the fatherly tutelage of the United States.

Racism and Segregation as U.S. Handicaps

Racism influenced U.S. relations with Third World countries. In 1955 G. L. Mehta, the Indian ambassador to the United States, was refused service in the whites-only section of a restaurant at Houston International Airport. The insult stung, as did similar indignities experienced by other Third World diplomats. Dulles apologized to Mehta and thought racial segregation in the United States was a "major international hazard," spoiling U.S. efforts to win friends in Third World countries and giving the Soviets a propaganda advantage.

Thus, as the U.S. attorney general noted race relations "furnished grist for the Communist propaganda mills." When the Court announced its *Brown* decision in 1954, the government quickly broadcast news of the desegregation order around the world in thirty-five languages on its *Voice of America* overseas radio network. But the problem did not go away. For example, after the 1957 Little Rock crisis, Dulles remarked that racial bigotry was "ruining our foreign policy." Still, when a Department of State office countered Soviet propaganda with a 1958 World's Fair exhibit in Brussels titled "The Unfinished Work"—on U.S. strides toward desegregation—southern conservatives kicked up such a furor that the Eisenhower administration closed the display.

U.S. hostility toward revolution also obstructed the quest for influence in the Third World. In the twentieth century, the United States opposed revolutions in Mexico, China, Russia, Cuba, Vietnam, Nicaragua, and Iran, among other nations. Many Third World revolutions arose against the United States's Cold War allies and threatened American investments, markets, and military bases. Preferring to maintain the status quo, the United States usually supported its European allies or the conservative, propertied classes in the Third World.

Development and Modernization

Yet idealism inspired U.S. policy. Believing that Third World peoples craved modernization and the U.S. economic model of private enterprise, U.S. policymakers launched various development projects. Such projects promised sustained economic growth, prosperity, and stability, which the benefactors hoped would undermine radicalism. In the 1950s, the Carnegie, Ford, and Rockefeller Foundations worked with the U.S. Agency for International Development (AID) to sponsor a Green Revolution promoting agricultural production. The Rockefeller Foundation supported foreign universities' efforts to train national leaders committed to nonradical development.

To persuade Third World peoples to abandon radical doctrines, U.S. leaders created propaganda campaigns. The United States Information Agency (USIA), founded in 1953, used films, radio broadcasts, the magazine *Free World*, exhibitions, and libraries (in 162 cities worldwide by 1961) to trumpet the theme of People's Capitalism. Citing the United States's economic success—contrasted with "slave-labor" conditions in the Soviet Union—it showcased well-paid U.S. workers, political democracy, and religious freedom. To counter ugly pictures of segregation, the USIA applauded success stories of individual African Americans, such as boxers Floyd Patterson and Sugar Ray Robinson. In 1960, some 13.8 million people visited U.S. pavilions abroad.

Undoubtedly the American way of life had appeal for some Third World peoples. Hollywood movies offered enticing glimpses of middle-class materialism, and American films dominated many overseas markets. Blue jeans, advertising billboards, and soft drinks flooded foreign societies. Foreigners envied and resented Americans for wasting so much while poorer peoples went without. The people of many countries, moreover, resented the profits that U.S. corporations extracted from them. Americans were often blamed for the persistent poverty of the developing world, even though the leaders of those nations made decisions hindering their own progress, such as pouring millions of dollars into their militaries while their people needed food. Nonetheless, anti-American resentments manifested in late 1950s' attacks on USIA libraries in Calcutta, India; Beirut, Lebanon; and Bogotá, Colombia.

Intervention in Guatemala

When the more benign techniques of containment—aid, trade, and cultural relations—proved insufficient to prompt Third World nations to side with the United States in the Cold War, the Eisenhower administration pressed harder. Guatemala was an early test case. In 1951 the leftist Jacobo Arbenz Guzmán was elected president of Guatemala, a poor country where the largest land-holder was the U.S.-owned United Fruit Company (UF). It owned 3 million acres across Latin America and operated railroads, ports, ships, and telecommunications facilities. Arbenz expropriated UF's uncultivated land and offered compensation. The company charged that Arbenz posed a communist threat. The CIA began a secret plot to overthrow Arbenz, who turned to Moscow for military aid, thus reinforcing U.S. suspicions. The CIA airlifted arms into Guatemala, and in mid-1954, CIA-supported Guatemalans struck from Honduras. U.S. planes bombed the capital city, driving Arbenz from power. The new pro-American regime returned UF's land, but an ensuing civil war staggered the nation for decades.

The Cuban Revolution and Fidel Castro

Eisenhower was apprehensive as turmoil gripped Cuba in the late 1950s. In early 1959, Fidel Castro's rebels, or *barbudos* ("bearded ones"), driven by anti-American nationalism, ousted Fulgencio Batista, a long-time U.S. ally whose corrupt, dictatorial regime turned Havana into a haven for gambling, prostitution, and organized crime. Cubans resented U.S. domination since the early twentieth century, when the Platt Amendment compromised their independence. Castro sought to break the U.S. grasp on Cuban trade and roll back American business, which had invested some $1 billion on the island.

In early 1960, after Cuba signed a trade treaty with the Soviet Union, Eisenhower ordered the CIA to organize Cuban exiles to overthrow the Castro government. The agency also plotted the Cuban leader's assassination. When the president drastically cut U.S. sugar purchases, Castro seized North American–owned companies that had not yet been nationalized. Castro appealed to the Soviet Union, which offered loans and expanded trade. Before leaving office in early 1961, Eisenhower broke diplomatic relations with Cuba and advised president-elect John F. Kennedy to advance plans for the invasion, which came—and failed—in early 1961.

Arab-Israeli Conflict

In the Middle East, meanwhile, ongoing tensions between Arabs and Jews posed additional challenges (see Map 33.2). Before the end of World War II, only France and Britain had been concerned with this region of the world. But the dissolution of empires and the rise of Cold War tensions drew Washington in, as did tensions in British-held Palestine. From 1945 to 1947, Britain tried to enlist U.S. officials to help resolve how to split Palestine between Arabs and Jews. The Truman administration declined, and the British in 1947 turned the issue over to the United Nations, which voted to partition Palestine into separate Arab and Jewish states. Arab leaders opposed the decision, but in May 1948 Jewish leaders announced the creation of Israel.

The United States, which lobbied to secure the U.N. vote, extended recognition to the new state mere minutes after its founding. A moral conviction that Jews deserved a homeland after the Holocaust and that Zionism would create a democratic Israel influenced Truman, as did the belief that Jewish votes might swing some states to the Democrats in the 1948 election. These beliefs trumped concerns that Arab oil producers might turn against the United States. The Soviet Union recognized the new nation, but Israel kept Moscow at arm's length. Palestinian Arabs, displaced from land they considered theirs, joined with Israel's Arab neighbors to make immediate war on the new state. The Israelis fought for six months until a U.N.-backed truce was called.

Thereafter, U.S. Middle East policy centered on ensuring Israel's survival and cementing ties with Arab oil producers. U.S. companies produced about half of the region's petroleum in the 1950s. Oil-rich Iran, became a special friend, as its shah granted U.S. oil companies a 40 percent interest in a new petroleum consortium in return for CIA help in the successful overthrow, in 1953, of his rival, Mohammed Mossadegh.

U.S. officials faced a more formidable foe in Egypt's Gamal Abdul Nasser, a towering figure in a pan-Arabic movement who vowed to expel the British from the Suez Canal and Israelis from Palestine. The United States wished neither to anger the Arabs, for fear of losing valuable oil supplies, nor to alienate its ally Israel, supported at home by politically active American Jews. When Nasser declared neutrality in the Cold War, Dulles lost patience.

Suez Crisis

In 1956 the United States reneged on its offer to help Egypt finance the Aswan Dam, which would provide inexpensive electricity and water for Nile valley farmland. Nasser responded by nationalizing the British-owned Suez Canal, intending to use its profits to build the dam. Fully 75 percent of western Europe's oil came from the Middle East, most of it via the Suez Canal. Fearing an interruption, the British and French conspired with Israel to bring down Nasser. On October 29, 1956, the Israelis invaded Suez, joined two days later by British and French forces.

Eisenhower fumed. The United States's allies had not consulted him, and the president feared the invasion would cause Nasser to seek help from the Soviets, inviting them into the Middle East. Eisenhower sternly demanded that London, Paris, and Tel Aviv pull their troops out, and they did. Egypt took possession of the canal, the Soviets built the Aswan Dam, and Nasser became a hero. The United States countered Nasser by supporting the notoriously corrupt conservative King Ibn Saud of Saudi Arabia, who renewed America's lease of an air base.

Eisenhower Doctrine

Washington officials worried that a power vacuum existed in the Middle East and that the Soviets might fill it. To protect U.S. interests, the president proclaimed in the 1957 Eisenhower Doctrine that the United States would intervene in the Middle East if any government threatened by a communist takeover asked for help. In 1958 fourteen thousand American troops scrambled to quell an internal political dispute in Lebanon that Washington feared might be exploited by pro-Nasser groups or communists.

Cold War concerns also drove Eisenhower's policy toward Vietnam. Despite substantial U.S. aid, the French lost steadily to the Vietminh. Finally, in early 1954, Ho's forces surrounded the French fortress at Dienbienphu in northwest Vietnam (see Map 30.2). The United States had advised and bankrolled the French, but had not committed troops to the war.

Eisenhower pressed the British to help form a coalition to address the Indochinese crisis, but they refused. At home, influential members of Congress—including Lyndon Baines Johnson of Texas, who as president would wage large-scale war in Vietnam—told Eisenhower they wanted no more Koreas and warned him against any U.S. military commitment. The issue became moot on May 7, when French defenders at Dienbienphu surrendered.

Geneva Accords on Vietnam

Peace talks, already under way in Geneva, brought Cold War and nationalist contenders together—the United States, the Soviet Union, Britain, the People's Republic of China, Laos, Cambodia, and the competing Vietnamese regimes of Bao Dai and Ho Chi Minh. The 1954 Geneva accords, signed by France and Ho's Democratic Republic of Vietnam, temporarily divided Vietnam at the 17th parallel; Ho's government was confined to the North, Bao Dai's to the South. The 17th parallel was meant as a truce line, not a national boundary; the country was scheduled to be reunified after national elections in 1956. Meanwhile, neither North nor South was to join a military alliance or permit foreign bases on its soil.

Confident that the Geneva agreements would mean communist victory, the United States tried to undermine them. Soon after the conference, a CIA team entered Vietnam and undertook secret operations against the North, including commando raids across the 17th parallel. In the South, the United States helped Ngo Dinh Diem push Bao Dai aside and inaugurate the Republic of Vietnam. Diem was a dedicated nationalist and anticommunist, but he had little mass support. When Ho and world leaders pressed for national elections, Diem and Eisenhower refused, fearing that the popular Vietminh leader would win. From 1955 to 1961, the Diem government received more than $1 billion in U.S. aid, most of it military. U.S. advisers trained Diem's army, and American agriculturalists improved crops. Diem's Saigon regime became dependent on the United States for its existence.

National Liberation Front

Diem proved a difficult ally. He abolished village elections and appointed people beholden to him. He threw dissenters in jail and shut down newspapers criticizing him. Noncommunists and communists alike struck back at Diem's repressive government. In Hanoi, Ho's government in the late 1950s sent aid to southern insurgents, who assassinated hundreds of Diem's village officials. In late 1960, southern communists, acting at Hanoi's direction, organized the National Liberation Front (NLF), known as the Vietcong. The Vietcong attracted other anti-Diem groups in the South. The Eisenhower administration, aware of Diem's shortcomings, affirmed its commitment to an independent, noncommunist South Vietnam.

Summary

The United States emerged from World War II as the preeminent world power. Washington officials nevertheless worried that the unstable international system, an unfriendly Soviet Union, and the decolonizing Third World could upset U.S. plans for the postwar peace. Locked with the Soviet Union in a Cold War, U.S. leaders marshaled their nation's superior resources to influence other countries. Foreign economic aid, atomic diplomacy, military alliances, client states, covert operations, propaganda, and cultural infiltration became the instruments of the Cold War, which began as a conflict over the Europe's future but soon encompassed the globe.

The United States's international leadership was welcomed by those who feared Stalin's intentions. The reconstruction of former enemies Japan and West Germany helped those nations recover swiftly and become staunch members of the western alliance. But U.S. policy also sparked resistance. Communist countries condemned financial and atomic diplomacy, while Third World nations sought to undermine the United States's European allies and sometimes identified the United States as an imperial coconspirator. Occasionally even the United States's allies bristled at a United States that boldly proclaimed itself economic master and global policeman.

At home, critics protested that Presidents Truman and Eisenhower exaggerated the communist threat, wasting U.S. assets on immoral foreign ventures. Still, these presidents and their successors held to creating a nonradical, capitalist, free-trade international order. Determined to contain Soviet expansion, fearful of domestic

The National Security State

For decades, the United States's Cold War religion has been national security; its texts, the Truman Doctrine, the X article, and NSC-68; and its cathedral, the national security state. The word *state* in this case means "civil government." During the Cold War, embracing preparedness for total war, the U.S. government essentially transformed itself into a huge military headquarters that interlocked with corporations and universities.

Overseen by the president and his National Security Council, the national security state's core, once called the National Military Establishment, in 1949 became the Department of Defense. This department is a leading employer; its payroll by 2007 included 1.4 million people on active duty and almost 600,000 civilian personnel. Almost 700,000 of these troops and civilians served overseas in 177 countries. Although national defense spending declined after the Cold War, it never fell below $290 billion. In the aftermath of the 9/11 terrorist attacks and the invasion of Iraq, the military budget rose again, reaching $439 billion in 2007. That does not include tens of billions of dollars in supplementary funds allocated by Congress to pay for operations in Afghanistan and Iraq.

Joining the Department of Defense as instruments of national security policy were the Joint Chiefs of Staff, the Central Intelligence Agency, and dozens more government bodies. The focus of these entities was finding the best means to combat real and potential threats from foreign governments. But what about threats from within? The terrorist attacks of September 2001 made starkly clear that enemies existed who, while perhaps beholden to a foreign entity, launched their attacks from inside the nation's borders.

In 2002 President George W. Bush created the Department of Homeland Security (DHS), with 170,000 employees encompassing all or part of twenty-two agencies, including the Coast Guard, the Customs Service, the Federal Emergency Management Administration (FEMA), and the Internal Revenue Service. It would involve the biggest overhaul of the federal bureaucracy since the creation of the Department of Defense, and it signified a more expansive notion of national security. By 2006, the number of DHS employees reached 190,000.

In 1961 President Eisenhower warned against a military-industrial complex, while others feared a warfare state. Still, the national security state remained vigorous in the early twenty-first century, a lasting legacy of the initial Cold War period for a people and a nation.

charges of being soft on communism, they enlarged the U.S. sphere of influence and held the line against the Soviet Union and the People's Republic of China and against revolution everywhere. One consequence was a dramatic increase in presidential power over foreign affairs—what the historian Arthur M. Schlesinger Jr. called "the Imperial Presidency."

The United States' globalist perspective prompted Americans to interpret troubles in the developing world as Cold War conflicts, inspired by Soviet-backed communists. The intensity of the Cold War obscured for Americans the indigenous roots of most Third World troubles, as the wars in Korea and Vietnam attested. Nor could the United States abide developing nations' drive for economic independence—for controlling their own raw materials and economies. Intertwined in the global economy as importer, exporter, and investor, the United States read challenges from this periphery as threats to the American standard of living. Overall, the rise of the Third World introduced new actors to the world stage, challenging the bipolarity of the international system. All the while, the threat of nuclear war unsettled Americans and foreigners alike.

Chapter Review

FROM ALLIES TO ADVERSARIES

Was the Cold War inevitable?

Historians aren't sure that it had to be. Aside from their alliance during World War II, the United States and Soviet Union had a tense relationship dating back to the 1917 Bolshevik Revolution. Since leaders of each country did not want war, their decades-old "cold peace" could have continued and inspired future cooperation. However, some believe that each nation's desire to fill the power vacuum left by the World War II defeat of Germany and Japan, along with their disparate goals and political ideologies, led individual leaders to make decisions that exacerbated tensions to the point of Cold War. While both nations clashed on most fronts by 1946, some argue that leaders could have done more to keep diplomatic negotiations open. Both countries backed different groups in Iran, could not agree on German reunification, and took many other opposing foreign policy positions. And the United States's nuclear monopoly only escalated strife first because the Soviets believed the United States used their nuclear superiority to bully them into concessions, and later when the Soviets had their own nuclear bomb, by advancing an arms race.

CONTAINMENT IN ACTION

Was the U.S. containment policy successful?

In 1947, Truman and his aides adopted what they called the containment policy, which meant forcefully confronting the Soviets every time they attempted to spread communism beyond their borders. The policy was successful in building an international network by aiding European reconstruction and having communists removed from governments, as in Italy and France. The policy also led the United States to a twelve-nation mutual defense treaty in 1949 and the establishment of NATO (the North Atlantic Treaty Organization). Truman hoped NATO would keep Europeans from turning communist and would deter Soviets from expansion. But containment failed when China, the world's most populous nation, became communist in 1949. Containment similarly could not keep the Soviet Union from becoming a nuclear power.

THE COLD WAR IN ASIA

How did the Cold War turn "hot" in Asia?

U.S. foreign policy focused on containing Soviet communism from spreading into Asia. That often led to decisions that alienated potential allies. The United States rejected an offer for diplomatic talks with China, and later refused diplomatic recognition to the People's Republic of China in 1949, fearing the nation was ultimately a likely Soviet ally. After the Sino-Soviet treaty of friendship in 1950, U.S. policy focused on keeping Indochina from falling to the communists. Rather than recognizing tensions in Vietnam as a rebellion against French colonial rule,

Truman and his aides blamed the Soviets for stirring up insurrection to expand communism. As such, the United States lent military aid, then arms, to the French, becoming increasingly engaged in what would develop into the Vietnam War, America's longest conflict.

THE KOREAN WAR

What were the consequences of the Korean War for the United States?

Along with heavy casualties (54,246 Americans died and 103,284 were wounded), the conflict greatly influenced politics in the United States. First, the powers of the U.S. president expanded, as Truman never sought congressional permission to declare war, believing that as commander-in-chief, he could dispatch troops at will. Consequently, he only turned to Congress for funding, and Congress also deferred to Truman rather than exercise its authority. As Republicans accused Truman of being soft on communism, he took an increasingly uncompromising position in negotiations for peace. He also engaged in a contest over military buildup with the Soviet Union. But public frustration over U.S. failure in the war led to Eisenhower's election in 1952. Finally, the war generated increased hostilities between the United States and China and strengthened the U.S. alliance with Japan.

UNRELENTING COLD WAR

How did Dulles and Eisenhower raise the stakes in the Cold War?

While President Eisenhower and Secretary of State Dulles continued the containment policy, they also added more aggressive tactics to their Cold War politics. Militarily, Eisenhower preferred increasing the nuclear arsenal, seeing it as a way to get more bang for the buck. Possessing the atomic bomb and the hydrogen bomb by 1952 enabled the United States to practice brinkmanship, not backing down against the spread of communism, even to the brink of war. Eisenhower also popularized the domino theory—that small, neighboring countries would fall to communism like dominoes without U.S. assistance. Despite his aggressive stand, however, Eisenhower was less likely to engage in war than other presidents. Instead, he increasingly utilized the Central Intelligence Agency, training foreign military officers in counterrevolutions, subverting Third World governments, and attempting to influence international opinion with disinformation and pro-U.S. campaigns. Brinkmanship and espionage prompted a similar Soviet response, as they tested their own H-bomb in 1953, fired the first intercontinental ballistic missile in 1957, and increased their intelligence operations—all of which made Americans feel increasingly vulnerable to attack.

THE STRUGGLE FOR THE THIRD WORLD

How did racism in America interfere with U.S. leaders' ability to win Cold War allies among developing nations?

Racism directly influenced U.S. relations with Third World countries, whose leaders were often people of color. With segregation and discrimination persisting in the United States, it was difficult for U.S. leaders to claim a moral advantage over communism and win friends in new and developing nations. Matters were made worse when there were incidents of discrimination against visiting leaders, as when Indian ambassador G. L Mehta was refused service in the whites-only section of a Houston restaurant. To counter this image, the U.S. government broadcast the positive news of the Supreme Court's desegregation ruling in the *Brown vs. Board of Education* in 1954, using its Voice of America overseas radio network to get the word out around the world in thirty-five languages.

SUGGESTIONS FOR FURTHER READING

Campbell Craig, *Destroying the Village: Eisenhower and Thermonuclear War* (1998)

Nick Cullather, *Secret History: The CIA's Classified Account of Its Operations in Guatemala, 1952–1954* (1999)

Mary L. Dudziak, *Cold War Civil Rights: Race and the Image of American Democracy* (2000)

John Lewis Gaddis, *Strategies of Containment*, 2d ed. (2005)

Walter LaFeber, *America, Russia, and the Cold War, 1945–2006*, 10th ed. (2006)

Douglas Little, *American Orientalism: The United States and the Middle East Since 1945* (2002)

Fredrik Logevall, *The Origins of the Vietnam War* (2001)

Robert J. McMahon, *The Limits of Empire: The United States and Southeast Asia Since World War II* (1999)

Geoffrey Roberts, *Stalin's Wars: From World War to Cold War, 1939–1953* (2007)

Marc Trachtenberg, *A Constructed Peace: The Making of the European Settlement, 1945–1963* (1999)

America at Midcentury

E venings after supper, when the sticky heat of Georgia summer days ebbed, families on Nancy Circle enjoyed a walk. Parents chatted as children played.

In 1959 the twenty houses on Nancy Circle were a couple of years old. Each stood on land that once belonged to the Cherokees, in a development carved from the old Campbell plantation, near where Confederate troops tried to stop General William Tecumseh Sherman's Union Army from attacking Atlanta. Slaves picked cotton there a century before, but no African Americans lived in those suburban homes.

Nancy Circle was part of a new suburban development in Smyrna, Georgia, northwest of Atlanta, but few of its residents worked in the city. Instead, most traveled to the massive Lockheed Georgia airplane plant created largely by Cold War defense spending. Born of the Cold War and the baby boom, this suburb's three-bedroom homes sold for about $17,000, making them affordable to young families.

Children played in each other's houses, and women gathered to drink coffee and gossip after men left for work. There were aerospace engineers, three career military men, an auto mechanic, and a musician. Only two women held paid jobs—one with almost-grown children taught second grade; the other was a divorced secretary. People were suspicious of her. Two war brides—one Japanese and one German—lived in the neighborhood. The Japanese woman spoke little English; the German woman taught the girls in the neighborhood to crochet.

The people who lived on Nancy Circle read magazines criticizing the homogeneity and conformity of suburban life, but it didn't feel that way to them. On this street, people from deep in Appalachia lived next to people who grew up in crowded city apartments, and women who'd done graduate work baked

This icon will direct you to interactive activities and study materials on A People And A Nation, Brief Edition website: **www.cengage.com/history/norton/ peoplenationbrief8e**

Chronology

1945	World War II ends.
1946	Marriage and birth rates skyrocket, creating baby boom.
	More than 1 million veterans enroll in colleges under GI Bill.
	More than 5 million U.S. workers go on strike.
1947	Taft-Hartley Act limits power of unions.
	Truman orders loyalty investigation of 3 million government employees.
	Mass-production techniques are used to build Levittown houses.
1948	Truman issues executive order desegregating armed forces and federal government.
	Truman is elected president.
1949	Soviet Union explodes atomic bomb.
	National Housing Act promises decent housing for all Americans.
1950	Korean War begins.
	McCarthy alleges communists in government.
	Treaty of Detroit creates model for new labor-management relations.
1951	Race riots occur in Cicero, Illinois, as white residents oppose residential integration.

1952	Eisenhower is elected president.
1953	Korean War ends.
	Congress adopts termination policy for Native American tribes.
	Rosenbergs are executed as spies.
1954	*Brown v. Board of Education* decision reverses separate-but-equal doctrine.
	Senate condemns McCarthy.
1955	Montgomery bus boycott begins.
1956	Highway Act launches interstate highway system.
	Eisenhower is reelected.
	Elvis Presley appears on *Ed Sullivan Show*.
1957	King is elected first president of Southern Christian Leadership Conference.
	School desegregation crisis occurs in Little Rock, Arkansas.
	Congress passes Civil Rights Act.
	Soviet Union launches *Sputnik*.
1958	Congress passes National Defense Education Act.
1959	Alaska and Hawai'i become forty-ninth and fiftieth states.

cookies with women who had not finished high school. These new suburbanites were creating a new middle-class culture. Having grown up with the Great Depression and world war, these new suburbanites believed they had found good lives.

The United States had emerged from World War II stronger and more prosperous. Europe and Asia had been devastated, but America's farms, cities, and factories were intact. U.S. production capacity increased during the war, and the fight against fascism gave Americans a unified purpose. But memories of sixteen years of depression and war would continue to shape the choices Americans made in their private lives, domestic policies, and relations with the world.

In the postwar era, the federal government's actions and individuals' choices profoundly reconfigured American society. Postwar social policies that sent millions of veterans to college on the GI Bill, linked the nation with high-speed interstate highways, fostered the growth of suburbs and the Sunbelt, and disrupted regional isolation helped to create a middle-class culture encompassing an unprecedented majority of citizens. Countless individual decisions—to go to college, marry young, have a large family, move to the suburbs, start a business—were made possible by federal initiatives.

Americans in the postwar era defined a new American Dream—one that centered on the family, material comfort and consumption, and a shared sense of belonging to a common culture. Nonetheless, almost one-quarter of Americans did not share in postwar prosperity, and they were nearly invisible to the middle-class majority. Rural poverty continued, and inner cities became increasingly impoverished as more-affluent Americans moved to the suburbs and new migrants—poor African American and white southerners, new immigrants from Mexico and Puerto Rico, and Native Americans resettled by the federal government from tribal lands—arrived.

As class and ethnicity became less important in suburbia, race continued to divide Americans. African Americans faced discrimination nationwide, but the war was a turning point in their struggle for equal rights. African American initiatives increasingly led to important federal actions, including the Supreme Court's school desegregation decision in *Brown v. Board of Education*. In 1955 the yearlong Montgomery bus boycott launched the modern civil rights movement.

The economic boom that began with the end of the war lasted twenty-five years, bringing new prosperity to America. Although fears—of nuclear war and of returning hard times—lingered, prosperity bred complacency by the late 1950s. The most significant domestic political ferment, in fact, was a byproduct of the Cold War: a ferocious anticommunism that narrowed the boundaries of acceptable dissent. At decade's end, people sought satisfaction in their families and the consumer pleasures newly available to so many.

- How did the Cold War affect American society and politics?
- How did federal government actions following World War II change the nation?
- During the 1950s, many people began to think of their country as a middle-class nation. Were they correct?

SHAPING POSTWAR AMERICA

At the end of World War II, many Americans feared the economy would plunge back into depression, and in the immediate aftermath of the war, unemployment rose and a wave of strikes rocked the nation. But dire predictions were wrong: the economy flourished, and Americans' standard of living improved. The GI Bill and other new federal programs created opportunities that fundamentally changed the nation.

Postwar Economic Uncertainty

As the end of the war approached, factories began to lay off workers. Ten days after the victory over Japan, 1.8 million people nationwide received pink slips, and 640,000 filed for unemployment compensation. More than 15 million GIs awaited demobilization, raising questions about jobs for them, too.

In spring 1944—a year before V-E Day—Congress, anticipating a postwar crisis, unanimously passed the Servicemen's Readjustment Act, known as the GI Bill of Rights. It showed the nation's gratitude to servicemen, but also attempted to keep demobilized veterans from swamping the U.S. economy: year-long unemployment benefits meant they could be gradually absorbed into civilian employment, and higher-education benefits would keep men in college and out of the job market.

In winter 1945, congressional Democrats introduced the Full Employment Act guaranteeing work through public-sector employment if necessary. By the time Truman signed the full Employment Act into law in early 1946, key provisions regarding guaranteed work virtually disappeared. But the act reaffirmed the federal government's responsibility for managing the economy and created a Council of Economic Advisers to help prevent downturns.

Postwar Strikes and the Taft-Hartley Act

Conversion to a peacetime economy hit workers hard, especially as inflation skyrocketed. More than 5 million workers walked off the job. Unions shut down the coal, automobile, steel, and electric industries and halted railroad and maritime transportation. The strikes were so disruptive that Americans began hoarding food and gasoline.

By spring 1946, Americans grew impatient with the strikes. When unions threatened a national railway strike, President Truman announced that if strikers in an industry deemed vital to national security refused a presidential order to return to work, he would ask Congress to draft them into the armed forces. The Democratic Party would not offer unlimited support to organized labor.

Then, in 1947 in an effort to restrict the power of labor unions, pro-business Republicans and conservative Democrats passed the Taft-Hartley Act. It permitted states to enact right-to-work laws outlawing closed shops, in which all workers were required to join the union if a majority favored a union shop. The law also mandated an eighty-day cooling-off period before unions initiated strikes imperiling national security. These restrictions limited unions' ability to expand their membership. Truman did not want to see union power so limited, but Congress passed the act over Truman's veto.

Economic Growth

Despite initial difficulties, the economy recovered quickly, fueled by consumer spending. Although Americans brought home steady paychecks during the war, there was little on which to spend them. No new cars, for example, had been built since 1942. Americans saved for four years, and when new cars and appliances appeared at war's end, they were ready to buy. Because most factories around the world were in ruins, U.S. corporations expanded their global dominance and increased in size. The United States's ten largest corporations were in automobiles (GM, Ford, and Chrysler), oil (Standard Oil of New Jersey, Mobil, and Texaco), and electronics and communications (GE, IBM, IT&T, and AT&T).

In the agricultural sector, new machines, such as mechanical cotton, tobacco, and grape pickers, and crop-dusting planes revolutionized farming, and the increased use of fertilizers and pesticides raised the total value of farm output from $24.6 billion in 1945 to $38.4 billion in 1961. Large investors were drawn to agriculture by its increased profitability, and the average farm size increased from 195 to 306 acres.

Economic growth was also fueled by government programs. By 1949, veterans received close to $4 billion in unemployment compensation. The GI Bill offered veterans low-interest loans to buy a house or start a business and stipends to cover college or technical school tuition and expenses.

*GI bill caused higher #
amount of people with
college/etc. education.*
*↳ more trained/educated
workers, boosting
economy*

Before the war, higher education was for the affluent; only about 7.5 percent of young Americans attended college. With GI benefits, almost half of America's returning veterans sought higher education. The resulting increase in the number of well-educated or technically trained workers benefited the U.S. economy. The flood of students and federal dollars into the nation's colleges and universities brought a golden age for higher education.

Education created social mobility: children of barely literate menial laborers became white-collar professionals. The GI Bill fostered the emergence of a national middle-class culture, for as colleges exposed students to new ideas and experiences, they became less rooted in ethnic or regional cultures.

Baby Boom

The end of the war brought a boom in marriage and birth rates. In 1946 the U.S. marriage rate was higher than that of any record-keeping nation (except Hungary). The soaring birth rate reversed the downward trend of the past 150 years. "Take the 3,548,000 babies born in 1950," wrote Sylvia F. Porter in her syndicated newspaper column, "bundle them into a batch, bounce them all over the bountiful land that is America. What do you get?" Porter's answer: "Boom. The biggest, boomiest boom ever known in history. Just imagine how much these extra people, these new markets, will absorb—in food, clothing, in gadgets, in housing, in services." Although the baby boom peaked in 1957, more than 4 million babies were born every year until 1965 (see Figure 29.1). As this vast cohort grew older, it had successive impacts on housing, schools, fads, popular music, the job market, and retirement funds, including Social Security.

*Massive amounts of
children affected
many aspects of
culture*

*Few new houses built
Many living with relatives*

Scarcely any new housing had been built since the 1920s. Almost 2 million families were doubled up with relatives in 1948; 50,000 lived in Quonset huts, and housing was so tight in Chicago that 250 used trolley cars were sold as homes.

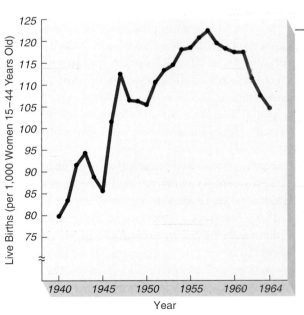

Figure 29.1   Birth Rate, 1945–1964

The birth rate began to rise in 1942 and 1943, but it skyrocketed during the postwar years beginning in 1946, reaching its peak in 1957. From 1954 to 1964, the United States recorded more than 4 million births every year.

(*Source:* Adapted from U.S. Bureau of the Census, *Historical Statistics of the United States, Colonial Times to 1970*, bicentennial ed. [Washington, DC: U.S. Government Printing Office, 1975], p. 49.)

TABLE 29.1   Geographic Distribution of the U.S. Population, 1930–1970 (in percentages)

Year	Central Cities	Suburbs	Rural Areas and Small Towns
1930	31.8	18.0	50.2
1940	31.6	19.5	48.9
1950	32.3	23.8	43.9
1960	32.6	30.7	36.7
1970	31.4	37.6	31.0

Source: Adapted from U.S. Bureau of the Census, *Decennial Censuses, 1930–1970* (Washington, DC: U.S. Government Printing Office).

Suburbanization

In the postwar years, white Americans moved to the suburbs. Some escaped crowded cities. People from rural areas moved closer to city jobs. Some white families left urban neighborhoods because African American families were moving in. Most, however, simply wanted to own their own home, and suburban developments were affordable. Although suburban development predated World War II, the massive migration of 18 million Americans to the suburbs between 1950 and 1960 was on a wholly different scale (see Table 29.1).

In 1947 the builder William Levitt adapted Henry Ford's assembly-line methods to revolutionize home building. By 1949, instead of 4 or 5 custom homes per year, Levitt's company built 180 houses a week. They were basic—four and a half rooms on a 60-by-100-foot lot, all with identical floor plans disguised by four different exteriors. By rotating seven paint colors, Levitt guaranteed that only 1 in 28 houses would be identical. The basic house sold for $7,990. Other homebuilders quickly adopted Levitt's techniques.

Suburban development happened on such a large scale because federal policies encouraged it. The Federal Housing Administration (FHA) offered low-interest GI mortgages and loans. Congress authorized construction of a 37,000-mile chain of highways in 1947 and in 1956 passed the Highway Act to create a 42,500-mile interstate highway system. Intended to facilitate commerce and rapid mobilization of the military, new highways allowed workers to live farther from their jobs in central cities, thereby fueling suburban construction.

Inequality in Benefits

Postwar federal programs did not benefit all Americans equally. First, federal policies often assisted men at the expense of women. As industry laid off civilian workers to make room for veterans, women lost their jobs at a rate 75 percent higher than men. Many women still worked but were pushed into lower-paying jobs. Universities made room for veterans on the GI Bill by excluding qualified women students.

Inequities were also based on race. Like European American veterans, African American, Native American, Mexican American, and Asian American veterans received educational benefits and hiring preference in civil service jobs. But war workers from these groups were among the first laid off. Federal loan officers and bankers often labeled African American or racially mixed neighborhoods high risk, denying mortgages to racial minorities regardless of individual creditworthiness. This practice, called redlining because such neighborhoods were outlined in red on lenders' maps, kept African Americans and many Hispanics from experiencing the postwar economic explosion. White families who bought homes with federally guaranteed mortgages saw their investments grow dramatically over the years.

DOMESTIC POLITICS IN THE COLD WAR ERA

The United States's social and economic transformations in the postwar era were largely due to federal policies, but politically, foreign affairs were paramount given the challenges of the expanding Cold War. Domestically, Truman attempted to build on the New Deal's liberal agenda, while Eisenhower sought balanced budgets and business-friendly policies. Neither administration approached the political and legislative activism of the 1930s New Deal.

Harry S Truman and Postwar Liberalism

Harry Truman, the plainspoken former haberdasher from Missouri, had never expected to be president. In 1944, when Franklin Roosevelt asked him to be his vice-presidential candidate, he almost refused. With the war in its fourth year, the president had little time for his new vice president and left Truman in the dark about everything from the Manhattan Project to plans for postwar domestic policy. When Roosevelt died suddenly in April 1945, Truman was unprepared to take his place.

Truman stepped forward, placing a sign on his desk that proclaimed, "The Buck Stops Here." Most of Truman's presidency focused on foreign relations, as he led the nation through the end of World War II and into the Cold War with the Soviet Union. Domestically, he oversaw reconversion from war to peace and attempted to keep a liberal agenda—the legacy of Roosevelt's New Deal—alive.

In his 1944 State of the Union address, President Roosevelt had offered Americans a Second Bill of Rights: the right to employment, healthcare, education, food, and housing. This declaration of government responsibility for citizens' welfare was the cornerstone of postwar liberalism. Truman's legislative program sought to maintain the federal government's active role: he supported an increase in the minimum wage and the Full Employment Act. To pay for social welfare programs, Truman gambled that full employment would generate sufficient tax revenue and that consumer spending would fuel economic growth.

The gamble paid off, but the conservative coalition of Republicans and southern Democrats that stalled Roosevelt's New Deal legislation in the late 1930s was even less inclined to support Truman. Congress gutted the Full Employment Act, refused to raise the minimum wage, and passed the anti-union Taft-Hartley Act. With powerful congressional opposition, Truman had few legislative accomplishments. But his inexperience contributed to the political impasse. "To err is Truman," people began to joke. As Truman presided over the rocky transition from wartime to peacetime economy, he faced massive inflation (briefly hitting 35 percent), shortages of consumer goods, and postwar strikes that slowed production and drove prices up. Truman's approval rating plunged from 87 percent in late 1945 to 32 percent in 1946.

1948 Election

By 1948 it seemed that Republicans would win the White House in November, and the party nominated Thomas Dewey, the man Roosevelt defeated in 1944, as its candidate. Republicans hoped schisms in the Democratic Party would ensure victory. The former New Dealer Henry A. Wallace ran for president on the Progressive Party ticket, advocating friendly relations with the Soviet Union, racial desegregation, and nationalization of basic industries. A fourth party, the Dixiecrats (States' Rights Democratic Party), was organized by white southerners who left the 1948 Democratic convention when it adopted a pro-civil rights plank. They nominated South Carolina's fiercely segregationist governor Strom Thurmond.

Truman refused to give up. He resorted to red-baiting, denouncing "Henry Wallace and his communists." Most important, he appealed to the burgeoning population of African American voters in northern cities, becoming the first presidential candidate to campaign in Harlem. In the end, Truman prevailed, with help from African American voters. Roosevelt's New Deal coalition—African Americans, union members, northern urban voters, and most southern whites—endured.

Truman's Fair Deal

In his 1949 State of the Union message, Truman stated, "I expect to give every segment of our population a fair deal." Unlike Roosevelt, Truman pushed legislation supporting the civil rights of African Americans, including antilynching laws. He proposed a national health insurance program and federal aid for education. Southern conservatives in Congress destroyed his civil rights legislation. The American Medical Association denounced his health insurance plan as socialized medicine, and the Roman Catholic Church opposed educational assistance because it would not include parochial schools.

When Truman ordered troops to Korea in June 1950, Americans grumbled as the nation again mobilized for war. People remembered the previous war's shortages and stocked up on sugar, coffee, and canned goods. Fueled by panic buying, inflation rose. An unpopular war and charges of influence peddling by Truman's cronies pushed the president's approval rating to an all-time low of 23 percent in 1951.

Eisenhower's Dynamic Conservatism

"It's Time for a Change" was the Republican presidential campaign slogan in 1952, and voters agreed. Americans hoped that the Republican candidate Dwight D. Eisenhower, the immensely popular World War II hero, could end the Korean War. And Eisenhower appealed to moderates in both parties (the Democrats tried to recruit him as their presidential candidate).

With a Republican in the White House for the first time in twenty years, conservatives hoped to roll back New Deal liberal programs such as Social Security.

A moderate, Eisenhower adopted what he called dynamic conservatism: being "conservative when it comes to money and liberal when it comes to human beings." In 1954 Eisenhower signed amendments to the Social Security Act that raised benefits and added 7.5 million workers, mostly self-employed farmers, to its rolls. Eisenhower's administration, motivated by Cold War fears, also increased government funding for education. When the Soviet Union launched *Sputnik,* the first earth-orbiting satellite, in 1957 (and the United States's first launch exploded seconds after liftoff), improving technology and education became an issue of national security. Congress responded in 1958 with the National Defense Education Act (NDEA), which funded enrichment of school programs in mathematics, foreign languages, and the sciences and offered fellowships and loans to college students.

Growth of the Military-Industrial Complex

Overall, Eisenhower was an ally of business and industry. The Eisenhower tax reform bill raised business depreciation allowances, and the 1954 Atomic Energy Act allowed private companies to own reactors and nuclear materials to produce electricity. Eisenhower balanced only three of his eight budgets, using deficit spending to cushion the impact of three recessions (1953–1954, 1957–1958, and 1960–1961) and fund America's global activities. In 1959 federal expenditures climbed to $92 billion, about half of which went to the military, mostly for developing new weapons.

Before leaving office in 1961 after his second term, Eisenhower delivered his farewell address. Because of the Cold War, he observed, the United States had a large standing army—3.5 million men—and devoted ever-greater percentages of its budget to developing weapons. Condemning the new "conjunction of an immense military establishment and a large arms industry," Eisenhower warned, "The total influence—economic, political, even spiritual—is felt in every city, every statehouse, every office of the federal government" and threatened the nation's democratic process. Eisenhower, the former five-star general, urged Americans to "guard against . . . the military-industrial complex."

COLD WAR FEARS AND ANTICOMMUNISM

International relations had a profound influence on America's domestic politics after World War II. Americans were frightened by Cold War tensions between the United States and the Soviet Union. Their legitimate fears inspired anticommunist demagoguery and witch hunts, allowing the trampling of civil liberties, the suppression of dissent, and the persecution of innocent Americans.

Anticommunism was not new: a Red Scare swept the United States following the 1917 Russian Revolution, and opponents of the United States's labor movement used charges of communism to block unionization through the 1930s. Many saw the Soviet Union's virtual takeover of eastern Europe in the late 1940s as an alarming parallel to Nazi Germany's takeover of neighboring states. People remembered the failure of appeasement at Munich and worried about being too soft toward the Soviet Union.

Espionage and Nuclear Fears

U.S. intelligence officers in a top-secret project, code-named "Venona," decrypted almost three thousand Soviet telegraphic cables that proved Soviet spies had infiltrated U.S. government agencies and nuclear programs. (The United States also had spies in the Soviet Union.) Intelligence officials withheld this evidence from the American public even as it prosecuted Soviet spies so that the Soviets would not realize their codes had been compromised.

Fear of nuclear war also contributed to American anticommunism. In 1949 when the Soviet Union joined the United States in possessing atomic weapons, President Truman initiated a national atomic civil defense program, advising Americans, "I cannot tell you when or where the attack will come or that it will come at all. I can only remind you that we must be ready when it does come." Children practiced duck-and-cover positions in school classrooms, learning how to shield their faces from the atomic flash. *Life* magazine featured backyard fallout shelters. Americans worried that the United States was newly vulnerable to attack.

Politics of Anticommunism

American leaders did not always draw a line between prudent attempts to prevent Soviet spies from infiltrating government agencies and anticommunist scare-mongering. Republican politicians red-baited Democratic opponents, eventually targeting the Truman administration. In 1947 President Truman ordered investigations into the loyalty of more than 3 million government employees. As anticommunist hysteria grew, the government discharged people deemed security risks, among them alcoholics, homosexuals, and debtors thought susceptible to blackmail. In most cases there was no evidence of disloyalty.

Leading the anticommunist crusade was the House Un-American Activities Committee (popularly known as HUAC). Created in 1938 to investigate "subversive and un-American propaganda," the committee lost credibility by charging that film stars—including eight-year-old Shirley Temple—were Communist Party dupes. In 1947, HUAC attacked Hollywood again, using Federal Bureau of Investigation (FBI) files and the testimony of people like Screen Actors Guild president Ronald Reagan (a secret FBI informant). Screenwriters and directors known as the Hollywood Ten were sent to prison when they refused to name names of suspected communists. At least a dozen others committed suicide. Studios blacklisted actors, screenwriters, directors, even makeup artists, suspected of communist affiliations. With no evidence of wrongdoing, people's lives and careers were ruined.

McCarthyism and the Growing Witch Hunt

University professors became targets of the growing witch hunt in 1949, when HUAC demanded lists of the textbooks used at eighty-one universities. When the board of regents at the University of California, Berkeley, instituted a loyalty oath and fired twenty-six faculty members resisting on principle, protests nationwide forced the regents to back down. But many professors began to downplay controversial material

[handwritten margin note: unions expelled from CIO]

in their courses. In the labor movement, the CIO expelled eleven unions, with more than 900,000 members, for alleged communist domination.

The red panic reached its nadir in February 1950, when Joseph R. McCarthy, a relatively obscure U.S. senator from Wisconsin, charged that the U.S. State Department was "thoroughly infested with Communists." Republican senator Joseph R. McCarthy of Wisconsin was not an especially credible source. He first claimed that there were 205 communists in the State Department, then 57, then 81. He had a severe drinking problem and a record of dishonesty as a lawyer and judge. But McCarthy crystallized Americans' anxieties, and anticommunist excesses came to be known as McCarthyism.

*[handwritten margin note: McCarthy
○ State department full of communists
– record of dishonesty
– americans believed
– McCarthyism → anti-communist to the excess]*

Anticommunism in Congress

In such a climate, most public figures found it risky to stand up against McCarthyist tactics. In 1950, with bipartisan support, Congress passed the Internal Security (McCarran) Act, which required members of Communist-front organizations to register with the government and prohibited them from holding government jobs or traveling abroad. In 1954 the Senate passed the Communist Control Act sponsored by Democratic senator Hubert H. Humphrey of Minnesota, which effectively made membership in the Communist Party illegal.

*[handwritten margin note: Internal Security Act (McCarran Act)
• communist front organizations to register w/ gov
• prohibited those people from having gov jobs + traveling abroad]*

*[handwritten margin note: Communist Control Act
○ membership of communist party illegal]*

In 1948 Congressman Richard Nixon of California, a member of HUAC, was propelled onto the national stage when he accused the former State Department official Alger Hiss of espionage. That same year, Ethel and Julius Rosenberg were arrested for passing atomic secrets to the Soviets; they were found guilty of treason and executed in 1953. For decades, many historians believed that the Rosenbergs were victims of a witch hunt, but there was evidence of Julius Rosenberg's guilt in cables decrypted by the Venona Project. This evidence was not presented at trial for national security reasons and remained top secret until 1995, when a Clinton administration initiative opened the files.

[handwritten margin note: Alger Hiss accused of espionage]

[handwritten margin note: Rosenbergs]

Waning of the Red Scare

The worst excesses of Cold War anticommunism waned when Senator McCarthy was discredited on national television in 1954. McCarthy was a master at using the press, making sensational accusations front-page material just before reporters' deadlines. When McCarthy's charges proved untrue, retractions appeared in the back pages of the newspapers.

[handwritten margin note: McCarthy discredited and condemned]

But McCarthy's crucial mistake was charging on television that the U.S. Army was shielding communists, citing the case of one army dentist. In the so-called Army-McCarthy hearings, held by a Senate subcommittee in 1954, McCarthy, apparently drunk, abused witnesses, ranted, and slurred his words. In December 1954, the Senate voted to condemn McCarthy for sullying the dignity of the Senate. He remained a senator, but exhaustion and alcohol took their toll and he died in 1957 at the age of forty-eight. With McCarthy discredited, the most virulent anticommunism had run its course. However, the use of fear tactics for political gain and the narrowing of American freedoms and liberties were chilling domestic legacies of the Cold War.

THE STRUGGLE FOR CIVIL RIGHTS

The Cold War also shaped African American struggles for social justice and the nation's responses to them. As the Soviet Union pointed out, the United States could hardly pose as the leader of the free world or condemn the denial of human rights in eastern Europe and the Soviet Union while practicing segregation. Nor could the United States convince new African and Asian nations of its dedication to human rights if African Americans were subjected to segregation, discrimination, disfranchisement, and racial violence. Many Americans viewed such criticism as a Soviet-inspired attempt to weaken the United States. The FBI and local law enforcement commonly used such anticommunist fears to justify attacking civil rights activists. In this heated environment, African Americans struggled to seize the political initiative.

Growing Black Political Power
African Americans who helped win World War II were determined to enjoy better lives in the postwar United States. Politicians like Harry Truman were heeding black aspirations, especially as black voters in some urban-industrial states began to influence the political balance of power.

President Truman had compelling political reasons for supporting African American civil rights. He genuinely believed that every American, regardless of race, should enjoy full citizenship. Truman was disturbed by a resurgence of racial terrorism, as a revived Ku Klux Klan burned crosses and murdered blacks seeking civil rights after World War II. But what really horrified Truman was the report that police in Aiken, South Carolina, gouged out the eyes of a black sergeant three hours after his army discharge. In December 1946, Truman signed an executive order establishing the President's Committee on Civil Rights. Its report, *To Secure These Rights,* would become the civil rights movement agenda for the next twenty years. It called for antilynching and antisegregation legislation and for laws guaranteeing voting rights and equal employment opportunity. For the first time since Reconstruction, a president acknowledged the government's responsibility to protect African Americans and strive for racial equality.

In 1948 Truman issued two executive orders ending racial discrimination in the federal government. One proclaimed a policy of "fair employment throughout the federal establishment" and created the Employment Board of the Civil Service Commission to hear discrimination charges. The other ordered the racial desegregation of the armed forces. Segregated units were being phased out by the Korean War.

Changing social attitudes and experiences in postwar America facilitated these changes. A new and visible African American middle class emerged, composed of college-educated activists, war veterans, and union workers. White awareness of social injustice was heightened by Gunnar Myrdal's social science study *An American Dilemma* (1944) and by Richard Wright's novel *Native Son* (1940) and autobiography *Black Boy* (1945). African Americans and whites worked together in CIO unions and service organizations, such as the National Council of Churches. In 1947 a black baseball player, Jackie Robinson, broke the major league color barrier and electrified Brooklyn Dodgers fans.

Supreme Court Victories and School Desegregation

African Americans were successfully challenging racial discrimination in the courts. In 1939 the NAACP had established its Legal Defense and Educational Fund under Thurgood Marshall. By the 1940s, Marshall (who in 1967 would become the first African American Supreme Court justice) and his colleagues worked to destroy the separate-but-equal doctrine established in *Plessy v. Ferguson* (1896). In higher education, the NAACP calculated, the cost of true equality in racially separate schools would be prohibitive. "You can't build a cyclotron for one student," the president of the University of Oklahoma acknowledged. Through NAACP lawsuits, African American students won admission to professional and graduate schools at several formerly segregated state universities. The NAACP also won victories through the Supreme Court in *Smith v. Allwright* (1944), which outlawed the whites-only primaries held by the Democratic Party in some southern states; *Morgan v. Virginia* (1946), which struck down segregation in interstate bus transportation; and *Shelley v. Kraemer* (1948), which held that racially restrictive covenants (private agreements among white homeowners not to sell to African Americans) could not legally be enforced.

Even so, African Americans continued to suffer disfranchisement, job discrimination, segregation, and violence. But in 1954 the NAACP won a historic Supreme Court victory, *Brown v. Board of Education of Topeka,* which Thurgood Marshall argued, incorporated school desegregation cases from several states. Written by Chief Justice Earl Warren, the court's unanimous decision concluded that "Separate educational facilities are inherently unequal." But the ruling that overturned *Plessy v. Ferguson* did not demand immediate compliance. A year later, the Court ordered school desegregation, but only "with all deliberate speed."

Montgomery Bus Boycott

By the mid-1950s, African Americans were increasingly engaged in a grassroots struggle for civil rights. In 1955 Rosa Parks, a department store seamstress and long-time NAACP activist, was arrested when she refused to give her seat to a white man on a public bus in Montgomery, Alabama. Her arrest enabled local black women's organizations and civil rights groups to organize a boycott of the city's bus system. They selected Martin Luther King Jr., a recently ordained minister, as their leader. King launched the boycott declaring, "If we are wrong, the Constitution is wrong. If we are wrong, God Almighty is wrong. . . . If we are wrong, justice is a lie."

Martin Luther King Jr. was a twenty-six-year-old Baptist minister with a recent Ph.D. from Boston University. Schooled in the teachings of India's leader Mohandas K. Gandhi, King believed in nonviolent civil disobedience as a vehicle to focus the nation's attention on the immorality of Jim Crow.

During the year-long Montgomery bus boycott, African Americans rallied in their churches. They maintained their boycott through heavy rains and the steamy summer heat, often walking miles a day. With the bus company near bankruptcy and downtown merchants suffering from declining sales, city officials adopted harassment tactics to end the boycott. But the African American people of Montgomery persevered: thirteen months later, the Supreme Court declared Alabama's bus segregation laws unconstitutional.

For leading the movement to gain equality for African Americans riding city buses in Montgomery, Alabama, Martin Luther King Jr. (1929–1968) and other African Americans, including twenty-three other ministers, were indicted by an all-white jury for violating an old law banning boycotts. In late March 1956, King was convicted and fined $500. A crowd of well-wishers cheered a smiling King (here with his wife, Coretta) outside the courthouse, where King proudly declared, "The protest goes on!" King's arrest and conviction made the bus boycott front-page news across the United States.   (© Bettmann/Corbis)

White Resistance

White reactions to civil rights gains varied. Some communities in border states like Kansas and Maryland quietly implemented the school desegregation order, and many southern moderates advocated a gradual rollback of segregation. But others urged defiance. The Klan experienced another resurgence, and white violence against African Americans increased. In 1955, Emmett Till, a fourteen-year-old from Chicago, was murdered by white men in Mississippi who took offense at the way he spoke to a white woman. Business and professional people created White Citizens' Councils (known familiarly as uptown Ku Klux Klans) to resist school desegregation and use economic power against civil rights activists. When FBI director J. Edgar Hoover briefed President Eisenhower on southern racial tensions in 1956, he warned of communist influences among civil rights activists and even suggested that, Citizens' Councils might "control the rising tension."

White resistance also mounted in large northern cities. Chicago's African American population increased from 275,000 in 1940 to 800,000 in 1960. These newcomers found good jobs and enjoyed political power, but faced racism and housing segregation. So racially divided was Chicago that the U.S. Commission on Civil Rights in

1959 described it as "the most residentially segregated city in the nation." Other northern cities were not far behind.

Federal Authority and States' Rights

Although President Eisenhower disapproved of racial segregation, he objected to "compulsory federal law," believing instead that race relations would improve "only if [desegregation] starts locally." He also feared that ugly public confrontations likely to follow rapid desegregation would jeopardize Republican inroads in the South. Thus Eisenhower did not state forthrightly that the federal government would enforce the *Brown* decision as the nation's law.

Events in Little Rock, Arkansas, forced the president to get involved. In September 1957, Arkansas governor Orval E. Faubus defied a court-supported desegregation plan for Little Rock's Central High School, saying on television that "blood would run in the streets" if black students tried to enter the high school. Eight black teenagers tried to enter Central High on the second day of school but were turned away by the Arkansas National Guard. The ninth was surrounded by jeering whites and narrowly escaped the mob with the help of a sympathetic white woman.

The Little Rock Nine entered Central High more than two weeks later after a federal judge intervened. Television broadcast the scene to the world. Eisenhower, fearing violence, nationalized the Arkansas National Guard (placing it under federal, not state, control) and dispatched one thousand army paratroopers to guard the students for the rest of the year. Eisenhower's use of federal power was a critical step toward racial equality, for he had directly confronted the conflict between federal authority and states' rights. However, state power triumphed the following year, when Faubus closed all public high schools in Little Rock rather than desegregate them.

In 1957 Congress passed the first Civil Rights Act since Reconstruction, creating the Commission on Civil Rights to investigate systemic discrimination, such as in voting. Although this measure was not fully effective, it lent further federal recognition to civil rights. Most important, however, was growing grassroots activism. In 1957 Martin Luther King Jr. became the first president of the Southern Christian Leadership Conference (SCLC), organized to coordinate civil rights activities. With the success in Montgomery and the gains through the Supreme Court, African Americans were poised to launch a national civil rights movement.

CREATING A MIDDLE-CLASS NATION

Despite resistance to civil rights during the 1950s, the United States was becoming increasingly inclusive. National prosperity offered greater numbers of Americans material comfort and economic security through entrance into an economic middle class. Old European ethnic identities faded, as an ever-smaller percentage of Americans were first- or second-generation immigrants.

In the new suburbs, people from different backgrounds created communities. Middle-class Americans increasingly looked to national media for advice on matters ranging from how to celebrate Thanksgiving to how to raise children. New opportunities for consumption—whether teenage fads or suburban ranch-style homes—also tied disparate Americans together. In the postwar years, a new middle-class way of life transformed the United States.

Prosperity for More Americans

During the 1950s, sustained economic growth created unprecedented prosperity and economic security. In great part the boom was driven by consumer spending. Americans eagerly bought goods unavailable during the war, and industries expanded production. As the Cold War deepened, government defense spending created jobs and further stimulated the economy.

Cold War military and aerospace spending fueled the need for highly educated scientists, engineers, and other white-collar professionals. Universities received billions of dollars to fund research, expanding the place of academia in the United States. Their research went beyond military applications and transformed society: the transistor, invented in the 1950s, was used in radios and sparked the computer revolution.

A new era of labor relations helped spread prosperity to more Americans. By 1950, the United Auto Workers (UAW) and General Motors led the way for other corporations in providing workers with health insurance, pension plans, and guaranteed cost-of-living adjustments (COLAs). The 1950 agreement gave GM's workers a five-year contract, with regular wage increases tied to corporate productivity. And with wage increases tied to corporate productivity, labor cast its lot with management: workplace stability and efficiency, not strikes, would bring higher wages. During the 1950s, wages and benefits propelled union families into the ranks of the economic middle class.

Sunbelt and Economic Growth

In the 1930s, Roosevelt called the South with its poverty "the nation's No. 1 economic problem." During World War II, new defense plants and military camps channeled federal money to the region, stimulating economic growth. In the postwar era, massive defense spending continued to shift economic development to the South and Southwest—the Sunbelt (see Map 29.1). Government actions—including generous tax breaks for oil companies, siting of military bases, and defense and aerospace contracts—were crucial to the region's new prosperity.

The Sunbelt's spectacular growth was fueled by agribusiness, the oil industry, real-estate development, and recreation. Sunbelt states aggressively and successfully sought foreign investment and drew industry with lower taxes and heating bills, along with right-to-work laws banning closed shops. The development of air conditioning was also crucial, making the hottest days bearable. Houston, Phoenix, Los Angeles, San Diego, Dallas, and Miami boomed, and by 1963 California was the most populous state in the United States.

A New Middle-Class Culture

By the 1950s, it seemed that the United States was becoming a middle-class nation. Unionized blue-collar workers gained middle-class incomes, and veterans with GI Bill college educations swelled the growing managerial and professional class. In 1956,

[handwritten margin notes:]
Economic growth/security

consumer goods available, people could afford it

Defense spending↑ jobs

Need for educated workers
Unis had gov.-funded research

corporations started to provide:
- health insurance
- pension plans
- cost-of-living adjustments
- some had wages tied to productivity

south had been an economic "problem"
Federal $ put into region
Sunbelt—south/southwest

Gov. Tax breaks for
- oil co. - military bases
- defense/aerospace contracts

drew industry

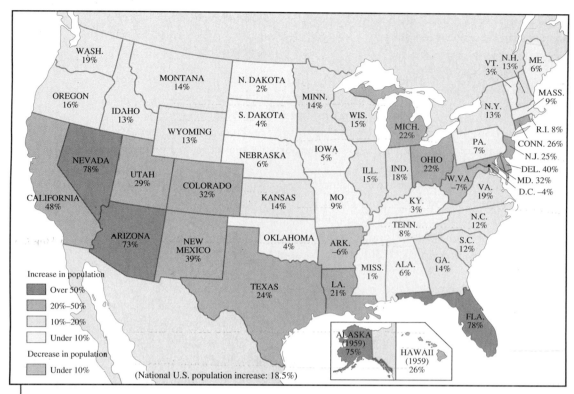

Map 29.1   Rise of the Sunbelt, 1950–1960

The years after World War II saw a continuation of the migration of Americans to the Sunbelt states of the Southwest and the West Coast.

for the first time, the United States had more white-collar than blue-collar workers, and 60 percent of families had incomes in the middle-class range (approximately $3,000 to $9,000 a year in the mid-1950s).

Paradoxically, the strength of unions in the postwar era contributed to a decline in working-class identity: as large numbers of blue-collar workers participated in suburban middle-class culture, the lines separating working class and middle class seemed less important. Increasingly, a family's standard of living mattered more than what sort of work made the standard possible. People of color did not share equally in the United States's postwar prosperity and were usually invisible in American representations of the good life. However, many middle-income African Americans, Latinos, and Asian Americans did participate in middle-class culture.

Whiteness and National Culture

The emergence of a national middle-class culture was possible in part because the United States's population was more homogeneous in the 1950s than before or since. In the nineteenth and early twentieth centuries, the United States restricted or prohibited immigration from Asia, Africa, and Latin America while accepting millions of Europeans. This large-scale European immigration was shut off in the 1920s, so by 1960 only 5.7 percent of Americans were foreign-born (compared with approximately 15 percent in 1910 and 12.4 percent in 2005). In 1950, 88 percent of Americans were of European ancestry (compared with 69 percent in 2000), 10 percent of the population was African American, 2 percent was Hispanic, and Native Americans and Asian Americans each accounted for about one-fifth of 1 percent. In 1959 the addition of two new states, Alaska and Hawai'i, brought more people of native, Asian, or Pacific origin into the U.S. population.

Although the new suburbs were peopled mostly by whites, these suburbs were more diverse than the communities from which their residents had come. The United States's small towns and urban ethnic enclaves were homogeneous and usually intolerant of challenges to tradition. In the suburbs, paradoxically, many people encountered different customs and beliefs. But new suburbanites often traded the provincial homogeneity of specific ethnic or regional cultures for a new sort of homogeneity: a national middle-class culture.

Television

Because many white Americans were new to the middle class, they were uncertain about what was expected of them. They found answers in the national mass media. Women's magazines helped housewives replace ethnic dishes with American recipes created from national brand name products, such as casseroles made with Campbell's cream of mushroom soup. Television also fostered a shared culture. Although television sets cost about $300—the equivalent of $2,000 today—almost half of American homes had TVs by 1953, and TV ownership rose to 90 percent by 1960, when more American households had a television set than a washing machine.

On television, suburban families like the Cleavers (*Leave It to Beaver*) ate dinner at a properly set dining room table. Every crisis was resolved through paternal wisdom. These popular family situation comedies reinforced the suburban middle-class ideal many American families sought.

The middle classness of television programming was due in part to advertising. Corporations buying airtime did not want to offend potential consumers. Thus, although the African American musician Nat King Cole drew millions of viewers to his NBC show, it never found a sponsor. National corporations feared that being linked to an African American performer would hurt sales among whites, especially in the South. Because African Americans made up only 10 percent of the population and many had little disposable income, they had little influence. The *Nat King Cole Show* was canceled within a year; it was a decade before the networks again anchored a show around an African American performer.

With only network television available—ABC, CBS, and NBC (and, until 1956, DuMont)—at any one time 70 percent or more of all viewers might be watching the same popular program. (In the early twenty-first century, the most popular shows might attract 12 percent of the audience.) Television gave Americans shared experiences and helped create a more homogeneous, white-focused, middle-class culture.

Consumer Culture

Americans also found common ground in a wealth of consumer goods. After decades of scarcity, Americans had a dazzling array of choices, and even utilitarian objects got two-tone paint jobs or rocket-ship details. People used purchases to express personal identities and to claim status. Cars more than anything embodied the consumer fantasies. Expensive Cadillacs were the first to develop tail fins, soon added to midrange Chevys, Fords, and Plymouths. Americans spent $65 billion on automobiles in 1955—a figure equivalent to almost 20 percent of the gross national product. To pay for cars, suburban houses and modern appliances, consumer debt rose from $5.7 billion in 1945 to $58 billion in 1961.

Religion

Church membership (primarily in mainline Christian churches) doubled between 1945 and the early 1960s. The media probably played a role, as preachers like Billy Graham created national congregations from television audiences with a message that combined the promise of salvation with Cold War patriotism. But local churches and synagogues offered new suburbanites a sense of community, celebrating life's rituals and supporting those far from their extended families.

MEN, WOMEN, AND YOUTH AT MIDCENTURY

Having survived the Great Depression and a world war, many Americans sought fulfillment in private life. They saw their familial commitment as an expression of faith in the future. Despite the satisfaction that many found in family life, both men and women felt limited by social pressures to conform to narrowly defined gender roles.

Marriage and Families

During the 1950s, few Americans remained single, and most people married young. By 1959, almost half of American brides were younger than nineteen; their husbands were usually only a year or so older. Early marriage was endorsed by experts and approved by most parents, partly to prevent premarital sex. As Americans accepted psychotherapeutic insights, they worried that premarital sex might leave the young woman pregnant or ruin her reputation, and also that it could damage her psychologically so she would never adjust to normal marital relations. One popular women's magazine argued, "When two people are ready for sexual intercourse at the fully human level they are ready for marriage. . . . And society has no right to stand in their way."

Many young couples found freedom from parental authority by marrying. Most newlyweds quickly had babies—an average of three—completing their families while still in their twenties. Birth control (condoms and diaphragms) was widely available and widely used, as couples planned family size. Two children were the American ideal in 1940; by 1960, most couples wanted four. About 88 percent of children under eighteen lived with two parents (in 2000, the figure was 69 percent), and fewer were born outside marriage; only 3.9 percent of births were to unmarried women in 1950 (compared with more than one-third of births in 2000). As late as 1960, there were only nine divorces per one thousand married couples.

Gender Roles in 1950s Families

In 1950s families, men and women usually took distinct roles, with male breadwinners and female homemakers. Contemporary commentators insisted this was based on essential differences between the sexes. In fact, the economic and social structure and the cultural values of the postwar United States determined the choices available to men and women.

During the 1950s, it was possible for many families to live in modest middle-class comfort on one (male) salary. There were strong incentives for women to stay home, especially while children were young. Good childcare was unavailable, and fewer families lived close to relatives. Childcare experts, including Dr. Spock, whose 1946 *Baby and Child Care* sold millions of copies, insisted that a mother's full-time attention was necessary for her children's well-being. Because of hiring discrimination, women who could afford to stay home often did not find the available jobs attractive enough to justify juggling cooking and housework, too. Instead, schools and religious institutions benefited immensely from women's volunteer labor.

Women and Work

Suburban domesticity left many women feeling isolated from the larger world their husbands inhabited. The popular belief that one should find complete emotional satisfaction in private life put unrealistic pressure on marriages. And despite near-universal celebration of women's domestic roles, many women were managing both job and family responsibilities (see Figure 29.2). Twice as many women were employed in 1960 as in 1940, including 39 percent of women with children between

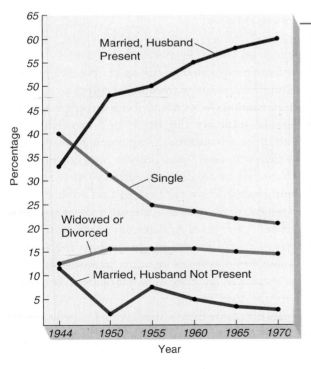

Figure 29.2   Marital Distribution of the Female Labor Force, 1944–1970

The composition of the female labor force changed dramatically from 1944 to 1970. In 1944, 41 percent of women in the labor force were single; in 1970, only 22 percent were single. During the same years, the percentage of the female labor force who had a husband in the home jumped from 34 to 59. The percentage who were widowed or divorced remained about the same from 1944 to 1970. (*Source:* Adapted from U.S. Bureau of the Census, *Historical Statistics of the United States, Colonial Times to 1970,* bicentennial ed. [Washington, DC: U.S. Government Printing Office, 1975], p. 133.)

age six and seventeen. Most worked part-time for a specific family goal like a new car. They saw their jobs as in service to the family, not a means to independence from it.

Women faced discrimination in the work force. Want ads were divided into Help Wanted—Male and Help Wanted—Female categories. Female full-time workers earned, on average, 60 percent of what men were paid and were restricted to lower-paid "female" fields: maids, secretaries, teachers, and nurses. A popular book, *Modern Woman: The Lost Sex,* claimed that ambitious women and feminists suffered from penis envy. College psychology textbooks warned women not to compete with men; magazine articles described career women as a third sex. Medical schools limited female admission to 5 percent of each class. In 1960 less than 4 percent of lawyers and judges were female. When the future Supreme Court justice Ruth Bader Ginsburg graduated at the top of her Columbia Law School class in 1959, she could not find a job.

"Crisis of Masculinity"

Academics and mass media critics devoted equal attention to the plight of the American male. American men faced a "crisis of masculinity," proclaimed the nation's mass-circulation magazines. In a bestselling book, the sociologist William H. Whyte explained that postwar corporate employees had become organization men, succeeding through cooperation and conformity, not initiative and risk. Experts claimed women's "natural" desire for security and comfort was stifling men's instinct for adventure. Men who did not conform to standards of male responsibility—husband, father, breadwinner—were forcefully condemned. Some linked concerns about masculinity to the Cold War, arguing that, unless the United States's men recovered masculinity diminished by white-collar work or a suburban, family-centered existence, the nation's future was at risk.

Sexuality

Sexuality was complicated terrain in the postwar United States. Only heterosexual intercourse within marriage was deemed acceptable. Women who became pregnant outside marriage were often ostracized by friends and family and expelled from school. Homosexuality was grounds for job dismissal, expulsion from college, even jail. In his major works on human sexuality, *Sexual Behavior in the Human Male* (1948) and *Sexual Behavior in the Human Female* (1953), Dr. Alfred Kinsey, director of the Institute for Sex Research at Indiana University, noted that while 80 percent of his female sample disapproved of premarital sex, half of them had had premarital sex. He also reported that 37 percent of American men had had "some homosexual experience." The *Chicago Tribune* called Kinsey a "menace to society." Although Kinsey's samples did not provide a completely accurate picture of American sexual behavior, they told many Americans that they were not alone in breaking certain rules.

Another challenge to the sexual rules came from Hugh Hefner, who launched *Playboy* magazine in 1953. Within three years, it had a circulation of 1 million. Hefner saw *Playboy* as an attack on the United States's "ferocious anti-sexuality" and his nude playmates as a means for men to combat the increasingly "blurred distinctions between the sexes" in suburban culture.

Youth Culture

The sheer numbers of baby boom youth made them a force in U.S. society. As this group moved from childhood to youth, a distinctive youth culture developed. Its customs and rituals were created within peer groups and were shaped by national media—teen magazines, movies, radio, advertising, and music. The United States's corporations quickly learned the power of youth, as children's fads launched multimillion-dollar industries. Mr. Potato Head—probably the first toy advertised on television—had $4 million in sales in 1952. In the mid-1950s, when Walt Disney's television show *Disneyland* featured Davy Crockett, "King of the Wild Frontier," every child in America (and more than a few adults) just *had* to have a coonskin cap. As baby-boom children grew up, their buying power shaped American popular culture.

By 1960, the United States's 18 million teenagers were spending $10 billion a year. Seventy-two percent of movie tickets in the 1950s were sold to teenagers, and Hollywood created a flood of teen films, ranging from forgettable B-movies to controversial films such as James Dean's *Rebel Without a Cause*. Adults worried that teens would copy the delinquency romanticized in *Rebel Without a Cause,* and teenage boys did emulate Dean's rebellious look. The film, however, blamed parents for teenage confusion, drawing heavily on popular psychological theories about sexuality and the "crisis of masculinity."

Nothing defined youth culture as much as music. Young Americans were electrified by the driving energy of Bill Haley and the Comets, Chuck Berry, Little Richard, and Buddy Holly. Elvis Presley's 1956 appearance on TV's *Ed Sullivan Show* touched off a frenzy of teen adulation and a flood of letters from parents scandalized by his "gyrations." Although few white musicians acknowledged it, the roots of rock 'n' roll lay in African American rhythm and blues. The raw energy and sometimes sexually suggestive lyrics of early rock music faded as the music industry sought white performers, like Pat Boone, to do blander, more acceptable "cover," or copycat, versions of music by African American artists.

The distinct youth culture of the 1950s made adults uneasy. Parents worried that going steady might encourage teens to "go too far" sexually. Juvenile delinquency was a major concern. Crime rates for young people rose dramatically after World War II, but much juvenile delinquency was status crimes—curfew violations, sexual experimentation, underage drinking—activities that were criminal only because of the person's age. Congress held hearings on juvenile delinquency, with experts testifying to the corrupting power of youth-oriented popular culture, comic books in particular. Most youthful behavior, however, fit squarely into the consumer culture that youth shared with their parents.

Challenges to Middle-Class Culture

The growth of middle-class culture inspired pockets of cultural dissent. *Beat* (a word that suggested both down and out and beatific) writers rejected middle-class social decorum and contemporary literary conventions. The Beat Generation

Handwritten margin notes:
Youth creating culture shaped by media fads

Rock derived from African-American music

Child crim rates rose (post WWII) -criminal because of age

Barbie

Barbie, the all-American doll, is—like many Americans—an immigrant. Although introduced in 1959 by the American toy company Mattel, Barbie's origins lie in Germany, where she was called Lilli.

The German Lilli doll was a novelty toy for adult men (as evidenced by her proportions, equivalent to 39-21-31 in human terms). She was based on a character that cartoonist Reinhard Beuthien drew for the German tabloid *Das Bild* in 1952. Lilli was so popular that she became a regular feature, later made three-dimensional as *Bild Lilli*, an eleven-and-a-half-inch-tall blonde doll with the figure Barbie would make famous.

Lilli came to the United States with Ruth Handler, one of the founders of the Mattel toy company. When she glimpsed Lilli while vacationing in Europe, Handler bought three and gave one to her daughter Barbara, after whom Lilli would be renamed. Mattel bought the rights to Lilli (the doll and the cartoon, which Mattel quietly retired) and unveiled Barbie in March 1959. Despite mothers' hesitations about a doll that looked like Barbie, within the year Mattel sold 351,000 Barbies at $3 each (or about $17 in 2000 dollars). The billionth Barbie was sold in 1997.

Within the United States, Barbie has been controversial. Some have worried that Barbie's wildly unrealistic figure fosters girls' dissatisfaction with their own body, potentially leading to eating disorders. Others claim that Barbie represents a model of empty-headed femininity. In 2002 international labor-rights groups called for a boycott of Barbie. They cited studies showing that half of all Barbies are made by exploited young women in mainland China: of the $10 retail, Chinese factories receive only 35 cents per doll to cover their costs, including labor. Saudi Arabia banned Barbie in 2003, arguing that her skimpy outfits and the values she represents are not suitable for a Muslim nation. Still, the eleven-and-a-half-inch doll remains popular worldwide, selling in more than 150 countries. For better or worse, Barbie continues to link the United States and the rest of the world.

Before Barbie became a U.S. child's toy, she was Lilli, a German sex symbol. Mattel transformed the doll into a wholesome American teenager with a new wardrobe to match. (Gareth Cattermole/Getty Images)

embraced spontaneity in their art, escape from the demands of everyday life, and enjoyed open sexuality and drug use. Perhaps the most significant beat work was Allen Ginsberg's angry poem "Howl" (1956), the subject of an obscenity trial whose verdict opened U.S. publishing to a broader range of works. The mainstream press ridiculed the beats, dubbing them *beatniks* (after *Sputnik*, suggesting their un-Americanness). Still, they laid the groundwork for the 1960s counterculture.

THE LIMITS OF THE MIDDLE-CLASS NATION

During the 1950s, the United States's popular culture and mass media celebrated new opportunities. But influential critics condemned middle-class culture as a wasteland of conformity, homogeneity, and ugly consumerism.

Critics of Conformity

These critics were not lone figures crying out in the wilderness. Americans, obsessed with self-criticism even as most participated wholeheartedly in the celebratory consensus culture of their age, rushed to books, such as J. D. Salinger's *The Catcher in the Rye* and Norman Mailer's *The Naked and the Dead*, which were profoundly critical of U.S. society. Americans even made bestsellers of difficult academic works, such as David Riesman's *The Lonely Crowd* (1950) and William H. Whyte's *The Organization Man* (1955), both of which criticized conformity in U.S. life. These critiques also appeared in mass-circulation magazines like *Reader's Digest*. Steeped in cultural criticism, many Americans understood *Invasion of the Body Snatchers*—a 1956 film in which zombielike aliens grown in pods gradually replace a town's inhabitants—as criticism of suburban conformity and postwar cultural homogeneity.

Many critics were attempting to understand large-scale and significant changes in U.S. society. Americans did lose some autonomy in work as large corporations replaced smaller businesses. They experienced the homogenizing force of mass production and a national consumer culture and saw distinctions among ethnic groups and socioeconomic classes fade. Critics, however, were often elitist and antidemocratic, seeing only bland conformity and sterility in the emerging middle-class suburban culture. But identical houses did not produce identical souls; instead, inexpensive suburban housing gave healthier—possibly happier—lives to millions raised in dank tenements or ramshackle farmhouses without indoor plumbing.

Environmental Degradation

The new consumer culture encouraged wasteful habits and harmed the environment. *Business Week* noted that corporations need not rely on planned obsolescence, purposely designing a product to wear out. Americans replaced products because they were out of date, not because they did not work. Hence, automakers

Handwritten margin notes:
Beats rejecting conformity

self-criticism present in popularity of critical books/movies

critics wanted to understand changes
large co. replaced small bus.
distinctions between class/ethnicity faded

products designed to wear out
people replaced because things were out of date

revamped designs annually. The United States's new consumer society used an ever-larger share of the world's resources. By the 1960s, the United States, with only 5 percent of the world's population, consumed more than one-third of its goods and services.

The rapid economic growth exacted environmental costs. Steel mills, coal-powered generators, and internal-combustion car engines burning lead-based gasoline polluted the atmosphere and imperiled people's health. As suburbanites commuted greater distances to work and neighborhoods were built without public transportation, Americans relied on private automobiles, consuming the nonrenewable resources of oil and gasoline and filling cities and suburbs with smog. Water was diverted from lakes and rivers to service burgeoning Sunbelt cities, including the swimming pools and golf courses that dotted parched Arizona and southern California.

Defense contractors and farmers were among the country's worst polluters. Refuse from nuclear weapons facilities at Hanford, Washington, and Colorado's Rocky Flats arsenal poisoned soil and water resources. Agriculture used pesticides and other chemicals. DDT, a chemical used on Pacific islands during the war to kill mosquitoes and lice, was used widely in the United States until after 1962, when wildlife biologist Rachel Carson indicted DDT for the deaths of mammals, birds, and fish in her bestselling book *Silent Spring*.

The nation was moving toward a postindustrial economy in which providing goods and services to consumers was more important than producing goods. Therefore, though union members prospered during the 1950s, membership grew slowly, because most new jobs were created in the union-resistant white-collar service trades. Technological advances increased productivity and also pushed people from well-paid blue-collar jobs into the growing and lower-paid service sector.

Continuing Racism

Racial discrimination stood unchallenged in most of the 1950s United States. Suburbs, both North and South, were almost always racially segregated. Many white Americans had little or no contact with people of different races, partly because the relatively small populations of nonwhite Americans were not equally dispersed nationwide. In 1960, 68 people of Chinese descent and 519 African Americans lived in Vermont; 181 Native Americans lived in West Virginia; and Mississippi had just 178 Japanese American residents. Most white Americans in the 1950s, especially those outside the South, gave little thought to race. Instead, they regarded the emerging middle-class culture not as white, but as American, marginalizing people of color in image as in reality.

In an age of abundance, more than one in five Americans still lived in poverty. One-fifth of the poor were people of color, including almost half of the nation's African Americans and more than half of all Native Americans. Two-thirds of the poor lived in households headed by a person with an eighth-grade education or less, one-fourth in households headed by a single woman. More than one-third were under age eighteen; one-fourth were over age sixty-five. Social Security payments helped, but many retirees were not yet covered, and medical costs drove many older Americans into poverty.

Medical costs problematt

Poverty in an Age of Abundance

As millions of Americans (most of them white) settled in suburbs, the poor concentrated in inner cities. African American migrants from the South were joined by poor whites from the southern Appalachians, moving to Chicago, Cincinnati, Baltimore, and Detroit. Latin Americans arrived in growing numbers from Mexico, the Dominican Republic, Colombia, Ecuador, and Cuba. According to the 1960 census, over a half-million Mexican Americans migrated to the Los Angeles–Long Beach area since 1940. And New York City's Puerto Rican population exploded from 70,000 in 1940 to 613,000 in 1960.

Because of the strong economy, many newcomers gained the higher standard of living they sought. But discrimination limited their advances, and they endured crowded and decrepit housing and poor schools. Federal programs that helped middle-class Americans sometimes made the poor's lives worse. For example, the National Housing Act of 1949, passed to make available "a decent home . . . for every American family," provided for urban redevelopment. Redevelopment meant slum clearance, replacing poor neighborhoods with luxury high-rise buildings, parking lots, or highways.

gained higher standard of living
discrimination limited them
Federal programs did not always help

The growth of large agribusinesses pushed more tenant farmers and owners of small farms off the land. From 1945 to 1961 the nation's farm population declined from 24.4 million to 14.8 million. When the harvesting of southern cotton was mechanized in the 1940s and 1950s, more than 4 million people were displaced. Southern tobacco growers dismissed tenant farmers, bought tractors, and hired migratory workers. In the West and Southwest, Mexican citizens served as cheap migrant labor under the *bracero* program. Almost 1 million Mexican workers came legally to the United States in 1959. Entire families labored, enduring conditions little better than in the Great Depression.

small farmers pushed off land
machines replaced farm labor
migrants provided cheap labor
bad conditions

Native Americans were America's poorest people, with an average annual income barely half that of the poverty level. Conditions were worsened by termination, a federal policy implemented during the Eisenhower administration. Termination reversed the Indian Reorganization Act of 1934, allowing Indians to terminate their tribal status and remove reservation lands from federal protection prohibiting their sale. Sixty-one tribes were terminated between 1954 and 1960. Termination could occur only with a tribe's agreement, but pressure was sometimes intense, especially when reservation land was rich in natural resources. Enticed by cash payments, almost four-fifths of the Klamaths of Oregon voted to sell their shares of forest land. Many Indians left reservation land for the city. By the time termination ceased in the 1960s, observers compared the situation of Native Americans to the devastation their forebears had endured in the nineteenth century.

Termination
• end tribal status
• removed land from protection (which prohibited sale)
• only w/ tribes agreement
– pressure to do this
– moved to cities

Many Americans enjoyed relative prosperity in the postwar era. But those who made it to the comfortable middle class often ignored the plight of those left behind. Their children—the baby-boom generation—would see racism, poverty, and the self-satisfaction of postwar suburban culture as a failure of American ideals.

The Pledge of Allegiance

The Pledge of Allegiance Americans recite today was shaped by the Cold War. Congress added the phrase "under God" to the pledge in 1954 to emphasize the difference between the god-fearing United States and the "godless communists" of the Soviet Union.

The Pledge of Allegiance was not always an important part of American life. The original version was written in 1892 by Francis Bellamy, editor of *The Youth's Companion*, to commemorate the four hundredth anniversary of Columbus's arrival in North America. In 1942 Congress officially adopted a revised version as an act of wartime patriotism. The Supreme Court ruled in 1943, however, that schoolchildren could not be forced to say the Pledge to the Flag.

During the Cold War years, the pledge became an increasingly important symbol of U.S. loyalty. Cold War fears fueled a campaign by the Knights of Columbus, a Catholic men's service organization, to include "under God" in the pledge. Supporting the bill, President Eisenhower proclaimed that

in this way we shall constantly strengthen those spiritual weapons which forever will be our country's most powerful resource in peace and war. From this day forward, the millions of our schoolchildren will daily proclaim in every city and town, every village and every rural schoolhouse, the dedication of our nation and our people to the Almighty.

Some Americans, citing the doctrine of separation of church and state, have protested including "under God." In June 2002, the Ninth District Court (covering California and eight western states) sparked a controversy by ruling that the 1954 pledge was unconstitutional because it conveyed "state endorsement" of a religious belief. Questions about the proper role of religion in the United States remain controversial, a legacy for a people and a nation becoming more diverse in the twenty-first century.

Summary

In the years following World War II, Americans married and had children in record numbers. Millions of veterans used the GI Bill to attend college, buy homes, and start businesses. Although U.S. leaders feared the nation would lapse back into economic depression after wartime government spending ended, consumer spending fueled growth. Sustained economic growth lifted a majority of Americans into an expanding middle class.

The Cold War presidencies of Truman and Eisenhower focused more on international relations than on domestic politics. Within the United States, Cold War fears provoked an extreme anticommunism that stifled political dissent and diminished Americans' civil liberties and freedoms.

The continuing African American struggle for civil rights drew national attention during the Montgomery bus boycott. African Americans won victories in the Supreme Court, including the landmark *Brown v. Board of Education* decision. Truman and Eisenhower used federal power to guarantee the rights of African Americans, as a national civil rights movement coalesced

Despite continued racial divisions, the United States became a more inclusive nation in the 1950s, as a majority of Americans participated in a national, consumer-oriented, middle-class culture. This culture largely ignored the poverty in the nation's cities and rural areas, but for the growing number in the middle-class, the American Dream seemed a reality.

Chapter Review

SHAPING POSTWAR AMERICA

What prompted the mass migration of Americans to the suburbs after World War II?

Two factors facilitated massive migration to the suburbs: first, demand for affordable, single-family homes, and second, federal policies. With the economic hardship of the Great Depression and World War II, few new homes were built, and many people moved in with relatives. But the prosperity of the postwar years joined with more economical housing developments to feed a growing demand for home ownership. At the same time, the Federal Housing Authority offered low-interest mortgages and loans, and Congress authorized the construction of major roadways and interstate highways in the late 1940s and 1950s. These roads enabled people to move further away from city jobs.

What happened to the U.S. economy after World War II?

Despite initial difficulties, the economy did not return to a depression, as many feared. Instead, it quickly recovered, driven by consumer spending. With the economic boom during the war, Americans had money to spend again, but rationing and war production meant few consumer goods to spend it on. At the end of the war, however, they were ready to buy. Manufacturing boomed as factories shifted production from war products to consumer goods. Government programs also encouraged growth. The GI Bill offered veterans low-interest loans to buy homes or launch businesses, as well as funds for education. The resulting increase in the number of well-educated or technically trained workers benefited the American economy.

DOMESTIC POLITICS IN THE COLD WAR ERA

What happened to New Deal style liberalism after World War II?

President Harry S. Truman embraced the same government responsibility for citizens' welfare that drove FDR's New Deal programs, but with limited success. He sought an increase in the minimum wage, national housing legislation offering mortgage loans, national health insurance, and federal aid for education. He additionally supported the Full Employment Act and civil rights legislation for African Americans. But conservative Republicans and southern Democrats in Congress gutted the Full Employment Act and refused to raise the minimum wage, while southern conservatives destroyed his civil rights legislation. His medical insurance and educational funding also met with resistance. A moderate Republican, Eisenhower signed amendments to the Social Security Act that increased benefits and made 7.5 million workers eligible for the program. He also increased government funding for education. Still, neither Truman nor Eisenhower came close to the liberalism of the New Deal.

COLD WAR FEARS AND ANTICOMMUNISM

How did Cold War fears inspire a Red Scare in the United States?

After World War II, Cold War tensions between the United States and the Soviet Union frightened Americans about the prospect of a communist invasion. People also prepared for nuclear attack once the Soviet Union had its own atomic weapons in 1949 by building backyard bomb shelters and teaching school children to shield their faces with duck-and-cover positions. As the hysteria grew, it fed anticommunist demagoguery and witch hunts, the trampling of civil liberties, the suppression of dissent, and the persecution of innocent Americans. The House Un-American Activities Committee (HUAC) was formed to investigate so-called subversive and un-American propaganda—even going so far as to charge that film stars (including eight-year-old Shirley Temple) were Communist Party dupes and to send ten screenwriters and directors to prison when they refused to name names of suspected communists. Studios blacklisted actors, screenwriters, directors, and makeup artists suspected of communist affiliations, and university professors were similarly targeted based on the books they used or their unwillingness to take a loyalty oath. In 1950, Senator Joseph R. McCarthy symbolized public fears when he charged that the U.S. State Department was "thoroughly infested with Communists." He was later discredited on national television.

THE STRUGGLE FOR CIVIL RIGHTS

How did changing social attitudes in the postwar era facilitate the burgeoning civil rights movement?

African Americans who helped win the World War II were determined to improve their status at home. Politicians such as President Harry S Truman agreed that they were entitled to full citizenship and equality. Truman's President's Committee on Civil Rights issued a report that would become the civil rights movement agenda for the next twenty years, calling for antilynching and antisegregation legislation, and for laws guaranteeing voting rights and equal employment opportunity. Truman also ordered desegregation of the military, which was completed by the Korean War. Cold War politics also aided the African American cause: the United States could not condemn other countries for denying human rights when it practiced segregation at home. At the same time, a new and visible black middle-class of college-educated activists, war veterans, and union workers emerged. Together this climate encouraged ongoing efforts to challenge racial discrimination through the courts and through grass roots activism.

CREATING A MIDDLE-CLASS NATION

What led to the emergence of a middle-class culture in the 1950s?

In the 1950s, the American population was more homogeneous than it had been before or would be later. Immigration restrictions in the 1920s meant that a small percent of Americans were foreign-born by the 1950s, and most Americans (88 percent) could trace their roots to Europe. The emergence of a national mass media—magazines, newspapers, film, and television—taught all Americans how to behave and live like the suburban middle-class—with American foods replacing ethnic dishes, national brands that replaced homemade products, and so on. Television shows even taught how to set the table or properly parent a child, thereby reinforcing middle-class ideals to those watching across class, racial, and ethnic lines.

MEN, WOMEN, AND YOUTH AT MIDCENTURY

| **How did the economic and social structure of the 1950s determine the choices and roles available to men and women?**

In the 1950s, middle-class families could survive on one income, typically the man's. That enabled experts and individuals to embrace the notion that it was better for women to stay at home, especially while children were young. Women's maternal roles were celebrated, and those who considered careers were considered abnormal. While many women did work, it was often part-time and for a specific goal, such as a new car. Hiring discrimination kept women out of high-paying jobs legally. Employment ads were sex segregated into Help Wanted Male and Help Wanted Female categories, and women earned only 60 percent of what men earned. The pressure to provide restricted the options available to men, too, with many choosing safer, corporate jobs that promoted conformity rather than risk.

THE LIMITS OF THE MIDDLE-CLASS NATION

| **What critiques emerged about middle-class America?**

Influential critics condemned middle-class culture as a wasteland of conformity, homogeneity, and crass consumerism. During the prosperity of the postwar era, an increasing number of Americans made it into the middle-class and answered the call to keep the economy thriving by partaking in an assortment of new consumer goods. Many corporations, however, built a limited lifespan into the goods they produced, designing them to wear out so they would need to be replaced, and hence continue to spark demand. Worse, critics noted as early as the 1960s that the United States, with only 5 percent of the world's population, consumed more than one-third of its goods and services. All of this production generated increased pollution and health concerns. Critics also noted that those who made it to the middle-class often failed to notice that poverty persisted, with one-fifth of Americans considered poor.

SUGGESTIONS FOR FURTHER READING

Taylor Branch, *Parting the Waters: America in the King Years, 1954–1963* (1988)

Lizabeth Cohen, *A Consumer's Republic: The Politics of Mass Consumption in Postwar America* (2003)

Stephanie Coontz, *The Way We Never Were: American Families and the Nostalgia Trap* (1992)

Mary Dudziak, *Cold War Civil Rights: Race and the Image of American Democracy* (2000)

James Gregory, *The Southern Diaspora: How the Great Migrations of Black and White Southerners Transformed the Nation* (2007)

Thomas Hine, *Populuxe* (1986)

Grace Palladino, *Teenagers* (1996)

James T. Patterson, *Grand Expectations: The United States, 1945–1974* (1996)

Ellen W. Schrecker, *Many Are the Crime: McCarthyism in America* (1998)

Thomas J. Sugrue, *The Origins of the Urban Crisis: Race and Inequality in Postwar Detroit* (1996)

The Tumultuous Sixties | 1960–1968

It was late, and Ezell Blair had an exam the next day. But he and his friends in the dormitory sat talking—as they often did—about injustice, about living in a nation that proclaimed equality for all but denied full citizenship to some because of the color of their skin. They were complaining about the do-nothing adults, condemning the African American community of Greensboro when Franklin McCain said, as if he meant it, "It's time to fish or cut bait." Joe McNeil and McCain's roommate, David Richmond, agreed. Blair hesitated. "I was thinking about my grades," he said later.

The next day, February 1, 1960, after their classes at North Carolina Agricultural and Technical College, the four freshmen walked into town. At the F. W. Woolworth's on South Elm Street, one of the most profitable stores in the national chain, each bought a few small things. Then, nervously, they sat down at the lunch counter and tried to order coffee. These seventeen- and eighteen-year-olds were prepared to be arrested, even physically attacked. But nothing happened. The counter help ignored them as long as possible; finally, one worker said, "We don't serve colored here." An elderly white woman told the boys how proud she was of them. Still nothing happened. The store closed the manager turned out the lights. After forty-five minutes, the four men who began the sit-in movement left the store.

The next day they returned with twenty fellow students. By February 3, sixty-three of the sixty-five seats were taken. On February 4, the sit-in spread to the S. H. Kress store across the street. By February 7, there were sit-ins in Winston-Salem; by February 8, in Charlotte; on February 9, in Raleigh. By the third week in February, students were picketing Woolworth's stores in the North. On July 26, 1960, F. W. Woolworth's ended segregation in all its stores.

This icon will direct you to interactive activities and study materials on *A People And A Nation*, Brief Edition website: **www.cengage.com/history/norton/peoplenationbrief8e**

Chronology

1960	Sit-ins begin in Greensboro.
	Birth-control pill is approved for contraceptive use.
	John F. Kennedy is elected president
	Young Americans for Freedom write Sharon Statement.
1961	Freedom Rides protest segregation in transportation.
1962	Students for a Democratic Society issues Port Huron Statement.
	Cuban missile crisis courts nuclear war.
1963	Civil rights March on Washington for Jobs and Freedom draws more than 250,000.
	South Vietnamese leader Diem is assassinated following U.S.-sanctioned coup d'état
	John F. Kennedy is assassinated; Lyndon B. Johnson becomes president.
1964	Civil Rights Act outlaws discrimination in hiring and public accommodations.
	Race riots break out in first of the long, hot summers.
	Gulf of Tonkin Resolution is passed by Congress.
	Free Speech Movement begins at University of California, Berkeley.
	Lyndon B. Johnson is elected president.

1965	Lyndon Johnson launches Great Society programs.
	United States commits ground troops to Vietnam and initiates Rolling Thunder bombing campaign.
	Voting Rights Act outlaws practices preventing most African Americans from voting in southern states.
	Immigration and Nationality Act lowers barriers to immigration from Asia and Latin America.
	Malcolm X is assassinated.
	Watts riot leaves thirty-four dead.
1966	National Organization for Women is founded.
1967	Summer of love occurs in San Francisco's Haight-Ashbury district.
	Race riots erupt in Newark, Detroit, and other cities.
1968	Tet Offensive deepens fear of losing war in Vietnam.
	Martin Luther King Jr. is assassinated.
	Robert Kennedy is assassinated.
	Antiwar protests escalate.
	Violence erupts at Democratic National Convention.
	Richard Nixon is elected president.

The sit-in at the Greensboro Woolworth's signaled the beginning of a decade of public activism rarely matched in U.S. history. During the 1960s, millions of Americans—many of them young—marched for civil rights or against the war in Vietnam. Passion over contemporary issues revitalized democracy and threatened to tear the nation apart.

John F. Kennedy, the nation's youngest president, told Americans as he took office in 1961, "The torch has been passed to a new generation." Despite his inspirational language, Kennedy had only modest success implementing his domestic agenda. In his third year as president, however, Kennedy offered greater support for civil rights and proposed ambitious domestic policies. When he was assassinated in November 1963, his death seemed to many the end of an era of hope.

Lyndon Johnson, Kennedy's successor, invoked the memory of the martyred president to launch an ambitious civil rights program and other liberal legislation. Calling his vision the Great Society, Johnson intended to use federal power to eliminate poverty and guarantee equal rights to all Americans.

Despite liberal triumphs and civil rights gains, social tensions escalated during the mid-1960s. A revitalized conservative movement emerged, and Franklin Roosevelt's old New Deal coalition fractured as white southerners abandoned the Democratic Party. Angry that poverty and discrimination persisted despite landmark civil rights laws, many African Americans rioted. White youth culture increasingly rejected the values and lifestyle of its elders, creating what Americans have called the generation gap.

Meanwhile, after the 1962 Cuban missile crisis brought the Soviet Union and the United States close to nuclear disaster, President John F. Kennedy and the Soviet leader Nikita Khrushchev deescalated tensions in 1963 and lessened Cold War pressures in Europe. Everywhere else, however, the superpowers competed frantically. Throughout the 1960s, the United States tried various approaches—including foreign aid, CIA covert actions, military assaults, cultural penetration, economic sanctions, and diplomacy—to win the Cold War. In Vietnam, Kennedy expanded U.S. involvement significantly. Johnson increased U.S. troops there to more than half a million in 1968.

By 1968 the Vietnam War divided Americans and undermined Johnson's Great Society. With the assassinations of Martin Luther King Jr. and Robert Kennedy—two of America's brightest leaders—with cities in flames and tanks on Chicago streets in August, the fate of the nation hung in the balance.

- **What were the successes and failures of American liberalism in the 1960s?**
- **Why did the United States expand its participation in the war in Vietnam and continue in the war so long?**
- **By 1968, many believed the fate of the nation hung in the balance. What did they think was at stake? What divided Americans, and how did they express their differences?**

KENNEDY AND THE COLD WAR

Young, handsome, and intellectually curious, John F. Kennedy brought wit and sophistication to the White House. His Irish American grandfather had been mayor of Boston, and his millionaire father, Joseph P. Kennedy, served as ambassador to Great Britain. In 1946 the young Kennedy returned from World War II a naval hero (the boat he commanded was sunk by a Japanese destroyer in 1943, and Kennedy saved his crew) and campaigned to represent Boston in the U.S. House of Representatives. He served three terms in the House, and in 1952 was elected to the Senate.

John Fitzgerald Kennedy

As a Democrat, Kennedy inherited the New Deal commitment to the United States's social welfare system. He generally voted with the pro-labor sentiments of his low-income, blue-collar constituents. But he avoided controversial issues, such as civil rights and the censure of Joseph McCarthy. Kennedy won a Pulitzer Prize for his *Profiles in Courage* (1956), a study of principled politicians, but he shaded the truth in claiming sole authorship, as it was written largely by aide Theodore Sorensen (from more than one hundred pages of notes dictated by Kennedy). In foreign policy, Senator Kennedy endorsed the Cold War policy of containment. Despite an unimpressive legislative record, he enjoyed an enthusiastic following, especially after his landslide Senate reelection in 1958.

Kennedy cultivated an image as a happy and healthy family man. But he was a chronic womanizer, even after his 1953 marriage to Jacqueline Bouvier. Nor was he the picture of physical vitality: as a child he nearly died of scarlet fever and later developed severe back problems, made worse by his participation in World War II. After the war, Kennedy was diagnosed with Addison's disease, an adrenalin deficiency that required daily cortisone injections and often left him in acute pain. As president he would require plenty of bed rest and frequent therapeutic swims in the White House pool.

Election of 1960

Kennedy beat Republican Richard Nixon for president in 1960 by a narrow 118,000 votes out of nearly 69 million cast. Kennedy achieved mixed success in the South but ran well in the Northeast and Midwest. His Roman Catholic faith hurt him in states where voters feared he would take direction from the pope, but helped in states with large Catholic populations. As the sitting vice president, Nixon had to answer for sagging economic figures and the Soviet downing of a U-2 spy plane. In televised debates against the telegenic Kennedy, Nixon looked nervous, and the camera made him appear unshaven. Perhaps worse, when asked to list Nixon's significant decisions as vice president, Eisenhower replied, "If you give me a week. I might think of one."

The new president surrounded himself with mostly young advisers whom writer David Halberstam called "the best and the brightest." Secretary of Defense Robert McNamara (age forty-four) was an assistant professor at Harvard at twenty-four and later the whiz-kid president of the Ford Motor Company Kennedy's special assistant for national security affairs, McGeorge Bundy (age forty-one) became a Harvard dean at thirty-four with only a bachelor's degree. Secretary of State Dean Rusk (fifty-two) had been a Rhodes scholar in his youth. Kennedy was only forty-three, and his brother Robert, the attorney general, was thirty-five.

Kennedy gave top priority to the Cold War In the campaign he accused Eisenhower of unimaginative foreign policy that failed to reduce the threat of nuclear war with the Soviet Union and weakened the United States's standing in the Third World.

Nation Building in the Third World

Kennedy in office understood sooner than his advisers the limits of U.S. power abroad. More than his predecessor, he proved willing to initiate dialogue with the Soviets, sometimes using his brother Robert as a secret channel to Moscow. Yet Kennedy also sought victory in the Cold War. After the Soviet leader Nikita Khrushchev endorsed wars of national liberation, such as the one in Vietnam, Kennedy called for peaceful revolution through nation building. The administration helped developing nations with aid to improve agriculture, transportation and communications. Kennedy thus oversaw the creation of the multibillion-dollar Alliance for Progress in 1961 to spur economic development in Latin America. That year, too, he created the Peace Corps, dispatching U.S. teachers, agricultural specialists, and health workers, many of them recent college graduates, to assist developing nations.

Alliance for Progress

Peace Corps

Cynics then and later dismissed the Alliance and the Peace Corps as Kennedy's Cold War tools for countering anti-Americanism and defeating communism in the developing world. True enough, but the programs were also born of genuine humanitarianism. As the historian Elizabeth Cobbs Hoffman has written, "the Peace Corps broached an age-old dilemma of U.S. foreign policy: how to reconcile the imperatives and temptations of power politics with the ideals of freedom and self-determination for all nations."

Although Kennedy and his aides were supportive of social revolution in the Third World, they could not see the legitimacy of communist involvement in these uprisings. Therefore, the administration also relied on counterinsurgency to defeat revolutionaries who challenged pro-U.S. Third World governments. U.S. military and technical advisers trained native troops and police to quell unrest.

The Alliance for Progress was only partly successful; infant mortality rates improved, but Latin American economies registered unimpressive growth and class divisions widened, exacerbating political unrest. Although many foreign peoples welcomed U.S. economic assistance and American material culture, they resented meddling. And because aid was usually funneled through a self-interested elite, it often never reached the poor. To people who preferred the quick solutions of a managed economy, moreover, the American emphasis on private enterprise seemed inappropriate.

Soviet-American Tensions

Nor did the new president succeed in relations with the Soviet Union. A summit meeting with the Soviet leader Nikita Khrushchev in Vienna in June 1961 went poorly, with the two leaders disagreeing over preconditions for peace and stability in the world. Consequently, the administration's first year witnessed little movement on controlling the nuclear arms race or getting a superpower ban on testing nuclear weapons in the atmosphere or underground. Instead, both superpowers accelerated their arms production. In 1961 the U.S. military budget shot up 15 percent; by mid-1964, U.S. nuclear weapons increased by 150 percent. Government advice to citizens to build fallout shelters in their backyards intensified public fear of devastating war.

If war occurred, many believed Berlin would be the cause. In mid-1961 Khrushchev demanded an end to western occupation of West Berlin and a reunification of East and West Germany, but Kennedy stood by U.S. commitment to West Berlin and West Germany. In August the Soviets, at the urging of the East German regime, erected a concrete and barbed-wire barricade to halt the exodus of East Germans into the prosperous and politically free West Berlin. The Berlin Wall inspired protests throughout the noncommunist world, but Kennedy privately sighed that "a wall is a hell of a lot better than a war."

Bay of Pigs Invasion

Kennedy knew that Khrushchev would continue to press elsewhere, and he was particularly rankled by growing Soviet assistance to Fidel Castro's Cuban government. The Eisenhower administration contested the Cuban revolution and bequeathed to the Kennedy administration a partially developed CIA plan to overthrow Castro: CIA-trained Cuban exiles would land and secure a beachhead; the Cuban people would rise up against Castro and welcome a new U.S.-backed government.

The attack took place on April 17, 1961, as twelve hundred exiles landed at the swampy Bay of Pigs in Cuba. Instead of discontented Cubans, they were greeted by Castro's troops and quickly captured. Kennedy tried to keep the U.S. participation in the operation hidden, but the CIA's role swiftly became public. Anti-American sentiment swept through Latin America. Castro, concluding that the United States might launch another invasion, looked increasingly toward the Soviet Union for military and economic assistance.

Embarrassed by the Bay of Pigs fiasco, Kennedy vowed to bring Castro down. The CIA soon hatched a project called Operation Mongoose to disrupt the island's trade, support raids on Cuba from Miami, and plot to kill Castro. The agency's assassination schemes included providing Castro with cigars laced with explosives and poison. The United States also tightened its economic blockade and undertook military maneuvers in the Caribbean. The Joint Chiefs of Staff sketched plans to spark a rebellion in Cuba that would be followed by an invasion of U.S. troops.

Cuban Missile Crisis Both Castro and Khrushchev believed an invasion was coming, which partly explains the Soviet leader's risky decision in 1962 to secretly deploy nuclear missiles in Cuba as a deterrent. But Khrushchev also hoped the move would improve the Soviet position in the nuclear balance of power and force Kennedy to finally resolve the German problem. Khrushchev worried that Washington might provide West Germany with nuclear weapons. He thought he could prevent it by putting Soviet missiles just 90 miles off the coast of Florida. The world soon faced brinkmanship at its most frightening.

In mid-October 1962, a U-2 plane flying over Cuba photographed the missile sites. The president immediately organized a special Executive Committee (ExComm) to force the missiles and their nuclear warheads out of Cuba. Options considered ranged from full-scale invasion to limited bombing to quiet diplomacy. Defense Secretary Robert McNamara proposed a solution acceptable to the president: a naval quarantine of Cuba.

Kennedy addressed the nation on television on October 22, demanding that the Soviets retreat. U.S. warships began crisscrossing the Caribbean, while B-52s with nuclear bombs took to the skies. Khrushchev agreed to withdraw the missiles if the United States pledged never to attack Cuba and removed Jupiter missiles aimed at the Soviet Union from Turkey. For several days the world teetered on the brink of disaster. Then, on October 28, came a compromise. The United States agreed to Soviet demands in exchange for the withdrawal of Soviet offensive forces from Cuba. Fearing Castro might make matters worse, Khrushchev settled without consulting the Cubans.

Many observers then and later called it Kennedy's finest hour. Critics, however, claimed Kennedy may have caused the crisis in the first place with his anti-Cuban projects. Either way, the Cuban missile crisis was a watershed in the Soviet-American relationship. Both Kennedy and Khrushchev acted with greater prudence in its aftermath, taking steps toward improved relations. In August 1963 the adversaries signed a treaty banning nuclear tests in the atmosphere, the oceans, and outer space. They also installed a coded wire-telegraph hot line staffed around the clock to allow near-instant communication between the capitals. Both sides refrained from further confrontation in Berlin.

Together these small steps began to build much-needed mutual trust. By autumn 1963, the Cold War in Europe was fading as both sides accepted the status quo of a divided continent and a fortified border. But the arms race continued and accelerated, and the superpower competition in the Third World remained intense.

MARCHING FOR FREEDOM

President Kennedy regarded the Cold War as the most important issue Americans faced. But in the early 1960s, young civil rights activists seized the national stage and demanded that the federal government mobilize behind them.

Students and the Movement

In 1960, six years after the *Brown* decision declared separate but equal unconstitutional, only 10 percent of southern public schools had begun desegregation. Fewer than one in four adult African Americans in the South could vote, and water fountains were still labeled White Only and Colored Only. One year after the young men sat down at the all-white lunch counter in Greensboro, more than seventy thousand Americans—mostly college students—had participated in sit-ins.

The young people who created the Student Nonviolent Coordinating Committee (SNCC) in spring 1960 to coordinate the sit-in movement were committed to nonviolence. In the years to come, SNCC stalwarts would risk their lives in the struggle for social justice.

Freedom Rides and Voter Registration

On May 4, 1961, thirteen members of the Congress of Racial Equality (CORE), a nonviolent civil rights organization formed during World War II, purchased bus tickets in Washington, D.C., for a 1,500-mile trip through the South to New Orleans. Calling themselves Freedom Riders, this racially mixed group meant to demonstrate that, despite Supreme Court rulings ordering the desegregation of interstate buses, Jim Crow still ruled in the South. They knew they were risking their lives. One bus was firebombed outside Anniston, Alabama. Riders were badly beaten in Birmingham. In Montgomery, a thousand whites attacked riders with baseball bats and steel bars. Police stayed away; the police commissioner called the freedom riders troublemakers.

News of the violent attacks made headlines worldwide. Soviet commentators highlighted the "savage nature of American freedom and democracy." One southern business leader, in Tokyo promoting Birmingham as a site for international business development, saw Japanese interest evaporate when photographs of the Birmingham attacks appeared in Tokyo newspapers.

In the United States, the violence forced many to confront racial discrimination and hatred in their nation. Middle- and upper-class white southerners resisted integration following the *Brown* decision. The Freedom Rides made some think differently. The *Atlanta Journal* editorialized: "[I]t is time for the decent people . . . to muzzle the jackals." The national and international outcry pushed a reluctant President Kennedy to send federal marshals to safeguard Freedom Riders in Alabama. But bowing to white southern pressure, he allowed the Freedom Riders to be arrested in Mississippi.

Beginning in 1961, thousands of SNCC volunteers, many of them high school and college students, risked their lives encouraging African Americans in rural Mississippi and Georgia to register to vote. Some SNCC volunteers were white, some were northerners, but many were African American southerners, often from low-income families. They experienced first-hand the intersection of racism, powerlessness, and poverty.

Kennedy and Civil Rights

Kennedy was sympathetic—though not terribly committed—to the civil rights movement, and he realized that racial oppression hurt the United States in the Cold War struggle for international opinion. However, like Franklin D. Roosevelt, he knew that if he alienated conservative southern Democrats in Congress, his legislative programs would founder. Thus he appointed five die-hard segregationists to the federal bench in the Deep South and delayed issuing an executive order forbidding segregation in federally subsidized housing (a pledge made in the 1960 campaign) until late 1962. He allowed the FBI director J. Edgar Hoover to harass Martin Luther King and other activists, using wiretaps and surveillance to gather personal information and circulating rumors of communist connections and personal improprieties to discredit them.

But grassroots civil rights activism—and the violence of white mobs—forced Kennedy's hand. In September 1962, the president ordered five hundred U.S. marshals to protect James Meredith, the first African American to attend the University of Mississippi. Thousands of whites attacked the marshals with guns, gasoline bombs, bricks, and pipes, killing 2 and seriously wounding 160. Neither the marshals nor James Meredith backed down.

Birmingham and the Children's Crusade

In 1961 the Freedom Riders captured the attention of the nation and the larger Cold War world. Martin Luther King Jr., having risen through the Montgomery bus boycott to leadership in the movement, concluded that only by provoking a crisis would the civil rights struggle advance. King and the SCLC planned a 1963 campaign in the most violently racist city in the United States: Birmingham, Alabama. Anticipating a violent response, they called their plan Project C—for confrontation. King wanted all Americans to see the racist hate and violence that marred their nation.

Through April 1963, nonviolent protests in Birmingham led to hundreds of arrests. Then, on May 2, in a controversial action, King and the parents of Birmingham put children on the front lines. As about a thousand African American children, some as young as six, marched, police commissioner Eugene "Bull" Connor ordered his police to train "monitor" water guns—powerful enough to strip bark from a tree at 100 feet—on them. The water guns mowed the children down, and police loosed attack dogs as the nation watched in horror on TV. President Kennedy demanded that Birmingham's white business and political elite negotiate a settlement. The Birmingham movement had won and, more importantly, pushed civil rights to the fore of Kennedy's agenda.

"Segregation Forever!"

On June 11, defiant Alabama governor George C. Wallace fulfilled a promise to "bar the schoolhouse door" himself to prevent the desegregation of the University of Alabama. Hearing echoes of Wallace's January 1963 inaugural pledge "Segregation now, segregation tomorrow, segregation forever!" and facing a nation rocked by civil rights protests, Kennedy committed the federal government to guarantee racial justice. In a televised address on June 12, Kennedy said, "Now the time has come for this nation to fulfill its promise." Hours later, the civil rights leader Medgar Evers was murdered in his driveway in Jackson, Mississippi. The next week, the president asked Congress to pass a comprehensive civil rights bill ending legal racial discrimination.

March on Washington

On August 28, 1963, a quarter-million Americans gathered on the Washington Mall to show support for Kennedy's civil rights bill. Behind the scenes, organizers from major civil rights groups—SCLC, CORE, SNCC, the NAACP, the Urban League, and A. Philip Randolph's Brotherhood of Sleeping Car Porters—grappled with growing tensions within the movement. SNCC activists saw Kennedy's proposed legislation as too little, too late. King and other older leaders counseled moderation. The movement was splintering.

What most Americans saw, however, was a celebration of unity. Black and white celebrities joined hands; folk singers sang freedom songs. Television aired Martin Luther King Jr.'s prophesy of a day when "all God's children, black men and white men, Jews and Gentiles, Protestants and Catholics, will be able to join hands and sing in the words of the old Negro spiritual, 'Free at last! Free at last! Thank God Almighty, we are free at last!'" The 1963 March on Washington for Jobs and Freedom was a triumph, powerfully demonstrating African Americans' commitment to equality and justice. Days later, white supremacists bombed the Sixteenth Street Baptist Church in Birmingham, killing four African American girls.

Freedom Summer

During summer 1964, more than one thousand white students joined the voter mobilization project in Mississippi. They formed Freedom Schools, teaching literacy and constitutional rights, and helped organize the Mississippi Freedom Democratic Party as an alternative to the whites-only Democratic Party. SNCC organizers also believed that

A historic moment for the civil rights movement was the March on Washington of August 28, 1963. The Reverend Martin Luther King Jr. (center) joined a quarter-million black people and white people in their march for racial equality. Addressing civil rights supporters and the nation from the steps of the Lincoln Memorial, King delivered his "I Have a Dream" speech. (R.W. Kelley / Getty Images)

large numbers of white volunteers would focus national attention on Mississippi's repression and violence. Project workers were arrested over a thousand times and were shot at, bombed, and beaten. On June 21, local black activist James Cheney and two white volunteers, Michael Schwerner and Andrew Goodman, were murdered by a Klan mob. That summer, black and white activists risked their lives together.

LIBERALISM AND THE GREAT SOCIETY

By 1963, Kennedy seemed to be taking a new path. Campaigning in 1960, he promised to lead Americans into a New Frontier, with the federal government working to eradicate poverty, guarantee healthcare to the elderly, and provide decent schools for all children. But few of Kennedy's domestic initiatives were passed into law. Lacking a popular mandate in the 1960 election, fearful of alienating southern Democrats in Congress, Kennedy let his social policy agenda languish.

Instead, Kennedy focused on the economy, believing that continued prosperity would solve the United States' social problems. Kennedy's vision was perhaps best realized in the United States's space program. As the Soviets drew ahead in the space race, Kennedy vowed in 1961 to put a man on the moon before decade's end. With billions in new funding, the National Aeronautics and Space Administration (NASA) began the Apollo program. And in February 1962, astronaut John Glenn orbited the earth in the space capsule *Friendship 7.*

Kennedy Assassination On November 22, 1963, Kennedy visited Texas, the home state of his vice president, Lyndon Johnson. In Dallas, riding with his wife, Jackie, in an open-top limousine, Kennedy was cheered by thousands along the motorcade's route. Suddenly shots rang out. The president crumpled, shot in the head. Tears ran down the cheeks of the CBS anchorman Walter Cronkite as he announced that the president was dead.

That same day police captured a suspect: Lee Harvey Oswald, a former U.S. marine (dishonorably discharged) who once attempted to gain Soviet citizenship. Two days later, television cameras rolled as Oswald was shot dead by the nightclub owner Jack Ruby. Shocked Americans wondered if Ruby was silencing Oswald to prevent him from implicating others. The seven-member Warren Commission, headed by U.S. Supreme Court chief justice Earl Warren, concluded that Oswald acted alone. But debates still rage over whether Oswald was a lone assassin.

Millions of Americans watched their president's funeral on television: the brave young widow, a riderless horse, three-year-old John-John saluting his father's casket. In one awful moment in Dallas, the reality of the Kennedy presidency had been transformed into myth, the man into martyr. In the post-assassination national grief, Lyndon Johnson invoked Kennedy's memory to push through the most ambitious legislative program since the New Deal.

Johnson and the Great Society Where Kennedy came from wealth and privilege and was educated at Harvard, Johnson grew up in modest circumstances in the Texas hill country and graduated from Southwest Texas State Teachers' College. He was as earthy as Kennedy was elegant, prone to colorful curses and willing to use his physical size to his advantage. Johnson had first come to Congress in 1937. As Senate majority leader from 1954 to 1960, he learned how to manipulate people and wield power. Now, as president, he used these skills to unite the nation.

Johnson, a liberal in the style of Franklin D. Roosevelt, believed that the federal government must actively improve the lives of Americans. In a 1964 commencement address at the University of Michigan, he described his vision of "abundance and liberty for all . . . demand[ing] an end to poverty and racial injustice . . . where every child can find knowledge to enrich his mind and to enlarge his talents." Johnson called this vision the Great Society.

Civil Rights Act

Johnson signed into law the Civil Rights Act of 1964, which ended *legal* discrimination on the basis of race, color, religion, or national origin, in federal programs, voting, employment, and public accommodation. The original bill did not include sex discrimination; that was introduced by a southern congressman who hoped it would engender enough opposition to torpedo the entire bill. But a bipartisan group of women members of the House of Representatives ensured it was passed with sex as a protected category. Significantly, the Civil Rights Act of 1964 gave the government authority to withhold federal funds from public agencies or federal contractors that discriminated and established the Equal Employment Opportunity Commission (EEOC) to investigate and judge claims of job discrimination. However, the EEOC largely ignored sex discrimination, prompting women's equality activists in 1966 to form the National Organization for Women (NOW).

Many Americans did not believe that it was the federal government's job to end racial discrimination or poverty. White southerners especially resented federal intervention in local customs, and millions of conservative Americans believed that since the New Deal the federal government had overstepped its constitutional boundaries. They sought a return to local control and states' rights. In the 1964 election, this vision was championed by the Republican candidate, Arizona senator Barry Goldwater.

Election of 1964

Goldwater not only voted against the 1964 Civil Rights Act, he also opposed the national Social Security system. Like many conservatives, he believed that individual *liberty,* not equality, mattered most. Goldwater further believed that the United States needed a more powerful national military to fight communism; in campaign speeches he suggested that the United States should use tactical nuclear weapons against its enemies.

Goldwater's campaign slogan, "In your heart you know he's right," was turned against him by Lyndon Johnson supporters: "In your heart you know he's right . . . far right," one punned. Johnson campaigned on an unemployment rate below 4 percent and economic growth above 6 percent. But his civil rights support severed the New Deal coalition, and he told an aide, "delivered the south to the Republican Party for my lifetime and yours."

Tensions mounted at the 1964 Democratic National Convention. Two delegations from Mississippi demanded to be seated. The Democratic Party's official delegation was exclusively white; the Mississippi Freedom Democratic Party's

(MFDP) was racially mixed. White southern delegates threatened to leave if the MFDP delegates were seated. Johnson sought a compromise, but the MFDP declined. "We didn't come all this way for no two seats." MFDP delegate Fannie Lou Hamer said, and the delegation walked out.

Johnson won the election by a landslide, but he lost the Deep South—the first Democrat since the Civil War to do so. Voters also elected the most liberal Congress in history. With a record 61.1 percent of the popular vote, Johnson launched his Great Society. Congress passed the most sweeping reform legislation since 1935.

In late 1964, the SCLC made voting rights its top priority. Martin Luther King Jr. and other leaders turned to Selma, Alabama, seeking another public confrontation that would mobilize national support and federal action. It came on March 6, when state troopers turned electric cattle prods, chains, and tear gas against peaceful marchers. On March 15, the president offered support for a second monumental civil rights bill, the Voting Rights Act. It outlawed practices that prevented most African American citizens in the Deep South from voting and provided for federal election oversight in districts with evidence of past discrimination. Within two years, African American registered voters in Mississippi jumped from 7 percent to more than 60 percent. African American elected officials became increasingly common in southern states over the following decade.

Improving American Life

Seeking to improve the quality of American life, the Johnson administration established new student loan and grant programs to help low- and moderate-income Americans attend college and created the National Endowment for the Arts and the National Endowment for the Humanities. The Immigration Act of 1965 ended racially based quotas. And Johnson supported consumer protection legislation, including the 1966 National Traffic and Motor Vehicle Safety Act, inspired by Ralph Nader's exposé of the automobile industry, *Unsafe at Any Speed* (1965). Johnson signed preservation legislation protecting the United States's wilderness and supported laws addressing environmental pollution.

War on Poverty

At the heart of Johnson's Great Society was the War on Poverty, which included major legislation beginning in 1964 (see Table 30.1). Johnson and other liberals believed that, in a time of affluence, the nation should use its resources to end "poverty, ignorance and hunger as intractable, permanent features of American society."

Johnson's goal was "to offer the forgotten fifth of our people opportunity, not doles." Municipalities and school districts received billions of federal dollars to improve opportunities for the poverty-stricken, from preschoolers (Head Start) to high schoolers (Upward Bound) to young adults (Job Corps). The Model Cities program offered federal funds to upgrade employment, housing, education, and health in targeted urban neighborhoods, and Community Action Programs involved poor Americans in creating local grassroots antipoverty programs.

The Johnson administration also expanded the Food Stamp program and earmarked billions for constructing public housing and subsidizing rents. Two new federal programs guaranteed healthcare: Medicare for those sixty-five and older, and

TABLE 30.1   Great Society Achievements, 1964–1966

	1964	1965	1966
Civil Rights	Civil Rights Act Equal Employment Opportunity Commission Twenty-fourth Amendment	Voting Rights Act	
War on Poverty	Economic Opportunity Act Office of Economic Opportunity Job Corps Legal Services for the Poor VISTA		Model Cities
Education		Elementary and Secondary Education Act Head Start Upward Bound	
Environment		Water Quality Act Air Quality Act	Clean Water Restoration Act

New Government Agencies		Department of
		  Housing and Urban
		  Development
		National Endowments for
		  the Arts and Humanities
			Department of
			  Transportation

Miscellaneous		Medicare and Medicaid Immigration and Nationality Act	

The Great Society of the mid-1960s saw the biggest burst of reform legislation since the New Deal of the 1930s.

Medicaid for the poor. Finally, Aid to Families with Dependent Children (AFDC), the welfare program created during the New Deal, broadened benefits and eligibility.

The War on Poverty was controversial. Leftists believed that the government was doing too little to change structural inequality. Conservatives argued that Great Society programs created dependency among the United States's poor. Policy analysts noted that specific programs were ill conceived and badly implemented. Decades later, most historians judge the War on Poverty a mixed success. Its programs improved the quality of housing, healthcare, and nutrition available to the poor. Federal spending for Social Security, healthcare, welfare, and education more than doubled between 1965 and 1975, with the number of Americans receiving food stamps increasing from 600,000 to 17 million. Poverty among the elderly fell from about 40 percent in 1960 to 16 percent in 1974, due largely to increased Social Security benefits and to Medicare. The War on Poverty improved many Americans' quality of life (see Figure 30.1).

But War on Poverty programs less successfully addressed the root causes of poverty. Neither the Job Corps nor Community Action Programs showed significant results. Economic growth largely sparked the dramatic decrease in poverty rates during the 1960s—from 22.4 percent of Americans in 1959 to 11 percent in 1973. Unchanged was the fact that 11 million Americans in female-headed households remained poor in 1969—the same number as in 1963.

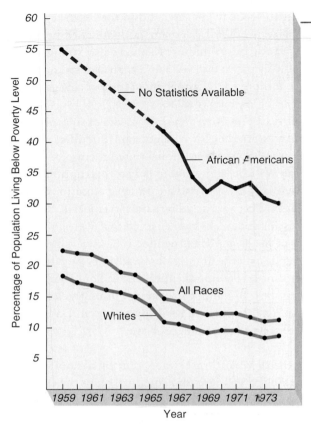

Figure 30.1 Poverty in America for Whites, African Americans, and All Races, 1959–1974

Because of rising levels of economic prosperity, combined with the impact of Great Society programs, the percentage of Americans living in poverty in 1974 was half as high as in 1959. African Americans still were far more likely than white Americans to be poor. In 1959 more than half of all African Americans (55.1 percent) were poor; in 1974 the figure remained high (30.3 percent). The government did not record data on African American poverty for the years 1960 through 1965.

Political compromises created long-term problems. For example, Congress accommodated doctors and hospitals in Medicare legislation by allowing federal reimbursements of hospitals' "reasonable costs" and doctors' "reasonable charges" in treating elderly patients. With no incentives for doctors or hospitals to hold prices down, national healthcare expenditures as a percentage of the gross national product rose by almost 44 percent from 1960 to 1971. Problems aside, Johnson's Great Society was a moment in which many Americans believed they could and should solve the problems of poverty, disease, and discrimination.

JOHNSON AND VIETNAM

In foreign policy, Johnson held firmly to ideas about U.S. superiority and the communist menace. International affairs held little interest for him, and he had little appreciation for foreign cultures. At the Taj Mahal in India, Johnson tested the monument's echo with a Texas cowboy yell. On a trip to Senegal, he ordered that an American bed, a special showerhead, and cases of Cutty Sark be sent with him. "Foreigners," Johnson quipped, only half-jokingly, "are not like the folks I am used to."

Kennedy's Legacy in Vietnam

Yet Johnson knew that foreign policy, especially regarding Vietnam, would demand his attention. Since the late 1950s, hostilities in Vietnam increased, as Ho Chi Minh's North assisted the Vietcong guerrillas in the South in reunifying the country under a communist government. President Kennedy increased aid to the Diem regime in Saigon, airdropped more raid teams into North Vietnam, and launched herbicide crop destruction to starve the Vietcong out of hiding. Kennedy also strengthened the U.S. military presence in South Vietnam: by 1963 more than sixteen thousand military advisers were there, some authorized to participate in combat alongside the U.S.-equipped Army of the Republic of Vietnam (ARVN).

Meanwhile, opposition to Diem's repressive regime increased. Peasants objected to being removed from their villages for their own safety, and Buddhist monks, protesting Roman Catholic Diem's religious persecution, ignited themselves in the streets of Saigon. Although Diem was honest, he countenanced corruption in his government and jailed critics. Eventually U.S. officials encouraged ambitious South Vietnamese generals to remove Diem. They murdered him on November 1, 1963.

The timing of Kennedy's assassination weeks later ensured that Vietnam would be the most controversial aspect of his legacy. He expanded U.S. involvement and approved a coup against Diem, but despite the urgings of top advisers, he refused to commit U.S. ground forces. Over time he became skeptical about South Vietnam's prospects and hinted he would end the U.S. commitment after winning reelection in 1964. Whether he would have can never be known. Kennedy arrived in Dallas that fateful day uncertain about how to solve the Vietnam problem.

Tonkin Gulf Incident and Resolution

Facing the 1964 election, Lyndon Johnson did not want to do anything in Vietnam that could cost him the election, so he kept Vietnam on the back burner. Yet Johnson also sought victory there, and throughout 1964 the administration secretly considered expanding the war to North Vietnam.

In early August 1964, U.S. destroyers reported coming under attack twice in three days from North Vietnamese patrol boats in the Gulf of Tonkin (see Map 30.1). Despite a lack of evidence that the second attack occurred, Johnson ordered retaliatory air strikes against North Vietnamese patrol boat bases and an oil depot. By a vote of 416 to 0 in the House and 88 to 2 in the Senate, Congress quickly passed the Gulf of Tonkin Resolution, giving the president the authority to "take all necessary measures to repel any armed attack against the forces of the United States and to prevent further aggression." In so doing, Congress essentially surrendered its war-making powers to the executive branch.

Decision for Escalation

President Johnson also appreciated how the Gulf of Tonkin affair boosted his public approval ratings and effectively removed Vietnam as a campaign issue for GOP presidential nominee Barry Goldwater. On the ground in South Vietnam, however, the outlook remained grim, as the Vietcong made gains. U.S. officials secretly planned to escalate U.S. involvement.

In February 1965, in response to Vietcong attacks on U.S. installations in South Vietnam which killed thirty-two Americans, Johnson ordered Operation Rolling Thunder, a bombing program that continued until October 1968. On March 8, the first U.S. combat battalions came ashore near Danang. The North Vietnamese responded by increasing infiltration into the South. In Saigon, meanwhile, coups and countercoups by self-serving military leaders undermined U.S. efforts.

CHINA

MYANMAR (BURMA)

Dienbienphu

Red R.

Black R.

Hanoi

Haiphong

Harbor mined, 1972

U.S. bombing begins, 1964
Communist–Pathet Lao victory, 1975

Gulf of Tonkin

PLAIN OF JARS

Maddox incident, 1964

LAOS

NORTH VIETNAM

Vinh

Mu Gia Pass

Vientiane

Mekong R.

Ca R.

U.S. Seventh Fleet operations during the war

Udon Thani

Nakhon Phanom

Demilitarized Zone

Quang Tri

17°   Demarcation Line, 1954

Khon Kaen

Khe Sanh

Sépone

A Chau

Hue

South China Sea

THAILAND

Kang Vei

Kham Duc

Da Nang

My Lai

Ta Khli

Ubon Ratchathani

Chu Lai

Quang Ngai

Rachasima

Dak To

Kontum

An Khe

Pleiku

Qui Nhon

Don Muang

Duc Co

Bangkok

CENTRAL HIGHLANDS

Tuy Hoa

CAMBODIA (KAMPUCHEA)

U.S. bombing begins, 1969

Ben Me Thuot

Nha Trang

Sattahip

U.S. invasion, 1975

Bu Dop

Dalat

Can Ranh Bay

Gulf of Siam

Vietnamese invasion, 1978

SOUTH VIETNAM

Communist–Khmer Rouge victory, 1975

Phnom Penh

Cholon

Bien Hoa

Tan Son Nhut

Long Binh

Chau Duc

Saigon

Vung Tau

Vietcong–North Vietnamese victory and U.S. withdrawal, 1975

Mayaguez incident, 1975

My Tho

Vinh Long

Ben Tre

Can Tho

Mekong Delta

Ca Mau

CA MAU PENINSULA

0   100   200 miles

0   100   200   300 kilometers

→ Ho Chi Minh Trail

⇨ Boat-people refugees after 1975

✬ Major battles of the Tet Offensive, January 1968

■ Major U.S. bases during the war

Map 30.1   Southeast Asia and the Vietnam War

To prevent communists from coming to power in Vietnam, Cambodia, and Laos in the 1960s, the United States intervened massively in Southeast Asia. The interventions failed, and the remaining U.S. troops made a hasty exit from Vietnam in 1975, as the victorious Vietcong and North Vietnamese took Saigon and renamed it Ho Chi Minh City.

In July 1965, Johnson convened a series of high-level discussions about U.S. war policy, partially so history would record that he agonized over a choice he had in fact already made about the United States's open-ended involvement. On July 28, Johnson publicly announced a significant troop increase, with others to follow. By the end of 1965, more than 180,000 U.S. ground troops were in South Vietnam. In 1966 the figure climbed to 385,000. In 1967 alone, U.S. warplanes flew 108,000 sorties and dropped 226,000 tons of bombs on North Vietnam. In 1968 U.S. troop strength reached 536,100. Each U.S. escalation brought a new North Vietnamese escalation and increased assistance to Hanoi from the Soviet Union and China.

Opposition to Americanization

Rolling Thunder and the U.S. troop commitment Americanized the war, transforming it from a civil war between North and South into a U.S. war against the communist Hanoi government. In the key months of decision, Democratic leaders in the Senate, major newspapers such as the *New York Times* and the *Wall Street Journal,* and prominent columnists such as Walter Lippmann warned against deepening involvement, as did Vice President Hubert H. Humphrey and Undersecretary of State George W. Ball. Abroad, virtually all of the United States's allies—including France, Britain, Canada, and Japan—cautioned against escalation and urged a political settlement. Remarkably, top U.S. officials knew that the odds of success were small but hoped the new measures would cause Hanoi to end the insurgency in the South.

U.S. leaders feared that if the United States failed in Vietnam, other countries would find U.S. power less credible. The Soviets and Chinese would challenge U.S. interests elsewhere, and allied governments might conclude they could not depend on Washington. Johnson worried that failure in Vietnam would harm his domestic agenda and feared personal humiliation. As for the stated objective of helping a South Vietnamese ally repulse external aggression, that did not figure into the equation as much as it would have had the Saigon government—racked with infighting and little popular support—done more in its own defense.

U.S. Soldiers in Vietnam

To minimize publicity about the war, Johnson refused to call up reserve units. This forced the military to rely heavily on the draft, which made Vietnam a young man's war; the average age of soldiers was twenty-two, compared with twenty-six in World War II. It also became a war of the poor and the working class. Through the years of heavy escalation (1965–1968), college students could get deferments, as could teachers and engineers. (In 1969 the draft was changed so that some students were called up through a lottery system.) The armed services recruited hard in poor communities, many of them heavily African American and Hispanic American, advertising the military as an avenue of training and advancement. Once in uniform, those with fewer skills were far more likely to see combat, and hence to die.

Infantrymen maneuvered into thick jungles, where booby traps and land mines were a constant threat. Boots and human skin rotted from the rains. The enemy was hard to find, often burrowed into elaborate underground tunnels or melded into the population, where any Vietnamese might be a Vietcong.

The entry of U.S. forces into the conflict in 1965 helped stave off a South Vietnamese defeat, thereby achieving Americanization's most immediate and basic

Wounded U.S. soldiers after a battle in Vietnam.
(Larry Burrows/Getty Images)

objective. But as the North Vietnamese matched each U.S. escalation with their own, the war became a stalemate. The U.S. commander, General William Westmoreland, mistakenly believed that a strategy of attrition represented the key to victory. Thus, the measure of success became the body count, the number of North Vietnamese and Vietcong corpses found after battle. But counts were manipulated by officers eager to demonstrate an operation's success. Worse, the U.S. reliance on massive military technology—including carpet bombing, napalm (jellied gasoline), and crop defoliants that destroyed forests—alienated many South Vietnamese and brought new recruits to the Vietcong.

Divisions at Home

As television coverage brought the war—its body bags, burned villages, and weeping refugees—into U.S. homes nightly, the number of opponents grew. College professors and students organized debates and lectures on U.S. policy, which became a form of protest, called teach-ins after the sit-ins of the civil rights movement. Pacifist groups, such as the American Friends Service Committee and the Women's International League for Peace and Freedom, organized early protests.

In early 1966 Senator William Fulbright held televised hearings on whether the national interest was served by pursuing the war. To the surprise of some, George F. Kennan testified that his containment doctrine was meant for Europe, not volatile Southeast Asia. The United States's preoccupation with Vietnam, Kennan asserted,

Handwritten margin notes:
stalemate
Attrition → Victory
body count = success
counts manipulated by officers
reliant on military technology
civilian opposition grew
teach-ins — debates / lectures on US policy/protest.
Pacifist groups organized protests

was undermining its global obligations. The Fulbright hearings provoked Americans to think about the conflict and the nation's role in it and revealed deep divisions on Vietnam among public officials.

Defense secretary Robert McNamara, who championed the Americanization of the war in 1965, became increasingly troubled by the killing and destructiveness of the bombing. In November 1965 he expressed skepticism that victory could ever be achieved. U.S. credibility was suffering grievous damage, McNamara feared. But Johnson was determined to prevail in Vietnam. Although he occasionally halted the bombing to encourage Ho Chi Minh to negotiate, such pauses often were accompanied by increases in U.S. troop strength. Hanoi demanded suspension of bombing raids before negotiating. And Ho rejected U.S. terms, which amounted to abandonment of his lifelong dream of an independent, unified Vietnam.

A NATION DIVIDED

As Johnson struggled in Vietnam, his Great Society faced challenges at home. The United States was fracturing not only over Vietnam but also along many different lines: black and white, youth and age, radical and conservative.

Urban Unrest

In 1964, shortly after President Johnson signed the landmark Civil Rights Act, racial violence erupted in northern cities. Angry residents of Harlem took to the streets after a white police officer shot an African American teenager. The following summer, in the predominantly African American Watts section of Los Angeles, crowds burned, looted, and battled police for five days. The riot, which began when a white police officer attempted to arrest an African American resident on suspicion of drunken driving, left thirty-four dead. In July 1967, twenty-six people were killed in street battles between African Americans and police and army troops in Newark, New Jersey. A week later, in Detroit, forty-three died as 3 square miles of the city went up in flames. In 1967 alone, there were 167 violent outbreaks in 128 cities.

The long, hot summers of urban unrest differed from previous race riots, which were typically started by whites. Here, African American residents exploded in anger and frustration over the conditions of their lives. They looted and burned stores, most of them white-owned, while also devastating their own neighborhoods.

In 1968 the National Advisory Commission on Civil Disorders, chaired by Governor Otto Kerner of Illinois, warned that the United States was "moving towards two societies, one white, one black—separate and unequal" and blamed white racism for the riots. "What white Americans have never fully understood—but what the Negro can never forget—is that white society is deeply implicated in the ghetto. White institutions created it, white institutions maintain it, and white society condones it," concluded the Kerner Commission. Some white Americans disagreed, while others wondered why African Americans were venting their frustration just when they were making real progress in civil rights.

The answer stemmed partly from regional differences. The civil rights movement focused mostly on fighting *legal* disenfranchisement and discrimination in the South and largely ignored problems in the North. Increasingly concentrated in the deteriorating inner-city ghettos, most northern African Americans faced discrimination in housing, credit, and employment. The median income of northern African Americans was roughly half that of northern whites, and their unemployment rate was twice as high. Many northern African Americans had given up on the civil rights movement and the Great Society.

Black Power

In this climate, a new voice urged African Americans to seize freedom "by any means necessary." Malcolm X, a onetime pimp and street hustler who converted in prison to the Nation of Islam faith, offered African Americans new leadership. Members of the Nation of Islam, known as Black Muslims, espoused black pride and separatism from white society. Their faith combined traditional Islam with a belief that whites were subhuman devils whose race would soon be destroyed and emphasized sobriety, thrift, and social responsibility. By the early 1960s, Malcolm X had become the Black Muslims' chief spokesperson. But his murder in 1965 by members of the Nation of Islam who felt betrayed when he started his own, more racially tolerant organization, transformed Malcolm X into a powerful symbol of black defiance and self-respect.

A year after Malcolm X's death, Stokely Carmichael, SNCC chairman, denounced "the betrayal of black dreams by white America." To end white oppression, Carmichael proclaimed, blacks had to "stand up and take over" by electing black candidates and organizing their own schools and institutions to embrace Black Power. That year, SNCC expelled its white members and repudiated nonviolence and integration. CORE followed in 1967.

The best-known black radicals were the Black Panthers, an organization formed in Oakland, California, in 1966. Blending black separatism and revolutionary communism, the Panthers focused on destroying capitalism and its "military arm," the police. Male Panthers dressed in commando gear, carried weapons, and talked about killing "pigs" and did kill eleven police officers by 1970. Police responded in kind; most infamously, Chicago police murdered the local Panther leader Fred Hampton in his bed. However, the Panthers also worked to improve life in their neighborhoods by instituting free breakfast and healthcare programs for ghetto children, offering courses in African American history, and demanding jobs and housing. Before the end of the decade, a vocal minority of the United States's young would join in calls for revolution.

Youth and Politics

By the mid-1960s, 41 percent of the U.S. population was under the age of twenty. These young people spent more time with peers than any previous generation, as three-quarters of them graduated from high school (up from one-fifth in the 1920s) and almost half of them went to college (up from 16 percent in 1940). As this large baby-boom generation came of age, many believed they must provide democratic leadership for their nation. Inspired by the sit-in movement at African American colleges, some white college students—from both political left and right—committed themselves to changing the system.

In fall 1960, a group of conservative college students met at William F. Buckley's estate in Sharon, Connecticut, to form Young Americans for Freedom (YAF). Their manifesto, the Sharon Statement, endorsed Cold War anticommunism and a vision of limited government directly opposed to New Deal liberalism. The YAF planned to capture the Republican Party and move it to the political right; Goldwater's selection as the Republican candidate for president in 1964 demonstrated their early success.

At the other end of the political spectrum, an emerging New Left also rejected liberalism. Whereas conservatives believed liberalism's activist government encroached on individual liberty, the New Left believed that liberalism was not enough to bring equality to all Americans. Meeting in Port Huron, Michigan, in 1962, founding members of Students for a Democratic Society (SDS) drafted their Port Huron Statement, condemning racism, poverty in the midst of plenty, and the Cold War. Calling for participatory democracy, SDS sought to wrest power from the corporations, the military, and the politicians and return it to the people.

Free Speech Movement The rise of activist white youth crystallized at the University of California, Berkeley. In the fall of 1964, the university administration banned political activity—including recruiting volunteers for civil rights work in Mississippi—from its traditional place along a university-owned sidewalk bordering the campus. When police tried to arrest a CORE worker who defied the order, four thousand students surrounded the police car. Berkeley graduate student and Mississippi Freedom Summer veteran Mario Savio encouraged the students: "You've got to put your bodies upon the levers . . . [and] you've got to indicate to the people who run it, to the people who own it, that unless you're free, the machine will be prevented from working at all."

Student political groups, left and right, united to create the Free Speech Movement (FSM). The FSM won back the right to political speech, but not before state police arrested almost eight hundred student protesters. Many saw the administration's actions as a failure of the United States's democratic promises, but the FSM's victory also demonstrated to students their potential power. By decade's end, the activism born at Berkeley would spread to hundreds of colleges and universities.

Student Activism Student protesters sought greater control over their education, demanding more relevant class offerings, more freedom in course selection, and a greater voice in the running of universities. Students protested against the doctrine of in loco parentis, which put universities legally "in the place of parents," allowing control over student behavior that went beyond the law. In loco parentis fell heaviest on women, who had strict curfew regulations called parietals, while men did not. Along with an end to sex discrimination, protesters like those at the University of Kansas wanted administrators to explain how statements that "college students are assumed to have maturity of judgment necessary for adult responsibility" squared with the minute regulation of students' nonacademic lives. One young man complained that "a high school dropout selling cabbage in a supermarket" had more rights and freedoms than successful university students.

Youth and the War in Vietnam It was the war in Vietnam, however, that mobilized a nationwide student movement. Believing that learning and speaking out about issues was their civic duty, in 1965 university students and faculty held teach-ins about U.S. involvement in Vietnam.

SDS sponsored the first major antiwar march that year, drawing twenty thousand protesters to Washington, D.C. On campuses everywhere, students borrowed civil rights movement tactics, picketing ROTC buildings and protesting military research and recruiting done on their campuses. Despite the antiwar protests visibility, most students did not yet oppose the war: in 1967, only 30 percent of male students were doves on Vietnam, while 67 percent were hawks. But as the war escalated, more students distrusted the government as well as the seemingly arbitrary authority of university administrations.

Youth Culture and the Counterculture

The large baby-boom generation changed the nation's culture more than its politics. Although many protested the war and marched for social justice, most did not. Fraternity and sorority life stayed strong even as radicalism flourished. And although there was some crossover, African American, white, and Hispanic American youth had different cultural styles, clothes, and music. Nonetheless, as potential consumers, young people exercised tremendous cultural authority and drove American popular culture in the late 1960s.

The most unifying element of youth culture was music. The Beatles electrified U.S. teenagers; 73 million viewers watched their first television appearance on the *Ed Sullivan Show* in 1964. Bob Dylan promised revolutionary answers in "Blowin' in the Wind," Janis Joplin brought the sexual power of the blues to white youth. James Brown and Aretha Franklin proclaimed black pride, and the psychedelic rock of Jefferson Airplane and the Grateful Dead—along with hallucinogenic drugs—redefined reality. At the Woodstock Festival in upstate New York in 1969, more than 400,000 people reveled in music and a world of their own making, living in rain and mud for four days without shelter or violence.

Some hoped to turn youth rebellion into social revolution, rejecting what they saw as hypocritical middle-class values. They crafted an alternative way of life, or counterculture, liberated from competitive materialism and celebrating pleasure. "Sex, drugs, and rock 'n' roll" became a mantra of sorts, offering these hippies a path to a new consciousness. Many did the hard work of creating communes and intentional communities, whether in cities or in hidden stretches of the rural United States. Although the New Left criticized the counterculture as apolitical, many hippies did envision revolutionary change through mind-altering drugs, sex, or music.

The nascent counterculture first entered the national consciousness during summer 1967, when tens of thousands poured into the Haight-Ashbury district of San Francisco, the heart of the United States's psychedelic culture, for the summer of love. As an older generation of "straight" (or establishment) Americans watched with horror, white youth looked like the counterculture. Coats and ties disappeared, as did stockings and bras. Young men grew long hair, and parents complained, "You can't tell the boys from the girls." Millions used marijuana or hallucinogenic drugs, read underground newspapers, and thought of themselves as alienated from straight culture even though as high school or college students, they were not completely dropping out.

Some of the most lasting cultural changes involved attitudes about sex. The mass media were fascinated with free love, and while some youth embraced promiscuous sexuality, it was most important that premarital sex no longer destroyed a

Hippies rejected middle-class culture/materialism

...dified cultural norms

The British Invasion

The British invasion began in earnest on February 7, 1964. Three thousand screaming American teenagers were waiting when Pan Am's *Yankee Clipper* touched down at Kennedy Airport with four British "moptops" aboard. "I Want to Hold Your Hand" was at the top of the U.S. charts, and seventy-three million people—the largest television audience in history—watched the Beatles on the *Ed Sullivan Show* the following Sunday night.

Although the Beatles led the invasion, they did not conquer the United States alone. The Rolling Stones' first U.S. hit single also came in 1964. The Dave Clark Five appeared on *Ed Sullivan* eighteen times. And there were many others: Herman's Hermits, the Animals, the Yardbirds, the Hollies, the Kinks, and Petula Clark.

The British invasion was, at least partly, the triumphal return of American music, a transatlantic exchange that reinvigorated both nations. American rock 'n' roll had lost much of its energy by the early 1960s, and the London-centered popular music industry was pumping out a saccharine version of American pop. But by the late 1950s, young musicians in England's provincial cities were listening to the music of the African American bluesmen Muddy Waters and Howlin' Wolf and the early rock 'n' roll of Buddy Holly and Chuck Berry. None of this music had a large following in the United States, where *Billboard* magazine's number one hit for 1960 was Percy Faith's "Theme from *A Summer Place*" (a movie starring Sandra Dee and Troy Donahue).

Young British musicians, including John Lennon, Eric Clapton, and Mick Jagger, re-created American musical forms and reinvented rock 'n' roll. By the mid-1960s, the British invasion bands were at the heart of a youth culture that transcended the boundaries of nations. This music connected Britain and America as well as young people throughout the world.

The Beatles perform on the *Ed Sullivan Show* in February 1964. Although Britain's Queen Mother thought the Beatles "young, fresh, and vital," U.S. parents were appalled when the long Beatles haircut swept the nation.
(AP Images)

woman's reputation. The birth-control pill, widely available to single women by the late 1960s, greatly lessened the risk of unplanned pregnancy, and venereal diseases were easily cured by a course of antibiotics. The number of couples living together increased 900 percent from 1960 to 1970. While many young people no longer tried to hide that they were sexually active, 68 percent of adults disapproved of premarital sex in 1969. The adult generation that grew up in the hard decades of depression and war and saw middle-class respectability as crucial to success and stability did not understand how promising young people could risk their futures by having sex without marriage, taking drugs, or protesting the war in Vietnam.

1968

By 1968, it seemed that the nation was coming apart. Divided over the war in Vietnam, frustrated by the slow pace of social change, or angry about racial violence, Americans faced the most serious domestic crisis of the postwar era.

The Tet Offensive

On January 31, 1968, the first day of the Vietnamese New Year (Tet), Vietcong and North Vietnamese forces struck South Vietnam, capturing provincial capitals (see Map 30.1). During the carefully planned offensive, the Saigon airport, the presidential palace, and the ARVN headquarters were attacked. The U.S. embassy was occupied by Vietcong soldiers for six hours. U.S. and South Vietnamese units eventually regained ground, inflicting heavy casualties and devastating villages.

Although the Tet Offensive was not the resounding battlefield victory its strategists sought, the heavy fighting called into question U.S. military leaders' predictions that the war would soon be won. Had not the Vietcong and North Vietnamese demonstrated that they could strike when and where they wished? If the United States's airpower, dollars, and half a million troops could not now defeat the Vietcong, could they ever do so? Top presidential advisers sounded notes of despair. Clark Clifford, the new secretary of defense, told Johnson the war could not be won, even with the 206,000 additional soldiers Westmoreland requested. Aware that the nation was suffering a financial crisis prompted by rampant deficit spending, Johnson's advisors knew that taking the initiative in Vietnam would cost billions more, further derail the budget, panic foreign owners of dollars, and wreck the economy.

Johnson's Exit

Controversy over the war split the Democratic Party, just as a presidential election loomed in November. Senator Eugene McCarthy of Minnesota and Robert F. Kennedy (now a senator from New York), both strong opponents of Johnson's war policies, forcefully challenged the president in early primaries. During a March 31 television address Johnson announced a halt to most of the bombing, asked Hanoi to negotiate, and stunned his listeners by withdrawing from the presidential race. His presidency had become a casualty of the war. Peace talks began in May in Paris, but the war ground on.

Assassinations

Days after Johnson's shocking announcement, Martin Luther King Jr. was murdered in Memphis. It remains unclear why James Earl Ray, a white forty-year-old drifter and petty criminal, shot King or whether he acted alone. By 1968 King, the senior states-man of the civil rights movement, was an outspoken critic of the Vietnam War and of U.S. capitalism. Most Americans mourned his death, and African American rage and grief exploded in 130 cities. The violence provoked a backlash from whites—primarily urban, working-class people who were had no sympathy for African Americans' increasing demands. In Chicago, Mayor Richard Daley ordered police to shoot rioters.

An already shaken nation watched in disbelief only two months later when the antiwar Democratic presidential candidate Robert Kennedy was shot and killed after winning the California primary. His assassin, Sirhan Sirhan, an Arab nationalist, tar-geted Kennedy because he supported Israel.

Chicago Democratic National Convention

Violence erupted again in August at the Democratic National Convention in Chicago. Thousands of protesters converged on the city: students who'd gone Clean for Gene, cutting long hair and donning "respectable" clothes to campaign for antiwar candidate Eugene McCarthy; members of the United States's counterculture, drawn by the anarchist Yippies' promise of a Festival of Life to counter the Convention of Death; and antiwar groups. Mayor Daley assigned twelve thousand police to twelve-hour shifts and had twelve thousand army troops with bazookas, rifles, and flamethrowers as backup. Police attacked peaceful antiwar protesters and journal-ists. "The whole world is watching," chanted protesters, as police beat people.

Global Protest

Upheavals spread around the world that spring and sum-mer. In France, university students protested rigid aca-demic policies and the Vietnam War. They received support from French workers, who occupied factories and paralyzed public transport; the turmoil contributed to the collapse of Charles de Gaulle's government the following year. In Italy, Germany, England, Ireland, Sweden, Canada, Mexico, Chile, Japan, and South Korea, students held similar protest. In Czechoslovakia, hundreds of thou-sands of demonstrators flooded Prague streets, demanding democracy and an end to Soviet repression. This so-called Prague Spring developed into a full-scale national rebellion before being crushed by Soviet tanks.

Why so many uprisings occurred simultaneously is unclear. The postwar baby boom produced by the late 1960s a huge mass of young adults, many who grew up in relative prosperity with high expectations for the future. Technological advances allowed the nearly instantaneous transmittal of televised images worldwide, so protests in one country could readily inspire similar actions in others.

Nixon's Election

The 1968 presidential election did not heal the nation. The Democratic nominee Hubert Humphrey, Johnson's vice president, seemed a continuation of old politics. The Republican candidate Richard Nixon appealed to those tired of social unrest. He reached out to those he called "the great, quite forgotten majority—the nonshouters and the nondemonstrators." On Vietnam, Nixon vowed he would "end the war and win the peace." Governor George Wallace of Alabama, a segregationist who proposed using nuclear weapons on Vietnam, ran as a third-party candidate. Wallace carried

The Immigration Act of 1965

When President Johnson signed the 1965 Immigration Act in a ceremony at the Statue of Liberty, he believed its importance was that it "repair[ed] a very deep and painful flaw in the fabric of American justice" by ending national-origins quotas that all but excluded "Polynesians, orientals, and Negroes." Nevertheless, the president mistakenly saw it as primarily symbolic. In fact, this act may have had greater long-term impact on Americans than any other Great Society legislation.

The 1965 Immigration Act ended blatant discrimination against potential immigrants from Asia, Africa, and Third World nations by substituting Eastern and Western Hemispheric caps for national quotas and allowing family reunification. The architects of the Immigration Act did not expect immigration to change, but world events decreed otherwise. Political instability along with rapidly growing populations in many poorer nations, created a large pool of potential immigrants drawn by U.S. prosperity.

Immigration rates skyrocketed, and by the 1990s, immigration accounted for almost 60 percent of the United States's population growth. By 2000, more Americans were foreign-born than at any time since the 1930s. The majority came from Mexico, the Philippines, Vietnam, China, the Dominican Republic, Korea, India, the Soviet Union, Jamaica, and Iran.

More than two-thirds of the new immigrants settled in six states—New York, California, Florida, New Jersey, Illinois, and Texas. By the late twentieth century, Spanish-language signs appeared in South Carolina, and Hmong farmers from the mountains of southeast Asia offered their produce at the farmers' market in Missoula, Montana. The legacy of the 1965 Immigration Act was unintended but profound: the Unites States is much more diverse than it otherwise would have been.

five southern states, drawing almost 14 percent of the popular vote, and Nixon was elected with the slimmest of margins.

On Christmas Eve 1968, *Apollo 8* entered lunar orbit. Looking down on a troubled world, the astronauts broadcast photographs of a fragile blue orb floating in darkness and read aloud the opening passages of Genesis, "In the beginning, God created the heaven and the earth . . . and God saw that it was good." Many listeners found themselves in tears.

Apollo 8 in orbit

Summary

The 1960s began with high hopes for a more democratic United States. Civil rights volunteers, often risking their lives, carried the quest for racial equality across the nation. The 1964 Civil Rights Act and the 1965 Voting Rights Act were major milestones. The United States was shaken by the assassination of President John Kennedy in 1963, but under President Johnson, the liberal vision of government working to improve citizens' lives inspired legislation designed to create a Great Society.

The Cold War between the United States and the Soviet Union intensified during the 1960s, and a nuclear war nearly happened in the 1962 Cuban missile crisis. Determined not to let Vietnam fall to communists, the United States sent military forces to prevent the victory of communist Vietnamese nationalists led by Ho Chi Minh. By 1968 there were more than half a million U.S. ground troops in Vietnam, which divided the United States at home, undermined Great Society domestic programs, and destroyed Lyndon Johnson's presidency.

Despite civil rights gains, many African Americans turned away from the movement, seeking more immediate change. Poor African American neighborhoods burned as riots spread through the nation. Vocal young people and some of their elders questioned whether democracy truly existed in the United States. Large numbers of the nation's white youth rebelled by embracing a counterculture that rejected white middle-class respectability. 1968 was a year of crisis, assassinations, and violence in the streets. The decade that started with promise ended in fierce political polarization.

Chapter Review

KENNEDY AND THE COLD WAR

How was the Cuban missile crisis a watershed in U.S.–Soviet relations?

Like his predecessors and his Soviet counterpart, President Kennedy wanted to win the Cold War. As such, he and Soviet leader Nikita Khrushchev disagreed over preconditions for peace and ultimately escalated (rather than controlled) nuclear arms production. Concerns about Khrushchev's relationships in Cuba tipped the balance toward war first in 1961 when Kennedy initiated a failed attempt in the Bay of Pigs to establish a U.S. beachhead in Cuba and spark an uprising. But in 1963 when the Soviets placed nuclear missiles in Cuba, just 90 miles from the Florida coast, these Cold War rivals were on the brink of a nuclear disaster. While Kennedy's steady handling eventually led the Soviets to remove the missiles, the event forced both leaders to take important small steps toward improving their relationship and operating with greater trust. In August 1963, they signed a treaty banning nuclear tests in the atmosphere, oceans, and outer space.

MARCHING FOR FREEDOM

What was Kennedy's reaction to growing civil rights activism?

President Kennedy was sympathetic to civil rights and recognized that U.S. racism damaged the nation's international reputation. But he also worried about alienating southern white Democrats in Congress. He initially thwarted civil rights by appointing segregationist judges to federal courts in the Deep South and held off an executive order forbidding segregation in federally subsidized housing. He also permitted the FBI to harass civil rights leaders—Martin Luther King Jr. in particular—with wiretaps, surveillance, and efforts to damage their reputations. But increasing grass roots activism in the form of sit-ins, the Freedom Rides, Freedom Summer, and the Montgomery Bus Boycott forced Kennedy to finally and formally support civil rights. He not only ordered U.S. marshals to protect James Meredith, the first African American to attend the University of Mississippi, but in 1963, he asked Congress to pass a comprehensive civil rights bill.

How did the protest in Birmingham make civil rights a priority for Kennedy?

Before Martin Luther King Jr. organized the 1963 protest against racism in Birmingham, Alabama, President Kennedy took a lukewarm position on civil rights. He thought the cause of equality was worthwhile, but did not want to alienate southern white voters. Then, in 1963, civil rights leader Martin Luther King Jr. and the SCLC planned a nonviolent campaign in one of the nation's most violently racist cities, Birmingham, Alabama, hoping to give Americans a true picture of the face of racial hatred. What made this protest different was that King and African American parents put young black children on the front lines of the march. When the children were mowed down by police using high-force water guns, the nation watched in horror on TV. From that point on, civil rights moved to the top of Kennedy's agenda, and he asked Congress to pass a comprehensive bill ending racial discrimination.

LIBERALISM AND THE GREAT SOCIETY

What made the War on Poverty controversial?

As part of his Great Society programs, President Johnson believed he could use the nation's prosperity to end poverty once and for all. War on Poverty programs included public housing and subsidized rents, Medicare and Medicaid, Food Stamps, Head Start, Job Corps, and Community Action Programs to involve the poor in creating antipoverty efforts. While a noble idea, the War on Poverty triggered intense reactions on both sides of the political spectrum. Those on the left felt the government had treated the surface-level problems resulting from poverty, without analyzing poverty's causes or addressing the structural inequalities that caused it in the first place. Those on the right feared the programs would create dependency rather than inspire initiative among the poor. Analysts, too, thought many of the programs were poorly implemented.

JOHNSON AND VIETNAM

How did the war in Vietnam become Americanized?

Two factors transformed the conflict in Vietnam from a civil war between the North and South into an American war against communism. First, Johnson dramatically expanded the number of U.S. troops from 180,000 to 385,000 in 1966 and 536,100 by 1968. Second, in 1965, Johnson responded to Vietcong attacks on American installations in South Vietnam with Operation Rolling Thunder, a bombing program that lasted for three years. As the U.S. presence grew, so did the response from North Vietnam, as well as assistance to that country from the Soviet Union and China.

A NATION DIVIDED

How did disillusionment with civil rights and the Great Society fuel political unrest in the sixties?

By the mid-1960s, a new breed of activist emerged, less willing to embrace the nonviolent, integrationist agenda of the past. Many northern blacks saw both civil rights and the Great Society as failing to eradicate inequality, especially with their unemployment rates for African Americans that were double that of whites while blacks', incomes were nearly half. Instead, these new African American leaders—among them Malcolm X, and later Stokely Carmichael and the Black Panthers—urged African Americans to seize freedom, expelled white members from civil rights organizations, and repudiated nonviolence and integration. At the same time, 41 percent of the population was under age twenty, and many young people, inspired by sit-ins and civil rights, wanted to change their country. This in turn fueled student movements on college campuses nationwide, among them the free speech movement, antiwar movement, and Students for a Democratic Society. By 1967, a youth counterculture emerged first in the Haight-Ashbury district of San Francisco, seeking to replace middle-class materialism with free love and a higher consciousness achieved through music and mind-altering drugs.

1968

What made 1968 unique?

Around the world, 1968 was a year of violent protest and political disillusionment. The heavy fighting during the Tet Offensive in Vietnam not only had leaders seriously doubting whether the war could be won quickly, but it also sparked antiwar protests. Two national leaders—Martin Luther King and Robert Kennedy—were assassinated, dousing the hopes held by African Americans, political activists, and young voters for a different, more progressive America. Protests at the Democratic National Convention in Chicago turned violent, as police and army troops attacked peaceful antiwar protesters and journalists. In France, students protested the war and rigid school policies, supported by workers who occupied factories and shut down public transportation. Within a year, similar student rebellions occurred in Italy, Germany, England, Ireland, Sweden, Canada, Mexico, Chile, Japan, and South Korea, while in Prague, Czechoslovakia, protesters democracy and an end to Soviet repression.

SUGGESTIONS FOR FURTHER READING

Beth Bailey, *Sex in the Heartland* (1999)

Lawrence Freedman, *Kennedy's Wars: Berlin, Cuba, Laos, and Vietnam* (2000)

David Farber, *Chicago '68* (1988)

George C. Herring, *LBJ and Vietnam: A Different Kind of War* (1994)

Michael Kazin and Maurice Isserman, *America Divided: The Civil War of the 1960s* (1999)

Fredrik Logevall, *Choosing War: The Lost Chance for Peace and the Escalation of War in Vietnam* (1999)

Lisa McGirr, *Suburban Warriors: The Origins of the New American Right* (2001)

Charles Payne, *I've Got the Light of Freedom: The Organizing Tradition and the Mississippi Freedom Struggle* (1995)

Continuing Divisions and New Limits

In 1969 Daniel Ellsberg was a thirty-eight-year-old former aide to Assistant Secretary of Defense John McNaughton. At the Pentagon, Ellsberg worked on a top-secret study of U.S. decision making in Vietnam. When he left office after Richard Nixon's election, he accessed a copy of the study stored at the Rand Corporation, where he would resume his pre-government research career. He spent the next six months poring over the seven thousand pages that made up the Pentagon Papers.

Initially supportive of U.S. military intervention in Vietnam, Ellsberg had grown disillusioned. A Harvard-trained Ph.D., former marine officer, and Cold Warrior, he spent from 1965 to 1967 in South Vietnam, assessing the war's progress for Washington. He had gone on combat patrols and interviewed military officials, U.S. diplomats, and Vietnamese leaders. The war, he concluded, was in military, political, moral respects a lost enterprise.

Loyal to the president, Ellsberg was initially reluctant to act on that conviction. But when in 1969 it became clear that Nixon had no intention of ending the war, Ellsberg boldly decided to risk imprisonment by making the Pentagon Papers public. The study, he believed, showed that presidents had escalated the United States's commitment in Vietnam despite pessimistic estimates from their advisers and that they had repeatedly lied to the public about their actions and the results. Ellsberg hoped disclosing this information would generate sufficient uproar to force a dramatic policy change.

Aided by a Rand colleague, Ellsberg surreptitiously photocopied the study, then spent months pleading with antiwar senators and representatives to release it. When they refused, he went to the press. On June 13, 1971, the *New York Times* published a front-page article on the Pentagon Papers. Other newspapers soon published excerpts as well.

This icon will direct you to interactive activities and study materials on A People And A Nation, Brief Edition
website: **www.cengage.com/history/norton/peoplenationbrief8e**

Chronology

1969	Stonewall Inn uprising begins gay liberation movement.		OPEC increases oil prices, creating U.S. energy crisis.
	Apollo 11 Astronaut Neil Armstrong becomes first person to walk on moon's surface.		*Roe v. Wade* legalizes abortion.
			Agnew resigns; Ford is named vice president.
	National Chicano Liberation Youth Conference is held in Denver.	**1974**	Nixon resigns under threat of impeachment; Ford becomes president.
	Indians of All Tribes occupy Alcatraz Island.	**1975**	In deepening economic recession, unemployment hits 8.5 percent.
	Nixon administration begins affirmative-action plan.		New York City is saved from bankruptcy by federal loan guarantees.
1970	United States invades Cambodia.		Congress passes Indian Self-Determination and Education Assistance Act in response to Native American activists.
	Students at Kent State and Jackson State Universities shot by National Guard troops.		
	First Earth Day is celebrated.	**1976**	Carter is elected president.
	Environmental Protection Agency is created.	**1978**	*Regents of the University of California v. Bakke* outlaws quotas but upholds affirmative action.
1971	Pentagon Papers are published.		
1972	Nixon visits China and Soviet Union.		California voters approve Proposition 13.
	CREEP stages Watergate break-in.	**1979**	Three Mile Island nuclear accident raises fears.
	Congress approves ERA and passes Title IX, which creates growth in women's athletics.		Camp David accords signed by Israel and Egypt.
1973	Peace agreement in Paris ends U.S. involvement in Vietnam.		American hostages are seized in Iran.
			Soviet Union invades Afghanistan.
			Consumer debt doubles from 1975 to hit $315 billion.

Ellsberg's leak became controversial. Nixon tried to stop the papers' publication—the first efforts to muzzle the press since the American Revolution—and to discredit Ellsberg and deter other leakers through the illegal actions of petty operatives. Many saw Ellsberg as a hero who acted to shorten an illegitimate war. To others, he was a publicity-seeking traitor.

The 1970s would be, for Americans, a decade of division and an age of limits. The chaos of 1968 continued in Nixon's early presidency. Antiwar opposition became more extreme, and, as government deceptions were exposed, Americans were increasingly divided over Vietnam. The movements for racial equality and social justice also became more radical by the early 1970s. Although some continued to work for racial integration, many embraced cultural nationalism, which sought separatist cultures and societies. Even the women's movement, the strongest social movement of the 1970s, had a polarizing effect. Opponents, many of them women, understood feminism as an attack on their way of life and mobilized a conservative grassroots movement that would gain political importance in subsequent decades.

This divided United States faced great challenges abroad. Richard Nixon and his national security adviser, Henry Kissinger, understood that the United States and the Soviet Union, weakened by the costs of their competition and challenged by other nations, faced a world where power was diffused. Accordingly, Nixon and Kissinger sought improved relations with the People's Republic of China and the Soviet Union to maintain world order.

Ultimately, Richard Nixon's illegal acts in the political scandal known as Watergate shook the faith of Americans. By the time Nixon, under threat of impeachment, resigned, Americans were cynical about politics. Neither of Nixon's successors, Gerald Ford or Jimmy Carter could restore that lost faith. Carter's presidency was undermined by international events beyond his control. In the Middle East—a region of increasing importance in U.S. foreign policy—Carter helped broker peace between Egypt and Israel but proved powerless to end a lengthy hostage crisis in Iran. Meanwhile, the Soviet invasion of Afghanistan in 1979 revived Cold War tensions.

A deepening economic crisis added to Carter's woes. In the 1970s, middle-class Americans saw their savings disappear to double-digit inflation, and unemployment skyrocketed. The downturn was largely caused by changes in the global economy and international trade, worsened by the oil embargo launched by Arab members of the Organization of Petroleum Exporting Countries in 1973. Americans realized their vulnerability to decisions made in far-off lands.

- How did U.S. foreign policy change as a result of involvement in Vietnam?
- Why did Americans see this era as an age of limits?
- Some historians describe the period between 1968 and 1980 as a time when many Americans lost faith—in their government, in the possibility of joining together in a society that offered equality to all, in the possibility of consensus instead of conflict. Do you agree, or were the struggles and divisions of this era similar to those of previous decades?

THE NEW POLITICS OF IDENTITY

By the end of the 1960s, divisions among Americans deepened. The civil rights movement, begun in a quest for equal rights and integration, splintered, as many young African Americans, rejected integration in favor of separatism and embraced a distinct African American culture. Mexican Americans and Native Americans, inspired by the civil rights movement, created powerful Brown Power and Red Power movements by the early 1970s. They too demanded equal rights and cultural recognition. These movements fueled a new identity politics, which saw group identity as the basis for political action and argued that social policy should be based on the needs not of individuals but of different identity-based groups.

African American Cultural Nationalism   By 1970, most African American activists no longer sought political power and racial justice by emphasizing the shared humanity of all people. Instead, they attracted a large following by highlighting the distinctiveness of black culture. Many African Americans, disillusioned by the racism that outlasted the end of legal segregation, believed that integration would mean subordination in a white-dominated society.

In the early 1970s, though mainstream groups such as the NAACP continued to seek equality through the courts and ballot boxes, many African Americans looked to culture for social change. Rejecting European American standards of beauty, young people let their hair grow into "naturals" and Afros. Seeking strength in their own histories, African American college students and faculty fought successfully to create black studies departments in American universities. African traditions were reclaimed or sometimes created. The new holiday, Kwanzaa, created in 1966 by Maulana Karenga, professor of black studies at California State University, Long Beach, celebrated African heritage.

Mexican American Activism

In 1970, the nation's 9 million Mexican Americans (4.3 percent of the United States's population) were concentrated in the Southwest and California. Although the federal census counted all Hispanics as white, discrimination in hiring, pay, housing, schools, and the courts was commonplace. Almost half of Mexican Americans were functionally illiterate, and in 1974, only 21 percent of Mexican American males graduated high school. Although more Mexican Americans were middle class, almost one-quarter remained below the poverty level in the 1970s.

The national Mexican American movement for social justice began with migrant farm workers. From 1965 through 1970, the labor organizers César Chávez and Dolores Huerta led migrant workers in a strike (*huelga*) against large grape growers in California's San Joaquin Valley. Chávez and the AFL-CIO–affiliated United Farm Workers (UFW) drew national attention to the working conditions of migrant laborers, who received 10 cents an hour (the minimum wage in 1965 was $1.25) and were often lodged by employers in squalid housing without running water or indoor toilets. A national consumer boycott of table grapes brought the growers to the bargaining table, and in 1970 the UFW won better wages and working conditions. The union resembled nineteenth-century Mexican *mutualistas,* or cooperative associations. Its members founded cooperative groceries, a Spanish-language newspaper, and a theater group.

Chicano Movement

During the same period, in northern New Mexico, Reies Tijerina created the Alianza Federal de Mercedes (Federal Alliance of Grants). The group wanted the return of land it claimed belonged to local *hispano* villagers, whose ancestors occupied the territory before the United States annexed it under the 1848 Treaty of Guadalupe Hidalgo. In Denver, former boxer Rudolfo "Corky" Gonzáles drew more than one thousand Mexican Americans for the National Chicano Liberation Youth Conference in 1969. They adopted a manifesto, *El Plan Espiritual de Aztlán,* condemning the "brutal 'Gringo' invasion of our territories."

These young activists called for the liberation of *La Raza* (from *La Raza de Bronze,* "the brown people") from oppressive U.S. society, not for equal rights. They also rejected a hyphenated Mexican-American identity. The "Mexican American," they explained in *El Plan Espiritual de Aztlán,* "lacks respect for his culture." Instead, they called themselves Chicanos or Chicanas—barrio slang associated with *pachucos,* the hip and sometimes criminal young men who symbolized much of what "respectable" Mexican Americans despised.

Many middle-class Mexican Americans and members of the older generations never embraced the term *Chicano* or the separatist agenda of *el movimiento.* Younger activists succeeded in introducing Chicano studies into local high school and college curricula and creating a unifying cultural identity for Mexican American youth. Politically, La Raza Unida (RUP), a Southwest-based political party, registered tens of thousands of voters and won local elections. Although never as influential as the

African American civil rights movement, the Chicano movement effectively challenged discrimination locally and created a basis for political action.

Native American Activism

Between 1968 and 1975, Native American activists forced American society to hear their demands and reform U.S. government policies toward native peoples. Young Native American activists were greatly influenced by cultural nationalist beliefs. Seeking a return to the old ways, they joined with traditionalists to challenge tribal leaders advocating assimilation.

In November 1969 a small group of activists, calling themselves Indians of All Tribes, occupied Alcatraz Island in San Francisco Bay, demanding that the land be returned to native peoples for an Indian cultural center. The protest, which lasted nineteen months and eventually involved more than four hundred people from fifty different tribes, marked the consolidation of pan-Indian activism. Before Alcatraz, protests were reservation-based and local. Although the protesters did not reclaim Alcatraz Island, they drew national attention to the growing Red Power movement. In 1972 the radical U.S. Indian Movement occupied a Bureau of Indian Affairs office in Washington, D.C., and then in 1973 a trading post in Wounded Knee, South Dakota, where U.S. Army troops massacred three hundred Sioux men, women, and children in 1890.

Meanwhile, moderate activists, working through such pan-tribal organizations as the National Congress of American Indians and the Native American Rights Fund, lobbied Congress for greater resources to govern themselves. In response, Congress and the federal courts returned millions of acres of land, and in 1975 Congress passed the Indian Self-Determination and Education Assistance Act. Still, during the 1970s and 1980s, American Indians had a higher rate of tuberculosis, alcoholism, and suicide than any other group. Nine of ten lived in substandard housing, with nearly 40 percent unemployment.

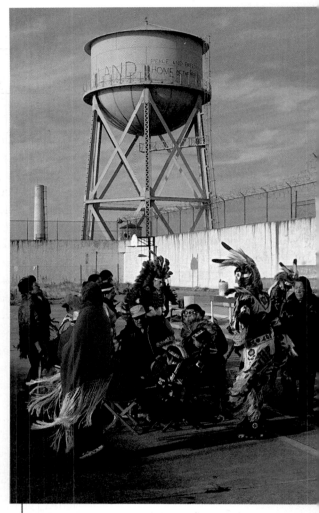

Calling their movement Red Power, these American Indian activists dance in 1969 "reclaiming" Alcatraz Island in San Francisco Bay. Arguing that an 1868 Sioux treaty entitled them to possession of unused federal lands, the group occupied the island until mid-1971. (Ralph Crane / Getty Images)

Affirmative Action

As activists made Americans aware of discrimination and inequality, policymakers struggled to frame remedies. As early as 1965, President Johnson acknowledged the limits of civil rights legislation, calling for "not just legal equality . . . but equality as a fact and equality as a result." Johnson joined his belief that the federal government must help *individuals* attain competitive skills to a new concept: equality could be measured by *group* outcomes.

Practical issues also contributed to the shift from individual opportunity to group outcomes. The 1964 Civil Rights Act outlawed discrimination but seemingly stipulated that action could be taken only when an employer "intentionally engaged" in discrimination against an individual. The tens of thousands of cases filed with the

[Handwritten margin notes: Hard to fight cases of job/education/etc. discrimination because its hard to prove it was intentional. Got job, still discrimination]

Equal Employment Opportunity Commission (EEOC) suggested a pervasive pattern of racial and sexual discrimination in education and employment, but each required proof of intentional actions against an individual. Some people argued that it was possible, instead, to prove discrimination by results—by the relative number of African Americans or women an employer hired or promoted.

In 1969 the Nixon administration implemented the first major government affirmative-action program. The Philadelphia Plan (so called because it targeted government contracts in that city) required businesses contracting with the federal government to show "affirmative action to meet the goals of increasing minority employment" and set specific numerical goals, or quotas, for employers. Affirmative action for women and racial and ethnic minorities was soon required by all major government contracts, and many corporations and educational institutions began their own programs.

[Handwritten margin note: Specific numbers/quotas of minorities for employees]

Supporters saw affirmative action as a remedy for the effects of past discrimination. Critics argued that creating proportional representation for women and minorities meant discrimination against others who had not created past discrimination and that group-based remedies violated the principle that individuals should be judged on their merits. As affirmative action affected hiring and university admissions, bringing members of underrepresented groups into college classrooms, law firms, and firehouses nationwide, a deepening recession made jobs scarce. Thus increasing the number of minorities and women hired often meant reducing the number of white men, which triggered resentment.

[Handwritten margin note: Recession   more opportunities for minorities]

THE WOMEN'S MOVEMENT AND GAY LIBERATION

During the 1960s, a second wave of the U.S. women's movement emerged, and by the 1970s, mainstream and radical activists waged a multi-front battle for women's liberation. In 1963, the popularity of Betty Friedan's *The Feminine Mystique* signaled that there was energy for a revived women's movement. Writing as a housewife and mother (though she had a long history of political activism), Friedan described "the problem with no name," the dissatisfaction of educated, middle-class wives and mothers, who—looking at their homes and families—wondered guiltily if that was all there was to life. Instead of blaming women for failing to adapt to women's proper role, as 1950s magazines often did, Friedan blamed the role itself and the society that created it.

Liberal and Radical Feminism

[Handwritten margin note: National Organization for Women (NOW) lobbyed for EEOC to hold Civil Rights Act (woman lower priority)]

The organized, liberal wing of the women's movement emerged in 1966 with the founding of the National Organization for Women (NOW). Consisting primarily of educated, professional women, NOW was a lobbying group seeking to pressure the EEOC to enforce the 1964 Civil Rights Act. With racial discrimination the EEOC's focus, sex discrimination became a low priority. By 1970, NOW had one hundred chapters with more than three thousand members nationwide.

[Handwritten margin note: Radical social justice mov. still less opportunity there]

Another strand of the women's movement developed from the nation's increasingly radical social justice movements. Many women working for civil rights or against the Vietnam War were treated as second-class citizens, making coffee, not policy. As they analyzed inequality, these women recognized women's oppression, too. In 1968 a group of women protested the "degrading mindless-boob girlie symbol" represented by the Miss America Pageant in Atlantic City. Although nothing was burned, the pejorative term for feminists, *bra-burners*, came from this event, in which women threw items of "enslavement" (girdles, high heels, curlers, and bras) into a Freedom Trashcan.

Second-wave feminism was never a single set of beliefs. Most radical feminists, however, practiced personal politics, believing that "there is no private domain of a person's life that is not political, and there is no political issue that is not ultimately personal." In the early 1970s, women meeting in suburban kitchens, college dorm rooms, and churches or synagogues, created consciousness-raising groups, where they explored topics such as power relationships in marriage, sexuality, abortion, healthcare, work, and family.

Accomplishments of the Women's Movement

During the 1970s, the women's movement claimed significant achievements: the right of a married woman to obtain credit in her own name, the right of an unmarried woman to obtain birth control, the right of women to serve on juries, the end of sex-segregated help-wanted ads. At the state and local level, they challenged understandings of rape that blamed the victim for the attack. By decade's end, activists established rape crisis centers, educated police and hospital officials about procedures for protecting survivors of rape, and changed laws.

In 1971, the Boston Women's Health Collective published *Our Bodies, Ourselves* to help women understand and take charge of their sexual and reproductive health. And women who sought the right to safe and legal abortions won a major victory in 1973 when the Supreme Court, in a 7-to-2 decision on *Roe v. Wade*, ruled that privacy rights protected a woman's choice to end a pregnancy.

Women's organizations united to revive the 1920s Equal Rights Amendment ending discrimination on the basis of sex. On March 22, 1972, Congress approved the amendment, which stated that "equality of rights under the law shall not be denied or abridged by the United States or by any State on account of sex." By the end of the year, twenty-two states (of the thirty-eight necessary to amend the Constitution) ratified the ERA. Also in 1972, Congress passed Title IX of the Higher Education Act, which barred federal funds from colleges or universities discriminating against women. Universities then began channeling money to women's athletics, and women's participation in sports boomed.

Women's applications to graduate programs also boomed. In 1970 only 8.4 percent of medical school graduates and 5.4 percent of law school graduates were women. By 1979, those figures climbed to 23 percent and 28.5 percent respectively. Colleges and universities established women's studies departments, and by 1980 more than thirty thousand college courses focused on women or gender relations. Women also increased their roles in religious organizations, and some denominations began to ordain women.

Opposition to the Women's Movement

The women's movement met with powerful opposition, much of it from women. Many had no desire to be equal if that meant giving up traditional gender roles in marriage or working at low-wage jobs. African and Hispanic American women, many of whom were active in movements for the liberation of their people and some of whom helped create second-wave feminism, often regarded feminism as a white movement that ignored their cultural traditions and diverted attention from the fight for racial equality.

Organized opposition to feminism came primarily from conservative, often religiously motivated men and women. As one conservative Christian writer claimed, "The Bible clearly states that the wife is to submit to her husband's leadership." Such beliefs, along with fears about changing gender roles, fueled the STOP-ERA movement led by Phyllis Schlafly, a lawyer and conservative political activist. Schlafly attacked the women's movement as "a total assault on the role of the American woman as wife and mother." Schlafly's group argued that the ERA would decriminalize rape, force Americans to use unisex toilets, and make women subject to the military draft.

In fighting the ERA, tens of thousands of women became politically experienced; they fed a growing grassroots conservative movement that would blossom in the 1980s. By the mid-1970s, the STOP-ERA movement stopped the Equal Rights Amendment. Despite Congress's deadline extension, the amendment fell three states short of ratification and expired in 1982.

Gay Liberation

In the early 1970s, gay men and lesbians faced widespread discrimination. Consensual same-sex sexual intercourse was illegal in almost every state, and until 1973 homosexuality was labeled a mental disorder by the American Psychiatric Association. Homosexual couples did not receive partnership benefits, such as health insurance; they could not marry or adopt children. Gay men and women remained targets of discrimination in hiring and endured public ridicule, harassment, and physical attacks.

There were small homophile organizations, such as the Mattachine Society and the Daughters of Bilitis, that worked for gay rights since the 1950s. But the symbolic beginning of the gay liberation movement came on June 28, 1969, when New York City police raided the Stonewall Inn, a gay bar in Greenwich Village, for violating a city law that made it illegal for more than three homosexual patrons to occupy a bar at the same time. That night, patrons stood up to the police, and hundreds joined them. The next morning, New Yorkers found a new slogan spray-painted on neighborhood walls: Gay Power.

Inspired by the Stonewall riot, some men and women worked openly and militantly for gay rights. They focused on a dual agenda: legal equality and the promotion of Gay Pride. Some rejected the notion of fitting into straight (heterosexual) culture and created distinctive gay communities. By 1973, there were about eight hundred gay organizations in the United States. Centered in big cities and on college campuses, most organizations created supportive environments for gay men and lesbians to come out of the closet and push for reform. By decade's end, gay men and lesbians were a political force in cities including New York, Miami, and San Francisco.

THE END IN VIETNAM

No issue divided Americans as pervasively as the Vietnam War. Although Richard Nixon said he was going to end the war fast so it would not ruin his political career as it had Johnson's, he did not. Like Johnson, he feared that a precipitous withdrawal would harm U.S. credibility on the world stage. Anxious to get U.S. troops out of Vietnam, Nixon was equally committed to preserving an independent, noncommunist South Vietnam. Hence, he adopted a policy that at once contracted and expanded the war.

Invasion of Cambodia

Nixon's policy centered on Vietnamization—building up South Vietnamese forces to replace U.S. forces. Accordingly, the president decreased U.S. troops from 543,000 in the spring of 1969 to 156,800 by the end of 1971, and to 60,000 by the fall of 1972. Vietnamization helped limit domestic dissent, but it did not end the stalemate in the Paris peace talks underway since 1968. Therefore, Nixon intensified the bombing of North Vietnam and enemy supply depots in neighboring Cambodia, hoping to pound Hanoi into concessions (see Map 30.2 on page 000).

The bombing of neutral Cambodia commenced in March 1969. For fourteen months, B-52 pilots flew 3,600 missions and dropped over 100,000 tons of bombs, initially in secret. When the North Vietnamese refused to buckle, Nixon turned up the heat: in April 1970 South Vietnamese and U.S. forces invaded Cambodia. The president announced that he would not allow "the world's most powerful nation" to act "like a pitiful, helpless giant."

Protests and Counterdemonstrations

Instantly, the antiwar movement emerged, as students on about 450 college campuses went out on strike and hundreds of thousands of demonstrators in various cities protested the administration's policies. The crisis atmosphere intensified on May 4, when National Guardsmen in Ohio fired into a crowd of fleeing students at Kent State University, killing four and wounding eleven. Ten days later, police armed with automatic weapons blasted a women's dormitory at the historic African American Jackson State University in Mississippi, killing two and wounding nine students. Police claimed they had been shot at, but no such evidence could be found. Nixon's widening of the war sparked congressional outrage, and in June the Senate terminated the 1964 Tonkin Gulf Resolution. After two months, U.S. troops withdrew from Cambodia.

Although a majority of Americans told pollsters they thought the original troop commitment to Vietnam was a mistake, 50 percent said they believed Nixon's claim that the Cambodia invasion would shorten the war, and some were angered by antiwar protests. In Washington, an Honor America Day program attracted 200,000 people who heard Billy Graham and Bob Hope laud administration policy. Nevertheless, the tumult over the invasion reduced Nixon's options on the war. Henceforth, solid majorities opposed any new missions for U.S. ground troops in Southeast Asia.

Morale Problems in Military

Equally troubling was that morale and discipline among troops was declining even before Nixon took office. There were growing reports of drug addiction, desertion, racial discord, even the murder of unpopular officers by enlisted men (called fragging). The 1971 court-martial and conviction of Lieutenant William Calley, charged with overseeing the killing of more than three hundred unarmed South Vietnamese civilians

Handwritten margin notes:
- Nixon expanded SV forces decreased US forces
- bombing - intensified when NV did not budge · supply depots
- Antiwar movement
- Kent State — National Guardsmen fired on students (killed + wounded)
- Jackson State — Police fired @ womens dorm (killing + wounding)
- Congress upset 2 months later US troops withdrew
- Many believed Nixon's tactics would shorten the war (~50%)
- Military having many morale issues

in My Lai in 1968, got particular attention when an army photographer captured the horror in graphic pictures.

Paris Peace Accords

The Nixon administration, meanwhile, stepped up its efforts to pressure Hanoi into a settlement. When the North Vietnamese launched a major offensive into South Vietnam in March 1972, Nixon responded with a massive aerial onslaught. In December 1972, after an apparent peace agreement collapsed, the United States launched another air strike on the North—the so-called Christmas bombing.

A diplomatic agreement was close, however. Months earlier, Kissinger and his North Vietnamese counterpart, Le Duc Tho, resolved many of the outstanding issues. Most notably, Kissinger agreed that North Vietnamese troops could remain in the South after the settlement, while Tho abandoned Hanoi's insistence that the Saigon government of Nguyen Van Thieu be removed. On January 27, 1973, Kissinger and Le Duc Tho signed a cease-fire agreement, and Nixon compelled a reluctant Thieu to accept it by threatening to cut off U.S. aid. The United States promised to withdraw its troops within sixty days. North Vietnamese troops could stay in South Vietnam, and a coalition government that included the Vietcong would be formed in the South.

The United States pulled its troops out of Vietnam, leaving behind some military advisers. Soon, full-scale war erupted again. Just before the South Vietnamese surrendered, hundreds of Americans and Vietnamese who had worked with the Americans were hastily evacuated from Saigon. On April 29, 1975, the South Vietnamese government collapsed, and Vietnam was reunified under a communist government in Hanoi. Saigon was renamed Ho Chi Minh City for the persevering patriot who died in 1969.

Costs of the Vietnam War

More than 58,000 Americans and between 1.5 and 2 million Vietnamese died in the war. Civilian deaths in Cambodia and Laos reached hundreds of thousands. The war cost the United States at least $170 billion, and billions more in subsequent veterans' benefits. With funds shifted from domestic programs during the war, the nation suffered inflation, political schism, and abuses of executive power. The war also delayed accommodation with the Soviet Union and the People's Republic of China, fueled friction with allies, and alienated Third World nations.

In 1975 communists established repressive governments in Vietnam, Cambodia, and Laos, but beyond Indochina the domino effect once predicted by U.S. officials never occurred. Acute hunger afflicted the people of those devastated lands. Soon refugees—boat people—crowded aboard unsafe vessels to escape. Many emigrated to the United States, where they were received with mixed feelings by Americans reluctant to be reminded of defeat and their responsibility for the plight of the southeast Asian peoples.

Debate over the Lessons of Vietnam

As the historian William Appleman Williams observed, Americans had had their overseas sphere of influence pushed back and were suffering from "empire shock."

Hawkish observers claimed that failure in Vietnam undermined the nation's credibility. They pointed to a Vietnam syndrome—an American suspicion of foreign entanglements—which they feared would inhibit the future exercise of U.S. power. The United States lost in Vietnam, they asserted, because Americans lost their guts at home.

first US loss→

Dovish analysts blamed the war on an imperial presidency that permitted strong-willed men to act without restraint and a weak Congress that conceded too much power to the executive branch. Make the president adhere to the checks-and-balances system—make him go to Congress for a declaration of war—these critics counseled. This view found expression in the War Powers Act of 1973, which limited the president's war-making freedom and required congressional approval before committing U.S. forces to combat lasting more than sixty days.

War. Powers Act
limited pres's war-making ability
required congress to approve anything
60th days

Vietnam Veterans

Veterans' calls for help in dealing with posttraumatic stress disorder, which afflicted thousands of the 2.8 million Vietnam veterans, stimulated public discussion. Doctors reported that the disorder, which included nightmares and extreme nervousness, stemmed from the soldiers' having seen many children, women, and elderly killed. Some GIs inadvertently killed these people; some killed them vengefully and later felt guilt. Other veterans publicized their deteriorating health from defoliant Agent Orange and other herbicides they had handled or were accidentally sprayed with in Vietnam.

Mental and Physical health issues
for veterans

NIXON, KISSINGER, AND THE WORLD

The difficulties of the Vietnam war signified to Nixon and Kissinger that U.S. power was limited and, in relative terms, in decline. This reality necessitated a new approach to the Cold War. In particular, they believed the United States had to adapt to a new, multipolar international system no longer defined simply by the Soviet-American rivalry. Western Europe was becoming a major player in its own right, as was Japan. The Middle East loomed increasingly large. Above all, Americans had to come to grips with China by rethinking the policy of hostile isolation.

They were an unlikely duo—the reclusive, ambitious Californian, born of Quaker parents, and the sociable, dynamic Jewish intellectual who fled Nazi Germany as a child. Nixon, ten years older, was a career politician, while Kissinger made his name as a Harvard professor and foreign policy consultant. What the two men shared was a paranoia about rivals and a capacity to think in large conceptual terms about the United States's place in the world.

Nixon Doctrine

In July 1969 Nixon and Kissinger acknowledged the limits of U.S. power and resources in the Nixon Doctrine. The United States, they said, would provide economic aid to allies, but these allies should not count on U.S. troops. Washington could no longer afford to sustain its overseas commitments and would have to rely on regional allies, including authoritarian regimes, to maintain an anticommunist world order. Nixon's doctrine partially retreated from the 1947 Truman Doctrine's promise to support noncommunist governments facing threats.

Would provide financial aid but
not troops to oversea allies
Rely on regional allies
(even regimes)

Handwritten margin notes (left column):

- check soviet expansion
- Limit soviets arms buildup
- curb revolution/radicalism in third world countries (to diminish threats of US interests)
- More trade w/ friendly Soviets/chinese

ABM treaty
- limited intercontinental missile defense

US/China thought USSR should not make gains in asia
↳ relations improved diplomatic recognition in '79

Détente

The other pillar of the new foreign policy was détente: measured cooperation with the Soviets through negotiations within an environment of rivalry. Détente's primary purpose, like that of the containment doctrine, was to check Soviet expansion and limit the Soviet arms buildup, but through diplomacy and mutual concessions. The second part of the strategy sought to curb revolution and radicalism in the Third World to quash threats to U.S. interests. More specifically, expanded trade with friendlier Soviets and Chinese might reduce the huge U.S. balance-of-payments deficit. And improving relations with both communist giants, at a time when Sino-Soviet tensions were increasing, might weaken communism.

The Soviet Union too found that the Cold War drained its resources, with defense needs and consumer demands at odds. Improved ties with Washington would allow the Soviet Union to focus on its increasingly fractious relations with China and might generate serious progress on outstanding European issues, including the status of Germany and Berlin. In May 1972 the United States and the Soviet Union agreed in the ABM Treaty to slow the arms race by limiting intercontinental ballistic missiles and antiballistic missile defenses.

Opening to China

Meanwhile, the United States took dramatic steps to end two decades of Sino-American hostility. The Chinese wanted to spur trade and hoped that friendlier Sino-American relations would make their onetime ally and now enemy, the Soviet Union, more cautious. In early 1972 Nixon made a historic trip to Red China, where he and the venerable Chinese leaders Mao Zedong and Zhou Enlai agreed to disagree on many issues, except one: the Soviet Union should not be permitted to make gains in Asia. Sino-American relations improved slightly, and official diplomatic recognition came in 1979.

The opening to communist China and the policy of détente with the Soviet Union reflected Nixon's and Kissinger's belief in the importance of maintaining stability among the great powers. In the Third World, too, Nixon and Kissinger sought stability, though there they hoped to get it by maintaining the status quo. As it happened, events in the Third World would provide the Nixon-Kissinger approach with its greatest test.

Wars in the Middle East

In the Middle East the situation grew more volatile after the Arab-Israeli Six-Day War in 1967. Israel scored victories against Egypt and Syria, seizing the Sinai Peninsula and the Gaza Strip from Egypt, the West Bank and East Jerusalem from Jordan, and the Golan Heights from Syria (see Map 33.2). Israel gained 28,000 square miles and could henceforth defend itself against invading forces. But with Gaza and the West Bank as the ancestral home to hundreds of thousands of Palestinians (see Chapter 28), Israel found itself governing people who wanted to see it destroyed. When the Israelis established Jewish settlements in their newly won areas, Arab resentment grew. Terrorists associated with the Palestinian Liberation Organization (PLO) made hit-and-run raids on Jewish settlements, hijacked jetliners, and murdered Israeli athletes at the 1972 Olympic Games in Munich, West Germany. The Israelis retaliated by assassinating PLO leaders.

OPEC and the 1973 Oil Embargo

If one date can mark the decline of U.S. power in the Cold War era and the arrival of the Arab nations of the Middle East as important players on the world stage, it would be October 20, 1973. That day, the Arab members of the Organization of Petroleum Exporting Countries (OPEC)—Saudi Arabia, Iraq, Kuwait, Libya, and Algeria—imposed an embargo on oil shipments to the United States and other Israeli allies. The move was in retaliation against U.S. support of Israel in the two-week-old Yom Kippur War. The embargo followed an OPEC price hike days earlier from $3.01 to $5.12 per barrel. In December, the five Arab countries, joined by Iran, raised prices again, to $11.65 per barrel, almost a fourfold increase from early October.

Gasoline prices surged across the United States, and some dealers ran low on supplies. Frustrated Americans endured endless lines at the pumps and shivered in underheated homes. When the embargo was lifted in April 1974, oil prices stayed high, and the aftereffects of the embargo would linger through the decade. It confirmed how much the United States's economic destiny was outside its control.

Just twenty years before, in the early 1950s, Americans produced at home all the oil they needed. By the early 1960s, the picture changed, as Americans depended on foreign sources for one out of every six barrels of oil. By 1972, the figure increased to about two out of six, or more than 30 percent. Few Americans worried, and all Americans were later shocked by the embargo. As author Daniel Yergin put it, "The shortfall struck at fundamental beliefs in the endless abundance of resources, . . . that a large part of the public did not even know, up until October 1973, that the United States imported any oil at all."

When the embargo ended, Americans resumed their wastefulness, but in a changed world. The United States had become a dependent nation, its economic future linked to decisions by Arab leaders half a world away.

In 1976 OPEC sharply raised the price of oil a second time, prompting this editorial cartoon by Don Wright of the Miami News.

(© Tribune Media Services, Inc. All Rights Reserved. Reprinted with permission)

In October 1973, on the Jewish High Holy Day of Yom Kippur, Egypt and Syria attacked Israel, primarily seeking revenge for the 1967 defeat. Surprised, Israel reeled before launching an effective counteroffensive. To punish the United States for its pro-Israel stance, the Organization of Petroleum Exporting Countries (OPEC), a group of mostly Arab nations that united to raise oil prices, embargoed oil shipments to the United States and other Israeli supporters. An energy crisis rocked the nation. Kissinger arranged a cease-fire in the war, but OPEC did not lift the oil embargo until March 1974. The next year Kissinger persuaded Egypt and Israel to accept a U.N. peacekeeping force in the Sinai. But Arabs still vowed to destroy Israel, and Israelis built more Jewish settlements in occupied lands.

Antiradicalism in Latin America and Africa

In Latin America, the Nixon administration thwarted radical leftist challenges to authoritarian rule. When voters in Chile elected a Marxist president, Salvador Allende, in 1970 the CIA secretly encouraged military officers to stage a coup. In 1973 a military junta ousted Allende and installed an authoritarian regime under General Augusto Pinochet. (Allende was subsequently murdered.) Washington publicly denied any role.

In Africa, too, Washington preferred the status quo, backing the white-minority regime in Rhodesia (now Zimbabwe) and activated the CIA in a failed effort to defeat a Soviet- and Cuban-backed faction in Angola's civil war. In South Africa, Nixon tolerated the white rulers who imposed segregationist apartheid on blacks and mixed-race "coloureds" (85 percent of the population), keeping them poor, disfranchised, and ghettoized in prisonlike townships. After the leftist government came to power in Angola, however, Washington paid attention to Africa, building economic ties and sending arms to friendly black nations, such as Kenya and the Congo, while distancing the United States from the white governments of Rhodesia and South Africa.

PRESIDENTIAL POLITICS AND THE CRISIS OF LEADERSHIP

Richard Nixon's foreign policy accomplishments were overshadowed by his domestic failures. He betrayed the public trust and broke laws. That, combined with Americans' belief that their leaders had lied repeatedly about the war in Vietnam, shook their faith in government. This new mistrust joined with conservatives' traditional suspicion of big, activist government to create a crisis of leadership and undermine liberal policies that had governed since the New Deal. Nixon's successors, Gerald Ford and Jimmy Carter, were limited by the public's suspicion of government.

Nixon's Domestic Agenda

Richard Nixon was brilliant, driven, politically cunning, yet also crude, prejudiced against Jews and African Americans, happy to use dirty tricks and presidential power against his enemies, and driven by a resentment that bordered on paranoia. The son of a grocer from an agricultural region of southern California, Nixon loathed the liberal establishment, which loathed him back, and his presidency was driven by that as much as by any strong philosophical commitment to conservative principles.

Much of Nixon's domestic policy initiatives seem liberal. The Nixon administration pioneered affirmative action. It doubled the budgets of the new National

Endowment for the Humanities (NEH) and National Endowment for the Arts (NEA). Nixon supported the ERA, signed major environmental legislation, created the Occupational Safety and Health Administration (OSHA), actively used deficit spending to manage the economy, and proposed a guaranteed minimum income for all Americans.

At the same time, Nixon pursued a conservative agenda that involved devolution, shifting federal government authority to states and localities. He promoted revenue-sharing programs that distributed federal funds back to the states, thus appealing to those who saw high taxes as supporting liberal giveaway programs for poor and minority Americans. Nixon worked to equate the Republican Party with law and order and the Democrats with permissiveness, crime, drugs, radicalism, and the hippie lifestyle. He used his outspoken vice president, Spiro Agnew, to attack war protesters and critics as "naughty children." He appointed four conservative justices to the Supreme Court: Warren Burger, Harry Blackmun, Lewis Powell Jr., and William Rehnquist.

But most of Nixon's liberal agenda was not so much liberal as it was tricky—a term commonly applied to Nixon at the time. Instead of attacking liberal programs and the entrenched government bureaucracies that administered them, he attempted to undermine them while appearing to offer support. For example, when the Nixon administration proposed a guaranteed minimum income for all Americans, his larger goal was to dismantle the federal welfare system and destroy its liberal bureaucracy of social workers.

Nixon additionally sought to attract white southerners to the Republican Party. He nominated two southerners to the Supreme Court, one of whom had a segregationist record. When Congress declined to confirm either nominee, Nixon protested angrily. After the Supreme Court upheld a school desegregation plan requiring a highly segregated North Carolina school system to achieve racial integration by busing both African American and white children throughout the county (*Swann v. Charlotte-Mecklenburg*, 1971), Nixon denounced busing.

Enemies and Dirty Tricks

Nixon was almost sure of reelection in 1972. His Democratic opponent was George McGovern, a progressive senator from South Dakota and strong opponent of the Vietnam War, who appealed to the left. Alabama governor George Wallace, running on a third-party ticket, withdrew from the race after an assassination attempt left him paralyzed. The Nixon campaign, however, took no chances. On June 17, five men from the Committee to Re-elect the President, known as CREEP, were caught breaking into the Democratic National Committee's offices at the Watergate apartment and office complex in Washington, D.C. The break-in got little attention, and Nixon was swept into office in November with 60 percent of the popular vote. McGovern carried only Massachusetts and the District of Columbia. But as Nixon triumphed, his downfall began.

From the beginning of his presidency, Nixon obsessively believed he was surrounded by enemies. He made enemies lists, hundreds of names long, that included all African American members of Congress and the presidents of most Ivy League universities. On Nixon's order, his aide Charles Colson formed a secret group called the Plumbers. Their first job was to break into the office of the psychiatrist treating

The Plumbers
- *Descrediting people*
- *Bugged phones*
- *false accusations*

Daniel Ellsberg, the former Pentagon employee who made the Pentagon Papers public, looking for material to discredit him. During the 1972 presidential campaign, the Plumbers bugged phones, infiltrated campaign staffs, and wrote anonymous letters falsely accusing Democratic candidates of sexual misconduct. They were going back to plant more surveillance equipment at the Democratic National Committee offices when they were caught by the D.C. police at the Watergate complex.

Watergate Cover-Up and Investigation

Nixon helped cover it up
- *ordered FBI to stop investigation*
  - *claimed NS*
  - *was obstruction of justice*
2 reporters followed $ trail to white house

Nixon was not directly involved in the Watergate affair. But instead of distancing himself and firing those responsible, he covered up their connection to the break-ins. He had the CIA stop the FBI's investigation, claiming national security. At this point, Nixon obstructed justice—a felony and an impeachable crime—but he also halted the investigation. However, two relatively unknown reporters for the *Washington Post,* Carl Bernstein and Bob Woodward, stayed on the story. Aided by an anonymous, highly placed government official whom they code-named Deep Throat (the title of a notorious 1972 X-rated film), they followed a money trail leading straight to the White House. (W. Mark Felt, second in command at the FBI in the early 1970s, identified himself as Watergate's Deep Throat in 2005.)

From May to August 1973, the Senate held televised hearings on the Watergate affair. White House Counsel John Dean, fearful that he was becoming the fall guy for the Watergate fiasco, gave damning testimony. On July 13, a White House aide told the Senate Committee that Nixon regularly recorded his conversations in the Oval Office. Nixon refused to turn the tapes over to Congress.

It was discovered Nixon recorded conversations in oval office
- *He refused to turn the tapes over*

Impeachment and Resignation

VP resigned on charges of accepting bribes

Nixon's staff worried about his excessive drinking

Nixon faced scandals on other fronts. In October 1973, Vice President Spiro Agnew resigned, following charges that he accepted bribes while governor of Maryland. Nixon appointed and Congress approved Michigan's Gerald Ford, the House minority leader, as Agnew's replacement. Meanwhile, Nixon's staff was increasingly concerned about his excessive drinking and seeming mental instability. Then, on October 24, 1973, the House of Representatives began impeachment proceedings.

edit tapes released
- *shock @ racist slurs / obscenities*
- *revealed nothing criminal*
other tapes released
- *grounds for impeachment*
resigned

Under court order, Nixon released edited portions of the Oval Office tapes. Although the first tapes revealed nothing criminal, the public was shocked by Nixon's obscenities and racist slurs. In July 1974, the Supreme Court ruled that Nixon must release all the tapes. Despite erasures on two key tapes, the House Judiciary Committee found evidence to impeach Nixon on three grounds: obstruction of justice, abuse of power, and contempt of Congress. On August 9, 1974, facing certain impeachment and conviction, Richard Nixon became the first president of the United States to resign.

The Watergate scandal shook Americans' confidence in government yet further and prompted Congress to pass several bills aimed at restricting presidential power, including the War Powers Act.

americans had doubts/ mistrust for/toward gov

Ford's Presidency

Gerald Ford, the nation's first unelected president, faced a cynical nation. The presidency was discredited. The economy was in decline. Ford was an honorable man who tried to end the long national nightmare. But when he issued a full pardon to Richard Nixon, his approval ratings plummeted from 71 to 41 percent. Some suggested, with no evidence, that he struck a deal with Nixon.

Ford accomplished little domestically during his two and a half years in office. The Democrats gained a large margin in the 1974 congressional elections, and after Watergate, Congress was willing to exercise its power. Ford almost routinely vetoed its bills—thirty-nine in one year— but Congress often overrode his veto. Ford was often portrayed as a buffoon and klutz in political cartoons, comedy monologues, and especially on the new hit television show *Saturday Night Live.* Ford caught the fallout of disrespect that Nixon's actions had unleashed. No longer would respect for the presidency prevent the media from reporting presidential stumbles or misconduct.

Carter as Outsider President

Jimmy Carter, who was elected in 1976 by a slim margin, initially benefited from Americans' suspicion of politicians. Carter was a one-term governor of Georgia, one of the new southern leaders committed to racial equality. He grew up on his family's peanut farm in the rural Plains, Georgia; graduated from the Naval Academy, then served as an engineer in the navy's nuclear submarine program. Carter, a born-again Christian, promised the United States, "I will never lie to you," underscoring his distance from Washington's recent political corruption.

From his inauguration, when he broke with the convention of a motorcade and walked down Pennsylvania Avenue holding hands with his wife and close adviser, Rosalynn, and their young daughter, Amy, Carter emphasized his populist, outsider appeal. But that status proved a problem as president. Though an astute policymaker, he scorned the deal making that was necessary to pass legislation in Congress.

Resigning in disgrace as impeachment for his role in the Watergate cover-up became a certainty, Richard Nixon flashed the V for victory sign as he left the White House for the last time.
(Nixon Presidential Materials Project, National Archives and Records Administration)

Carter faced problems that would have challenged any leader: continued economic decline, unabated energy shortages, and public distrust of government. More than any other postwar U.S. leader, Carter was willing to tell Americans things they did not want to hear. As shortages of natural gas forced schools and businesses to close during the bitterly cold winter of 1977, Carter, wearing a cardigan sweater, called for sacrifice and implemented energy conservation measures at government buildings. In the defining speech of his presidency, Carter told Americans that the nation suffered from a crisis of the spirit. He talked about the false lures of self-indulgence and consumption. He called for a "new commitment to the path of common purpose." But he offered few solutions for the national malaise.

Carter did ease burdensome government regulations without destroying consumer and worker safeguards and created the Departments of Energy and Education. He also established a $1.6 billion superfund to clean up abandoned chemical-waste sites and placed more than 100 million acres of Alaskan land under federal protection as national parks, forests, and wildlife refuges.

ECONOMIC CRISIS

Since World War II, except for a few brief downturns, prosperity dominated American life. Prosperity made possible the great liberal initiatives of the 1960s and improved the lives of the United States's poor and elderly. But in the early 1970s, that long period of economic expansion ended. In 1974 alone, the gross national product dropped 2 percentage points. Industrial production fell 9 percent. Inflation—the increase in costs of goods and services—skyrocketed, and unemployment grew.

Stagflation and Its Causes

Throughout most of the 1970s, the U.S. economy floundered in what economists dubbed stagflation: a stagnant economy characterized by high unemployment combined with out-of-control inflation. Stagflation was almost impossible to manage with traditional economic remedies. When the federal government increased spending to stimulate the economy and reduce unemployment, inflation grew. When it tried to control inflation by cutting government spending or tightening the money supply, the recession deepened and unemployment escalated.

The causes of the economic crisis were complex. President Johnson created inflationary pressure by waging an expensive war in Vietnam while greatly expanding domestic spending in his Great Society programs. But fundamental problems also came from the United States' changing role in the global economy. By the early 1970s, both of the United States's wartime adversaries, Japan and Germany, had become major economic powers and competitors in global trade that the United States once dominated. In 1971, for the first time since the nineteenth century, the United States imported more than it exported, beginning an era of U.S. trade deficits.

Corporate actions also contributed to the growing trade imbalance. During the years of global dominance, few U.S. companies improved production techniques or educated workers. Consequently, U.S. productivity—the average output of goods per hour of labor—declined. But wages rarely did. The combination of falling productivity and high labor costs meant that U.S. goods became increasingly expensive. Worse, U.S. companies allowed the quality of their goods to decline. From 1966 to 1973, for example, U.S. car and truck manufacturers recalled almost 30 million vehicles because of serious defects.

The United States's global economic vulnerability was driven home by the energy crisis in 1973. The country depended on imported oil for almost one-third of its energy. When OPEC cut off shipments to the United States, prices rose 350 percent and increased heating costs, shipping costs, and manufacturing costs, as well as the cost of goods and services. Inflation jumped from 3 percent in 1973 to 11 percent in 1974. Sales of gas-guzzling U.S. cars plummeted as people switched to energy-efficient subcompacts from Japan and Europe. GM laid off 6 percent of its domestic work force and put larger numbers on rolling unpaid leaves. As the ailing automobile industry quit buying steel, glass, and rubber, manufacturers of these goods laid off workers, too.

Attempts to Fix the Economy

U.S. leaders tried desperately to manage the economic crisis, but their actions often exacerbated it instead. As the United States's rising trade deficit undermined international confidence in the dollar, the Nixon administration ended the dollar's link to the gold standard; free-floating exchange rates increased the price of foreign goods in the United States and stimulated inflation. Following monetary theory, which held that, with less money available to chase the supply of goods, price increases would slow, ending the inflationary spiral, Ford curbed federal spending and encouraged the Federal Reserve Board to tighten credit, prompting the worst recession in forty years. In 1975 unemployment climbed to 8.5 percent.

many failed attempts @ fixes

Carter's larger economic policies, including his 1978 deregulation of airline, trucking, banking, and communications industries, would eventually foster economic growth, but not soon enough. After almost a decade of decline, Americans were losing faith in the economy and the ability of their leaders to manage it.

Impacts of the Economic Crisis

The economic crisis of the 1970s accelerated the transition from an industrial to a service economy. During the 1970s, the United States deindustrialized, as automobile companies laid off workers and steel plant closings left communities devastated. Other manufacturing concerns moved overseas, seeking lower labor costs and fewer government regulations. New jobs were created—27 million of them—overwhelmingly in what economists called the service sector: retail sales, restaurants, and other service providers. These jobs—such as warehouse work or retail sales, for example—paid much lower wages than union manufacturing positions and often lacked healthcare and other benefits.

sped industrial → service economy

some moved labor overseas

↑service sector paid ↓ than manufacturing lacked healthcare/benefits

Formerly successful blue-collar workers saw their middle-class standards of life slipping away. More married women joined the work force because they had to. High school or college graduates in the 1970s, raised with high expectations, found limited possibilities, if they found jobs at all.

As the old industrial regions of the North and Midwest declined, people headed for the Sunbelt, which was booming (see Map 31.1). The federal government invested heavily in the South and West during the postwar era, especially in military and defense industries. The Sunbelt was primed for the rapid growth of modern industries and services—aerospace, defense, electronics, transportation, research, banking and finance, and leisure. City and state governments competed for business dollars, partly by preventing the growth of unions. Atlanta, Houston, and other southern cities marketed themselves as cosmopolitan and racially tolerant; they bought sports teams and built museums.

Sunbelt more jobs + people went there

The population shift south and west created disaster in northern and midwestern cities. New York City, near financial collapse by late 1975, was saved only when the House and Senate Banking Committees approved federal loan guarantees. Cleveland defaulted on its debts in 1978, the first major city to do so since Detroit declared bankruptcy in 1933.

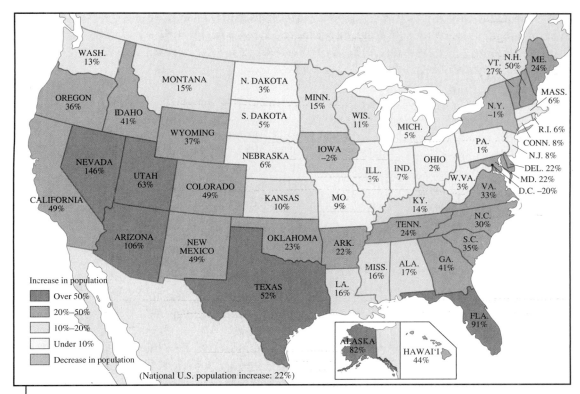

Map 31.1   The Continued Shift to the Sunbelt in the 1970s and 1980s

Throughout the 1970s and 1980s, Americans continued to leave economically declining areas of the North and East in pursuit of opportunity in the Sunbelt. States in the Sunbelt and in the West had the largest population increases.   (*Source:* "Shift to the Sunbelt," *Newsweek*, September 10, 1990.)

Tax Revolts

Meanwhile, a tax revolt movement emerged in the West. In California, inflation had driven property taxes up rapidly, hitting middle-class taxpayers hard. Instead of calling for wealthy citizens and major corporations to pay a larger share, voters rebelled against taxation itself. California's Proposition 13, passed by a landslide in 1978, rolled back property taxes and restricted future increases. Thirty-seven states similarly cut property taxes, and twenty-eight lowered their state income taxes.

The impact of Proposition 13 and similar initiatives was initially cushioned by state budget surpluses, but as those turned to deficits, states cut services—closing fire stations and public libraries and ending or limiting mental health services and programs for the disabled. Public schools were hit especially hard.

Credit and Investment

Before the runaway inflation of the 1970s, home mortgages and auto loans were the only major debt most Americans had. National credit cards had become common only in the late 1960s, and few Americans—especially those who remembered the Great Depression—were willing to spend money they did not have. In the 1970s, however, double-digit inflation rates made it economically smarter to buy goods before prices went up, even if it meant borrowing the money. Because debt was paid

↑ property tax
voters angry @ taxes
some states ↓ property or
    incom taxes

budget surplus ran out
    state gov ↓ jobs/etc.

people started buying before
prices↑. whether or not
they had $.

off later with devalued dollars, the consumer came out ahead. In 1975 consumer debt hit a high of $167 billion; it almost doubled to $315 billion by 1979.

In the 1970s, Americans became investors rather than savers. Because banking regulations capped interest paid on individual savings accounts, with inflation, a savings account bearing 5 percent interest actually *lost* more than 20 percent of its value from 1970 through 1980. That same money, invested at market rates, would have grown dramatically. Fidelity Investments, a mutual fund company, saw an opportunity: its money market accounts combined many smaller investments to purchase large-denomination Treasury bills and certificates of deposit, thus providing small investors the high interest rates normally available only to major investors. Money market investments grew from $1.7 billion in 1974 to $200 billion in 1982. Deregulation of the New York Stock Exchange spawned discount brokerage houses, whose low commission rates were affordable for middle-class investors.

AN ERA OF CULTURAL TRANSFORMATION

As Americans struggled with economic recession, governmental betrayal, and social division, major strands of late-twentieth-century culture were developed. The current environmental movement, the growth of technology, the rise of born-again Christianity and a therapeutic culture, contemporary forms of sexuality and the family, and the United States's emphasis on diversity all have roots in this odd decade sandwiched between the political vibrancy of the 1960s and the conservatism of the 1980s.

Environmentalism

A series of ecological crises drove home the fragility of the environment. In 1969 a major oil spill took place off the coast of Santa Barbara, California; that same year, the polluted Cuyahoga River, flowing through Cleveland, caught fire. In 1979 human error contributed to a nuclear accident at the Three Mile Island nuclear power plant near Harrisburg, Pennsylvania, and in 1980 President Carter declared a federal emergency at New York State's Love Canal, a dump site for a local chemical manufacturer, after it was discovered that 30 percent of local residents had suffered chromosome damage. Public activism produced major environmental initiatives, from the Environmental Protection Agency (EPA), created (under strong public pressure) in 1970 by the Nixon administration, to eighteen major environmental laws enacted by Congress during the decade.

When almost 20 million Americans—half of them schoolchildren—celebrated the first Earth Day on April 22, 1970, they signaled the triumph of a new understanding of environmentalism. Central to this movement was a recognition that the earth's resources were finite and must be conserved and protected. Many also identified rapid global population growth as a problem, and state public health offices frequently dispensed contraceptives to stem this new "epidemic."

Technology

During these years, Americans became increasingly uneasy about the science and technology that had been one source of the United States's might. Americans watched with pride as the astronaut Neil Armstrong stepped onto the lunar surface on July

20, 1969, saying, "That's one small step for a man, one giant step for mankind." But technology seemed unable to cope with earthbound problems of poverty, crime, pollution, and urban decay. The failure of technological warfare to deliver victory in Vietnam came as antiwar protesters were questioning the morality of such technology. But in the 1970s, the foundation was laid for the United States's computer revolution, with the creation of the integrated circuit in 1970, and by 1975 the MITS Altair 8800, boasting 256 bytes of memory and requiring thirty hours to assemble.

Religion and the Therapeutic Culture

Americans increasingly sought spiritual fulfillment. Methodist, Presbyterian, and Episcopalian churches lost members during this era, while evangelical and fundamentalist Christian churches grew dramatically. Protestant evangelicals, describing themselves as born again, emphasized the immediate, daily presence of God in their lives. Even some Catholics, such as the Mexican Americans who embraced the *cursillo* movement (a "little course" in faith), sought a more personal relationship with God. The New Age movement, which drew from and combined non-western spiritual and religious practices, including Zen Buddhism, yoga, and shamanism, along with insights from western psychology and spiritually oriented environmentalism, also drew adherents.

During the 1970s, the United States saw the emergence of a therapeutic culture. Although some were disgusted with the self-centeredness of the Me-Decade, best-selling books by therapists and self-help gurus insisted that individual feelings offered the ultimate measure of truth. Self-help books with titles like *I'm OK—You're OK* made up 15 percent of all bestselling books.

Sexuality and the Family

Sex became much more visible in U.S. culture during the 1970s, as network television loosened its regulation of sexual content. Early in the 1960s, married couples in television shows were required to occupy twin beds; in the 1970s, hit television shows included *Three's Company,* a situation comedy based on the then-scandalous premise that a single man shared an apartment with two female roommates and got away with it by pretending that he was gay. Donna Summers's 1975 disco hit "Love to Love You Baby" contained sixteen minutes of sexual moaning. And though few Americans participated in heterosexual orgies at New York City's Plato's Retreat, many read about them in *Time* magazine.

Sexual behaviors also changed. The seventies were the era of singles bars and gay bathhouses, but for most Americans, the sexual revolution meant a broader public acceptance of premarital sex and a limited acceptance of homosexuality, especially among more educated Americans. More heterosexual young people lived together without marriage during the 1970s; the census bureau even coined the term *POSSLQ* (persons of opposite sex sharing living quarters) to describe the relationship.

Changes in sexual mores and in women's roles altered the U.S. family as well. Men and women married later and had fewer children. By 1979, the birth rate had dropped almost 40 percent from its 1957 peak. Almost one-quarter of young single women in 1980 said they did not plan to have children. And a steadily rising percentage of babies were born to unmarried women, as the number of families headed by never-married women rose 400 percent. The divorce rate also rose, in part because states implemented no-fault divorce, which did not require evidence of adultery, physical cruelty, abandonment, or other wrongdoing. Americans also developed a greater acceptance of various family forms, symbolized by the blended family of television's *Brady Bunch*.

Diversity

The racial justice and identity movements of the late 1960s and 1970s made Americans more aware of differences among the nation's peoples—an awareness strengthened by new immigrants from Latin America and Asia. The challenge was figuring out how to acknowledge the new importance of difference in public policy. The 1970s solution was the idea of diversity. Difference was not a problem but a strength; the nation should seek to foster the diversity of its schools, workplaces, and public culture.

The 1978 Supreme Court decision in *Regents of the University of California v. Bakke* was a crucial early step. Allan Bakke, a thirty-three-year-old white man with a strong academic record, was denied admission to the medical school of the University of California at Davis. Bakke sued, charging that he had been denied equal protection because the medical school's affirmative-action program reserved 16 percent of its slots for racial-minority candidates, who were held to lower standards than other applicants. In 1978 the Supreme Court, in a split decision, decided in favor of Bakke. Four justices argued that any race-based decision violated the Civil Rights Act of 1964; four saw affirmative-action programs as constitutionally acceptable. The deciding vote, though for Bakke, contained an important qualification. A "diverse student body," Justice Lewis Powell wrote, is "a constitutionally permissible goal for an institution of higher education." To achieve diversity, educational institutions could consider race in admissions.

[handwritten margin note: schools allowed to factor race in decision-making to ↑ diversity]

RENEWED COLD WAR AND MIDDLE EAST CRISIS

When Jimmy Carter took office in 1977, he asked Americans to abandon their "inordinate fear of Communism." Carter vowed to reduce the U.S. military presence overseas, to cut back arms sales, and slow the nuclear arms race. More than 400,000 U.S. military personnel were stationed abroad, the United States had military links with ninety-two nations, and the CIA was active on every continent. Carter promised to avoid new Vietnams and give more attention to environmental issues. He especially determined to improve human rights abroad—the freedom to vote, worship, travel, speak out, and get a fair trial. Like his predecessors, however, Carter identified revolutionary nationalism as a threat to the United States's global prominence.

Carter's Divided Administration

Carter spoke and acted inconsistently, partly because in the post-Vietnam years no consensus existed in foreign policy and partly because his advisers squabbled among themselves. One source of the problem was the stern-faced Zbigniew Brzezinski, a Polish-born political scientist who became Carter's national security adviser. An old-fashioned Cold Warrior, Brzezinski blamed foreign crises on Soviet expansionism. Carter gradually listened more to Brzezinski than to Secretary of State Cyrus Vance, an experienced public servant who advocated quiet diplomacy.

[handwritten margin note: Diffrent foreign policy views within administration]

Under Carter, détente deteriorated and the Cold War deepened. Initially, Carter maintained fairly good relations with Moscow and secured some foreign policy successes. The United States signed two treaties with Panama in 1977. One provided for the return of the Canal Zone to Panama in 2000, and the other guaranteed the United States the right to defend the canal after that time. With conservatives denouncing the deal as a sellout, the Senate narrowly endorsed both agreements in 1978. The majority agreed with Carter's argument that relinquishing the canal would improve U.S. relations with Latin America.

Camp David Accords

The crowning accomplishment of Carter's presidency was the Camp David accords, the first mediated peace treaty between Israel and an Arab nation. In September 1978, the president persuaded Israel and Egypt to agree to a peace treaty, gained Israel's promise to withdraw from the Sinai Peninsula, and forged a provisional agreement that provided for continued negotiations on the future status of Palestinians living in the occupied territories of Jordan's West Bank and Egypt's Gaza Strip. Other Arab states denounced the agreement for not requiring Israel to relinquish all occupied territories and not guaranteeing a Palestinian homeland. But the accord, signed on March 26, 1979, by Israeli prime minister Menachem Begin and Egyptian president Anwar al-Sadat, at least ended warfare along one frontier.

Soviet Invasion of Afghanistan

Meanwhile, relations with Moscow deteriorated. U.S. and USSR officials sparred over the Kremlin's reluctance to lift restrictions on Jewish emigration and over the Soviet decision to deploy new intermediate-range ballistic missiles aimed at western Europe. Then, in December 1979, the Soviets invaded Afghanistan, a remote country whose strategic position made it a source of great-power conflict. Following World War II, Afghanistan struggled with ongoing ethnic and factional squabbling; in the 1970s, it spiraled into anarchy. In late 1979, the Red Army entered Afghanistan to shore up a faltering communist government under siege by Muslim rebels. Moscow officials calculated they could be in and out of the country before anyone noticed, including the Americans.

Carter not only noticed but reacted forcefully. He suspended shipments of grain and high-technology equipment to the Soviet Union, withdrew a major arms control treaty from Senate consideration, and initiated an international boycott of the 1980 Summer Olympics in Moscow. He also secretly authorized the CIA to distribute aid, including arms and military support, to the Mujahidin (Islamic guerillas) fighting the communist government and sanctioned military aid to their backer, Pakistan. Announcing the Carter Doctrine, the president asserted that the United States would intervene, unilaterally and militarily, should Soviet aggression threaten the petroleum-rich Persian Gulf. Carter warned aides that the Soviets, unless checked, would likely attack elsewhere in the Middle East, but declassified documents confirm what contemporary critics said: that the Soviet invasion was limited and did not presage a push into the Persian Gulf.

Iranian Hostage Crisis

Carter simultaneously faced a tough foreign policy test in neighboring Iran. The shah, long favored by the United States, was dethroned by a coalition of Iranians, who resented the dislocation of their traditional ways by the shah's attempts at modernization. Riots led by anti-American Muslim clerics erupted in late 1978. The shah went into exile, and in April 1979 Islamic revolutionaries, led by the Ayatollah Khomeini, an elderly cleric who denounced the United States as the stronghold of capitalism and western materialism, proclaimed a Shi'ite Islamic Republic. In November, with the exiled shah in the United States for medical treatment, mobs stormed the U.S. embassy in Teheran. They took American personnel as hostages, demanding the return of the shah to stand trial. The Iranians eventually released a few American prisoners, but fifty-two others suffered solitary confinement, beatings, and terrifying mock executions.

Unable to gain the hostages' freedom through diplomatic intermediaries, Carter took steps to isolate Iran economically, freezing Iranian assets in the United States. When the hostage takers paraded their blindfolded captives before television cameras, Americans felt taunted and humiliated. In April 1980, Carter broke diplomatic relations with Iran and ordered a daring rescue mission. But equipment failed and two aircraft collided, killing eight American soldiers. The hostages were not freed until January 1981, after Carter left office.

The Iranian revolution, together with the rise of the Mujahidin in Afghanistan, signified the emergence of Islamic fundamentalism as a force in world affairs. Socialism and capitalism, the answers that the two superpowers offered to the problems of modernization, failed to solve the problems in Central Asia and the Middle East. Consequently, Islamic orthodoxy found growing support for its message: that secular leaders such as Nasser in Egypt and the shah in Iran had taken their people down the wrong path, necessitating a return to conservative Islamic values and Islamic law. The Iranian revolution expressed a complex mixture of discontents within Islamic societies.

Rise of Saddam Hussein

U.S. officials took some consolation from the avowedly secular government in neighboring Iraq. Ruled by the Ba'athist Party, Iraq won favor in Washington for its pursuit and execution of Iraqi communists. When a Ba'athist leader named Saddam Hussein took over as president of Iraq in 1979 and threatened the Teheran government, U.S. officials thought Saddam could offset the Iranian danger in the Persian Gulf. As border clashes between Iraqi and Iranian forces escalated into war in 1980, Washington policymakers were officially neutral but soon tilted toward Iraq.

Carter earned some diplomatic successes in the Middle East, Africa, and Latin America, but the revived Cold War and prolonged Iranian hostage crisis hurt the administration politically. Contrary to Carter's goals, more U.S. military personnel were stationed overseas in 1980 than in 1976; the defense budget climbed and arms sales grew to $15.3 billion in 1980. On human rights, the president practiced a double standard, applying the human-rights test to some nations (the Soviet Union, Argentina, and Chile) but not to U.S. allies (South Korea, the shah's Iran, and the Philippines). Still, Carter's human-rights policy saved the lives of some political prisoners and institutionalized concern for human rights worldwide. But his inability to restore economic and military dominance dashed his reelection prospects. He lost in 1980 to the hawkish Ronald Reagan, former Hollywood actor and governor of California.

The All-Volunteer Force

On In 1973, the United States ended the draft and turned to an all-volunteer force (AVF). The draft had been in effect, with only a brief interruption in the late 1940s, since the United States began mobilizing for World War II. Never before had the United States had a peacetime draft. But as the country embraced global leadership and faced a heightened Cold War, the draft became an accepted part of American life. By 1973 more than 50 million American men had been inducted into the military since World War II.

Richard Nixon promised to end the draft during his 1968 presidential campaign, realizing that the draft was a focus for widespread protest against the Vietnam War. Ending the draft was not feasible during the war, but Nixon began planning for an all-volunteer force once in office. Many Americans supported the shift because they believed a president could not rely on a draft to compel people to fight a war they did not support.

The military, however, disliked Nixon's plan. The war in Vietnam shattered morale and left the military, particularly the army, in disarray. With public opinion of the military at an all-time low, how would it attract volunteers?

The largest of the four services, the army required the most volunteers. To draw volunteers, the army ended make-work ("chickenshit") tasks and enhanced military professionalism. It also turned to market research and advertising. Discovering that many young men were afraid to lose their individuality, the army launched a campaign that told potential volunteers, "Today's Army Wants to Join You."

The army needed about 225,000 recruits annually (compared to about 80,000 per year in 2006) and had difficulty attracting them. Within a decade, however, the United States's military boasted a higher rate of high school graduates than the comparable age population. During an era of relative peace, many young people found opportunities for education and training through military service, particularly the economically disadvantaged—a high percentage of whom were African American.

The military understood that, without a draft, it would need women to fill the ranks. The proportion of women in the military increased from 1.9 percent in 1972 to about 15 percent currently, with a wider range of available roles. The nation's understanding of military service changed from an obligation of (male) citizenship to a voluntary choice. The implications seemed less urgent in peacetime. But in wartime, the volunteer force raises the question: What does it mean when only a small number of volunteers bears the burden of warfare and most Americans do not have to consider the possibility of going to war?

Summary

From the crisis year of 1968 on, Americans were highly polarized—over the war in Vietnam, over the best path to racial equality and equal rights, over the meaning of the United States itself. As many activists turned to cultural nationalism, or group-identity politics, notions of American unity seemed a relic of the past. And though a new women's movement won victories against sex discrimination, powerful opposition arose in response.

During this era, Americans became increasingly disillusioned with politics and presidential leadership. Richard Nixon's abuses of power in the Watergate scandal and cover-up, combined with growing awareness that the administration had lied repeatedly about the United States's role in Vietnam, produced a profound suspicion of government. A major economic crisis ended the post–World War II expansion, and Americans struggled with the effects of stagflation: rising unemployment rates coupled with high inflation.

Overseas, a string of setbacks—defeat in Vietnam, the oil embargo, and the Iranian hostage crisis—signified the waning of U.S. power. Détente with the Soviet Union had flourished for a time; however, by 1980 Cold War tensions escalated. And the Middle East became an increasing focus of U.S. foreign policy.

Plagued by political, economic, and foreign policy crises, at the end of the 1970s, the United States's age of liberalism was over; the elements for a conservative resurgence were in place.

Chapter Review

THE NEW POLITICS OF IDENTITY

What defined political activism in the late 1960s and 1970s?

A new identity politics, in which groups stressed and celebrated their racial and ethnic differences, became the hallmark of activism by the 1970s. African Americans no longer sought equality via their shared humanity with white society. Instead, they—as well as Native Americans and Mexican Americans—looked to first validate what made them culturally unique and use that as the starting point for their demands for social and political equality. Through the Black Power movement, African Americans embraced a black standard of beauty, celebrated their heritage, and founded black studies programs in universities. Native Americans began a Red Power movement similarly to seek the return of native lands, validate tribal customs, and ensure greater power to self-govern. Hispanics likewise embraced their cultural distinctiveness while seeking better pay and conditions for migrant farm workers and establishing cooperative societies and ethnically-focused businesses.

THE WOMEN'S MOVEMENT AND GAY LIBERATION

What were the successes of the women's movement?

The women's movement made major gains in the 1960s and 1970s: the right of a married woman to obtain credit in her own name; the right of an unmarried woman to obtain birth control; the right to serve on juries; and the end of sex-segregated help wanted ads. Activists established rape crisis centers, educated law enforcement, and challenged definitions of rape that blamed the victim for the attack. They worked for legalized abortion at the state level and won a major victor with the 1973 Supreme Court decision in *Roe v. Wade*, which ruled that privacy rights protected a woman's decision not to continue a pregnancy. The women's movement also achieved greater opportunities for women in sports via passage of Title IX of the Higher Education Act, which barred federal funds from colleges or universities discriminating against women. Likewise, the movement sparked the creation of women's studies programs in colleges nationwide.

THE END IN VIETNAM

What kept Nixon from ending the Vietnam War as quickly as he had hoped?

Nixon's policy in Vietnam was driven by a goal to end the war fast, partly so that it would not ruin his political career as it had Johnson's. But at the same time, he did not want to hurt American credibility as a world leader, and he refused to allow South Vietnam to fall to the communists. Consequently, although he dramatically decreased the number of American troops from 543,000 in 1969 to 60,000 in 1970, he increased bombing of North Vietnam and neutral Cambodia, hoping to force the enemy into concessions. This failed even after invading Cambodia. A cease-fire was agreed to in 1973, and shortly after U.S. troops left, a full-scale war developed between North and South Vietnam, with the latter falling and the two countries reunifying as a communist nation in 1975.

NIXON, KISSINGER, AND THE WORLD

How did Vietnam influence Nixon's approach to foreign policy?

The failure in Vietnam forced Nixon to rethink the Cold War containment policy of providing military aid to anticommunist revolutions and wars. Instead, he adopted the Nixon Doctrine, which said the United States would provide economic aid but not troops to allies. Second, he implemented détente, a policy of minimizing Soviet expansion and arms buildup through diplomacy and mutual concessions. Détente also focused on improving trade relations with the Soviets and other communist giants, such as China, to help minimize communism's reach. And Chinese leaders Mao Zedong and Zhou Enlai agreed with Nixon that the Soviet Union should be kept from making gains in Asia.

PRESIDENTIAL POLITICS AND THE CRISIS OF LEADERSHIP

How did Watergate bring down the Nixon administration?

Sometimes paranoid, Nixon kept long lists of so-called enemies and directed aide Charles Colson to form a secret group called the Plumbers to dig up dirt on various groups and individuals. During Nixon's 1972 reelection campaign, the Plumbers were arrested while breaking into the Democratic National Campaign headquarters in the Watergate complex to plant surveillance equipment. While Nixon was not directly involved in this effort, he made the mistake of blocking the CIA and FBI investigations into it—which constituted an obstruction of justice. He also initially refused to turn over his audiotape conversations to congressional hearings. Eventually, he relinquished the tapes, although several contained significant gaps. Congress began impeachment hearings, and facing certain conviction and impeachment, Nixon became the first U.S. president to resign on August 9, 1974.

ECONOMIC CRISIS

What were the long-term effects of the 1970s recession?

The 1970s recession accelerated the nation's shift from an industrial to a service-based economy. As manufacturers in leading industries, such as automobiles and steel, laid off large numbers of workers or shifted to cheaper production, new jobs opened in the lower-paid service sector, such as cashiers and waiters. Increasing numbers of married women went to work to keep their families afloat. Older industrial cities suffered decay, while the Sunbelt was well-positioned to prosper with the growth of modern industries such as defense, aerospace and finance. Double-digit inflation in the 1970s led people to buy up goods before prices would rise, often on credit, fueling a major rise in consumer indebtedness. Finally, with interest rates capped on savings accounts, people increasingly shifted to investments via mutual funds and the stock market.

AN ERA OF CULTURAL TRANSFORMATION

How did the openness of the 1970s impact family life?

The tolerance and openness about sex in the 1970s facilitated major changes in traditional notions of what constituted a family. As norms against premarital sex ebbed, more young couples were opting to live together rather than get married. Those who wed, tended to do so later in life and had fewer children. By decade's end, the birth rate dropped nearly 40 percent from its all-time high, and nearly 25 percent of single women said they did not intend to have children at all. Divorce rates also shot up as a result of new no fault laws that enabled couples to end bad relationships without proving adultery, abandonment, or other cause.

RENEWED COLD WAR AND MIDDLE EAST CRISIS

What was Carter's record regarding the Middle East?

On the one hand, Carter achieved great success in mediating a peace treaty between Israel and Egypt in 1978. While the move was a major first step toward future negotiations, Arab states felt it fell short in not providing a Palestinian homeland and allowing Israel to maintain some of its occupied territories. On the other hand, Carter aided Islamic guerillas to fight Soviets in Afghanistan, which he mistakenly feared was the communist country's first step toward the Persian Gulf. Second, Carter angered Iranians when he provided protection for the exiled shah in the United States to seek medical treatment. Mobs stormed the U.S. embassy in Iran and took hostages to press for the shah to stand trial. While some were released, fifty-two other hostages were imprisoned and beaten or paraded before television cameras for the world to see. Carter's inability to free the U.S. hostages contributed to his political downfall and defeat in his reelection bid in 1980.

SUGGESTIONS FOR FURTHER READING

Donald T. Critchlow, *Phyllis Schlafly and Grassroots Conservatism: A Woman's Crusade* (2005)

Daniel Ellsberg, *Secrets: A Memoir of Vietnam and the Pentagon Papers* (2002)

David Farber, *Taken Hostage: The Iran Hostage Crisis and America's First Encounter with Radical Islam* (2004)

Ian F. Haney-Lopez, *Racism on Trial: The Chicano Fight for Justice* (2003)

Richard Reeves, *President Nixon: Alone in the White House* (2001)

Ruth Rosen, *The World Split Open: How the Modern Women's Movement Changed America* (2000)

Hal Rothman, *The Greening of a Nation: Environmentalism in the U.S. Since 1945* (1997)

Bruce Schulman, *The Seventies: The Great Shift in American Culture, Society, and Politics* (2001)

John D. Skrentny, *The Minority Rights Revolution* (2002)

Odd Arne Westad, *The Global Cold War: Third World Interventions and the Making of Our Times* (2005)

Conservatism Revived

"It was hot and there was a lot of desert," Luisa Orellana remembered about crossing the Mexican border into the United States in the early 1980s. "All of us started running, each one with a child in our arms. . . . It rained so hard we couldn't see where we were going, but it helped because the Border Patrol couldn't see us either."

Three months earlier Luisa's father was murdered. Tanis Stanislaus Orellana worked in El Salvador with Archbishop Óscar Romero, the most powerful critic of the ruling military dictatorship whose death squads killed thirty thousand Salvadorans between 1979 and 1981. In 1980 Romero was shot and killed as he consecrated the Eucharist during Mass. The civil war that followed lasted twelve years, leading an estimated 1 million Salvadorans to seek refuge elsewhere from the torture, rape, and murder increasingly commonplace in their homeland.

After Orellana's murder, his widow fled with their children, leaving almost everything behind. They took the bus through Guatemala, crossed illegally into Mexico, and, sheltered by churches, made their way from Chiapas to Mexico City to Agua Prieta, on the U.S.-Mexico border.

There, Luisa and her family ran 2 miles through blinding rain. Cold, hungry, and scared, they were met in Douglas, Arizona, by the Sanctuary movement, Americans who believed that the U.S. government's refugee policy, which offered asylum to those fleeing violent repression and possible death or torture, must include people who escaped the deadly civil wars ravaging Central America in the 1980s. Officially, the U.S. government designated them economic refugees and denied them asylum.

The originators of the U.S. Sanctuary movement used church networks and human-rights groups throughout Central America to investigate refugees' stories of abuse and murder. Their mission

This icon will direct you to interactive activities and study materials on A People And A Nation, Brief Edition
website: **www.cengage.com/history/norton/ peoplenationbrief8e**

Chronology

1980	Reagan is elected president.	1986	Iran-contra scandal erupts.
1981	AIDS is first observed in United States.	1987	Stock market drops 508 points in one day.
	Economic problems continue; prime interest rate reaches 21.5 percent.		Palestinian *intifada* begins.
	Reagan breaks air traffic controllers' strike.	1988	George H. W. Bush is elected president.
	Reaganomics plan of budget and tax cuts is approved by Congress.	1989	Tiananmen Square massacre occurs in China.
			Berlin Wall is torn down.
1982	Unemployment reaches 10.8 percent, highest rate since Great Depression.		U.S. troops invade Panama.
			Gulf between rich and poor is at highest point since 1920s.
	ERA dies after Stop-ERA campaign prevents ratification in key states.	1990	Americans with Disabilities Act is passed.
1983	Reagan introduces SDI.		Communist regimes in eastern Europe collapse.
	Terrorists kill U.S. Marines in Lebanon.		Iraq invades Kuwait.
	U.S. invasion of Grenada occurs.		South Africa begins to dismantle apartheid.
1984	Reagan aids contras despite congressional ban.	1991	Persian Gulf War occurs.
	Economic recovery; unemployment rate drops and economy grows without inflation.		Soviet Union dissolves into independent states.
			United States enters recession.
	Reagan is reelected.	1992	Annual federal budget deficit reaches high of $300 billion at end of Bush presidency.
	Gorbachev promotes reforms in Soviet Union.		

was to protect human rights and to save those they could from torture and death. Many members belonged to faith-based communities, although secular institutions, including some universities and the state of New Mexico, also participated. Some movement members went to prison, charged with transporting or harboring fugitives.

Luisa and her family moved from the sanctuary offered by Tucson churches, which were at the center of the movement, to live in the basement of a Spokane, Washington, Catholic church. In 1989 the U.S. government granted protection and work permits to Central American refugees. Luisa stayed in Washington, where she became a teacher of English as a second language.

Luisa Orellana and her family were part of the new immigration that began in the early 1970s and grew throughout the 1980s, as record numbers of immigrants came to the United States from Asia, Mexico, Central and South America, and the Caribbean. Many from Central America, Vietnam, the Soviet Union, and Cuba were political refugees. The Orellanas found safety and peace in the United States, but not all immigrants—or all Americans—fared so well in the 1980s, when divisions between rich and poor widened dramatically. While the urban poor struggled with social problems—drugs, violence, homelessness, the growing AIDS epidemic— those on the other side of the economic divide enjoyed an era of luxury and ostentation.

The election of Ronald Reagan in 1980 began twelve years of Republican rule, as Reagan was succeeded by his vice president, George Bush, in 1988. Reagan was a popular president who seemed to restore the confidence shaken by the social, economic, and political crises of the 1970s. Wealthy people liked Reagan's pro-business economic policies; the religious New Right shared his vision of God's America; white middle- and working-class Americans admired Reagan's charisma and embrace of old-fashioned values.

Reagan supported New Right social issues: he was anti-abortion, embraced prayer in schools, and reversed the GOP's support of the Equal Rights Amendment. Most important, Reagan appointed Supreme Court and federal judges whose rulings strengthened social-conservative agendas. Reagan's primary focus was on the conservative issues of reducing the size and power of the federal government and creating favorable conditions for business. The U.S. economy recovered from the 1970s stagflation and boomed through much of the 1980s. But corruption flourished in financial institutions freed from government oversight. By the end of the Reagan-Bush era, a combination of tax cuts and massive increases in defense caused the budget deficit to jump fivefold.

In a single decade, the Cold War intensified, then ended. The key figure in the intensification was Reagan, who promised to stand up to the Soviet Union. The key figure in ending the Cold War was Soviet leader Mikhail Gorbachev, who came to power in 1985 determined to end the Soviet Union's economic decline, which required a more amicable superpower relationship. Gorbachev hoped to reform the Soviet system, but lost control of events as revolutions in eastern Europe toppled one communist regime after another. In 1991 the Soviet Union disappeared, and the Persian Gulf War demonstrated the United States's unrivaled world power and the unprecedented importance of the Middle East.

- Ronald Reagan, campaigning for president in 1984, told voters, "It's morning again in America." How would Americans from different backgrounds judge the accuracy of his claim?
- What issues, beliefs, backgrounds, and economic realities divided Americans in the 1980s, and how did those divisions shape the culture and politics of contemporary America?
- Why did the Cold War intensify and then wane during the decade of the 1980s?

Reagan and the Conservative Resurgence

The 1970s were hard for Americans: defeat in Vietnam, the resignation of a president in disgrace, the energy crisis, economic stagflation, and the Iranian hostage crisis. In 1980, President Carter's approval rating stood at 21 percent, lower than Richard Nixon's during the Watergate crisis. The time was ripe for a challenge to Carter's leadership, the Democratic Party, and the liberalism that had basically governed the United States since Franklin Roosevelt's New Deal.

Ronald Reagan

In 1980 several conservative Republican politicians ran for the White House, including Ronald Reagan, former movie star and two-term California governor. In the 1940s, as president of the Hollywood Screen Actors Guild, Reagan was a New Deal Democrat. But in the 1950s, as a corporate spokesperson for General Electric, he became increasingly conservative. In 1964 Reagan's televised speech supporting Republican presidential candidate Barry Goldwater catapulted him to the forefront of conservative politics.

Elected governor of California two years later, Reagan became known for his right-wing rhetoric: The United States should "level Vietnam, pave it, paint stripes on it, and make a parking lot out of it." And in 1969, when student protestors occupied People's Park near the University of California in Berkeley, he threatened a "bloodbath," dispatching National Guard troops. Reagan was often pragmatic; he denounced welfare but presided over reform of the state's social welfare bureaucracy. And he signed one of the nation's most liberal abortion laws.

The New Conservative Coalition

In the 1980 election, Reagan contrasted Carter with an optimistic vision for the United States's future. With his Hollywood charm, he forged different kinds of conservatives into a new coalition. Strongly anticommunist, many wanted to strengthen national defense, limit federal power and roll back the liberal programs of the 1930s New Deal and 1960s Great Society. Reagan similarly attracted economic conservatives who sought deregulation and tax policies benefiting corporations, wealthy investors, and entrepreneurs. He also drew neoconservatives, a small but influential group of intellectuals—typically former Democrats disillusioned with the party after Vietnam.

Reagan further tapped into the sentiments that fueled the tax revolt of the 1970s, drawing voters from traditionally Democratic constituencies, such as labor unions and urban ethnic groups. Many middle- and working-class whites resented what they saw as tax-funded welfare for people who did not work. These Reagan Democrats found the Republican critique of tax-funded social programs and big government appealing, even though Reagan's policies would benefit the wealthy at their expense.

Finally, Reagan drew the increasingly powerful, religiously based New Right. "When political conservative leaders began to . . . strike an alliance with social conservatives—the pro-life people, the anti-ERA people, the evangelical and born-again Christians, the people concerned about gay rights, prayer in the schools, sex in the movies or whatever," explained conservative fundraiser Richard Viguerie, "that's when this whole movement began to come alive."

Reagan's Conservative Agenda

Reagan won with 51 percent of the popular vote. Jimmy Carter carried only six states. Reagan served two terms as president, and, like Franklin Roosevelt, defined the era over which he presided. Reagan was not especially focused on the details of governing. When Carter briefed him on foreign and domestic policy, Reagan took no notes. Critics argued that his lack of knowledge could prove dangerous—as when he insisted that intercontinental ballistic missiles carrying nuclear warheads could be called back once launched.

But supporters insisted that Reagan focused on the big picture. When he spoke to the American people, he offered what seemed to be simple truths. While even supporters winced at his willingness to reduce complex policy issues to basic (and often misleading) stories, Reagan was to most Americans the Great Communicator. He won admiration for his courage after he was seriously wounded in an assassination attempt sixty-nine days into his presidency. Most important, Reagan had a clear vision for the

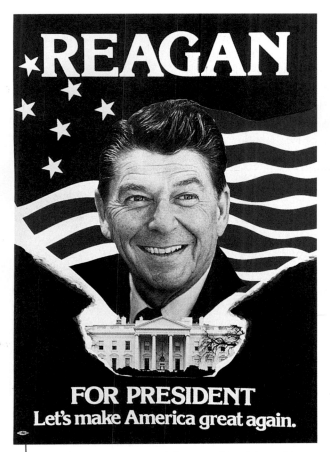

REAGAN

FOR PRESIDENT
Let's make America great again.

Ronald Reagan, the Republican presidential candidate in 1980, campaigned for fam ly values, an aggressive anti-Soviet foreign and military policy, and tax cuts. He also exuded optimism and appealed to Americans' patriotism. This poster issuec by the Republican National Committee included Reagan's favorite campaign slogan, "Let's make America great again." (Collection of David J. and Janice L. Frent)

United States's future. He wanted to roll back the liberalism of the past fifty years that made government responsible for the nation's economic health and the social welfare of its citizens.

Attacks on Social Welfare Programs

Reagan, like traditional conservatives, believed that the federal government could not solve social problems. He also tapped into a backlash against Great Society social programs. Many Americans who struggled to make ends meet during the economic crises of the 1970s and early 1980s resented paying taxes that, they believed, funded government handouts. Lasting racial tensions also fueled public resentment: Reagan fed a stereotype of welfare recipients as unwed, black, teenage mothers who kept having babies to collect larger checks.

In 1981 the administration cut social welfare funding by $25 billion. But welfare programs benefiting the poor (Aid to Families with Dependent Children and food stamp programs) were small compared with Social Security and Medicare—welfare programs benefiting Americans across income levels. The Reagan administration did shrink the *proportion* of the federal budget devoted to social welfare programs (including Social Security and Medicare) from 28 to 22 percent by the late 1980s, but only because of a $1.2 trillion increase in defense spending.

Pro-Business Policies and the Environment

Reagan also attacked federal environmental, health, and safety regulations as reducing business profits and discouraging economic growth. Administration officials claimed that removing government regulation would restore the creativity of the United States's free-market system. However, they did not so much end government's role as deploy government power to aid corporate America. The president even appointed opponents of federal regulations to head agencies charged with enforcing them.

Environmentalists were appalled when Reagan appointed James Watt, a well-known antienvironmentalist, as secretary of the interior. Watt was a leader in the Sagebrush Rebellion, which sought the return of publicly owned lands in the West, such as national forests, to state control. The federal government controlled more than half of western lands, including 83 percent of the land in Nevada, 66 percent in Utah, and 50 percent in Wyoming. But state control was not the sole issue; Watt's group wanted to open western public lands to businesses for logging, mining, and ranching.

Telling Congress in 1981, "I don't know how many generations we can count on until the Lord returns," Watt dismissed concerns about protecting resources and public lands for future generations and allowed private corporations to acquire oil, mineral, and timber rights to federal lands for minuscule payments. He was forced to resign in 1983 after he referred to a federal advisory panel as "a black . . . a woman, two Jews, and a cripple." Even before Watt's resignation, his appointment backfired, as his actions reenergized the nation's environmental movement and even provoked opposition from business leaders who understood that uncontrolled strip-mining and clear-cut logging could destroy lucrative tourism and recreation industries in western states.

Attacks on Organized Labor

The pro-business Reagan administration undercut organized labor's ability to negotiate wages and working conditions. Union power was already waning; labor union membership declined in the 1970s as jobs in heavy industry disappeared and efforts to unionize the high-growth electronics and service sectors of the economy failed. Reagan intervened in an August 1981 strike by the Professional Air Traffic Controllers Organization (PATCO). The air traffic controllers—federal employees, for whom striking was illegal—protested working conditions they believed compromised the safety of air travel. Forty-eight hours later, Reagan fired the 11,350 strikers, stipulating they could never be rehired by the Federal Aviation Administration.

With the support of Reagan appointees to the National Labor Relations Board, businesses took an increasingly hard line with labor during the 1980s, and unions failed to mount effective opposition. Yet roughly 44 percent of union families voted for Reagan in 1980, drawn to his espousal of old-fashioned values and vigorous anticommunist rhetoric.

The New Right

It is surprising that the religious New Right was drawn to Reagan, a divorced man without strong ties to religion or, seemingly, his own children. But Reagan supported New Right social issues: the anti-abortion cause and prayer in public schools.

Reagan's judicial nominations also pleased the religious New Right. The Senate, in a bipartisan vote, refused to confirm Supreme Court nominee Robert Bork. Congress eventually confirmed Anthony M. Kennedy. Reagan also appointed Anton Scalia, who would become a key conservative force, and Sandra Day O'Connor (the first woman appointee), and elevated Nixon appointee William Rehnquist to chief justice.

These appointments made the Court more conservative. In 1986, for example, the Supreme Court upheld a Georgia law that punished consensual anal or oral sex between men with up to twenty years in jail (*Bowers v. Hardwick*); in 1989 justices ruled that a Missouri law restricting the right to an abortion was constitutional (*Webster v. Reproductive Health Services*), thus encouraging further challenges to *Roe v. Wade*. Overall, however, the Reagan administration did not push a conservative social agenda as strongly as some in the new Republican coalition hoped.

REAGANOMICS

The centerpiece of Reagan's domestic agenda was the economic program that took his name: Reaganomics. The U.S. economy was faltering in the early 1980s. Stagflation proved resistant to traditional remedies: when the government increased spending to stimulate the economy, inflation skyrocketed; when it cut spending or tightened the money supply to reduce inflation, the economy plunged deeper into recession, and unemployment increased.

Reagan offered a simple answer. Instead of focusing on the complexities of global competition, deindustrialization, and OPEC's control of oil, Reagan argued that U.S. economic problems were caused by intrusive government regulation of business and industry, expensive social programs, high taxes, and deficit spending—in short, government itself. Reagan sought to unshackle the free-enterprise system from government regulation, slash social programs, and balance the budget by reducing the role of the federal government.

Supply-Side Economics

Reagan's economic policy was based largely on supply-side economics, the theory that tax cuts (rather than government spending) stimulate growth. Economist Arthur Laffer proposed one hypothesis—his soon-to-be-famous Laffer curve. It stated that at some point rising tax rates discourage people from engaging in taxable activities (such as investing). As people invest less, the economy slows, and there is less tax revenue to collect. Cutting taxes, in contrast, reverses the cycle.

Although economists accepted the larger principle behind Laffer's curve, almost none believed U.S. tax rates approached the point of disincentive. Even conservative economists were suspicious of supply-side principles. Reagan and his staff, however, sought a massive tax cut, arguing that U.S. corporations and individuals would invest funds freed up by lower tax rates, producing new plants, new jobs, and new products. And as prosperity returned, the profits at the top would trickle down to the middle classes and even the poor.

David Stockman, head of the Office of Management and Budget, proposed a five-year plan to balance the federal budget through economic growth (created by tax cuts) and deep spending cuts, primarily in social programs. Congress cooperated with a three-year, $750 billion tax cut, the largest in American history. Stockman's plan assumed $100 billion in cuts from government programs, including Social Security and Medicare, which Congress rejected. Reagan, meanwhile, canceled out gains from domestic spending cuts by dramatically increasing defense spending.

With major tax cuts, big increases in defense spending, and small cuts in social programs, the federal budget deficit exploded from $59 billion in 1980 to more than $100 billion in 1982 to almost $300 billion by the end of George W. H. Bush's presidency in 1992. The federal government borrowed money to make up the difference, transforming the United States from the world's largest creditor to its largest debtor (see Figure 32.1). The national debt grew to almost $3 trillion.

Harsh Medicine for Inflation

In 1981, the Federal Reserve Bank, an autonomous federal agency, raised interest rates for bank loans to an unprecedented 21.5 percent, battling inflation by tightening the money supply and slowing the economy. The nation plunged into recession. By year's end, the gross national product (GNP) fell 5 percent, and sales of cars and houses dropped sharply. Unemployment soared to 8 percent.

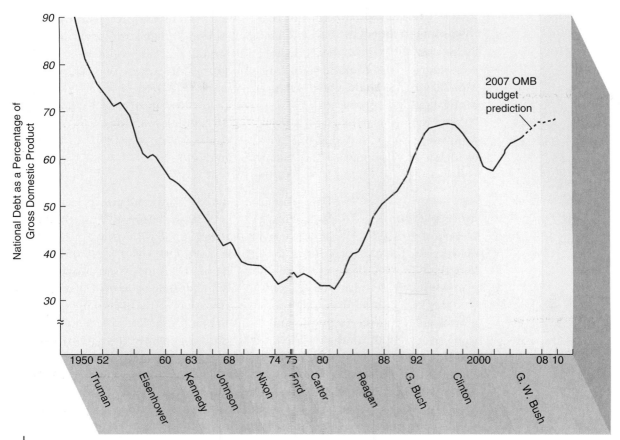

Figure 32.1   The United States's Rising National Debt, 1974–1989

The United States's national debt, which rose sporadically throughout the 1970s, soared to record heights during the 1980s. Under President Reagan, large defense expenditures and tax cuts caused the national debt to grow by $1.5 trillion.   (*Source:* Adapted from U.S. Bureau of the Census, *Statistical Abstract of the United States* [Washington, DC: U.S. Government Printing Office, 1992], p. 315.)

By late 1982, unemployment reached 10.8 percent, the highest rate since 1940. For African Americans, it was 20 percent. Reagan promised that consumers would lift the economy from the recession by spending their tax cuts. But as late as April 1983, unemployment remained at 10 percent, and people were angry. Along with industries such as steel and automobiles, agriculture, too, was faltering as farmers suffered from falling crop prices, floods, droughts. and burdensome debts at high interest rates. Many lost their property through mortgage foreclosures; others filed for bankruptcy. As the recession deepened, poverty rose to its highest level since 1965.

It was harsh medicine, but the Federal Reserve Bank's plan to end stagflation worked. High interest rates helped drop inflation from 12 percent in 1980 to less than 7 percent in 1982. The economy also benefited from OPEC's 1981 decision to increase oil production, thus lowering prices. In 1984 the GNP rose 7 percent, the sharpest increase since 1951, and midyear unemployment fell to a four-year low of 7 percent.

everyone in a bad position
poverty ↑

inflation dropped

unemployment fell

First female VP candidate

"Morning in America"

Reagan got credit for the recovery, though it had little to do with his supply-side policies. Insisting that the escalating budget deficit would have dire consequences for the economy, 1984 Democratic presidential candidate and former vice president Walter Mondale said he would raise taxes. Mondale emphasized fairness; not all Americans, Mondale said, were prospering in Reagan's America. Reagan, in contrast, proclaimed, "It's morning again in America." Reagan won in a landslide, with 59 percent of the vote. Mondale, with running mate Geraldine Ferraro—the first woman vice-presidential candidate—carried only his home state of Minnesota.

↓ Prices,

Deregulation

Deregulation, begun under Carter and expanded by Reagan, created new opportunities for business. The 1978 deregulation of the airline industry lowered ticket prices; airline tickets cost almost 45 percent less in the early twenty-first century (in constant dollars) than in 1978. Deregulation of telecommunications industries created serious competition for the giant AT&T, and long-distance calling became inexpensive.

savings and-loans problems

The Reagan administration loosened regulation of the banking and finance industries and purposely cut the enforcement ability of the Securities and Exchange Commission (SEC). In the early 1980s, Congress deregulated the nation's savings-and-loan institutions (S&Ls), organizations previously required to invest depositors' savings in thirty-year, fixed-rate mortgages secured by property within a 50-mile radius of the S&L's main office. By ending government oversight of investment practices, while covering losses from bad S&L investments, Congress left no penalties for failure. S&Ls increasingly put depositors' money into high-risk investments and engaged in shady—even criminal—deals.

Junk Bonds and Merger Mania

Risky investments typified Wall Street as well, as Michael Milken, a reclusive bond trader, pioneered the junk bond industry and created lucrative investment possibilities. Milken offered financing to debt-ridden corporations unable to get traditional, low-interest bank loans, using bond issues that paid investors high interest rates because they were high-risk (thus junk bonds). Many of these corporations were attractive targets for takeover by other corporations or investors, who, in turn, could finance takeovers with junk bonds. Such predators could use the first corporation's existing debt as a tax write-off, sell off unprofitable units, and lay off employees to create a more profitable corporation.

*Junk bonds
- high-risk, high-interest
Merger Mania
- debt ridden co's
taken over (for profit)*

By the mid-1980s, hundreds of major corporations, including giants Walt Disney and Conoco—fell prey to merger mania and hostile takeovers. Profits for investors were staggering, and by 1987 Milken, the guru of junk bonds, was earning $550 million a year, about $1,046 a minute.

economy boomed

Deregulation helped smaller corporations challenge the virtual monopolies of giant corporations in fields like telecommunications. And the U.S. economy boomed. Although the stock market plunged 508 points on a single day in October 1987—losing 22.6 percent of its value, or almost double the loss of value in the 1929 crash—it rebounded quickly. But the high-risk boom of the 1980s had significant costs. Corporate downsizing meant layoffs for white-collar workers and management personnel, many of whom had difficulty finding comparable positions. The wave of mergers and takeovers left U.S. corporations increasingly burdened by debt. It also helped consolidate sectors of the economy, such as the media, under the control of fewer players.

The Rich Get Richer

The 1980s boom, furthermore, was rotten with corruption. By the late 1980s, insider trading scandals, in which people used inside information not available to the public to make huge profits trading stocks, rocked financial markets and sent some of the most prominent Wall Street figures to jail. Savings and loans lost billions in bad investments, sometimes turning to fraud to cover them up. Scandal reached to the White House: Vice President Bush's son Neil was involved in shady S&L deals. The Reagan-Bush administration's bailout of the S&L industry cost taxpayers half a trillion dollars.

corruption

During the 1980s, the rich got richer, and the poor got poorer (see Figure 32.2). The number of Americans reporting an annual income of $500,000 increased tenfold between 1980 and 1989. The average compensation of corporate executive officers increased from 35 times an average worker's pay in 1978 to 71 times workers' average pay in 1989 (in 2005 the ratio was 262 to 1). In 1987 the United States had forty-nine billionaires—up from one in 1978. Middle-class incomes, however, remained stagnant.

rich ↑ middle = poor ↓

Reagan's economic policies benefited the wealthy at the expense of other Americans. Reagan's tax policies decreased the total effective tax rates—income taxes plus Social Security taxes—for the top 1 percent of American families by 14.4 percent. But they increased taxes for the poorest 20 percent of families by 16 percent. By 1990, the richest 1 percent controlled 40 percent of the nation's wealth; with 80 percent of wealth controlled by the top 20 percent.

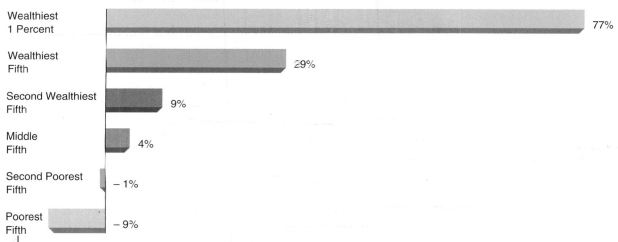

Percentage Increase in Pretax Income, 1977–1989

Wealthiest 1 Percent	77%
Wealthiest Fifth	29%
Second Wealthiest Fifth	9%
Middle Fifth	4%
Second Poorest Fifth	– 1%
Poorest Fifth	– 9%

Figure 32.2   Poverty in America by Race.

Between 1977 and 1989, the richest 1 percent of American families reaped most of the gains from economic growth. In fact, the average pretax income of families in the top 1 percent rose 77 percent. At the same time, the typical family saw its income edge up only 4 percent. And the bottom 40 percent of families had actual declines in income. (*Source:* Data from the *New York Times,* March 5, 1992)

REAGAN AND THE WORLD

A key element in Reagan's winning strategy in the 1980 election was his call for the United States to assert itself in the world. Though lacking a firm grasp of world issues, history, and geography, Reagan adhered to a few core principles. One was a deep anticommunism; a second was an underlying optimism about the United States's power and ability to positively affect the world. Together, these elements help explain Reagan's aggressive anticommunist foreign policy and his positive response in his second term to Soviet leader Mikhail Gorbachev's call for "new thinking" in world affairs.

Soviet-American Tension

Initially embracing the strident anticommunism of early Cold War foreign policy, Reagan rejected Nixon's détente and Carter's focus on human rights. Where Nixon and Carter perceived an increasingly multipolar international system, the Reagan team reverted to a bipolar perspective defined by the Soviet-American relationship. When Poland's pro-Soviet leaders in 1981 cracked down on an independent labor organization, Solidarity, Washington restricted Soviet-American trade and hurled angry words at Moscow. In March 1983, Reagan told evangelical Christians in Florida that the Soviets were "an evil empire." That year, Reagan restricted commercial flights to the Soviet Union after a Soviet fighter pilot mistakenly shot down a South Korean commercial jet straying 300 miles off course into Soviet airspace, and killed 269 passengers.

Reagan believed that substantial military buildup would thwart the Soviet threat. Accordingly, the administration launched the largest peacetime arms buildup in history. In 1985, when the military budget hit $294.7 billion (a doubling since 1980), the Pentagon spent an average $28 million an hour. Assigning low priority to arms control talks, Reagan announced in 1983 his desire for a space-based defense shield against incoming ballistic missiles: the Strategic Defense Initiative (SDI). His critics tagged it Star Wars and said such a system could never work; some enemy missiles would get through. Moreover, critics warned, SDI would elevate the arms race to dangerous levels. SDI research and development ultimately consumed tens of billions of dollars.

Reagan Doctrine

Because he attributed Third World disorders to Soviet intrigue, the president declared the Reagan Doctrine: the United States would openly support anticommunist movements—freedom fighters battling the Soviets or Soviet-backed governments. In Afghanistan, Reagan continued providing covert assistance, through Pakistan, to the Mujahidin rebels fighting Soviet occupation. When the Soviets stepped up the war in 1985, the Reagan administration sent more high-tech weapons, particularly anti-aircraft Stinger missiles. Easily transportable and fired by a single soldier, the Stingers turned the tide in Afghanistan by making Soviet jets and helicopters vulnerable below fifteen thousand feet.

Senior officials believed that the Soviets and Castro's Cuba were fomenting disorder in the region (see Map 32.1). In October 1983 the president sent troops into the tiny Caribbean island of Grenada to oust a pro-Marxist government. In El Salvador, he provided military and economic assistance to a military-dominated government

600 miles
600 kilometers

ATLANTIC OCEAN

Soviet military aid

Commonwealth status, 1952
Operation Bootstrap, 1950s

VIRGIN IS. (U.S)
ST. KITTS
AND NEVIS (1983)
ANTIGUA AND
BARBUDA (1981)
GUADELOUPE (Fr.)
DOMINICA (1978)
MARTINIQUE (Fr.)
ST. LUCIA (1979)
BARBADOS
(1966)
TRINIDAD AND
TOBAGO (1962)
(until 1967)
ST.
VINCENT
(1979)

San
Juan
 Cieba
PUERTO
RICO
(U.S.)

GUYANA
(1966)

BRAZIL

VENEZUELA

Vice President Nixon attacked by
mob, 1958
Founding member of OPEC, 1960

GRENADA (1974)
CURAÇAO
(Netl.)
Caracas

U.S. invasion, 1983

Drug War, 1989–

U.S. intervention, 1965

U.S. invasion,
1994

Raney

DOMINICAN
REP.

Santo
Domingo

HAITI
Port-au-Prince

Bay of Pigs invasion, 1961

JAMAICA
(1962)

Caribbean Sea

COLOMBIA

Bogotá

Norfolk

VA.
Ft. Bragg
N.C.
Charleston
S.C.
Savannah
GA.

CUBA
Guantánamo Bay
Kingston

Bay of Pigs invasion, 1931

Sandinistas oust Somoza, 1979
U.S.–Contra war against, 1981–1990
Sandinistas defeated in elections, 1990

Canal Zone
Panamá

PANAMA

UNITED STATES

TENN.
ALA.
MISS.
Montgomery
Atlanta
Columbus
Orlando
Tampa
FLA.
Miami
Homestead
Refugees
Key West
Havana

Castro to power, 1959
Cuba ousted from
OAS, 1962
Missile crisis, 1962
Helms-Burton Act, 1996

U.S. trade and travel
restrictions against Cuba

HONDURAS
Tegucigalpa

NICARAGUA
Managua

COSTA
RICA
San José

Anti-U.S. riots, 1959, 1964
Canal treaties, 1978
U.S. invasion, 1989

ARK.
LA.
New Orleans

Gulf of Mexico

BELIZE (1981)
Belize

GUATEMALA
Guatemala
San Salvador
EL SALVADOR

U.S. military advisors and aid, since 1979
Civil war ends, 1992

PACIFIC OCEAN

OKLA.
Dallas
Houston
San Antonio
TEXAS
N. MEX.
El Paso

Disputes over migrants
and drug trade
North American Free
Trade Agreement
signed with U.S., 1992

MEXICO
Mexico City

U.S. intervention, 1954
CIA trained Cuban exiles,
1960–1961
Civil war ends, 1996

□ U.S. military sites
⊢ U.S. Naval quarantine, 1962
| Soviet missile sites
▨ Members of Organization of American States (OAS) and
   participants in U.S.-sponsored Alliance for Progress
(1959) Dates of independence

Map 32.1 The United States in the Caribbean and Central America

The United States has often intervened in the Caribbean and Central America. Geographic proximity, economic stakes, political disputes, security links, trade in illicit drugs, and Cuba's alliance with the Soviet Union and defiance of the United States have kept North American eyes fixed on events in the region.

struggling with left-wing revolutionaries. The regime used right-wing death squads, from which Luisa Orellana and her family fled. By decade's end, the death squads had killed forty thousand dissidents and citizens, as well as several U.S. missionaries. By the late 1980s, the United States spent more than $6 billion there in a counterinsurgency war. In January 1992 the Salvadoran combatants negotiated a U.N.-sponsored peace.

Contra War in Nicaragua

The Reagan administration also meddled in the Nicaraguan civil war. In 1979 leftist insurgents in Nicaragua overthrew Anastasio Somoza, a long-time U.S. ally. The revolutionaries called themselves Sandinistas in honor of César Augusto Sandino, who headed the anti-imperialist Nicaraguan opposition against U.S. occupation in the 1930s and was finally assassinated by Somoza supporters. When the Sandinistas aided rebels in El Salvador, bought Soviet weapons, and invited Cubans to help reorganize the Nicaraguan army, Reagan officials charged that Nicaragua was becoming a Soviet client. In 1981 the CIA began to train, arm, and direct more than ten thousand counterrevolutionaries, known as contras, to overthrow the Nicaraguan government.

Many Americans, including Democratic leaders in Congress, were skeptical about the communist threat and warned that Nicaragua could become another Vietnam. Congress in 1984 voted to stop U.S. military aid to the contras. Secretly, the Reagan administration lined up other countries, including Saudi Arabia, Panama, and South Korea, to funnel money and weapons to the contras, and in 1985 Reagan imposed an economic embargo against Nicaragua. Reagan rejected a plan by Costa Rica's president Oscar Arias Sánchez in 1987 to obtain a cease-fire in Central America through negotiations and cutbacks in military aid to rebel forces. (Arias won the 1987 Nobel Peace Prize.) Three years later, Central American presidents brokered a settlement; in the national election that followed, the Sandinistas lost to a U.S.-funded party. After nearly a decade of civil war, thirty thousand Nicaraguans were dead and the ravaged Nicaraguan economy was one of the poorest in the hemisphere.

Iran-Contra Scandal

Reagan's obsession with defeating the Sandinistas almost caused his political undoing. In November 1986 it became known that the president's national security adviser, John M. Poindexter, and an aide, Marine lieutenant colonel Oliver North, in collusion with CIA director Casey, covertly sold weapons to Iran in an unsuccessful attempt to win the release of Americans held hostage by Islamic fundamentalist groups. Washington condemned Iran as a terrorist nation and demanded that America's allies cease trading there. More damaging was the revelation that money from the Iran arms deal had been illegally diverted to the contras. North later admitted that he illegally destroyed government documents and lied to Congress to keep the operation clandestine.

Although Reagan survived the scandal, his popularity declined, and Congress reasserted its authority over foreign affairs. In late 1992, outgoing president George W. H. Bush pardoned several former government officials convicted of lying to Congress. Critics smelled a cover-up, for Bush himself, as vice president, participated in high-level meetings on Iran-contra deals. As for North, his conviction was overturned on a technicality.

U.S. Interests in the Middle East

U.S. foreign policy placed increased importance on the Middle East and terrorism (see Map 33.2). The main U.S. goals in the Middle East were preserving access to oil and supporting its ally Israel, while checking Soviet influence. In the 1980s, though, American leaders faced new pressures from a deepened Israeli-Palestinian conflict and an anti-American and anti-Israeli Islamic fundamentalist movement that spread after the ouster of the shah of Iran in 1979.

The 1979 Camp David accords between Israel and Egypt raised hopes of a lasting settlement involving self-government for the Palestinian Arabs living in the Israeli-occupied Gaza Strip and West Bank. Instead, Israel and the Palestinian Liberation Organization (PLO) remained at odds. In 1982, in retaliation for Palestinian shelling of Israel from Lebanon, Israeli troops invaded Lebanon. The beleaguered PLO and various Lebanese factions called on Syria to contain the Israelis. Thousands of civilians died. Soon after Reagan sent Marines to Lebanon to join a peacekeeping force, U.S. troops became embroiled in a war between Christian and Muslim factions. In October 1983, terrorist bombs demolished a barracks, killing 241 U.S. servicemen. Four months later, Reagan pulled the remaining Marines out.

Terrorism

The attack on the Marine barracks showed the growing danger of terrorism to the United States and other western countries. In the 1980s, numerous otherwise powerless groups, many of them associated with the Palestinian cause or with Islamic fundamentalism, relied on terrorism to further their aims. Often they targeted U.S. citizens and property, because of Washington's support of Israel and U.S. involvement in the Lebanese civil war. Of the 690 hijackings, kidnappings, bombings, and shootings around the world in 1985, for example, 217 were against Americans, most originating in Iran, Libya, Lebanon, and the Gaza Strip. Three years later, a Pan American passenger plane was destroyed over Scotland, and many suspected pro-Iranian terrorists.

Washington proposed peace plans for the Israelis to give back occupied territories and the Arabs to stop trying to push the Jews out of the Middle East. As the peace process stalled in 1987, Palestinians living in the West Bank began an *intifada* (Arabic for "uprising") against Israeli forces. Israel refused to negotiate, but the United States talked with PLO chief Yasir Arafat after he renounced terrorism and accepted Israel's right to live in peace. For the PLO to recognize Israel and the United States to recognize the PLO were major developments in the Arab-Israeli conflict.

In South Africa, too, American diplomacy became more aggressive. At first, the Reagan administration followed a policy of constructive engagement, asking the increasingly isolated government to reform its white supremacist apartheid system. But many Americans demanded cutting off imports from South Africa and pressuring 350 U.S. companies to cease operations there. Some U.S. cities and states passed divestment laws, withdrawing dollars from U.S. companies active in South Africa.

Public protest and congressional legislation forced the Reagan administration in 1986 to impose economic restrictions. Within two years, about half of the U.S. companies in South Africa left.

Enter Gorbachev

Many on the right disliked the South Africa sanctions policy; they believed the main black opposition group, the African National Congress (ANC), was dominated by communists, and they doubted the efficacy of sanctions. They also balked when Reagan, his popularity declining, entered negotiations with the Soviet Union. At a 1985 Geneva summit meeting, Reagan agreed in principle with new Soviet leader Mikhail S. Gorbachev's contention that strategic weapons should be substantially reduced, and at a 1986 Reykjavik, Iceland, meeting, they came close to a major reduction agreement. SDI stood in the way: Gorbachev insisted it should be shelved, and Reagan refused.

But Reagan and Gorbachev got along well. As General Colin Powell commented, though the Soviet leader was far superior to Reagan in mastery of specifics, he understood that Reagan was, as Powell put it, "the embodiment of his people's down-to-earth character, practicality, and optimism." And Reagan toned down his strident anti-Soviet rhetoric.

Perestroika and *Glasnost*

The turnaround in Soviet-American relations stemmed more from changes abroad than from Reagan's decisions. Under Gorbachev, a younger generation of Soviet leaders came to power in 1985. They modernized the highly bureaucratized, decaying economy through a reform program known as *perestroika* ("restructuring") and liberalized the authoritarian political system through *glasnost* ("openness"). For these reforms to work, Soviet military expenditures had to be reduced.

In 1987 Gorbachev and Reagan signed the Intermediate-Range Nuclear Forces (INF) Treaty banning all land-based intermediate-range nuclear missiles in Europe. About 2,800 missiles were destroyed. Gorbachev also reduced his nation's armed forces, helped settle regional conflicts, and began the withdrawal of Soviet troops from Afghanistan. The Cold War was coming to an end.

AMERICAN SOCIETY IN THE 1980s

As the Cold War waned, the belief in a United States united by shared middle-class values also lost its force. By the 1980s, after years of social struggle and division, few Americans believed in the reality of that vision; many rejected it as undesirable. Although the 1980s were never as contentious as the 1960s and 1970s, deep social divides split Americans. A newly powerful group of Christian conservatives challenged the secular majority. A growing class of affluent Americans seemed a society apart from the urban poor, whom sociologists and journalists began calling the underclass. And the composition of the U.S. population was changing dramatically, as people immigrated to the United States from more and different nations than ever before.

Growth of the Religious Right

Since the 1960s, the United States's liberal Protestant churches—Episcopalian, Presbyterian, Methodist—had been losing members, while Southern Baptists and other denominations offering the experience of being born again through belief in Jesus Christ and the literal truth of the Bible (fundamentalism) grew rapidly. Fundamentalist preachers reached out through television: by the late 1970s, televangelist Oral Roberts was drawing 3.9 million viewers. Nearly 20 percent of Americans self-identified as fundamentalist Christians in 1980.

Most fundamentalist Christian churches stayed out of the social and political conflicts of the 1960s and early 1970s. But in the late 1970s, some influential preachers mobilized for political struggle against the United States's increasing permissiveness. In a 1980 Washington for Jesus rally, fundamentalist leader Pat Robertson told crowds, "We have enough votes to run the country." The Moral Majority, founded in 1979 by Jerry Falwell, sought to create a Christian America, partly by supporting political candidates. Falwell's defense of socially conservative family values and his condemnation of feminism (he called NOW the National Order of Witches), homosexuality, pornography, and abortion resonated with many Americans.

Throughout the 1980s, conservative Christians known as the New Right campaigned against the United States's secular culture. Rejecting multiculturalism—that different cultures and lifestyles were equally valid—the New Right wanted God's law to be the basis for American society. Concerned Women for America, founded by Beverly LaHayes in 1979, wanted elementary school readers containing "unacceptable" religious beliefs (including excerpts from *The Diary of Anne Frank* and *The Wizard of Oz*) removed from classrooms. The Reagan administration frequently turned to James Dobson, founder of the conservative Focus on the Family organization, for policy advice. Conservative Christians also joined with Roman Catholics, Mormons, and other groups in the anti-abortion, or prolife, movement.

Culture Wars

Many Americans vigorously opposed the New Right's seeming intolerance and threat to basic freedoms, including freedom of religion for those whose beliefs differed from the conservative Christianity of the New Right. In 1932 politically progressive television producer Norman Lear, influential former congresswoman Barbara Jordan, and other prominent figures from the fields of business, religion, politics, and entertainment founded People for the American Way to support American civil liberties, the separation of church and state, and the values of tolerance and diversity. The struggle between the religious right and their opponents for the nation's future came to be known as the culture wars.

Many beliefs of Christian fundamentalists ran counter to the way most Americans lived, especially regarding women's roles. By the 1980s, a generation of girls had grown up with the gains of the women's movement, expecting freedoms and opportunities that their mothers never had. Legislation such as the Civil Rights Act of 1964 and Title IX opened academic and athletic programs to females. By 1985, more than half of married women with children under three worked outside the home, many from economic necessity. The religious right's insistence that women's place was in the home, subordinated to her husband, contradicted the gains made toward sexual equality and the reality of many women's lives.

The New Inequality

A 1988 national report on race relations looked back to the 1968 Kerner Commission report to claim, "America is again becoming two separate societies," white and black. It argued that African Americans endured poverty, segregation, and crime in inner-city ghettos while whites lived comfortably in suburbia. The majority of the United States's poor were white, and the black middle class was expanding. But people of color were disproportionately poor. In 1980, 33 percent of African Americans and 26 percent of Hispanic Americans lived in poverty, compared with 10 percent of whites (see Figure 32.3).

Reasons for poverty varied. The legacies of racism played a role. The changing job structure was partly responsible, as well-paid jobs decreased, replaced by lower-paid service jobs. In addition, families headed by a single mother were five times more likely to be poor than families maintained by a married couple. By 1992, 59 percent of African American children and 17 percent of white children lived in female-headed households, and almost half of African American children lived in poverty.

Social Crises in American Cities

In impoverished inner-city neighborhoods, violent crime—particularly homicides and gang warfare—grew alarmingly, as did school dropout rates, crime rates, and child abuse. Some people sought escape in hard drugs, especially crack, a derivative of cocaine, which first struck New York City's poorest neighborhoods in 1985. Gang shootouts over drugs were deadly: the toll in Los Angeles in 1987 was 387 deaths, more than half

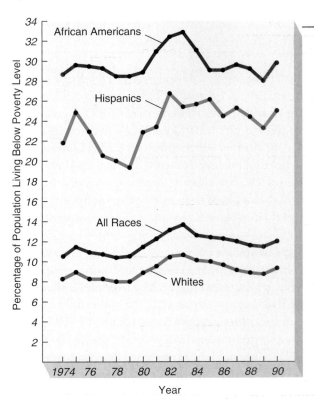

Figure 32.3   Poverty in the United States by Race, 1974–1990

Poverty in the United States rose in the early 1980s but subsided afterward. Many people of color, however, experienced little relief during the decade. Notice that the percentage of African Americans living below the poverty level was three times higher than that for whites. It was also much higher for Hispanic Americans. (*Source:* Adapted from U.S. Bureau of the Census, *Statistical Abstract of the United States* [Washington, DC: U.S. Government Printing Office, 1992], p. 461.)

of them innocent bystanders. Many states instituted mandatory prison sentences for possessing small amounts of crack equivalent to those for 100 grams of cocaine, the drug favored by more affluent, white Americans. Such policies increased the United States's prison population almost fourfold from 1980 to the mid-1990s, with African and Hispanic American youth arrested in disproportionate numbers. By 2000, young African American men were more likely to have been arrested than to have graduated from college.

Homelessness also grew during the 1980s. Some homeless were impoverished families; many had drug or alcohol problems. About one-third of the homeless were former psychiatric patients. By 1985, 80 percent of the beds in state mental hospitals were eliminated on the claim that neighborhood programs would serve people better. Such local programs never materialized. Consequently, many of the United States's mentally ill citizens wandered the streets.

In the 1980s there was an alarming spread of sexually transmitted diseases, especially acquired immune deficiency syndrome (AIDS). Campaigns for safe sex, such as this New York City subway ad, urged people to use condoms. (Sandro Tucci/Time Life Pictures/Getty Images)

The AIDS Epidemic

Another social crisis in the 1980s was the global spread of acquired immune deficiency syndrome, or AIDS. Caused by the human immunodeficiency virus (HIV), AIDS leaves its victims susceptible to deadly infections and cancers. The human immunodeficiency virus is spread through the exchange of blood or body fluids, often through sexual intercourse or needle sharing by intravenous drug users.

AIDS was first diagnosed in the United States in 1981. Between 1981 and 1988, of the 57,000 AIDS cases reported, nearly 32,000 resulted in death. Politicians were slow to devote resources to AIDS, partly because it was initially perceived as a gay man's disease. "A man reaps what he sows," declared the Reverend Jerry Falwell of the Moral Majority. AIDS, along with other sexually transmitted diseases, such as genital herpes and chlamydia, ended an era defined by penicillin and the pill, in which sex was freed from the threat of serious disease or unwanted pregnancy.

An Era of Ostentation

For the rich, the 1980s were an era of ostentation. "Greed is all right," the Wall Street financier Ivan Boesky told students at the University of California, Berkeley, the center of 1960s campus protest, and he was met with cheers and laughter. The New York entrepreneur Donald Trump's $29 million yacht had gold-plated bathroom fixtures. The publisher Malcolm Forbes flew eight hundred guests to Morocco for his seventieth birthday; the party cost $2 million.

Nineteen eighty-four was the Year of the Yuppie—Young Urban Professional—proclaimed *Newsweek* magazine. A derogatory term, *Yuppie* (and *Buppie*, for Black Urban Professional) described ambitious and successful young Americans in demanding careers who enjoyed a consumer-driven lifestyle: BMWs, Armani suits, Häagen-Dazs ice cream. Americans seemed fascinated with the superrich (making *Dallas* a top-rated television show) and with Yuppie lifestyles. But Yuppies also represented those who got ahead without caring about those left behind. As Yuppies gentrified urban neighborhoods, displacing poorer residents, graffiti, like "Die, Yuppie Scum," appeared in New York.

New Immigrants from Asia

Social divisions were further complicated by the arrival of new immigrants from regions barely represented in the United States. Between 1970 and 1990 the United States absorbed more than 13 million new arrivals, most from Latin America and Asia. Before the 1965 immigration reforms Americans of Asian ancestry made up less than 1 percent of the population; by 1990 that figure tripled.

Before 1965, most Asian Americans were of Japanese ancestry (about 52 percent in 1960), followed by Chinese and Filipino. In the 1960s and 1970s, the highest rates of immigration were from nations not previously represented in the U.S. population. There were only 603 Vietnamese residents of the United States in 1964. By 1990, the United States absorbed almost 800,000 refugees from Indochina, casualties of the Vietnam War. Immigrants flooded in from South Korea, Thailand, India, Pakistan, Bangladesh, Indonesia, Singapore, Laos, Cambodia, and Vietnam. Japanese Americans were now only 15 percent of the Asian American population.

Immigrants from Asia were typically either highly skilled or unskilled. Unsettled conditions in the Philippines in the 1970s and 1980s created an exodus of well-educated Filipinos to the United States. India's overabundance of physicians and healthcare workers increasingly emigrated, as did educated, skilled workers from Korea, Taiwan, and China. Other Chinese immigrants, however, had few job skills and spoke little English. Many crowded into neighborhoods like New York City's Chinatown, where women worked under terrible conditions in the city's nonunion garment industry. But even highly educated immigrants had limited options. A 1983 study found that Korean Americans owned three-quarters of the approximately twelve hundred greengroceries in New York City. Though often cited as a success story, Korean greengrocers usually descended the professional ladder: 78 percent had college or professional degrees.

The Growing Hispanic American Population

Unprecedented immigration coupled with a high birth rate made Hispanic Americans the fastest-growing group of Americans. In 1970 Hispanic Americans made up 4.5 percent of the nation's population; that jumped to 9 percent by 1990, when one out of three Los Angelenos and Miamians were Hispanic. Mexican Americans, concentrated in California and the Southwest, made up most of this population, but Puerto Ricans, Cubans, Dominicans, and other Caribbean immigrants also lived in the United States, clustered principally in East Coast cities.

During the 1980s, people from Guatemala and El Salvador, like Luisa Orellana, fled civil war and government violence for the United States. Although the U.S. government commonly refused them political asylum (about 113,000 Cubans received political refugee status during the 1980s, compared with fewer than 1,400 El Salvadorans), a national Sanctuary movement of Christian churches defied the law to protect refugees from deportation. Economic troubles in Mexico and throughout

Central and South America also produced a flood of undocumented workers who crossed the poorly guarded 2,000-mile border between the United States and Mexico, seeking economic opportunities. Some were sojourners, who moved back and forth across the border. A majority meant to stay.

Many Americans believed new arrivals threatened jobs and economic security, and nativist violence and bigotry increased. In 1982 twenty-seven-year-old Vincent Chin was beaten to death in Detroit by an unemployed auto worker and his uncle. U.S. automobiles were losing to Japanese imports, and the two men seemingly mistook the Chinese American Chin for Japanese. In New York, Philadelphia, and Los Angeles, inner-city African Americans boycotted Korean groceries. Riots broke out in Los Angeles schools between African American students and newly arrived Mexicans. In Dade County, Florida, voters passed an antibilingual measure that removed Spanish-language signs on public transportation, while at the state and national level people debated declaring English the official U.S. language. Concerned about illegal aliens, Congress passed the Immigration Reform and Control (Simpson-Rodino) Act in 1986. The act's purpose was to discourage illegal immigration by imposing sanctions on employers who hired undocumented workers, but it also provided amnesty to millions who immigrated illegally before 1982.

THE END OF THE COLD WAR AND GLOBAL DISORDER

The end of Ronald Reagan's presidency coincided with world events that brought the dawn of a new international system. Reagan's vice president, George Herbert Walker Bush, would become president and oversee the transition. The scion of a Wall Street banker and U.S. senator from Connecticut, Bush attended an exclusive boarding school and then Yale. He had the advantage in seeking the Republican presidential nomination in having been a loyal vice president. And he possessed a formidable résumé, including ambassador to the United Nations, chairman of the Republican Party, special envoy to China, and director of the CIA. He had also been a war hero, flying fifty-eight combat missions in the Pacific in World War II and receiving the Distinguished Flying Cross.

George Herbert Walker Bush

Bush entered the 1988 presidential campaign trailing his Democratic opponent, Massachusetts governor Michael Dukakis. Republicans turned that around by waging one of the most negative campaigns in U.S. history. Most notoriously, the Bush camp aired a television commercial featuring an African American convicted murderer, Willie Horton, who terrorized a Maryland couple, raping the woman, while on weekend furlough from prison—a temporary release program begun under Dukakis's Republican predecessor but attributed in the ad to Dukakis's being soft on crime. The Republicans also falsely suggested that Dukakis had a history of psychiatric problems. Dukakis, while not personally attacking Bush, ran an uninspired campaign. Bush won by 8 percentage points in the popular vote and received 426 electoral votes to Dukakis's 112. The Democrats, however, retained control of both houses of Congress.

Bush focused on foreign policy, though naturally cautious and reactive in world affairs, much to the chagrin of neoconservatives. Mikhail Gorbachev's reforms in the Soviet Union were now stimulating reforms in eastern Europe that ultimately led to revolution. In 1989 thousands in East Germany, Poland, Hungary, Czechoslovakia, and Romania startled the world by repudiating their communist governments and staging mass protests for increased freedom. In November 1989, Germans scaled the Berlin Wall and tore it down; the following October, the two Germanys reunited. By then other eastern European communist governments had fallen or were near collapse.

Pro-Democracy Movements

Other communist challenges were less successful. In June 1989, Chinese armed forces slaughtered hundreds—perhaps thousands—of unarmed students and citizens holding peaceful pro-democracy rallies in Beijing's Tiananmen Square. The Bush administration, anxious to preserve influence in Beijing, simply denounced the action, allowing the Chinese government to emphatically reject political liberalization.

Elsewhere, however, democratization efforts proved too powerful to resist. In South Africa, a new government under F. W. de Klerk began a cautious retreat from apartheid. In February 1990, de Klerk legalized all political parties in South Africa, including the ANC, and released Nelson Mandela, a hero to black South Africans, after a twenty-seven-year imprisonment. Then, the government repealed its apartheid laws over several years, allowing all citizens to vote. Mandela, who became South Africa's first black president in 1994, called the transformation a small miracle.

Collapse of Soviet Power

In 1990 the Soviet Union began to disintegrate. First the Baltic states of Lithuania, Latvia, and Estonia declared independence from Moscow. The following year, the Soviet Union ceased to exist, disintegrating into successor states—Russia, Ukraine, Tajikistan, and many others (see Map 32.2). Muscled aside by Russian reformers who thought he was moving too slowly toward democracy and free-market economics, Gorbachev lost power. The breakup of the Soviet empire, the dismantling of the Warsaw Pact (the Soviet military alliance formed in 1955 with communist countries of eastern Europe), the repudiation of communism by its leaders, German reunification, and a significantly reduced risk of nuclear war signaled the end of the Cold War.

The United States and its allies had won. The containment policy followed by nine presidents—from Truman through Bush—had many critics over the years, but succeeded at containing communism for four-plus decades without blowing up the world or obliterating freedom at home. Over time, the Soviet socialist economy proved less able to compete with the U.S. free-market one, less able to cope with the demands of the Soviet and eastern European citizenry.

Yet the Soviet empire might have survived longer had it not been for Gorbachev, one of the most influential figures of the twentieth century. Through unexpected overtures and decisions, Gorbachev fundamentally transformed the superpower relationship in ways that could scarcely have been anticipated before. Ronald Reagan's role was less central but still important because of his later willingness to negotiate and treat Gorbachev more as a partner than as an adversary. Just as personalities mattered in starting the Cold War, they mattered in ending it.

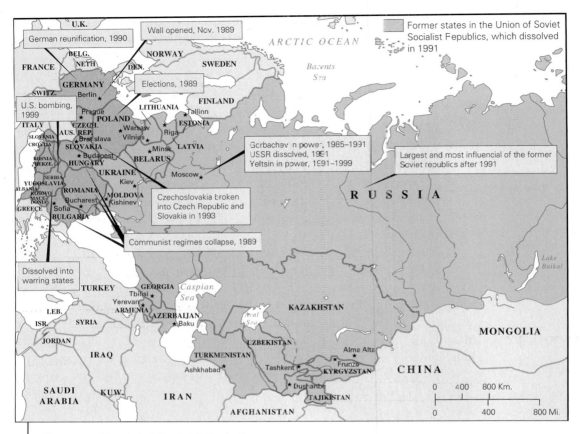

Map 32.2   The End of the Cold War in Europe

When Mikhail Gorbachev came to power in the Soviet Union in 1985, he initiated reforms that ultimately undermined the communist regimes in eastern Europe and East Germany and led to the breakup of the Soviet Union itself, ensuring an end to the Cold War.

Costs of Victory

The victory in the Cold War elicited little celebration among Americans. The confrontation may never have become a hot war globally, but the period after 1945 nevertheless witnessed numerous Cold War–related conflicts claiming millions of lives In the Vietnam War alone, up to 2 million people died, more than 58,000 of them Americans. Military budgets ate up billions of dollars, shortchanging domestic programs. Some Americans wondered whether the communist threat was ever as grave as officials had claimed.

Bush proclaimed a new world order and signed important arms reduction treaties with the Soviet Union in 1991 and with the post-breakup Russia in 1993. But the United States sustained a large defense budget and stationed large numbers of military forces overseas. As a result, Americans were denied the peace dividend that they hoped would reduce taxes and free up funds for domestic problems.

In Central America, the Bush administration cooled the zeal with which Reagan meddled, but showed no reluctance to intervene to further U.S. aims. In December 1989, U.S. troops invaded Panama to oust military leader Manuel Noriega. A long-time drug trafficker, Noriega stayed in Washington's favor in the mid-1980s by providing logistical support for the Nicaraguan contras. In the early 1990s, exposés of his sordid record changed Bush's mind. Noriega was captured and taken to Miami, where, in 1992, he was convicted of drug trafficking and imprisoned. Devastated Panama, meanwhile, became increasingly dependent on the United States.

Saddam Hussein's Gamble

The strongest test of Bush's foreign policy came in the Middle East. The Iran-Iraq War ended inconclusively in August 1988, after eight years and almost 400,000 dead. The Reagan administration assisted the Iraqis with weapons and intelligence, as had many NATO countries. In mid-1990 Iraqi president Saddam Hussein, facing massive war debts, invaded neighboring Kuwait, hoping to enhance his regional power and oil revenues. George Bush condemned the invasion and vowed to defend Kuwait, partly fearing that Iraq might threaten U.S. oil supplies in Kuwait and petroleum-rich Saudi Arabia.

Within weeks, Bush convinced every important government, including most Arab and Islamic states, to economically boycott Iraq. Then, in Operation Desert Shield, Bush dispatched more than 500,000 U.S. forces to the region, joined by more than 200,000 from allied countries. Likening Saddam to Hitler and declaring it the first post–Cold War "test of our mettle," Bush rallied a deeply divided Congress to authorize "all necessary means" to oust Iraq from Kuwait (a vote of 250 to 183 in the House and 52 to 47 in the Senate). Many Americans believed that economic sanctions should be given more time to work, but Bush would not wait. Victory would come swiftly and cleanly.

Operation Desert Storm

Operation Desert Storm began on January 16, 1991, with the greatest air armada in history pummeling Iraqi targets. U.S. missiles reinforced round-the-clock bombing raids on Baghdad, Iraq's capital. It was a television war, in which CNN reporters broadcast live from a Baghdad hotel as bombs fell. In late February, coalition forces under General Norman Schwartzkopf launched a ground war that quickly routed the Iraqis from Kuwait. When the war ended on March 1, at least 40,000 Iraqis had been killed, while allied troops lost 240 (148 of them Americans).

Bush rejected suggestions from advisers to take Baghdad and topple Hussein's regime. Coalition members would not have agreed to such a plan, and it was unclear who would replace Iraq's dictator. So Saddam Hussein remained, though with his authority curtailed. The United Nations maintained an arms and economic embargo, and the Security Council issued Resolution 687, demanding full disclosure of Iraq's program to develop weapons of mass destruction and ballistic missiles. In Resolution 688, the Security Council condemned the Iraqi regime's brutal crackdown against Kurds in northern Iraq and Shi'ite Muslims in the south and demanded access for humanitarian groups. The United States, Britain, and France seized on Resolution 688 to create a northern no-fly zone, prohibiting Iraqi aircraft flights. A similar no-fly zone was set up in southern Iraq in 1992 and expanded in 1996.

Domestic Problems

Although many would later question President Bush's decision to stop short of Baghdad, initially there were few objections. In the wake of Desert Storm, the president's

CNN

When Ted Turner launched CNN, his Cable News Network, on June 1, 1980, few people took it seriously. With a staff of three hundred—mostly young, mostly inexperienced—CNN operated from the basement of a converted Atlanta country club. CNN was initially known for its on-air errors, as when a cleaning woman emptied anchor Bernard Shaw's trash during his live newscast. But by 1992, CNN was seen in more than 150 nations, and *Time* magazine named Ted Turner its Man of the Year.

Throughout the 1980s, CNN built relations with local news outlets worldwide. CNN reported live from Tiananmen Square and from the Berlin Wall in 1989. Millions watched as CNN reporters broadcast live from Baghdad in the 1991 Gulf War. When the Soviet Union wanted to denounce the 1989 U.S. invasion of Panama, officials called CNN's Moscow bureau instead of the U.S. embassy. During the Gulf War, Saddam Hussein reportedly kept televisions in his bunker tuned to CNN, and U.S. generals used its broadcasts to judge the effectiveness of missile attacks. Despite its global mission, CNN's U.S. origins were often apparent. During the U.S. invasion of Panama, CNN cautioned correspondents not to refer to the U.S. military forces as "our" troops. What CNN offered was a global experience: people throughout the world watching the major moments in contemporary history as they unfolded. The United States's CNN created new links among the world's people. But, as *Time* magazine noted (while praising Turner as the Prince of the Global Village), such connections "did not produce instantaneous brotherhood, just a slowly dawning awareness of the implications of a world transfixed by a single TV image."

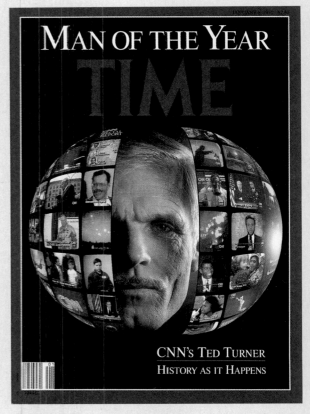

"I am the right man in the right place at the right time," Ted Turner declared at the time of CNN's founding in 1980. "Not me alone, but all the people who think the world can be brought together by telecommunications." Just over a decade later, Turner was rewarded for his visionary ideas by being named *Time* magazine's Man of the Year for 1991.

(Time Life Pictures/Getty Images)

---

popularity soared to 91 percent, beating the record 89 percent set by Harry Truman in June 1945 after Germany surrendered. Cocky advisers thought Bush could ride his popularity through the 1992 election.

Bush could also claim domestic achievements that seemed to affirm his pledge to lead a "kinder, gentler nation." In 1990, for example, Bush signed the Americans with Disabilities Act. Also in 1990, the president signed the Clean Air Act, which sought to reduce acid rain by limiting factory and automobile emissions.

[handwritten margin note: Clean Air Act → to reduce acid rain by limiting factory/auto emissions]

Yet Bush's poll numbers started falling and kept falling, largely because of his ineffectual response to the weakening economy. He was slow to grasp the implications of the heavy national debt and massive federal deficit. When the nation entered into a full-fledged recession after the Gulf War, Bush merely proclaimed that things were not *that* bad.

Business shrank, despite low interest rates that theoretically should have encouraged investment. Real-estate prices plummeted. U.S. products faced tougher overseas competitors, especially in Japan and elsewhere in Asia. As unemployment climbed to 8 percent, consumer confidence sank. By late 1991, fewer than 40 percent of the American people felt comfortable about the nation's direction.

Clarence Thomas's Nomination

Bush's credibility was diminished further in fall 1991 by the confirmation hearings for Clarence Thomas, his Supreme Court nominee. The Bush administration hoped that those who opposed the nomination of another conservative to the high court might support an African American justice. But in October, Anita Hill, an African American law professor at the University of Oklahoma, charged that Thomas had sexually harassed her when she worked for him during the early 1980s. The televised Judiciary Committee hearings turned ugly, and some Republican members suggested that Hill was either lying or mentally ill. Thomas described himself as the "victim" of a "high-tech lynching." However, Hill's testimony focused the nation's attention on issues of power, gender, race, and the workplace. And the Senate's confirmation of Thomas, along with the attacks on Hill, angered many, further increasing the gender gap in American politics.

Summary

When Ronald Reagan left the White House in 1988, the *New York Times* wrote: "Ronald Reagan leaves no Vietnam War, no Watergate, no hostage crisis. But he leaves huge question marks—and much to do." George H. W. Bush met the foreign policy promises of the 1980s, as the Soviet Union collapsed and the United States won the Cold War. He also led the United States into war with Iraq, which ended swiftly and left Saddam Hussein in power.

During the 1980s, the United States moved from recession to economic prosperity. However, deep tax cuts and massive increases in defense spending increased the national debt from $994 billion to more than $2.9 trillion. Pro-business policies, such as deregulation, created opportunities for economic growth but also opened the door for corruption. Policies that benefited the wealthy at the expense of middle-class or poor Americans widened the gulf between the very rich and everyone else. Drug addiction, crime, and violence grew, especially in the most impoverished areas. The 1980s also saw the beginning of culture wars between fundamentalist Christians who sought to "restore" America to God and those who championed separation of church and state. The nation shifted politically to the right, though the coalitions of economic and social conservatives who supported Reagan were fragile.

Finally, during the 1980s, the nation's Hispanic population grew. New immigrants from Asia arrived in large numbers, too. During the Reagan-Bush years, the United States became both more divided and more diverse.

The Americans with Disabilities Act

The Americans with Disabilities Act (ADA), passed by large bipartisan majorities in Congress and signed into law by President George H. W. Bush on July 26, 1990, built on the legacy of the United States's civil rights movement. Beyond prohibiting discrimination, it mandated that public and private entities—schools, stores, restaurants and hotels, government buildings, and public transportation authorities—provide "reasonable accommodations" allowing people with disabilities to participate fully in their communities and the nation.

The equal-access provisions of the ADA have changed the U.S. landscape. Steep curbs and stairs once blocked access to wheelchair users; now ramps and lifts are common. Buses "kneel" for passengers with limited mobility; crosswalks and elevators use audible signals for the sight-impaired; colleges and universities offer qualified students a wide range of assistance. People with various disabilities have traveled into the Grand Canyon and other parks, thanks to the National Park Service's accessibility programs.

At the same time, ADA employment regulations have generated difficult legal questions. Which conditions are covered by the ADA? (The Supreme Court ruled that asymptomatic HIV infection is a covered disability and carpal tunnel syndrome is not.) Employers may not discriminate against qualified people who can, with "reasonable" accommodation, perform the "essential" tasks of a job—but what is "reasonable" and what is "essential"? The specific provisions of the ADA will likely continue to be contested and redefined in the courts. But as Attorney General Janet Reno noted, as she celebrated the ADA's tenth anniversary, its true legacy is the determination "to find the best in everyone and to give everyone equal opportunity."

Chapter Review

REAGAN AND THE CONSERVATIVE RESURGENCE

How did Ronald Reagan unify conservatives into a powerful political coalition?

In his 1980 and 1984 presidential campaigns (and as president), Ronald Reagan appealed to, and ultimately united, a broad range of previously fragmented groups nationwide, transforming them into a strong, unified conservative Republican base. First, Reagan drew those who wanted to strengthen the military, minimize federal power, and weaken liberal social programs of the 1930s New Deal and 1960s Great Society. Second, Reagan attracted economic conservatives with his stand on deregulation, weaker unions, and tax policies benefiting corporations and investors. Third, Reagan drew support from disillusioned Democrats—intellectual neoconservatives who fell away from the party after Vietnam and members of unions and ethnic groups who resented their hard-earned tax dollars funding welfare handouts to those who did not work. Finally, though divorced, Reagan also drew the religious New Right into his coalition by embracing causes that were important to them: the anti-abortion cause and prayer in public schools.

REAGANOMICS

Which policies helped transform the economic recession into an economic boom?

Reaganomics—President Ronald Reagan's supply-side economic policy—is often credited with ending stagflation and promoting economic recovery. This theory held that by cutting taxes, businesses and the wealthy would invest in the economy, and the growth produced by this investment would, in turn, ultimately trickle down to benefit all Americans. In truth, Federal Reserve policies actually deserve the credit for ending stagflation and reversing the downturn. This autonomous governmental body raised interest rates on loans to an all-time high of 21.5 percent and tightened money supply. While this policy initially took the nation deeper into a slump, as foreclosures, bankruptcy, and unemployment rates skyrocketed, it ultimately lowered inflation and raised the Gross National Product, triggering an economic resurgence by 1984.

Why was the 1980s' economic boom a mixed blessing?

On the one hand, by 1984, the Federal Reserve's policy of increasing interest rates and tightening money supply ended stagflation and reversed the economic downturn. And President Reagan's pro-business policies and deregulation helped smaller companies make inroads into fields previously dominated by major corporations. On the other hand, deregulation allowed many businesses—particularly the financial services industry—to operate without accountability to governing authorities such as the SEC. Consequently, corruption was widespread, as some investors became rich via insider trading, the illegal practice of buying stocks with information not available to the public. Shady deals in the savings and loan industry caused its collapse and required a federal bail-out of half a trillion dollars. The high-risk investment climate of the latter half of the decade not only fueled a stock market crash in 1987, but also led to corporate downsizing and layoffs for middle managers. Finally, Reagan's tax cuts and other policies benefited the rich at the expense of other Americans, enabling the rich to get richer while the poor became poorer.

REAGAN AND THE WORLD

What characterized Reagan's approach to foreign policy?

In foreign policy, Reagan was both aggressive and optimistic. In dealing with the Soviets, he initially adopted a strident anticommunist position, implementing the Reagan Doctrine to aid anticommunist freedom fighters around the world. He even branded the Soviet Union as "an evil empire" and helped arm counter-revolutionaries to overthrow the Nicaraguan government when he thought it was becoming communist. Believing that a solid defense would thwart the Soviet threat, Reagan launched the largest peacetime arms buildup in U.S. history, spending $294.7 billion in 1985 (twice as much as in 1980). But his optimism about the power of the United States to positively affect world events also led him in his second term to accept Soviet leader Mikhail Gorbachev's call for disarmament and new thinking in world affairs that led to the end of the Cold War.

AMERICAN SOCIETY IN THE 1980S

What divided Americans in the 1980s?

Americans continued to feel the tug of unresolved racial and ethnic tensions, especially as the immigrant groups who arrived in the 1960s and 1970s (particularly Asians and Hispanics) began to claim their place in society. In addition, a growing class of rich Americans were farther removed from the so-called under-class, as journalists referred to urban poor. New lines were also being drawn between secular and religious forces, as a powerful new group of Christian conservatives sought to reverse what they regarded as society's increased permissiveness, restore conservative family values, and shape the nation's future around their core Christian beliefs. The resulting battle, dubbed the culture wars, pitted those who supported the separation of church and state and celebrated tolerance and diversity against the religious right's seeming intolerance, antifeminism, and homophobia.

THE END OF THE COLD WAR AND GLOBAL DISORDER

What were the highs and lows of Bush's presidency?

George H. W. Bush's popularity ratings soared to 91 percent after the United States's success in Operation Desert Storm. He scored kudos for passing the Americans with Disabilities Act, banning job discrimination against those with disabilities who can reasonably perform a job's task with minor accommodations. He also signed the Clean Air Act in 1990, which sought to reduce acid rain by restricting factory and auto emissions. But his blind-spot about the weakening economy and recession that emerged after the Gulf War turned voters off. He dismissed the rising jobless rates, shrinking number of businesses, and plummeting real estate prices as not that bad, leading many Americans to distrust the nation's future in Bush's hands.

SUGGESTIONS FOR FURTHER READING

Elijah Anderson, *Streetwise: Race, Class, and Change in an Urban Community* (1992)

A. J. Bacevich et al., *The Gulf War of 1991 Reconsidered* (2003)

Lou Cannon, *President Reagan: The Role of a Lifetime* (2000)

Robert M. Collins, *Transforming America: Politics and Culture During the Reagan Years* (2006)

Jack F. Matlock, *Reagan and Gorbachev: How the Cold War Ended* (2004)

John Micklethwait and Adrian Wooldridge, *The Right Nation: Conservative Power in America* (2004)

James A. Morone, *Hellfire Nation: The Politics of Sin in American History* (2003)

James Patterson, *The Restless Giant: The United States from Watergate to Bush vs. Gore* (2005)

For a more extensive list for further reading, go to college.cengage.com/pic/norton8e.

Into the Global Millennium

At 8:46 A.M. on that fateful Tuesday morning, Jan Demczur, a window washer, stepped into an elevator in the North Tower of the World Trade Center in New York City. Before the elevator reached its next landing, one of the six occupants recalled, "We felt a muted thud. The whole building shook. And the elevator swung from side to side like a pendulum." None of the occupants knew it, but American Airlines Flight 175 had just crashed into the building at 440 miles per hour.

The elevator started plunging. Someone pushed the emergency stop button. Then a voice came over the intercom: there had been an explosion. As smoke seeped into the elevator, several men used the wooden handle of Demczur's squeegee to force open the doors but discovered they were on the fiftieth floor, where this elevator did not stop. In front of them was a wall.

Demczur, a Polish immigrant who once worked as a builder, saw that the wall was made of Sheetrock, a plasterboard that could be cut. Using the squeegee, the six men took turns scraping and poking, and finally burst through to a men's bathroom. Startled firefighters guided them to a stairwell. They finally reached the street at 10:23 A.M. Five minutes later the tower collapsed.

It was September 11, 2001.

Later that day Demczur learned that terrorists had hijacked four airliners and turned them into missiles. Two were flown into the World Trade Center; one slammed into the Pentagon in Washington, D.C.; and one crashed in a Pennsylvania field after passengers tried to retake the plane from the hijackers. Both World Trade Center towers collapsed, killing nearly three thousand people.

It was the deadliest attack the United States ever suffered on its soil, and it would dramatically change American life. The events sent shock waves around the globe, revealing how

This icon will direct you to interactive activities and study materials on A People And A Nation, Brief Edition
website: **www.cengage.com/history/norton/peoplenationbrief8e**

Chronology

1992	Violence erupts in Los Angeles over Rodney King verdict.		Antiglobalization demonstrators disrupt World Trade Organization (WTO) meeting in Seattle.
	Major economic recession occurs.	**2000**	Nation records longest economic expansion in its history.
	Clinton is elected president.		Supreme Court settles contested presidential election in favor of Bush.
	United States sends troops to Somalia.		
1993	Congress approves North American Free Trade Agreement (NAFTA).	**2001**	Economy dips into recession; period of low growth and high unemployment begins.
	United States withdraws from Somalia.		Bush becomes president.
1994	Contract with America helps Republicans win majorities in House and Senate.		Al Qaeda terrorists attack World Trade Center and Pentagon.
	Genocide occurs in Rwanda.		PATRIOT Act is passed by Congress.
	U.S. intervenes in Haiti.		United States attacks Al Qaeda positions in Afghanistan, topples ruling Taliban regime.
1995	Domestic terrorist bombs Oklahoma City federal building.	**2003**	United States invades Iraq, ousts Saddam Hussein regime.
	U.S. diplomats broker peace for Bosnia.	**2004**	Bush is reelected.
1996	Welfare reform bill places time limits on welfare payments.	**2005**	Hurricane Katrina strikes Gulf Coast.
	Clinton is reelected.	**2006**	Iraq War continues; by end of year U.S. deaths reach three thousand.
1998	House votes to impeach Clinton.		Democrats take both houses of Congress in midterm elections.
1999	Senate acquits Clinton of impeachment charges.		
	NATO bombs Serbia over Kosovo crisis.		

interconnected the world had become in the early twenty-first century. At the World Trade Center, almost five hundred foreigners from more than eighty countries perished: sixty-seven Britons, twenty-one Jamaicans, twenty-seven Japanese, seventeen Mexicans, thirty-four Indians, sixteen Canadians, fifteen Australians, and seven Haitians. Many of the victims were, like Demczur, immigrants who came to New York seeking a better life; others were on temporary work visas. But all made the World Trade Center a kind of global city within a city, where some 50,000 people worked and another 140,000 visited daily.

A symbol of U.S. financial power, the World Trade Center towers also represented the globalization of world trade that marked the 1980s and 1990s. The towers housed the offices of more than four hundred businesses, including some of the world's leading financial institutions—Bank of America, Switzerland's Credit Suisse Group, Germany's Deutsche Bank, and Japan's Dai-Ichi Kangyo Bank.

Globalization was a 1990s buzzword and went beyond trade and investment to include connections in commerce, communications, and culture. While the terrorists—tied to the radical Islamic group Al Qaeda—sought to bring down that globalization, their attack used the same international technological, economic, and travel infrastructure that fueled global integration. Cell phones, computers, intercontinental air travel—all instruments of globalization—were crucial in the terrorists plot to turn four jetliners into lethal weapons.

Islamic militants had struck the World Trade Center before, bombing its underground parking garage in 1993. But Americans at the time paid only fleeting attention. President Bill Clinton took office in 1993 and concentrated less on foreign policy and more on domestic issues such as healthcare and deficit reduction. Clinton also sought to harness globalization to the United States's benefit.

For most Americans, the 1990s brought good times. The stock market soared, unemployment dropped, and more Americans owned homes. But the 1990s were also marked by violence and cultural conflict—the first multiethnic uprising in Los Angeles, domestic terrorism in Oklahoma City, school shootings, and hate crimes.

These were also politically volatile years. Republicans blocked the Democrats' legislative programs. With a conservative agenda of limited government and family values, the GOP routed Democrats in the 1994 midterm elections. But Republicans alienated voters by shutting down the federal government during the winter of 1995–1996 in a budget standoff, and Clinton was reelected in 1996. However, scandal plagued the Clinton White House, and in 1999 the House of Representatives voted to impeach Clinton, alleging he committed perjury and obstructed justice. The Senate failed to convict him, and his popularity remained high, but his leadership was compromised.

Clinton's successor, George W. Bush, successful in an extremely controversial election, responded to the 9/11 attacks by declaring a war on terrorism. Bush ordered U.S. forces into large-scale military action, first in Afghanistan, where Al Qaeda was headquartered with the blessing of the Taliban regime, then in Iraq to oust Saddam Hussein's government. Militarily, the Taliban and Iraqi governments were quickly beaten. Al Qaeda, however, remained a threat, and in Iraq, U.S. occupying forces battled a large-scale insurgency. Bush's high approval ratings dropped, and though he won reelection in 2004, his second term was undermined by continued bloodshed in Iraq and scandal at home.

- **What was the New Economy of the 1990s, and how did it contribute to the globalization of business?**
- **Did the attacks of September 11, 2001, change the United States in fundamental ways? Explain**
- **Why did the United States invade Iraq in 2003, and why did its occupying forces subsequently face a drawn-out and bloody insurgency?**

SOCIAL STRAINS AND NEW POLITICAL DIRECTIONS

Although the 1990s would be remembered for relative peace and prosperity, the decade did not start that way. Scourges of drugs, homelessness, and crime plagued U.S. cities. Racial tensions worsened; the gulf between rich and poor became more pronounced. The economy tipped into recession. Public disillusionment with political leaders ran strong. As the 1992 presidential election began, Americans wanted a change.

4 white cops acquitted on african american beating case

Violence in Los Angeles

Racial tensions erupted in Los Angeles in 1992. A jury (with no African American members) acquitted four white police officers charged with beating an African American man, Rodney King, who fled a pursuing police car at speeds exceeding 110 miles per hour. A bystander's video of the beating played so often on CNN, the new twenty-four-hour news network, that the local event became major national news. Within hours of the verdict, fires were burning in South Central Los Angeles.

The roots of this violence, however, went deeper. Well-paid jobs disappeared in the deindustrialization of the 1970s and 1980s, as more than a hundred manufacturing and industrial plants shut their doors. By the early 1990s, almost one-third of South Central residents lived in poverty—a rate 75 percent higher than the entire city.

Tensions increased as new immigrants arrived—Hispanics from Mexico and Central America, who competed with African Americans for scarce jobs, and Korean immigrants, who established small businesses such as grocery stores. Street gangs struggled over territory in South Central as the crack epidemic further decimated the neighborhood and homicide rates soared. Many African and Hispanic American residents saw high prices in Korean-owned shops as exploitation, while Korean shopkeepers complained of frequent shoplifting, robberies, and even beatings.

The violence in Los Angeles left at least fifty-three people dead. Almost a billion dollars in property was destroyed, including 2,300 stores owned by Koreans or Korean Americans. More than sixteen thousand people were arrested, many of them recent immigrants.

Economic Troubles and the 1992 Election

During the Bush administration, the economy grew slowly or not at all. Some city and thirty state governments faced bankruptcy. In 1978 California's Proposition 13—the first in a series of tax revolts nationwide—cut property taxes while the population boomed, and the state government, out of money in mid-1992 paid workers and bills in ICUs. Many businesses closed down or cut back. Factory employment plummeted, and corporate downsizing cost well-educated white-collar workers their jobs as well. In 1991 median household incomes hit the most severe decline since the 1973 recession; in 1992 the number of poor people in America reached the highest level since 1964.

As economic woes continued, President George H. W. Bush's approval rating fell to half of its high of 91 percent after the Persian Gulf War. Despite the credit Bush gained for ending the Cold War and the quick victory in the Gulf War, economic woes and the belief that he was out of touch with the problems most Americans faced left him vulnerable in the 1992 presidential election.

The Democratic nominee, Arkansas governor Bill Clinton, offered a profound contrast to Bush. Clinton's campaign headquarters bore signs with the four-word reminder "It's the economy stupid." In a town hall–format presidential debate, a woman asked how the economic troubles affected each candidate, and Clinton replied, "Tell me how it's affected you again?" George Bush was caught on camera looking at his watch.

On election day, Americans denied George Bush a second term. Ross Perot, a Texas billionaire who claimed he would bring economic common sense to the federal government, claimed almost 20 percent of the popular vote—the highest percentage for a third-party candidate in eighty years—but did not carry a single state. Clinton, with 43 percent of the popular vote, swept New England, the West Coast, and much of the industrial Midwest, even making inroads into the South and drawing Reagan Democrats back to the fold. Although Democrats controlled both houses, incumbents did not fare well. The 103rd Congress had 110 new representatives and 11 new senators.

William Jefferson Clinton

A journalist described the paradoxical Bill Clinton in a 1996 *New York Times* article as "one of the biggest, most talented, articulate, intelligent, open, colorful characters ever to inhabit the White House," while also noting that Clinton can be "an undisciplined, fumbling, obtuse, defensive, self-justifying rogue." Larger than life, Clinton was a born politician from a small town called Hope who wanted to be president most of his life. At Georgetown University in Washington, D.C., during the 1960s he protested the Vietnam War and maneuvered to keep himself out of it. Clinton won a Rhodes scholarship to Oxford, earned his law degree from Yale, and returned to his home state of Arkansas, where he was elected governor in 1978 at age thirty-two.

In 1975 Clinton married Hillary Rodham, whom he met when both were law students at Yale. Rodham Clinton was the first First Lady to have a significant career of her own, and she spoke of balancing her professional and family life. Rodham Clinton was attacked by conservatives and antifeminists. After she told a hostile interviewer, "I suppose I could have stayed home and baked cookies and had teas," the *New York Post* called her "a buffoon, an insult to most women."

A New Democrat's Promise and Pitfalls

Politically, Bill Clinton was a new Democrat, advocating a more centrist—though still socially progressive—position for the Democratic Party. Clinton and his colleagues emphasized private-sector economic development, focusing on job training and other policies to promote opportunity, not dependency. Some Democrats found Clinton too conservative. However, the political right vehemently attacked Clinton, making the political struggles of the 1990s exceptionally partisan.

Clinton began his presidency with an ambitious program of reform and revitalization, including appointing a cabinet that "looks like America" in all its diversity. But Republicans, determined not to allow Clinton the traditional honeymoon period, maneuvered him into fulfilling his pledge to end the ban on gays in the military before he secured congressional or military support. Amid great controversy, Clinton accepted a "don't ask, don't tell" compromise that alienated liberals and conservatives, the gay community and the military.

Clinton's major goal was to make healthcare affordable and accessible for all Americans. But special interests mobilized in opposition: the insurance industry worried about lost profits; the business community feared higher taxes; the medical community worried about more regulation, lower government reimbursement rates, and reduced healthcare quality. The healthcare task force, cochaired by Hillary Rodham Clinton, could not defeat these forces. Within a year, the centerpiece of Clinton's fledgling presidency failed.

Republican Revolution

New-style Republicans challenged the beleaguered new Democrat. In September 1994, more than three hundred Republican candidates for the House of Representatives endorsed the Contract with America. Developed under the leadership of Georgia representative Newt Gingrich, the Contract promised "the end of [big] government . . . [and] the beginning of a Congress that respects the values and shares the faith of the American family." It called for a balanced-budget amendment to the Constitution, reduction of the capital gains tax, a two-year limit on welfare payments (while making unmarried mothers under eighteen ineligible), and increased defense spending.

In the midterm elections, the Republican Party mobilized socially conservative voters and took control of both houses of Congress for the first time since 1954. Ideological passions ran high, and many Republicans believed that their attempts to weaken federal power and to dismantle the welfare state would succeed.

Although many Americans applauded cutting government spending, they opposed cuts to specific programs, including Medicare and Medicaid, education and college loans, highway construction, farm subsidies, veterans' benefits, and Social Security. Republicans made a bigger mistake when they issued Clinton an ultimatum on the federal budget and forced the government to suspend all nonessential action during the winter of 1995–1996.

Political Compromise and the Election of 1996

Such struggles led Clinton to make compromises that moved U.S. politics to the right. For example, he signed the 1996 Personal Responsibility and Work Opportunity Act, a welfare reform measure that eliminated cash assistance for poor children (Aid to Families with Dependent Children). The law mandated that heads of families on welfare must find work within two years—though states could exempt 20 percent of recipients—and limited welfare benefits to five years over an individual's lifetime. The Telecommunications Act of 1996, signed by Clinton, reduced diversity in media by permitting companies to own more television and radio stations.

Clinton was reelected in 1996 (defeating Republican Bob Dole and Reform Party candidate Ross Perot), partly because Clinton stole some of the conservatives' thunder. He declared that "the era of big government is over" and invoked family values, a centerpiece of the Republican campaign. Sometimes Clinton's actions were true compromises; other times he attempted to reclaim issues from the conservatives, as when he redefined family values as "fighting for the family-leave law." And despite scandal and gridlock, Clinton's election-year promise to "build a bridge to the future" seemed plausible as prosperity increased.

THE NEW ECONOMY AND GLOBALIZATION

Just how much credit Clinton deserved for the improved economy is debatable. The roots of the 1990s boom were in the 1970s, when U.S. corporations began investing in new technologies, retooling plants to become more energy-efficient, and cutting labor costs. Specifically, companies reduced the influence of organized labor by moving operations to the union-weak South and West and to countries such as China and Mexico, where labor was cheap and pollution controls were lax.

Digital Revolution

The rapid development of what came to be called information technology—computers, fax machines, cell phones, and the Internet—had a huge economic impact in the 1980s and 1990s. New companies and industries sprang up, many headquartered in the Silicon Valley near San Francisco. By the second half of the 1990s, the *Forbes* list of the 400 Richest Americans featured high-tech leaders such as Microsoft's Bill Gates, who became the wealthiest person in the world with worth approaching $100 billion, as his company produced the operating software for most personal computers. The high-tech industry had considerable spillover effects, generating improved productivity, new jobs, and sustained economic growth.

The heart of this technological revolution was the microprocessor. Introduced in 1970 by Intel, the microprocessor miniaturized the central processing unit of a computer, meaning small machines could now perform calculations previously requiring large machines. Computing chores that took a week in the early 1970s took only a minute by 2000; the cost of storing one megabyte of information fell from more than $5,000 in 1975 to $.17 in 1999.

Analysts dubbed this technology-driven sector the New Economy, and it would have emerged no matter who was in the White House. Yet Clinton and his advisers had some responsibility for the dramatic upturn. With the U.S. budget deficit topping $500 billion, they made the politically risky move of abandoning the middle-class tax cut and making deficit reduction a top priority. White House officials rightly concluded that, if the deficit could be brought under control, interest rates would drop and the economy would rebound. And that is what happened. The budget deficit decreased (by 1997 it had been erased); this lowered interest rates, and this boosted investment. Stock prices soared, and the gross national product rose by an average of 3.5 to 4 percent annually.

Globalization of Business

Clinton perceived early on that the technology revolution would make the world more interconnected. He was convinced that, with the demise of Soviet communism, capitalism—or at least the introduction of market forces, freer trade and deregulation—was spreading around the globe.

The journalist Thomas L. Friedman asserted that the post–Cold War world was the age of globalization, characterized by the integration of markets, finance, and technologies. U.S. officials lowered trade and investment barriers, completing the North American Free Trade Agreement (NAFTA) with Canada and Mexico in 1993, and in 1994 concluding the Uruguay Round of the General Agreement on Tariffs and Trade (GATT), which lowered tariffs for the seventy member nations that accounted for about 80 percent of world trade. The administration also endorsed the 1995 creation of the World Trade Organization (WTO), to administer and enforce agreements made at the Uruguay Round. Finally, the president formed a National Economic Council to promote trade missions around the world.

Multinational corporations were the hallmark of this global economy. By 2000 there were 63,000 parent companies worldwide and 690,000 foreign affiliates. Some, such as Nike and Gap, Inc., subcontracted production of certain merchandise to whichever developing countries had the lowest labor costs. Such arrangements created a new international division of labor and generated a boom in world exports, which, at $5.4 trillion in 1998, had doubled in two decades. U.S. exports reached $680 billion in 1998, but imports rose even higher, to $907 billion (for a trade deficit of $227 billion). Sometimes the multinationals affected foreign policy, as when Clinton in 1995 extended full diplomatic recognition to Vietnam under pressure from such corporations as Coca-Cola, Citigroup, General Motors, and United Airlines, which wanted to enter that emerging market.

[handwritten margin notes: ↑ world exports (imports even ↑) / affected foreign policy / full diplomatic recognition of Vietnam]

Critics of Globalization While the administration promoted open markets, labor unions argued that free-trade agreements exacerbated the trade deficit and exported U.S. jobs. Average real wages for U.S. workers declined steadily after 1973, from $320 per week to $260 by the mid-1990s. Other critics maintained that globalization widened the gap between rich and poor countries, creating a mass of "slave laborers" in poor countries working under conditions that would never be tolerated in the West. Environmentalists charged that globalization also exported pollution to countries unprepared to deal with it. Still other critics warned about the power of multinational corporations and the global financial markets over traditional cultures.

Antiglobalization fervor reached a peak in fall 1999, when thousands of protesters disrupted the WTO meeting in Seattle. In the months that followed, there were sizable protests at meetings of the International Monetary Fund (IMF) and the World Bank. In July 2001, fifty thousand demonstrators protested an IMF and World Bank meeting in Genoa, Italy.

Target: McDonald's Activists also targeted corporations, such as the Gap, Starbucks, Nike, and, especially, McDonald's, which by 1995 was serving 30 million customers daily in twenty thousand franchises in over one hundred countries. Critics assailed the company's slaughterhouse techniques, alleged exploitation of workers, its high-fat menu, and its role in creating an increasingly homogeneous and sterile world culture. For six years starting in 1996, McDonald's endured hundreds of often-violent protests, including bombings in Rome, Prague, London, Macao, Rio de Janeiro, and Jakarta.

[handwritten note: people upset @ McDonald's protests/bombing]

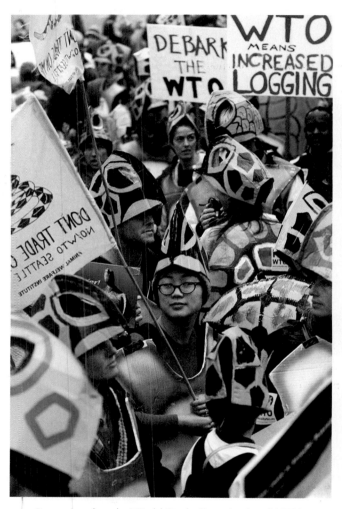

Protesting that the World Trade Organization (WTO) possessed the dangerous power to challenge any nation's environmental laws if the WTO deemed them barriers to trade, charting demonstrators marched in the streets of Seattle on November 30, 1999. Critics of the WTO claimed that sea turtles and dolphins have already been victimized by the WTO. Demonstrators identified the WTO as an example of globalization gone wrong. The WTO meeting went on, but the results proved meager because nations could not agree on rules governing dumping, subsidies for farm goods, genetically altered foods, and lower tariffs on high-tech goods. (Beth A. Keiser/AP Images)

Others decried the violence and the underlying arguments of the antiglobalization campaigners. True, some economists acknowledged, statistics showed that global inequality had grown in recent years. But if one included quality-of-life measurements, such as literacy and health, global inequality had declined. Some studies found that wage and job losses for U.S. workers were caused not primarily by globalization factors, such as imports, production outsourcing, and immigration, but by technological change that made production more efficient, that used less labor. Other researchers saw no evidence that governments' sovereignty had been seriously compromised or that there was a "race to the bottom" in environmental standards from globalization.

As for creating a homogeneous global culture, McDonald's, others said, tailored its menu and operating practices to local tastes. And although American movies, TV programs, music, computer software, and other intellectual property often dominated world markets, foreign competition also arrived in the United States. Millions of American children were gripped by the Japanese fad Pokemon, and satellite television established a worldwide following for European soccer teams.

Clinton's Diplomacy

Still, it remained true that the United States occupied a uniquely powerful position on the world stage. The demise of the Soviet Union created a one-superpower world, in which the United States stood far above other powers in political, military, and economic might. Yet in his first term Clinton was more wary in traditional aspects of foreign policy—great-power diplomacy, arms control, regional disputes—than in facilitating American cultural and trade expansion. Recalling the public's impatience in the Vietnam debacle, he was deeply suspicious of foreign military involvements.

Clinton's mistrust of foreign interventions was cemented by the difficulties he inherited from Bush in Somalia. In 1992 Bush sent U.S. Marines to the East African nation as part of a U.N. effort to ensure that humanitarian supplies reached starving Somalis. But in summer 1993, when Americans came under deadly attack, Clinton withdrew U.S. troops. And he did not intervene in Rwanda, where in 1994 the majority Hutus butchered 800,000 of the minority Tutsis in a brutal civil war.

Balkan Crisis

Many administration officials argued for using the United States's power to contain ethnic hatreds, support human rights, and promote democracy worldwide. Humanitarian intervention faced a test in the Balkans, where Bosnian Muslims, Serbs, and Croats were killing one another. Clinton talked tough against Serbian aggression and atrocities in Bosnia-Herzegovina, especially the Serbs' ethnic cleansing of Muslims through massacres and rape camps. He occasionally ordered air strikes, but he primarily emphasized diplomacy. In late 1995, U.S. diplomats brokered a fragile peace.

But Yugoslav president Slobodan Milosevic continued the anti-Muslim and anti-Croat fervor. When Serb forces moved to violently rid Kosovo of its majority ethnic Albanians, reports of Serbian atrocities and a major refugee crisis stirred world opinion and pressed Clinton to intervene. In 1999 U.S.-led NATO forces launched a massive aerial bombardment of Serbia. Milosevic withdrew from Kosovo, where U.S. troops joined a U.N. peacekeeping force.

Agreements in the Middle East

In the Middle East, Clinton took an active role in trying to bring the PLO and Israel together to settle their differences. In September 1993 the PLO's Yasir Arafat and Israel's prime minister Yitzhak Rabin signed an agreement at the White House for Palestinian self-rule in the Gaza Strip and the West Bank's Jericho. The following year Israel signed a peace accord with Jordan, further reducing the chances of another full-scale Arab-Israeli war. Radical anti-Arafat Palestinians, however, continued terrorist attacks on Israelis, while extremist Israelis killed Palestinians and, in November 1995, Rabin himself. With American-conducted negotiations and renewed violence in the West Bank, Israel agreed in early 1997 to withdraw troops from the Palestinian city of Hebron. Thereafter, the peace process alternately lagged and spurted.

International environmentalism also gathered pace in the 1990s. The George H. W. Bush administration had opposed many provisions of the 1992 Rio de Janeiro Treaty protecting the diversity of plant and animal species and resisted stricter rules to reduce global warming. Clinton, urged on by his environmentalist vice president Al Gore, signed the 1997 Kyoto protocol, which aimed to combat emissions of carbon dioxide and other gases. But facing strong opposition, Clinton never submitted the protocol for ratification to the Republican-controlled Senate.

Bin Laden and Al Qaeda

Meanwhile, the administration was increasingly concerned about the threat to U.S. interests by Islamic fundamentalism. Senior officials worried Al Qaeda (Arabic for "the base"), an international terrorist network led by Osama bin Laden, wanted to purge Muslim countries of what it considered the profane influence of the West.

The son of a Yemen-born construction tycoon in Saudi Arabia, bin Laden supported the Afghan Mujahidin—also backed by the United States—against Soviet occupation. He then founded Al Qaeda and financed terrorist projects with his substantial inheritance. U.S. officials grew more concerned, particularly as bin Laden focused on U.S. targets. In 1995 a car bomb in Riyadh killed 7 people, 5 of them Americans. In 1998 simultaneous bombings at the American embassies in Kenya and Tanzania killed 224 people, including 12 Americans. In Yemen in 2000, a boat laden with explosives hit the destroyer USS *Cole*, killing 17 American sailors. Although bin Laden masterminded and financed these attacks, he eluded U.S. attempts to apprehend him. In 1998 Clinton approved a plan to assassinate bin Laden, but it failed.

PARADOXES OF PROSPERITY

For most Americans, the late 1990s marked unprecedented peace and prosperity, fueled by the dizzying rise of the stock market. Between 1991 and 1999, the Dow Jones Industrial Average climbed from 3,169 to a high of 11,497. The booming market benefited the middle class and the wealthy, as mutual funds, 401(k) plans, and other new investment vehicles drew a majority of Americans into the stock market. In 1952 only 4 percent of U.S. households owned stocks; by 2000, almost 60 percent did.

At the end of the 1990s, the unemployment rate stood at 4.3 percent. That made it easier to implement welfare reform, and welfare rolls declined 50 percent. Both the richest 5 percent and the least well-off 20 percent of U.S. households saw their incomes rise almost 25 percent. But that translated to an average $50,000 gain for the top 5 percent and only $2,880 for the bottom, further widening the gap between rich and poor. Still, by decade's end, more than two-thirds of Americans were homeowners—the highest proportion in history.

Oklahoma City Bombing

New crises emerged. On April 19, 1995, 168 people were killed in a bomb blast that destroyed the nine-story Alfred P. Murrah Federal Building in Oklahoma City. At first, many blamed Middle Eastern terrorists. But a charred piece of truck axle two blocks away, with the vehicle identification number still legible, revealed that the bomber was Timothy McVeigh, a white American and Persian Gulf War veteran. He sought revenge for the deaths of Branch Davidian religious sect members, whom he believed the FBI had deliberately slaughtered in a standoff over firearms charges two years before in Waco, Texas.

In subsequent months, reporters and investigators discovered militias, tax resisters, and white-supremacist groups nationwide. United by distrust of the federal government, many saw gun control laws as a dangerous usurpation of citizens' right to bear arms. They believed that the federal government was controlled by sinister forces, including Zionists, cultural elitists, Queen Elizabeth, and the United Nations.

Violence and Hate Crimes

On April 20, 1999, eighteen-year-old Eric Harris and seventeen-year-old Dylan Klebold opened fire on classmates and teachers at Columbine High School in Littleton, Colorado, killing thirteen before killing themselves. No clear reason why two academically successful students in a middle-class suburb would commit mass murder ever emerged. Students in Paducah, Kentucky; Springfield, Oregon; and Jonesboro, Arkansas, also massacred classmates.

In the late 1990s, two hate crimes shocked the nation. In 1998 James Byrd Jr., a forty-nine-year-old African American, was murdered by three white supremacists who dragged him with a chain from the back of a pickup truck in Jasper, Texas. Later that year, Matthew Shepherd, a gay college student, was beaten unconscious and left tied to a wooden fence in freezing weather outside Laramie, Wyoming. His killers said they were humiliated when he flirted with them at a bar. To some, these murders signified the strength of racism and homophobia in the United States. Others saw the horror Americans expressed at these murders as a sign of positive change.

Scandal in the Clinton White House

Scandals plagued the Clinton White House. The independent counsel would eventually spend $72 million investigating allegations of wrongdoing by Hillary and Bill Clinton. Independent counsel Kenneth Starr, a conservative Republican and former judge, was originally charged with investigating Whitewater, a 1970s Arkansas real-estate deal in which the Clintons had invested. He never found any evidence against the Clintons, but expanded the range of his investigation.

Early in Clinton's presidency, former Arkansas state employee Paula Jones brought charges of sexual harassment against him, which were eventually dropped.

But when asked before a grand jury whether he had sexual relations with twenty-two-year-old White House intern Monica Lewinsky, Clinton said no. Speaking to the American people, Clinton angrily declared, "I did not have sexual relations with that woman, Miss Lewinsky." Starr produced DNA evidence: a navy blue dress of Lewinsky's, stained with Clinton's semen.

proven to have lied on sexual harrasment charges

Impeachment

In a 445-page report to Congress, Starr outlined eleven possible grounds for impeachment, accusing Clinton of lying under oath, obstruction of justice, witness tampering, and abuse of power. On December 19, 1998, the House voted on four articles of impeachment; largely along party lines, the House passed two of the articles, one alleging the president committed perjury in his grand jury testimony, the other that he obstructed justice. Clinton became only the second president to face a trial in the Senate, which has the constitutional responsibility to decide (by two-thirds vote) whether to remove a president from office.

But the American people did not want Clinton removed from office. Polls showed that large majorities approved of his job performance, even while condemning his personal behavior. And many did not believe that his actions constituted "high crimes and misdemeanors" (normally acts such as treason) required by the Constitution for impeachment. The Republican-controlled Senate, responding partly to popular opinion, voted against the charges of perjury and obstructing justice, thus clearing Clinton.

Political Partisanship, the Media, and Celebrity Culture

Clinton was not the first president to engage in illicit sex. President John F. Kennedy had numerous and well-known sexual affairs, including one with a nineteen-year-old intern. But after the 1970s Watergate scandals, the mass media no longer turned a blind eye to presidential misconduct. The fiercely competitive news networks relied on scandal, spectacle, and crisis to lure viewers.

The 1990s partisan political wars created a take-no-prisoners climate. Both Republican Speaker of the House Newt Gingrich and his successor, Robert Livingston, resigned when evidence of their extramarital affairs surfaced. Finally, as the former Clinton aide Sidney Blumenthal writes, the impeachment struggle was part of the culture wars: "a monumental battle over . . . cultural mores and the position of women in American society, and about the character of the American people."

Clinton's Legislative Record

Clinton's legislative accomplishments during his two terms included the Family and Medical Leave Act, guaranteeing 91 million workers the right to take time off to care for ailing relatives or newborn children. The Health Insurance Portability and Accountability Act ensured that, when Americans changed jobs, they would not lose health insurance because of preexisting medical conditions. The federal government operated efficiently with 365,000 fewer employees. Clinton created national parks and monuments that protected 3.2 million acres of U.S. land and made unprecedented progress cleaning up toxic waste dumps.

The Bush-Gore Race

Vice President Al Gore was the favorite in the 2000 presidential election. The son of a prominent senator from Tennessee, Gore graduated cum laude from Harvard in 1969 and served in Vietnam despite his reservations about the war. He had served six terms in Congress and played a greater role than any vice president in American history. After eight years of prosperity and relative peace, he had a strong platform. Earnest and highly intelligent, Gore appeared to be a policy wonk rather than a charismatic leader.

Gore's Republican opponent was the son of George H. W. Bush, the forty-first president of the United States. An indifferent student, George W. Bush graduated from Yale in 1968 and pulled strings to jump ahead of a one-and-a-half-year waiting list for the Texas Air National Guard, thus avoiding service in Vietnam. He had a rocky career in the oil business. At age forty, after years of hard drinking, Bush gave up alcohol and embraced Christianity. In 1994 he was elected to the first of two terms as governor of Texas.

As a presidential candidate, Bush made up for his limited foreign policy knowledge, often garbled syntax, and lack of interest in the intricacies of public policy with a confident style that connected with many Americans. Bush spoke of his relationship with God and his commitment to conservative social values, styling himself a "compassionate conservative." Supported by Republican business leaders, Bush amassed the largest campaign war chest in history ($67 million, compared with Gore's $28 million).

The consumer rights activist Ralph Nader ran on the Green Party ticket. Condemning globalization and environmental despoliation, he attacked Bush and Gore, calling them Tweedledee and Tweedledum. Nader drew support from left-liberal voters who might have voted for Gore and so possibly helped tip some states to Bush.

The Contested Election of 2000

On election day 2000, Al Gore narrowly won the popular vote, but not the presidency. It all came down to Florida (where Bush's brother Jeb was governor) and its twenty-five electoral votes. According to the initial tally, Bush narrowly edged Gore out in Florida, but by a close margin that legally required a recount. In several heavily African American counties, tens of thousands of votes went uncounted because voters failed to fully dislodge the chads, small perforated squares, when punching the paper ballots. Lawyers struggled over whether hanging chads (partially detached) and pregnant chads (punched but not detached) were sufficient signs of voter intent. In Palm Beach County, many elderly Jewish residents were confused by a poorly designed ballot and accidentally selected the allegedly anti-Semitic Pat Buchanan instead of Gore. After thirty-six days, with court cases at the state and federal levels, the Supreme Court voted 5 to 4 along narrowly partisan lines to end the recount process. Florida's electoral votes—and the presidency—went to George Bush.

Gore won the West Coast, Northeast, and industrial Midwest. The South, Rocky Mountain West (except New Mexico), and heartland went to Bush. More than 90 percent of African American voters selected Gore, as did 63 percent of Hispanic Americans and 55 percent of Asian Americans. Bush won 60 percent of the white vote, and, overall, 95 percent of his supporters were white. The gender gap was 12 points: 54 percent of women voted for Gore, 42 for Bush. The struggles over the election outcome further polarized the nation.

SEPTEMBER 11 AND THE WAR ON TERRORISM

With the close election and bitter controversy, many believed Bush would govern from the center. Some also thought he, like his father, moved to the right during the election only to secure conservative evangelical Christian voters. But Bush governed from the right, arguably further to the right than any other modern administration.

Bush's Tax Plan

The centerpiece of the Bush agenda was a massive tax cut, to be financed by the predicted budget surplus. Critics believed that a massive cut would wipe out the surplus and that the Bush plan favored the wealthy, but Bush used his party's control of Congress to push through the largest tax cut in U.S. history—$1.3 trillion. To the dismay of environmentalists, he also reiterated his plan to drill for oil in America's last wilderness, the Arctic National Wildlife Refuge.

In international affairs, the administration charted a unilateralist course. Given the United States's preponderant power, senior Bush officials reasoned, it did not need other countries' help. Accordingly, Bush withdrew the United States from the 1972 Anti-Ballistic Missile Treaty with Russia to develop a National Missile Defense system similar to Reagan's Star Wars. The White House also renounced the 1997 Kyoto protocol on controlling global warming and opposed a carefully negotiated protocol to strengthen the 1972 Biological and Toxin Weapons Convention. These decisions and the administration's hands-off policy toward the Israeli-Palestinian peace process caused consternation in Europe.

9/11

Then came September 11. On that sunny Tuesday morning, nineteen hijackers seized control of four commercial jets departing from East Coast airports. At 8:46 A.M. one plane crashed into the 110-story North Tower of the World Trade Center in New York City. At 9:03 A.M., a second plane flew into the South Tower. In less than two hours, both buildings collapsed, killing thousands of office workers, firefighters, and police officers. At 9:43, a third plane crashed into the Pentagon, leaving a huge hole in its west side. The fourth plane was also headed toward Washington, but several passengers, learning of the World Trade Center attacks through cell-phone conversations, stormed the cockpit; in the scuffle, the plane crashed in Somerset County, Pennsylvania, killing all aboard.

More than three thousand people died in the deadliest act of terrorism in history. The hijackers—fifteen Saudi Arabians, two Emiratis, one Lebanese, and, leading them, an Egyptian—had ties to Al Qaeda, Osama bin Laden's radical Islamic organization. Some officials in the Clinton and Bush administrations warned that an Al Qaeda attack was inevitable, but neither administration made counterterrorism a foreign policy priority.

Afghanistan War

September 11 made counterterrorism priority number one. President Bush responded quickly with military force. Al Qaeda operated out of Afghanistan with the blessing of the ruling Taliban, a repressive Islamic fundamentalist group that gained power in 1996. In early October, the United States launched a sustained bombing campaign against Taliban and Al Qaeda positions and sent special operations forces to help a resistance organization in northern Afghanistan. Within two months, the Taliban was driven from power, although bin Laden and top Taliban leaders eluded capture.

As administration officials acknowledged, military victory did not end the terrorist threat. Bush spoke of a long struggle against evil forces, in which the nations of the world were either with the United States or against it. Some questioned whether a war on terrorism could ever be won in a meaningful sense, given that the foe was a nonstate actor with little to lose. Most Americans, however, were ready to believe. Stunned by September 11, they experienced a renewed sense of national unity and pride. Flag sales soared, and Bush's approval ratings skyrocketed.

PATRIOT Act

But the new patriotism had a dark side. Congress passed the USA PATRIOT Act (Uniting and Strengthening America by Providing Appropriate Tools Required to Intercept and Obstruct Terrorism), making it easier for law enforcement to conduct searches, wiretap telephones, and obtain electronic records on individuals. Attorney General John Ashcroft approved giving FBI agents new powers to monitor the Internet, mosques, and rallies. Civil libertarians charged that the Justice Department overstepped, and some judges ruled against the tactics. Yet, according to a June 2002 Gallup poll, 80 percent of Americans were willing to exchange some freedoms for security.

In surveys weeks after the attacks, 71 percent of respondents said that they felt depressed, and one-third had trouble sleeping. The discovery of anthrax-laden letters in several East Coast cities heightened fears, particularly after post offices and government buildings were closed and five people died. Investigators found no evidence to connect the letters to the 9/11 hijackings, but also no good clues as to who the perpetrator might be.

Yet people continued shopping in malls, visiting amusement parks, and working in skyscrapers. Although airline bookings dropped significantly in the early weeks (causing severe problems for many airlines), people still took to the skies. In Washington, the partisanship that disappeared after 9/11 returned, as Democrats and Republicans sparred over judicial appointments, energy policy, and the proposed new Department of Homeland Security. Approved by Congress in November 2002, the department incorporated parts of eight cabinet departments and twenty-two agencies to coordinate intelligence and defense against terrorism.

Economic Uncertainty

Economically, the months before September 11 witnessed a collapse of the dot-coms, Internet companies that were the darlings of Wall Street in the 1990s. In 2001 some five hundred dot-coms declared bankruptcy or closed. There were other economic warning signs as well, notably a meager 0.2 percent growth rate in goods and services for the second quarter. Corporate revenues were also down.

Economic concerns deepened after 9/11 with a four-day closing of Wall Street and a subsequent sharp drop in stock prices. The Dow Jones Industrial Average plunged 14.26 percent. The markets eventually rebounded, but questions remained about the economy's overall health. Neither economic uncertainty nor the failure to capture Osama bin Laden and top Taliban leaders dented Bush's post-9/11 popularity. In the 2002 midterm elections, Republicans retook the Senate and increased their majority in the House.

International Responses

Immediately after September 11, there was an outpouring of support from people everywhere. "We are all Americans now," said the French newspaper *Le Monde* after the attacks. Governments worldwide announced they would work with Washington against terrorism. But within a year, attitudes changed dramatically. Bush's good-versus-evil stance put off foreign observers, but they initially swallowed their objections. When the president hinted that the United States might unilaterally strike Saddam Hussein's Iraq or deal forcefully with North Korea or Iran—Bush's "axis of evil"—many allied governments strongly objected.

Bush and other top officials argued that in an age of terrorism, the United States would not wait for a potential security threat to become real; henceforth, it would strike first. Americans, Bush declared had to be "ready for preemptive action when necessary to defend our liberty and to defend our lives." Critics, among them many world leaders, called it recklessly aggressive and contrary to international law.

The attacks on 9/11 brought forth an outpouring of sympathy for the victims and their families, and for the United Sates generally, from people around the world. Here firefighters in Taipei, Taiwan, attend a prayer service during a global day of mourning.   (Sam Yeh/Getty Images)

WAR AND OCCUPATION IN IRAQ

But Bush was determined, particularly on Iraq. Several of his top advisers, including Secretary of Defense Donald Rumsfeld and Vice President Dick Cheney, wanted to oust Saddam Hussein since the end of the Gulf War in 1991. After the Twin Towers fell, they folded Iraq into the larger war on terrorism even though counterterrorism experts saw no link between Saddam and Al Qaeda. For a time, Secretary of State Colin Powell, the first African American in that post, kept the focus on Afghanistan, but gradually the thinking in the White House shifted. In November 2001 Bush ordered the Pentagon to initiate war planning for Iraq; by spring 2002 a secret consensus was reached: Saddam Hussein would be removed by force.

Why Iraq?

In September 2002 Bush challenged the United Nations to enforce its resolutions against Iraq, or the United States would act on its own. In subsequent weeks, he and his aides offered shifting reasons for getting tough with Iraq. They said Saddam was a major threat to the United States and its allies, a leader who possessed and would use banned biological and chemical "weapons of mass destruction" (WMDs) and who sought to acquire nuclear weapons. They claimed, contrary to intelligence estimates, that he had ties to Al Qaeda and could be linked to the 9/11 attacks.

Beneath the surface lurked other motivations. Neoconservatives claimed that ousting Saddam would enhance the security of Israel, the United States's key Middle East ally, and start a chain reaction that would extend democracy throughout the region. White House political strategists believed a swift removal of a hated dictator would assure Bush's reelection. And Bush wanted to prevent an Iraq armed with WMDs from destabilizing an oil-rich region.

Congressional Approval

Bush claimed he did not need congressional authorization for military action against Iraq but sought it anyway. In early October 2002, the House of Representatives voted 296 to 133 and the Senate 77 to 23 to authorize him to use force against Iraq. Many who voted in favor were unwilling to defy a president so close to a midterm election, even though they opposed military action without U.N. sanction. Critics complained that the president had not presented evidence that Saddam Hussein constituted an imminent threat or was connected to the 9/11 attacks. Bush switched to a less hawkish stance, and in early November, the U.N. Security Council unanimously approved Resolution 1441, imposing rigorous new arms inspections on Iraq.

But the Security Council was divided over the next move. In late January 2003, the weapons inspector's report castigated Iraq for failing to complete "the disarmament that was demanded of it" but also said it was too soon to tell whether inspections would succeed. Whereas U.S. and British officials said the time for diplomacy was up, France, Russia, and China called for more inspections. As the U.N. debate continued, Bush sent about 250,000 soldiers to the region. Britain sent about 45,000 troops.

Fall of Baghdad

In late February, the United States floated a draft resolution to the United Nations that proposed issuing an ultimatum to Iraq, but only three of the fifteen Security Council members affirmed support. Bush abandoned the resolution and diplomatic efforts on March 17, when he ordered Saddam Hussein to leave Iraq within forty-eight hours or face an attack. Saddam ignored the ultimatum, and on March 19 the United States and Britain launched an aerial bombardment of Baghdad and other areas. A ground invasion followed (see Map 33.1). The Iraqis initially offered stiff resistance, but on April 9, Baghdad fell.

The military victory was swift, the result of sixteen months of planning. But senior policymakers showed scant interest in readying for postwar Iraq. Top officials who voiced worst-case scenarios in urging war, emphasized best-case outcomes in preparing for peace, expecting that Iraqis would embrace "liberation" with joy, that stability would emerge quickly, and that few U.S. troops would be required to secure the country.

Insurgency

Thus, when violence and lawlessness soon erupted, U.S. planners seemed powerless to respond. The plight of ordinary Iraqis deteriorated as the occupation authority proved unable to maintain order. In Baghdad, electricity worked only a few hours each day, and telephone service was nonexistent. Decisions by the Coalition Governing Council (CPA), headed by Ambassador Paul Bremer, made matters worse, notably Bremer's move in May to disband the Iraqi army. A multisided insurgency of Saddam loyalists, Iraqi nationalists, and foreign Islamic revolutionaries took shape; soon, U.S. occupying forces faced frequent ambushes. By October 2003 more troops had died from these attacks than had perished in the initial invasion.

The chaos in Iraq and the failure to find weapons of mass destruction had critics questioning the war's validity. Sanctions and U.N. inspections had clearly been successful. Prewar claims of a "rush to war" resounded again. Even defenders of the invasion castigated the administration for its failure to anticipate the occupation problems. In spring 2004, photos showing Iraqi detainees being abused by American guards at Abu Ghraib prison were broadcast worldwide, generating international condemnation.

Election of 2004

Facing reelection, President Bush expressed disgust at Abu Ghraib and fended off charges that he and his top aides condoned the abuse. The White House also claimed the dissolution of the CPA in late June and the transfer of sovereignty to an interim Iraqi government would flatten the insurgency. Bush's Democratic opponent, Senator John Kerry of Massachusetts, a Vietnam veteran who had voted for the Iraq resolution, never articulated a clear alternative strategy on the war. Bush won reelection with 51 percent of the popular vote to Kerry's 48 percent and 279 electoral votes to Kerry's 252. The GOP also increased its majorities in the House and Senate.

Bush and his aides took the victory as a mandate to make major domestic policy changes, including partially privatizing Social Security. This plan failed, as Democrats and Republicans in Congress argued that it would not work. The president succeeded, however, in reshaping the Supreme Court. The conservative U.S. Circuit Court judge John Roberts was confirmed as chief justice following the death of Chief Justice

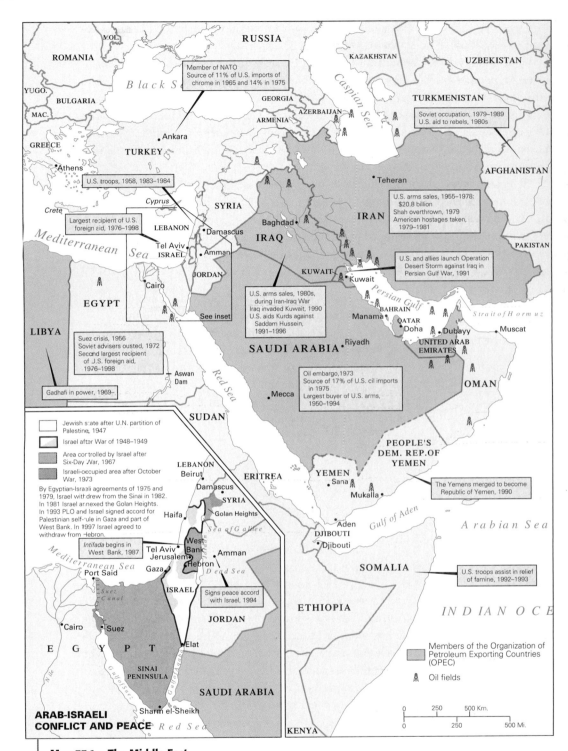

Map 33.1   The Middle East

Extremely volatile and often at war, the nations of the Middle East maintained precarious relations with the United States. To protect its interests, the United States extended large amounts of economic and military aid and sold huge quantities of weapons to the area. At times, Washington ordered U.S. troops to the region. The Arab-Israeli dispute particularly destabilized order, although the peace process moved forward intermittently.

William Rehnquist, and another strong conservative, Samuel Alito, became junior associate justice following the resignation of Sandra Day O'Connor.

The increasing evidence that the war in Iraq had little chance of success undermined Americans' confidence in President Bush. Growing perceptions of administrative incompetence were exacerbated when Hurricane Katrina, the sixth most powerful Atlantic hurricane on record, hit the Gulf Coast and New Orleans in late August 2005. The high winds and storm surge destroyed the levees that kept low-lying parts of New Orleans from being swamped by Lake Pontchartrain and surrounding canals. Floodwaters covered 80 percent of the city, and more than eighteen hundred people died.

Tens of thousands of people who lacked the resources to evacuate the city sought shelter at the Superdome. Food and water supplies quickly ran low, and toilets backed up; people wrapped the dead in blankets and waited for rescue. Those outside the Gulf region, watching the suffering of poor, African American New Orleanians, discussed what Democratic Party leader Howard Dean called the ugly truth: that poverty remains linked to race. The public also worried about administrative mismanagement and the president's seeming indifference. Despite the federal government's failure in handling the crisis, President Bush told Federal Emergency Management Association (FEMA) director Michael Brown, "Brownie, you're doing a heck of a job." Within a few weeks, Brown resigned amid criticism, and Bush distanced himself from him.

America Isolated

Internationally, too, Bush faced criticism because of Iraq, Abu Ghraib, and his administration's lack of engagement in the Israeli-Palestinian dispute. The White House, critics said, rightly sought to prevent North Korea and Iran from joining the nuclear club but seemed incapable of working imaginatively and multilaterally to make it happen. In Europe, Bush continued to be depicted as a gun-slinging cowboy whose aggressive policies threatened world peace.

The bill for the Iraq war now exceeded $1 billion per week. In March 2005, the U.S. war dead reached 1,500; in December 2006, it reached 3,000; in September 2008, it topped 4,100. Meanwhile by mid-2006, estimates of Iraqi civilian deaths since the invasion ranged from 60,000 to 655,000. These Iraqi casualties resulted from insurgent suicide attacks, U.S. bombing of suspected insurgent hideouts, and increased sectarian violence between Sunnis and Shi'ites.

The Bush administration denied that Iraq had degenerated into civil war or that the struggle had become a Vietnam-like quagmire, but it seemed uncertain how to end the fighting. Far from reducing the terrorist threat, the Iraq invasion seemed to have increased it, as the Al Qaeda presence in the United States (nonexistent before the war) became pronounced.

In Congress and the press, calls for withdrawal from Iraq multiplied, but skeptics cautioned it could make things worse, triggering sectarian bloodshed and a collapse of the Baghdad government. The power and regional influence of neighboring Iran would increase, and U.S. credibility would be undermined throughout the Middle East. Some commentators instead called for a major increase of U.S. forces in Iraq. The 2006 midterm election was partly a referendum on the war, and the voters were clear: 55 percent voted for Democratic candidates, and the party seized control of both houses of Congress.

AMERICANS IN THE FIRST DECADE OF THE NEW MILLENNIUM

At the beginning of the twenty-first century, the United States is a nation of extraordinary diversity. Immigration reform in the mid-1960s opened U.S. borders to people from a wider variety of nations than previously. New technologies—the Internet and cable and satellite television—replaced mass markets with niche markets. Everything from television shows to cosmetics to cars could be targeted toward specific groups defined by age, ethnicity, class, gender, or lifestyle choices. These changes helped to make Americans' understandings of identity more fluid and complex.

Race and Ethnicity in Recent America

[handwritten note: gov census allowd for multiple races]

In the 2000 U.S. government census, for the first time Americans could identify themselves as belonging to more than one race. The change acknowledged the growing number of Americans born to parents of different racial backgrounds. Critics, however, worried that, because census data are used to gather information about social conditions to allocate resources, the new multiracial option would reduce the clout of minority groups. Thus, the federal government counted those who identified both as white and as a racial or ethnic minority as belonging to the minority group. Consequently, the official population of some groups increased. Others rejected racial and ethnic categories: 20 million people identified themselves simply as American.

[handwritten note: info gathering issues]
[handwritten note: part minority race = all minority race]
[handwritten note: ↑ official pop. of some groups]

On October 17, 2006, the United States passed the 300 million population mark (100 million in 1915 and 200 million in 1967). During the 1990s, the population of people of color grew twelve times as fast as the white population, fueled by immigration and birth rates. In 2003 Hispanic Americans passed African Americans to become the second largest ethnic or racial group (after non-Hispanic whites) (see Figure 33.1). Immigration from Asia also remained high, and in 2006, 5 percent of the U.S. population was Asian or Asian American.

These rapid demographic changes have altered the face of the United States. At a Dairy Queen in the far southern suburbs of Atlanta, teenage children of Indian and

Figure 33.1 The Growth of the U.S. Hispanic Population
The Hispanic category combines people from a wide variety of national origins or ancestries—including all the nations of Central and South America, Mexico, Cuba, Puerto Rico, the Dominican Republic, and Spain—as well as those who identify as Californio, Tejano, Nuevo Mexicano, and Mestizo. (*Source:* Adapted from the U.S. Department of Commerce, Economics and Statistics Information, Bureau of the Census, 1993 report "We, the American . . . Hispanics"; also recent census bureau figures for the Hispanic population)

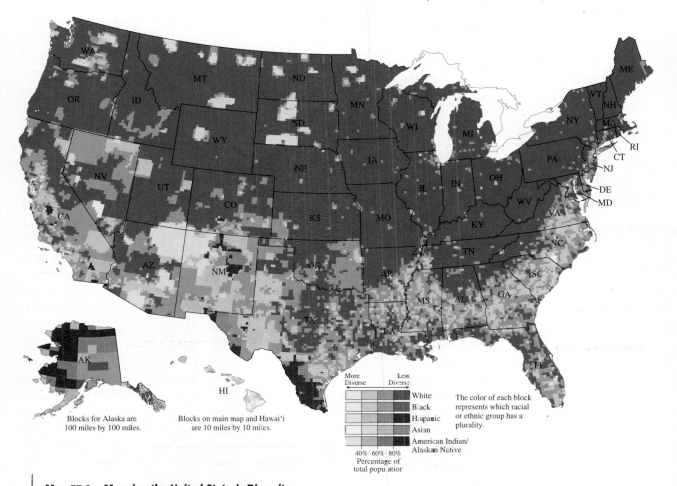

Map 33.2   Mapping the United States's Diversity

Aggregate figures (more than 12 percent of the U.S. population was African American and about 4 percent Asian American in 2000, for example) convey the United States's ethnic and racial diversity. However, as this map shows, members of racial and ethnic groups are not distributed evenly throughout the nation.   (*Source:* Adapted from the *New York Times* National Edition, April 1, 2001, "Portrait of a Nation," p. 18. Copyright © 2001 by The New York Times Co. Reprinted with permission.)

Pakistani immigrants serve Blizzards. In the small town of Ligonier, Indiana, the formerly empty main street now boasts three Mexican restaurants; Mexican immigrants cross paths with the newest immigrants, Yemenis, some in traditional dress, and with Amish families in horse-drawn buggies.

American popular culture embraced this new multiethnic population. Hispanic Americans' buying power exceeded $798 billion in 2006, and average income for Asian American households topped all other ethnic groups. But audiences also crossed racial and ethnic lines. Golfer Tiger Woods became a symbol of this new hybrid, multiethnic nation: of African, European, Native American, Thai, and Chinese descent, he calls himself Cablinasian (CAucasian-BLack-INdian-ASIAN).

The Changing American Family

Americans were divided over the meaning of changing family structure (see Figure 33.4). The median age at marriage continued to rise, reaching 27.1 for men and 25.8 for

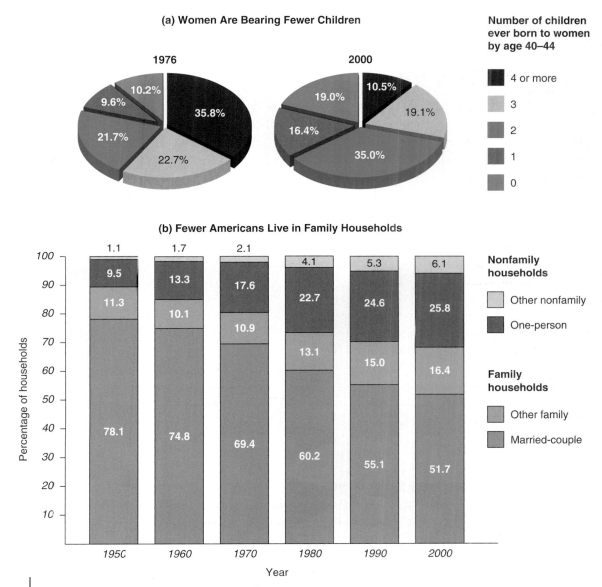

(a) Women Are Bearing Fewer Children

Figure 33.4 The Changing American Family

American households became smaller in the latter part of the twentieth century, as more people lived alone and women had, on average, fewer children. (*Source:* Adapted from U.S. Bureau of the Census, http://www.census.gov/prod/2002pubs/censr-4.pdf and http://www.census.gov/population/pop-profile/2000/chap04.pdf)

women in 2006. In 2006, when households composed of married couples slipped below 50 percent for the first time, unmarried, opposite-sex partners were about 5 percent of households, and same-sex couples accounted for just under 1 percent. One-third of female-partner households and one-fifth of male-partner households had children, and in 2002 the American Academy of Pediatrics endorsed adoption by gay couples. A vocal antigay movement coexisted with support for the legal equality of gay, lesbian, transgendered, and bisexual Americans. Although many states and corporations extended domestic-partner benefits to gay couples, the federal Defense of Marriage Act, passed in 1996, defined marriage only as a union between one man and one woman.

Early in the twenty-first century, one-third of all children and more than two-thirds of African American children were born to unmarried women. In the majority of married-couple families with children under eighteen, both parents held jobs. Although almost one-third of families with children had only one parent present—usually the mother—children also lived in blended families created by second marriages. For couples marrying in the mid-1990s, the woman's educational level was the clearest predictor of divorce: if the woman graduated from a four-year college, the couple had a 25 percent likelihood of divorce if she had not, the rate jumped to 50 percent.

In 2006 the leading edge of the baby-boom generation turned sixty. As life expectancy increases, the growing number of elderly Americans will put enormous pressure on the nation's healthcare system and family structure and strain the Social Security and Medicare systems.

More than 65 percent of American adults are now overweight or obese—conditions linked to hypertension, cardiovascular disease, and diabetes. In 1995 no state had an adult obesity rate that hit 20 percent. By 2005, only four states were under that 20 percent marker. Cigarette smoking continues to slowly decline. About one-fifth of U.S. adults smoked in 2005, down from about one-third of adults in 1980. Approximately 440,000 people die annually from smoking-related illnesses, and medical costs and lost productivity total about $157 billion a year. Local governments have increasingly banned smoking in public spaces.

Medicine, Science, and Religion   Rapid advances in biogenetics offer great new possibilities and raise ethical conundrums. During in vitro fertilizations—in which sperm and egg combine in a sterile dish and the fertilized egg or eggs are then transferred to the uterus—five- or six-cell blastocytes are formed. These blastocytes contain stem cells, unspecialized cells that can be induced to become cells with specialized functions. For example, stem cells might become insulin-producing cells of the pancreas, and thus a cure for diabetes.

President Bush in 2001 called embryonic stem cell research "the leading edge of a series of moral hazards," because extracting stem cells destroys the blastocyte's "potential for life," and limited federally funded research to the existing seventy-eight stem cell lines, most of which proved not viable for research. In 2006 he vetoed a bipartisan congressional bill that expanded the number of stem cell lines available for federally funded research. Often treated as a conflict between religion and science, stem cell research is supported by most Americans, who believe the moral good of curing diseases outweighs preserving the potential life of blastocytes.

Still, many Americans see a conflict between religious belief and scientific study. Fundamentalist Christians sought to prevent the teaching of evolution in the nation's science classes or to introduce parallel instruction of biblical creationism or intelligent design, which hold that an intelligent creator is behind the development of life on earth. The percentage of Americans who accept scientific evidence for evolution is lower than that in any other major nation except Turkey.

Century of Change

The twentieth century witnessed momentous changes, some bringing enormous benefits, others threatening the existence of the human species. Research in the physical and biological sciences provided insight into the structure of matter and the universe. Technology—the application of science—made startling advances that benefited Americans in nearly every aspect of life.

Consequently, Americans at the start of the new century were more connected to other people worldwide than ever before. This was perhaps the most powerful result of globalization. The world had shrunk to the size of an airplane ticket. In 1955, 51 million people a year traveled by plane. By the turn of the century, 1.6 billion were airborne annually, and 530 million—about 1.5 million each day—crossed international borders. This permeability of national boundaries brought many benefits, as did the integration of markets and the global spread of information that occurred with it.

Globalization and World Health

On the flip side, the rapid increase in international air travel was a potent force for the spread of global disease, as flying enabled people to reach the other side of the world in less time than the incubation period for many ailments. In early 2003, a respiratory illness known as severe acute respiratory syndrome (SARS) emerged in China and threatened to spread across the globe. Thirteen labs in ten countries worked to map the genome, followed by efforts to devise a diagnostic test for it. SARS did not develop into a worldwide epidemic, but health authorities recognized that international cooperation would be essential to combat the health threats intensified by globalization.

In 2003 the World Health Organization (WHO) estimated that nearly one-quarter of the global burden of disease and injury was related to environmental disruption and decline. For example, some 90 percent of diarrheal diseases (such as cholera), which were killing 3 million people a year, resulted from contaminated water. WHO also noted that in the final two decades of the twentieth century, more than thirty infectious diseases were identified in humans for the first time—including AIDS, Ebola virus, hantavirus, and hepatitis C and E. Environmentalists insisted that the growing global interaction was having a deleterious impact on the ecosystem through climate change, ozone depletion, hazardous waste, and damage to fisheries.

Confronting Terrorism

In diplomatic terms, the 9/11 attacks brought home what Americans had previously only dimly perceived: that globalization shrunk the natural buffers that distance and two oceans provided the United States. Al Qaeda used the increasingly open, globalized world to give itself new power and reach. It had shown that small terrorist cells could become transnational threats without a state sponsor or home base. According to U.S. intelligence, Al Qaeda operated in more than ninety countries.

The Global AIDS Epidemic

AIDS, first reported in the United States in 1981, has become a global epidemic. Researchers now believe that the first infection with HIV, the human immunodeficiency virus that causes AIDS, may have appeared in West Africa around 1930. HIV/AIDS spread rapidly in the late 1970s, partly as a byproduct of globalization. Increased international travel allowed for sexual transmission of HIV between populations; the international heroin trade stimulated intravenous drug use, another means of transmission; and the international circulation of blood for medical transfusions also contributed to the virus's spread. In 2003 the World Health Organization estimated that 58 million people worldwide were living with HIV/AIDS and 23 million had died from the disease.

Globally, AIDS claims 350 lives per hour, and though altered behavior and new drug therapies have slowed the disease's progress in North America and western Europe, infection and death rates continue to escalate in sub-Saharan Africa, Thailand, eastern Europe and the former Soviet Union, and Latin America, especially the Caribbean. In the African nation of Malawi, one in six adults is HIV-positive, and the nation expects to lose almost one-quarter of its work force to AIDS in the next decade.

U.S. worries about the global spread of AIDS are not solely humanitarian. In 2000 the U.S. National Intelligence Council concluded that "these diseases will endanger U.S. citizens at home and abroad, threaten U.S. armed forces deployed overseas, and exacerbate social and political instability in key countries and regions in which the United States has significant interests." In nations already facing shortages of food and clean water and rife with conflict, AIDS has further undermined government ability to cope with crisis, triggering political instability.

In 2002 U.N. secretary general Kofi Annan estimated that between $7 billion and $10 billion are needed annually to combat the spread of AIDS and tuberculosis and malaria, which have reemerged as threats to world health. President Bush called for increases in U.S. AIDS spending internationally, but many believe the United States should do more. With globalization, diseases do not stop at borders. The links between Americans and the rest of the world cannot be denied.

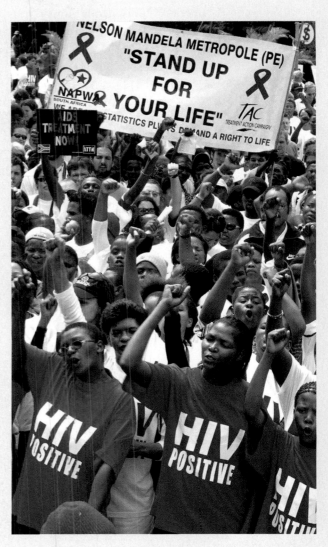

Activists protest outside Parliament in Cape Town, South Africa, calling on South African president Thabo Mbeki to make the struggle against AIDS a national priority. An estimated 20 percent of South Africans between the ages of fifteen and forty-nine are HIV-positive.
(Benny Goo/AP Images)

903

How would one go about vanquishing such a foe? Was a decisive victory even possible? These remained open questions five years after the World Trade Center collapsed. Unchallenged militarily, the United States felt few constraints about intervening in Afghanistan and then Iraq. It continued to spend colossal sums on its military. (In 2006 the Pentagon spent more than $500 billion, or roughly $60 million per hour.) The United States had military commitments around the globe, from the Balkans and Iraq to Afghanistan and Korea (see Table 33.1).

TABLE 33.1 U.S. Military Personnel on Active Duty in Foreign Countries, 2005*

Region/Country[†]	Personnel	Region/Country[†]	Personnel
United States and Territories		**North Africa, Near East, and South Asia**	
Continental U.S.	894,921	Bahrain	1,482
Alaska	18,980	Diego Garcia	773
Hawai'i	33,816	Egypt	424
Guam	2,931	Iraq	207,000
Puerto Rico	211	Israel	43
		Oman	36
Europe		Pakistan	195
Belgium[‡]	1,388	Qatar	387
Bosnia and Herzegovina	261	Saudi Arabia	269
France[‡]	56	United Arab Emirates	72
Germany[‡]	66,000	**Sub-Saharan Africa**	
Greece[‡]	431	Kenya	32
Greenland[‡]	144	South Africa	33
Iceland[‡]	1,257		
Italy[‡]	11,428	**Western Hemisphere**	
Macedonia	40	Brazil	39
Netherlands[‡]	579	Canada	145
Norway[‡]	74	Chile	29
Portugal[‡]	990	Colombia	96
Russia	44	Cuba (Guantanamo)	950
Serbia (includes Kosovo)	1,909	Honduras	416
Spain[‡]	1,634	Peru	36
Turkey[‡]	1,738	Venezuela	21
United Kingdom[‡]	10,536		
East Asia and Pacific		Total foreign countries[†]	271,381
Australia	140	Ashore	247,341
China (includes Hong Kong)	71	Afloat	24,040
Japan	35,050	Total worldwide[†]	1,605,414
Korea, Rep. of	29,982	Ashore	1,249,616
Philippines	44	Afloat	128,398
Singapore	159		
Thailand	116		

*Only countries with 35 or more U.S. military personnel are listed.
[†]Includes all regions/countries, not simply those listed.
[‡]NATO countries.
Source: U.S. Department of Defense, Defense Manpower Data Center.

The Internet

"Google it"—the phrase, essentially unknown before the new century, had within its first years become a household expression. Google was the hugely popular Internet search engine that went from obscurity in the mid-1990s to responding almost instantly to 200 million queries daily from around the world—almost 40 percent of all Internet searches.

While widespread use of the Internet was a recent phenomenon, its history went back four decades. In the mid-1960s, the U.S. military's Advanced Research Projects Agency (ARPA) wanted a communications network for government and university researchers across the nation. In 1969 early portions of the experimental system, called ARPANET, went online at UCLA; the University of California, Santa Barbara; Stanford Research Institute; and the University of Utah. By 1971, twenty-three computers were connected, and the numbers reached nearly a thousand by 1984. Renamed the Internet, this system transmitted only words, but in 1990 computer scientists developed the World Wide Web to send graphic and multimedia information. Then in 1993 the first commercial browser for Web navigation hit the market, followed in 1994 and 1995 by two superior browsers: Netscape and Internet Explorer.

By 2003, there were almost half a billion Internet users worldwide, including 140 million Americans. Thanks to technological advances and to new forms of broadband access with high-speed connections, users could send and receive e-mail, join online discussion groups, read newspapers, book vacations, download movies and music, shop, and even do their banking—all through a small computer at home. For Americans in the new globally connected millennium, the Internet was a fitting legacy of the twentieth century.

Election of 2008

On many levels, the 2008 election proved historic. During primary season, it looked like Americans might get their first female presidential party nominee when New York Senator and former First Lady Hillary Rodham Clinton made a strong showing for the Democrats. While she fought until the end of the primaries in June 2008, newcomer and little-known Illinois Senator Barrack Obama garnered more of the necessary delegates and advanced to the general election, making him the first African American presidential candidate from either party. He selected popular Delaware Senator Joseph Biden as his running mate. The Republicans made history, too, nominating long-time Arizona Senator and Vietnam veteran and POW John McCain, who, at age 72, would have become the nation's oldest elected president if he should win, and his running mate, Alaska Governor Sarah Palin, the country's first woman vice president.

The nation's economic turmoil soon surpassed the War in Iraq as the number one issue. Until September, McCain was leading in the polls, but with one Wall Street firm after another in trouble, the stock market tumbling, a banking and credit crisis looming, unemployment increasing, and housing foreclosures at record numbers, Americans feared an impending depression worse than the Great Depression of the 1930s. Two missteps by McCain—telling reporters that "the fundamentals of the nation's economy are strong" and

Newly elected President of the United States, Barack Obama, and Vice President-Elect, Joe Biden.
(© Jason Reed/Reuters/Corbis)

economy becoming the priority
(over Iraq)

promising to put his campaign on hold until a $700 billion bailout plan could be approved—made many question his leadership. That, combined with Palin's poor showing in several television interviews and incumbent president George Bush's record low approval rating of 25%, undermined McCain's candidacy. Obama, meanwhile, merged his skills as a community organizer with the Internet age to marshal support and win young voters. He turned away from public financing to build a massive private campaign fund of over $600 million, which enabled him to run a half-hour infomercial during the World Series, and he convinced many middle and working class voters that McCain was out of touch with their economic anxieties. Record numbers of voters (roughly 125 million or 61.7%*) turned out to elect Barack Obama with 365 electoral votes to McCain's 173. The popular vote totals were 66,882,230 (53%) for Obama and 58,343,671 (46%) for McCain. Obama would take his oath of office in January 2009 on the Capitol steps that were installed by African slaves over 200 years ago. But the significance of his election went beyond race: along with being America's first African American president, Obama is also the first post-Vietnam generation president. At age 47, he was too young to have served there, and his election makes military service in that war unlikely to be a necessary credential for future presidential candidates.

First African-American president [handwritten margin note]

Summary

The 1990s were good times for most Americans. A digitized revolution in communications and information generated prosperity and transformed life in the United States and worldwide. The longest economic expansion in U.S. history—from 1991 to 2001—meant that most Americans who wanted jobs had them, that the stock market boomed, that the nation had a budget surplus, and that more Americans owned homes. And with no other formidable rival, the United States stood as the world's lone superpower.

Yet, unsettling events troubled the nation. Ethnic conflicts in the Balkans, the Middle East, Central Asia, and Africa crowded the international agenda, as did human rights and the environment. At home, violence—the 1995 domestic terrorist attack in Oklahoma City and a rash of school shootings—captured headlines, even as the crime rate dropped. And scandal further undermined Americans' faith in their government, as President Bill Clinton was caught lying about having a sexual relationship with an intern, and later the House of Representatives voted to impeach him.

Minutes before midnight on December 31, 1999, President Clinton had called on Americans not to fear the future, but to "welcome it, create it, and embrace it." The challenges ahead would include the contested presidential election in 2000 that was decided by the Supreme Court in a partisan 5-to-4 vote, and in 2001 the end of the ten-year economic expansion.

Then, on September 11, 2001, radical Islamic terrorists attacked the World Trade Center and the Pentagon, killing thousands. The new president, George W. Bush,

---

* While the number of voters broke records this year, the percentage of eligible voters did not. The record was set in 1960, when 67% of voters cast their ballots.

declared a war on terrorism. While U.S. forces went after targets in Afghanistan, Congress created the Department of Homeland Security and passed the PATRIOT Act, expanding the federal government's surveillance powers. In March 2003, Bush initiated a war in Iraq, not expecting an insurgency by disaffected Iraqis against U.S. occupying forces and sectarian violence between Sunnis and Shi'ites. To counter a troubled economy, Bush pushed through tax cuts each of his first three years in office.

The world that Americans found in the first years of the twenty-first century was different from the one they imagined for the new millennium. The horror of the September 11 terror attacks made people declare that life would never be the same. But, their resilience saw them through, as they continued to struggle over the nation's future with the passion and commitment that keeps democracy alive.

Chapter Review

SOCIAL STRAINS AND NEW POLITICAL DIRECTIONS

What undermined Bill Clinton's first presidency?

As a "New Democrat" or centrist, Bill Clinton faced members of his own party who found some of his policies—such as his emphasis on private sector economic development—too conservative. Worse, from the start, a new breed of conservative Republicans challenged many of Clinton's campaign goals, and ultimately took control of both houses of Congress after the mid-term elections in 1994. This group successfully blocked Clinton's attempts at nationalized healthcare and ending the ban on gays in the military. These increasing partisan roadblocks led the beleaguered president to make compromises that pushed the nation further to the right—most notably, signing the 1996 Personal Responsibility and Work Opportunity Act (also known as "Welfare Reform") which limited federal assistance for the needy to two years, and the Telecommunications Act, which allowed greater concentration of media ownership in fewer hands.

"THE NEW ECONOMY" AND GLOBALIZATION

What concerns did critics raise about globalization?

The so-called "age of globalization" that emerged in the late 1990s was characterized by greater worldwide integration of markets, finance and technology. Labor unions feared losing jobs to less expensive overseas production, while critics argued that globalization widened the gap between rich and poor nations. Environmentalists charged that globalization resulted in greater pollution of developing countries, and others feared the power of multinational corporations over traditional cultures. Anti-global protests targeted McDonalds as symbolizing the creation of a homogeneous global culture, and demonstrations turned violent at World Trade Organization meetings in 1999 and those of the International Monetary Fund in 2001.

PARADOXES OF PROSPERITY

Why was the presidential election in 2000 so hotly contested?

While vice president Al Gore narrowly won the popular vote, in the end, it all came down to Florida. Republican George W. Bush had a slight lead there, which, by state law, required a recount. Because of a flawed paper ballot, tens of thousands of African American votes went uncounted, and Jewish voters in Palm Beach County accidentally voted for anti-Semitic candidate Pat Buchanan. After thirty-six days with no president and legal challenges pending, the Supreme Court voted 5 to 4 along partisan lines to give the state's 25 electoral votes—and thereby the election—to George W. Bush. Some people also felt that third party candidate Ralph Nader drew support from left-liberal voters who might have voted for Gore.

SEPTEMBER 11 AND THE WAR ON TERRORISM

How did the events of Sept. 11 change America's relationship to the world?

The terrorist attacks in which hijackers forced two planes to deliberately crash into each of the twin World Trade Center towers claimed more than 3000 American lives. Another plane targeted the Pentagon and a fourth plane crashed in rural Pennsylvania when passengers attempted to wrest control of it away from hijackers. Initially, the world community united in support of the United States. But within a year, as President Bush took a hard line in the battle against terrorism that dictated countries were either with the US or against it, he began to alienate former allies. International relations further soured when he hinted he might strike Saddam Hussein's Iraq or deal forcefully with North Korea or Iran.

WAR AND OCCUPATION IN IRAQ

What challenges did the War in Iraq pose?

The U.S. and Britain moved forward (with some support from a few other countries) in March 2003 with an attack on Iraq, claiming that the country harbored biological and chemical weapons of mass destruction (WMD) and that— despite intelligence reports to the contrary—it provided refuge for Al Qaeda terrorists. Other countries and the United Nations felt diplomacy and weapons inspections were working and wanted to hold off on military action. While U.S. and British forces won the early military battle within a few months, they did not anticipate the insurgency and anti-Western ambushes it would inspire among Iraqis on the ground. Five years later, the war cost $1 billion a week, with no end in sight. Bush also faced sharp international criticism for Iraq and the US military's abuse of war prisoners at Abu Ghraib.

AMERICANS IN THE FIRST DECADE OF THE NEW MILLENNIUM

What demographic changes are Americans beginning to face in the 21st century?

As the American population reached the 300 million mark in 2006, the country was more racially and ethnically diverse than ever. The population of people of color grew 12 times faster than that of whites. Family structure has become increasingly varied, with households composed of married couples representing less than 50% of the population, and one third of all children are born to single women. The country also faces an aging population, as the leading edge of the baby boom generation turned 60 in 2006. That, combined with greater life expectancy, presents new concerns of healthcare and additional family pressures. Meanwhile, debates about medical technology and balancing science and religion—particularly over the question of stem cell research—continues to divide the nation.

SUGGESTIONS FOR FURTHER READING

Daniel Benjamin and Steven Simon, *The Sacred Age of Terror* (2002)

Barbara Ehrenreich, *Nickled and Dimed: On (Not) Getting by in America* (2002)

David Halberstam, *War in a Time of Peace: Bush, Clinton, and the Generals* (2001)

John F. Harris, *The Survivor: Bill Clinton in the White House* (2005)

Jennifer L. Hochschild, *Facing up to the American Dream: Race, Class, and the Soul of the Nation* (1995)

James Mann, *Rise of the Vulcans: The History of Bush's War Cabinet* (2004)

Alejandro Portes and Reuben G. Rumbaut, *Immigrant America: A Portrait*, 3d ed. (2006)

Thomas E. Ricks, *Fiasco: The American Military Adventure in Iraq* (2006)

Joseph E. Stiglitz, *Globalization and Its Discontents* (2002)

For a more extensive list for further reading, go to college.cengage.com/pic/norton8e.

DECLARATION OF INDEPENDENCE
IN CONGRESS, JULY 4, 1776

When, in the course of human events, it becomes necessary for one people to dissolve the political bonds which have connected them with another, and to assume, among the powers of the earth, the separate and equal station to which the laws of nature and of nature's God entitle them, a decent respect to the opinions of mankind requires that they should declare the causes which impel them to the separation.

We hold these truths to be self-evident: That all men are created equal; that they are endowed by their Creator with certain unalienable rights; that among these are life, liberty, and the pursuit of happiness; that, to secure these rights, governments are instituted among men, deriving their just powers from the consent of the governed; that whenever any form of government becomes destructive of these ends, it is the right of the people to alter or to abolish it and to institute new government, laying its foundation on such principles, and organizing its powers in such form, as to them shall seem most likely to effect their safety and happiness. Prudence, indeed, will dictate that governments long established should not be changed for light and transient causes; and accordingly all experience hath shown that mankind are more disposed to suffer, while evils are sufferable, than to right themselves by abolishing the forms to which they are accustomed. But when a long train of abuses and usurpations, pursuing invariably the same object, evinces a design to reduce them under absolute despotism, it is their right, it is their duty, to throw off such government, and to provide new guards for their future security. Such has been the patient sufferance of these colonies; and such is now the necessity which constrains them to alter their former systems of government. The history of the present King of Great Britain is a history of repeated injuries and usurpations, all having in direct object the establishment of an absolute tyranny over these states. To prove this, let facts be submitted to a candid world.

He has refused his assent to laws, the most wholesome and necessary for the public good.

He has forbidden his governors to pass laws of immediate and pressing importance, unless suspended in their operation till his assent should be obtained; and, when so suspended, he has utterly neglected to attend to them.

He has refused to pass other laws for the accommodation of large districts of people, unless those people would relinquish the right of representation in the legislature, a right inestimable to them, and formidable to tyrants only.

He has called together legislative bodies at places unusual, uncomfortable, and distant from the depository of their public records, for the sole purpose of fatiguing them into compliance with his measures.

He has dissolved representative houses repeatedly, for opposing, with manly firmness, his invasions on the rights of the people.

He has refused for a long time, after such dissolutions, to cause others to be elected; whereby the legislative powers, incapable of annihilation, have returned to the people at large for their exercise; the state remaining, in the mean time, exposed to all the dangers of invasions from without and convulsions within.

He has endeavored to prevent the population of these states; for that purpose obstructing the laws for naturalization of foreigners; refusing to pass others to encourage their migration hither, and raising the conditions of new appropriations of lands.

He has obstructed the administration of justice, by refusing his assent to laws for establishing judiciary powers.

He has made judges dependent on his will alone, for the tenure of their offices, and the amount and payment of their salaries.

He has erected a multitude of new offices, and sent hither swarms of officers to harass our people and eat out their substance.

He has kept among us, in times of peace, standing armies, without the consent of our legislatures.

He has affected to render the military independent of, and superior to, the civil power.

He has combined with others to subject us to a jurisdiction foreign to our constitution, and unacknowledged by our laws, giving his assent to their acts of pretended legislation:

For quartering large bodies of armed troops among us;

For protecting them, by a mock trial, from punishment for any murders which they should commit on the inhabitants of these states;

For cutting off our trade with all parts of the world;

For imposing taxes on us without our consent;

For depriving us, in many cases, of the benefits of trial by jury;

For transporting us beyond seas, to be tried for pretended offenses;

For abolishing the free system of English laws in a neighboring province, establishing therein an arbitrary government, and enlarging its boundaries, so as to render it at once an example and fit instrument for introducing the same absolute rule into these colonies;

For taking away our charters, abolishing our most valuable laws, and altering fundamentally the forms of our governments;

For suspending our own legislatures, and declaring themselves invested with power to legislate for us in all cases whatsoever.

He has abdicated government here, by declaring us out of his protection and waging war against us.

He has plundered our seas, ravaged our coasts, burned our towns, and destroyed the lives of our people.

He is at this time transporting large armies of foreign mercenaries to complete the works of death, desolation, and tyranny already begun with circumstances of cruelty and perfidy scarcely paralleled in the most barbarous ages, and totally unworthy the head of a civilized nation.

He has constrained our fellow-citizens, taken captive on the high seas, to bear arms against their country, to become the executioners of their friends and brethren, or to fall themselves by their hands.

He has excited domestic insurrection among us, and has endeavored to bring on the inhabitants of our frontiers the merciless Indian savages, whose known rule of warfare is an undistinguished destruction of all ages, sexes, and conditions.

In every stage of these oppressions we have petitioned for redress in the most humble terms; our repeated petitions have been answered only by repeated injury. A prince, whose character is thus marked by every act which may define a tyrant, is unfit to be the ruler of a free people.

Nor have we been wanting in our attentions to our British brethren. We have warned them, from time to time, of attempts by their legislature to extend an unwarrantable jurisdiction over us. We have reminded them of the circumstances of our emigration and settlement here. We have appealed to their native justice and magnanimity; and we have conjured them, by the ties of our common kindred, to disavow these usurpations, which would inevitably interrupt our connections and correspondence. They, too, have been deaf to the voice of justice and of consanguinity. We must, therefore, acquiesce in the necessity which denounces our separation, and hold them, as we hold the rest of mankind, enemies in war, in peace friends.

We, therefore, the representatives of the United States of America, in General Congress assembled, appealing to the Supreme Judge of the world for the rectitude of our intentions, do, in the name and by the authority of the good people of these colonies, solemnly publish and declare, that these United Colonies are, and of right ought to be, FREE AND INDEPENDENT STATES; that they are absolved from all allegiance to the British crown, and that all political connection between them and the state of Great Britain is, and ought to be, totally dissolved; and that, as free and independent states, they have full power to levy war, conclude peace, contract alliances, establish commerce, and do all other acts and things which independent states may of right do. And for the support of this declaration, with a firm reliance on the protection of Divine Providence, we mutually pledge to each other our lives, our fortunes, and our sacred honor.

ARTICLES OF CONFEDERATION

(The text of the Articles of Confederation can be found at cengage.com/ history/norton/peoplenationbrief8e)

CONSTITUTION OF THE UNITED STATES OF AMERICA AND AMENDMENTS*

Preamble

We the people of the United States, in order to form a more perfect union, establish justice, insure domestic tranquillity, provide for the common defense, promote the general welfare, and secure the blessings of liberty to ourselves and our posterity, do ordain and establish this Constitution for the United States of America.

Article I

Section 1 All legislative powers herein granted shall be vested in a Congress of the United States, which shall consist of a Senate and a House of Representatives.

---

* Passages no longer in effect are printed in italic type.

Section 2 The House of Representatives shall be composed of members chosen every second year by the people of the several States, and the electors in each State shall have the qualifications requisite for electors of the most numerous branch of the State Legislature.

No person shall be a Representative who shall not have attained to the age of twenty-five years, and been seven years a citizen of the United States, and who shall not, when elected, be an inhabitant of that State in which he shall be chosen.

Representatives and direct taxes shall be apportioned among the several States which may be included within this Union, according to their respective numbers, *which shall be determined by adding to the whole number of free persons, including those bound to service for a term of years and excluding Indians not taxed, three-fifths of all other persons.* The actual enumeration shall be made within three years after the first meeting of the Congress of the United States, and within every subsequent term of ten years, in such manner as they shall by law direct. The number of Representatives shall not exceed one for every thirty thousand, but each State shall have at least one Representative; *and until such enumeration shall be made, the State of New Hampshire shall be entitled to choose three, Massachusetts eight, Rhode Island and Providence Plantations one, Connecticut five, New York six, New Jersey four, Pennsylvania eight, Delaware one, Maryland six, Virginia ten, North Carolina five, South Carolina five, and Georgia three.*

When vacancies happen in the representation from any State, the Executive authority thereof shall issue writs of election to fill such vacancies.

The House of Representatives shall choose their Speaker and other officers; and shall have the sole power of impeachment.

Section 3 The Senate of the United States shall be composed of two Senators from each State, *chosen by the legislature thereof,* for six years; and each Senator shall have one vote.

Immediately after they shall be assembled in consequence of the first election, they shall be divided as equally as may be into three classes. The seats of the Senators of the first class shall be vacated at the expiration of the second year, of the second class at the expiration of the fourth year, and of the third class at the expiration of the sixth year, so that one-third may be chosen every second year; *and if vacancies happen by resignation or otherwise, during the recess of the legislature of any State, the Executive thereof may make temporary appointments until the next meeting of the legislature, which shall then fill such vacancies.*

No person shall be a Senator who shall not have attained to the age of thirty years, and been nine years a citizen of the United States, and who shall not, when elected, be an inhabitant of that State for which he shall be chosen.

The Vice-President of the United States shall be President of the Senate, but shall have no vote, unless they be equally divided.

The Senate shall choose their other officers, and also a President *pro tempore,* in the absence of the Vice-President, or when he shall exercise the office of President of the United States.

The Senate shall have the sole power to try all impeachments. When sitting for that purpose, they shall be on oath or affirmation. When the President of the United States is tried, the Chief Justice shall preside: and no person shall be convicted without the concurrence of two-thirds of the members present.

Judgment in cases of impeachment shall not extend further than to removal from the office, and disqualification to hold and enjoy any office of honor, trust or profit under the United States: but the party convicted shall nevertheless be liable and subject to indictment, trial, judgment and punishment, according to law.

Section 4 The times, places and manner of holding elections for Senators and Representatives shall be prescribed in each State by the legislature thereof; but the Congress may at any time by law make or alter such regulations, except as to the places of choosing Senators.

The Congress shall assemble at least once in every year, and such meeting *shall be on the first Monday in December, unless they shall by law appoint a different day.*

Section 5 Each house shall be the judge of the elections, returns and qualifications of its own members, and a majority of each shall constitute a quorum to do business; but a smaller number may adjourn from day to day, and may be authorized to compel the attendance of absent members, in such manner, and under such penalties, as each house may provide.

Each house may determine the rules of its proceedings, punish its members for disorderly behavior, and with the concurrence of two-thirds, expel a member.

Each house shall keep a journal of its proceedings, and from time to time publish the same, excepting such parts as may in their judgment require secrecy; and the yeas and nays of the members of either house on any question shall, at the desire of one-fifth of those present, be entered on the journal.

Neither house, during the session of Congress, shall, without the consent of the other, adjourn for more than three days, nor to any other place than that in which the two houses shall be sitting.

Section 6 The Senators and Representatives shall receive a compensation for their services, to be ascertained by law and paid out of the treasury of the United States. They shall in all cases except treason, felony and breach of the peace, be privileged from arrest during their attendance at the session of their respective houses, and in going to and returning from the same; and for any speech or debate in either house, they shall not be questioned in any other place.

No Senator or Representative shall, during the time for which he was elected, be appointed to any civil office under the authority of the United States, which shall have been created, or the emoluments whereof shall have been increased, during such time; and no person holding any office under the United States shall be a member of either house during his continuance in office.

Section 7 All bills for raising revenue shall originate in the House of Representatives; but the Senate may propose or concur with amendments as on other bills.

Every bill which shall have passed the House of Representatives and the Senate, shall, before it become a law, be presented to the President of the United States; if he approve he shall sign it, but if not he shall return it with objections to that house in which it originated, who shall enter the objections at large on their journal, and proceed to reconsider it. If after such reconsideration two-thirds of that house shall agree to pass the bill, it shall be sent, together with the objections, to the other house, by which it shall likewise be reconsidered, and, if approved by two-thirds of that house, it shall become a law. But in all such cases the votes of both houses shall be determined by yeas and nays, and the names of the persons voting for and against the bill shall be entered on the journal of each house respectively. If any bill shall not be returned by the President within ten days (Sundays excepted) after it shall have been presented to him, the same shall be a law, in like manner as if he had signed it, unless the Congress by their adjournment prevent its return, in which case it shall not be a law.

Every order, resolution, or vote to which the concurrence of the Senate and House of Representatives may be necessary (except on a question of adjournment) shall be presented to the President of the United States; and before the same shall take effect, shall be approved by him, or being disapproved by him, shall be repassed by two-thirds of the Senate and House of Representatives, according to the rules and limitations prescribed in the case of a bill.

Section 8 The Congress shall have power

To lay and collect taxes, duties, imposts, and excises, to pay the debts and provide for the common defense and general welfare of the United States; but all duties, imposts and excises shall be uniform throughout the United States;

To borrow money on the credit of the United States;

To regulate commerce with foreign nations, and among the several States, and with the Indian tribes;

To establish an uniform rule of naturalization, and uniform laws on the subject of bankruptcies throughout the United States;

To coin money, regulate the value thereof, and of foreign coin, and fix the standard of weights and measures;

To provide for the punishment of counterfeiting the securities and current coin of the United States;

To establish post offices and post roads;

To promote the progress of science and useful arts by securing for limited times to authors and inventors the exclusive right to their respective writings and discoveries;

To constitute tribunals inferior to the Supreme Court;

To define and punish piracies and felonies committed on the high seas and offenses against the law of nations;

To declare war, grant letters of marque and reprisal, and make rules concerning captures on land and water;

To raise and support armies, but no appropriation of money to that use shall be for a longer term than two years;

To provide and maintain a navy;

To make rules for the government and regulation of the land and naval forces;

To provide for calling forth the militia to execute the laws of the Union, suppress insurrections, and repel invasions;

To provide for organizing, arming, and disciplining the militia, and for governing such part of them as may be employed in the service of the United States, reserving to the States respectively the appointment of the officers, and the authority of training the militia according to the discipline prescribed by Congress;

To exercise exclusive legislation in all cases whatsoever, over such district (not exceeding ten miles square) as may, by cession of particular States, and the acceptance of Congress, become the seat of government of the United States, and to exercise like authority over all places purchased by the consent of the legislature of the State, in which the same shall be, for erection of forts, magazines, arsenals, dockyards, and other needful buildings;—and

To make all laws which shall be necessary and proper for carrying into execution the foregoing powers, and all other powers vested by this Constitution in the government of the United States, or in any department or officer thereof.

Section 9 The migration or importation of such persons as any of the States now existing shall think proper to admit shall not be prohibited by the Congress prior to the year 1808; but a tax or duty may be imposed on such importation, not exceeding $10 for each person.

The privilege of the writ of habeas corpus shall not be suspended, unless when in cases of rebellion or invasion the public safety may require it.

No bill of attainder or ex post facto law shall be passed.

No capitation, or other direct, tax shall be laid, unless in proportion to the census or enumeration herein before directed to be taken.

No tax or duty shall be laid on articles exported from any State.

No preference shall be given by any regulation of commerce or revenue to the ports of one State over those of another; nor shall vessels bound to, or from, one State, be obliged to enter, clear, or pay duties in another.

No money shall be drawn from the treasury, but in consequence of appropriations made by law; and a regular statement and account of the receipts and expenditures of all public money shall be published from time to time.

No title of nobility shall be granted by the United States: and no person holding any office of profit or trust under them, shall, without the consent of the Congress, accept of any present, emolument, office, or title, of any kind whatever, from any king, prince, or foreign state.

Section 10 No State shall enter into any treaty, alliance, or confederation; grant letters of marque and reprisal; coin money; emit bills of credit; make anything but gold and silver coin a tender in payment of debts; pass any bill of attainder, ex post facto law, or law impairing the obligation of contracts, or grant any title of nobility.

No State shall, without the consent of Congress, lay any imposts or duties on imports or exports, except what may be absolutely necessary for executing its inspection laws: and the net produce of all duties and imposts, laid by any State on imports or exports, shall be for the use of the treasury of the United States; and all such laws shall be subject to the revision and control of the Congress.

No State shall, without the consent of Congress, lay any duty of tonnage, keep troops or ships of war in time of peace, enter into any agreement or compact with another State, or with a foreign power, or engage in war, unless actually invaded, or in such imminent danger as will not admit of delay.

Article II

Section 1 The executive power shall be vested in a President of the United States of America. He shall hold his office during the term of four years, and, together with the Vice-President, chosen for the same term, be elected as follows:

Each State shall appoint, in such manner as the legislature thereof may direct, a number of electors, equal to the whole number of Senators and Representatives to which the State may be entitled in the Congress; but no Senator or Representative, or person holding an office of trust or profit under the United States, shall be appointed an elector.

The electors shall meet in their respective States, and vote by ballot for two persons, of whom one at least shall not be an inhabitant of the same State with themselves. And they shall make a list of all the persons voted for, and of the number of votes for each; which list they shall sign and certify, and transmit sealed to the seat of government of the United States, directed to the President of the Senate. The President of the Senate shall, in the presence of the Senate and House of Representatives, open all the certificates, and the votes shall then be counted. The person having the greatest number of votes shall be the President, if such number be a majority of the whole number of electors appointed; and if there be more than one who have such majority, and have an equal number of votes, then the House of Representatives shall immediately choose by ballot one of them for President; and if no person have a majority, then from the five highest on the list said house shall in like manner choose the President. But in choosing the President the votes shall be taken by States, the representation from each State having one vote; a quorum for this purpose shall consist of a member or members from two-thirds of the States, and a majority of all the States shall be necessary to a choice. In every case, after the choice of the President, the person having the greatest number of votes of the electors shall be the Vice-President. But if there should remain two or more who have equal votes, the Senate shall choose from them by ballot the Vice-President.

The Congress may determine the time of choosing the electors and the day on which they shall give their votes; which day shall be the same throughout the United States.

No person except a natural-born citizen, *or a citizen of the United States at the time of the adoption of this Constitution,* shall be eligible to the office of President; neither shall any person be eligible to that office who shall not have attained to the age of thirty-five years, and been fourteen years a resident within the United States.

In cases of the removal of the President from office or of his death, resignation, or inability to discharge the powers and duties of the said office, the same shall devolve on the Vice-President, and the Congress may by law provide for the case of removal, death, resignation, or inability, both of the President and Vice-President, declaring what officer shall then act as President, and such officer shall act accordingly, until the disability be removed, or a President shall be elected.

The President shall, at stated times, receive for his services a compensation, which shall neither be increased nor diminished during the period for which he shall have been elected, and he shall not receive within that period any other emolument from the United States, or any of them.

Before he enter on the execution of his office, he shall take the following oath or affirmation:—"I do solemnly swear (or affirm) that I will faithfully execute the office of the President of the United States, and will to the best of my ability preserve, protect and defend the Constitution of the United States."

Section 2 The President shall be commander in chief of the army and navy of the United States, and of the militia of the several States, when called into the actual service of the United States; he may require the opinion, in writing, of the principal officer in each of the executive departments, upon any subject relating to the duties of their respective offices, and he shall have power to grant reprieves and pardons for offenses against the United States, except in cases of impeachment.

He shall have power, by and with the advice and consent of the Senate, to make treaties, provided two-thirds of the Senators present concur; and he shall nominate, and by and with the advice and consent of the Senate, shall appoint ambassadors, other public ministers and consuls, judges of the Supreme Court, and all other officers of the United States, whose appointments are not herein otherwise provided for, and which shall be established by law: but Congress may by law vest the appointment of such inferior officers, as they think proper, in the President alone, in the courts of law, or in the heads of departments

The President shall have power to fill up all vacancies that may happen during the recess of the Senate, by granting commissions which shall expire at the end of their next session.

Section 3 He shall from time to time give to the Congress information of the state of the Union, and recommend to their consideration such measures as he shall judge necessary and expedient; he may, on extraordinary occasions, convene both houses, or either of them, and in case of disagreement between them, with respect to the time of adjournment, he may adjourn them to such time as he shall think proper; he shall receive ambassadors and other public ministers; he shall take care that the laws be faithfully executed, and shall commission all the officers of the United States.

Section 4 The President, Vice-President and all civil officers of the United States shall be removed from office on impeachment for, and on conviction of, treason, bribery, or other high crimes and misdemeanors.

Article III

Section 1 The judicial power of the United States shall be vested in one Supreme Court, and in such inferior courts as the Congress may from time to time ordain and establish. The judges, both of the Supreme and inferior courts, shall hold their offices during good behavior, and shall, at stated times, receive for their services a compensation which shall not be diminished during their continuance in office.

Section 2 The judicial power shall extend to all cases, in law and equity, arising under this Constitution, the laws of the United States, and treaties made, or which shall be made, under their authority;—to all cases affecting ambassadors, other public ministers and consuls;—to all cases of admiralty and maritime jurisdiction;—to controversies to which the United States shall be a party;—to controversies between two or more States;—*between a State and citizens of another State;*—between citizens of different States;—between citizens of the same State claiming lands under grants of different States, and between a State, or the citizens thereof, and foreign states, citizens or subjects.

In all cases affecting ambassadors, other public ministers and consuls, and those in which a State shall be party, the Supreme Court shall have original jurisdiction. In all the other cases before mentioned, the Supreme Court shall have appellate jurisdiction, both as to law and fact, with such exceptions, and under such regulations, as the Congress shall make.

The trial of all crimes, except in cases of impeachment, shall be by jury; and such trial shall be held in the State where said crimes shall have been committed; but when not committed within any State, the trial shall be at such place or places as the Congress may by law have directed.

Section 3 Treason against the United States shall consist only in levying war against them, or in adhering to their enemies, giving them aid and comfort. No person shall be convicted of treason unless on the testimony of two witnesses to the same overt act, or on confession in open court.

The Congress shall have power to declare the punishment of treason, but no attainder of treason shall work corruption of blood, or forfeiture except during the life of the person attainted.

Article IV

Section 1 Full faith and credit shall be given in each State to the public acts, records, and judicial proceedings of every other State. And the Congress may by general laws prescribe the manner in which such acts, records, and proceedings shall be proved, and the effect thereof.

Section 2 The citizens of each State shall be entitled to all privileges and immunities of citizens in the several States.

A person charged in any State with treason, felony, or other crime, who shall flee from justice, and be found in another State, shall on demand of the executive authority of the State from which he fled, be delivered up, to be removed to the State having jurisdiction of the crime.

No person held to service or labor in one State, under the laws thereof, escaping into another, shall, in consequence of any law or regulation therein, be discharged from such service or labor, but shall be delivered up on claim of the party to whom such service or labor may be due.

Section 3 New States may be admitted by the Congress into this Union; but no new State shall be formed or erected within the jurisdiction of any other State; nor any State be formed by the junction of two or more States, or parts of States, without the consent of the legislatures of the States concerned as well as of the Congress.

The Congress shall have power to dispose of and make all needful rules and regulations respecting the territory or other property belonging to the United States; and nothing in this Constitution shall be so construed as to prejudice any claims of the United States, or of any particular State.

Section 4 The United States shall guarantee to every State in this Union a republican form of government, and shall protect each of them against invasion; and on application of the legislature, or of the executive (when the legislature cannot be convened), against domestic violence.

Article V

The Congress, whenever two-thirds of both houses shall deem it necessary, shall propose amendments to this Constitution, or, on the application of the legislatures of two-thirds of the several States, shall call a convention for proposing amendments, which, in either case, shall be valid to all intents and purposes, as part of this Constitution, when ratified by the legislatures of three-fourths of the several States, or by conventions in three-fourths thereof, as the one or the other mode of ratification may be proposed by the Congress; provided *that no amendments which may be made prior to the year one thousand eight hundred and eight shall in any manner affect the first and fourth clauses in the ninth section of the first article;* and that no State, without its consent, shall be deprived of its equal suffrage in the Senate.

Article VI

All debts contracted and engagements entered into, before the adoption of this Constitution, shall be as valid against the United States under this Constitution, as under the Confederation.

This Constitution, and the laws of the United States which shall be made in pursuance thereof; and all treaties made, or which shall be made, under the authority of the United States, shall be the supreme law of the land; and the judges in every State shall be bound thereby, anything in the Constitution or laws of any State to the contrary notwithstanding.

The Senators and Representatives before mentioned, and the members of the several State legislatures, and all executive and judicial officers, both of the United States and of the several States, shall be bound by oath or affirmation to support this Constitution; but no religious test shall ever be required as a qualification to any office or public trust under the United States.

Article VII

The ratification of the conventions of nine States shall be sufficient for the establishment of this Constitution between the States so ratifying the same.

Done in Convention by the unanimous consent of the States present, the seventeenth day of September in the year of our Lord one thousand seven hundred and eighty-seven and of the Independence of the United States of America the twelfth. In witness whereof we have hereunto subscribed our names.

AMENDMENTS TO THE CONSTITUTION*

Amendment I

Congress shall make no law respecting an establishment of religion, or prohibiting the free exercise thereof; or abridging the freedom of speech, or of the press; or the right of the people peaceably to assemble, and to petition the government for a redress of grievances.

Amendment II

A well-regulated militia being necessary to the security of a free State, the right of the people to keep and bear arms shall not be infringed.

Amendment III

No soldier shall, in time of peace, be quartered in any house without the consent of the owner, nor in time of war, but in a manner to be prescribed by law.

Amendment IV

The right of the people to be secure in their persons, houses, papers, and effects, against unreasonable searches and seizures, shall not be violated, and no warrants shall issue but upon probable cause, supported by oath or affirmation, and particularly describing the place to be searched, and the persons or things to be seized.

---

*The first ten Amendments (the Bill of Rights) were adopted in 1791.

Amendment V

No person shall be held to answer for a capital, or otherwise infamous crime, unless on a presentment or indictment of a grand jury, except in cases arising in the land or naval forces, or in the militia, when in actual service in time of war or public danger; nor shall any person be subject for the same offense to be twice put in jeopardy of life or limb; nor shall be compelled in any criminal case to be a witness against himself, nor be deprived of life, liberty, or property, without due process of law; nor shall private property be taken for public use without just compensation.

Amendment VI

In all criminal prosecutions, the accused shall enjoy the right to a speedy and public trial, by an impartial jury of the State and district wherein the crime shall have been committed, which district shall have been previously ascertained by law, and to be informed of the nature and cause of the accusation; to be confronted with the witnesses against him; to have compulsory process for obtaining witnesses in his favor, and to have the assistance of counsel for his defense.

Amendment VII

In suits at common law, where the value in controversy shall exceed twenty dollars, the right of trial by jury shall be preserved, and no fact tried by a jury shall be otherwise reexamined in any court of the United States, than according to the rules of the common law.

Amendment VIII

Excessive bail shall not be required, nor excessive fines imposed, nor cruel and unusual punishments inflicted.

Amendment IX

The enumeration in the Constitution, of certain rights, shall not be construed to deny or disparage others retained by the people.

Amendment X

The powers not delegated to the United States by the Constitution, nor prohibited by it to the States, are reserved to the States respectively, or to the people.

Amendment XI

[Adopted 1798]

The judicial power of the United States shall not be construed to extend to any suit in law or equity, commenced or prosecuted against one of the United States by citizens of another State, or by citizens or subjects of any foreign state.

Amendment XII

[Adopted 1804]

The electors shall meet in their respective States, and vote by ballot for President and Vice-President, one of whom, at least, shall not be an inhabitant of the same State with themselves; they shall name in their ballots the person voted for as President, and in distinct ballots the person voted for as Vice-President, and they shall make distinct lists of all persons voted for as President, and of all persons voted for as Vice-President, and of the number of votes for each, which lists they shall sign and certify, and transmit sealed to the seat of government of the United States, directed to the President of the Senate;—the President of the Senate shall, in the presence of the Senate and House of Representatives, open all the certificates and the votes shall then be counted;—the person having the greatest number of votes for President shall be the President, if such number be a majority of the whole number of electors appointed; and if no person have such majority, then from the persons having the highest numbers not exceeding three on the list of those voted for as President, the House of Representatives shall choose immediately, by ballot, the President. But in choosing the President, the votes shall be taken by States, the representation from each State having one vote; a quorum for this purpose shall consist of a member or members from two-thirds of the States, and a majority of all the States shall be necessary to a choice. And if the House of Representatives shall not choose a President whenever the right of choice shall devolve upon them before *the fourth day of March* next following, then the Vice-President shall act as President, as in the case of the death or other constitutional disability of the President.

The person having the greatest number of votes as Vice-President shall be the Vice-President, if such number be a majority of the whole number of electors appointed; and if no person have a majority, then from the two highest numbers on the list the Senate shall choose the Vice-President; a quorum for the purpose shall consist of two-thirds of the whole number of Senators, and a majority of the whole number shall be necessary to a choice. But no person constitutionally ineligible to the office of President shall be eligible to that of Vice-President of the United States.

Amendment XIII

[Adopted 1865]

Section 1 Neither slavery nor involuntary servitude, except as a punishment for crime whereof the party shall have been duly convicted, shall exist within the United States, or any place subject to their jurisdiction.

Section 2 Congress shall have power to enforce this article by appropriate legislation.

Amendment XIV

[Adopted 1868]

Section 1 All persons born or naturalized in the United States, and subject to the jurisdiction thereof, are citizens of the United States and of the State wherein they reside. No State shall make or enforce any law which shall abridge the privileges or immunities of citizens of the United States; nor shall any State deprive any person of life, liberty, or property, without due process of law; nor deny to any person within its jurisdiction the equal protection of the laws.

Section 2 Representatives shall be apportioned among the several States according to their respective numbers, counting the whole number of persons in each State, excluding Indians not taxed. But when the right to vote at any election for the choice of Electors for President and Vice-President of the United States, Representatives in Congress, the executive and judicial officers of a State, or the members of the legislature thereof, is denied to any of the male inhabitants of such State, being twenty-one years of age and citizens of the United States, or in any way abridged, except for participation in rebellion, or other crime, the basis of representation therein shall be reduced in the proportion which the number of such male citizens shall bear to the whole number of male citizens twenty-one years of age in such State.

Section 3 No person shall be a Senator or Representative in Congress, or Elector of President and Vice-President, or hold any office, civil or military, under the United States, or under any State, who, having previously taken an oath, as a member of Congress, or as an officer of the United States, or as a member of any State legislature, or as an executive or judicial officer of any State, to support the Constitution of the United States, shall have engaged in insurrection or rebellion against the same, or given aid or comfort to the enemies thereof. Congress may, by a vote of two-thirds of each house, remove such disability.

Section 4 The validity of the public debt of the United States, authorized by law, including debts incurred for payment of pensions and bounties for services in suppressing insurrection or rebellion, shall not be questioned. But neither the United States nor any State shall assume or pay any debt or obligation incurred in aid of insurrection or rebellion against the United States, or any claim for the loss of emancipation of any slave; but all such debts, obligations, and claims shall be held illegal and void.

Section 5 The Congress shall have power to enforce, by appropriate legislation, the provisions of this article.

Amendment XV

[Adopted 1870]

Section 1 The right of citizens of the United States to vote shall not be denied or abridged by the United States or by any State on account of race, color, or previous condition of servitude.

Section 2 The Congress shall have power to enforce this article by appropriate legislation.

Amendment XVI

[Adopted 1913]

The Congress shall have power to lay and collect taxes on incomes, from whatever source derived, without apportionment among the several States, and without regard to any census or enumeration.

Amendment XVII

[Adopted 1913]

Section 1 The Senate of the United States shall be composed of two Senators from each State, elected by the people thereof, for six years; and each Senator shall have one vote. The electors in each State shall have the qualifications requisite for electors of [voters for] the most numerous branch of the State legislatures.

Section 2 When vacancies happen in the representation of any State in the Senate, the executive authority of such State shall issue writs of election to fill such vacancies: Provided, that the Legislature of any State may empower the executive thereof to make temporary appointments until the people fill the vacancies by election as the Legislature may direct.

Section 3 This amendment shall not be so construed as to affect the election or term of any Senator chosen before it becomes valid as part of the Constitution.

Amendment XVIII

[Adopted 1919; Repealed 1933]

Section 1 After one year from the ratification of this article the manufacture, sale, or transportation of intoxicating liquors within, the importation thereof into, or the exportation thereof from the United States and all territory subject to the jurisdiction thereof, for beverage purposes, is hereby prohibited.

Section 2 The Congress and the several States shall have concurrent power to enforce this article by appropriate legislation.

Section 3 This article shall be inoperative unless it shall have been ratified as an amendment to the Constitution by the legislatures of the several States, as provided by the Constitution, within seven years from the date of the submission thereof to the States by the Congress.

Amendment XIX

[Adopted 1920]

Section 1 The right of citizens of the United States to vote shall not be denied or abridged by the United States or by any State on account of sex.

Section 2 The Congress shall have power to enforce this article by appropriate legislation.

Amendment XX

[Adopted 1933]

Section 1 The terms of the President and Vice-President shall end at noon on the 20th day of January, and the terms of Senators and Representatives at noon on the 3rd day of January, of the years in which such terms would have ended if this article had not been ratified; and the terms of their successors shall then begin.

Section 2 The Congress shall assemble at least once in every year, and such meeting shall begin at noon on the 3d day of January, unless they shall by law appoint a different day.

Section 3 If, at the time fixed for the beginning of the term of the President, the President-elect shall have died, the Vice-President-elect shall become President. If a President shall not have been chosen before the time fixed for the beginning of his term, or if the President-elect shall have failed to qualify, then the Vice-President-elect shall act as President until a President shall have qualified; and the Congress may by law provide for the case wherein neither a President-elect nor a Vice-President–elect shall have qualified, declaring who shall then act as President, or the manner in which one who is to act shall be selected, and such persons shall act accordingly until a President or Vice-President shall have qualified.

Section 4 The Congress may by law provide for the case of the death of any of the persons from whom the House of Representatives may choose a President whenever the right of choice shall have devolved upon them, and for the case of the death of any of the persons from whom the Senate may choose a Vice-President whenever the right of choice shall have devolved upon them.

Section 5 Sections 1 and 2 shall take effect on the 15th day of October following the ratification of this article.

Section 6 This article shall be inoperative unless it shall have been ratified as an amendment to the Constitution by the Legislatures of three-fourths of the several States within seven years from the date of its submission.

Amendment XXI [Adopted 1933]

Section 1 The eighteenth article of amendment to the Constitution of the United States is hereby repealed.

Section 2 The transportation or importation into any State, Territory, or Possession of the United States for delivery or use therein of intoxicating liquors, in violation of the laws thereof, is hereby prohibited.

Section 3 This article shall be inoperative unless it shall have been ratified as an amendment to the Constitution by conventions in the several States, as provided in the Constitution, within seven years from the date of submission thereof to the States by the Congress.

Amendment XXII [Adopted 1951]

Section 1 No person shall be elected to the office of President more than twice, and no person who has held the office of President, or acted as President, for more than two years of a term to which some other person was elected President shall be elected to the office of President more than once. But this article shall not apply to any person holding the office of President when this article was proposed by the Congress, and shall not prevent any person who may be holding the office of President, or acting as President, during the term within which this article becomes operative from holding the office of President or acting as President during the remainder of such term.

Section 2 This article shall be inoperative unless it shall have been ratified as an amendment to the Constitution by the legislatures of three-fourths of the several States within seven years from the date of its submission to the States by the Congress.

Amendment XXIII

[Adopted 1961]

Section 1 The District constituting the seat of Government of the United States shall appoint in such manner as the Congress may direct:

A number of electors of President and Vice-President equal to the whole number of Senators and Representatives in Congress to which the District would be entitled if it were a State, but in no event more than the least populous State; they shall be in addition to those appointed by the States, but they shall be considered for the purposes of the election of President and Vice-President, to be electors appointed by a State; and they shall meet in the District and perform such duties as provided by the twelfth article of amendment.

Section 2 The Congress shall have the power to enforce this article by appropriate legislation.

Amendment XXIV

[Adopted 1964]

Section 1 The right of citizens of the United States to vote in any primary or other election for President or Vice-President, for electors for President or Vice-President, or for Senator or Representative in Congress, shall not be denied or abridged by the United States or any State by reason of failure to pay any poll tax or other tax.

Section 2 The Congress shall have the power to enforce this article by appropriate legislation.

Amendment XXV

[Adopted 1967]

Section 1 In case of the removal of the President from office or of his death or resignation, the Vice-President shall become President.

Section 2 Whenever there is a vacancy in the office of the Vice-President, the President shall nominate a Vice-President who shall take office upon confirmation by a majority vote of both Houses of Congress.

Section 3 Whenever the President transmits to the President pro tempore of the Senate and the Speaker of the House of Representatives his written declaration that he is unable to discharge the powers and duties of his office, and until he transmits to them a written declaration to the contrary, such powers and duties shall be discharged by the Vice-President as Acting President.

Section 4 Whenever the Vice-President and a majority of either the principal officers of the executive departments or of such other body as Congress may by law provide, transmit to the President pro tempore of the Senate and the Speaker of the House of Representatives their written declaration that the President is unable to discharge the powers and duties of his office, the Vice-President shall immediately assume the powers and duties of the office as Acting President.

Thereafter, when the President transmits to the President pro tempore of the Senate and the Speaker of the House of Representatives his written declaration that no inability exists, he shall resume the powers and duties of his office unless the Vice-President and a majority of either the principal officers of the executive department[s] or of such other body as Congress may by law provide, transmit within four days to the President pro tempore of the Senate and the Speaker of the House of Representatives their written declaration that the President is unable to discharge the powers and duties of his office. Thereupon Congress shall decide the issue, assembling within forty-eight hours for that purpose if not in session. If the Congress, within twenty-one days after receipt of the latter written declaration, or, if Congress is not in session, within twenty-one days after Congress is required to assemble, determines by two-thirds vote of both Houses that the President is unable to discharge the powers and duties of his office, the Vice-President shall continue to discharge the same as Acting President; otherwise, the President shall resume the powers and duties of his office.

Amendment XXVI

[Adopted 1971]

Section 1 The right of citizens of the United States, who are eighteen years of age or older, to vote shall not be denied or abridged by the United States or by any State on account of age.

Section 2 The Congress shall have power to enforce this article by appropriate legislation.

Amendment XXVII

[Adopted 1992]

No law, varying the compensation for the services of the Senators and Representatives, shall take effect, until an election of Representatives shall have intervened.

Presidential Elections

Year	Number of States	Candidates	Parties	Popular Vote	% of Popular Vote	Electoral Vote	% Voter Participation[a]
1789	10	George Washington	No party			69	
		John Adams	designations			34	
		Other candidates				35	
1792	15	George Washington	No party			132	
		John Adams	designations			77	
		George Clinton				50	
		Other candidates				5	
1796	16	John Adams	Federalist			71	
		Thomas Jefferson	Democratic-Republican			68	
		Thomas Pinckney	Federalist			59	
		Aaron Burr	Democratic-Republican			30	
		Other candidates				48	
1800	16	Thomas Jefferson	Democratic-Republican			73	
		Aaron Burr	Democratic-Republican			73	
		John Adams	Federalist			65	
		Charles C. Pinckney	Federalist			64	
		John Jay	Federalist			1	
1804	17	Thomas Jefferson	Democratic-Republican			162	
		Charles C. Pinckney	Federalist			14	
1808	17	James Madison	Democratic-Republican			122	
		Charles C. Pinckney	Federalist			47	
		George Clinton	Democratic-Republican			6	
1812	18	James Madison	Democratic-Republican			128	
		DeWitt Clinton	Federalist			89	
1816	19	James Monroe	Democratic-Republican			183	
		Rufus King	Federalist			34	
1820	24	James Monroe	Democratic-Republican			231	
		John Quincy Adams	Independent Republican			1	

Presidential Elections (*continued*)

Year	Number of States	Candidates	Parties	Popular Vote	% of Popular Vote	Electoral Vote	% Voter Participation[a]
1824	24	**John Quincy Adams**	Democratic-Republican	108,740	30.5	84	26.9
		Andrew Jackson	Democratic-Republican	153,544	43.1	99	
		Henry Clay	Democratic-Republican	47,136	13.2	37	
		William H. Crawford	Democratic-Republican	46,618	13.1	41	
1828	24	**Andrew Jackson**	Democratic	647,286	56.0	178	57.6
		John Quincy Adams	National Republican	508,064	44.0	83	
1832	24	**Andrew Jackson**	Democratic	701,780	54.2	219	55.4
		Henry Clay	National Republican	484,205	37.4	49	
		Other candidates		107,988	8.0	18	
1836	26	**Martin Van Buren**	Democratic	764,176	50.8	170	57.8
		William H. Harrison	Whig	550,816	36.6	73	
		Hugh L. White	Whig	146,107	9.7	26	
1840	26	**William H. Harrison**	Whig	1,274,624	53.1	234	80.2
		Martin Van Buren	Democratic	1,127,781	46.9	60	
1844	26	**James K. Polk**	Democratic	1,338,464	49.6	170	78.9
		Henry Clay	Whig	1,300,097	48.1	105	
		James G. Birney	Liberty	62,300	2.3		
1848	30	**Zachary Taylor**	Whig	1,360,967	47.4	163	72.7
		Lewis Cass	Democratic	1,222,342	42.5	127	
		Martin Van Buren	Free Soil	291,263	10.1		
1852	31	**Franklin Pierce**	Democratic	1,601,117	50.9	254	69.6
		Winfield Scott	Whig	1,385,453	44.1	42	
		John P. Hale	Free Soil	155,825	5.0		
1856	31	**James Buchanan**	Democratic	1,832,955	45.3	174	78.9
		John C. Frémont	Republican	1,339,932	33.1	114	
		Millard Fillmore	American	871,731	21.6	8	
1860	33	**Abraham Lincoln**	Republican	1,865,593	39.8	180	81.2
		Stephen A. Douglas	Democratic	1,382,713	29.5	12	
		John C. Breckinridge	Democratic	848,356	18.1	72	
		John Bell	Constitutional Union	592,906	12.6	39	
1864	36	**Abraham Lincoln**	Republican	2,206,938	55.0	212	73.8
		George B. McClellan	Democratic	1,803,787	45.0	21	
1868	37	**Ulysses S. Grant**	Republican	3,013,421	52.7	214	78.1
		Horatio Seymour	Democratic	2,706,829	47.3	80	

Presidential Elections (*continued*)

Year	Number of States	Candidates	Parties	Popular Vote	% of Popular Vote	Electoral Vote	% Voter Partici- pation[a]
1872	37	**Ulysses S. Grant**	Republican	3,596,745	55.6	286	71.3
		Horace Greeley	Democratic	2,843,446	43.9	[b]	
1876	38	**Rutherford B. Hayes**	Republican	4,036,572	48.0	185	81.8
		Samuel J. Tilden	Democratic	4,284,020	51.0	184	
1880	38	**James A. Garfield**	Republican	4,453,295	48.5	214	79.4
		Winfield S. Hancock	Democratic	4,414,082	48.1	155	
		James B. Weaver	Greenback- Labor	308,578	3.4		
1884	38	**Grover Cleveland**	Democratic	4,879,507	48.5	219	77.5
		James G. Blaine	Republican	4,850,293	48.2	182	
		Benjamin F. Butler	Greenback- Labor	175,370	1.8		
		John P. St. John	Prohibition	150,369	1.5		
1888	38	**Benjamin Harrison**	Republican	5,447,129	47.9	233	79.3
		Grover Cleveland	Democratic	5,537,857	48.6	168	
		Clinton B. Fisk	Prohibition	249,506	2.2		
		Anson J. Streeter	Union Labor	146,935	1.3		
1892	44	**Grover Cleveland**	Democratic	5,555,426	46.1	277	74.7
		Benjamin Harrison	Republican	5,182,690	43.0	145	
		James B. Weaver	People's	1,029,846	8.5	22	
		John Bidwell	Prohibition	264,133	2.2		
1896	45	**William McKinley**	Republican	7,102,246	51.1	271	79.3
		William J. Bryan	Democratic	6,492,559	47.7	176	
1900	45	**William McKinley**	Republican	7,218,491	51.7	292	73.2
		William J. Bryan	Democratic; Populist	6,356,734	45.5	155	
		John C. Wooley	Prohibition	208,914	1.5		
1904	45	**Theodore Roosevelt**	Republican	7,628,461	57.4	336	65.2
		Alton B. Parker	Democratic	5,084,223	37.6	140	
		Eugene V. Debs	Socialist	402,283	3.0		
		Silas C. Swallow	Prohibition	258,536	1.9		
1908	46	**William H. Taft**	Republican	7,675,320	51.6	321	65.4
		William J. Bryan	Democratic	6,412,294	43.1	162	
		Eugene V. Debs	Socialist	420,793	2.8		
		Eugene W. Chafin	Prohibition	253,840	1.7		
1912	48	**Woodrow Wilson**	Democratic	6,296,547	41.9	435	58.8
		Theodore Roosevelt	Progressive	4,118,571	27.4	88	
		William H. Taft	Republican	3,486,720	23.2	8	
		Eugene V. Debs	Socialist	900,672	6.0		
		Eugene W. Chafin	Prohibition	206,275	1.4		

Presidential Elections (*continued*)

Year	Number of States	Candidates	Parties	Popular Vote	% of Popular Vote	Electoral Vote	% Voter Participation[a]
1916	48	**Woodrow Wilson**	Democratic	9,127,695	49.4	277	61.6
		Charles E. Hughes	Republican	8,533,507	46.2	254	
		A. L. Benson	Socialist	585,113	3.2		
		J. Frank Hanly	Prohibition	220,506	1.2		
1920	48	**Warren G. Harding**	Republican	16,143,407	60.4	404	49.2
		James M. Cox	Democratic	9,130,328	34.2	127	
		Eugene V. Debs	Socialist	919,799	3.4		
		P. P. Christensen	Farmer-Labor	265,411	1.0		
1924	48	**Calvin Coolidge**	Republican	15,718,211	54.0	382	48.9
		John W. Davis	Democratic	8,385,283	28.8	136	
		Robert M. La Follette	Progressive	4,831,289	16.6	13	
1928	48	**Herbert C. Hoover**	Republican	21,391,993	58.2	444	56.9
		Alfred E. Smith	Democratic	15,016,169	40.9	87	
1932	48	**Franklin D. Roosevelt**	Democratic	22,809,638	57.4	472	56.9
		Herbert C. Hoover	Republican	15,758,901	39.7	59	
		Norman Thomas	Socialist	881,951	2.2		
1936	48	**Franklin D. Roosevelt**	Democratic	27,752,869	60.8	523	61.0
		Alfred M. Landon	Republican	16,674,665	36.5	8	
		William Lemke	Union	882,479	1.9		
1940	48	**Franklin D. Roosevelt**	Democratic	27,307,819	54.8	449	62.5
		Wendell L. Willkie	Republican	22,321,018	44.8	82	
1944	48	**Franklin D. Roosevelt**	Democratic	25,606,585	53.5	432	55.9
		Thomas E. Dewey	Republican	22,014,745	46.0	99	
1948	48	**Harry S Truman**	Democratic	24,179,345	49.6	303	53.0
		Thomas E. Dewey	Republican	21,991,291	45.1	189	
		J. Strom Thurmond	States' Rights	1,176,125	2.4	39	
		Henry A. Wallace	Progressive	1,157,326	2.4		
1952	48	**Dwight D. Eisenhower**	Republican	33,936,234	55.1	442	63.3
		Adlai E. Stevenson	Democratic	27,314,992	44.4	89	
1956	48	**Dwight D. Eisenhower**	Republican	35,590,472	57.6	457	60.6
		Adlai E. Stevenson	Democratic	26,022,752	42.1	73	
1960	50	**John F. Kennedy**	Democratic	34,226,731	49.7	303	62.8
		Richard M. Nixon	Republican	34,108,157	49.5	219	
1964	50	**Lyndon B. Johnson**	Democratic	43,129,566	61.1	486	61.7
		Barry M. Goldwater	Republican	27,178,188	38.5	52	
1968	50	**Richard M. Nixon**	Republican	31,785,480	43.4	301	60.6
		Hubert H. Humphrey	Democratic	31,275,166	42.7	191	
		George C. Wallace	American Independent	9,906,473	13.5	46	

Presidential Elections (*continued*)

Year	Number of States	Candidates	Parties	Popular Vote	% of Popular Vote	Electoral Vote	% Voter Participation[a]
1972	50	Richard M. Nixon	Republican	47,169,911	60.7	520	55.2
		George S. McGovern	Democratic	29,170,383	37.5	17	
		John G. Schmitz	American	1,099,482	1.4		
1976	50	James E. Carter	Democratic	40,830,763	50.1	297	53.5
		Gerald R. Ford	Republican	39,147,793	48.0	240	
1980	50	Ronald W. Reagan	Republican	43,904,153	50.7	489	52.6
		James E. Carter	Democratic	35,483,883	41.0	49	
		John B. Anderson	Independent	5,720,060	6.6		
		Ed Clark	Libertarian	921,299	1.1		
1984	50	Ronald W. Reagan	Republican	54,455,075	58.8	525	53.3
		Walter F. Mondale	Democratic	37,577,185	40.6	13	
1988	50	George H. W. Bush	Republican	48,886,097	53.4	426	50.1
		Michael S. Dukakis	Democratic	41,809,074	45.6	111[c]	
1992	50	William J. Clinton	Democratic	44,909,326	43.0	370	55.2
		George H. W. Bush	Republican	39,103,882	37.4	168	
		H. Ross Perot	Independent	19,741,048	18.9		
1996	50	William J. Clinton	Democratic	47,402,357	49.2	379	49.1
		Robert J. Dole	Republican	39,196,755	40.7	159	
		H. Ross Perot	Reform	8,085,402	8.4		
		Ralph Nader	Green	684,902	0.7		
2000	50	George W. Bush	Republican	50,455,156	47.9	271	51.2
		Albert Gore	Democratic	50,992,335	48.4	266	
		Ralph Nader	Green	2,882,955	2.7		
2004	50	George W. Bush	Republican	62,039,073	50.7	286	55.3
		John F. Kerry	Democratic	59,027,478	48.2	251	
		Ralph Nader	Independent	240,896	0.2		
2008	50	Barack Obama	Democratic	66,832,230	53.0	365	61.7
		John McCain	Republican	58,343,671	46.0	173	
		Ralph Nader	Independent	705,200	0.55		

Candidates receiving less than 1 percent of the popular vote have been omitted. Thus the percentage of popular vote given for any election year may not total 100 percent.
  Before the passage of the Twelfth Amendment in 1804, the electoral college voted for two presidential candidates; the runner-up became vice president.
  Before 1824, most presidential electors were chosen by state legislatures, not by popular vote.

[a]Percent of voting-age population casting ballots.
[b]Greeley died shortly after the election; the electors supporting him then divided their votes among minor candidates.
[c]One elector from West Virginia cast her electoral college presidential ballot for Lloyd Bentsen, the Democratic Party's vice-presidential candidate.

Presidents and Vice Presidents

1. President	**George Washington**	1789–1797	18. President	**Ulysses S. Grant**	1869–1877
Vice President	John Adams	1789–1797	Vice President	Schuyler Colfax	1869–1873
2. President	**John Adams**	1797–1801	Vice President	Henry Wilson	1873–1877
Vice President	Thomas Jefferson	1797–1801	19. President	**Rutherford B. Hayes**	1877–1881
3. President	**Thomas Jefferson**	1801–1809	Vice President	William A. Wheeler	1877–1881
Vice President	Aaron Burr	1801–1805	20. President	**James A. Garfield**	1881
Vice President	George Clinton	1805–1809	Vice President	Chester A. Arthur	1881
4. President	**James Madison**	1809–1817	21. President	**Chester A. Arthur**	1881–1885
Vice President	George Clinton	1809–1813	Vice President	None	
Vice President	Elbridge Gerry	1813–1817	22. President	**Grover Cleveland**	1885–1889
5. President	**James Monroe**	1817–1825	Vice President	Thomas A. Hendricks	1885–1889
Vice President	Daniel Tompkins	1817–1825	23. President	**Benjamin Harrison**	1889–1893
6. President	**John Quincy Adams**	1825–1829	Vice President	Levi P. Morton	1889–1893
Vice President	John C. Calhoun	1825–1829	24. President	**Grover Cleveland**	1893–1897
7. President	**Andrew Jackson**	1829–1837	Vice President	Adlai E. Stevenson	1893–1897
Vice President	John C. Calhoun	1829–1833	25. President	**William McKinley**	1897–1901
Vice President	Martin Van Buren	1833–1837	Vice President	Garret A. Hobart	1897–1901
8. President	**Martin Van Buren**	1837–1841	Vice President	Theodore Roosevelt	1901
Vice President	Richard M. Johnson	1837–1841	26. President	**Theodore Roosevelt**	1901–1909
9. President	**William H. Harrison**	1841	Vice President	Charles Fairbanks	1905–1909
Vice President	John Tyler	1841	27. President	**William H. Taft**	1909–1913
10. President	**John Tyler**	1841–1845	Vice President	James S. Sherman	1909–1913
Vice President	None		28. President	**Woodrow Wilson**	1913–1921
11. President	**James K. Polk**	1845–1849	Vice President	Thomas R. Marshall	1913–1921
Vice President	George M. Dallas	1845–1849	29. President	**Warren G. Harding**	1921–1923
12. President	**Zachary Taylor**	1849–1850	Vice President	Calvin Coolidge	1921–1923
Vice President	Millard Fillmore	1849–1850	30. President	**Calvin Coolidge**	1923–1929
13. President	**Millard Fillmore**	1850–1853	Vice President	Charles G. Dawes	1925–1929
Vice President	None		31. President	**Herbert C. Hoover**	1929–1933
14. President	**Franklin Pierce**	1853–1857	Vice President	Charles Curtis	1929–1933
Vice President	William R. King	1853–1857	32. President	**Franklin D. Roosevelt**	1933–1945
15. President	**James Buchanan**	1857–1861	Vice President	John N. Garner	1933–1941
Vice President	John C. Breckinridge	1857–1861	Vice President	Henry A. Wallace	1941–1945
16. President	**Abraham Lincoln**	1861–1865	Vice President	Harry S Truman	1945
Vice President	Hannibal Hamlin	1861–1865	33. President	**Harry S Truman**	1945–1953
Vice President	Andrew Johnson	1865	Vice President	Alben W. Barkley	1949–1953
17. President	**Andrew Johnson**	1865–1869	34. President	**Dwight D. Eisenhower**	1953–1961
Vice President	None		Vice President	Richard M. Nixon	1953–1961

35. President	**John F. Kennedy**	1961–1963	40. President	**Ronald W. Reagan**	1981–1989
Vice President	Lyndon B. Johnson	1961–1963	Vice President	George H. W. Bush	1981–1989
36. President	**Lyndon B. Johnson**	1963–1969	41. President	**George H. W. Bush**	1989–1993
Vice President	Hubert H. Humphrey	1965–1969	Vice President	J. Danforth Quayle	1989–1993
37. President	**Richard M. Nixon**	1969–1974	42. President	**William J. Clinton**	1993–2001
Vice President	Spiro T. Agnew	1969–1973	Vice President	Albert Gore	1993–2001
Vice President	Gerald R. Ford	1973–1974	43. President	**George W. Bush**	2001–2009
38. President	**Gerald R. Ford**	1974–1977	Vice President	Richard Cheney	2001–2009
Vice President	Nelson A. Rockefeller	1974–1977	44. President	**Barack Obama**	2009–
39. President	**James E. Carter**	1977–1981	Vice President	Joseph Biden	2009–
Vice President	Walter F. Mondale	1977–1981			

For a complete list of Presidents, Vice Presidents, and Cabinet Members, go to cengage.com/history/norton/peoplenationbrief8e

Justices of the Supreme Court

	Term of Service	Years of Service	Life Span		Term of Service	Years of Service	Life Span
John Jay	1789–1795	5	1745–1829	William Strong	1870–1880	10	1808–1895
John Rutledge	1789–1791	1	1739–1800	Joseph P. Bradley	1870–1892	22	1813–1892
William Cushing	1789–1810	20	1732–1810	Ward Hunt	1873–1882	9	1810–1886
James Wilson	1789–1798	8	1742–1798	*Morrison R. Waite*	1874–1888	14	1816–1888
John Blair	1789–1796	6	1732–1800	John M. Harlan	1877–1911	34	1833–1911
Robert H. Harrison	1789–1790	–	1745–1790	William B. Woods	1880–1887	7	1824–1887
James Iredell	1790–1799	9	1751–1799	Stanley Mathews	1881–1889	7	1824–1889
Thomas Johnson	1791–1793	1	1732–1819	Horace Gray	1882–1902	20	1828–1902
William Paterson	1793–1806	13	1745–1806	Samuel Blatchford	1882–1893	11	1820–1893
*John Rutledge**	1795	–	1739–1800	Lucius Q. C. Lamar	1888–1893	5	1825–1893
Samuel Chase	1796–1811	15	1741–1811	*Melville W. Fuller*	1888–1910	21	1833–1910
Oliver Ellsworth	1796–1800	4	1745–1807	David J. Brewer	1890–1910	20	1837–1910
Bushrod Washington	1798–1829	31	1762–1829	Henry B. Brown	1890–1906	16	1836–1913
Alfred Moore	1799–1804	4	1755–1810	George Shiras Jr.	1892–1903	10	1832–1924
John Marshall	1801–1835	34	1755–1835	Howell E. Jackson	1893–1895	2	1832–1895
William Johnson	1804–1834	30	1771–1834	Edward D. White	1894–1910	16	1845–1921
H. Brockholst Livingston	1806–1823	16	1757–1823	Rufus W. Peckham	1895–1909	14	1838–1909
Thomas Todd	1807–1826	18	1765–1826	Joseph McKenna	1898–1925	26	1843–1926
Joseph Story	1811–1845	33	1779–1845	Oliver W. Holmes	1902–1932	30	1841–1935
Gabriel Duval	1811–1835	24	1752–1844	William D. Day	1903–1922	19	1849–1923
Smith Thompson	1823–1843	20	1768–1843	William H. Moody	1906–1910	3	1853–1917
Robert Trimble	1826–1828	2	1777–1828	Horace H. Lurton	1910–1914	4	1844–1914
John McLean	1829–1861	32	1785–1861	Charles E. Hughes	1910–1916	5	1862–1948
Henry Baldwin	1830–1844	14	1780–1844	Willis Van Devanter	1911–1937	26	1859–1941
James M. Wayne	1835–1867	32	1790–1867	Joseph R. Lamar	1911–1916	5	1857–1916
Roger B. Taney	1836–1864	28	1777–1864	*Edward D. White*	1910–1921	11	1845–1921
Philip P. Barbour	1836–1841	4	1783–1841	Mahlon Pitney	1912–1922	10	1858–1924
John Catron	1837–1865	28	1786–1865	James C. McReynolds	1914–1941	26	1862–1946
John McKinley	1837–1852	15	1780–1852	Louis D. Brandeis	1916–1939	22	1856–1941
Peter V. Daniel	1841–1860	19	1784–1860	John H. Clarke	1916–1922	6	1857–1945
Samuel Nelson	1845–1872	27	1792–1873	*William H. Taft*	1921–1930	8	1857–1930
Levi Woodbury	1845–1851	5	1789–1851	George Sutherland	1922–1938	15	1862–1942
Robert C. Grier	1846–1870	23	1794–1870	Pierce Butler	1922–1939	16	1866–1939
Benjamin R. Curtis	1851–1857	6	1809–1874	Edward T. Sanford	1923–1930	7	1865–1930
John A. Campbell	1853–1861	8	1811–1889	Harlan F. Stone	1925–1941	16	1872–1946
Nathan Clifford	1858–1881	23	1803–1881	*Charles E. Hughes*	1930–1941	11	1862–1948
Noah H. Swayne	1862–1881	18	1804–1884	Owen J. Roberts	1930–1945	15	1875–1955
Samuel F. Miller	1862–1890	28	1816–1890	Benjamin N. Cardozo	1932–1938	6	1870–1938
David Davis	1862–1877	14	1815–1886	Hugo L. Black	1937–1971	34	1886–1971
Stephen J. Field	1863–1897	34	1816–1899	Stanley F. Reed	1938–1957	19	1884–1980
Salmon P. Chase	1864–1873	8	1808–1873	Felix Frankfurter	1939–1962	23	1882–1965

	Term of Service	Years of Service	Life Span		Term of Service	Years of Service	Life Span
William O. Douglas	1939–1975	36	1898–1980	Abe Fortas	1965–1969	4	1910–1982
Frank Murphy	1940–1949	9	1890–1949	Thurgood Marshall	1967–1991	24	1908–1993
Harlan F. Stone	1941–1946	5	1872–1946	*Warren C. Burger*	1969–1986	17	1907–1995
James F. Byrnes	1941–1942	1	1879–1972	Harry A. Blackmun	1970–1994	24	1908–1998
Robert H. Jackson	1941–1954	13	1892–1954	Lewis F. Powell Jr.	1972–1987	15	1907–1998
Wiley B. Rutledge	1943–1949	6	1894–1949	*William H. Rehnquist*	1972–2005	33	1924–2005
Harold H. Burton	1945–1958	13	1888–1964	John P. Stevens III	1975–	—	1920–
Fred M. Vinson	1946–1953	7	1890–1953	Sandra Day O'Connor	1981–	—	1930–
Tom C. Clark	1949–1967	18	1899–1977	Antonin Scalia	1986–	—	1936–
Sherman Minton	1949–1956	7	1890–1965	Anthony M. Kennedy	1988–	—	1936–
Earl Warren	1953–1969	16	1891–1974	David H. Souter	1990–	—	1939–
John Marshall Harlan	1955–1971	16	1899–1971	Clarence Thomas	1991–	—	1948–
William J. Brennan Jr.	1956–1990	34	1906–1997	Ruth Bader Ginsburg	1993–	—	1933–
Charles E. Whittaker	1957–1962	5	1901–1973	Stephen Breyer	1994–	—	1938–
Potter Stewart	1958–1981	23	1915–1985	John G. Roberts	2005–	—	1955–
Byron R. White	1962–1993	31	1917–	Samuel A. Alito, Jr.	2006–	—	1950–
Arthur J. Goldberg	1962–1965	3	1908–1990				

Note: Chief justices are in italics.

*Appointed and served one term, but not confirmed by the Senate.